Philosophy Before Socrates

Second Edition

Philosophy Before Socrates

An Introduction with Texts and Commentary

Second Edition

Richard D. McKirahan

Hackett Publishing Company, Inc.
Indianapolis/Cambridge

Copyright © 2010 by Hackett Publishing Company, Inc.

Printed in the United States of America

20   19   18   17   16   2   3   4   5   6   7

For further information, please address
  Hackett Publishing Company, Inc.
  P.O. Box 44937
  Indianapolis, Indiana 46244-0937
  www.hackettpublishing.com

Interior design by Dan Kirklin
Composition by Scribe, Inc. (www.scribenet.com)

Library of Congress Cataloging-in-Publication Data

McKirahan, Richard D.
    Philosophy before Socrates : an introduction with texts and
  commentary / Richard D. McKirahan—2nd ed.
        p.   cm.
    Includes bibliographical references (p.) and indexes.
    ISBN 978-1-60384-182-5 (pbk.)—ISBN 978-1-60384-183-2 (cloth)
    1. Pre-Socratic philosophers. I. Title.
  B187.5.M35 2010
  182—dc22   2009040711

The paper used in this publication meets the minimum requirements of American
National Standard for Information Sciences—Permanence of Paper for Printed Library
Materials, ANSI Z39.48–1984.
                                        ∞

for Voula again, as always

Contents

Preface to the First Edition

Greek philosophy had been flourishing for over a century when Socrates was born (469 BCE). Socrates' thought, as well as that of all later Greek philosophers, was strongly influenced by the work of the early pioneers in the field, both the philosopher-scientists known as "Presocratics" and the fifth-century Sophists. The theories, arguments, and concepts of the early Greek philosophers are also important and interesting in their own right. And yet this seminal period of philosophical and scientific activity is much less familiar than the work of Socrates, Plato, and Aristotle.

This state of affairs is partly, perhaps principally, due to the nature of the evidence about thinkers before the time of Plato and Aristotle. In contrast with these two great philosophers, many of whose works survive in entirety, not a single work of any of the "Presocratic" philosophers has been preserved from antiquity to the present, and we have only a few short writings of the Sophists. We are confronted instead with a variety of quotations and paraphrases of their words, summaries of their theories, biographical information (much of it fabricated), in some cases adaptations and extensions of their views, and also parodies and criticisms. These materials come from a wide range of authors who write with different purposes and biases, and whose reliability and philosophical and historical acumen vary enormously.

These circumstances have led some scholars to despair of the possibility of reaching the truth about the early philosophers. The present book, however, is founded on the belief that it is possible to sift through the information and develop interpretations which, though incomplete and not demonstrably correct, have a high degree of internal coherence, mutually reinforce one another, have some historical plausibility, and may be approximations to the original ideas and intentions of the thinkers in question.

Four features of this book deserve comment and explanation. First, since much of the fascination in dealing with early Greek philosophy comes from working out one's own interpretations of the evidence, I have made it a principle to present most, and in many cases all, of the fragments of the philosophers discussed, as well as other important evidence on their thought. Except in the few cases that are noted, the translations are my own. I have aimed to provide translations that are as literal as possible, given the differences between Greek and English. Readers are thus in a position to formulate their own understanding of the early philosophers and to form their own judgments of the interpretations I have put forward.

Second, since our knowledge of these philosophers is largely based on source materials other than their own writings, and since these materials are of unequal value, I have made a point of identifying the source of each passage and (in Chapter 1) of discussing the principal sources and commenting on their strengths and weaknesses. In this way readers can assess the value of the evidence and decide for themselves how to weigh it and how confidently to base an interpretation on it.

Third, during the period covered in this book, knowledge had not yet been divided into the separate categories of philosophy, science, and their subfields. Most of the Presocratic "philosophers" treated topics which we find more scientific than philosophical, and none of them drew clear lines between his philosophical and his scientific oeuvre. In fact, the earliest Presocratics focused mainly on issues that we assign to the fields of cosmology, meteorology, biology, and matter theory. Thus, in order to be faithful to the thought of the sixth- and fifth-century philosophers, "philosophy before Socrates" must include scientific issues as well; to omit topics *we* consider unphilosophical would be to amputate vital portions of their thought without which the remainder would make little sense. Accordingly, I have devoted rather more space to scientific topics than is usual in books of this sort, though in many cases much of the interest the scientific ideas have for us lies in the level of philosophical sophistication on which they are founded.

Fourth, the thinkers treated in this book lived in, and to some extent were the products of, particular times and places. Where possible and appropriate I have said something about their lives and their cultural environment; for these circumstances had important effects on the early Greek philosophers, just as the ideas of these men had important effects on Greek civilization.

Acknowledgments to the First Edition

My interest in early Greek philosophy and science began with graduate seminars on the Presocratics given at Harvard by the late G. E. L. Own, and my work owes a deep debt to his inspiring teaching and writings, even though I have come to disagree with some of his interpretations. John Murdoch's courses on ancient and medieval science which I attended at the same time were models of clear exposition and of history of science at its best. A National Endowment for the Humanities Seminar—"The Exact Sciences in Antiquity"—taught at Yale by Asger Aaboe opened my eyes to pre-Greek mathematics and astronomy and gave me a wider scientific context in which to situate Greek science. My education in the interpretation of texts in ancient philosophy has been advanced by attending for the past twenty years the meetings of the West Coast Aristotelian Society led by Julius Moravcsik and, for almost as long, the meetings of the Southern California Readers of Ancient Philosophy. I have benefited greatly from the revolutionary work on Greek science done by G. E. R. Lloyd, who has set for me an example of what is possible in this field. I should like to thank him for his friendship and support, which have meant a great deal to me.

I offer my thanks to Professors A. A. Long, John Malcolm, Henry Mendell, Michael Wedin, and Mary Whitlock Blundell for their helpful comments on drafts of the book and for their encouragement. In addition, I am grateful to the students in my courses at Pomona College for their willingness to use the manuscript in lieu of a textbook and for their many valuable suggestions. Finally, I am deeply indebted to Paul Coppock for his generous editorial assistance and to Patricia Curd, who commented on more than one version of the manuscript as I was revising it for publication, and whose suggestions in many cases prompted significant alterations and, I believe, improvements.

Claremont, California
December 1993

Preface to the Second Edition

Interest in the field of Presocratic studies had grown in the generation before the publication of the first edition of *Philosophy Before Socrates* in 1994, but in the past sixteen years it has expanded out of all recognition. Two series of international colloquia on specific Presocratic topics have taken place in Europe (beginning in 2000). Two conferences on individual Presocratic thinkers have been held in Latin America. The International Society for Presocratic Studies was founded. Books devoted to the Presocratic thinkers have appeared in standard series such as the *Cambridge Companions* and the *Oxford Handbooks*.[1] Important earlier books have been reprinted.[2] Significant new editions of the texts of many of the Presocratics have been published.[3] A project is underway to publish for the first time complete collections of the Presocratic testimonia.[4] Ambitious Web-based projects have been planned. Even more important, significant new interpretations have been proposed for many of the individual Presocratics and for the trajectory of Presocratic philosophy as a whole. Old paradigms and models have come under heavy attack and at present there is less consensus than a generation ago.

These circumstances have made it both important to update this book and difficult to do so. My decision to propose a second edition was initially due to the discovery of important new material on Empedocles,[5] which in my opinion rendered almost all previous interpretations obsolete. Also, the ever increasing amount of new scholarship was making a book published in 1994 increasingly out of date; even in many places where my views had not changed it was necessary to engage with more recent literature. And inevitably I found that I had changed my mind on a number of issues since writing the first edition.

I began work on the present edition in summer 2006 and finished in spring 2009. The biggest changes from the first edition occur in the chapters on the Pythagoreans, Parmenides, Zeno, Anaxagoras and Empedocles, and in the new chapter on Philolaus, but almost every chapter contains changes. I have included additional source materials, and I have changed the translations of some passages. On topics where I now think differently than I did twenty years ago, I have changed the discussion accordingly. I have also referred to some of the

---

1. Long (1999), and Curd and Graham (2008).

2. For example, Mourelatos (1970/2008), Coxon (1986/2009).

3. Notably Conche (1996), Mouraviev (1999–), Pendrick (2002), Taylor (1999), Curd (2007).

4. This multi-volume series (*Traditio Praesocratica*) published by De Gruyter will contain translations as well as original texts of the testimonia. The first volume, on Thales, has recently appeared (Wöhrle [2009]).

5. Martin and Primavesi (1999).

most important new interpretations that are different from mine. (I have not aimed for completeness here, and considerations of space have prevented me from mentioning more views and frequently from doing justice to the views I mention.) I have added an Appendix containing translations of three Hippocratic writings and the Derveni papyrus.

Acknowledgments to the Second Edition

I want to express my thanks to Hackett Publishing Company for enthusiastically accepting my proposal for a second edition and subsequently agreeing to include an Appendix of texts related in various ways to the Presocratic tradition. In particular I want to thank Deborah Wilkes for her help at every stage. The book also owes a great deal to Pomona College, where I have had the opportunity to develop my thinking about the Presocratics and to try out new ideas and preliminary versions of new material each year in my courses in front of bright and interested students. My thinking has benefited from conferences I have attended—in particular conferences sponsored by the Institute of Philosophical Research in Patras, Greece in 2003, 2005, and 2008, from which I learned much about Empedocles, Heraclitus, the Pythagoreans and Philolaus, and the Derveni papyrus. I was also privileged to be invited to attend a workshop on the Derveni papyrus at the University of Crete in 2006, which gave me my first serious introduction to that important and fascinating text. A lively session at the Cambridge University B Club in 2006 and discussions with Carl Huffman and others at the first conference of the International Association for Presocratic Studies in 2008 helped me clarify my thoughts on Philolaus. The individuals whose comments have helped my thinking are too many to list, but I want to thank the authors of reviews of the first edition for pointing out some of its faults as well as its good features, and Michael Frede, Charles Kahn, Bob Lamberton, Tony Long, Henry Mendell, Alex Mourelatos, Apostolos Pierris, Oliver Primavesi, Malcolm Schofield, David Sedley, Vassileia Tzaligopoulou, and Voula Tsouna for their comments and suggestions. Finally, I want to express my appreciation and gratitude to Pat Curd, who was the referee for this edition (as for the first) and whose insightful comments and criticisms of the manuscript right up to the end led to improvement in many places.

This second edition, completed after twenty years of marriage, like the first, which I began exactly twenty-one years ago during our engagement, is dedicated with deep gratitude to my dearest wife Voula, who has given me a wonderful child, a lovely home, a life rich in experiences and interests, and always her unbounded love.

Athens
January 2010

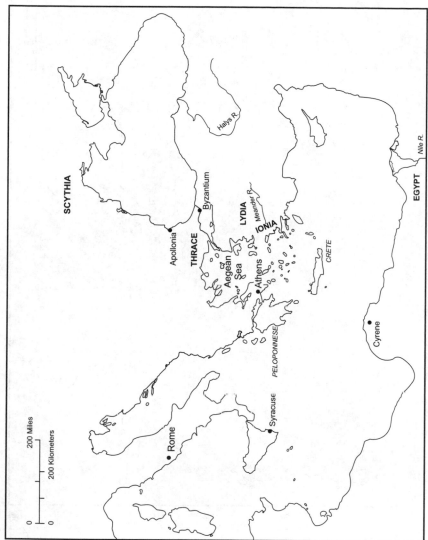

SCYTHIA

Halys R.

Apollonia

Byzantium

THRACE

LYDIA

IONIA

Meander R.

Aegean Sea

Athens

CRETE

EGYPT

Nile R.

Cyrene

PELOPONNESE

Syracuse

Rome

200 Miles

200 Kilometers

0

0

The Eastern
Mediterranean

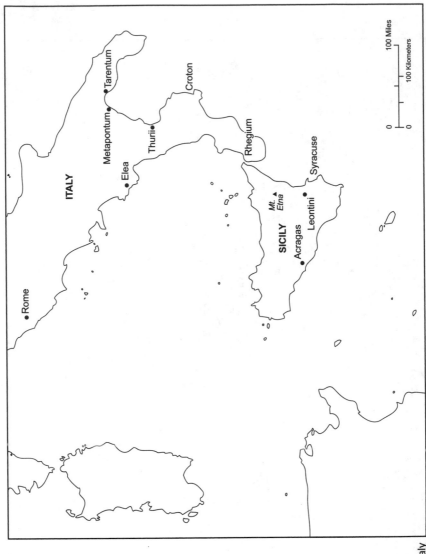

Sicily and
Southern Italy

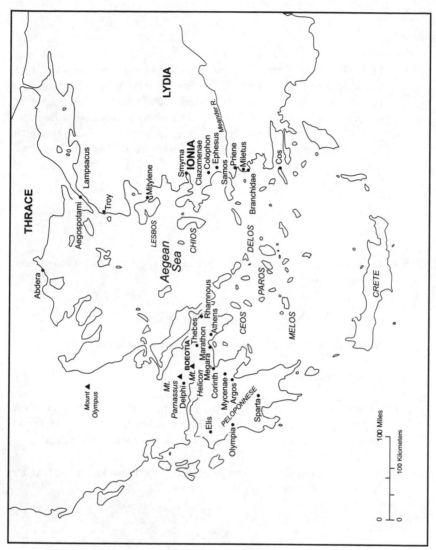

THRACE

Abdera

Aegospotami
Lampsacus
Troy

LESBOS
Mitylene

LYDIA

Smyrna
IONIA
Clazomenae
Colophon
Ephesus
Meander R.
Samos
Priene
Miletus
Branchidae
Cos

CHIOS

Aegean
Sea

PAROS
DELOS

CEOS

MELOS

CRETE

Mount
Olympus

Mt.
Parnassus
Delphi
Mt.
Helicon
BOEOTIA
Thebes
Rhamnous
Marathon
Megara
Athens
Corinth
Mycenae
Argos
PELOPONNESE
Sparta

Elis
Olympia

0   100 Miles
0   100 Kilometers

Greece and
Western Asia Minor

Abbreviations

DK   H. Diels and W. Kranz, *Die Fragmente der Vorsokratiker*, 6th ed., Berlin, 1951 and later editions. The standard edition of the Presocratic Philosophers. Each Presocratic is assigned a number. The fragments of each Presocratic are also assigned numbers preceded by the letter "B." Thus, the number for Heraclitus is 22, and Heraclitus's fragment 101 is referred to as DK 22B101. Testimonia are likewise identified by numbers preceded by the letter "A." The DK references are used widely in books and articles on the Presocratics.

KR   G. S. Kirk and J. E. Raven, *The Presocratic Philosophers*, Cambridge, 1957.

KRS   G. S. Kirk, J. E. Raven, and M. Schofield, *The Presocratic Philosophers*, 2nd edn., Cambridge, 1983.

Note on Use of Brackets

I use the following conventions in quoted passages from ancient authors.

(. . .)   parenthetical comment in the ancient text

<. . .>   supplements to the text (in some cases these are supplements to the text that have been proposed by scholars, in others they are additions I have made in order for the translations to make sense in English)

[. . .]   alternative possible translations, explanatory remarks, or context for the quoted passage

1

The Sources of Early Greek Philosophy

When we read a work by a modern author, we usually have no trouble about an accurate complete text. Reliable editions are easily found. It may be useful to read what others say, but we are in a position to judge the work ourselves and accept or reject the opinions of others according as they square with our own. It is very different with ancient authors.

Before printing was invented in the fifteenth century, the original version of a work was a document hand written by the author or dictated to a scribe. "Publication" consisted in having copies made (again, by hand) and distributing them to interested people.

No ancient prototypes survive, so ancient works come to us only through copies, or rather, copies of copies an unknown number of removes from the original. The earliest complete surviving text of Plato, for example, was written in the late ninth century CE, some 1,250 years after Plato's death, and, in fact, closer in time to us than to him. In the best cases, then, we have one or more complete manuscripts of the text, from which scholars known as textual critics attempt to determine what the author actually wrote.

Each time a text was copied by hand, the copyist might introduce errors, especially since the Greek language and the way it was written changed over the centuries. As a result, the manuscripts of a work disagree at those points where different errors were introduced. A modern printed text of an ancient work is based on the determination by its editor as to which of the different manuscript readings or alternatives proposed by scholars is most likely to be correct at each point. The uncertainty of the text is a factor constantly to keep in mind.

The situation of the philosophers covered in this book is worse than the case just described, since, except for two short writings by Gorgias, not only the prototypes but all the copies of their works have perished. We know these thinkers first through quotations or close paraphrases of what they wrote contained in surviving works of other authors who either had access to the lost writings or relied on other authors who did, and second through information about them preserved in other authors. These surviving works too underwent the process of copying described above with its attendant possibility for introducing errors. We must consider the interests, prejudices, approaches, and purposes of the authors and texts containing information on the early Greek philosophers in order to decide how far we can trust them and how they may have distorted the original. The problematic nature of the evidence entails that there is ample room to disagree with any selection and interpretation of ancient evidence on early Greek philosophy, including the present one, and further that a book of this length and nature must presuppose solutions to issues still under debate.

Only rarely can we be certain that an interpretation is correct. In fact, beliefs about particular views and about the overall nature and importance of a thinker's contributions can vary widely, depending on which sources are accepted and which are preferred over others. For each early philosopher the information is like a jigsaw puzzle with many pieces missing and to which some of the pieces at hand may not really belong. The project is to put the pieces together as best we can, throwing away the ones that do not fit, and, on the basis of the partial picture that results, to sketch in the missing area of the puzzle. Among the most fascinating features of studying early Greek philosophy are the possibilities of assigning different weights to different pieces and putting the pieces together in different ways. In this field there is no unanimity among experts, and those who disagree with this book's interpretation of a text or who find another arrangement of the evidence more satisfying are encouraged to see how well their ideas agree with information not included in this book and with other interpretations that have been proposed. The bibliography at the end of this book can be used as a starting point for such research.

The two most important types of sources for the Presocratics are known as fragments (quotations containing the philosopher's actual words) and testimonia (passages providing information about the thinker without quoting his words).

Fragments. Quotations vary in length from a single word to an extract of over fifty lines of Parmenides. In some cases a considerable number of fragments are preserved: there are some three hundred fragments attributed to Democritus, for example. Some fragments are found in works as early as the writings of Plato, who lived only a generation or two after the original works were written, while others come from works as late as the tenth century CE.

Dealing with purported fragments is not always straightforward. In the first place, they may not really be genuine fragments; since it was common for ancient authors to quote from memory, the words they claim to quote may actually be a misremembered paraphrase.[1] Second, in addition to paraphrases there are also misattributions, imitations, and outright forgeries. Another problem is that fragments are frequently taken out of their original contexts, most obviously in the anthologies of quotations that became widespread from the last three centuries BCE. As a result, the quoted words and even sentences are deprived of much of their meaning. Their literal meaning may be left uncertain, or their intended application, or the reasons why their author believed them. Further, the people who quote the Presocratics do not always understand them and frequently embed the fragments in alien, sometimes hostile, contexts. It is wrong to think that the earlier the source the more accurate the quotation[2] or interpretation.

Testimonia. Much material on the early Greek philosophers—their lives, writings and theories—varying from the reliable to the fictitious, comes from sources that range from the near-contemporary (including some of the Presocratics themselves)

1. A related problem is where a quotation begins and ends, since the ancients did not use quotation marks and it can be uncertain what is fragment and what is context.

2. Plato and Aristotle, who are among the earliest sources of quotations, tend to quote from memory, also the widely-read Plutarch (c.100 CE).

to authors closer in time to us than to the philosophers they discuss. Since fragments are frequently embedded in testimonia, the same kinds of concerns apply to the latter as to the former. Many sources of testimonia have particular axes to grind, whether philosophical, religious, or other. Antiquity did not have the notion of the history of philosophy in the sense of a careful attempt to understand earlier philosophers in their own terms simply for the sake of understanding them. Many quarried the writings of earlier thinkers in order to find support for philosophical or scientific views of their own; others did so in order to prove other kinds of points. Consequently it is imperative to take into account the interests, biases, and limitations of the sources of testimonia in order to evaluate their worth and to deploy them appropriately in constructing an interpretation.

In order to offer some help on this critical matter, I shall briefly survey the authors and writings that contribute most to our knowledge of early Greek philosophy by providing fragments and/or testimonia.[3]

Plato (427–347 BCE), who may have known personally some of the thinkers treated here, must be used with caution, since his interests in quoting and discussing the views of other philosophers are not historical but philosophical, and he frequently treats them with humor or irony. Also important is the fact that Plato wrote dialogues rather than systematic treatises. His purposes do not require a fair reconstruction of views in their original context. He was downright hostile to the Sophists, whom he considered the antithesis of philosophers, and what he tells us about them appears in an unfriendly light. Because of the powerful influence of Plato and his student, Aristotle, who shared his hostility, the Sophists were largely ignored by later sources interested in preserving early thought.

Aristotle (384–322 BCE), however, had a serious interest in the theories of his predecessors, and it is to him that we owe, directly or indirectly, practically all of our knowledge of the Presocratics. Aristotle's standard practice in discussing a topic is to survey the relevant evidence, including the opinions of earlier thinkers, then to explore their differences and the problems they raise, and to attempt to find out where the truth lies.[4] He takes these views seriously because he tends to think that all or most of them can make some contribution toward discovering the truth. Again, Aristotle's motives are not what we would call historical. He does not aim to give complete expositions of the theories of others but selects and surveys views he finds useful for his purposes. He can fail to mention some writers who treated the topics under discussion, and he does not systematically survey as many topics as we might wish. In spite of his limitations as a historian and source, the accounts he gives of his predecessors[5] have irreplaceable value. To some extent—

---

3. See below pp. 80–81 and 375 for discussion of the source materials on Pythagoras and the Pythagoreans and on the Sophists, and p. 400 for Hippias the Sophist as the first doxographer.

4. Aristotle describes his method in *Nicomachean Ethics* 7.1.

5. Especially in *Metaphysics* 1 and *Physics* 1.

and this for better or for worse—Aristotle invented the concept of "Presocratic" philosophy as we still think of it (although he did not use that term).

Following Aristotle's approach, three of his immediate followers in the Peripatetic school, which he founded, produced important historical surveys. Eudemus compiled a history of mathematics, astronomy, and theology, Meno a history of medicine, and most importantly for us, Theophrastus wrote extensively on earlier philosophers from Thales to Plato (that is, those earlier than Aristotle). If all of Theophrastus's material had survived, our knowledge of early Greek philosophy would be much improved. As it is, we have a good deal of only a single book, *On Sensation*, which does, however, enable us to form an opinion of his methods and value as a historian. He treats his subject topic by topic (e.g., theories that declare that like is perceived by like), not chronologically or thinker by thinker and was influenced by Aristotle in his choice of topics. He judges the views he reports from an Aristotelian perspective. His longest and most important historical survey, the *Opinions of the Natural Philosophers* (or *Opinions on Nature*), is entirely lost, but it was abridged and summarized in later times. A great deal of our information on Presocratic "natural philosophy" (the ancient term corresponding to what we call natural science) comes either from Theophrastus himself or from these summaries. Hence his great importance to the "doxographic tradition" (the name given to the ancient works recording the opinions of philosophers).

Two important surviving doxographical works deserve mention. One is the *Placita*[6] *Philosophorum*, or *Opinions of the Philosophers*, attributed to Plutarch (c.50–120 CE) but probably written in the second century CE by someone else (hence its author is called pseudo-Plutarch). It is a summary of earlier views on each of over one hundred philosophical topics. The second text is the *Eclogae Physicae*, or *Selections on Natural Philosophy*, of John of Stobi, otherwise known as Stobaeus (fifth century CE). This is a collection of quotations and summaries of over five hundred poets and prose writers. The content of the information about the Presocratics in these two works is very similar because they were based on a common source, now lost, which was composed around 100 CE by an otherwise unknown author named Aëtius. This work, which has been partially reconstructed mainly from the materials in pseudo-Plutarch and Stobaeus,[7] is an updated version of earlier collections of *Placita* going back to Theophrastus and Meno.

---

6. "Placita" is the title given to ancient doxographic collections.

7. The detective work on the origin of these materials and the reconstruction of Aëtius's text is due to H. Diels in his fundamental work (in Latin) *Doxographi Graeci* (Diels [1879] in the Bibliography). Diels identified Aëtius as the author of the common source of pseudo-Plutarch and Stobaeus on the basis of Theodoret, a fifth-century bishop, who both quotes and names Aëtius. In recent times Diels's interpretation has been challenged (some even deny the existence of Aëtius). It is currently being studied intensively and refined by J. Mansfeld, D. Runia, and others, who support Diels's construction in

Cicero, the Roman orator and statesman of the mid-first century BCE wrote important accounts of post-Aristotelian Greek philosophy which contain historical surveys of philosophical views going back to the Presocratics.

The learned *Natural Questions* of **Seneca the Elder** (first century BCE) employs doxographic sources other than Theophrastus and far from simply copying or rearranging what he found, he examined them with his active and independent mind.

Sextus Empiricus (?second century CE), a proponent of a form of philosophical skepticism, quotes some Presocratics to show that they held views related to his own and quotes others to show that their dogmatic views are false.

Hippolytus, a bishop of Rome in the late second or early third century, wrote a work (in ten books) entitled *Refutation of All Heresies*, which argues that Christian heresies coincide with views of Greek philosophers.[8] Book 1 contains doxographical accounts of fourteen Presocratics whom Hippolytus describes as "natural philosophers." Moreover, the comparisons of the heresies with pagan philosophers in the later books are an important source of fragments, since Hippolytus frequently quotes the Presocratics to help make his points.[9]

Diogenes Laertius's (third century CE) work, *Lives of the Philosophers*, is an ambitious but undiscriminating collection of a wide variety of materials on philosophers from Thales on down to centuries after the end of our period. Among the over two hundred sources he used, three sorts of materials need to be mentioned. First, biographies of the philosophers that began to be written in the third century BCE, frequently with unreliable or fabricated information. Second, philosophical "successions" of a kind that began to appear in the second century BCE, which identify one philosopher as the student, associate, or follower of another. Third, chronological writings, especially the *Chronica* of Apollodorus (second century BCE). In this verse work Apollodorus attempted to record the dates of significant events and people from the fall of Troy to his own times. His dating was extremely influential in ancient times, but his methods involved shaky assumptions,[10] and his research must have been based in many cases on sparse materials.

---

large measure, and have re-edited much of the text of Aëtius. The study of the sources has fundamental importance for our understanding of the beginnings of our philosophical tradition. Runia gives a good picture of its current state (see Runia [2008]).

8. Exactly how this strategy makes for a refutation is disputed. It is usually thought to be a smear-campaign: pagan views are false, or at least unchristian, so the evidence that Hippolytus presents establishes that the heresies are false or unchristian too.

9. Hippolytus's value as a doxographic source is considered by most to be low despite Osborne's attempt (Osborne [1987b]) to raise his stock.

10. For example, he assumes that a philosopher is forty years old at the time of his most important work and that a pupil is forty years younger than his teacher.

In the sixth century CE, **Simplicius**, a Neoplatonist philosopher and the author of extensive commentaries on Aristotle's works, quoted earlier philosophers in discussing Aristotle's remarks on them and added other material whose ultimate source is Theophrastus. Simplicius is of special interest to us because he wished to understand the early thinkers as well as Aristotle. He occasionally gives long and apparently accurate extracts from works that had become rare. The same is true of other commentators on Aristotle, notably Simplicius's rival and contemporary **John Philoponus** and **Alexander of Aphrodisias** (second century CE).

The nature of our sources might lead a reasonable person to despair. Indeed some scholars have challenged the value of the information in Aristotle and Theophrastus[11]—and if these two cannot be used, we are in truly desperate straits. Nevertheless, in some cases we have enough fragments to form a fair judgment of a philosopher's views on at least some topics. And in many cases the evidence of testimonia can be used, once allowance is made for the authors' methods, sources, interests, and prejudices. It is reasonable to suppose that in some cases at least we can attain an approximation to what the philosopher actually thought.

---

11. Cherniss (1935) and McDiarmid (1953) are notable skeptics.

2

Hesiod and the Beginnings of
Greek Philosophy and Science

Since antiquity the beginning of Greek philosophy has been placed in Miletus in the early sixth century BCE. The first philosophers—Thales, Anaximander, and Anaximenes—the story goes, invented and made rapid developments in a new way of looking at and thinking about the world. This claim is largely true, but it is not the whole truth. These men gave a new direction to ways of thought found much earlier in Greece, and proposed new kinds of answers to questions that had been asked and answered long before. A look at Thales' precursors will enable us to see better why the early philosophers were interested in the particular issues they took up and to form a more accurate appreciation of their achievement.

The present chapter will concentrate on Hesiod, who lived in the late eighth or early seventh century, a century before Thales. Though he presents himself as a poor farmer from rustic Ascra in Boeotia, Hesiod was a widely recognized poet whose chief works, *Theogony* ("Birth of the Gods") and *Works and Days*, permit us to grasp some important points of difference and similarity between pre-philosophical and Presocratic Greek thought.

A principal difference between them is that traditional Greek mythology, focusing on the Olympian gods, is omnipresent in Hesiod yet absent from the Presocratics. For Hesiod, the world is full of gods. These gods range from what we think of as physical components of the world (Heaven, Earth, Hills, etc.) to anthropomorphic beings (including the Olympian gods) who combine superhuman powers with human feelings, emotions, desires, motivation, and reasoning, as well as such human qualities as favoritism, ambition, and inconsistency. Some gods, especially the earliest born, are less anthropomorphic, and some verge on allegory (such as Blame, Distress, Quarrels, Famine, Work, and Lies[1]), but the chief figures have incipient personalities (supportive Gaia, crafty Kronos, wise Zeus, wily Prometheus), and are doers of deeds. This large assemblage of gods is in keeping with the broadly inclusive Greek notion of the divine.

The anthropomorphic gods control the events in the world that fall into their various departments. Since the gods are competitive and jealous of their prerogatives, and since their departments are not wholly separate, the world does not have perfect order. The gods can be capricious, and phenomena occur through their arbitrary will. Further, gods can help and harm humans, so individuals and states must try to keep them favorably disposed by prayers and gifts, although even pious behavior does not guarantee the assistance of these notoriously fickle deities.

---

1. Cf. *Theogony* lines 226–32 (not in DK).

Hesiod's view of the gods and their relation to the world stemmed from tradition, which commanded belief. *Theogony* does not claim to contain either new ideas or Hesiod's own ideas. Here too he differs from the Presocratics, whose accounts of the world were their own inventions and so were not isolated from criticism as well-entrenched traditional material can be.[2]

At the same time, Hesiod is not just a teller of familiar myths. Even *Theogony* endeavors to shape the traditional material on which it is based according to discernible principles of order. Hesiod's belief that the world is ordered in a way that humans can understand—in other words that it is a *kosmos* (world order, ordered world)—is a fundamental article of faith for the Presocratics, as is his operating principle: that it can be correctly described and communicated to others in language.[3] Another common feature is the importance of the divine in the world, although the Presocratics' notion of divinity is no longer anthropomorphic, arbitrary, or competitive. Finally, Hesiod and the Presocratics share an interest in certain features of the world, both physical (notably in its history and composition, as well as in astronomical and meteorological phenomena) and moral (above all, in justice).

Theogony presents its main theme, the ascendancy of Zeus to secure and lasting power, in a definite chronological sequence:

1. Origin of early divinities down to and including the Titans, children of Gaia (Earth) and Ouranos (Heaven); as soon as the Titans are born Ouranos conceals them in a hiding place within Gaia.
2. Kronos, the youngest Titan, assisted by Gaia, castrates Ouranos and assumes command.
3. Origin of the Olympian gods, who are children of Titans Kronos and Rhea; Kronos eats the gods as soon as they are born, except for Zeus, who escapes through the help of Gaia and Rhea.
4. The Olympians, led by Zeus, defeat the Titans in battle; Zeus assumes command.
5. Zeus alone defeats Typhoeus, child of Gaia and Tartaros (Underworld).
6. The Olympians proclaim Zeus their ruler; he gives out rank and privileges to each.

---

2. Hesiod's assertion that he received his song directly from the Muses (*Theogony* lines 22–34 [not in DK]) is matched by Parmenides' attribution of his poem to an unnamed goddess (**11.1**, especially lines **24–32**). Empedocles (**14.38** and **14.45**) and Heraclitus (cf. **10.46** and **10.44** with **10.28** and **10.30**; also **10.47** and **10.1**) also claim divine warrant for their philosophy. But here too Hesiod has a stronger claim on his audience's belief: the non-Olympian deities of the Presocratics will not have carried the same degree of conviction.

3. The completeness and consistency of the accounts of the world offered by Hesiod and the Presocratics are open to question, though, as the discussion of their views will make plain.

7. Zeus swallows his consort Metis (Counsel, Wisdom) to prevent her having
    a child who would usurp his place as king of the gods; thus Zeus's rule will
    last forever.

The central element of this sequence is the story of divine rulership, held in turn
by Ouranos, Kronos, and Zeus. Hesiod gives a distinctive version of this myth,
which existed in various forms throughout the eastern Mediterranean and Near
East, notably in the Babylonian succession myth *Enuma Elish*, which probably
goes back a thousand years before Hesiod, and in the Derveni papyrus (translated below pages 460–68).

But the succession myth makes up only about one-fourth of *Theogony*. About
one-third of the poem consists of material that fits the title—the births of gods
from the beginning down to the children and grandchildren of the Olympian
gods—and displays an interest in issues the Presocratic philosophers would take
up. Hesiod's account of the earliest gods bears this out.

2.1 First of all Chaos came into being. Next came   *(116)*
      broad-breasted Gaia [Earth], the secure dwelling place forever
          of all
      the immortals who hold the peak of snowy Olympus.
      And murky Tartaros [Underworld] in a recess of the
          broad-roaded Earth,
      and Eros [Love], who is the most beautiful among
          the immortal gods,   *(120)*
      who loosens the limbs and overpowers the intentions and
          sensible plans
      of all the gods and all humans too.
      From Chaos there came into being Erebos [Darkness] and
          black Night.
      From Night, Aithēr [bright upper air] and Hēmerē [Day]
          came into being,
      which she conceived and bore after uniting in love with Erebos.   *(125)*
      Gaia first brought forth starry Ouranos [Heaven]
      equal to herself, to cover her all about
      in order to be a secure dwelling place forever for the blessed gods.
      She brought forth long mountains, beautiful shelters of divine
      Nymphs who live in wooded mountains,   *(130)*
      and also, without delightful love, gave birth to the barren sea,
      Pontos, raging with its swelling waves. Then,
      bedded by Ouranos, she gave birth to deep-swirling Ocean
      and Koios and Kreios and Hyperion and Iapetos
      and Theia and Rhea and Themis and Mnemosyne   *(135)*
      and Phoebe with a golden wreath and lovely Tethys.
      After them, last of all, was born crafty-minded Kronos,
      the most terrible of the children, and he hated his mighty father.
          (Hesiod, *Theogony* lines 116–38 [not in DK])

This passage begins the theogonic myths and ends with an ominous note that
foretells the first struggle for mastery of the world. Several features need comment. First, Chaos. Although in later antiquity the word meant what it means for
us, it has been argued convincingly[4] that here it refers to a gap. But a gap between
what? The most common view is that it is the gap between earth and heaven: the
first stage in the development of the present world was the separation of heaven
and earth. But since Earth gives birth to Heaven at a later developmental phase
(line 126), the original gap must result from the separation of Earth and Tartaros, the two entities mentioned immediately after Chaos.[5] On either interpretation the first event in the process that led to our world is the differentiation of an
already existing thing. The world did not arise out of nothing, and there was no
creator. Hesiod explains neither how the sum total of existence came into being
nor how it came to be divided.

Second, Hesiod's theogony is also a cosmogony ("birth of the ordered world").
Many of the primordial gods have the names of regions of the physical world
and are conceived as identical with those regions. The births of Gaia, Tartaros,
and Ouranos, for example, are the origins simultaneously of three divine figures
and the three largest areas of the universe: Earth, Underworld, and Heaven.
Theogony thus gives us a picture of the structure of the physical world as Hesiod
understood it. The world is a divine place, literally full of, made up of, gods,
although many of Hesiod's divinities had no myths or worship, and anthropomorphism is so slight or altogether lacking that it is difficult to know even
whether to capitalize the names. As to the physical structure of the universe,
Hesiod shows an interest in large-scale geographical features of the earth, the
large-scale cosmic features, and in astronomical and meteorological phenomena,
all of which he treats as divine. But his interest here does not go beyond naming
them, identifying their parentage, and asserting their existence.

Third, Hesiod's *kosmos* contains more than just things we regard as physi-
cal. Passage 2.1 mentions Love and Mnemosyne (Memory). Elsewhere we have
Death, Sleep, the Fates, Deceit, Quarrels, Lies, Power, Right, Order, Peace, and
Justice, among others.

Fourth, Hesiod accounts for the origin of most of the gods by means of a
process found in the realm of humans and animals. Eros (Love) appears early on
the scene, and afterwards parenting occurs through sexual reproduction, though
there is inconsistency even here; some gods are born of only one parent and the
earliest few, including Eros, come into being without parents at all. Hesiod offers
no explanations of these exceptional cases.

Fifth, in Hesiod's hands parentage becomes a device for ordering the diverse
world, making it a *kosmos*. In the beginning all is dark, and from dark Chaos
emerge Night and Erebos (Darkness). Dark Night produces Hemera (Day) and

---

4. On philological grounds: the root "cha-" in "chaos" being the same as in "chasm."

5. For the original view, see KRS, pp. 36–41. The alternative view is that of Miller
(1983).

bright Aither. Earth and Heaven produce geographical entities. These genealogies and others manifest organizing principles or patterns of order: like produces like, opposite produces opposite.

The following lines give us a rough picture of the *kosmos*.

2.2   . . . as far beneath Earth as Heaven is from Earth.   *(720)*
For that is the distance from Earth to murky Tartaros.
For a bronze anvil falling nine days and nights
from Heaven would reach Earth on the tenth.
And a bronze anvil falling nine days and nights
from Earth would reach Tartaros on the tenth.   *(725)*
Around Tartaros a fence of bronze has been built. Night is
    poured round
its throat in three layers. Above it
grow the roots of Earth and of the barren Sea.
There the Titans are hidden away beneath the murky
darkness through the plans of cloud-gathering Zeus,   *(730)*
in a dark place at the ends of the huge Earth.
They have no way out, since Poseidon has set bronze
doors upon it and a wall runs in both directions. . . .
There are the sources and limits   *(736)*
of dark Earth and murky Tartaros,
and the barren Sea and starry Heaven, one after the next,
unpleasant and dank, and the gods loathe them.
It is a huge chasm, and not within an entire complete year   *(740)*
would a person reach its floor if he first came to be within its gates,
but gust after hard gust would bring him this way and that. . . .
And the dread house of dark Night
stands covered in black clouds.   *(745)*
In front of these things the son of Iapetos [Atlas] stands and holds
the broad heaven on his head and tireless arms
without moving, where Night and Day draw near
and greet each other as they cross the great threshold
of bronze. The one will descend while the other   *(750)*
goes out, and the chamber never contains both at once,
but one is always outside,
wandering over the earth, while the other is within
and waits for the time of her own journey to arrive.
The one holds far-seeing light for those who live on the earth,   *(755)*
while deadly Night holds in her hands Sleep,
brother of Death, and is covered in murky cloud.
There the children of black Night have their homes—
Sleep and Death, dreadful gods, nor does
shining Helios [Sun] ever look upon them with his rays   *(760)*
as he ascends the Heaven or as he descends from Heaven.
(Hesiod, *Theogony* lines 720–33, 736–42, 744–61 [not in DK])

These verses do not present a coherent description from which we could draw a map. For example, it is hard to see how Atlas, who stands in the Underworld, can hold up the Heavens. But the *kosmos* is given a definite size and a roughly symmetric structure:

1. Heaven at the top;
2. The gap between Heaven and Earth, which is bright by day and dark by night;
3. Earth surrounded by the river Ocean, which flows back into itself;[6]
4. A similar gap between Earth and Tartaros,[7] which is always dark, gloomy, and stormy;
5. Tartaros at the bottom.

A crude sketch of Hesiod's *kosmos* might look like this, where the sides of Heaven bend down at the edges to touch the Ocean and something symmetrical happens below. Gates to the Underworld allow the passage of Day and Night. On the other hand, since the Sun never sees the Underworld, it is in Heaven during the day and at night is carried around Ocean from west to east, to rise again the next day.

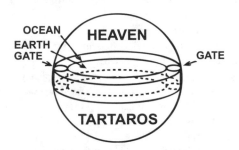

In the more familiar myths of the succession stories, by contrast, anthropomorphism prevails. Gods have the same bodily parts that humans do, the same motivations and feelings (for example, hate, pain, fear, revenge, sexual desire, lust for power), and they and their actions are evaluated in terms that apply to humans (they are called wicked, clever, shameful, just, etc.). Ouranos, Kronos, and Zeus (up to the overthrow of Kronos) derive their supremacy from strength and violence, but the rule of Zeus introduces a different kind of administration of the world.

2.3   But when the blessed gods had completed their labor   (*881*)
        and decided by force the dispute about the Titans' powers and
            privileges,

---

6. *Theogony* line 776 (not in DK).
7. This gap is also called Chaos (line 814 [not in DK]).

> then by the advice of Gaia they urged
> wide-seeing Olympian Zeus to be king and to rule
> the immortals. And he distributed well the powers and
>   privileges among them.
>   (Hesiod, *Theogony* lines 881–85 [not in DK])

When the Olympians defeat the Titans, they follow the advice of their grand-mother Gaia and urge Zeus to rule. His supreme strength and his mighty weapon the thunderbolt make him an obvious choice. But he does not simply seize power; his rule is legitimated by a kind of election by acclamation. Moreover, he delegates some of his power, assigning duties and privileges to the other gods so that Demeter becomes goddess of agriculture, etc.

Further, Zeus's rule is wise and good. By swallowing his consort Metis (Counsel, Wisdom), he receives her attributes. His second consort is Themis (Order, Right). His offspring include Eunomia (Good Order), Dikē (Justice), Eirēnē (Peace).

In *Works and Days*, Hesiod stresses Zeus's justice.

2.4   Those who give straight judgments to foreigners   *(225)*
     and citizens and do not step at all aside from justice
     have a flourishing city and the people prosper in it.
     There is Peace, the nurse of children, throughout the land,
        and wide-seeing Zeus
     never ordains harsh war for them.
     Famine and Disaster never attend men of straight judgment,   *(230)*
     but with good cheer they feed on the fruits of their labors.
     For these the Earth bears the means of life in abundance. In the
        mountains the oak tree
     bears acorns at the top and bees in the middle.
     Their woolly sheep are heavy with fleece.
     Women give birth to children who are like their fathers.   *(235)*
     They flourish continuously with good things and do not go
     on boats, but their fertile fields bear fruit.
     But for those who have thoughts of evil violence and cruel deeds,
     wide-seeing Zeus son of Kronos has ordained justice.
     Often indeed the entire city of an evil man suffers,   *(240)*
     when he sins and plans wicked deeds.
     The son of Kronos brings a great disaster on them from heaven,
     Famine and Disease together, and the people perish.
     Women do not give birth, but houses are diminished
     through the cunning of Olympian Zeus. Again, on
        another occasion   *(245)*
     the son of Kronos either destroys their broad army or their
        city wall
     or takes vengeance on their ships at sea.
             (Hesiod, *Works and Days* lines 225–47 [not in DK])

The just Zeus rewards justice in humans and punishes their injustice, and so stands as the guarantor of a moral order in the *kosmos* as a whole and specifically in the human sphere.

Theogony surprisingly says little about humans. (It would be less surprising if it said either much or nothing at all.) The Pandora myth (lines 535–616) recounts the origin of woman (fashioned out of earth by Hephaistos) and, through her, of many of the troubles that men endure, but already "mortal men" (line 535) existed and had dealings with the gods. *Works and Days* also accounts for the grim conditions of human life. It does so both in another version of Pandora and in the myth of five generations of humans.

2.5   First of all, the immortals who dwell on Olympus   *(109)*
    created a golden race of humans endowed with speech.   *(110)*
    They lived under Kronos when he reigned in heaven.
    They lived like gods with carefree hearts
    far from toil and grief. Wretched old age
    did not afflict them, but unchanged in legs and arms
    they delighted in feasting apart from all evils.   *(115)*
    They died as if overcome by sleep. They had all
    good things. Of its own accord the fertile land
    bore fruit bounteous and in plenty. They lived off their fields
    as they pleased, in peace, with many good things . . . [8]
    But since the earth covered this race,   *(121)*
    through the counsels of Zeus they are noble
    spirits dwelling on earth, protectors of mortal humans . . .
    givers of wealth; indeed they got this royal privilege.   *(126)*
    Afterwards, those who dwell on Olympus created
    a second race, of silver, one much worse,
    and resembling the golden race in neither body nor thought.
    A child was brought up by its dear mother for a hundred years,   *(130)*
    a complete baby, playing in its house.
    But when they grew up and reached the measure of their age,
    they lived for only a brief time, suffering pains
    through their folly. For they could not keep from treating
       each other
    with violence and outrage and were unwilling to worship   *(135)*
    the immortals or to perform sacrifices at the holy altars of
       the blessed ones,
    which local custom declares right for humans to do. Then Zeus,
    the son of Kronos, put them away in anger because they
       would not pay
    honors to the blessed gods who dwell on Olympus.
    But when the earth had covered this race too,   *(140)*
    the second one, they are called blessed mortals beneath the earth

---

8. I omit lines 120, 124–25, whose authenticity is doubtful.

and honor attends these too nevertheless.
Father Zeus created out of ash trees yet a third,
bronze, race of humans endowed with speech, wholly
   different from the silver race,
terrible and mighty. They devoted themselves   *(145)*
to the grievous works of Ares and to violence. They did not eat
grain, but had a powerful spirit of adamant;
crude people. Their might was great and invincible arms
grew from their shoulders on their stout limbs.
Their armor was bronze, their houses were bronze,   *(150)*
and they worked with bronze tools. There was no dark iron.
And overcome by their own hands,
nameless, they went to the dank house of cold Hades.
Black death took them even though they were
terrible, and they left the shining light of the sun.   *(155)*
But when earth had covered this race too,
Zeus, the son of Kronos, created yet a fourth one
upon the fertile earth, one more just and good,
the divine race of heroic men who are called
demigods, the race before the present one upon
   the boundless earth.   *(160)*
Evil war and dread battle destroyed
some of them fighting for the flocks of Oedipus
at seven-gated Thebes, the land of Cadmus.
Others it killed after bringing them in ships over the great gulf
of the sea to Troy for the sake of fair-haired Helen.   *(165)*
There the end of death covered some,
while father Zeus, the son of Kronos, established others
at the ends of the earth and bestowed on them life and a
   place to live apart from humans.   *(168)*
And they dwell with carefree hearts   *(170)*
in the Islands of the Blest near deep-swirling Ocean,
blessed heroes, for whom the fertile land
bears honey-sweet fruit flourishing three times a year,   *(173)*
far from the immortals, and Kronos rules over them . . .   *(169a)*
Then Zeus made another race of humans endowed with
   speech, who now are upon the earth.   *(169b)*
I wish I were not among the men of the fifth generation,   *(174)*
but either had died earlier or were born afterwards.   *(175)*
For now it is a race of iron. Never will they
cease being worn down by distress and sorrow
day and night. The gods will give them harsh troubles.
But even so, these too will have good things mixed with their evils.
(Hesiod, *Works and Days* lines 109–19, 121–23, 126–79 [not in DK])

In this picture of overall decline, the race of heroes between those of bronze and iron is exceptional. This anomaly suggests that the account is based on different traditions about human history. Hesiod adapts the myth of the metallic races to accommodate the tradition of the godlike heroes of Troy and Thebes, too important to omit. Faced by a problem comparable to a theory that fails to fit obvious facts, he refuses to settle for a simple, uniform pattern conflicting with important data.

In Hesiod's account the races are all created by the gods, but their ends come about variously. The Golden Race just died out. The Bronze Race destroyed itself in war. The fate of the Heroic Race was as the mythological tradition required. Zeus destroyed the Silver Race for refusing to worship the gods, and he will destroy the Iron Race because of its moral degeneracy.

2.6   Zeus will destroy this race too of humans endowed with speech,   (*180*)
    when they come to have gray hair at birth.
    A father will not be like his children nor will they be at all like him,
    nor will a guest be friendly to his host
    or comrade with comrade or brother with brother as before.
    They will quickly come to dishonor their parents
        as they grow old,   (*185*)
    and will find fault with them, speaking with bitter words,
    abominable people and ignorant of the gods' vengeance . . .
    There will be no thanks for one who keeps his oath or is just   (*190*)
    or good, but men will rather praise the evildoers
    and violence. Justice and reverence will be based
    in strength. The evil person will harm the better man,
    addressing him with crooked words, and he will swear an
        oath upon them.
    Ugly-mouthed envy, with a hateful look, delighting in evil,   (*195*)
    will accompany all miserable men.
    Then Aidōs [Reverence] and Nemesis [Righteous Indignation],
        their fair skin
    covered with white robes, will abandon humanity
    and go to Olympus from the broad-roaded earth, to be
    among the tribe of immortals. Bitter greed will be left   (*200*)
    for mortal humans, and there will be no defense from evil.
        (Hesiod, *Works and Days* lines 180–87, 190–201 [not in DK])

Viewed broadly, Hesiod's poems present a history of the world from its origins to the present, and forecast its future. The present world order is governed by the Olympian gods under Zeus, the most powerful and potentially ruthless. As the champion of order and justice, he firmly enforces a system of values in the universe, however far the ideal of a justice which punishes an entire city for the transgressions of a single individual may be from our own notion of justice.

The traditional mythological picture did not encourage speculation about nature without reference to the gods. Many events are due to the gods—not only episodes of myth, but ordinary everyday occurrences. Rain is the doing of Zeus the sky-god. When crops grow or fail to grow, Demeter is responsible.

In a sense, this account of events posits unvarying relations between them and their divine causes, but the gods' willfulness and inconstancy tend to undermine attempts to understand or control events that affect us. Interest will focus more on individual events and the gods responsible for them than on general regularities, relationships, and laws.

This attitude underlies even the parts of *Works and Days* in which Hesiod gives practical advice. He advocates work as the key to success,[9] but is keenly aware of obstacles to the generalization that hard work ensures success. First, injustice (one's own or that of one's fellow citizens) may be punished by famine and plague, regardless of how hard one works (**2.4**). Second, the gods' inconsistency means that sometimes the sluggish will be as successful as the hard worker.[10] Not hard work but Demeter fills one's barn with food.[11] Even when work brings wealth it is because the gods favor those who work, and when idleness brings poverty it is because the gods are angry at the idle.[12] The favoritism of the Olympians is present here even where we would look for regularities and explanations of a mundane sort.

Hesiod's world ruled by the Olympians has limited potential as a well-ordered *kosmos* governed by intelligible principles. Even if the possibilities of chaotic disorder are tempered by Zeus's overall commitment to rule and justice, Hesiod is far from achieving a complete and consistent account of how chaos is avoided. On the other hand, his view of the world as a *kosmos* would remain an essential part of Greek philosophical thought along with his goal of producing a coherent unified understanding of the structure, origins, and operations of the *kosmos*. His practice of employing different sources of information and using one to correct or supplement another was also important in later philosophical and scientific method. There is even a kind of critical stance toward sources in the Muses' address to Hesiod:

> **2.7**   We know enough to make up lies that are convincing,
> but we also have the skill, when we've a mind, to speak the truth.
> (Hesiod, *Theogony* lines 27–28 [not in DK])

The philosophers of sixth century Miletus managed to take the decisive steps of abandoning mythological ways of thought and rejecting traditional ways of looking at the world. To them we will turn, after a short discussion of the conditions in Miletus in the early sixth century which may have contributed to this decisive revolution in thought.

---

9. Hesiod's chief concern is the farmer's life, where success is measured mainly by the extent and quality of one's fields and flocks, the bounty of the harvest, and the possession of the qualities in oneself and one's family that help attain these material goals.

10. *Works and Days* lines 479–90 (not in DK).

11. *Works and Days* lines 298–301 (not in DK).

12. *Works and Days* lines 302–9 (not in DK).

3

Miletus in the Sixth Century: The Cultural
Setting for the Beginnings of Philosophy

Western philosophy and science trace their beginnings to the Ionian Greek city of Miletus, on the Aegean coast of Asia Minor, in the early years of the sixth century BCE. Thales of Miletus, whom Aristotle calls "the founder of this kind of philosophy,"[1] reputedly predicted the eclipse of the sun which occurred May 28, 585, and his fellow countrymen Anaximander and Anaximenes maintained an apparently unbroken tradition until the late sixth or early fifth century. The distinctive Milesian approach was also pursued in the sixth and fifth centuries by philosophers who, although not from Miletus, tended to have Ionian connections, notably Anaxagoras and Democritus. (Ionia is the district comprising the central part of the west coast of Asia Minor.) The questions these men posed and their answers are more the subject matter of science than of philosophy as we think of those fields, but their speculation prompted others to raise what we recognize as philosophical issues, and their intellectual attitudes and methods were adopted by the thinkers who pursued those issues philosophically.

Miletus and numerous other Greek cities in the Aegean islands and on the west coast of Asia Minor were established around 1000 BCE after the collapse of the Bronze Age culture of the Greek mainland known as Mycenaean civilization. From the eighth century the Greeks both from the homeland and from these newer settlements came into contact with other peoples and founded colonies, either to establish permanent trading posts or to shed excess population. These colonies were established around the coast of the Black Sea, in Southern Italy and Sicily, and elsewhere on the Mediterranean seaboard. The founder of many colonies, Miletus developed into a prominent and wealthy community active in shipping, trade, and industry, and enjoying commercial relations with other Greek cities from the Black Sea to Sicily and with non-Greek civilizations, notably Egypt, Mesopotamia, and the Lydian people of inland Asia Minor.

Miletus was a *polis* (plural *poleis*), a city-state, neither a country nor a nation in any modern sense. Greece existed neither as a political entity nor even as a concept until long after our period. The Milesians shared with other Greeks the Greek language, a social structure, and a cultural heritage that can loosely be called Homeric, in the sense that they accepted the oral epics which we know as the *Iliad* and *Odyssey* as their own tradition and recognized the Olympian gods. Much of the cultural life and all of the political life of a *polis* was under its own control.

The society of Miletus was aristocratic and secular. Unlike the older and more culturally prestigious civilizations of Egypt and Mesopotamia, the Greeks tended

---

1. See **4.8**.

to keep their religious institutions separate from administrative and military matters. There were state religious cults and practices, but much religious activity took place at the level of the family or other social groups within or transcending the *polis*. Moreover, unlike the older civilizations, the Greeks did not have sacred texts or an official class of hereditary, professional priests, much less an Egyptian-style divine monarch. Religious practices varied from place to place and from individual to individual. Even if the Homeric epics were the common property of all Greeks, the stories they told of the gods did not amount to dogma in which everyone was expected or compelled to believe. To this extent the claim that Homer was the Bible of the Greeks is wrong. In fact, possibly in Homer himself and certainly in Hesiod, Homer's approximate contemporary, we find a speculative attitude toward the gods which tends in the opposite direction from dogma.

The spread of political authority to an aristocratic class required a measure of cooperation and discussion. Written law codes, too, introduced in this period, called for reasoned argument. Cases at law would in principle be won or lost according as the facts of the case were established and shown by argument to conform or conflict with the laws. In principle, decisions would not be made on arbitrary or personal grounds, but according to rational criteria. How far these principles were carried out in practice is another question. Still, the existence of the principles as principles will have exerted some pressure in actual cases and made available an ideal or standard which could be applied elsewhere.

Contact with Egypt and Mesopotamia had powerful effects seen clearly in the "orientalizing" art of the eighth and seventh centuries and in some of the ideas and discoveries attributed to the Milesian philosophers. Some early Greek philosophers are reported to have learned from sages of the East—evidence that the Greeks of the period were open to ideas from foreigners, although they never simply copied, but adapted foreign elements and made them their own. This adaptive borrowing may even have played a decisive role in the rise of Greek science and philosophy.

Why the kind of inquiry that led to philosophy and science started in early sixth century Miletus is likely to remain without a definitive answer. Several factors were doubtless relevant: the relative freedom of thought (including speculative thought) and expression possible in the absence of a monolithic centralized religion and political administration; a sufficient accumulation of wealth to provide to some the leisure for speculative thought; the fact that literacy was not restricted to a certain caste of the population and to bureaucratic purposes; the beginnings of the practice of reaching decisions through discussion (whether public debate or in discussions among closed groups of aristocrats) conducted according to rational principles; contact with several other cultures and openness to foreign ideas. Recently the advent of coinage has been proposed as an important influence.[2]

---

2. Seaford (2004, Chs. 9–13).

Since these social, economic, and political circumstances were found equally in other Greek cities, they are insufficient by themselves to account for the origin of philosophy and science in Miletus. Nor does Aristotle's opinion—that people are in a position to study philosophy only when their practical needs are taken care of and in addition they have leisure time available for speculation[3]—point to Miletus alone among Greek cities as the starting place of theoretical thought. In the present case, the decisive reason for the beginning of philosophy and science is that individuals with the intellectual interests and vigor of Thales, Anaximander, and Anaximenes were born and nurtured in Miletus under conditions that allowed their genius to be expressed in certain ways.

---

3. Aristotle, *Metaphysics* 1.1 981b13–25 (not in DK).

4

Thales of Miletus

Thales of Miletus, famed as the originator of Greek philosophy and science, lived in the first part of the sixth century, as is shown by the stories of his prediction of the solar eclipse of 585 BCE. Thales is a figure of legendary wisdom in many fields, from engineering to politics, from applied economics to science. He was known as the founder of Greek mathematics and astronomy as well as of philosophy. He was also reputed as a sage, a kind of combination of Solomon and Benjamin Franklin who authored short sayings of practical advice. ("The man's a Thales!" exclaims a character in one of Aristophanes' comedies[1] written a century and a half after Thales lived.) He is unique among the early philosophers in being associated with so wide a range of activities. In fact, many scholars doubt that Thales actually was responsible for so many deeds and discoveries, and for good reason, as we will see. But how far can skepticism reasonably go? There are three general approaches to interpreting Thales: the credulous, the skeptical, and the historically tempered. On the first, Thales is a genius who actually accomplished all that antiquity reports. On the second, he is truly a man of legend: a historical person to whom various exploits and accomplishments (some of them genuine, but achieved by others) have been falsely attributed. On the third, he is a gifted but historically plausible person whose actual accomplishments were transformed by tradition into works of genius. Which of these approaches (or what combination of them) we decide is correct has crucial importance for our understanding of the beginning of Greek philosophy. I shall return to this issue at the end of the chapter and also in Chapter 8. But first I will present Thales' achievements as they are reported and some of the interpretations they have received.

In an oft-told story,[2] King Croesus of Lydia asked Thales for help in transporting his army across the river Halys, and Thales made it passable by diverting its course upstream from the army's position, so that some or all the water flowed behind the camp, rejoining the original riverbed downstream. Here we have a practical Thales involved in engineering projects, whose reputation was so great that foreign monarchs consulted him. However, the military expedition in question, Croesus's attack on the Persian army, took place almost forty years after the eclipse, a date that seems to some impossibly (or improbably) late for Thales' active participation. (We do not know when he was born or died.) He is said to have advised the Ionian cities of Asia Minor to form a political union with a centrally located common governing council,[3] advice which if taken might have

---

1. Aristophanes, *Birds* line 1009 (not in DK).

2. The earliest source is Herodotus, *Histories* 1.75 = DK 11A6. Other sources are cited as well at DK 11A6.

3. Herodotus, *Histories* 1.170 = DK 11A4.

made the Ionian cities better able to resist Persian expansion. However, this story is rendered historically implausible by the same considerations, namely the time when the Persians were threatening the Ionian Greeks seems too late to have occurred in the period of Thales' activity.

Further, he has a reputation as a sage. Later ages assembled a list of the Seven Sages, like the Seven Wonders of the World, and various deeds and pieces of proverbial wisdom are assigned to them. They are all historical personages who lived in the sixth century. Thales is the only Presocratic named among the Seven Sages,[4] a clear indication of his fame as a wise man in later generations. One author credits a number of sayings to each of the Seven, including the following, which he ascribes to Thales.

4.1 Remember friends both present and absent. Don't beautify your face, but be beautiful in what you do. Don't acquire wealth immorally. Don't hesitate to flatter your parents. Don't take your father's bad points. However many feasts you hold in honor of your parents, your children will hold for you. It is difficult to know oneself. The sweetest thing is to get what you desire. Laziness is incurable. Incontinence is harmful. Lack of education is a burden. Teach and learn what is better. Don't be late, even if you are wealthy. Keep evil things hidden at home. It is better to be envied than pitied. Be moderate. Don't believe everyone.

(Demetrius of Phaleron, *Sayings of the Seven Sages*,
quoted in Stobaeus, 3.1.172 = DK 10, 3)

However, it would be a mistake to accept these alleged quotations at face value. The content of the sayings reveals a good deal about traditional attitudes and beliefs, but most people agree that these maxims were well known and were assigned to the Seven Sages by later compilers for want of more information about their authors.

As the earliest subject of both an "absent-minded professor" story and a defense of philosophy against charges of uselessness, Thales is emblematic of the different responses philosophy provoked in its cultural setting.

4.2 They say that once when Thales was gazing upwards while doing astronomy, he fell into a well, and that a witty and charming Thracian serving-girl made fun of him for being eager to know the things in the heavens but failing to notice what was just behind him and right by his feet.

(Plato, *Theaetetus* 174a = DK 11A9)

4.3 The story goes that when they were reproaching him for his poverty, supposing that philosophy is useless, he learned from his astronomy that the olive crop would be large. Then, while it was still winter, he obtained a little

---

4. The earliest reference to the Seven Sages includes Thales among their number. It is found in Plato, *Protagoras* 343a = DK 10,2.

money and made deposits on all the olive presses both in Miletus and in Chios, and since no one bid against him, he rented them cheaply. When the time came, suddenly many requested the presses all at once, and he rented them out on whatever terms he wished, and so he made a great deal of money. In this way he proved that philosophers can easily be wealthy if they wish, but this is not what they are interested in.

(Aristotle, *Politics* 1.11 1259a9–18 = DK 11A10)

Astronomy

These no doubt fictitious stories portray Thales as an astronomer, which chimes with his prediction of the eclipse. But here we run across the central problem in understanding Thales. Did he really found Western science and philosophy? Or did he simply parrot the theories and discoveries of others? Or is the story a total fabrication? First, what did his prediction actually say? We do not have his words; the earliest report is given by the fifth-century historian Herodotus. In recounting a war between the Medes and the Lydians he says:

4.4 As they were having equal success in the war, it happened that in the sixth year, when a battle was being fought, the day suddenly became night. Thales of Miletus had foretold to the Ionians that this loss of daylight would occur, setting as a limit the very year in which the event occurred.

(Herodotus, *Histories* 1.74 = DK 11A5)

Two things should be noticed in Herodotus's account. Thales predicted the year of the eclipse, not the date or time of day, and he is not said to have predicted that the eclipse would be visible at any specific place. If Herodotus is an accurate guide, Thales' prediction, if it existed, did not resemble modern ones, which specify not just the year but the day and the path of the eclipse and the time of partial and total eclipse at different places along its path. Modern predictions require much precise knowledge that was not available until much later (for example, the elliptical orbits of earth and moon were determined in the 17th century), and although some needed facts, such as the sphericity of the earth, were known in later antiquity, there is no reason to suppose that Thales knew them.[5] It is clear that Thales could not have predicted the eclipse in the same way that astronomers do today.

But this does not necessarily mean that he did not predict the eclipse in some other way. An attractive alternative is that he based his prediction on Babylonian astronomy. Here the idea is that if solar eclipses are recorded over a sufficiently long time—longer than a single person's lifetime—patterns of their

---

5. The evidence for this assertion is the astronomy of Thales' immediate successors, which does not recognize a spherical earth and which was in other ways grossly unsuited to making accurate predictions of celestial phenomena.

occurrences emerge which can be used to make rough predictions even without modern astronomical knowledge. The Babylonians, keenly interested in eclipses and other astronomical phenomena for astrological and religious purposes, kept meticulous records from the mid-eighth century and so had a data base sufficient for such limited predictions. Thales is said to have traveled to Egypt, and given Miletus's international connections he may have visited Babylon too. Alternatively, people versed in Babylonian astronomy may have visited Miletus. In these circumstances, Thales may have learned to make predictions himself or may merely have reported a Babylonian prediction. But this approach is doomed as well. Babylonian astronomy was never capable of predicting when an eclipse would occur at a specific location. Eventually it could say when an eclipse might occur (which is a matter of predicting when the moon is in the same place in the sky as the sun[6]) but the determination of whether it would occur in a particular place was not achieved prior to Ptolemy's *Almagest* (c.150 CE).

On the other hand, there is some more concrete evidence that Thales was interested in eclipses.

> **4.5**   Thales said that the sun suffers eclipse when the moon comes to be in front
> of it, the day in which the moon produces the eclipse being marked by its
> concealment.
>
> (P.Oxy. 53.3710, col. 2, 37–40 [not in DK])

This information is taken from a quotation of Aristarchus (third century BCE) in a commentary on Homer's *Odyssey*.[7] According to this text, Thales knew the cause of solar eclipses: that the moon is between the sun and the earth and so blocks the sun's light. But this knowledge does not amount to a method of predicting eclipses. Since the concealment referred to is most likely to be not the concealment of the sun (namely, the eclipse) but that of the moon, Aristarchus is asserting that Thales knew that eclipses occur at new moon (the phase when the moon is invisible), which is the period when its celestial longitude is very near to that of the sun. This is not improbable. A person interested in solar and lunar phenomena, including the apparent motion of the moon relative to the sun, and who observed one or more solar eclipses could be expected to note that the eclipse took place at new moon. From here it would be but a small step to the conclusion that eclipses always take place at this phase of the moon's cycle—in other words, that a necessary condition for a solar eclipse is that it occur at new moon—and it would be a larger but not unimaginably larger step to the conclusion that the position of the moon in the sky during an eclipse coincides with

------

6. That is, when the celestial longitude and latitude of the moon and sun are identical, which occurs when the moon and sun are in conjunction (have the same longitude) at a lunar node (when the moon is at the ecliptic). See Aaboe (1972).

7. This text is discussed in Bowen and Goldstein (1994).

that of the sun. From here it would be natural to infer the correct account of solar eclipses as due to the moon's interposition between the earth and the sun. I see no reason against thinking that Thales could have gone so far (although I am cautious about asserting that he actually did), but I remain skeptical about the possibility of his being able to predict when an eclipse will actually occur.[8]

In any case it is likely that Thales had an interest in astronomical phenomena. In addition to the eclipse, he is plausibly said to have investigated the solstices and equinoxes, the seasons of the year, and the number of days in the year and month. These phenomena have to do with the sun and moon, and their investigation requires careful and sustained observations but nothing that could not have been done at any time by a person interested in understanding the phenomena in question.[9]

Mathematics

In his *History of Geometry*, Aristotle's follower Eudemus reports that Thales introduced geometry to Greece from Egypt, made discoveries of his own, and transmitted to posterity the principles of many theorems, "attacking some more generally and others more perceptually."[10] Among other achievements[11] he is credited with the theorem that triangles with one side and the two adjacent angles equal are congruent, for "he must have used this theorem to show the distance of ships at sea in the way he did."[12] This statement gives a clue to how later historians of geometry approached their subject, and also leads us once more to question Thales' originality.

Greek geometry, as canonized in Euclid's *Elements* (c.300 BCE), proceeds by proofs based on definitions and other unproved principles. It deals more with general theorems than with specific problems and is not primarily devoted to calculations. In these respects it differs from earlier mathematics, including Egyptian geometry. Ancient historians of mathematics from Eudemus on assumed that Greek geometry had this distinctive character from the start and that it developed cumulatively, with successive mathematicians contributing proofs of new theorems or organizing existing knowledge into a comprehensive system of proofs. Accordingly, they said that Thales, the founder of Greek mathematics, passed on the principles of many theorems to posterity, and they sought to attribute particular theorems to him. Recent historians of Greek mathematics reject this approach.

---

8. For a more optimistic account of Thales as eclipse-predictor, see Panchenko (1994).

9. For further discussion, see White (2008).

10. Eudemus, cited in Proclus, *Commentary on the First Book of Euclid's* Elements 65.7–11 = DK 11A11.

11. He is also said to have "demonstrated" that a circle is bisected by its diameter, that the base angles of an isosceles triangle are equal, and that if two straight lines intersect, the vertical angles are equal (ibid., 157.10, 250.20, 299.1 = DK 11A20).

12. Ibid., 352.14–18 = DK 11A20.

The notion of proving results is unlikely to have sprung full grown from the head of the first Greek geometer like Athena from the head of Zeus, but more probably developed over an extended period of time, perhaps influenced by the use of proofs in philosophy, which are not found before Parmenides.[13]

The mention of Thales' use of the angle–side–angle congruence theorem to show the distance of ships at sea indicates the following method or something equivalent to it. From two points on the shore (*A*, *B*) determine the angles between shore and ship (*a*, *b*). Construct equal angles on the shoreward side of those points and continue the lines until they intersect (*C*). The distance from *C* to the line between *A* and *B* will be equal to the distance from that line to the ship.

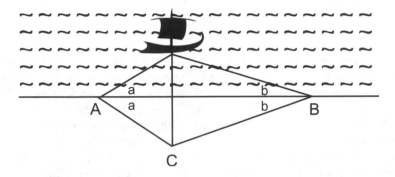

This application of geometry does presuppose knowing certain properties of triangles, but contrary to Eudemus's inferences it implies nothing about Thales' inventing a proof of the angle–side–angle theorem or of his having a concept of proof. It does not even make it certain that he stated the theorem generally or that he had the technical vocabulary ("angle," "congruent") to do so.

Eudemus's vague assertion that Thales attacked some theorems "more generally and others more perceptually" may give insight into the nature of Thales' "proofs." His proof that a circle is bisected by its diameter,[14] perhaps involved folding or cutting a drawn circle and showing that the two pieces match. Such an argument might be called perceptual. Nowadays this kind of procedure would not count as a legitimate proof, and even by Euclid's day it had fallen out of favor. But it does contain the germ of the idea of mathematical proof (showing one fact to follow from others and seeing that the result applies generally to all circles and their diameters, not just to the one used in the actual proof) and constitutes a decisive step away from the practical and empirical mathematics of the Egyptians.

On the other hand, skeptics argue, if we are dubious about the claims that Thales discovered these theorems, we should be equally dubious about the proof

13. Parmenides is the subject of Ch. 11.

14. Eudemus, cited in Proclus, *Commentary on the First Book of Euclid's* Elements 157.10–11 = DK 11A20.

he is said to have found. It would be simple enough for someone at a later date who wanted to attribute some specific mathematical discoveries to Thales to have credited him with a few simple theorems that anyone with a little geometry would know and to have credited him with a simple and primitive sounding proof for one of them. Thales' claim to be the founder of Greek mathematics is as uncertain as his credentials as the first Greek astronomer.

So far Thales is an ambiguous figure. He may have made original scientific discoveries (inventing the notion of proof would make him one of the most important figures in the entire history of human thought); he may have simply imported the scientific knowledge of other peoples; and he may have done nothing at all in these areas. His speculations about water, however, belong to quite a different area of endeavor.

Water

Aristotle's survey of some of the opinions of his philosophical forebears contains the most important testimonium about Thales, which I divide into several sections.

> **4.6** Causes are spoken of in four ways, of which . . . one is matter. . . . Let us take as associates in our task our predecessors who considered the things that are and philosophized about the truth, for it is clear that they too speak of certain principles and causes, and so it will be useful to our present inquiry to survey them: either we will find some other kind of cause or we will be more confident about the ones now being discussed.
>
> (Aristotle, *Metaphysics* 1.3 983a26–b6 [not in DK])

Aristotle's purposes are clear. He does not aim to discuss the complete theories of former philosophers sympathetically and in context; he wants only to see if they contain anything relevant to his own philosophical project of identifying different types of causes. His starting points are his own notion of "cause" and his view that there are precisely four kinds of causes, and despite his assertion in the final sentence, he proves reluctant to acknowledge additional kinds, let alone to admit any radically different approach to the subject of causes. He continues with a strongly Aristotelian account of what a "material cause" is.

> **4.7** Of those who first pursued philosophy, the majority believed that the only principles of all things are principles in the form of matter. For that of which all existing things are composed and that from which they originally come to be and that into which they finally perish—the substance persisting but changing in its attributes—this they state is the element and principle of the things that are. . . . For there must be one or more natures from which the rest come to be, while it is preserved.
>
> (Aristotle, *Metaphysics* 1.3 983b6–18 = DK 11A12)

This notion of underlying matter was Aristotle's invention. Even though earlier thinkers regarded one or more kinds of things as somehow primary, Aristotle is anachronistic in assuming that their notions of primacy coincided with his (in particular with his developed notion of "substance"), or even that their theories addressed the problems that engaged him. He goes on to mention Thales.

> 4.8   However, they do not all agree about how many or what kinds of such prin-
> ciples there are, but Thales, the founder of this kind of philosophy, stated it
> to be water. (This is why he declared that the earth rests on water.) He may
> have got this idea from seeing that the nourishment of all things is moist,
> and that even the hot itself comes to be from this and lives on this (the
> principle of all things is that from which they come to be)—getting this idea
> from this consideration and also because the seeds of all things have a moist
> nature; and water is the principle of the nature of moist things.
>
> > (Aristotle, *Metaphysics* 1.3 983b18–27 = DK
> > 11A12) (continuation of 4.7)

This passage tells us three things. (a) Thales says the earth floats on water, (b) Aristotle interprets Thales as declaring that water is the "material cause" as defined in 4.7, and (c) Aristotle has to guess Thales' reasons for giving primacy to water. If Aristotle infers (b) from (a), we must question Thales' originality again. For in discussing another passage which attributes (a) to Thales, Simplicius remarks:

> 4.9   Aristotle speaks quite strongly against this view, which was prevalent per-
> haps because the Egyptians recounted it in mythological form and Thales
> may have imported the doctrine from there.
>
> > (Simplicius, *Commentary on Aristotle's* On the
> > Heavens 522.16–18 = DK 11A14)

Again, we may have borrowing from Egypt; this time the borrowing is not of science but of myth. Aristotle himself is aware of Greeks who advanced mythical ways of thought, but makes it clear that Thales was not one of them.

> 4.10   Some believe that the people of remote antiquity, long before the present
> generation, who were the first to speculate about the gods, had this idea
> about nature too. For they made Ocean and Tethys parents of coming to be
> and made water, which the poets called Styx, the oath by which the gods
> swore. For the most ancient is the most honored, and the most honored
> thing is what is used to swear by.
>
> > (Aristotle, *Metaphysics* 1.3 983b27–33 = DK
> > 11A12) (continuation of 4.8)

For Aristotle, Thales is a philosopher, not a speculator about the gods, and I think that this is one interpretation that we are bound to accept. Thales was said to have contributed to many areas of thought, but mythology is not one of them.

Thales' claim that the earth rests on water may have been intended to explain natural phenomena. One source tells us that Thales held that the motion of this subterranean water was the cause of earthquakes.[15] If this was his view, Thales made a decisive break with the traditional belief that earthquakes are caused by Poseidon.[16] Moreover, in hypothesizing an unobserved natural state of affairs (no one had seen the earth resting on water) to explain an observed phenomenon, Thales made an intellectual move which has remained a principal part of scientific thinking to this day.

It is unlikely that Thales wrote down his views on water as a cosmological principle. If Aristotle had any such book he would not have been so vague and so quickly driven to guesswork. Still, he regards Thales as the founder of his own philosophical and scientific tradition, not just an importer of foreign ideas or a teller of myths like Homer and Hesiod (who are behind the reference to Ocean and Tethys in **4.10**). Even if Thales' ideas stem from mythology, at the very least he demythologizes them, and this is a crucial move for philosophy and science. How, then, did he present the demythologized ideas? There are two main lines of interpretation.

First, the traditional view, which follows Aristotle, is that for Thales in some way all things are water; they are made or composed of water. Thus, Thales' main question is "What are all things made of?" and as far as we know he was the first to ask this question, and his answer is of the same type as those given by later Presocratics and by physicists up to the present day.

The idea that everything is water is open to a number of objections which not only seem obvious to us, but which Thales' immediate successors avoid in their theories—objections such as, "If everything is composed of water, how can there be different kinds of things in the world, some of them, such as fire, seemingly opposed to water?" and "Even if (as Aristotle indicates) water is necessary for the origin and maintenance of other things, why should we think that water is their only constituent?" It is unclear what if any response Thales would make to these criticisms. But in this period it is not surprising if theories are open to obvious objections, and the mere fact that there are decisive reasons to reject a theory is no reason at all to think it was not actually held.

On the second interpretation, towards which I incline and which is actually better supported than the first by Aristotle's discussion in **4.8**, Thales' principal question is, "What is the origin of all things?"[17] In identifying water as the origin he harks back to Greek and Near Eastern mythological accounts of the origin of the earth, with which his assertion that the earth floats on water fits nicely. On this view, Thales' interests are somewhat different from those of his successors, although many of them were concerned with the origin

---

15. Seneca, *Natural Questions* 3.14 = DK 11A15.

16. Since Poseidon was also the god of the sea, it is possible that by attributing earthquakes to the movement of water, Thales was offering a naturalistic account of phenomena that eliminated the need to refer to this Olympian god at all.

17. The key word, *arkhē* can mean "origin" and "beginning" as well as "principle."

of the world as well as its physical constitution. Thales' question stems from the past, but his answer, grounded in the nature of the world around us rather than in the family history of the gods, rejected tradition and provided a starting point for his successors.

Souls and Gods

Aristotle reports that Thales believed magnets possess soul because they move iron, and infers that he judged the soul to be a thing that causes motion.[18] Thales also held that amber (which has magnetic properties when rubbed or heated) possesses soul.[19]

It is hard to know what to make of these statements. The idea that the soul is the principle of life was widespread in Greek thought. The presence of soul makes a thing alive; when a living thing dies, it no longer has a soul. Thus, Aristotle held that plants and animals possess souls. He held further that motion is characteristic of life, especially in his broad sense of "motion," which includes growth and changes in quality—"motions" which even plants possess. Thus, the presence of soul, and therefore of life, implies motion.

Thales attributes soul to things not normally thought to be alive. Is he proposing a version of hylozoism, the view that matter has life, so that life is found in all things whatever? Also, since magnets and amber cause other things to move, is Thales' point that the notion of soul should be extended to include things that themselves are motionless but make other things move? Or instead of moving in these exciting new directions does he just want to reinforce (in a nonmythological context) a pre-philosophical animistic conception that many parts of what we regard as inanimate nature are actually alive?

The following passage may help resolve these questions.

4.11   Some declare that it [the soul] is mixed in the whole [the universe], and this
        may be why Thales thought all things are full of gods.
                                    (Aristotle, *On the Soul* 1.5 411a7–8 = DK 11A22)

Here Aristotle says that Thales believes all things are full of gods and suggests, without asserting confidently, that he believes soul pervades the whole world and that these two ideas are related. If the link between souls and gods is valid (an assumption which is possible, though not certain), Thales' most important surviving doctrines can be connected as follows, though the interpretation is speculative and the elements of Thales' thought it pulls together may have been separate.

---

18. Aristotle, *On the Soul* 1.2 405a19 = DK 11A22.
19. Diogenes Laertius, *Lives of the Philosophers* 1.24 = DK 11A1.

Water is primary since it is prominent in the physical makeup of the world (occurring not only on the earth but also above it in the form of rain and below it as the water on which the earth floats), and it is needed for the generation and maintenance of living things and of some apparently nonliving things. Thales conceives of water not as a chemically pure substance but as moisture quite generally—in the sea, in rain, in sperm. Water's unceasing mobility, seen especially in the continuous movement of the sea, rivers, and rain, reveals it to be living and so possessing a soul. Since everything is made of water or ultimately arises from water, the life-force of water pervades the whole world, showing up in some things more than others (just as some things are wetter than others). Moreover, as a living thing with no beginning in time (everything else owes its beginning to *it*) and apparently no end in time either, water is divine (since for the Greeks the primary characteristics of the divine are immortality and power independent of human will). Hence all things, being composed of or arising from water, are full of the divine. (This is not to say that they have any relation to the Olympian gods; in fact, the claim that all things are full of gods is to be understood in the context of Thales' demythologized world view.)

Thales is a threshold figure, standing at the beginning of the Western scientific and philosophical tradition, but strongly influenced by the past. Of the little we know about him, much fits both the picture of Thales as the brilliant innovator and also that of Thales as the importer of others' ideas. While skepticism is appropriate, it must be kept within bounds, and few would be so skeptical as to say that Thales did nothing (although some not unreasonably say that we cannot be at all sure about what he did); there must be a reason why all those stories were attributed to Thales and not to someone else. But even if we reject his credentials as the first Greek astronomer and geometer, his views on water as the material principle and his apparent rejection of the Olympian gods and traditional Greek mythology are harder to dismiss, and they are what led Aristotle to name him the first philosopher. Although Thales remains a Janus-faced figure, the same cannot be said of Anaximander, the second Milesian philosopher, whose originality and imagination are beyond doubt.

5

Anaximander of Miletus

If Anaximander was sixty-four in 546, as our best source[1] says, he was twenty-five at the time of Thales' eclipse, which agrees with the tradition that he was Thales' successor in investigating nature. His picture of the *kosmos* and his ways of thought can be gleaned from the surviving information on his physical speculations. He may have been the first Greek to write in prose. One fragment of his book survives.

Inventions

Anaximander is credited with important inventions: the gnomon, the celestial sphere, the map. He is also said to have predicted an earthquake. As with Thales, we must be cautious about these claims.

> 5.1 He was the first to discover the gnomon and set one up on the sundials at Sparta . . . indicating the solstices and equinoxes, and he constructed hour markers.
>
> (Diogenes Laertius, *Lives of the Philosophers* 2.1 = DK 12A1)

A gnomon is the raised piece of a sundial whose shadow indicates the sun's position. Most ancient sundials indicated not only the time of day by the direction of the shadow but also the season of the year as a function of the sun's elevation in the sky (higher in summer, lower in winter) marked by the length of the shadow. At the summer and winter solstices the shadow is respectively shortest and longest; on the equinoxes, the sun rises and sets due east and west and the path of the shadow during the course of the day is a straight line. (On other days it traces a curved arc of a hyperbola.) With appropriate markings a sundial will show both time of day and distance from the solstices and equinoxes.

5.1 attributes all this to Anaximander. However, since Herodotus says that the Greeks learned the use of the gnomon and the twelve parts of the day from the Babylonians,[2] Anaximander may have introduced sundials to Greece (without inventing them). On the other hand, some sources[3] credit Thales with determining solstices, which may point to his knowing about the gnomon. The matter is unclear, but I am inclined to suppose that Thales had nothing to do with sundials and that as with other matters he here receives credit for the achievements of others. Also, Anaximander's association with a particular set of sundials in a

---

1. Diogenes Laertius, *Lives of the Philosophers* 2.2 = DK 12A1.

2. Herodotus, *Histories* 2.109 = DK 12A4.

3. Diogenes Laertius, *Lives of the Philosophers* 1.23 = DK 11A1 and Dercyllides, cited in Theon of Smyrna p.198, 16–17 (Hiller) = DK 12A26.

particular city far from Miletus may be based on a visit to Sparta that Anaximander actually made and that was preserved in local Spartan tradition.

Anaximander was called the first Greek map maker: he "was the first to draw the inhabited world on a tablet"[4]—an achievement that could have a basis in knowledge gained from his own travels (we have already seen him in Sparta; he also led an expedition to found a colony on the Black Sea) and also from consultations with merchants and other travelers. His fellow Milesian, Hecataeus, who was active around 500, is also credited with an improved map, which Herodotus ridiculed in the mid-fifth century in a passage that gives us an idea of the design of such early maps.

> 5.2 I laugh when I consider that before now many have drawn maps of the world, but no one has set it out in a reasonable way. They draw Okeanos [the river Ocean] flowing around the earth, which is round as if made by a compass, and they make Asia equal to Europe.
>
> (Herodotus, *Histories* 4.36 [not in DK])

Anaximander is also said to have been the first to construct a sphere,[5] that is, a celestial globe or map of the heavens.

Anaximander is reported to have warned the Spartans of an impending earthquake and to have advised them to abandon the city and sleep in the fields.[6] If there is any truth to the story, the successful prediction was at best based on some lore about the behavior of animals before earthquakes.

So far, the information on Anaximander is no more secure than the testimony on Thales and it is equally easy to dismiss. However, the situation changes decisively when we come to his views on the origin of the world, its structure, and the processes that occur in it.

Physical Theories

The *Apeiron* as *Arkhē*

Anaximander's views on the *arkhē* (starting point, basic principle, originating source) are preserved in three sources, each derived from Theophrastus. I combine them as follows.

> 5.3 Of those who declared that the *arkhē* is one, moving and *apeiron*, Anaximander . . . said that the *apeiron* was the *arkhē* and element of things that are, and he was the first to introduce this name for the *arkhē* [that is, he was

---

4. Agathemerus 1.1 = DK 12A6.

5. Diogenes Laertius, *Lives of the Philosophers* 2.2 = DK 12A1.

6. Cicero, *On Divination* 1.50.112 = DK 12A5a.

the first to call the *arkhē apeiron*].[7] (In addition he said that motion is eternal, in which it occurs that the heavens come to be.[8]) He says that the *arkhē* is neither water nor any of the other things called elements, but some other nature which is *apeiron*, out of which come to be all the heavens and the worlds in them. This is eternal and ageless and surrounds all the worlds.

(Simplicius, *Commentary on Aristotle's* Physics 24. 13–18 = DK12A9; Hippolytus, *Refutation* 1.6.1–2 = DK 12A11; pseudo-Plutarch, *Stromata* 2 = DK 12A10)

According to this account, for Anaximander the *apeiron* is the stuff of which all things are composed. On this influential view, Anaximander's *apeiron* replaces Thales' water as the Aristotelian "material cause" of all things. I have already called this way of interpreting Thales into question; as we will see, for Anaximander it cannot stand. Theophrastus says Anaximander was the first to use the word *apeiron* in this context and that the *apeiron* differs from water, fire, and other familiar materials identified by others as the basic stuff, but he does not describe it except to say that it is eternal, ageless, and in motion, and that a plurality of heavens and worlds arise or are born out of it and are surrounded by it.

The word *apeiron* is a compound of the prefix *a-*, meaning "not" and either the noun *peirar* or *peiras*, "limit, boundary," so that it means "unlimited, boundless, indefinite," or the root *per-*, "through, beyond, forward," so that it means "unable to be got through," "what cannot be traversed from end to end." Either etymology (or both together) are plausible for Anaximander's use of the word. Although in Aristotle it can mean "infinite," in dealing with the Presocratic period it is misleading to understand the word in this relatively technical sense.[9]

Passage 5.3 contains three hints about what *apeiron* means for Anaximander. Since it surrounds the heavens and worlds, it is (1) indefinitely (though not necessarily infinitely) large, spatially unlimited. Since it is eternal and ageless, it is (2) temporally unlimited. Since it is no definite substance like water, it is (3) an indefinite kind of material. All three interpretations have ancient authority. The first two correspond to reasons Aristotle cites for believing that something exists which is *apeiron*,[10] while the third results from an argument for making the original substance *apeiron*, which Aristotle cites and later writers attribute to Anaximander:

---

7. This phrase is also translated "he was the first to introduce this very term of *arkhē*," i.e., the first to use the term "*arkhē*" itself. Simplicius makes this point at *Commentary on Aristotle's* Physics 150.22–25 (not in DK) and he may have meant to make it in the current passage (ibid., 24.13–18) too, but the translation given in the text best suits the Greek of the current passage.

8. This obscure sentence probably means that the heavens come to be in the *apeiron* by means of its eternal movement.

9. In this book, I usually translate *apeiron* as "unlimited," except for passages from Aristotle and later sources (such as 5.4) in which "infinite" is appropriate.

10. Aristotle, *Physics* 3.4 203b23–26, b16–17 (both = DK 12A15).

5.4 The infinite [*apeiron*] body cannot be one and simple, nor can it be as some say it is: that which is apart from the elements, and from which they generate the elements. . . . For some make the infinite [*apeiron*] this [namely, something aside from the elements], rather than air or water, so that the others are not destroyed by the one of them that is infinite. For they contain oppositions with regard to one another, for example, air is cold, water wet, fire hot. If any one of them were infinite, the rest would already have been destroyed. But as it is, they declare that the thing from which all come to be is different.

(Aristotle, *Physics* 3.3 204b22–29 = DK 12A16)

If the Aristotelian ideas (especially the concept of elements and the identification of air, etc. as elements and the use of *apeiron* in the sense of "infinite") are discounted, **5.4** may record Anaximander's own proof that the originative material differs from any definite substance. Water and other familiar materials possess definite properties, yet there is no property that all things have and some properties have opposites: hot and cold, for example. But if everything is made of or arose from water, everything must have the properties of water. Further, since, as Anaximander thinks, opposites conflict with one another, an unlimited amount of a material with definite characteristics would long since have destroyed things with opposite characteristics (even supposing that they existed in the first place), swamping them by the vastly larger quantity of their opposites. Thus Thales is refuted, whether he held that all things are composed of water or that all things have their ultimate origin in water.

This is a powerful argument for an originative substance with no definite characteristics. The *apeiron*, then, is neither water nor fire, neither hot nor cold, nor heavy nor light, nor wet nor dry, nor light nor dark. As the ultimate source of all the things and all the characteristics in the world, it can be none of those things, can have none of those characteristics. This makes it difficult to describe. (Ancient complaints that he failed to specify what kind of material the *apeiron* is are off the mark.[11]) When Anaximander says it is eternal, ageless and in motion and that it surrounds and is the source of everything else, he may be describing it as fully as his language and concepts permitted.

Since it is eternal and in motion, the *apeiron* possesses characteristics which, as we saw in discussing Thales, qualify it as divine.

---

11. Likewise Aristotle's (inconsistent) suggestions that Anaximander considered it a substance intermediate between two of the four Aristotelian elements (e.g., *On Generation and Corruption* 2.5 332a19–23 (not in DK); Aristotle does not name Anaximander, but he is widely thought to have Anaximander in mind) and that it is a mixture of the four elements (*Physics* 1.4 187a20–21 = DK 12A9) are sheer guesswork. Aristotle flounders because Anaximander's *apeiron* simply does not fit well into his system.

5.5   This does not have an *arkhē*, but this seems to be the *arkhē* of the rest, and to contain all things and steer all things,[12] as all declare who do not fashion other causes aside from the infinite . . . and this is the divine. For it is deathless and indestructible, as Anaximander says and most of the natural philosophers.
(Aristotle, *Physics* 3.4 203b10–15 = DK 12A15)

Being divine, immortal, and in motion, it is alive, like Thales' water, and capable of generating a (living) world. What kind of motion does it have? Three answers given by modern scholars are that it has a vortex motion like a whirlpool, in which the heavier parts move to the center and the lighter to the edge; that it has a circular motion; and that its motion is "shaking and sifting as in a sieve."[13] None of these interpretations has substantial support and it is best not to press the question. If the *apeiron* had a definite type of motion, an analogous argument to the one above would apply: how could all the different kinds of motion we observe have arisen out of a primordial substance endowed with only one specific kind of movement? It is best to suppose that Anaximander thought the *apeiron* was in motion because otherwise no change could occur and the world could never have originated, but that he said nothing definite about the nature of the motion.

Cosmogony: The Origin of the World

For Anaximander the existence and the interaction of opposites need to be accounted for. This outlook is intelligible as a reaction to Thales' problem of accounting for the existence of fire, given the priority of water. Anaximander believes that the opposites hot and cold are equally important in the structure and operation of the world and gives them a prominent position in his cosmogony.

5.6   He declares that what arose from the eternal and is productive of [or, "capable of giving birth to"] hot and cold was separated off at the coming to be of this kosmos, and a kind of sphere of flame from this grew around the dark mist[14] about the earth like bark about a tree. When it was broken off and enclosed in certain circles, the sun, moon, and stars came to be.
(pseudo-Plutarch, *Stromata* 2 = DK 12A10) (continuation of **5.11**)

---

12. It is tempting to add "governing" or "steering" all things to the list of the *apeiron*'s attributes given just above, but it is not certain from **5.5** that Aristotle has Anaximander in mind when he uses this word, which he may have taken from other early philosophers, such as Heraclitus (**10.44**), Parmenides (**11.12** line 3), Diogenes of Apollonia (**17.5** sec. 1).

13. Burnet (1930: 61).

14. *aēr*, the Greek word translated here as "dark mist," is discussed below p. 49 n. 3.

Since the *apeiron* is neither hot nor cold, it does not favor either opposite over the other, but how can something neither hot nor cold generate both opposites? Anaximander's solution is to declare that hot and cold arose from something capable of giving birth to hot and cold, and this thing is "separated off" from the *apeiron*. We have no evidence on how he understood "arising" and "giving birth" to occur or the nature of those events, but it is likely that he considered the generation of the *kosmos* to be a kind of birth. Neither hot nor cold will overwhelm the other since they are created at the same time and have equal power.

Other problems arise regarding the thing that generates hot and cold. It arises from the undifferentiated, uniform mass of the *apeiron* through "separating off," a process found elsewhere in Anaximander's system, in which part of an existing thing is isolated so as to take on an identity separate from the original thing, and as such behave differently from the thing from which it arose. But (perhaps because Anaximander said little about these crucial issues) we have no clues about how "separating off" takes place, what the thing is that produces hot and cold, or how it produces them.[15]

5.6 identifies several stages in the formation of the world. First there is the *apeiron*, referred to here as "the eternal." From the *apeiron*, through the process of "separating off," arises something capable of giving birth to hot and cold.[16] The hot and cold which arise from this are described concretely as flame and dark mist. The flame is a spherical shell that tightly encloses the mist "like bark about a tree" (a simile possibly due to Anaximander himself). Since at this stage there are only two things, fire and mist, corresponding to hot and cold, the mention of earth refers to a later stage of differentiation which may occur simultaneously with the breakup of the sphere of flame into circles to make the sun, moon, and stars (see **5.8**).

Anaximander's approach to his fundamental problem, which can be rephrased as "How does the determinate diversity of the world come out of the indeterminate uniformity of the *apeiron*?" is already clear. The *apeiron* appears only at the beginning of the process; afterwards things take their own course. (For possibilities of what happens to the *apeiron* after generating the *kosmos*, see below page 47.) The world's diversity is due not to the intervention of the *apeiron*, let alone to the Olympian gods, but to a small number of processes such as differentiation of one thing into many and "separation off" of one thing from another. The dark mist is differentiated into the air we breathe and the earth we stand on, which was originally moist. Its currently dry state is due to a further process of differentiation.

---

15. The alternate translation in **5.6**, "capable of giving birth," has led some to think that hot and cold were produced through some sort of biological process; but biological processes are inexplicable at this primitive stage of the world. At any rate, the word (which in any case was not Anaximander's) can mean "productive" without any biological overtones.

16. For the status of "hot" and "cold," see below pp. 45–46.

5.7   They[17] claim that at first all the region about the earth is wet. When it is dried
       by the sun, that which evaporated causes winds and turnings of the sun and
       moon, and what remains is the sea. This is why they believe that it is being
       dried and becoming smaller and finally that it will all some day be dry.
                                (Aristotle, *Meteorologica* 2.1 353b6–11 = DK 12A27)

"Separating off" is invoked again to account for the breakup of the sphere of
flame to form the heavenly bodies (**5.8**).

Despite Anaximander's unclarity on some important points, his overall picture is impressive, as is his understanding of the logical requirements of generating a complex world out of a simple originative material.

Cosmology: The Articulation of the World

5.8   The stars come to be as a circle of fire separated off from the fire in the kos-
       mos and enclosed by dark mist. There are vents, certain tube-like passages
       at which the stars appear. For this reason, eclipses occur when the vents are
       blocked. The moon appears sometimes waxing sometimes waning as the
       passages are blocked or opened. The circle of the sun is twenty-seven times
       <that of the earth and> that of the moon <eighteen times>, and the sun is
       highest, and the circles of the fixed stars are lowest.
                                   (Hippolytus, *Refutation of All Heresies* 1.6.4–5
                                            = DK 12A11) (continuation of **5.12**)

5.9   Anaximander says that the sun is equal to the earth, and the circle where it has its
       vent and on which it is carried is twenty-seven times <the size> of the earth.
                                                      (Aëtius 2.21.1 = DK 12A21)

5.10   Anaximander says that the stars are borne by the circles and spheres on
       which each one has mounted.
                                                      (Aëtius 2.16.5 = DK 12A18)

5.11   He says that the earth is cylindrical in shape, and its depth is one-third its
       breadth.
                                         (pseudo-Plutarch, *Stromata* 2 = DK 12A10)

5.12   The earth's shape is curved, round, like a stone column. We walk on one of
       the surfaces and the other one is set opposite.
                                      (Hippolytus, *Refutation of All Heresies* 1.6.3
                                            = DK 12A11) (continuation of **5.13**)

---

17. Aristotle does not give the names of these people. However, the overall picture fits what we know of Anaximander's theory and Theophrastus explicitly says that
Anaximander held this view (in Alexander, *Commentary on Aristotle's Meteorologica*
67.11 = DK 12A27).

There are many interesting points here. First, there is no appearance of mythology or mention of the traditional divinities; eclipses, traditionally held to indicate impending disaster, become mere facts of astronomy. Second, the heavenly bodies are made of fire, a substance familiar from human experience. Third, Anaximander boldly decrees the size of the universe and adopts a terrestrial standard as its measure. Fourth, he assumes that the sizes and distances of the earth and heavenly bodies are related by simple proportions, based on the number 3. Fifth, he assumes that the *kosmos* has a geometrical structure. Sixth, he uses a single mechanism to account for different phenomena (eclipses, phases of the moon).

Anaximander's universe has a simple symmetric structure. At the center is the earth, a cylinder one-third as high as it is broad. We live on one of the flat surfaces. Around the cylinder are rings of fire surrounded by mist, which makes them invisible except where a hole in the mist lets the fire shine through. The stars are closest to the earth, the sun is farthest, with the moon in between. (Anaximander may have reasoned that since fire rises upwards, the purest fire must be furthest from the earth; the sun's brightness and heat are greatest; so the sun is made of the purest fire and so is furthest from the earth. By similar reasoning the feeble light of the stars places them closest.) The sun is the same size as the earth. (Quite possibly he held that the moon has this size too; sun and moon appear roughly the same size in the sky.) Approximately once a day each star is carried around its circular path: either the mist together with the hole moves around the ring of fire, or the mist, hole and fire all rotate together. The diameter of the moon's circle is eighteen times the size of the earth, that of the sun's is twenty-seven times.[18] These figures make it likely that he put the distance of the stars from the earth at nine times the earth's size. Anaximander describes the sun and moon as "lying aslant,"[19] which shows that he knew of the obliquity of the ecliptic. As the sun and moon are different distances from the earth their orbits can be oblique to those of the stars without colliding with each other or with the stars. The circles of the stars do not intersect, so there is no possibility of collision.[20] The essential features of this system can be represented in a simple diagram,[21] and perhaps the "sphere" he is said to have constructed was a model of his astronomical ideas.

---

18. In fact the value of eighteen times for the moon is not attested. Aëtius gives the value of twenty-eight times for the sun (2.20.1 = DK 12A21) and nineteen times for the moon (2.25.1 = DK 12A22), figures which may be due to an attempt to refine the system to take into account the thickness of the sun and moon.

19. Aëtius 2.25.1 = DK 12A22.

20. Whether Anaximander had anything to say about the motions of the planets (which were well known to the Babylonians, for whom see p. 24) is unknown. Planetary motions could have raised problems for his simple model.

21. The diagram below is only one possible representation of Anaximander's system. The information we have supports a number of others, including that the circles of the stars do not combine to form a sphere but a segment of a cylinder.

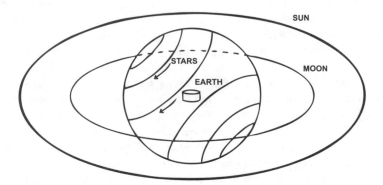

Anaximander might have explained how the sun and moon can be seen through the mist surrounding the stars by pointing out that mist can render some things invisible and yet not others. It can hide a nearby object from view while permitting a bright light much farther away to be seen clearly.

Anaximander holds that the earth is immobile at the center of the universe, a view shared by most of his successors[22] until the birth of modern astronomy with Copernicus (1543). The sophisticated argument on which he bases this belief is remarkable.

> 5.13   The earth is aloft and is not supported by anything. It stays at rest because
>   its distance from all things is equal.
>   (Hippolytus, *Refutation of All Heresies* 1.6.3 = DK 12A11)

Aristotle expands this statement into the following argument.

> 5.14   Some, like Anaximander . . . declare that the earth stays at rest because of
>   equality. For it is no more fitting for what is situated at the center and is
>   equally far from the extremes to move up rather than down or sideways.
>   And it is impossible for it to move in opposite directions at the same time.
>   Therefore, it stays at rest of necessity.
>   (Aristotle, *On the Heavens* 2.13 295b11–16 = DK 12A26)

This too can be understood as a criticism of Thales, who had the earth resting on water (**4.8**). What, then, did the water rest on? As long as one thing needs to be supported by another, there is no end. Anaximander cuts off this infinite regress at the start with the first known application of the Principle of Sufficient Reason, according to which, in Leibniz' formulation, "no fact can be real or existent . . . unless it has a sufficient reason why it should be thus and not otherwise."[23] In

---

22. Notable exceptions for our purposes are the Atomists and Philolaus. See below pp. 104–5, 324 and 358–59.

23. Leibniz, *Monadology* sec. 32. Aristotle criticizes Anaximander's argument from the standpoint of Aristotelian physics at *On the Heavens* 2.13 295b16–296a22 (not in DK),

the present case, Anaximander reasons that the earth is at rest since its equal distance from the extremes implies that there is no sufficient reason for it to move in one direction rather than any other.

Further, the presuppositions underlying this argument have great methodological interest. On the basis of the senses we believe that all things move downwards and also that the earth, on which we stand, is at rest. Anaximander accepts the latter of these conflicting judgments and rejects the former as applying to the earth, and does so on the basis of symmetry and geometrical structure. On this account of his reasoning, Anaximander is intolerant of contradiction, adopts a critical stance toward sensory information, is ready to reject some sense-based judgments in favor of others, and appeals to mathematical and logical considerations in constructing his theory.

Anaximander is interested in meteorological as well as astronomical phenomena and sees no distinction between the two but accounts for both by the same processes.

> **5.15** Winds occur when the finest vapors of dark mist are separated off and collect together and then are set in motion. Rain results from the vapor arising from the earth under the influence of the sun. Lightning occurs whenever wind escapes and splits the clouds apart.
>
> (Hippolytus, *Refutation of All Heresies* 1.6.7 = DK 12A11)

> **5.16** Anaximander says that these [thunder, lightning, thunderbolts, waterspouts, and hurricanes] all result from wind. For whenever it [wind] is enclosed in a thick cloud and forcibly escapes because it is so fine and light, then the bursting [of the cloud] creates the noise and the splitting creates the flash against the blackness of the cloud.
>
> (Aëtius 3.3.1 = DK 12A23)

Once again "separating off" is responsible for generation. The finest vapors become wind, leaving the thicker remains to become cloud. This time "separating off" originates change not only in what is separated off but also in the remainder. The resemblance between this process and that which generates the sea and winds at the beginning of the world (**5.7**) makes it likely that that process, too, occurs through "separating off."

Anaximander's belief that thunder and lightning result from wind being enclosed in cloud and then breaking out is reminiscent of his account of the origin of the heavenly bodies. (If, as seems likely, lightning is fire bursting out from the cloud, it resembles the celestial bodies, which are fire surrounded by dark

---

comparing it to "a hair, which, it is said, however great the tension, will not break under it, if it is evenly distributed, or the man who, being extremely hungry and thirsty, and both equally, is equidistant from food and drink, and therefore bound to stay where he is."

mist.) Once again, the break from tradition is apparent. The cause of lightning and thunder is no longer Zeus, only wind.

5.15 and **5.16** make it clear that for Anaximander the world arose from the same processes that maintain it. He therefore deserves the title of the first uniformitarian, as the eighteenth- and nineteenth-century geologists were called who held that processes found today, such as erosion and volcanic activity, are responsible for the geological features of the earth.

Anaximander used his understanding of present-day phenomena to project future events (**5.7**). His belief that the earth is drying up could well have been based on the silting up of the harbor of Miletus.[24]

Anaximander also has an account of the origin of living creatures, including humans.

5.17   Anaximander says that the first animals were produced in moisture, enclosed in thorny barks. When their age advanced they came out onto the drier part, their bark broke off, and they lived a different mode of life for a short time.
(Aëtius 5.19.4 = DK 12A30)

5.18   He also declares that in the beginning humans were born from animals of a different kind, since other animals quickly manage on their own and humans alone require lengthy nursing. For this reason they would not have survived if they had been like this at the beginning.
(pseudo-Plutarch, Stromata 2 = DK 12A10) (continuation of **5.6**)

5.19   Anaximander . . . believed that there arose from heated water and earth either fish or animals very like fish. In these, humans grew and were kept inside as embryos up to puberty. Then finally they burst, and men and women came forth already able to nourish themselves.
(Censorinus, *On the Day of Birth* 4.7 = DK 12A30)

The origin of animals is explained similarly to the origin of the universe and to meteorological events: more complex things arise out of simpler things, and new things come into existence after being enclosed tightly in something else and breaking out of the container.

The distinction we feel between living animals and inanimate matter (such as heated water) is inappropriately applied to Anaximander, whose originative material is in some sense alive (see above page 36), so that all its products, including earth and water, inherit its vital force. Animals and humans, with a greater concentration of vitality, differ in degree, not in kind, from the rest of the *kosmos*.

---

24. This process, which is due to alluvial deposits of the river Meander at whose mouth the city was situated, has continued to the present, advancing the shoreline so far that the Aegean cannot now even be seen from the site of ancient Miletus.

Particularly striking is Anaximander's recognition and solution of a problem arising from the helplessness of human infants. The first humans could not have come into this world as babies or they would have died before reaching an age at which they could propagate the race. How, then, did they come into being? This "first generation problem" can be answered by positing a god who creates adult humans or by asserting that the world and the human race have always been in existence. However, both these solutions conflict with basic features of Anaximander's system. Accordingly he takes an original and ingenious approach, having the first humans nurtured in other animals until self-sustaining.

For his claims that animals arose in the sea before they emerged to live on dry land and that they developed from fish, and for recognizing the need for a different original form for humans and the difficulties of adapting to different habitats (perhaps implicit in the short lives of the animals who first moved onto dry land), Anaximander is sometimes called the father of evolution. This interpretation is wrong, however, since he says nothing about the evolution of species. His problem of how to account for the first generation of each kind of animal, how to get each kind of animal established once and for all, is different from Darwin's. Moreover, he makes no mention of such Darwinian mechanisms as natural selection.

Anaximander's Fragment

How the World Works

Aside from a few words in the testimonia that have an early ring, all that survives of Anaximander's writings is one fragment which seems to have been quoted out of its correct context.

5.20   The things that are perish into the things from which they come to be, according to necessity, for they pay penalty and retribution to each other for their injustice in accordance with the ordering of time, as he says in rather poetical language.

(Simplicius, *Commentary on Aristotle's* Physics
24.18–21 = DK 12B1 + 12A9)

The last words of **5.20** show that some of the preceding is in Anaximander's own words, but the extent of the fragment is uncertain.[25] I think it most likely that the words from "according to necessity" to "time" are Anaximander's and that the preceding words either quote or paraphrase his words. We have a picture of a world full of change—things coming to be and in turn perishing. These changes are ordered in two ways: (1) when a thing (*a*) perishes *a* turns into something definite—the same sort of thing that perished when *a* came to be; (2) each thing

---

25. For discussion, see Kahn (1960: 168–78, 193–96), and KRS p. 118, which summarizes Kirk (1955/1970).

has a determinate time span. In addition, comings–to–be and perishings are acts of injustice which one thing (*a*) commits against another (*b*) and for which *a* is compelled to make restitution to *b*.

The process here described seems to have nothing to do with the *apeiron* but can easily apply to the opposites hot and cold, which we have seen are important both at the beginning of the world and at the present state of things. The alternation of the seasons is an obvious case in point. In the region of Miletus it is reasonable to say that hot prevails in summer, cold prevails in winter, and spring and fall mark an even balance between hot and cold. When summer comes, hot commits injustice by driving out cold and occupying some of its territory. In due time hot must pay a penalty in which cold is recompensed for this injustice first by a return to an even balance (in the fall) and then by a period in which cold drives out hot (winter). But by doing so cold commits injustice against hot and so must make recompense in turn. Hence there occurs an endless cycle of regular alternation between states where first one and then the other opposite dominates.

Deployment of other pairs of opposites such as wet and dry, light and dark, rare and dense, either singly or in combination, can account for many features of the world. The change of the seasons is also marked by orderly alternation between wet and dry and between light and dark (reflecting the longer periods of daylight in summer). Day and night can be analyzed in terms of light and dark; a more detailed account will also bring in hot and cold. The alternation of rare and dense can perhaps be seen in successive periods of wind ("the finest vapors" of **5.15**) and cloudy or stormy weather (the "thick cloud" of **5.16**). There is also a broad contrast between the sun as hot, dry, light, rare, and at the edge of the universe, and the earth (together with the sea), which is cold, wet, dark, dense, and at the center. Moreover weather can be seen as the interplay of these two groups of opposites.

This account of the fragment focuses on the opposites, which have special importance for Anaximander, but the fragment may be meant to describe other "things that are" as well, for example, animals and humans (along the lines of "ashes to ashes and dust to dust"). However, Anaximander recognized that there are difficulties in extending it to cover the origin of certain entities, including the *kosmos* (see below page 47).

The fragment occupies an important place in the history of philosophy and science. It contains a general account that applies to a wide variety of phenomena. It contains the germs of the ideas of the conservation of matter and of a dynamic equilibrium in which opposed principles prevail alternately in regularly repeated cycles such as we find, for example, in a swinging pendulum and in a spring with a weight attached to it moving indefinitely up and down. Although the predominance of hot over cold or of cold over hot changes from time to time, the system has an overall stability that continues without external interference. The fragment also contains the beginning of the idea of a law of nature which operates uniformly and impersonally and also holds inevitably ("according to necessity"): things not only do happen in accordance with this law, they *must*.

A notable feature of the fragment is its legal language: "pay penalty and ret-ribution," "injustice," and "the ordering of time" (as if time plays the role of a judge assessing penalties in criminal trials). The legal language may strike us as no more than a colorful metaphor, but that response reveals our distance from Anaxi-mander. To assume that it is a metaphor presupposes a radical difference between the world of nature (where injustice and the like are not really found) and the world of humans (where they are): humankind is somehow distinct from nature and the two realms operate according to different principles. This interpretation, though congenial to those who hold that social, moral, and evaluative language applies only in the human sphere, is inappropriate for Anaximander and other Pre-socratics, who place humans squarely in the natural world. The injustice which hot commits on cold is the same kind as that which a robber commits on a victim—taking something which is by right not its own—and the penalty assessed by a judge according to the law is of the same sort as that assessed by time according to necessity—restoration of what was taken and payment of an additional amount as a fine. In Greek, *dikē* ("justice") and its opposite have descriptive as well as evalu-ative force. Descriptively, injustice is taking something not one's own; evaluatively it is bad. This evaluation applies to all acts which, descriptively, are unjust, regard-less of the nature of the agent. Further, the idea that justice or retribution comes inevitably accords with a view of justice expressed by other authors of the Archaic period,[26] and the notion that the cosmic principle of justice is fair to the rival con-tenders is doubtless due to the ideal of justice on which the legal system known to Anaximander was based. In the case of human judges, justice in the normative sense is not always served; but in the case of the cosmic law, justice is necessary. Not only is the way events occur good, but they also cannot happen otherwise.

All Greek philosophers assume that the world we perceive is a world of change and motion. Anaximander expresses this idea in describing the world as the scene of opposites in a continuous conflict governed by necessity and justice. Although hot and cold are the only opposites the sources mention, the fragment equally well accounts for the interaction of others. As other pairs of opposites are prominent in Pythagoras and Heraclitus,[27] it would be excessively cautious to hold that Anaximander had only the one pair in mind.

One more feature of this interpretation calls for explanation—the claim that hot commits injustice against cold. It is strange to see "hot" used as the subject of a sentence rather than the predicate, as in "the food is hot," and equally odd for "hot" to *do* something, that is, to perform the role of an agent—committing injustice, for example. We tend to think of opposites like hot and cold as attributes or qualities of *things;* the things are subjects to which the qualities are somehow attached. There is something that is hot or cold—food, for example. In thinking this way, we are

---

26. For example, Hesiod, *Works and Days* lines 213–73, 280–85, 320–34; Solon, frs. 1, 3; Theognis, lines 197–208 (none of these passages in DK).

27. See 9.38 and 10.48, 10.49, 10.52–73.

unconsciously following Aristotle, who was the first to distinguish clearly between qualities (such as hot) and substances (such as fire), and to say that (except in special contexts) when we think or talk, we think or talk about substances. Something (some substance) can be hot and can become cold. As he points out,[28] one quality can be opposite to another quality, but substances do not have opposites. Hot is the opposite of cold, but fire is not the opposite of water. Calling fire and water opposites is just shorthand for saying that they have opposite qualities.

However, to apply this analysis to Anaximander would distort his thought. Before Aristotle, hot food might have been conceived in various ways. For example, the hot might have been thought a part of the food, or something (some ingredient) in the food.[29] Before Plato and Aristotle, it was possible to talk of hot and cold (or the hot and the cold) as constituents or elements of bodies (as in the fifth-century Hippocratic treatise *The Nature of Man*.[30]) Likewise Anaxagoras considers hot, cold, and colors to be basic things, ingredients of macroscopic objects, alongside flesh, blood, and bone.[31] Evidently in making a clear distinction between substances and qualities Aristotle was not simply expressing what everyone had previously believed, however obvious his views may seem to us.

Returning now to Anaximander, we may easily imagine that he thought of the hot and the cold not as qualities of substances but as things in their own right. That is not to say that they occur apart from other "things"—the issue what kinds of things have independent or separate existence was not raised as early as this. But whatever else Anaximander might have thought, he will have recognized that there is a special relation between the hot and fire: among the hot things Anaximander could have experienced, fire is preeminently hot. In discussing the early stages of his cosmogony it would have been natural for him to say that the newly generated hot is manifested in the form of fire and likewise to have thought of dark, cool mist as the embodiment of the cold.

Finally, the fragment apparently describes the world around us as a stable, ongoing system which maintains itself without any limit in time. Summer and winter, it suggests, will alternate forever. The *apeiron* may have acted only once, at the beginning of the world; once generated, the world went on without further dependence on it. Alternatively, the *apeiron* may play an ongoing role in the world, if the governing or "steering" function that 5.5 refers to is correctly assigned to it. In that case there will be some link between the *apeiron* and the necessity mentioned in the fragment. In any case, Anaximander focuses on the world around him. He

---

28. Aristotle, *Categories* 5 3b24–25 and 8 10b12–15 (neither passage in DK).

29. Plato develops these ideas in connection with his theory of Forms (*Phaedo* 96–107 [not in DK]). They constitute an important part of the background for his treatment of the differences between statements like "the food is hot" and those like "the food is [identical with the] hot" (*Sophist* 250–57 [not in DK]).

30. Translated below pp. 431–39.

31. See Ch. 13, especially p. 204.

describes its origin (perhaps because Thales had given such an account, or because Hesiod had done so, or because of a more widespread Greek concern with origins and parentage) but not its destruction. Rather, on the present interpretation the fragment, at least, suggests that the world will never perish.

One World or Many?

This interpretation of the fragment leaves some problems. A created but indestructible *kosmos* requires a sharp distinction between the one-time cosmogonic process and the ever-repeating processes of the developed world, a distinction which sits uneasily with the uniformities Anaximander posits between these two stages of the history of the universe. It thus requires a conspicuous exception to the symmetry which is so prominent in his accounts of cosmic phenomena. It also entails that the fragment's account of "things that are" fails to apply to such conspicuous things as the earth, sun, and other members of the *kosmos* which form the setting in which the regular changes take place.

Some of these problems can be solved by interpreting the fragment to cover the origin and perishing of the world as well as of things in the world, but at the price of abandoning the long-term stability the fragment favors and of leaving it unclear why the world will perish. On the other hand, if the argument in 5.7, that the world is drying up, implies that when it is completely dry it will stay that way forever, it does not agree with the fragment. And if the stage of total dryness immediately precedes the destruction of the world, the fragment simply does not apply to all stages of cosmic history.

Modern opinion is divided on this issue, and the ancient sources are too. Three interpretations have emerged: first, that Anaximander is concerned with only a single world, our world; he tells of its origin, but (perhaps inconsistently) says nothing about its end and leaves the impression that it will go on forever. Second, that he believed in a limitless succession of worlds: at any time there is only one world in existence; it is generated from the *apeiron*, and when it perishes it perishes back into the *apeiron*, after which time another world is generated from the *apeiron* in the same way. Third, that he believed that at any time there are a limitless number of coexistent worlds, each of which has been generated from the *apeiron* and which will in due course perish. I favor the third, a minority view, but the one which I find most consistent with the bulk of the ancient evidence on the point and also with Anaximander's other theories and his way of thinking. For example, since our world was generated at a particular place in the *apeiron* at a particular time, the Principle of Sufficient Reason would require other worlds to be generated at other times and places.[32] If this is correct, then Anaximander is even more comprehensive and systematic a thinker than has generally been appreciated, a man of genius some of whose ideas proved too bold for his immediate followers to accept.

---

32. McKirahan (2001).

6

Anaximenes of Miletus

Anaximenes was called Anaximander's pupil and associate. That and the fact that he was from Miletus are practically all that we know about his life. Even his date is uncertain, though he was probably somewhat younger than Anaximander. Aristotle and the doxographical tradition speak of his theory that air is the basic substance and provide some details of his cosmology, but that is about all. Anaximenes was less bold a thinker than his teacher, but it was to his theory rather than Anaximander's that later Presocratics looked back for the details of their views on astronomy and meteorology. Like Anaximander he wrote in prose. One fragment and a few other words of his book survive.

Air, the Material Principle

6.1   Anaximenes . . . like Anaximander, declares that the underlying nature is one and unlimited [*apeiron*] but not indeterminate, as Anaximander held, but definite, saying that it is air. It differs in rarity and density according to the substances <it becomes>. Becoming finer it comes to be fire; being condensed it comes to be wind, then cloud, and when still further condensed it becomes water, then earth, then stones, and the rest come to be from these. He too makes motion eternal and says that change also comes to be through it.

(Theophrastus, quoted by Simplicius, *Commentary on Aristotle's* Physics 24.26–25.1 = DK 13A5)

6.2   Anaximenes . . . declared that the principle is unlimited [*apeiron*] air, from which come to be things that are coming to be, things that have come to be, and things that will be, and gods and divine things. The rest come to be out of the products of this. The form of air is the following: when it is most even, it is invisible, but it is revealed by the cold and the hot and the wet, and by its motion. It is always moving, for all the things that undergo change would not change if it were not moving. For when it becomes condensed or finer, it appears different. For when it is dissolved into a finer condition it becomes fire, and on the other hand air being condensed becomes winds. Cloud comes from air through felting,[1] and water comes to be when this happens to a greater degree. When condensed still more it becomes earth, and when it reaches the absolutely densest stage it becomes stones.

(Hippolytus, *Refutation* 1.7.1–3 = DK 13A7)

---

1. Felting is the production of nonwoven fabric by the application of heat, moisture, and pressure, as felt is produced from wool. The term here is extended to describe another process in which the product is denser than and so has different properties from the ingredients.

By making the originative material be of a definite kind, Anaximenes seems at first sight to take a step backward. Anaximander accounted for opposites by positing a neutral principle with no definite properties of its own. If this was Anaximander's response to the objection to Thales' theory—"if all things are (or originated from) water, why isn't everything wet?"—Anaximenes' theory seems open to a similar objection: if everything is made of air, why doesn't everything have the specific characteristics of air? How can he account for the diversity in the world on the basis of a single originative principle of a definite kind?

Anaximenes could reply by pointing out weaknesses in Anaximander's theory. Theories, he might say, should be based on principles that are familiar, understandable, known to exist, and found in the world around us, but there is no evidence that the *apeiron* exists, only Anaximander's reasoning. It is unfamiliar and alien to our experience, barely describable or comprehensible; it is not found in our *kosmos*. Air is a better principle than the *apeiron* in these respects. In fact, there can be no objection to theories based on a single principle of a definite kind as long as they generate the wide variety of things found in the *kosmos* in an acceptable way. Further, Anaximander's account of the generation of the *kosmos* is itself crucially flawed in precisely this way, since it depends on something whose origin from the *apeiron* is left obscure.[2]

Whether or not Anaximenes actually criticized Anaximander this way, he accounts for the origin of this world's diversity out of a single substance, air. Air can take on different appearances, and when conditions are right it even becomes different types of substances. When rarefied it becomes fire, and when condensed it becomes wind, earth, etc. This idea may have come from reflection on the melting of ice to form water, the freezing of water to form ice, and the evaporation of air to form mist, events in which apparently different materials are seen to be forms of the same thing. In this way the question "Why doesn't everything have the properties of air?" receives a straightforward answer: everything does have the properties of air; its properties include being fire (in certain conditions), being water (in other conditions), etc. Also, the processes by which air takes on these properties are comprehensible. Rarefaction and condensation simply mean that there is more or less air in a given region—notions more familiar than Anaximander's obscure processes.

Several details of Anaximenes' theory require closer examination. "Air" translates the Greek word *aēr*, which in earlier writers, including Anaximander,[3] means dark mist. The bright, clear part of the atmosphere, as distinct from the misty lower part, was called *aithēr*. 6.2 shows that for Anaximenes *aēr* is much closer to our notion of air, close enough to justify translating it by its English derivative. In its most "even" state, air lacks any perceptible properties. Since we cannot perceive it, we must infer its existence, but the inference is not difficult.

---

2. See above pp. 36–37, on "that which is productive of hot and cold."

3. The word occurs in **5.6**, **5.8**, and **5.15**, where it is translated "dark mist."

Anaximenes associates breath and air, and he knows that our breath (which is like a feeble wind) can be hot or cold, properties that "reveal" air. If what we breathe out is the same as what we breathe in, what we inhale is air even if it is imperceptible, as on a dry, windless day that is neither hot nor cold.

Like Anaximander's *apeiron*, Anaximenes' air is (or can be) imperceptible. But the fact that air has an imperceptible state is not crucial. From one point of view, there is so far no reason for making air the principle. Ice is a form of water, but equally water is a form of ice; water is condensed air, and air is rarefied water. From this point of view any (or all) of the "phases" of air can serve as the basic substance. Anaximenes had other reasons for making air primary.

Anaximenes accounts for Anaximander's principal opposites, hot and cold, in terms of the most important pair of opposites in his own system, rare and dense.

> 6.3   Or as Anaximenes of old believed, let us leave neither the cold nor the hot
>   in the category of substance, but <hold them to be> common attributes of
>   matter which come as the results of its changes. For he declares that the
>   contracted state of matter and the condensed state is cold, whereas what is
>   fine and "loose" (calling it this way with this very word) is hot. As a result he
>   claimed that it is not said unreasonably that a person releases both hot and
>   cold from his mouth. For the breath becomes cold when compressed and
>   condensed by the lips, and when the mouth is relaxed, the escaping breath
>   becomes warm because of rareness.
>   (Plutarch, *The Principle of Cold* 7 947F = DK 13B1)

This passage is important in many ways. First, it shows how Anaximenes related two pairs of opposites which appear unrelated. Because breath is rare, it is warm; because it is dense, it is cold. Thus, hot and cold depend on, can be explained in terms of, or reduced to rare and dense. In this way Anaximenes advances our understanding of the world by reducing the range of independent phenomena through increasing the number of intelligibly connected features. The world becomes more intelligible as the range of related phenomena is increased.

Second, rarity and density are quantitative notions: more or less of the same stuff in the same place. Hot and cold, qualitative notions, are accounted for in terms of quantitative notions. Anaximenes thus frequently receives credit for being the ancestor of a basic attitude of science—the desire to express concepts quantitatively.[4] However, there is no reason to think that he conceived of analyzing rarity and density in numerical terms (for example, that a cubic meter of air if condensed to half a cubic meter becomes water, and if condensed to one-tenth a cubic meter becomes stone), much less that he had a notion of mass which would enable him to "weigh" fire, wind, and cloud, and so compare the amount of air in them to the amount in water or stone. Moreover, though "more" and "less" are

––––––––––––––––––––

4. See below pp. 92–102 for further discussion of this point with reference to the Pythagoreans.

quantitative concepts, it is not clear that Anaximenes understood rare and dense in that way. For us, rarity and density depend on how much of something there is in a given volume, but the idea of "a given volume" is rather sophisticated, and dense and rare themselves can be thought of as qualities (something like "thick" and "thin") just as well as hot and cold can. Anaximenes had the idea of analyzing one feature in terms of another, but it is anachronistic to see him as the originator of the belief that science is essentially quantitative.

Third, **6.3** reports the first piece of reasoning preserved from Greek philosophy, and enables us to form an impression of Anaximenes' way of thinking. The account of the relation between hot and rare and between cold and dense is based on familiar phenomena easily observable by anyone who follows Anaximenes' directions. Anaximenes derives his theory from the evidence by describing the observed phenomena and generalizing on the basis of that description. He notes that the breath feels cold when blown through pursed lips, describes the situation as air feeling cold when condensed, and states the general claim that matter which is condensed is cold and apparently that condensation makes it cold, not vice versa.

It is going too far to say that Anaximenes conducted a scientific experiment, but it is apparent that he did base the account on repeatable observational evidence. On the other hand, the observation admits of other explanations, as the following criticism points out.

> **6.4**   A person who blows out air does not move the air all at once but blows through a narrow opening of the lips, and so he breathes out just a little air but moves much of the air outside his body, in which the warmth from his body is not apparent because of its small amount.
>
> (pseudo-Aristotle, *Problems* 34.7 964a13–16 [not in DK])

Nor does Anaximenes explain how to deal with obvious counter examples to his theory. Wind, which as slightly condensed air should be cool, can be hot. Mist can be cool (fog) or hot (steam). Rocks, which as the densest things should be coldest, can be hot. (This is not to say that such cases would defeat him. For example, he might say that rocks are very cold when they are being formed, though afterwards they can become warm.) It is noteworthy too that Anaximenes' conclusion is exactly wrong, although a theory's mere rightness or wrongness is no appropriate gauge of whether it is reached scientifically. In general, putting a substance under pressure makes it hotter, not colder, as Boyle's law asserts for gases and as also happens for most liquids and solids.

Other substances are products of the rarefaction and condensation of air. What status do rarefaction and condensation have? Are they causal principles of motion and change, so that Anaximenes' system in fact has three principles? Apparently not. Aristotle, who was interested in this question, asserts that Empedocles was the first to distinguish principles of change[5] and that Anaximenes had only a material principle.[6] Even if Aristotle is wrong to interpret Anaximenes' air as a material principle, it remains that Anaximenes did not identify separation and condensation as causes separate from air. Condensation and rarefaction, then, seem not to be separate principles but rather describe what happens to air: fire is air in a state of rarefaction, water is condensed air.[7]

The following passage, which describes some of air's properties, suggests how air becomes rarefied and condensed.

> **6.5**   Anaximenes determined that air is a god and that it comes to be and is
> without measure, infinite, and always in motion.
>   (Cicero, *On the Nature of the Gods* 1.10.26 = DK 13A10)

This passage is written in Latin, but "without measure" perhaps and "infinite" certainly represent *apeiron*, which **6.1** and **6.2** use to describe air. The assertion that "it comes to be" probably means that air comes to be—say, when water is rarefied. Here the key attribute of air is its unceasing motion, which is an indication of its divinity. This need mean only that as a whole or in general air is characterized by motion, not that every bit of air is always in motion. When air moves enough to be noticed, it is a breeze, which is already a condensed form of air. Thus, it seems that air by its own mobile nature is condensed in some places and rarefied in others, and so other substances come into being.

What are these substances? The sources agree that air becomes fire when rarefied, and when condensed more and more it becomes in turn wind, cloud, water, earth, and stones. Although this list includes fire, air, water, and earth, the appearance of other substances shows that these four were not yet canonical.[8] After giving this list, **6.1** notes briefly "the rest come to be from these." This statement corresponds to **6.2**'s assertion "the rest come to be out of the products of this." Anaximenes must have said something about the origin of other substances than the ones so far mentioned. How detailed a treatment did he provide?

At one extreme, he could have given an extended treatment of how different substances arise from the sorts of matter identified. At the other extreme, he may have said no more than the sources. Either reading supports two significantly different theories: (a) a two-tier system, with fire, air, etc. serving equally as ingredients of other substances, and (b) a three-tier system, with fire, wind, etc.

---

5. Aristotle, *Metaphysics* 1.4 985a29–31 = DK 31A37.

6. Aristotle, *Metaphysics* 1.3 984a5–6 = DK 13A4, cf. 983b6–8 = DK 11A12.

7. Evidence against this interpretation can be found at Aristotle, *Physics* 1.6 189b12–14 (not in DK), which may identify Anaximenes' "dense" and "rare" as active principles which affect passive air. I give this passage little weight since it ignores air's own active nature in Anaximenes.

8. Empedocles was the first to make just these four his elements; they are prominent also in Plato and Aristotle.

being formed out of air, and other things being formed of these (fire, wind, etc.) but not of air. In (b) air corresponds roughly to protons, neutrons, and electrons in classical chemistry; fire, water, etc., correspond to elements such as hydrogen and oxygen; and other substances like wood correspond to compounds such as water and carbon dioxide. On interpretation (a) air is an "element" alongside fire, etc., and nothing corresponds to the subatomic level.

Can we decide between the possibilities? **6.2** more clearly points to the three-tier system than **6.1** does, but **6.1**, which is neutral between the two interpretations, probably stays closer to the original Theophrastean account. Thus, as far as the sources go, either interpretation is possible. However, the following considerations tip the balance in favor of the two-tier view. Not only are fire, etc. formed of air, but air can come to be out of the others, as is implied in the statement that air comes to be (**6.5**). But the process of air coming to be out of water, as when, for example, mist rises from the sea and eventually becomes so thinned out as to be invisible air, seems more like a phase change (water to ice) than like a dissolution of something into its constituent parts (water being broken up into hydrogen and oxygen). Also, air seems to be a constituent of the world on the same level as fire, wind, etc., and equally able to join in forming compounds.

The question remains whether Anaximenes offered a detailed account of how compounds are formed. The absence of information on the matter favors a negative reply. If he had gone much further than the vague statements preserved in **6.1** and **6.2**, Aristotle and Theophrastus, who had interests in these issues, would surely have said so.

The only surviving sentence of Anaximenes' works[9] describes another role of air.

> **6.6** Just as our soul, being air, holds us together and controls[10] us, so do breath and air surround the whole kosmos.
>
> (Anaximenes, DK 13B2)

6.6 identifies the soul with air, following a well-attested pre-philosophical view that the air we breathe is our soul, or vital principle—that which distinguishes the living from the nonliving and from the dead. When we stop breathing not only do we die but also our body decomposes. Thus, the air which is our soul maintains us in existence; it "holds us together." It also "controls us," though just what it controls and how it exercises control are unclear.

Anaximenes continues Anaximander's tendency to see humans as part of the *kosmos*, subject to the same principles as the rest of nature. In comparing humans and

---

9. The authenticity of this fragment is disputed, but even if some of the words it contains were not in the original, it is at least a close paraphrase.

10. I follow KRS (p. 159 n.) in translating *sunkratein* as "hold together and control." If this is an overtranslation and the Greek means only "hold together," then my following remarks must be weakened accordingly.

the universe, **6.6** contains the first explicit use of the microcosm–macrocosm analogy, the view that humans and the universe are constructed or function similarly,[11] which would be developed further by later Presocratics. The exact point of the comparison is unclear, since "surrounding" is different from "holding together" and "controlling," but it asserts that in some sense air functions similarly in the universe as it does in humans. It follows that we can use what we know about humans to understand the universe and vice versa. The function of air in the universe is, then, to hold it together, surrounding it, pervading it, and keeping everything in its right place. To take the simile further, air controls the *kosmos*, presumably by regulating astronomical and meteorological events and perhaps others too, through its controlling motions. Moreover, because air plays the same role in the universe as it does in humans and it makes humans alive, it seems to follow that the universe is alive. This interpretation finds support in the Milesian tendency already found in Thales and Anaximander to imbue all things with life force. Air gives life to its offspring, including the entire *kosmos*. In any case, by identifying the animating substance with the primary material substance, Anaximenes incorporates the "breath soul" into the scientific tradition while using this traditional belief as a prop for his own theory and perhaps as a reason for choosing air as the basic type of matter.

The Gods

Although **6.5** may imply only that air has divine attributes, **6.2** reports that gods come into being from air[12]—which may reflect an attempt to link physical theory with Olympian religion. Air is the substance out of which all other things are ultimately made, therefore gods arise out of air. Not only do the gods have a beginning, they are physical beings subject to the same conditions of existence as other entities. This view accords with evidence that Anaximenes held that the rainbow (traditionally the Olympian goddess Iris) is caused by the sun's rays striking a dense, black cloud.[13] It becomes explicit that Anaximenes believes the gods and goddesses of myth have nothing to do with the origin or maintenance of the universe. Air does that. Any divinities there are, aside from divine air, must have a vastly diminished role. This conclusion had vast importance for the history of Greek natural philosophy. It was picked up and given great emphasis by Xenophanes and seems to have been accepted without question by most of the Presocratic philosophers after that.

---

11. "Microcosm" derives from the Greek *mikros*, "small" + *kosmos*.

12. Saint Augustine attributes this view to Anaximenes as well (*City of God* 8.2 = DK 13A10).

13. Aëtius 3.5.10 and Scholia on Aratus p. 515, 27 M (both = DK 13A18).

Cosmogony and Cosmology

6.7   When the air was being felted the earth was the first thing to come into
       being, and it is very flat. This is why it rides upon the air, as is reasonable.
                                     (pseudo-Plutarch, *Stromata* 3 = DK 13A6)

6.8   Anaximenes, Anaxagoras, and Democritus say that its flatness is the cause
       of its staying at rest. For it does not cut the air below but covers it like a lid,
       as bodies with flatness apparently do; they are difficult for winds to move
       because of their resistance. They say that the earth does this same thing with
       respect to the air beneath because of its flatness. And the air, lacking sufficient
       room to move aside, stays at rest in a mass because of the air beneath.
                         (Aristotle, *On the Heavens* 2.13 294b13–20 = DK 13A20)

6.9   Likewise the sun and moon and all the other heavenly bodies, which are
       fiery, ride upon the air on account of their flatness.
                         (Hippolytus, *Refutation of All Heresies* 1.7.4 = DK 13A7)

Like Anaximander, Anaximenes tackles the problems of the origin of the earth and
the reasons for its stability. The earth resulted from "felting"[14] (the word is likely
to be Anaximenes' own), an appropriate term to use in describing the thickening of
air into earth. Again we find cosmic events explained in terms of familiar processes
(this time a technological process) with no reference to the supernatural.

Anaximenes agrees with Anaximander that the earth is flat, but does not follow his predecessor's hypothesis that it stays motionless without support. The
earth and the celestial bodies are supported by and "ride upon" the air, an
account evidently meant to explain why they do not fall, not why the one is at
rest while the others move. The air's constant motion accounts for the movements of the celestial bodies; what needs explanation is the non-movement of
the earth. Anaximenes proposes that the earth somehow sits atop the air beneath
it and keeps it from moving out of the way to let the earth fall. It is difficult to
make sense of this theory, since air surrounds the earth on all sides. Anaximenes
may have been thinking of leaves, which fall more slowly than more compact
objects because of their wind resistance—but they do fall, precisely because the
air beneath them does move around them out of their way.

6.10   The stars came into being from the earth because moisture rises up out
       of it. When the moisture becomes fine, fire comes to be and the stars are
       formed of fire rising aloft. There are also earthen bodies in the region of the
       stars carried around together with them.
                         (Hippolytus, *Refutation of All Heresies* 1.7.5 = DK 13A7)
                                                        (continuation of **6.9**)

---

14. See above p. 48 n. 1.

The fiery stars did not come to be from the original air, but resulted from exhalation of moisture from the earth, perhaps as it was originally being condensed out of air. How earthen bodies could reach the starry vicinity is unclear. The moist exhalation may have played a role. These bodies were presumably posited to account for meteorites, possibly also for eclipses.

> **6.11**   He says that the stars do not move under the earth as others have supposed, but around it, as a felt cap turns around our head. The sun is hidden not because it is under the earth but because it is covered by the higher parts of the earth and on account of the greater distance it comes to be from us. Because of their distance the stars do not give heat.
>
> (Hippolytus, *Refutation of All Heresies*
> 1.7.6 = DK 13A7) (continuation of **6.10**)

> **6.12**   Many of the ancient speculators on the heavens believed that the sun is not borne under the earth, but around the earth and in this region, and that it disappears and causes night because the earth is high toward the north [or, "toward the pole star"].
>
> (Aristotle, *Meteorologica* 2.1 354a28–33 = DK 13A14)

If Anaximenes envisaged the earth as supported on a sea of air, he might have thought that the heavenly bodies, especially the sun, could not pass under the earth without disturbing its serene poise. The felt cap analogy neatly solves this problem. To serve as a model for the region of sky from the north celestial pole to the sun's path through the stars, the felt cap will be a segment of a spherical shell, whose diameter is large enough not to intersect the sea of air beneath the earth and which rotates on an axis extending from the north celestial pole through the earth. The sun does not move under the earth, but around it. The fixed stars move in circles around the celestial pole, all at the same speed, maintaining the same positions relative to one another. The cap is a handy model, because as it turns, the various points on its surface maintain constant relative positions. The north part of the earth is tilted toward the celestial pole, or rather the celestial pole is tilted toward the north part of the earth, and this is why the sun, moon, and some of the stars go beneath the horizon as they revolve about the pole. This tilt could be the source of calling the northern parts of the earth "higher."[15]

The *kosmos* will look something like the following diagram.[16]

The view that the stars give no warmth because of their great distance (**6.11**) contradicts Anaximander's theory that the stars are closer to the earth than the moon and sun are. It is also correct. Other correct views attributed to Anaximenes

---

15. This model cannot account for all the visible stars, unless the spherical segment cuts through the column of air beneath the earth. Worse, it cannot account for the sun's and moon's motions. In this respect it is an important step back from Anaximander's circles.

16. Miletus's latitude is 38 degrees north; the sun's positions at the summer and winter solstices are 23 1/2 degrees north and south of the celestial equator, respectively.

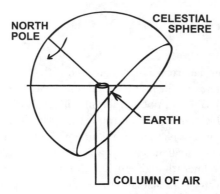

are that the seasons are due to the sun,[17] and that the moon is illuminated by the sun. He also gave the correct account of lunar eclipses.[18] One source credits him instead of Anaximander for discovering the use of the gnomon and placing the hour-markers at Sparta.[19]

Like other early Presocratics Anaximenes gave accounts of meteorological phenomena. Unsurprisingly, his accounts emphasize the role of air.

> **6.13** Anaximenes stated that clouds occur when the air is further thickened. When it is condensed still more, rain is squeezed out. Hail occurs when the falling water freezes, and snow when some wind is caught up in the moisture.
>
> (Aëtius 3.4.1 = DK 13A17)

He explains earthquakes differently from Thales.

> **6.14** Anaximenes declares that when the earth is being drenched and dried out it bursts, and earthquakes result from these hills breaking off and collapsing. This is why earthquakes occur in droughts and also in heavy rains. For in the droughts, as was said, the earth is broken while being dried out, and when it becomes excessively wet from the waters, it falls apart.
>
> (Aristotle, *Meteorologica* 2.7 365b6–12 = DK 13A21)

Though Anaximenes is a less adventurous theorizer than Anaximander and his cosmology differs from his predecessor's in important details, the two men have much in common—an interest in natural phenomena and the goal of accounting for these phenomena in terms of the intelligible behavior of natural substances. These features of their systems, together with some of their accounts of meteorological phenomena, are their legacy to the Greek philosophical and scientific tradition and were followed by the later Presocratics.

---

17. Aëtius 2.19.1.2 = DK 13A14.

18. Theon of Smyrna p. 198.19–p. 199.2 (Hiller) = DK 13A16.

19. Pliny, *Natural History* 2.187 = DK 13A14, cf. 5.1.

7

Xenophanes of Colophon

Born in Colophon, not far from Miletus, around 570, Xenophanes was a poet with wide-ranging interests. The literary tradition[1] remembers him more for his poetry (some of which ridicules poets and philosophers [for example, **9.1**]) than for his philosophy. However, he has an important place in the story of Presocratic philosophy. In the first place, he is the first philosopher for whom we have a significant amount of original material: some forty fragments of his poetry survive, over one hundred lines (though much of this material is not on philosophical subjects), and we can get a sense of his style and the range of his intellectual interests—considerably wider than we find in the Milesians and extending into areas that we regard as more philosophical. A few of his remaining lines reflect on the possibility of knowledge and how it is attained. Plato identifies him (incorrectly, in the view of recent interpreters) as the founder of monism.

> **7.1**   Our own Eleatic tribe, which began from Xenophanes and even earlier, proceeds in its stories on the supposition that all things, as they are called, are one.
>
> (Plato, *Sophist* 242d4–5 = DK 21A29)

Aristotle repeats this view and reports that he was called Parmenides' teacher (**7.14**). His innovations in cosmology are at present receiving closer study than ever before. Unlike Anaximander and Anaximenes, Xenophanes made proposals about the right way to live. There are special problems connected with the doxography of Xenophanes,[2] but despite these difficulties we can form some opinion of his ideas through his surviving verses. In what follows I will discuss his ideas on the divine,

---

1. I refer to such non-doxographic sources as Strabo (DK 21A20), Apuleius (DK 21A21), Proclus's *Commentary on Hesiod* (DK 21A22), Scholia on Homer's *Iliad* (DK 21A23) and Athenaeus (DK 21A27).

2. Plato (*Sophist* 242d = DK 21A29) and Aristotle (*Metaphysics* 1.5 986b21–23 = DK 21A30) call Xenophanes the first Eleatic philosopher and the teacher of Parmenides because Xenophanes's description of god in ways resembles the Eleatic account of what-is. Some scholars have adopted this interpretation, but I side with those who see him as following the lead of the Milesians. Theophrastus (in Simplicius, *Commentary on Aristotle's* Physics 22.26–30 = DK 21A31), following Aristotle (*On the Heavens* 3.1 298b14–20 = DK 28A25), regards Xenophanes' doctrines as irrelevant to the study of nature and therefore says little about him. Consequently, the normal doxographic sources are poor on Xenophanes. *On Melissus, Xenophanes, and Gorgias* offers a fabricated and erroneous account of Xenophanes' doctrines (Chs. 3–4 = DK 21A28). Though written a few centuries after Aristotle, this treatise somehow found its way into the corpus of Aristotle's writings and in turn confused other sources, which use it to supplement the meager information in Theophrastus.

the natural world, the possibility of knowledge, and the possible relations among these views. In Chapter 19 I will briefly discuss two of his fragments[3] that contain recommendations for the best way to live one's life.

As is the case with most of the early thinkers, we know practically nothing definite about Xenophanes' life. In one fragment he says he was still composing verse at the age of ninety-two.

7.2 (8)[4] Already there are sixty-seven years
tossing my speculation throughout the land of Greece,
and from my birth there were twenty-five in addition to these,
if indeed I know how to speak truly about these matters.

"Tossing throughout" may indicate that for all those years he had no fixed residence, possibly a result of the Persian conquest of Colophon, c.546. This interpretation places his birth c.570 and his death not before 478.[5]

Critique of the Greek Gods

The Milesians were unanimous in recognizing the divine nature of their primary substances but accounted for the world in terms of natural processes. This approach to the universe has devastating implications for the Olympian religion. There is no room left for anthropomorphic gods governing natural phenomena and human destiny or for stories of strife among the gods which imply that the divine realm is itself not well ordered and so is incapable of regulating our world in an ordered, comprehensible manner. These conclusions are implicit in Milesian natural speculation but were first drawn by Xenophanes, who lashes the Olympians with vigor and points the way to a rational theology. He mounts his attack on the traditional religion on five fronts.

First, the Olympian gods are immoral. They live a disorderly existence on a lower moral level even than humans.

7.3[6] (1) <Praise the man who> does not relate battles of Titans or Giants
or Centaurs—the fictions of our fathers—

---

3. 19.3 and 19.4.

4. The numbers in parentheses are the numbers of the fragments in DK. (1) = DK 21B1.

5. These dates are compatible with other evidence—principally Xenophanes' references to others (Thales, Pythagoras, and Epimenides), a reference to him in Heraclitus, and later (not necessarily correct) reports that he was Anaximander's pupil and Parmenides' teacher and that he composed an epic on the foundation of Elea (540 BCE).

6. The complete poem is given in **19.4**.

> nor violent conflicts, in which there is no use,
> but it is good always to have high regard for the gods.
>
> (lines 21–24)

7.4   (11) Both Homer and Hesiod have ascribed to the gods all deeds
            which among men are matters of reproach and blame:
            thieving, adultery, and deceiving one another.

Second, beliefs that gods physically resemble humans are questionable.

7.5   (14) Mortals believe that the gods are born
            and have human clothing, voice, and bodily form.

7.6   (16) Ethiopians say that their gods are snub-nosed and black,
            Thracians that theirs are blue eyed and red haired.

7.7   (15) But if oxen or horses or lions had hands
            or were able to draw with their hands and accomplish the
                same works as men,
            horses would draw the figures of gods as resembling horses
            and oxen as resembling oxen, and each would make the
            gods' bodies have the same bodily form as they themselves had.

7.6, which may represent extremes among human conceptions of the gods
(Thrace being the northernmost region well known to the Greeks and Ethiopia
the southernmost), is an early instance of Greek curiosity about other peoples
which is a delightful part of Herodotus's *Histories* and an important ingredient
of the fifth-century *nomos–phusis* debate.[7] More relevant to our purposes is the
argument which **7.6** implies: we Greeks think the gods have the appearance of
Greeks (something visible in Greek art), yet all other peoples portray the gods
as having the distinctive characteristics of themselves;[8] but a god cannot simultaneously have the characteristics of all human peoples, and there is no reason to
prefer one anthropomorphic account to another. More radically, by like reasoning **7.7** challenges the very conception of anthropomorphic gods. In this case
too, the belief stems from humans projecting their own nature onto the divine.
Xenophanes rejects religious tradition in favor of rational considerations. Greek,
"barbarian," and hypothetical bovine views of the gods are put on an even footing and cancel each other out, leaving no grounds to prefer one over the others.
This brings them all equally into question.

---

7. See Ch. 19, especially p. 406.

8. This claim overlooks the God of the Hebrews and also the theriomorphic (having
the appearance of animals) gods of the Egyptians, who were known to the Greeks of
Xenophanes' time.

Third, gods are not born and do not die. This criticism, implicit in 7.5, is made explicit in the following passage.

7.8   Xenophanes used to say that those who say that the gods are born are just as impious as those who say that they die, since either way it follows that there is a time when the gods do not exist.

(Aristotle, *Rhetoric* 2.23 1399b6–9 = DK 21A12)

It was impious to deny the Olympians' immortality (although some pre-Olympian survivals, such as the cult of Zeus's grave in Crete, did so). Xenophanes maintains that the divine is eternal (it was not born and it will not die), not just immortal (it will not die), and so declares accounts of the births of the gods, including Hesiod's *Theogony*, equally impious.

Fourth, there is no divine hierarchy.

7.9   It is unholy for any of the gods to have a master.

(pseudo-Plutarch, *Stromata* 4 = DK 21A32)

Zeus's preeminent rank among the gods here falls under attack. Though elsewhere Zeus's rule is a basis of order among the potentially unruly Olympians and in the world, Xenophanes finds it intolerable for anything divine to be constrained.

Fifth, the gods do not meddle in human affairs.

7.10   (26) He always remains in the same place, moving not at all,
            nor is it fitting for him to come and go to different places at
            different times.

7.10 contrasts strongly with Homer's gods, who move from Olympus to their sanctuaries to the battlefield of Troy, their minds often on human events in which they actively participate.

Positive Theology

Like the Milesians, Xenophanes does not question the presence of the divine in the universe, only the way it was conceived. His attacks imply that god is not immoral or responsible for evil, is not anthropomorphic, is eternal, self-sufficient, independent, master of everything, and unmoving.

God is described in a number of fragments as well as 7.10.

7.11   (23) God is one,[9] greatest among gods and men,
            not at all like mortals in bodily form or thought.

---

9. Or, "One god."

7.12   (24) All of him sees, all of him thinks,[10] all of him hears.

7.13   (25) But without effort he shakes all things by the thought of his mind.[11]

Abandoning religious tradition as a source of truth about god, Xenophanes turns to reason, appealing to the rational criterion of "what is fitting" to determine god's nature and attitudes. In keeping with the Milesian conception of the divine, god is deanthropomorphized and impersonal but not isolated from the universe, of which he[12] is fully aware (though not through human sense organs) and over which he exercises control ("shakes all things"), though not by physical might but effortlessly and through his thought, without having to move from place to place. God is eternal. Most important, and contrary to earlier Greek views, Xenophanes is a monotheist, as **7.11** emphatically proclaims.[13]

It is natural for us to think that Xenophanes' god must be immaterial, but the fragments do not say so much. "Not at all like mortals in bodily form or thought" (**7.11**) is consistent with his having no body, but it does not imply so much any more than it implies that he does not think—and he does think (**7.12**). He has no limbs or special sense organs, but this, too, does not prove that he has no body. As we shall see the idea of an immaterial entity came only with difficulty.

Like Anaximenes' air, Xenophanes' god controls the world; is he identical with the whole universe, as some interpreters believe, or with one of its major components, as is the case for the divine basic entities of the Milesians? An argument against these views would go like this. The world is full of motion, but Xenophanes' god does not move (**7.10**); therefore, he is not part of the world. A counterargument would go as follows. Xenophanes' god always remains in the

---

10. The translation "thinks" undersells the range of the word it translates (*noein*), which covers knowing, recognizing, understanding, realizing, planning, foreseeing, conceiving, devising, remembering, thinking, imagining, intending, etc. (See Lesher [1992: 103–4]). The same range applies to *noos* and *noēma*, translated "thought" in **7.11** and **7.13**.

11. "With the *phrēn* of his *noos*." Both words have a range of meanings. *Phrēn* can mean not only "thought" but also the location where thought occurs; *noos* can mean the capacity or faculty of thought, or it can mean mind, or it can mean a particular thought. A paraphrase that perhaps gives Xenophanes' sense is "by the active exercise of the thought from his mind" (Lesher [1992]: 109).

12. In describing god, Xenophanes uses masculine forms of adjectives.

13. I take the phrase "among gods and men" in **7.11** as a "polar" expression, which emphasizes a point by mentioning extreme cases ("polar opposites"), which need not be actual. Since "among gods" contradicts Xenophanes' monotheistic message, either the expression had wholly lost its original associations (cf. "navy blue") or else Xenophanes mischievously employs it to describe his unique god. It follows from Xenophanes' fourth objection to the traditional religion that no god is greater than others. However, the phrase is taken by many to show that Xenophanes was *not* a monotheist but believed that one of the gods is supreme to the others.

same place (**7.10**); therefore, he occupies some place, so that he has a location in the world. Moreover, motion requires contact. Therefore, if without moving he causes all things to move, he must be in contact with all things—he is present everywhere. The conclusions of these arguments need not contradict one another. They point to a conception of god as a divinity that permeates the world and causes change in it but that is distinct from the things it affects. This picture requires a distinction between god and the world such that the former is an active principle and the latter is passive, and it calls for an account of how the one can act on the other and how the other can be affected by it. That Xenophanes failed to address these questions is suggested by the silence of the sources and confirmed by the remark (**7.14**, below) that he "made nothing clear," which Aristotle makes with this sort of issue in mind.[14] To judge by what we know of his predecessors and immediate successors, though, it would be entirely anachronistic to expect Xenophanes to provide such accounts or even to have thought it important to provide them.

Though there are gaps, Xenophanes' view of the relation between god and the world amounts to the following. The world for all its diversity and change possesses an underlying unity. All its movements are controlled by the unitary divinity that pervades it. Moreover, god controls things through thought: his complete awareness of the world (implied in **7.12**), gives him insight or complete understanding, and on the basis of this understanding he thinks, decides, and wills things to happen. More explicitly than in the Milesians, intelligence, not the whims of the Olympians, governs the world. This is perhaps the most important feature of Xenophanes' theology and of his world-view.

The Natural World

Xenophanes was interested in the same issues as the Milesians: the basic materials, astronomical and meteorological phenomena, and the origin of life. He made original contributions on all of these topics. Unlike his predecessors,

---

14. There are other interpretations of Xenophanes' theology, notably that of Guthrie (1962: 376–83), who believes Xenophanes' god is spherical and identical with the *kosmos*. Guthrie relies heavily on **7.14**, the dramatic concluding words of which, however, could equally well have come from a person whom the sight of the heaven inspired to believe not that the heaven is divine but that it is moved by god. Also, it is a difficulty for this view that Xenophanes' god causes motion in the world (**7.13**). First, if god is motionless (**7.10**), he cannot be identical with a world containing motion. (Even if the world as a whole does not move, still, parts of it do, and there are obvious problems in holding that parts of god move.) Second, since Xenophanes holds that there is motion in the world, Aristotle is wrong to associate him with the Eleatics who deny that motion exists. I therefore dismiss **7.14** along with other testimonia Guthrie cites, on the grounds that they incorrectly represent Xenophanes as a proto-Eleatic.

Xenophanes did not have a cosmogony. Aristotle implies that he held that the world is ungenerated and therefore eternal.[15]

> 7.14   Some declared the universe to be a single substance . . . not supposing, like
>   some of the natural philosophers, that what-is is one and generating <the
>   universe> out of the one as out of matter, but speaking differently. For the
>   others add change, since they generate the universe, but these people say it is
>   unchangeable . . . Xenophanes, who was the first of these to preach monism
>   (Parmenides is said to have been his student) made nothing clear . . . but
>   looking off to the whole heaven he declares that the one is god.
>   (Aristotle, *Metaphysics* 1.5 986b10–25, part in DK 21A30)

Positing an eternal *kosmos* brings advantages. Xenophanes needs to account only for how the world functions, not for how it arose, and does not need to distinguish differences between the cosmogonic process and the processes that maintain the world order. His task in describing the world is reduced to discussing its present composition and operation.

He was the first dualist, positing earth and water as the basic substances from which all other things are made.

> 7.15   (29) All things that come into being and grow are earth and water.

> 7.16   (33) We all come into being out of earth and water.

> 7.17   (30) Sea is the source of water and the source of wind.
>   For not without the wide sea would there come to be
>   in clouds the force of wind blowing out from within,
>   nor streams of rivers nor rain water from the sky,
>   but the great wide sea is the sire of clouds and winds and rivers.

> 7.18   (27) For all things are from the earth and all return to the earth in the end.

> 7.19   (28) The earth's upper limit is seen here at our feet
>   touching the air. But the lower part goes down without limit.

> 7.20   He says that the sun is gathered together from many small fires . . . He
>   declares that the earth is without limit and is not surrounded by air in
>   every direction, that all things come into being from the earth. And he
>   says that sun and stars come into being from the clouds.
>   (pseudo-Plutarch, *Stromata* 4 = DK 21A32)

---

15. The principle is widespread in Greek philosophy that things not subject to generation are not subject to perishing either.

7.21 The sun <is constituted> out of incandescent clouds.[16]

(Stobaeus 2.20.3 = DK 21A40)

7.22 <The stars> are constituted out of ignited clouds that die down every day but become fiery again by night, just like coals.

(Aëtius 2.13.13 = DK 21A38)

7.23 All things of this sort [comets, shooting stars, etc.] are aggregations of incandescent clouds.

(Aëtius 3.2.11 = DK 21A44)

7.24 He declared that the sea is salty because many mixtures flow together in it . . . Xenophanes believes that earth is being mixed into the sea and over time it is dissolved by the moisture, saying that he has the following kinds of proofs: sea shells are found in the middle of earth and in mountains, and imprints of fish and seals have been found at Syracuse in the quarries, and the imprint of coral [or, "of a laurel leaf"] in the depth of the stone in Paros, and on Malta flat impressions of all forms of marine life. He says that these came about when all things were covered with mud long ago and the impressions were dried in the mud. All humans perish when the earth is carried down into the sea and becomes mud, and then there is another beginning of generation, and this change occurs in all the *kosmoi* [that is, in every such cycle].

(Hippolytus, *Refutation of All Heresies* 1.14.4–6 = DK 21A33)

This information can be interpreted in several ways, of which the following is perhaps the simplest. First, earth and water are the basic forms of matter. Both are abundant in the world around us: earth in the ground on which we walk, and water in rain, rivers, lakes, and especially in the sea. Other things derive from them and are composed of them, some from earth alone, some from water alone, and some from both together. Clouds, wind, rain, and rivers come from the sea, as do the celestial bodies. (This can be seen as a correction of Anaximenes' view that wind, cloud, and water are forms of air.) It is a reasonable inference that Xenophanes held that air and fire are generated from the sea as well, since the sun and stars are fiery and since wind is generally thought to be a form of air.

Second, the earth (the physical entity) is largely constituted of earth (the material) and the sea. We touch the upper surface of the earth, and when we are on land we touch the upper surface of its earthen part. The earth (and therefore its earthen part, conceivably also the sea) "is without limit" (**7.19**) The word for "without limit" is *apeiron*, which later came to mean "infinite" but in Xenophanes' time had no such precise meaning; "indefinitely far" is a possible paraphrase. One implication of its being unlimitedly deep is that there is nothing beneath it to limit it in that direction. So the air, which is *above* the earth, cannot entirely surround it.

---

16. The translation of this and the following two passages is indebted to Mourelatos (2008).

Further, since the sea is part of the earth and is the ultimate source of the weather cycle in which rain returns to the earth, and since plants and animals can be said to be "from" the earth and to return to the earth when they die, Xenophanes might well have felt justified in generalizing these facts to the claim of 7.18.

Third, Xenophanes seems to have adopted a theory that the history of the world is cyclical, a series of successive arrangements of existing material into *kosmoi*, possibly going back into the past and forward into the future "without limit." If this is right, then he was the first Greek to do so. The cycle is sketched in 7.17. Each cycle begins and ends in a state of complete mixture of the two basic materials: a mass of mud. There follows a period in which earth and water are separated from one another to some degree and another period in which they are mixed again until they return to the primordial muddy state. The original state does not support life; generation of living things occurs when earth and water are sufficiently separated. The phase in which we live is that of increasing mixture: "earth is being mixed into the sea and over time it is dissolved by the moisture," which accounts for the salty nature of the sea.

This fragment is interesting for its reasoning and use of evidence. Particularly impressive is Xenophanes' marshaling of facts to support his thesis, which indicates a belief that the best way to prove a theory is to provide the greatest amount and widest variety of evidence possible. Thus, he does not simply say that there used to be less mixture than now; he assembles evidence that once there was more mixture. From this evidence for a period of increasing separation followed by one of increasing mixture he concludes not that the history of the world consists of only one swing from wet to dry and back to wet, but apparently that there is alternation between states of total mixture and some degree (perhaps not total) of separation, with life being extinguished in each period of extreme mixture and then regenerated as the world dries out. This may (but does not necessarily) imply a belief in a principle of causation according to which in some sense similar conditions lead to similar results.

Xenophanes' explanations of astronomical and meteorological phenomena are fascinating, especially the prominent role played by clouds (7.21, 7.22, 7.23), but cannot be pursued here.[17] The only feature that I will mention is his deliberate practice of identifying phenomena traditionally associated with the gods as natural phenomena, in this way continuing his attacks on traditional Greek ways of explaining events in the world by reference to the gods. In this he was practicing a kind of interpretation previously proposed by Anaximenes.[18] His accounts of the rainbow and St. Elmo's fire go as follows.

7.25   (32) What they call Iris, this thing too is in reality a cloud,
             purple and red and yellow to behold.

---

17. See Mourelatos (2008) for an excellent account.
18. See above p. 54.

7.26   <Concerning the stars that are called the Dioscuri[19]> Xenophanes says that
the things like stars that appear on boats [that is, St. Elmo's fire] are small
clouds that glimmer as a result of a certain kind of motion.

(Aëtius 2.18.1 = DK 21A39)

Human Knowledge

As the first Presocratic to reflect on the frailty of our ability to gain knowledge,
Xenophanes is the father of epistemology. He was also hailed in antiquity as the
father of skepticism for the following fragment.

7.27   (34) No man has seen nor will there be anyone
     who knows the clear truth about the gods and about all the things I speak of.
     For even if a person should in fact say what has come to pass,
     nevertheless he himself does not know, but in all cases it is opinion that
        has been wrought.

Xenophanes assumes that only what is true or is the case can be known, but he
claims that merely stating what happens to be true does not guarantee knowledge. Far from it. He contrasts knowledge and opinion and maintains that true
opinion falls short of knowledge. Simply saying something true (and presumably
believing it) is no guarantee that you know it. Thus, he distinguishes between
(1) p is true, (2) A correctly believes that p is true, and (3) A knows that p. These
distinctions are fundamental for epistemology, and it is remarkable to find them
in the earliest Presocratic author to discuss the subject of knowledge. Something
can be true without anyone's knowing it. (A famous example is that it is either
true or false that the number of hairs on a person's head at any moment is even,
but unless the person is almost bald no one knows whether this is true or false.)
Likewise, nothing can be known unless it is true. (It is impossible to know that
$2 + 2 = 5$. Likewise, since the world is round, it is impossible to know that it is
flat—even if many people in the past were so convinced that this is true that they
said that they knew it.) On the other hand, it is possible to believe things that
are false as well as things that are true, but true belief (true opinion) falls short
of knowledge. (For example, I am not a meteorologist and I have not seen the
weather forecast for tomorrow, but I believe it will not rain tomorrow; still, the
absence of rain tomorrow will not be enough to guarantee that I knew it would
not rain.) What the difference is between true belief and knowledge has been
one of the central problems of epistemology since antiquity, and Xenophanes'
fragment does not suggest any answer.

---

19. Literally, "sons of Zeus;" the term was used to refer to Castor and Polydeuces
(Pollux).

According to 7.27, beliefs can be had on all subjects (or can be had by all people), but on at least some subjects humans cannot attain knowledge. These subjects include all the things Xenophanes speaks of. He recognizes the difficulty of his subject matter but evidently thinks that there is some point in his stating and promoting his own beliefs on those subjects. Perhaps (in view of his own use of evidence[20]) the point is that on these subjects we cannot amass enough evidence to guarantee us knowledge as opposed to mere belief.

7.27 does not present Xenophanes as a thoroughgoing skeptic who denies all possibility of knowledge, but it places his confident assertions and clever reasoning in a different light. If knowledge is unattainable on the subjects Xenophanes studies (the nature of the divine, the basic materials of the world, the origin and future of the world, as well as the nature and behavior of the things in the heavens), he cannot claim to have proved his own views. His claims are possible, maybe even nearer the truth than previous ones. This interpretation accords with a short fragment which has been taken to be the conclusion of his philosophical book.

7.28 (35) Let these things be believed as resembling the truth.

Further, although his views about god count as opinion, not knowledge, still there is a reason why his theory, which is the product of rational inquiry, is superior to the traditional view, which is accepted without reflection.

7.29   (18) By no means did the gods intimate all things to mortals from the
             beginning,[21]
         but in time, by searching, they discover better.

7.29 unsurprisingly rejects divine revelation as a source of knowledge. That is not the sort of thing Xenophanes' god (note the plural in the fragment) does. Diligent research as pursued by Xenophanes leads to better discoveries. The best knowledge, that is, full knowledge, has been ruled out by 7.27, so in the context, "discover better" means doing a better job than believing in divine revelation can, and in fact doing the best job possible under our limited circumstances.

Finally, a fragment, perhaps related to Xenophanes' views on the frailty of human knowledge, introduces the notion of the relative nature of judgments, which Heraclitus would take up.[22]

7.30   (38) If god had not created yellow honey, they would say that figs are far
             sweeter.

---

20. See above p. 66.

21. I take the point of this line to be that knowledge does not come from divine revelation, not that there are gods which reveal things to mortals.

22. See below pp. 131–34.

Conclusion

Xenophanes' interests are wider than those of his Milesian predecessors. His physical speculations place him in the Milesian tradition, but his abandonment of the Milesian attempt to find a single basic substance is noteworthy. His views on the divine crystallized the dissatisfaction with the Olympian deities implicit in the naturalistic accounts of phenomena proposed by Anaximander and Anaximenes. In fact after Xenophanes there was little or no serious defense of a literal understanding of traditional Greek mythology by any major philosopher. His interest in human knowledge—its nature and limitations, and how to attain it—was taken up in the following generations and lay at the heart of much of the treatment of knowledge in antiquity. Together with his contemporary Heraclitus, Xenophanes introduced concerns about method and the theoretical limits of human knowledge, which altered the course of Presocratic thought from speculating about nature to theorizing about the basis for such speculation. In this change of direction we have in an important sense the birth of Western philosophy.

8

The Early Ionian Achievement

We are now in a position to assess the difference between the thought of the early Ionians (I shall use this label for Thales, Anaximander, Anaximenes, and Xenophanes) and what went before and to identify some features of the new way of thought.[1]

In the opening chapters of the *Metaphysics*, Aristotle says

> 8.1   That it [wisdom] is not concerned with making things is . . . clear from the examples of the earliest philosophers. People both now start and in the beginning started to do philosophy out of wonder. At first they wondered about the obvious difficulties, and then they gradually progressed to puzzle about the greater ones, for example, the behavior of the moon and sun and stars and the coming to be of the universe. Whoever is puzzled and in a state of wonder believes he is ignorant. (This is why the lover of myths too is in a sense a philosopher, since myths are made up of wonders.) And so, if indeed they pursued philosophy to escape ignorance, they were obviously pursuing scientific knowledge in order to know and not for the sake of any practical need.
>
>   (Aristotle, *Metaphysics* 1.2 982b12–21 [not in DK])

Aristotle stresses philosophy's impractical nature and hints at the difference between philosophy and myth. A little later he identifies Thales as the founder of the philosophical tradition and marks him off from those like Homer who were "terribly ancient, long before our own times . . . the first to speculate about the gods."[2]

In considering Hesiod we saw that even that early "speculat[or] about the gods" did not simply retell familiar tales. His two principal works, broadly speaking, present overviews of the external world and the human world—the former at the end of the *Theogony*, after Zeus has secured his rule, and the latter in the *Works and Days*—with some attempt to provide an integrated picture. The world is ordered to some extent on a rationally comprehensible basis. The *Theogony* puts traditional myths together into a unified story of the development of the world up to the rule of Zeus, which still prevails and will continue forever. Like humans and animals, the chief physical parts of the differentiated world (sky, earth, underworld, mountains, rivers, etc.) and such other prominent features of existence as love, day, and night, are born, most of them from the union of a male and a female parent. Hesiod accounts for the present world by telling

---

1. Several treatments of this and related topics are collected in Furley and Allen (1970). G. E. R. Lloyd has written extensively on these issues, most notably in Lloyd (1979) and Lloyd (1987). More recently Graham (2008, Ch. 1) has identified a pattern common to the Ionian cosmologies, which he claims remained influential throughout the Presocratic period and afterward.

2. Aristotle, *Metaphysics* 1.3 983b27–29 = DK 1B10.

its history—how it developed from a simpler, earlier situation into its present complex state. The world is characterized by order, with the inferior divinities performing the functions assigned to them by Zeus. In fact, it is a moral order, since Zeus is closely associated with Justice, Peace, etc., and (in *Works and Days*) is the guarantor of justice through a system of rewards and punishments.

The early Ionians took over much from Hesiod. Most important is the concept of an ordered world comprehensible to human intelligence. But their manner of expression and reasoning was dramatically different, as was their conception of order. It is certainly wrong to say that they were the first Greeks to ask all the questions they did and to regard Hesiod as a primitive mythologist, but it is also incorrect to deny all value to Aristotle's distinction between philosophy and mythology, even mythology of Hesiod's sophisticated kind.

Xenophanes' theological fragments show most strikingly the departure from earlier ways of thinking. Xenophanes criticizes mythological stories for attributing to the gods shameful actions like theft, adultery, and deceit, which are frequent events in the Homeric epics and the *Theogony* (7.4). Such behavior is inappropriate to the divine and so is wrongly ascribed to the gods. Xenophanes rejects tradition as a reliable source of knowledge about divine things; he substitutes human thought and in particular the application of the criterion "what is fitting" (7.10). Humans can determine the nature of god as Xenophanes does, first finding reasons to question traditional ideas (7.3–7.9) and then constructing an acceptable view of the divine. In developing his theology along rational lines, Xenophanes does not simply bowdlerize Homer; he discards the Olympians altogether. On the interpretation I adopt, there is only one god, who governs the world by the thought of his mind (7.13)—a far cry from the boisterous polytheism of Mount Olympus, where jealous gods frequently come into conflict and rule the world according to their whims and ambitions, through physical might and intimidation.

Do away with gods governed by human passions, emotions, and caprices, and the world takes on a different face. No longer is the thunderbolt the weapon Zeus hurls at objects of his wrath. No longer can puzzling events be shrugged off as due to the will of the gods. There is a rational order in the world, knowledge of which can be attained, for just as we can understand the single god who rules the world, so, since god rules the world rationally, as rational beings we can hope to understand how it works. Early Ionian philosophy sought after this understanding.

The early Ionians share with Homer and Hesiod a belief in the divine governance of the world as has already been shown for Xenophanes. In addition, Thales roundly declares that all things are full of gods (4.11), and Anaximander and Anaximenes claim for their originative substances the attributes of being eternal and eternally in motion, in effect making them divine. (5.5, 6.1, and 6.2)

The early Ionians and Hesiod have the common aim of understanding the history of the world, its present constitution, and the principles on which it functions. Anaximander, whose interest in origins is most evident, begins his account with the eternal *apeiron*, from which the world took its start. He describes the origin largely in terms of entities and processes still found in the developed *kosmos* and which are prominent in his treatment of its present state, although it is unclear how his principle of cosmic justice in which opposites in turn commit injustice upon and make reparation to one another (**5.20**) is related to the *apeiron* or to the way the world came to be. Nevertheless, this principle can explain many diverse phenomena, including the regular succession of day and night, of winter and summer, of flood and drought. It plays the role of a general scientific law, like Newton's Law of Universal Gravitation, which is applied to a wide variety of events; we explain those events by showing that they fall under the law and how they do so. Further, this principle not only accounts for much of the order observed in the world around us but also guarantees that it will last. Xenophanes takes a different approach, declaring the world's history to be a perhaps unlimited sequence of cycles (**7.24**), so that the materials of which it consists have always been and will always be.

The world presents itself as a chaotic diversity of things and events. In order to comprehend it we need to locate order in the chaos, unity in the multiplicity, limit in the unlimited. The traditional world-view found its principle of order, unity, and limit in the gods. Lightning might strike here or there, now or then, but it is always caused by a single thing: the will of Zeus. There are limits on the amount of order the Olympians could bring, and there is something unsatisfactory about explaining the apparently random behavior of lightning by reference to a capricious being. Laws of nature do not explain events in such terms. Anaximander's law makes reference to "the ordering of time" (**5.20**), and some translators capitalize "Time" as if Anaximander intended some measure of personification. Even if they are correct, there is no suggestion that Time acts capriciously in establishing order or in dealing out penalties for injustice.

Explaining events through universal laws is one way to order the universe. Another is to show that things are more closely related than their bewildering variety suggests. Hesiod's genealogical account is one way of relating entities to one another. The early Ionians adopted another strategy—identifying a small number of basic principles and claiming that other things can be explained in terms of these. Thales and Anaximenes each posited a single principle, water and air respectively (**4.8, 6.1, 6.2**). Anaximenes thought that all things are composed of air in its various phases (which include fire, wind, water, etc.). Thales may have held that all things are made of water, but may instead have offered a cosmogony in which the present-day world developed out of (rather than is composed of) water as a single original substance. Anaximander proposed a cosmogony beginning with a single substance of indefinite nature, the *apeiron* (**5.3, 5.6**). Xenophanes identified earth and water as the basic substances (**7.15**).

The types of explanation the early Ionians used mark a further break from their predecessors. Homer's epics portray individual humans in particular sets of circumstances, with their own individual goals and individual deeds, and much of Hesiod's *Theogony* treats the (unique) history of Zeus's rise to power and the particular events which preceded and attended it. Cosmological matters receive attention largely because of this interest in individual events. It is quite otherwise with the early Ionians, whose interests center on the *kosmos* rather than on particular people and for whom the individual is to a large extent seen as an instance of a universal. The principal questions now are: How did the whole world come into being? How did animal life arise? What are all things made of? Why do eclipses occur? What is lightning? rather than Why was that tree struck by lightning? What is the significance of that eclipse? or What is my (or Achilles') ancestry? The universality of the answers implicit in the theories of the early Ionians is another consequence of abandoning modes of explanation in terms of personified deities. Thunder is due to a natural principle which operates uniformly and impersonally. Every thunderclap is caused by a certain specifiable set of natural circumstances, and whenever those circumstances occur, thunder will result. The focus on the universal and impersonal rather than the particular and personal forms an important feature of the philosophical and scientific tradition which the early Ionians began. Aristotle says explicitly that philosophy and science deal primarily with universals,[3] and modern science still has as one of its main tasks the description and explanation of particular events through universal laws.

Another point of difference between the early Ionians and Homer and Hesiod is their attitude toward tradition. Put very crudely, where Homer and Hesiod worked within traditional frameworks,[4] the early Ionians rejected tradition as a source of knowledge and set rational criteria in its place. It is hard to underrate either the intellectual courage it took to make this step or the profound and continuing effects it has had on human civilization. In doing away with the Olympians and accounting for the world in other ways, the early Ionians forfeited the only previously available means of justifying many of their basic beliefs. (This assertion should not be misunderstood. No doubt rational considerations and argument had frequently been used in the past, in Greece and elsewhere. What is new is the application of intellectual tools to cosmology and theology, and the belief that these tools are sufficient for the task.) They rejected Homer's and Hesiod's authority and challenged a way of looking at the world that was universal both among the Greeks and among all the foreign peoples known to the Greeks at the time. Xenophanes discarded Homeric theology because "it is not fitting," and his authority for doing so was his own reasoning. It is hard to think of a bolder move.

Moreover, once tradition is rejected as an authoritative source of knowledge, theories must stand or fall on their own merits. This approach has been followed

---

3. Aristotle, *Metaphysics* 1.1, cf. *Posterior Analytics* 1.31 and 2.19 (none of these passages in DK).

4. This is not to say that they followed tradition blindly. In Ch. 2 I suggested that Hesiod put traditional myths together in new ways for his own purposes. Homer too may well have innovated. The absence of earlier and contemporaneous evidence makes certainty impossible, but in general the Greeks tolerated variations and innovations in their myths more than we might expect; tradition was flexible up to a point. My claim is that Homer and Hesiod remained within the Olympian tradition, whereas the early Ionians abandoned it.

by philosophy and science to this very day, and in assessing the early Ionian theories we have been employing the method they invented. But what are appropriate grounds for judging theories? The early Ionians show increasing sophistication in this area too.

Some of the methods used by Hesiod and the early Ionians have already been mentioned. I shall now describe another aspect of Ionian rationality which some interpreters consider possibly the most important feature of Ionian speculation. I call it rational criticism. The idea is that the early Ionians developed their theories partly in response to their predecessors. Anaximander and Anaximenes, for example, reflected on earlier theories, identified objections, and produced new theories immune to those objections. They rejected theories because they failed to fit observed facts or to satisfy rational criteria. This way of criticizing old theories and proposing new ones is public in a certain sense. Theories are not accepted or rejected through mysterious processes controlled by a few experts or otherwise privileged individuals. This was much truer in the Greek world than in ours. During the period covered by this book, when science and philosophy were not the specialized disciplines they later became, theories were accessible to all intelligent people, and philosophical and scientific debates at least sometimes took place in public settings. The evidence for or against a theory and the criteria by which theories are judged were capable of being stated publicly and understood by a general audience. Others were then in a position to evaluate the theory and criteria for themselves, to decide whether the criteria are cogent, how far a theory satisfies those criteria and how well it fits the empirical facts. Moreover, the same sort of examination could be applied to the new theories. So it happened that the process of rational criticism led to successive theories, each improving on its predecessors. The level of sophistication and the plausibility of the theories advanced rapidly. Traditional accounts of the world were driven from the scene, for mythology is hard put to withstand critical scrutiny or mount a rational defense.

We can also hazard an account of why this method might have begun in sixth century Ionia. The Greeks of the Archaic period were open to new ideas. In art they borrowed and assimilated motifs from a variety of foreign cultures; elements of Greek architecture of the period have evident Egyptian influence; most important the idea of alphabetic writing was borrowed from the Phoenicians, and the Greek alphabet itself is an adaptation of the Phoenician script. However, the same was not possible in philosophy or religion. Faced with rival systems of gods and religious traditions going back so far into antiquity as to make incredible Homer's stories of gods walking on earth only a few centuries previously, the Greeks could not simply keep their own gods and also accept others. But they were not in the position of nineteenth-century South Sea islanders confronted by just one prestigious civilization with its ancient and well-established religion. They faced at least two such civilizations, the Egyptian and the Mesopotamian, each with its own pantheon, mythology, and views on the origin of the world. In this unusual if not historically unique situation, it is understandable that a few highly intelligent and reflective people should have come to question their own religious tradition and the others as well, inventing and developing ways of examining beliefs for their plausibility and intelligibility. It is also understandable that this examination should have led to dissatisfaction with all known religions, mythologies, and world systems and to a desire to replace them with more satisfactory accounts, and that it should have been applied to the new theories in their turn.

Another feature of early Ionian speculation is its propensity toward bold generalizations based on little evidence. Such readiness to generalize beyond carefully controlled limits is nowadays unacceptable in science and philosophy, but in the Presocratic era, on the contrary, speculation needed this degree of recklessness for progress to be made at all. As there was no agreement on a general theory of how the world works, it is not surprising that attention was paid mainly to finding the outline of an acceptable overall theory and not to working out details within a single theory. It is premature to proceed to details until such an overall theory is adopted; in fact detailed explanations make no sense except in the context of a general theory.[5] And since all the theories of the early Ionians had obvious shortcomings, it was too soon to begin the careful, controlled work we associate with science and philosophy. Further, the notion of working out details was as yet hardly known to the intellectual tradition the Milesians began.

The word that best suits the theorizing of the early Ionians is *historiē*, "inquiry," a general term which is different from "science" and "philosophy" as we understand them in that it does not prescribe a specific subject matter or method. (The historian Herodotus used this word to describe his own work; hence it came to have the meaning "history.") Xenophanes contrasts this approach with divine revelation as a source of knowledge (**7.29**). Indeed, the early Ionians offered accounts of an astonishing range of topics—from the origin and constitution of the *kosmos* to the nature of change, to the origin of life, to questions of astronomy, meteorology, geology, and theology. They did not recognize any disciplinary boundaries and had no conception of specialization. They are justifiably said to have invented "the conception of nature as an all-inclusive system ordered by immanent law,"[6] although they had no single word for "nature."[7]

The experimental method, characteristic of science since the Renaissance, was unknown in the sixth century. In fact, very few experiments are recorded for the thousand-year history of Greek science. Further, many of the theories of the early Ionians and of the Presocratics in general are not subject to empirical testing. It is difficult or impossible to think of evidence that could be observed with techniques or technology available in sixth-century Greece that would

---

5. These remarks are made with the early Ionians' treatments of cosmogony and the material principle mainly in mind. In areas such as meteorology, where there was more agreement, more attention was paid to details.

6. Cherniss (1935: 10).

7. *Phusis* came to be used in this sense no earlier than the late fifth century.

conclusively prove the theories right or wrong. And there is no reason to think that the theories were stated with any notion that they might be or should be subject to such verification or falsification. Still, that is not to deny altogether that they are based on observation of the world. In some sense they must have been, since their aim was to account for the observed world and to do so in terms of processes and substances that are either familiar from observation or somehow analogous to or extrapolated from observed phenomena.[8]

Another methodological approach largely missing in the thought of the early Ionians is that of deductive proof. As far as we can tell, they tended not to argue for their views but to proclaim them.[9] To a very large extent, accounts of the history of early Greek thought, including the present one, involve attempts to reconstruct reasoning that could have led to the theories which the testimonia assert that individual thinkers proposed; the reasoning they actually employed is lost—perhaps it was never recorded, perhaps they did not think it an important thing to record.

The Ionian scientist-philosophers, then, did not use the sorts of evidence and argument we associate above all with science (experimental evidence, inductive method) or philosophy. Their approach is not well described as either a priori or empirical. Rather, the style of thought characteristic of the early Ionians is frequently called "speculation," and this word, or rather what it represents in their thought, requires some comment. To speculate means, primarily, to think up ideas, especially new ideas. The word does not suggest any specific procedure of thinking, as perhaps do words such as "investigate" and "prove," though it does tend to exclude irrational fancies. I suggested above (pages 74–75) that the early Ionians employed rational criticism to evaluate others' theories and support their own, but this is a general approach rather than a definite method. Different theories conflicted with different empirical facts, and different theories fared better or worse according to which rational criteria might be adopted. The standard for accepting a theory seems to be the vague criterion of what is plausible. Each of the early Ionians had a story to tell of the nature and history of the universe, and their goal was to tell the most plausible story, as measured by an incompletely specified set of rational criteria.

The Milesians developed an increasingly sophisticated set of rational criteria along with their increasingly sophisticated theories, and progress in both areas went hand in hand. Before long some thinkers began to take a conscious interest

---

8. Xenophanes' use of fossil evidence (**7.24**) is the best known case of empiricism among the early Ionians.

9. Here there is need for great caution in view of the almost complete absence of original texts for the early Ionians and our consequent dependence on the doxographical tradition. The doxographers tended to be interested in what was believed, not why it was believed or with what reservations.

in method. Xenophanes raised questions in this area, which became more central for the Pythagoreans, Heraclitus, and the Eleatics. The heightened interest in philosophical issues which we find in the first half of the fifth century stems in part from these reflections on the nature of knowledge, its limitations, and how it can be attained.

The final question I shall take up is whether there was a Milesian school of philosophy. There is a long-standing tradition of referring to Thales, Anaximander, and Anaximenes as the Milesian school. The sources link Anaximander with Thales as his "pupil and successor," "hearer" (that is, student), and "associate," and Anaximenes is said to be related in all these ways to Anaximander. They have much in common. Not only were they all from Miletus, but they also shared an attitude of mind and an intellectual approach. They worked on many of the same problems and were in close agreement on methods and theories, although they differed significantly in details. Each of them learned from his predecessors and continued their work. This much can be stated with reasonable confidence, but is it enough to constitute them as a school?

A standard book on the post-Aristotelian period of Greek philosophy describes a philosophical school as "not, in general, a formally established institution, but a group of like-minded philosophers with an agreed leader and a regular meeting place, sometimes on private premises, but normally in public. School loyalty meant loyalty to the *founder* of the sect . . . and it is in that light that the degree of intellectual independence within each school must be viewed. It was generally thought more proper to present new ideas as interpretations or developments of the founder's views than as criticisms of him. . . . The virtually unquestioned authority of the founder within each of the schools gave its adherents an identity as members of a 'sect.'"[10]

Some elements of this account, which was written to describe the Stoic, Epicurean, and other Hellenistic philosophical schools, can be adapted to the Milesians. The independence and critical stance we have seen in Anaximander and Anaximenes do not count against the existence of a Milesian school nor does the absence of evidence that there was a formally established institution or a regular meeting place. We may be inclined to question whether the later Milesians felt any particular loyalty to Thales or thought of themselves as being under his authority and merely interpreting or developing his views, but it would be risky to base a decision on this doubt, since we know nothing about Anaximander's or Anaximenes' attitudes and motives.

The Milesian school is sometimes compared to the Pythagorean school or society, which existed by the end of the sixth century. But there are important features the Pythagoreans share with the Stoics and other later philosophical schools which the Milesians lacked, and their absence is a strong reason to deny

---

10. Long and Sedley (1987: vol. 1, pp. 5–6).

that there was a Milesian school of philosophy.[11] Throughout the entire course of the sixth century we hear of only three active figures in Miletus. They have a succession of teacher-student relations, but we know of only one student for each teacher. With the Pythagoreans, by contrast, there was kind of religious society and even for the early years we have several names of people associated with Pythagoras and his sect. The Milesian "school" therefore seems to be an invention of the doxographers who wrote at a time when philosophy was largely associated with "schools" and who assumed that the association which evidently took place between Thales and Anaximander and between Anaximander and Anaximenes must have taken place in a school.

---

11. The case is similar for the so-called Eleatic School, consisting of Parmenides, Zeno, and Melissus. But Melissus was from Samos, an island next to modern Turkey, which lies at the other end of the Greek world from Elea, a town on the west coast of Italy, and there is no reason to suppose that he ever visited Elea. Zeno was Parmenides' pupil and defended his teacher's views (12.1). But one follower does not make a school.

9

Pythagoras of Samos and the Pythagoreans

Pythagoras's Life and the Pythagorean Movement

Although details of Pythagoras's life and work are unclear, even mysterious, and the sources disagree on many points, the following brief account may be not far from the truth. Born on the island of Samos c.570, he left c.530 on account of disagreement with the policies of the tyrant[1] Polycrates. At this time or before, he visited Egypt and Babylonia, where he became acquainted with the religious beliefs and cultural practices of those peoples. He settled in Croton, a Greek city in southern Italy. Won over by his personality and his conservative views on morality (emphasizing moderation, piety, respect of elders and of the state, and a monogamous family life), the Council of Croton put him in charge of the education of the children and of the women of the city. In this way he came to have great influence, which extended to other Greek cities in southern Italy and in Sicily and possibly even to Rome. In the first half of the fifth century Croton rose to an unprecedented position of military and economic importance, a development which has been attributed to the presence of Pythagoreans in the region, although the evidence is not certain. In Croton Pythagoras established an exclusive community of his followers that was characterized by a distinctive way of life, based on certain religious and philosophical views. The community, which is frequently called a school or brotherhood, bears some resemblance to a secret cult. Cylon, a young man of an aristocratic family, whose request to become a follower of Pythagoras had been rejected, gathered anti-Pythagorean support and (c.500) led an attack on Pythagoras, who subsequently abandoned Croton and moved to Metapontum, where he died shortly after.

Pythagoras was far more than a politician. He was a religious and moral reformer whose Pythagorean way of life was a long-lasting legacy which survived the dissolution of the movement. His followers were devoted to his sayings, which they collected, memorized, and passed down and many of which were collected and have survived. He was a charismatic figure who became the subject of legends: he killed a poisonous snake by biting it; a river hailed him by name; he made predictions; he appeared simultaneously in two different places; he had a golden thigh. The people of Croton addressed him as Hyperborean[2] Apollo.[3] Pythagoreans identified three types of rational beings: gods, humans, and beings like Pythagoras.[4]

---

1. For this term, see below pp. 373–74.

2. Literally, "beyond the North Wind." Several myths associate Apollo with this distant place.

3. Aristotle, fr. 191 (Rose), Aelian, *Varia Historia* 2.26 (both = DK 14, 7).

4. Aristotle, fr. 192 (Rose) (= DK 14, 7).

After the Founder's death the Pythagorean communities in Croton and elsewhere continued to function. However, mid-century saw anti-Pythagorean uprisings throughout the area. At Croton, a house where the Pythagoreans were gathered was set on fire and all but two were burned alive. Their meeting houses elsewhere were destroyed too, their leaders killed, and there was widespread violence and destruction. Afterwards the character of the movement changed. Some fled to mainland Greece. Those who stayed were centered in Rhegium, but some time later, perhaps about 400 BCE, almost all left Italy, with the notable exception of Archytas, who became an able monarch at Tarentum, where Plato visited him in the early fourth century. The Pythagorean movement effectively died out in the fourth century, as the scattered remnants of this persecution were unable or unwilling to organize and establish active Pythagorean centers again.

Even so, the influence of Pythagoras continued throughout antiquity. Empedocles, who refers to him with respect (**9.6**), was influenced by his doctrine of reincarnation, but his most important philosophical legacy is the strong stamp it left on Plato's thought, as found notably in the myths of the afterlife at the end of *Gorgias*, *Phaedo*, and *Republic*, in the cosmology of the *Timaeus*, and possibly in Plato's belief in the importance of harmony and mathematics and in some fundamental aspects of his theory of Forms.

Later on, "Neopythagoreans" from the mid-first century BCE to the third century CE emphasized the religious, superstitious, and numerological aspects of Pythagoreanism, and followed some of Plato's successors from 300 years before in combining Pythagorean ideas with elements of Plato's thought. These Neopythagoreans followed the common ancient practice of ascribing their own doctrines to the Founder in order to gain authority for their views, which they regarded as implicit in or extensions of his teachings. Neopythagorean beliefs were absorbed from the third century CE by the Neoplatonists, and it is to Neoplatonist writings based largely on Neopythagorean works that most of our information about Pythagoras is due.[5]

Sources

Information about Pythagoras and Pythagorean philosophy in our period presents special difficulties. Pythagoreans in subsequent generations and even into the Neopythagorean period tended to ascribe to Pythagoras their own developments of his ideas. There are few contemporary or near-contemporary references to him. The Pythagorean influence present in many of Plato's dialogues is of some help but cannot be the basis of a detailed historical treatment because of the difficulties in distinguishing Pythagorean ideas from Platonic developments of them. Aristotle wrote two (lost) works on the Pythagoreans. His surviving writings give valuable information about Pythagorean doctrines but rarely mention Pythagoras, more frequently speaking of "those who are called Pythagoreans" or

---

5. For good recent treatments of Pythagoras and Pythagoreanism, see Kahn (2001) and Riedweg (2005).

"the Italians," as though he is unwilling to attribute the doctrines he reports to Pythagoras himself. Moreover, Aristotle's information is hard to interpret since he is out of sympathy, even impatient, with Pythagorean doctrines, which do not fit well into his own system. Neopythagorean and Neoplatonic writings provide abundant materials on Pythagoras's life and teachings, but most of them are unhistorical and therefore are worthless for reconstructing the thought of Pythagoras and his followers in the fifth century. The wry observation that the further in time we get from Pythagoras the more people knew about him reminds us to exercise extreme care in dealing with the source material.

We are no better off regarding original writings. Although Pythagoras and his early followers may have composed written works, none survive. There are many references to Pythagorean secrecy, an unsurprising feature of a religious brotherhood, and reports of the evil end that befell one early follower for revealing a secret, a discovery in geometry.[6] The earliest Pythagoreans for whom there are authentic fragments are Philolaus (who lived in the late fifth and early fourth centuries) and his pupil Archytas (early to middle fourth century) although some of the oral sayings (*akousmata*) may go back to Pythagoras himself. In this situation the only safe thing to say is that although we know a lot about Pythagorean beliefs, we can be sure of practically nothing about the life and teachings of Pythagoras. But extreme skepticism is inappropriate too. Cautious handling of the evidence gives a picture of Pythagoras which is plausible though not demonstrably correct.

The following account of Pythagoreanism down to the time of Philolaus is divided into two parts. First I will treat Pythagoras himself and what appear to be features of Pythagorean thinking that may go back to the Founder. This part is based as far as possible on sources prior to Aristotle. Second I will discuss the cosmology and metaphysics which Aristotle ascribes to the Pythagoreans. The second part stresses the philosophical and scientific elements of Pythagoreanism rather than the religious and political, but the many facets of Pythagorean thought are closely tied and it is important to bear in mind the fundamental religious strand that pervades them all. The philosophy of the Pythagorean Philolaus, which is known from his surviving fragments, is treated separately in Chapter 18.

Early Source Material on Pythagoras

Most of the contemporary and near-contemporary evidence on Pythagoras and fifth-century Pythagoreanism is found in the following passages. Xenophanes mocks Pythagoras's belief in the transmigration of souls.

9.1 Once he passed by as a puppy was being beaten,
  the story goes, and in pity said these words:
  "Stop, don't beat him, since it is the soul of a man, a friend of mine,
  which I recognized when I heard it crying."
               (Xenophanes DK 21B7)

---

6. See below pp. 97–98.

Heraclitus, whose life overlapped Pythagoras's, comments sarcastically about Pythagoras and others.

> **9.2**   Much learning ["polymathy"] does not teach insight. Otherwise it would have taught Hesiod and Pythagoras and moreover Xenophanes and Hecataeus.
>
> (Heraclitus DK 22B40)

> **9.3**   Pythagoras the son of Mnesarchus practiced inquiry (*historiē*[7]) more than all other men, and making a selection of these writings constructed his own wisdom, polymathy, evil trickery.
>
> (Heraclitus DK 22B129)

Some interpret the references to Pythagoras's learning and practice of inquiry as evidence that he followed the Ionian thinkers in investigating nature.[8] (Samos is located quite close to Miletus.) Others take the sneer in **9.3** as a charge that he was a plagiarist; his research was not into nature, but into the discoveries of others.

Ion of Chios (born c.490), in describing Pherecydes, a sixth-century mythographer and author of a *Theogony*, associates Pythagoras with the view that the soul has an afterlife.

> **9.4**   Thus he excelled in both manhood and reverence
> and even in death has a delightful life for his soul,
> if indeed Pythagoras was truly wise about all things,
> he who truly knew and had learned thoroughly the opinions of men.
>
> (Ion of Chios DK 36B4)

Ion also refers to some writings of Pythagoras, indicating that they contain Orphic doctrine—and it is plausible to regard Pythagoras as having some connection with the Orphic religion, which flourished in southern Italy during and after his lifetime and which promised its initiates a happy existence after death.

> **9.5**   Ion of Chios in his work *The Triads* says that he [Pythagoras] composed some poems and attributed them to Orpheus.
>
> (Ion of Chios DK 36B2)

Empedocles, who adopted some Pythagorean beliefs, describes Pythagoras[9] as follows.

---

7. See above p. 75.

8. Some think that **9.2** pairs Pythagoras with Hesiod *as opposed to* Xenophanes and Hecataeus, the former as religious thinkers, the latter as representing the new ways of thought, and that the writings **9.3** refers to are writings of Orphic sects, which believed in an afterlife and the immortality of the soul. This is the interpretation of Burkert (1972).

9. Most interpreters believe that these verses praise Pythagoras, but there was doubt even in antiquity. According to Diogenes Laertius, *Lives of the Philosophers* 8.54 = DK 31A1, some held that they describe Parmenides.

9.6　There was a certain man among them who knew very
　　　　holy matters,
　　　who possessed the greatest wealth of mind,
　　　mastering all sorts of wise deeds.
　　　For when he reached out with all his mind
　　　easily he would survey every one of the things that are,
　　　yea, within ten and even twenty generations of humans.
　　　　　　　　　　　　　　　　　(Empedocles DK 31B129)

Herodotus (485/4–c.430) reports the story that Greeks in the region of the Black
Sea told of Pythagoras's Thracian slave Zalmoxis.

9.7　After being set free, he [Zalmoxis] returned to Thrace. He decided to
　　　civilize his compatriots, who were primitive and stupid, since through
　　　his contact with Greeks and especially with Pythagoras, who was "not the
　　　weakest Sophist [wise man] of the Greeks," he had become acquainted
　　　with the Ionian way of life and with more profound sorts of people
　　　than could be found among the Thracians. "He built a hall in which he
　　　received and feasted leading Thracians and taught them the better view,
　　　that neither he nor his guests nor any of their descendants would die but
　　　would come to a place where they would live forever and have all good
　　　things." To convince them of his teaching, Zalmoxis disappeared for three
　　　years, living in a secret underground chamber, while everyone thought
　　　him dead. In the fourth year he reappeared above ground, and since then
　　　the Thracians believe in immortality.
　　　　　　　　　　　　(Paraphrase of Herodotus, *Histories* 4.95 = DK 14, 2;
　　　　　　　　　　　　　　　　　　the words in quotation marks are
　　　　　　　　　　　　　　　　an adaptation of Godley's translation)

Herodotus also reports that Egyptian religious customs forbade people to wear
wool into temples and to be buried in woolen clothing, and he links those practices with the Pythagoreans.

9.8　The Egyptians agree in this with those called Orphics . . . and with the
　　　Pythagoreans; for it is likewise unholy for anyone who takes part in these
　　　rites to be buried in woolen garments.
　　　　　　　　　　　　　　　(Herodotus, *Histories* 2.81 = DK 14, 1)

Finally, a somewhat later quotation referring to the Pythagorean communities
and their way of life.

9.9　Is Homer said to have been during his life a guide in education for people
　　　who delighted in associating with him and passed down to their followers a
　　　Homeric way of life? Pythagoras himself was greatly admired for this, and
　　　his followers even nowadays name a way of life Pythagorean and are con-
　　　spicuous among others.
　　　　　　　　　　　　　　　(Plato, *Republic* 10 600a–b = DK 14, 10)

The contemporary references (**9.1–9.3**) are ambivalent at best. As Heraclitus criticizes many of his predecessors but not the Milesian philosophers,[10] the charges in **9.2** and **9.3** may be addressed to aspects of Pythagoras's thought that differ from Milesian-style investigations. The charge of lacking insight may mean only that he did not see eye to eye with Heraclitus, but there may be something specific in the claims that his wide knowledge is plagiarized or based on the ideas of others and is "evil trickery."[11] Heraclitus may be expressing his contempt for Pythagoras's mystical, religious views or possibly for some physical doctrines which he found seriously wrong.

9.1, **9.4**, **9.7**, and **9.6** associate Pythagoras with a belief in an afterlife. The soul upon death might enter the body of a lower animal or a human. **9.4** suggests that one's fate after death is a reward or punishment for one's character in the previous life and perhaps refers to the later-attested view that the reward for an outstandingly good life is eternal happiness untouched by the need for rebirth. **9.7** is a patent attempt by some Greeks[12] to claim a Greek origin for a native Thracian belief (Zalmoxis was a Thracian god, not a human). The portrait of Zalmoxis as an impostor may be meant to reflect negatively on Pythagoras himself. The remark in **9.9** on Pythagoras's disciples and way of life illustrates the special nature of the Pythagorean "brotherhood," whose principal beliefs, many of them bound closely to the belief in reincarnation, were traced back to the Founder.

Immortality and Reincarnation

The religious message of Pythagoras is based on the doctrine of the immortality of the individual soul, which along with other related beliefs, is recounted in the following passage.

> **9.10** First he declares that the soul is immortal; then that it changes into other kinds of animals; in addition that things that happen recur at certain intervals, that nothing is absolutely new, and that all things that come to be alive must be thought akin. Pythagoras seems to have been the first to introduce these opinions into Greece.
>
> (Porphyry, *Life of Pythagoras* 19 = DK 14, 8a)

The final statement in **9.10** is disputed,[13] but the views mentioned are certainly Pythagorean. In declaring the soul immortal, Pythagoras obliterated the barrier that the Olympian religion placed between humans and gods. "Immortal" is, for the Greeks, tantamount to "divine."

---

10. See **10.5**, **10.16**, **10.71**, and discussion below p. 127.

11. The word is also rendered "worthless artifice" (Guthrie 1962: 157), "artful knavery" (KRS: 217), and "imposture" (Burnet 1930: 134).

12. Not including Herodotus himself, who is skeptical about the whole tale.

13. Many give priority to Orphism. (See above p. 82 n. 8 and below p. 430.)

The doctrine can be seen as a development of ideas of the Milesian philosophers, who made their originative substances immortal and divine and held that divinity was widespread in the *kosmos*. According to Anaximenes (**6.4**), the human soul is composed of the divine originative substance, air. It is no great leap to infer that the soul is immortal. The Pythagoreans gave special importance to breath in their cosmogony (**9.30, 9.31**), and some Pythagoreans identified the soul with air.

9.11   Some of them [the Pythagoreans] declared that the soul is the motes in the air, and others that it is what makes the motes move.

(Aristotle, *On the Soul* 1.2 404a17 = DK 58B40)

Pythagoras represents a new and radical challenge to the Olympian tradition. To promote each human, or *part* of each human, to the level of the gods simultaneously devalues the gods and their worship and raises the importance of our care for ourselves, or more precisely for our *selves*, where our selves are our souls as opposed, say, to our bodies. Moreover, this doctrine is not anthropocentric. Not only human souls are at stake; all living things possess souls. Only thus can transmigration of souls take place. Our concern is for all ensouled things, with whom we are in a literal sense related.

The doctrines of the immortality and transmigration (otherwise called metempsychosis) of souls imply a major restructuring of values. Our interests, even our egoistic interests, now extend beyond our mortal selves and beyond this lifetime. Further, if what we do and how we live in this life affect our soul's next incarnation, as **9.4** suggests, we have strong prudential reasons to choose certain actions and ways of life over others. The Pythagorean way of life (**9.9**) aimed to improve the soul and to attain for it the best possible destiny, which consists either in attaining the best of reincarnations or in complete freedom from the necessity of continued rebirth through reunion with the divine universal soul.[14]

The following passages say more about this doctrine.

9.12   The Egyptians were the first to declare this doctrine too, that the human soul is immortal, and each time the body perishes it enters into another animal as it is born. When it has made a circuit of all terrestrial, marine, and winged animals, it once again enters a human body as it is born. Its circuit takes three thousand years. Some Greeks have adopted this doctrine, some earlier and some later, as if it were peculiar to them. I know their names, but do not write them.

(Herodotus, *Histories* 2.123 = DK 14, 1)

9.13   Heraclides of Pontus says that Pythagoras said the following about himself. Once he had been born Aethalides and was believed to be the son of Hermes. When Hermes told him to choose whatever he wanted except immortality, he asked to retain both alive and dead the memory of what happened

---

14. A case for the latter view is made on the basis of little evidence by Guthrie (1962: 203).

> to him. . . . Afterwards he entered into Euphorbus and was wounded by
> Menelaus. Euphorbus said that once he had been born as Aethalides and
> received the gift from Hermes, and told of the migration of his soul and
> what plants and animals it had belonged to and all it had experienced in
> Hades. When Euphorbus died his soul entered Hermotimus, who, wishing
> to provide evidence, went to Branchidae, entered the sanctuary of Apollo,
> and showed the shield Menelaus had dedicated. (He said that when Mene-
> laus was sailing away from Troy he dedicated the shield to Apollo.) The
> shield had already rotted away and only the ivory facing was preserved.
> When Hermotimus died, it [the soul] became Pyrrhus the Delian fisher-
> man and again remembered everything. . . . When Pyrrhus died it became
> Pythagoras and remembered all that had been said.
>
> (Diogenes Laertius, *Lives of the Philosophers* 8.4–5 = DK 14, 8)

The Greeks whom Herodotus infuriatingly refuses to name in **9.12** are generally thought to include Pythagoras. **9.13**, which is attributed to a good source,[15]
differs from **9.12** in important points. According to **9.12** but not **9.13** the soul
spends time in Hades as well as in living things. In **9.13** but not **9.12** the soul
sometimes animates plants in addition to animals and humans. In **9.13** but not in
9.12 the soul occupies all animals in between human incarnations, as if all souls
have the same fate. Finally, the three thousand-year span between successive
human incarnations in **9.12** is incompatible with the three human incarnations
of Pythagoras's soul, which **9.13** places after the Trojan War.[16] Some of the discrepancies may stem from the fact that **9.12** claims to be giving an account not
of Pythagorean beliefs but of Egyptian ones (although the Egyptians, who had
an elaborate doctrine of the afterlife, did not believe in transmigration). The
Greeks referred to allegedly borrowed beliefs from the Egyptians, but there is
no guarantee that they did not alter them. In any case, neither passage proves
that the Pythagorean belief in reincarnation involved rewards and punishments
for previous lives. Still, the likelihood is great that it did. First, there is the evidence of **9.4**. Also, Empedocles, who was influenced by Pythagoreanism, held
that the best sort of animal for a soul[17] to occupy is a lion and the best sort of
plant a laurel (**14.34**) and that the best souls become outstanding men and even
blessed gods (**14.35**, **14.36**). Poems from the early fifth century, which may have
been written for people with Pythagorean beliefs, refer to judgment after death
leading to rewards in subsequent lives for outstanding success in this one[18] and
to everlasting happiness in the Islands of the Blest as the reward of "all those
who have had the courage to keep their soul completely away from unjust deeds

---

15. Heraclides of Pontus was a pupil of Plato and a contemporary of Aristotle and had
a special interest in the Pythagorean movement.

16. The date of the Trojan War was disputed in antiquity, but it was usually put at
about 1200 BCE.

17. Empedocles speaks of the *daimōn* instead of the soul. For the equivalence of the
two notions in Empedocles, see below p. 286.

18. Pindar, fr. 133 (not in DK).

for three stays in each place [on earth and in the underworld]."[19] Also, later Pythagoreans held these beliefs.

This evidence makes it plausible that Pythagoras taught not only that the soul is immortal and passes into one living being after another (directly or after a time in Hades), but also that some incarnations are preferable to others and that the next kind of being a soul will inhabit is determined by a postmortem judgment of its previous life. These beliefs are related to the beliefs of the ancient Greek religion or cult known as Orphism, after the myth of Orpheus, who descended to Hades and returned to the world of the living. This religion was prominent in Southern Italy in the sixth century BCE, where Pythagoras will have come into contact with it after settling at Croton. Our knowledge of Orphism is based in part on original documents—in some cases inscriptions on stone, gold leaves, and bone plaques, found in places as diverse as Olbia, on the Black Sea and Cumae, in western Italy. An important document for Orphism is the Derveni papyrus,[20] which was discovered in northern Greece and dates to the second half of the fourth century BCE. It contains an Orphic theogony which has connections with Hesiod's work of that name but distinctive elements of its own. Orphism was a mystery religion, in effect a society requiring secret rites of initiation. It held that after death the soul is reborn (a belief not widely accepted among the ancient Greeks), reincarnated into other bodies both animal and human. The Orphics viewed the cycle of death and rebirth as a "dire cycle of deep grief"[21] from which they were promised eventual release as well as communion with the gods in consequence of their being initiated into the cult, practicing vegetarianism, and living an ascetic life. We know too little about both Orphism and early Pythagoreanism to determine the exact links between the two movements, even which movement was influenced by which. In any case, as with the Orphics, the Pythagorean belief in reincarnation was connected to a set of practices known as the Pythagorean way of life.

Prohibition on Killing; Dietary Restrictions

Important features of the Pythagorean life can be understood from this perspective. The aim of life is to ensure a good future for the soul. Vegetarianism, prominent in the Pythagorean life, results from the belief in transmigration and the kinship of all living things. Bluntly put,[22] what you kill and eat for dinner may have the soul of your dear departed mother or father. More generally, since all living beings are related, it is an equal offense to kill anything, without reference to the possibility that its soul might once have ensouled a human. If it is alive it is at least a distant relative. Any killing is tantamount to murder; eating animals amounts to cannibalism. Empedocles developed this idea in much greater

---

19. Pindar, *Olympians* 2.56–77 (not in DK).
20. A translation of this document is given on pp. 460–68.
21. Quoted in Parker (1995: 500).
22. With Empedocles, **14.27**.

detail[23] than can be attributed to the Pythagoreans from early sources, but there is no reasonable doubt that violating this prohibition was the premier form of injustice, which merited punishment after death.

There are difficulties about this doctrine, which amounts to a rationalization of the instinctive pre-philosophical Greek horror of incurring pollution by bloodshed. First, if all living things are related, then killing and eating plant life including fruits and vegetables should be prohibited too, so that Pythagoreans could eat only a very few things, such as milk and honey; yet there was no general ban on vegetable foods. Quite likely only some plants, such as laurels,[24] were thought to have souls. Second, there is conflicting evidence about the prohibition on eating meat, some sources declaring that all meat was prohibited, others that only certain kinds were (typically, kinds of animals not used for sacrifice), still others denying that any such prohibition existed. A sensible approach to this contradictory information is to see in it traces of variations in Pythagoreanism. Possibly some Pythagoreans were more "orthodox" than others and ate no meat at all while others ate the meat of certain animals; possibly there was initially a ban on all meat but it ceased to be observed rigorously in the fifth-century diaspora, when there were only scattered remnants of the Pythagoreans and hence the likelihood of local deviations from the original norm.

Another notorious practice of the Pythagoreans was their refusal to eat beans. The amount of ancient speculation about this dietary aberration proves that the custom was found odd and that there was no obvious reason for it. We are told that beans were banned because their flatulent tendency disturbs our sleep and our mental tranquillity; because they resemble testicles, or the gates of Hades, or the shape of the universe; because they are used in allotting political offices (a reference to anti-democratic Pythagorean politics); because if buried in manure they take on a human shape; or because their stems are hollow so that they are connected directly to the underworld, and so on.[25] On a plausible recent interpretation,[26] Pythagoras introduced this prohibition because eating beans can be bad for your health: some people grow ill upon eating fava beans, which are common in south Italy, so the ban on beans might be a practical expedient, not a ritual abstention.

Akousmatikoi and *Mathēmatikoi*

After Pythagoras's death there were disputes about his teachings.

9.14   There are two kinds of the Italian philosophy called Pythagorean, since two
        types of people practiced it—the *akousmatikoi* and the *mathēmatikoi*. Of these,
        the *akousmatikoi* were admitted to be Pythagoreans by the others, but they, in
        turn, did not recognize the *mathēmatikoi* but claimed that their pursuits were

---

23. See below pp. 284–90.

24. See above p. 86.

25. These and other explanations are discussed by Guthrie (1962: 184–85).

26. Brumbaugh and Schwartz (1980).

> not those of Pythagoras, but of Hippasus . . . The philosophy of the *akousma-tikoi* consists of unproved and unargued *akousmata* to the effect that one must act in appropriate ways, and they also try to preserve all the other sayings of Pythagoras as divine dogma. These people claim to say nothing of their own invention and say that to make innovations would be wrong. But they suppose that the wisest of their number are those who have got the most *akousmata*.
>
> (Iamblichus, *Life of Pythagoras* 81, 82 = DK 18, 2, 58C4)

The claim of the *akousmatikoi* (the word derives from *akousma*, "oral saying") to be preserving Pythagoras's teachings unchanged and to be following them is unchallenged by the *mathēmatikoi* and so may be taken as broadly true (allowing for the likelihood of additions, subtractions, and alterations). In contrast to the *akousmatikoi*, who learned and accepted Pythagoras's sayings simply on the strength of Pythagoras's having said them, the *mathēmatikoi* (from *mathēma*, "learning" or "studying," not specifically mathematical learning and studying, although the study these Pythagoreans pursued was largely mathematical) promoted the scientific studies Pythagoras allegedly began (and which even the *akousmatikoi* admitted went back as far as Pythagoras's early pupil Hippasus [9.14]), while acknowledging the religious side of Pythagoreanism, even though the *akousmatikoi* refused to recognize continued mathematical and scientific research as part of the Founder's intentions. This split between the religious, conservative, dogmatic *akousmatikoi* and the scientific, progressive, intellectually active *mathēmatikoi*, which resembles the sectarianism often found in the early history of religious movements, continued until the end of the Pythagorean movement in the fourth century, when on the one hand Archytas was engaged in advanced work in mathematics and on the other we hear of pious Pythagoreans who continued to follow the life prescribed in the *akousmata* by practicing Pythagorean silence, dressing simply, and avoiding meat, in hopes for a privileged afterlife.

The *Akousmata*

The *akousmata* were oral sayings attributed to Pythagoras. Some may well go back to him. Their role is described thus.

9.15   All the *akousmata* referred to in this way fall under three headings. (a) Some indicate what something is, (b) others indicate what is something in the greatest degree, and (c) others what must or must not be done. (a) The following indicate what something is. What are the Isles of the Blest? Sun and Moon. What is the oracle at Delphi? The tetractys, which is the harmony in which the Sirens sing. (b) Others indicate what is something in the greatest degree. What is most just? To sacrifice. What is the wisest? Number, and second wisest is the person who assigned names to things. What is the wisest thing in our power? Medicine. What is most beautiful? Harmony.

     (Iamblichus, *Life of Pythagoras* 82 = DK 58C4) (continuation of 9.14)

Examples of the third type of *akousmata* are found in the following passages.

9.16 <Pythagoras ordered his followers> not to pick up <food> which had
fallen, to accustom them not to eat self-indulgently or because it fell on
the occasion of someone's death . . . not to touch a white rooster, because
it is sacred to the Month and is a suppliant; it is a good thing, and is sacred
to the Month because it indicates the hours . . . white is of the nature of
good, while black is of the nature of evil, not to break bread, because friends
long ago used to meet over a single loaf just as foreigners still do, and not
to divide what brings them together. Others <explain this practice> with
reference to the judgment in Hades, others say that it brings cowardice in
war, and still others that the whole universe begins from this.

(Aristotle, fr. 195 (Rose), quoted in Diogenes Laertius,
Lives of the Philosophers 8.34–35 = DK 58C3)

9.17 Do not stir the fire with a knife.
Rub out the mark of a pot in the ashes.
Do not wear a ring.
Do not have swallows in the house.
Spit on your nail parings and hair trimmings.
Roll up your bedclothes on rising and smooth out
the imprint of the body.
Do not urinate facing the sun.

(a selection from Iamblichus, *Protrepticus* 21 = DK 58C6)

Some of the justifications in **9.16** are moral precepts (behave with moderation,
respect the gods), but others reek of pre-philosophical ways of thought. Still
others point to an aspect of Pythagoreanism which remains to be discussed—the
study of the *kosmos* with the aid of mathematics. The *akousmata* make it clear
that to be a Pythagorean required conducting one's life by a closely prescribed
set of rules. Many of them reflect the importance the Pythagoreans attributed to
ritual purity and to moral behavior toward the gods and toward other humans.
Doubtless they believed that following these rules was beneficial to the future of
our soul in its next reincarnation.

So far, Pythagoreanism hardly deserves space in a treatment of early Greek philosophy. The religious side is in many ways the antithesis of the rational approach
to nature. Not only does it contain superstitions and other taboos, it makes no
attempt to justify or systematize them. The *akousmatikoi* followed Pythagoras differently from the way Anaximenes followed Thales and Anaximander. They aimed
to preserve his ideas, not to criticize or enlarge them. Their acceptance of the
akousmata unproved and unargued (**9.14**) is unphilosophical and unscientific.

On the other hand, some of the *akousmata* have connections with interests of
the Ionian philosophers. **9.15** can be seen as rationalizing a myth, identifying the
Isles of the Blest with the sun and the moon. The evidence tantalizingly hints at
the possibility of an allegorical cosmology. More generally, the interest in "what
something is" can be put into the context of some fragments of Heraclitus, who

also declared what wisdom is (**10.44**), what "things taken together" are (**10.48**) and what "all things" are (**10.80**).

The *Mathēmatikoi*

The interests of the *mathēmatikoi* are more central to Greek philosophy. In fact, Pythagoras is most famous today for the geometrical theorem that bears his name. Aristotle declares that the Pythagoreans were the first to advance mathematics. Other "mathematical" ideas associated with Pythagoras or the early Pythagoreans are the mathematical analysis of the harmonic musical intervals, an interest in number theory and the theory of proportions, and the definition of a number of mathematical "means" (such as the arithmetic, geometric, and harmonic means). They claimed that all things are numbers and constructed a cosmogony generating the world from numbers and a cosmology which removed the Earth from the center of the universe and made it move together with the other planets, the sun, and the moon in orbits around a central fire in such as way as to create a celestial harmony. How much of this goes back to Pythagoras himself remains a controversial, but it seems reasonable to suppose that there was something in Pythagoras behind these Pythagorean developments.

Harmonia

One of the *akousmata* states that *harmonia* is the most beautiful thing (**9.15**). If it goes back to Pythagoras, it gives an important clue to his interest and involvement in things mathematical, but in order to understand it we need know what is meant by *harmonia*. The word originally meant a fitting together, connection, or joint. Later it meant the string of a lyre, and then a way of stringing the lyre, that is, a tuning or scale. But the claim that *harmonia* is the most beautiful thing is not simply about music. It refers to the discovery (which may be due to Pythagoras) that concordant musical intervals can be expressed mathematically. The musical intervals of the octave (C–C′), fifth (C–G) and fourth (C–F) were basic to Greek music. In the seven-stringed lyre, four of the strings were tuned to pitches separated by these intervals (for example, C, F, G, C′) and the other three were put at different pitches depending on the "mode" desired. In a lyre the strings all have the same length, so it is clear that the higher notes come from the tauter strings, but no obvious numerical relation is detectable between pitch and tension. In a monochord, a single-stringed instrument with a movable bridge, changing the position of the bridge changes the pitch produced by plucking or bowing the string, which remains under the same tension. There are a limitless number of possible positions the bridge can have and so an unlimited number of possible pitches. When the bridge is placed exactly halfway between the fixed ends of the string, the note produced is an octave higher than is produced by the entire length of the string. This is the case no matter how long the string is, what the string is made of, or how taut it is (as long as it is taut enough to produce a tone). The essence of the octave is the numerical ratio 2:1, not the actual length or the material involved in making the sound. Since the intervals of the fifth and fourth are also expressible in terms of the ratios of small whole numbers (3:2 and 4:3, respectively) music appears to result from the imposition, by means of number, of order and limit on the unlimited continuum of possible tones.

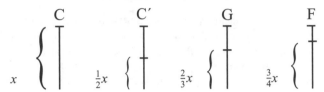

It is difficult for us to imagine how wonderful and surprising it must have been to learn that fundamental features of music could be expressed numerically. After all, we are used to expressing qualitative notions in quantitative, numerical terms. We measure and count color, sound, weight, and speed in wavelengths, grams, and feet per second. In fact, we regard quantitative treatment as one of the hallmarks of science. This discovery was the first time any quality was reduced to a quantity, and so it stands at the beginning of this central aspect of our scientific tradition. Also within Pythagorean thought the discovery had important effects on mathematics, cosmology, and the doctrine of the soul.

Kosmos is another important concept in Pythagoreanism. Pythagoras was said to be the first to apply this word to the universe. It has two basic meanings: orderly arrangement and ornament, and so it combines regularity, tidiness, and arrangement with beauty, perfection, and positive moral value. The Ionians had already treated the world as a *kosmos*, but the Pythagoreans enlarged and deepened this idea to apply to the mathematical structure and religious significance that they found in the world around them. The essence of the order in the world, the Pythagoreans believed, is located in the connections of its parts, that is, *kosmos* depends on *harmonia*, especially on *harmonia* based on number. This doctrine was first applied to musical *harmonia* but was later extended more widely.

The following diagram, which the Pythagoreans called "the tetractys of the decad" and by which they swore their most solemn oaths, represents the numbers involved in the analysis of the three principal harmonic intervals.

$$\bullet$$
$$\bullet \quad \bullet$$
$$\bullet \quad \bullet \quad \bullet$$
$$\bullet \quad \bullet \quad \bullet \quad \bullet$$

The tetractys was called "the harmony in which the Sirens sing" and was mystically identified with the oracle at Delphi (see **9.15**). The following passage mentions some of its other associations.

9.18   The tetractys is a certain number, which being composed of the four first numbers produces the most perfect number, ten. For 1 and 2 and 3 and 4 come to be 10. This number is the first tetractys and is called the source of ever-flowing nature since according to them the entire *kosmos* is organized according to *harmonia*, and *harmonia* is a system of three concords, the fourth, the fifth, and the octave, and the proportions of these three concords are found in the aforementioned four numbers.

          (Sextus Empiricus, *Against the Mathematicians* 7.94–95 [not in DK])

We will come back to the statement that the *kosmos* is arranged according to *harmonia* in discussing Pythagorean cosmology, but the general nature of Pythagorean thought can be gathered from this passage. The concordant musical intervals are accounted for in terms of the numbers 1, 2, 3, and 4. These are assumed to explain the structure of the universe, and a particular way of exhibiting them takes on a sacred character, as does their sum.

Numbers and Things

The same *akousma* that identifies *harmonia* as the most beautiful thing says that the wisest thing is number. This may mean that number is the key to wisdom and knowledge. There was great interest in identifying numerical properties of things, perhaps stemming from the numerical analysis of the concordant intervals.

9.19   In numbers they thought they observed many resemblances to the things that are and that come to be . . . such and such an attribute of numbers being justice, another being soul and intellect, another being decisive moment, and similarly for virtually all other things . since all other things seemed to be made in the likeness of numbers in their entire nature.

          (Aristotle, *Metaphysics* 1.5 985b28–33 = DK 58B4)

Further insight into this aspect of Pythagoreanism is found in the following passages, of which the first comments on **9.19**.

9.20   They supposed that requital and equality were characteristic of justice and found these features in numbers, and so declared that justice was the first number that is equal-times-equal . . . They said that decisive moment is the number 7, since things which are natural appear to have their decisive moments of fulfillment in birth and growth by sevens. Humans, for example. They are born in the seventh month and teethe in as many months, and reach adolescence in the second span of seven years and get a beard in the third. . . . They said that marriage is the number five, because marriage is the union of male and female, and according to them the odd is male and the even is female, and this number is the first which has its origin from two, the first even number, and three, the first odd . . . They declared intellect and essence to be the one, since he spoke of the soul as the intelligence. They said that because it is stable and similar in every way and sovereign, the intelligence is the unity and one.

(Alexander, *Commentary on Aristotle's*
Metaphysics 38.10–39.20 [not in DK])

9.21   Concerning what things are, they began to make statements and definitions but treated the matter too simply. For they would define superficially and thought that the first thing an indicated term applies to was the essence of the thing, as if one were to suppose that double and the number two are the same because two is the first thing double applies to. But surely to be double and to be two are not the same; otherwise one thing will be many—a consequence they actually drew.

(Aristotle, *Metaphysics* 1.5 987a20–27 = DK 58B8)

Some of these cases reveal the reductionist reasoning found elsewhere, but the association of "decisive moment" with the number 7 (**9.20**) is based on the wildest sort of speculative association.[27] One Pythagorean extended this approach to concrete substances.

9.22   Eurytus [late fifth century] assigned what was the number of what, for example, this is the number of a human, that is the number of a horse, like those who bring numbers into triangular and square figures, fashioning with pebbles the forms of plants.

(Aristotle, *Metaphysics* 14.5 1092b10–13 = DK 45, 3)

9.23   For example, suppose the number 250 is the definition of human being . . . After positing this, he would take 250 pebbles, some green, some black, others red, and generally pebbles of all colors. Then he smeared a wall with lime and drew a human being in outline . . . and then fastened some of these pebbles in the drawn face, others in the hands, others elsewhere, and he completed the drawing of the human being there represented by means of pebbles equal to the units which he declared define human being. As a result of this procedure he would state that just as the particular sketched human being is composed of, say, 250 pebbles, so a real human being is defined by so many units.

(Alexander, *Commentary on Aristotle's* Metaphysics 827.9–19 = DK 45, 3)

In a procedure only distantly related to the reasoning given in **9.20**, Eurytus displays the number of a human being by placing pebbles on his diagram, thus showing that they are the smallest number that can fill in the shape of a human. Whether he went on to claim that the number so found is the definition of a

---

27. Iamblichus, *Theologoumena Arithmeticae* contains much of this kind of material, which formed an important part of Neopythagorean speculation. Some of the material in **9.20** may be due to Neopythagorean sources too.

human being, as **9.23** asserts, is less certain, but the association of things with numbers in this way must have been felt to indicate something fundamental about their nature.

The material presented thus far indicates that the Pythagoreans, and possibly Pythagoras himself, were interested in numbers, but it does nothing to show that they advanced mathematics in any notable way. However, their interests went further. Some were interested in classifying numbers, and were the first to make the distinction between even and odd numbers and perhaps between prime and composite numbers. Eurytus's practice may have extended a more mathematically respectable practice of representing numbers by arrangements of pebbles, which the Pythagoreans probably pursued by Eurytus's time. Thus the number 9 can be represented by nine pebbles arranged in three rows of three pebbles each, thus forming a square. The same holds for any "square" number. Numbers were called oblong if they can be represented by pebbles arranged into a rectangle one of whose sides exceeded the other by one pebble. Thus 6 (= 2 x 3) and 12 (= 3 x 4) are oblong numbers.

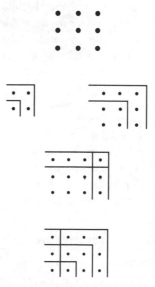

Classification of numbers as even, odd, square, composite, and the like is basic to number theory as it came to be practiced by the ancient Greeks, and so the Pythagoreans can reasonably be granted an important place in its history. Moreover, Euclid's *Elements*, which is largely a compilation of earlier materials, contains a treatment of elementary number theory (Books 7–9), an important part of it concerning the properties of even and odd integers (Book 9, Propositions 22–34).[28]

---

28. Knorr (1975) argues that a good deal of material from Books 7 and 9 is Pythagorean in origin.

Various mathematical properties of such numbers can be easily derived by inspecting the pebble diagrams and generalizing from them. For example, if we take one pebble and place three more pebbles around it, we have a square with two pebbles on a side. If we then place five more pebbles around that square, we have another square. The L-shaped addition in each case was called a *gnōmōn* (carpenter's square). It is clear that all square numbers can be derived this way and also that the number of pebbles in each successive gnomon is two more than in the previous one, which entails that the sum of any sequence of odd numbers beginning with the number 1 is a square number. Unfortunately it is not at all clear how early these important contributions were made.[29] In what follows I discuss views reported by Aristotle, and other material that is plausibly dated before the end of the fifth century.

The relation between numbers and things is described in various ways. **9.19** says both that things resemble numbers and that things are attributes of numbers, **9.20** that things are numbers, **9.21** that a thing is the first number that it applies to, and **9.23** that numbers are the definitions of things. Elsewhere Aristotle says that elements of numbers are the elements of all things, that the principles of numbers are the principles of all things, and that number is the substance (or essence) of all things.[30] The easiest explanation for this variety is that there were a variety of Pythagorean views[31] on this important subject and that Aristotle, who provides most of this information, based his accounts on several sources and did not think it important to identify differences within the Pythagorean tradition. One interpretation of the evidence is that the early discovery that number is the basis of the concordant musical intervals quickly led to the claim that all things are somehow based on numbers. The resemblances noted in **9.19** and **9.20** may be regarded as support for this claim cobbled together from human experience. The interest in principles and elements will be later. It fits well into the milieu of the second half of the fifth century, when thinkers like Anaxagoras, Empedocles, and the Atomists were developing theories about the nature and constitution of the world in response to the arguments of Parmenides, Zeno, and Melissus.

Geometry

The claim in **9.25** that the Pythagoreans were "first to advance" the study of mathematics is frequently understood to refer to their contributions to geometry, although their interest in number theory and their belief that numbers are the key to the *kosmos* would be by themselves enough to justify the statement. The Pythagorean theorem is one of the most famous geometrical propositions, and

---

29. Knorr makes a good case for dating these developments to the fifth century (Knorr 1975: Ch. 5).

30. See below pp. 100–102.

31. For clear indications that the Pythagoreans did not always agree, see **9.11** and **9.38**.

ancient sources attribute its discovery to Pythagoras himself.[32] But Pythagoras did not discover Euclid's proof (which could not have been worked out before the late fifth century), and if all he did was to state the theorem, he may have merely been reporting something he learned when (and if) he visited Babylon, where it had been known for well over a thousand years, though it had not been proved. There are other ways than Euclid's of proving this theorem, but in my judgment it is most likely that Pythagoras did not discover any proof of it, and that he was later associated with this famous theorem by people (perhaps later Pythagoreans) who wanted to credit him with an important place among the founders of geometry.

In evaluating the Pythagoreans' contributions to geometry, three pieces of evidence are crucial: first and earliest, Aristotle's statement in **9.25**, second, the history of mathematics composed by Aristotle's pupil Eudemus, of which important extracts are preserved in Proclus's *Commentary on the First Book of Euclid's* Elements (fifth century CE), and third, attributions of particular geometrical results by Eudemus to the Pythagoreans. The difficulty here is that Aristotle is positive but vague, Eudemus gives no prominence to Pythagoras or anyone known to be a Pythagorean, and the specific attributions, while showing that Eudemus and others did acknowledge a Pythagorean contribution to geometry, do not provide enough evidence to understand the nature and extent of Pythagorean geometry. On the basis of this evidence it would be imprudent to assign any important role in the history of geometry to Pythagoras himself or to be confident what, if any, role the fifth-century Pythagoreans played in the development of geometry.

Two questions in particular remain open. Did the early (pre-Platonic) Pythagoreans discover the incommensurability of the side and diagonal of the square, and did they invent the notions of mathematical proof and the arrangement of theorems into a deductive system?

The first question, which many have thought important both for Pythagoreanism and for the history of mathematics, asks whether the Pythagoreans discovered that if a square has sides of length A and diagonals of length B, then there are no whole numbers m, n such that $A:B = m:n$. We would express this fact by saying that the ratio $A:B$ is irrational, or equivalently (but anachronistically) that $\sqrt{2}$ is irrational. This discovery preceded the work of Theodorus of Cyrene,[33] who extended it in the late fifth century, proving in effect which square roots are irrational up to $\sqrt{17}$.[34] Euclid presents two different theories of proportion, of which one is a theory of ratios of whole numbers which can be applied to ratios of any magnitudes (lengths, weights, areas, times, etc.) that are "rational" in the sense that their ratios are ratios of whole numbers; and the other works for magnitudes generally (including "irrational magnitudes," those which cannot be

---

32. Diogenes Laertius, *Lives of the Philosophers* 8.12 (not in DK); Porphyry, *Life of Pythagoras* 36 (not in DK); Athenaeus, *Table Talk* 10.13 (not in DK). But it is far from certain that Pythagoras actually made the discovery. See Heath (1921: vol. 1, pp. 144–49).

33. Iamblichus, *Life of Pythagoras* 36 asserts that Theodorus was a Pythagorean.

34. Plato, *Theaetetus* 147d (not in DK).

represented as ratios of whole numbers). The obvious inference is that the former theory was worked out before the discovery of the irrational and the latter, which is due to the fourth-century mathematical genius Eudoxus, was developed afterwards. Some attribute the earlier theory to the Pythagoreans (recall their interest in the ratios of whole numbers in connection with the musical intervals), and hold in addition that the discovery of the irrational caused a crisis for the Pythagoreans since it showed that the world could not be entirely accounted for through whole numbers. Some have even declared that a story that Hippasus, an early Pythagorean, was drowned at sea for revealing a secret of geometry relates to this theorem,[35] as if divulging the existence of the irrational and making public the shortcomings of the Pythagorean numerical conception of the world was a great scandal. While these speculations give a good story, the support for them is too weak to give certainty, and most scholars now reject them.[36]

The second question is equally important for the history of mathematics and philosophy. What distinguishes Greek mathematics from Babylonian and Egyptian mathematics is the notion and prominence of proofs. The earlier cultures developed methods of doing arithmetic and calculating areas over a millennium before the rise of Greek mathematics, and the Babylonians' interest in the relations of numbers was not entirely practical, but it was the Greeks who discovered and developed the idea of showing how one fact follows from others and arranging facts into a logically ordered system. This is the practice of Euclid's *Elements* (c.300 BCE), parts of which are familiar to anyone who has studied geometry. Euclid was by no means the first person to prove theorems. Eudemus names several writers of "Elements" before Euclid beginning with the fifth-century mathematician Hippocrates of Chios (active c.430 BCE), and the practice of proving theorems (in some sense of the word "prove") must have been well established before Hippocrates, who will have arranged and systematized existing theorems and proofs. To whom, then, do we owe the discovery of proofs? Did the idea of proof come from mathematics, or did it start elsewhere? And why did it arise at all?

One consideration[37] is that rigorous proofs are more likely to have arisen in connection with negative than with positive results. With positive results—say that the sum of the angles of a triangle is equal to two right angles—you can "see" that they hold by inspecting a few cases, perhaps with the help of cutting or folding the figure. This sort of procedure makes no pretense to rigor, but it does establish the result (at least for reasonably obvious facts in arithmetic and geometry). With negative results it is quite different. To take as an example a problem discussed in the fifth century, if you want to show that if A, B are the side and diagonal of a square, then there are no whole numbers m, n such that $A:B = m:n$, you cannot examine all possible pairs of whole numbers and show

---

35. Others identify the secret in question as the construction of the dodecahedron (a regular solid with twelve identical regular pentagons as its faces).

36. See especially Knorr (1975: 306–14) and Fowler (1987: 302–8).

37. Szabó (1978: 185–216).

that none of them has the property in question. But if your only way of showing that a proposition is true is to examine specific cases, you can never prove this result, only that none of the pairs so far considered has the property. Establishing a negative result in arithmetic or geometry therefore requires a proof, and in fact such problems, perhaps the one involving the side and diagonal of the square, may have given rise to the idea of proving theorems.

This consideration has led some to propose that the idea of rigorous proof was first developed in philosophy and then applied to mathematics.[38] On this view, the sophisticated arguments of the Eleatic philosophers Parmenides and Zeno,[39] who proved negative results (e.g., that there is no motion), came first and mathematical proofs came second. (The author of the most thorough study of the discovery of the incommensurability of the side and diagonal of a square dates the discovery to not much earlier than c.430.[40] This is a plausible account, but it has been challenged by evidence that mathematics in the fifth and fourth centuries shows no particular influence of philosophy,[41] and it is best to admit that our evidence does not allow us to say for certain whether the priority goes to mathematics or to philosophy, Pythagorean philosophy in particular.[42]

It is nevertheless certain that the Pythagoreans were interested in geometry. Their interest in reducing things to numbers naturally led them to do the same for geometry. The relations between the two fields are seen in the definitions of the basic entity in each field—the unit and the point. (A unit is a point lacking position, and a point is a unit having position.[43]) Numbers are pluralities of units, and lines, planes, and solids are determined by pluralities of points. One way in which one-, two-, and three-dimensional space depend on points is indicated in the following fragment of *Pythagorean Numbers*, a work by Plato's nephew Speusippus.

9.24 <The number 10 contains> formulas for lines, surfaces and solids; for 1 is a point, 2 a line, 3 a triangle, and 4 a pyramid, and all these are primary and the starting points for the other figures of each kind.

(Speusippus, fr. 4 (Lang) = DK 44A13)

---

38. Ibid., 216–20.

39. See Chs. 11 and 12.

40. Knorr (1975: 38). I believe that the evidence Knorr uses for this conclusion is compatible with a date somewhat earlier still, say c.450.

41. Knorr (1982).

42. It cannot be excluded that the inspiration for deductive proofs came from the Ionian geometrical tradition, which made important contributions well into the fourth century, even though this method of argument was not characteristic of early Ionian philosophy. See Guthrie (1962: 218–19) for a statement of the pro-Ionian, anti-Pythagorean view. Van der Waerden advocates the view that Thales invented the notion of mathematical proof (van der Waerden [1954: 87–90]).

43. Aristotle, *Metaphysics* 13.9 1084b26–27 (not in DK) and *On the Soul* 1.5 409a6 (not in DK).

Here we are to think of the number 10 as represented in the tetractys of the decad (see above page 92), composed of the numbers 1, 2, 3, and 4 in that order. Two points determine a straight line, three points not in a straight line mark the corners of a triangle, and four points not in the same plane the vertices of a pyramid. These are the simplest one-, two-, and three-dimensional figures.

This is another example of Pythagorean reductionism. In each situation we treat the minimal case, and that is supposed to take care of the more complicated cases. How it does so is vague; there is no reason to suppose that the Pythagoreans believed that, for example, all plane figures (including ones with curved sides) are triangles or can be formed out of or approximated by triangles.[44] It also skips over the facts that geometrical points are different from arithmetical units, and straight lines are determined by two points in a different way from that in which the number 2 is composed of two units.

Principles of Number

A prominent feature of Presocratic thought is the desire to identify a small number of principles from which the world is constructed or out of which it has grown: the world depends on a small number of principles and can be accounted for in terms of them. The Pythagoreans were no exception. As we have seen, they believed that number is fundamental to the world, that somehow the world can be understood in terms of number. But there is no end to the number of numbers. They therefore needed to account for numbers in terms of a small number of principles and to generate the *kosmos* from numbers so that the principles of number ultimately serve as the principles of all things. From mid-fifth century this project gained prominence in the agenda of the *mathēmatikoi*.

> **9.25**   At the same time as these [Leucippus and Democritus] and before them, those called Pythagoreans took hold of mathematics and were the first to advance that study; and being brought up in it, they believed that its principles are the principles of all things that are. Since numbers are naturally first among these, and in numbers they thought they observed many

---

44. This last result and the fact that all plane figures with straight sides can be broken up into triangles were known to Euclid (they are obvious extensions of proof techniques that Euclid uses in *Elements* book 12 proposition 1 and book 1 proposition 46, respectively) and so may have been known to the Pythagoreans, but there is nothing to indicate that these theorems had anything to do with the generation of lines, planes, and solids out of points.

resemblances to things that are and that come to be . . . and since they saw the attributes and ratios of musical scales in numbers, and other things seemed to be made in the likeness of numbers in their entire nature, and numbers seemed to be primary in all nature, they supposed the elements of numbers to be the elements of all things that are.

(Aristotle, *Metaphysics* 1.5 985b23–986a2 = DK 58B4)

9.26   The elements of number are the even and the odd, and of these the latter is limited and the former unlimited. The one is composed of both of these (for it is both even and odd) and number springs from the one; and numbers, as I have said, constitute the whole universe.

(Aristotle, *Metaphysics* 1.5 986a17–21 = DK 58B5)

9.27   The Pythagoreans similarly posited two principles, but added something peculiar to themselves, not that the limited and the unlimited are distinct natures like fire or earth or something similar, but that the unlimited itself and the one itself are the substance of what they are predicated of. This is why they call number the substance of all things.

(Aristotle, *Metaphysics* 1.5 987a13–19 = DK 58B8)

9.28   They say that the unlimited is the even. For when this is surrounded and limited by the odd it provides things with the quality of unlimitedness. Evidence of this is what happens with numbers. For when gnomons are placed around the one, and apart, in the one case the shape is always different, and in the other it is always one.

(Aristotle, *Physics* 3.4 203a10–15 = DK 58B28)

9.28 refers to the gnomon-wrapping described above and shows how even is linked with unlimited, and odd with one. The successive figures formed by wrapping gnomons with odd numbers of dots "around the one" are all square and so have the same shape, whereas in the sequence of oblong figures formed by wrapping gnomons with even numbers of dots around the two,[45] no two shapes are the same (since the ratios of their sides are different).

9.25 says that the Pythagoreans thought the elements of numbers are the elements of all things, and **9.26** identifies the elements of number as the even and the odd, which compose the one, from which springs number, of which the universe is composed. The generation implied by **9.26** is:

even and odd → the one → number → the universe

---

45. The text says merely "and apart." Perhaps this refers to a diagram Aristotle drew as he gave the lectures for which the *Physics* is the notes. What is "apart" is the extra row of dots, which when added to the square numbers makes oblong numbers.

On the other hand, **9.27** does not mention even and odd, but makes it clear that the limited and the unlimited are the two principles, and associates unity with the limited, whereas **9.26** makes the one composed of both odd and even. Here the generation seems to be:

> unlimited and limited (= the one) → number → all things

Again, the discrepancy is probably due to Aristotle's use of different sources.

Generation of the Physical World

Other passages provide further information on the origin of the *kosmos*.

> **9.29** It is absurd to construct an account of the generation of things that are eternal, or rather it is an impossibility. There is no need to doubt whether or not the Pythagoreans construct such an account, since they say clearly that when the one had been constructed—whether from planes or surfaces or seed or from something they are at a loss to specify—the nearest parts of the unlimited at once began to be drawn in and limited by the limit. But since they are constructing a *kosmos* . . .
> (Aristotle, *Metaphysics* 14.3 1091a12–18 = DK 58B26)

> **9.30** The Pythagoreans also said that void exists and enters the universe from the unlimited breath, the universe being supposed in fact to inhale the void, which distinguishes things. For void is that which separates and distinguishes things that are next to each other. This happens first in numbers; the void divides their nature.
> (Aristotle, *Physics* 4.6 213b22–27 = DK 58B30)

> **9.31** The universe is unique, and from the unlimited it draws in time, breath, and void, which distinguishes the places of separate things.
> (Aristotle, fr. 201 [Rose] = DK 58B30)

This account has both early and late elements. The idea that unlimited breath surrounds the *kosmos* recalls Anaximenes (**6.4**), and the picture of the *kosmos* growing by inhaling this breath is at home among early Ionian ideas, while the conception of this breath as void and the role it plays (**9.30** and **9.31**) cannot antedate the fifth-century Atomists. The overall picture is that the universe is formed by the imposition of limit on the unlimited. Limit, determinacy, definiteness, and number are associated with order and intelligibility. As the musical scale is formed by imposing determinate numerical relations on the indefinite and continuous spectrum of sound, and as numbers are generated as the products of limit and the unlimited, the *kosmos* too is formed when the one (representing limit) operates on the unlimited. Order begins in the center of the universe and expands by assimilating unordered, unlimited stuff into the ordered universe.

The material presented establishes a close connection between numbers and the *kosmos*. The first thing generated in the cosmogony of **9.29** is the number 1, which **9.26** declares to be composed of even (unlimited) and odd (limit), the two elements of number (without specifying how those two elements combine to form it). In **9.26** number "springs from" the one; in **9.29** the *kosmos* does: the number one draws in the unlimited (which **9.30** specifies as "void" and unlimited breath) and limits it, thus making possible the differentiation of individual things and the articulation of the *kosmos*. The same process that generates numbers also generates the *kosmos*, so in a sense numbers *are* the *kosmos*. An important feature of the order in the *kosmos* is that its parts are separate. The *kosmos* is an arrangement of distinct individual things. The void keeps things apart and performs an analogous function in the ordered realm of discrete, whole numbers, separating each from the rest and guaranteeing to each its identity and uniqueness. **9.31** adds that time was also drawn in from the unlimited. This doctrine may reflect Philolaus's ideas (see below page 357). The *kosmos* has both spatial and temporal order, which are both imposed in analogous ways by the limiting principle.

Cosmology

The Pythagorean account of the *kosmos*, which may be due to Philolaus,[46] contains three noteworthy features: its rejection of the geocentric picture, the role of the number 10, and the harmony of the spheres.

> **9.32**   Although most say that the earth is situated at the center <of the universe> . . . those in Italy called Pythagoreans assert the contrary opinion. For they declare that fire is at the center and the earth is one of the stars and by being carried in a circle around the center it causes night and day. Further, opposite to this one they construct another earth, which they name "counter-earth." In this they are not inquiring for theories and causes with a view to the phenomena but are forcing the phenomena to fit certain theories and opinions of their own and trying to bring them into line. Many others agree that the earth should not be put at the center, finding reliability on the basis not of the phenomena but rather of their theories. For they believe that the most honorable thing deserves to have the most honorable region and that fire is more honorable than earth and that the limit is more honorable than what is intermediate and that the extremity and the center are limits. So, reasoning from these premises they think that not it but fire is situated at the center of the sphere. Moreover, the Pythagoreans call the fire occupying this region Zeus's guardhouse because the most important part of the universe should be the best guarded, and the center is most important, as if "center" had a single meaning and the center of the spatial

---

46. See below pp. 358–59. I have chosen to present this material here rather than in Ch. 18, partly because many sources attribute this cosmology to the Pythagoreans in general, and partly since Ch. 18 is mainly devoted to Philolaus's views on the nature of reality.

extension and of the thing itself were also the natural center. But just as in animals the center of the animal is not the same as the center of its body, we must suppose the same to hold concerning the whole heaven.

(Aristotle, *On the Heavens* 2.13 293a18–b8 = DK 58B36)

9.33   Philolaus says that there is fire in the middle around the center, which he calls the hearth of the universe and the house of Zeus and the mother of the gods and altar, bond, and measure of nature. Moreover, he says that what surrounds the universe at the furthest extreme is another fire. The center is by nature first. Around it ten divine bodies dance—the heaven, the five planets; after them the sun; beneath it the moon; beneath it the earth; beneath it the counter-earth; after them all the fire of the hearth, which maintains its position around the center. He calls the highest part of the surrounding <region> Olympus, in which <he says> is <located> the pure form of the elements. The <region> below the motion of Olympus, in which the five planets are positioned together with the sun and moon <he calls> *kosmos*. The sublunary and earthly <region> below these <he calls> Heaven, in which <are located> the entities involved in change-loving generation. He <declares that> wisdom is concerned with the order found in the things above, while *aretē* is concerned with the disorderly behavior of things that come to be, and that of these the former [wisdom] is complete and the latter [*aretē*] is incomplete.

(Aëtius 2.7.7 = DK 44A16)

9.34   Philolaus the Pythagorean <says that> fire is in the middle (for this is the hearth of the universe); the counter-earth is second, the inhabited earth is third and is situated and revolves opposite the counter-earth. This is why the people on the counter-earth cannot be seen by those on this one.

(Aëtius 3.11.3 = DK 44A17)

9.35   They supposed . . . the entire heaven to be a *harmonia* and a number. And all the characteristics of numbers and *harmoniai* [plural of *harmonia*] they found corresponding to the attributes and parts of the heaven and to the entire ordering, they collected and made them fit. If anything was missing anywhere they eagerly filled in the gaps to make their entire system coherent. For example, since they think the number 10 is something perfect and encompasses the entire nature of numbers, they declare that the bodies that move in the heaven are also ten. But since only nine are visible, they invent the counter-earth as the tenth.

(Aristotle, *Metaphysics* 1.5 986a2–12 = DK 58B4) (continuation of **9.25**)

In the middle of the *kosmos* there is a huge fire, which is orbited by the counter-earth, earth, moon, sun, Mercury, Venus, Mars, Jupiter, Saturn, and the fixed stars, in that order.[47] Aristotle objects strongly to this picture of the world (**9.30,**

---

47. The Pythagoreans are said to have been "first to discover the order of the positions of the planets" (Eudemus, quoted in Simplicius, *Commentary on Aristotle's* On the

9.35) on the grounds that the central fire is posited for unscientific reasons and because of the failure to understand that "center" can have two meanings. The counter-earth is posited simply because of the Pythagorean prejudice in favor of the number 10, though modern physicists, who are used to positing the existence of entities on the basis of theory, might be more sympathetic. Some ancient sources say that the Pythagoreans used the counter-earth to account for lunar eclipses.[48] And it is worth mentioning that they offered an explanation of why the central fire is never observed (**9.34**).

The Pythagoreans were the first to remove the earth from the center of the *kosmos*, and their reasons as reported in **9.32** and **9.33** are not astronomical but metaphysical ("the center is most important") and religious ("house of Zeus"). It is not surprising that this idea was not adopted by most other ancient astronomers, who retained the traditional geocentric view.[49] However, the proponents of this theory defended it against the astronomical objection that the circular-appearing orbits of the heavenly bodies imply that the earth is in the center of the *kosmos*.[50]

> **9.36** Since the earth's surface is not in fact the center but is distant from the center by its whole hemisphere [that is, radius], the Pythagoreans feel no difficulty in supposing that although we do not occupy the center the phenomena are the same as if the earth were at the center. For they hold that even on the current view [that the earth is at the center] there is nothing to show that we are distant from the center by half the earth's diameter.
>
> (Aristotle, *On the Heavens* 2.13 293b25–30 [not in DK])

It is not true that the Pythagoreans discovered that the earth is a planet, seeing that they held the false view that the earth (as well as the sun, moon, etc.) goes around a central fire rather than around the sun. Nevertheless, the fact that they could conceive of the earth's not being at the center is an important conceptual advance, and from this perspective "the identification of the central fire with the sun is a detail in comparison."[51] For Philolaus's distinctive views on the nature of the sun and moon, see below page 359.

The Pythagorean doctrine of the harmony of the spheres, based on several basic features of Pythagoreanism—harmonics, cosmology, and mathematics,

---

Heavens 471.5–6 = DK 12A19). The outer planets are invisible to the naked eye and were only discovered in 1781 (Uranus), 1846 (Neptune), and 1930 (Pluto).

48. Aristotle, *On the Heavens* 2.13 293b21–25 (not in DK), Aëtius 2.29.4 = DK 58B36.

49. An important ancient exception is Aristarchus of Samos (first half of the third century) who hypothesized that "the fixed stars and the sun remain unmoved and that the earth revolves about the sun on the circumference of a circle, the sun lying in the middle of the orbit" (Archimedes, *The Sand-Reckoner* 4–5 [not in DK]).

50. This objection was also made by Tycho Brahe against the heliocentric hypothesis of Copernicus in the 15th century.

51. Burnet (1930: 299).

and the basic belief in an intimate connection between *kosmos* and *harmonia*—caught the fancy of literary authors in later antiquity and the Renaissance. It should be mentioned that there is no good evidence that this doctrine is due to Philolaus. The clearest and most sober account is given by Aristotle.[52]

> 9.37   Although the assertion that a harmony arises from the motion of the heavenly bodies, since the sounds that are produced are concordant, is expressed cleverly and remarkably by its proponents, it does not contain the truth. For some think a sound must be produced when bodies of such great size are in motion, since it happens with bodies on earth too which do not have so great a bulk and do not move with so great speed. And when the sun and moon and the stars, which are so great in number and size, move so quickly, there must be a noise overwhelming in loudness. Assuming these things and that the speeds, which depend on the distances, have the ratios of the concords, they declare that the sound of the stars in circular motion is harmonious. But since it appeared illogical that we do not hear this sound, they declare that the reason is that the sound is present to us from birth and so is not evident in contrast to the opposing silence, for noise and silence are recognized by contrast to one another. And so the same thing happens to humans as to bronzesmiths: as a result of habituation there seems to be no difference.
>
>   (Aristotle, *On the Heavens* 2.9 290b12–29 = DK 58B35)

This gives some meaning to the statement that "they supposed . . . the entire heaven to be a *harmonia* and a number" (9.35). The pitches of the various notes correspond to their speeds, which depend on their distances (from the central fire). Indeed the Pythagoreans are said to have been "first to discover the order of the positions of the planets."

Opposites

The importance of the notion of opposition, already present in Anaximander and Anaximenes, continues in later philosophers, including the Pythagoreans, some of whom developed it in a distinctive way.

> 9.38   Others of this same school declare that there are ten principles arranged in parallel columns:
>
> | | |
> |---|---|
> | limit | unlimited |
> | odd | even |
> | one | plurality |
> | right | left |
> | male | female |
> | at rest | moving |
> | straight | bent |

---

52. The first appearance of the doctrine is in Plato (*Republic* 10 616b–617d [not in DK]).

light   darkness
good   evil
square   oblong

> This is how Alcmaeon of Croton too seems to have understood things, and either he took this theory from them or they from him. . . . He says that most human matters are pairs, identifying as the oppositions not definite ones like the Pythagoreans . . . but the Pythagoreans described how many and what the oppositions are.
> (Aristotle, *Metaphysics* 1.5 986a22–b2 = DK 58B5) (continuation of **9.26**)

The table of opposites contains twenty opposites but ten principles, each pair counting as one principle. The table manifests interest in a wide range of aspects of the world, including moral values, which accords with the Pythagoreans' use of numbers to account for features of the physical universe and also for qualities like justice (**9.19**).

The table displays many Pythagorean ideas. First, the number of pairs of basic opposites is ten. Second, the prominence of limit and unlimited, followed by odd and even, recalls the accounts of the generation of number in **9.25–9.28**. One and plurality, lined up respectively with limit and unlimited and with square and oblong bring to mind the properties of square and oblong numbers discussed above (pages 95–96). The remaining pairs of opposites are diverse and not in all cases clearly related.

From the point of view of logic, each pair seems intended to consist of mutually exclusive items. Some pairs seem intended to exhaust their fields of application (all animals are either male or female, all whole numbers are either odd or even) and some do not (some numbers are neither square nor oblong). Some items admit degrees (moving, bent), while others do not. From the point of view of Pythagorean metaphysics, some of the pairs are basic (odd and even, compare **9.25** and **9.26**; alternatively, limit and unlimited, compare **9.27**), and some are derivative (one and plurality, compare **9.26**). But the table leaves some important issues open. No effort is made to distinguish the types of opposition involved, and there is no explanation of the way in which these opposites are principles or of why these particular pairs of opposites are chosen instead of those which figure conspicuously in earlier cosmologies, such as dense and rare, hot and cold, or wet and dry. Indeed, if odd and even (or limit and unlimited) are the principles of all things, how can there be any other principles?

Numbers in the World

The Pythagorean cosmogony is different from the Ionian ones—so different, in fact, that it is hard to believe that the *kosmos* that results is the world around us. Further, the account fails to address a number of crucial issues. As the following passage shows, Aristotle, who wrote a (no longer extant) treatise on the Pythagoreans and so must have had access to relevant materials, shared these feelings.

9.39   Those called Pythagoreans use stranger principles and elements than the
natural philosophers do. The reason is that they did not take their principles
from perceptible things . . . yet everything they discuss and treat has to do
with nature; for they generate the heaven and observe what happens regarding its parts, its attributes, and the events in it and use up the principles
and causes on these as if they agreed with the others—the natural philosophers—that what exists is precisely all that is perceptible and contained by
what they call the heaven. . . . However, they say nothing about how there
can be motion if limit and unlimited and odd and even are the only things
assumed, or how without motion and change there can be generation and
perishing, or the behavior of the bodies that move through the heavens.
                              (Aristotle, *Metaphysics* 1.8 989b29–990a12 = DK 58B22)

It is possible, then, that what the Pythagoreans said really was unclearly or incompletely stated, so perhaps the broad sketch I have given of how they founded
their *kosmos* on numbers and on the principle of imposing limit on the unlimited
is as far as it is reasonable to go. There remains the question how they could
have thought that the principles of the *kosmos* could be numbers rather than of
something physical. The answer to this question depends on our view of how
they conceived the relation between numbers and things.

We have seen that Aristotle states several Pythagorean opinions on this point,
including that things are identical with numbers, that things are composed of
numbers, that things resemble numbers and that the principles of numbers are
the principles of all things.

Aristotle criticizes Pythagorean philosophy on the grounds that it leads to
absurd consequences, and he is surely correct if the theory asserts that numbers
are identical with things or that things are composed of numbers. However, the
claim that things resemble numbers is not open to these objections and also has
links with central features of Pythagorean thought.[53] There are many ways in
which things may resemble numbers. **9.20** points out some ways in which qualities such as justice can be thought of as resembling numbers, that is, by having
some of the same properties as a particular number. More generally, numbers,
geometrical figures, the physical *kosmos*, and musical scales are generated similarly: all come to be when limit is imposed on the unlimited. All are instances
of order, perhaps even of sequential order, which exists in different realms. And
they all have numerical aspects that are basic: the number of sides of a triangle,
the number and distances of the heavenly bodies, the ratios of the lengths of
strings. Moreover, the analysis of the generation of all these things in terms of

---

53. The Pythagorean doctrine that things resemble numbers is a probable forerunner
of Plato's doctrine that sensible things resemble or imitate Forms. Many of the philosophical problems inherent in the Pythagorean conceptions of the relations between things
and numbers—issues of identity, resemblance, and predication—also arise for Plato, who
struggles with them in such dialogues as *Phaedo*, *Parmenides*, and *Sophist*.

limit being imposed on the unlimited gives a clear sense to the claim that the principles of number are the principles of all things.

I prefer to see these claims as ways of asserting that number is fundamental to all things, that the basic features of all things are numerical, that numerical considerations are basic in understanding all things, and that all things are generated in a similar way to numbers. These statements are all ways of claiming primacy for numbers, but they are different ways. The Pythagoreans noticed all these ways, but instead of keeping them distinct gathered them together into a single thought. One way of expressing the point is to say that they did not think that number is fundamental in many distinct and perhaps unrelated ways, some of which apply here and others there, but simply thought that number is fundamental and looked for evidence to support this claim. The difference is important. The Pythagoreans piled up evidence without calling attention to how different the bits of evidence are. They were not interested in analyzing different ways numbers are primary, only in establishing that numbers are in fact primary. They formulated their thesis vaguely, to accommodate the different relations they found between things and numbers, and they phrased it differently on different occasions. Also, to judge by Aristotle's criticisms,[54] their vague notion of priority does not stand up to analysis, but as soon as people ask in what way numbers are primary and in what way all things are numbers it becomes necessary to specify once again all the different ways in which different things are numbers, imitate numbers, resemble numbers, etc.

These problems arise for the Pythagoreans because they based their physical system on numbers. How numbers are basic to the universe and things around us is less straightforward a matter than how a substance like air is, and the Ionian background offered little help toward drawing the necessary distinctions and analyzing connections at a sufficiently abstract level to identify the issues involved or offer a philosophically satisfactory account. What does it mean, for example, to say that the one is generated out of odd and even, or that the universe is composed of numbers, or that justice is the number 4? What notions of generation, composition, and identity are in play—and if these are not precisely the notions in play, what relations are meant?

In fact, the Pythagoreans probably could not express their ideas accurately, given the state of the Greek language and the primitive state of philosophical analysis in their time. In the fifth century Greek lacked most of the philosophical vocabulary needed to distinguish between sameness and resemblance (the same Greek word *homoios* means both "same" and "similar"), identity and composition, or origin and metaphysical structure. (In Greek, to say that one thing (*A*) is or comes "out of" another (*B*) can mean that *B* is identical with *A*, or that what was once *B* is now *A*, or that *A* is made up of *B*, or that *A* depends on *B*, or that *A*

---

54. Aristotle frequently criticizes the Pythagorean views on number in ways that show how far his own way of thinking was from theirs. Representative passages are *Metaphysics* 13.8 1083b8–19 = DK 58B10; 14.3 1090a32–35 (not in DK); and 14.6 1093a1–13 = DK 58B27.

can be analyzed into *B*.) These ambiguities need to be resolved before statements like the ones the Pythagoreans made about number can be fully understood, but nothing in earlier philosophy encouraged Pythagoras or his early followers to make fine distinctions. In fact, the philosophical work needed for the task was not undertaken before Socrates, Plato, and Aristotle, whose evident frustration with the Pythagoreans reflects the intellectual distance that separates him from ideas formulated only two or three generations before.

The Unity of Pythagoreanism

A general problem for understanding the Pythagoreans is why a religious movement dedicated to purifying the soul should have promoted mathematics and the study of the *kosmos*. In other words, how are the two sides of the movement related? Do they form a unity? I believe they do, and the connection between them may go back to the Founder. Other Greek cults promised their devotees immortality, but how can some souls be immortal while others are mortal, and how can attending or performing religious rites make souls immortal? Milesian speculation on the nature of the *kosmos* and the composition of things including souls pointed to the view that souls are made up of the basic stuff of the universe and so, immortal. The issue is thus not how to gain immortality, but how best to use it. Pythagoras taught that the best and most important thing to do is to purify the soul, to rid it of pollution, disorder, and immorality, because pure souls have the best afterlife, and perhaps ultimately attain a kind of divinity.

Distinctive to Pythagoreanism is idea that purification is not achieved solely by ritual means. It requires more than abstaining from meat and beans and more than obedience to the *akousmata*. It also requires eliminating the disorder that affects our soul when we have a bad character and, importantly, when we lack clear knowledge of the *kosmos*. For the Pythagoreans (more precisely, the *mathēmatikoi*), this clear knowledge is not simply a matter of parroting a set of beliefs, saying a catechism of fixed doctrine without understanding. It involves the study of mathematics and the *kosmos*. The numerical basis of the *kosmos* implies that the *kosmos* is comprehensible to humans, and the knowledge of it which benefits our soul demands thought and understanding. Our soul becomes orderly (*kosmios*) when it understands the order (*kosmos*) in the universe.[55] This is the inspiration that underlies the developments in Pythagorean thought and gives them much common ground with their Ionian predecessors as well as with their successors in mathematics, science, and philosophy.

---

55. Plato, *Republic* 6 500c (not in DK). The idea is nicely developed in Guthrie (1962: 206–12).

Conclusion

Pythagoreanism was a two-faced movement that combined primitive ingredients with ideas still current today into a doctrine at home in the Presocratic period. Its breadth of interest is typified by its concern with the individual soul on the one hand and with the structure of the universe on the other and is represented by the ten pairs of fundamental opposites. The Pythagoreans shared with their Ionian predecessors an interest in the physical world and the goal of explaining it through a small number of basic principles as well as the confidence to base a theory on a breathtaking generalization from a limited range of evidence. Different was their proclamation of the fundamental importance of number in the world. Instead of basing other things on a material substance such as water or air, they explained them in terms of numbers. For this they are given credit for recognizing the importance of the quantitative aspects of phenomena and for the first reduction of quality to quantity (in their numerical account of the concordant musical intervals). On the other hand the clear distinction between quantity and quality was not made until Aristotle, and in the absence of this and other relevant philosophical distinctions the Pythagoreans literally did not know what they were doing. Some of their statements even seem to entail that numbers are substances and form the material composition of other things. However, their mathematical explorations made a lasting contribution. They were concerned to define mathematical concepts and invented the field of number theory. They were also involved in the development of geometry, and it is possible, but no more than that, that they created the notion of mathematical proof. Their cosmology is a blend of their mathematics, their musical theory, their religious ideas, and their numerology. In its details it is noteworthy for removing the earth from the center of the universe and for postulating the harmony of the spheres. The main philosophical interest of their discussion of the universe is in its account of the origin, in which the *kosmos* resembles number, geometrical figures, and the musical intervals by being the product of the imposition of limit on the unlimited. Their failure to distinguish between the nature of numbers and the nature of material objects, however, leaves them open to charges that their cosmogony attempts the impossible—to make numbers the physical constituents of material things. Their doctrines of the soul's immortality, its rebirth into different living things, and the possibility of its ultimate release into a better existence have practical implications for how Pythagoreans should live their lives. The assumption that a living being is composed of a body and a soul and the belief that the soul is more important than the body would have an important legacy in ethical and metaphysical as well as religious thought. Finally, the bold conception of the universe in all its aspects—including the living and nonliving, the cosmological, musical, and mathematical, and the ethical—as an intelligible, ordered whole—in a word a *kosmos*—was the ultimate basis of their thought and life.

10

Heraclitus of Ephesus

The Fragments of Heraclitus[1]

Group I. Contempt for the Lack of Understanding of the Many

10.1 (1)[2] This *Logos* holds always,[3] but humans always prove unable to understand it both before hearing it and when they have first heard it. For although all things come to be [or, "happen"] in accordance with this *Logos*, humans are like the inexperienced when they experience such words and deeds as I set out, distinguishing each in accordance with its nature and saying how it is. But other people fail to notice what they do when awake, just as they forget what they do while asleep.

10.2 (2) For this reason it is necessary to follow what is common. But although the *Logos* is common, most people live as if they had their own private understanding.

10.3 (17) For many, in fact all that come upon them, do not understand such things, nor when they have noticed them do they know them, but they seem to themselves <to do so>.

10.4 (29) The best renounce all for one thing, the eternal fame of mortals, but the many stuff themselves like cattle.

10.5 (56) People are deceived about the knowledge of obvious things, like Homer, who was wiser than all the Greeks. For children who were killing lice deceived him by saying "All we saw and caught we have left behind, but all we neither saw nor caught we bring with us."

---

1. I translate all the fragments agreed to be authentic (except for DK 22B122, which is a single word without any context) and a few whose authenticity is disputed (which I mark with an asterisk). The wording of some fragments is disputed, as are their meaning and their proper order. General books on early Greek philosophy, including the present one, lacking much room to treat the problems or offer alternative readings, make things seem more certain than they are. For discussion of individual fragments, I recommend Kahn (1979), Marcovich (1967), and Kirk (1954).

2. The numbers in parentheses are the numbers of the fragments in DK. (1) = DK 22B1.

3. The word "always," which occurs only once in the Greek, can go grammatically with either "holds" or "prove." Since Heraclitus holds both that the *Logos* is eternal and that other people do not understand it when he explains it to them, I have translated it twice. I believe the ambiguity is intentional. Heraclitus often exploits language in ways like this. Also the first words, which I render as an absolute clause, can also be the object of "unable to understand." An alternative translation is "Humans always prove unable to understand this *Logos*, which holds always."

10.6* (70) [Heraclitus judged human opinions to be] children's playthings.

(Context from Stobaeus, *Eclogae* 2.1.16)

10.7 (74) We should not be children of our parents.

10.8* (72) They are at odds with the *Logos*, with which above all they are in continuous contact, and the things they meet every day appear strange to them.[4]

10.9* (71) . . . the person who forgets which way the road leads.

10.10 (86) Divine things for the most part escape recognition because of unbelief.

10.11 (87) A fool is excited by every word (*logos*).

10.12 (97) Dogs bark at everyone they do not know.

10.13 (104) What understanding (*noos*) or intelligence (*phrēn*[5]) have they? They put their trust in popular bards and take the mob for their teacher, unaware that most people are bad, and few are good.

10.14 (108) Of all those whose accounts (*logoi*, plural of *logos*) I have heard, no one reaches the point of recognizing that what is wise is set apart from all.[6]

10.15 (11) Every beast is driven to pasture by blows.

Also **10.20**, **10.22**.

Group II. Contempt for Predecessors

9.2 (40) Much learning ["polymathy"] does not teach insight. Otherwise it would have taught Hesiod and Pythagoras and moreover Xenophanes and Hecataeus.

9.3 (129) Pythagoras the son of Mnesarchus practiced inquiry [*historiē*] more than all other men, and making a selection of these writings constructed his own wisdom, polymathy, evil trickery.

---

4. Probably a recollection of **10.3**. Marcus Aurelius gives **10.9**, **10.8**, and **10.23**, one after the other. He is probably relying on his memory and may be intentionally paraphrasing.

5. See above p. 62 n. 11.

6. Grammatically, "all" can mean either "all humans" or "all things."

10.16   (42) Heraclitus said that Homer deserved to be expelled from the contests and flogged, and Archilochus likewise.

10.17   (28) The knowledge of the most famous persons, which they guard, is but opinion. Justice will convict those who fabricate falsehoods and bear witness to them.

10.18   (39) In Priene was born Bias, son of Teutames, whose worth (*logos*) is greater than the others'.

Also **10.5, 10.71.**

Group III. Method

A. Misuse of the Senses

10.19*   (46) [He said that] conceit is a holy disease[7] [and that] sight tells falsehoods.

10.20   (19) [Rebuking some for their unbelief, Heraclitus says,] Knowing neither how to hear nor how to speak.

10.21   (107) Eyes and ears are bad witnesses to people if they have barbarian[8] souls.

10.22   (34) Uncomprehending when they have heard, they are like the deaf. The saying describes them: though present they are absent.

B. Sleep and Death

10.23*   (73) One ought not to act and speak like people asleep.

10.24   (89) For the waking there is one common world, but when asleep each person turns away to a private one.

10.25   (26) A man in the night kindles a light for himself when his sight is extinguished; living he touches[9] the dead when asleep, when awake he touches the sleeper.

10.26*   (75) Sleepers are workmen and fellow-workers in what goes on in the world.[10]

---

7. A reference to epilepsy, which was called the holy disease.

8. A *barbaros* was originally anyone who did not speak Greek. Perhaps in Heraclitus's lifetime it began to have the negative overtones of "barbarian." Heraclitus probably uses the word here of people who do not understand the *Logos*.

9. The Greek word for "kindles" and "touches" is the same.

10. At best this is a paraphrase of Heraclitus's actual words.

10.27   (21) What we see when awake is death, what we see asleep is sleep.

Also **10.1, 10.74, 10.76, 10.89, 10.90, 10.103, 10.106, 10.107, 10.108, 10.109, 10.110, 10.112**.

C. Wisdom and Insight

10.28   (78) Human nature has no insight, but divine nature has it.

10.29   (79) A man is called infantile by a divinity as a child is by a man.

10.30   (32) The wise is one alone; it is unwilling and willing to be called by the name of Zeus. [or, "The wise is one; it alone is unwilling . . ." or, "One thing, the only wise . . ."]

10.31   (113) Thinking is common to all.[11]

10.32   (116) It belongs to all people to know themselves and to think rightly.

Also **10.14, 10.44, 10.46**.

D. Experience and Inquiry

10.33   (101) I searched myself.

10.34   (35) Men who are lovers of wisdom must be inquirers into many things indeed.

Also **9.2**.

E. The Senses

10.35   (55) All that can be seen, heard, experienced—these are what I prefer.

10.36   (101a) Eyes are more accurate witnesses than the ears.

10.37   (7) If all things were smoke, nostrils would distinguish them.

10.38   (98) Souls smell [that is, use the sense of smell] in Hades.

---

11. See above p. 113 n. 6.

F. DIFFICULTY OF THE SUBJECT

10.39   (18) Unless he hopes for the unhoped for, he will not find it, since it is not to be hunted out and is impassable.[12]

10.40   (22) Those who seek gold dig up much earth but find little.

10.41   (84b) It is weariness to labor at the same things and <always> to be beginning [or, "It is weariness to labor for the same <masters> and to be ruled"].

10.42   (123) Nature loves to hide.

10.43   (93) The Lord whose oracle is at Delphi neither speaks nor conceals but gives a sign.

G. THE GOAL

10.44   (41) Wisdom is one thing, to be skilled in true judgment, how all things are steered through all things.

10.45   (47) Let us not make random conjectures about the greatest matters.

10.46   (112) Right thinking is the greatest excellence, and wisdom is to speak the truth and act in accordance with nature while paying attention to it.

Group IV. The *Logos*

10.1, 10.2, 10.8.

10.47   (50) Listening not to me but to the *Logos*, it is wise to agree that all things are one.

10.48   (10) Things taken together are whole and not whole, <something that is> being brought together and brought apart, in tune and out of tune; out of all things there comes a unity and out of a unity all things.

10.49   (51) They do not understand how, though at variance with itself, it agrees with itself [or, "how by being at variance with itself it agrees with itself"; more literally, "how (by) being brought apart it is brought together"]. It is a backwards-turning [or, "backward-stretching"][13] attunement like that of the bow and lyre.

---

12. *Aporon* ("without a path"), related to *aporia*, ("perplexity").

13. *Palintropos* or *palintonos*. The sources disagree here, and there is no scholarly consensus on which word Heraclitus used.

10.50 (54) An unapparent connection (*harmonia*) is stronger than an apparent one.

10.51 (114) Those who speak with understanding (*noos*) must rely firmly on what is common to all[14] as a city must rely on [its?] law, and much more firmly. For all human laws are nourished by one law, the divine law; for it has as much power as it wishes and is sufficient for all[15] and is still left over.

10.52 (8) What is opposed brings together; the finest harmony [*harmonia*] is composed of things at variance, and everything comes to be [or, "occurs"] in accordance with strife.

Group V. Fragments on Opposition

A. X Has Contrary Properties from Different Points of View

10.53 (61) The sea is the purest and most polluted water: to fishes drinkable and bringing safety, to humans undrinkable and destructive.

10.54 (13) Pigs rejoice in mud more than in pure water.

10.55 (9) Asses would choose rubbish rather than gold.

10.56 (4) We would call oxen happy when they find bitter vetch to eat.

10.57 (37) Pigs wash themselves in mud, birds in dust or ash.

10.58 (82) The most beautiful of apes is ugly in comparison with the human race.[16]

10.59 (83) The wisest of humans will appear as an ape in comparison with a god in respect to wisdom, beauty, and all other things.

10.60 (124) The most beautiful *kosmos* is a pile of things poured out at random.

Also **10.88**.

---

14. See above p. 113 n. 6.

15. Grammatically, "all" can mean either "all humans," "all things," or "all human laws."

16. Some consider this fragment spurious.

B. X Has Contrary Properties to the Same Observer
Simultaneously, in Different Respects

10.61   (58) Physicians who cut and burn complain that they receive no worthy pay, although they do these things.[17]

10.62   (59) The track of writing [or, "the path of the carding wheels"[18]] is straight and crooked.

10.63   (60) The road up and the road down are one and the same.

10.64   (12) Upon those who step into the same rivers, different and again different waters flow.

10.65   (91) [It is not possible to step twice into the same river][19]. . . . It scatters and again comes together, and approaches and recedes.

10.66* (49a) We step into and we do not step into the same rivers. We are and we are not.[20]

10.67   (103) The beginning and the end are common on the circumference of a circle.

---

17. The text of this fragment is problematic. Another version (which is further removed from the manuscript readings) is "Physicians . . . demand pay, but deserve nothing." In any case, the point is that physicians cure painful ailments by inflicting pain and consider it right to be paid on the grounds that they alleviate the pains of physical ailments (which are bad for the patient) by inflicting more pain (which is in this case good for the patient).

18. The manuscript reading *gnapheiōn* ("carding wheels") is emended by some editors to *grapheiōn* ("writing").

19. The first clause of **10.65** contradicts **10.64**, which sees no difficulty about stepping into the "same" river. I follow KRS in thinking that the first clause of **10.65** follows Plato's interpretation (see below pp. 137–38). (KRS print **10.64** together with **10.65** minus its first clause as a single fragment.) Since **10.66** is probably a paraphrase of Heraclitean ideas, not a direct quotation (see Kahn [1979: 288]), **10.64** is probably the only authentic river fragment. Much depends on whether the first clause of **10.65** is genuine, since **10.64** is the best evidence for Herclitus's fundamental doctrine that identity is preserved by change. For the view that all three fragments are genuine and represent a succession of reflections on the nature of a river, and for a proposal to read Heraclitus as not simply making obscure pronouncements but arguing dialectically, see Mackenzie (1988).

20. See previous note.

10.68   (48) The name of the bow [*bíos*] is life [*bíos*], but its work is death.[21]

Also **10.47, 10.48, 10.49, 10.52, 10.78**.

C. Opposite Qualities That Occur Successively

10.69   (126) Cold things grow hot, a hot thing cold, a moist thing withers, a parched thing is wetted.

10.70   (88) The same thing is[22] both living and dead, and the waking and the sleeping, and young and old; for these things transformed are those, and those transformed back again are these.

10.71   (57) Most men's teacher is Hesiod. They are sure he knew most things—a man who could not recognize day and night; for they are one.[23]

Also **10.86, 10.89**.

D. Opposites Contrasted by Each Other; Each Is
Necessary for the Recognition of the Other

10.72   (23) They [people in general] would not have known the name of justice if these things [unjust things] did not exist.

10.73   (111) Disease makes health pleasant and good, hunger [does the same for] satiety, weariness [for] rest.

E. Transmutation of Elements

10.74   (36) It is death to souls to come to be water, death to water to come to be earth, but from earth water comes to be and from water soul.

---

21. The fragment exploits the identical spelling of the Greek words for bow (*bíos*) and life (*bíos*); they differed in the accented syllables, but in Heraclitus's time accents were not yet written. Also, the fragment does not contain the word *bíos*, but uses the more common word *toxon*, thus requiring his readers (or hearers) to make the essential association themselves.

22. The word translated "is" more commonly means "is in." Perhaps Heraclitus means "the same thing is in us as both living and dead."

23. The verbs translated "are sure," "knew," and "recognize" are almost synonyms and can all be translated "know," a translation which would emphasize the paradoxical suggestion of the fragment. Mackenzie (1988) emphasizes the paradoxes.

10.75   (31) The turnings of fire: first, sea; and of sea, half is earth and half fiery waterspout. . . . Earth is poured out as sea, and is measured according to the same ratio (*logos*) it was before it became earth.

10.76*   (76) Fire lives the death of earth and *aēr* lives the death of fire, water lives the death of *aēr*, earth that of water.

Everliving fire

10.77   (30) The *kosmos*, the same for all, none of the gods nor of humans has made, but it was always and is and shall be: an ever-living fire being kindled in measures and being extinguished in measures.

Group VI. Cosmological Principles: The *Logos* at Work

All fragments in **Group V.E**.

10.78   (84a) Changing [or, "by changing"], it is at rest.

10.79   (125) Even the posset[24] separates if it is not being stirred.

10.80   (90) All things are an exchange for fire and fire for all things, as goods for gold and gold for goods [or, "as money for gold and gold for money"].

10.81   (64) Thunderbolt steers all things.

10.82   (53) War is the father of all and king of all, and some he shows as gods, others as humans; some he makes slaves, others free.

10.83   (80) It is necessary to know that war is common and justice is strife and that all things happen in accordance with strife and necessity.

10.84*   (66) For fire will advance and judge and convict all things.

10.85   (65) Fire is want and satiety.

10.86   (67) God is day and night, winter and summer, war and peace, satiety and hunger, but changes the way <fire,> when mingled with perfumes, is named according to the scent of each.

10.87   (33) It is law,[25] too, to obey the counsel of one.

---

24. *Kukeōn* a potion made of ground barley, grated cheese, wine, and sometimes honey.

25. *Nomos* "law," "custom."

10.88　(102) To God all things are beautiful and good and just, but humans have supposed some unjust and others just.

10.89　(62) Immortal mortals, mortal immortals [or, "immortals are mortal, mortals are immortal"], living the death of the others and dying their life.

10.90　(20) When they are born, they are willing to live and to have their destinies, and they leave children behind to become their destinies.

Also **10.70, 10.103**.

Group VII. Cosmology: Details

10.91　(3 + 94) The sun by its nature is the width of a human foot, not exceeding in size the limits of its width. Otherwise, the Erinyes, ministers of Justice, will find him out.[26]

10.92　(6) The sun is new each day.

10.93　(99) If there were no sun, as far as concerns all the other stars[27] it would be night.

10.94　(100) Seasons which bring everything. . . .

10.95　(120) Limits of dawn and evening are the Bear and opposite the Bear,[28] the limit of bright Zeus.

Also **10.71**.

Group VIII. Religion

10.96　(5) They vainly purify themselves with blood when defiled with it, as if a man who had stepped into mud were to wash it off with mud. He would be thought mad if anyone noticed him acting thus.

10.97　(15) If it were not for Dionysus that they hold processions and sing hymns to the shameful parts [phalli], it would be a most shameless act; but Hades

---

26. I adopt the text in the Derveni papyrus, column IV. See below p. 460.

27. The clause "as far . . . stars" is omitted in one of the sources and may not be authentic.

28. The Bear is the constellation Ursa Major (the Big Dipper), and "opposite the Bear" refers to the star Arcturus, which was used as an indicator of the seasons.

and Dionysus are the same, in whose honor they go mad and celebrate the Bacchic rites.

10.98   (14) Nightwalkers, Magi, Bacchoi, Lenai, and the initiated. [These people Heraclitus threatens with what happens after death. . . .] For the secret rites practiced among humans are celebrated in an unholy manner.

(Context from Clement, *Protrepticus* 22)

10.99*   (69) [I posit two kinds of sacrifices: those made by people who are wholly purified, which may take place] rarely, in the case of a single man [as Heraclitus says] or of so few that they can easily be counted.[29]

10.100   (92) The Sibyl with raving mouth uttering mirthless [and unadorned and unperfumed phrases, reaches a thousand years in her voice on account of the god].[30]

(Context from Plutarch, *On the Oracles at Delphi* 397A)

10.101   (68) [Things seen and heard in sacred rites are introduced to the soul in us and to keep within bounds the evils which birth has caused to grow about it, to set us free and release us from bonds. Hence Heraclitus rightly called them] cures [as tending to cure our troubles and the disasters attendant on generation.][31]

(Context from Iamblichus, *On the Mysteries* 1.11)

Also **10.43**.

Group IX. The Soul

10.102*   (67a) As a spider standing in the middle of its web notices as soon as a fly breaks any of its threads and quickly runs there as if grieved by the breaking of the thread, so the soul of a man, when any part of his body is harmed, rushes there quickly as if unable to endure the harm of the body, to which it is joined firmly and proportionally.

10.103   (77) It is death for souls to become wet.

10.104   (118) A gleam of light is a dry soul, wisest, and best.

---

29. This alleged fragment is thought by many to be a reminiscence of **10.117**.

30. The bracketed material may contain Heraclitean ideas, although the wording is probably not authentic.

31. This is a testimonium containing only one word from Heraclitus.

10.105 (117) A man when drunk is led by a boy, stumbling and not knowing where he goes, since his soul is moist.

10.106* (136) Souls slain in war are purer than those that perish in diseases.

10.107 (24) Gods and humans honor those slain in war.

10.108 (25) Greater deaths win greater destinies.

10.109 (27) Things unexpected and unthought of await humans when they die.

10.110 (63) They arise and become vigilant guardians of the living and the dead.

10.111 (16) How could one fail to be seen by that which does not set?

10.112 (96) Corpses are more fit to be thrown out than dung.

10.113 (45) You would not discover the limits of the soul although you traveled every road: so deep a *Logos* does it have.

10.114* (115) The soul has a self-increasing *Logos*.

Also **10.21, 10.74, 10.124**.

Group X. Politics

10.115 (121) Every grown man of the Ephesians should hang himself and leave the city to the boys; for they banished Hermodorus, the best man among them, saying "let no one of us excel, or if he does, be it elsewhere and among others."

10.116 (125a) May wealth never leave you, Ephesians, lest your wickedness be revealed.

10.117 (49) One person is ten thousand to me if he is best.

10.118 (52) A lifetime [or, "eternity"] is a child playing, playing checkers; the king-dom belongs to a child.

10.119 (44) The people must fight for the law[32] as for the city wall.

---

32. *Nomos* "law," "custom."

Group XI. Moral Thought

10.120   (43) Willful violence [*hubris*] must be quenched more than a fire.

10.121   (119) A person's character [or, "individuality"] is his divinity [or, "guardian spirit"].

10.122   (110) It is not better for humans to get all they want.

10.123   (95) It is better to conceal ignorance.

10.124   (85) It is difficult to fight against anger, for whatever it wants it buys at the price of the soul.

Also **10.4**, **10.13**, **10.32**, **10.46**, **10.51**, **10.87**.

Heraclitus, Dates and Life

Heraclitus was reportedly born c.540 and lived sixty years—dates consistent with his references to Xenophanes, Pythagoras and Hecataeus of Miletus (c.500 BCE).[33] He belonged to an aristocratic family in Ephesus and was entitled to hold a hereditary and possibly largely honorary "kingship," which he resigned to his brother. Xenophanes and Pythagoras had both left Ionia, the one probably before Heraclitus's birth and the other before Heraclitus was grown, so Heraclitus, as the only known Presocratic philosopher in the Ionian regions during his time, seems to have been an isolated figure, and this fact may have something to do with his idiosyncrasies and evident arrogance.

Many biographical anecdotes about Heraclitus are preserved, but practically all of them are spurious and based on his own fragments. For example, the story that he died in a pile of cow manure where he had put himself when suffering from dropsy, thinking that the warmth of the manure would evaporate the disease from him, is based on his statement "it is death for souls to become wet" (**10.103**) and on his doctrine of exhalations or evaporations by which water becomes fire (**10.75**).

Source Materials

Like the other Presocratics, Heraclitus is known to us through accounts of his philosophy and fragments preserved in later sources. Although his book, whose beginning is preserved (**10.1**) and which he deposited in the temple of Artemis at Ephesus, has not survived as a whole, over one hundred fragments survive. We are consequently better able to approach him through his own words and on his

---

33. **9.2**, cf. **10.16** and **10.18**.

own terms than we are his predecessors. This is fortunate since the reports of Heraclitus's ideas in ancient writers are wildly different from one another. Plato (in *Theaetetus* and *Cratylus*) found in Heraclitus the doctrine that "all things flow" (a statement not found in any of Heraclitus's genuine fragments, though related to two important ones), which he interpreted as meaning that all things are always changing in all respects—the world is in continuous flux and there is no stability or permanence in it. Aristotle, followed by Theophrastus, placed him in the tradition of the Ionian theorists, with fire as his basic substance. The Stoics saw him as a forerunner of their own philosophy, in which fire is primary, the universe is governed by *Logos*, and in some sense fire, *Logos*, and god are identical, and so they interpreted him through their own system, attributing their views to him. In the third century CE, Bishop Hippolytus of Rome found in him certain doctrines which he regarded as the origin of a Christian heresy.

The preserved fragments make it clear how Heraclitus could be interpreted in so many ways, all of them with a basis in the original but all of them partial and influenced by their authors' interests and beliefs. Most fragments are short, balanced, powerfully expressed. They have the ring of prophesies, riddles, similes, and metaphors which stand alone and demand careful attention, each individually and in relation to one another. Many can be understood both metaphorically and literally or as applying to more than one subject (**10.74** talks of changes; it also tells about the human soul). In many cases words and images are echoed vividly from fragment to fragment. The fragments cry out to be considered in each other's light, and the meaning that emerges is greater than the meanings of the fragments taken separately. They do not, in general, give the impression of being parts of a continuous prose exposition, but have much in common with the sayings of the Seven Sages and other maxims which survive in abundance in the literature of the Archaic period (although Heraclitus's fragments exhibit more unity and probe more deeply than is common in such cases). A book of Heraclitus's writings in three sections (The Universe, Politics, Theology) circulated in later antiquity,[34] but may have been a compilation of Heraclitean materials rather than his original book. In any case, the divisions seem arbitrary[35] and untrue to Heraclitus, part of whose profound insight was that all things are one, which implies that such divisions are fundamentally incorrect.

In these circumstances some have decided to base their interpretations on the fragments alone (or virtually alone), ignoring the ancient testimonia or holding them guilty until proved innocent. This approach is flawed. First, many of the fragments considered genuine are preserved in the same ancient reports that are considered dubious. But the authors of those reports had Heraclitus's book (or at least more information than we do), and so to reject the testimony is to suppose that we understand Heraclitus better than the ancients did, although we have less information than they had, and that we can reject their interpretations

---

34. Diogenes Laertius, *Lives of the Philosophers* 9.5 = DK 22A1.
35. How would **10.51** and **10.86**, for example, be classified?

on the basis of the evidence they selected to support them. Second, if the ancient testimonia are misleading about Heraclitus, what becomes of our knowledge of the earlier Presocratics, which in the absence of abundant fragments depends almost entirely on the same authors? Further, the fragments occur in contexts determined by the interests of the writers who preserve them. To take them out of context and treat them as independent entities to be manipulated on their own risks losing valuable clues about their original context and meaning, and presupposes that the contexts in which they are preserved are so misleading that we do better without them.[36]

Heraclitus appears different to virtually everyone who spends time with him, and the formidable and unique problems associated with his fragments and the ways they have been preserved do not encourage the hope that there will ever be a consensus about how to present the material, let alone about its meaning.[37] I have chosen to print the fragments in most cases without context and to arrange them by the topics I have chosen to discuss, with no pretense that they are in anything like the original order. This arrangement promotes brevity and focuses attention on Heraclitus but is no substitute for close study of the source materials.[38] Further, though problems regarding text and meaning arise with most of the fragments, a treatment of this scope cannot hope to mention them all, let alone treat them fully. The discussion that follows is meant to be merely suggestive, not exhaustive or authoritative.

Attitude toward Others

Heraclitus often expresses his low opinion of his fellow human beings (**Group I**). He complains that people fail to understand him (**10.1**) and perhaps that they are hostile to his unfamiliar ideas (**10.12**), also that they care more about their bellies than the truth (**10.4**). They do not use their senses (**10.1, 10.3, 10.20, 10.22, 10.13**) or intelligence (**10.3, 10.13**) correctly, they unreflectively and inconsistently (**10.1, 10.11**) listen to tradition, authority, and one another (**10.13**), and in the end they all make up their own mind and are content with their own thoughts (**10.2, 10.3**), which are for the most part worthless (**10.6, 10.20**), instead of recognizing that a single truth is present everywhere (**10.1, 10.8**) and common to all (**10.2**).

---

36. The testimonia and fragment contexts have been collected by Mouraviev as part of his monumental work on Heraclitus (Mouraviev [1999–]).

37. To cite three approaches: DK abandons all hope of recovering the original arrangement and prints the fragments in the alphabetical order of the names of the authors who quote them; Kahn believes that the fragments "were originally arranged in a significant order" and "it is the interpreter's task to present these incomplete and shattered fragments in the most meaningful order he can find" (Kahn [1979: 8]); Osborne argues in favor of reading the fragments in the context in which they are preserved (Osborne [1987b]).

38. Osborne (1987b) translates much of Hippolytus. A good deal of ancient context is given in the chapter on Heraclitus in Barnes (2001).

Heraclitus also attacks notable intellectual figures for their ignorance (**Group II**). Bias of Priene, one of the Seven Sages, is excepted from abuse (**10.18**), perhaps because he declared "most people are bad" (**10.13**). It is interesting and perhaps significant that (in surviving fragments) Heraclitus does not attack the Milesian philosophers, to whom he is in fact indebted for many of his views.

Remarks on Method

As **10.1** makes clear, Heraclitus claims to have made a discovery of colossal importance—no less than the key to understanding everything. His notion of "everything" extends further than the Ionians', since it covers in addition to the physical world the practical world of ethics and politics, religion, and some more strictly philosophical realms as well. He calls this fundamental discovery the *Logos*, and believes that understanding the *Logos* is the most important thing a person can do. The chief task of this chapter will be to determine what he means by the *Logos* and how he understands it to account for all phenomena. Before turning to these questions it will be useful to consider his remarks on how to learn the *Logos*, which constitute the most extensive surviving reflections on philosophical method up to his time.[39]

Most people act as if asleep (**10.1**, **10.23**), each with a private dream world, different from the common, public world we live in (**10.24**). Although surrounded by a part of the real world, which is common to all (the *Logos* is common [**10.2**]), they do not apprehend it (**10.3**, **10.2**, **10.1**, **10.8**, **10.10**) or comprehend it (**10.1**, **10.3**, **10.13**). Heraclitus suggests that we can escape from this state. For he contrasts sleeping and the dream world with waking and the real world, and the contrast suggests that we can wake up; the question is how.

In contrast to the normal human state of ignorance and unbelief, the divine has knowledge and insight (**10.28**) and is the only truly wise being (**10.30**). Neither this claim nor the observation that we are like babies in comparison with god (**10.29**) means that we must remain wholly ignorant any more than the thesis that understanding is common to all (**10.31**) means that we all possess the very insight Heraclitus denies we have (**10.28**). Rather, as children grow to maturity, we may grow in insight. Our ultimate goal is thinking (**10.31**), self-knowledge, and thinking rightly (**10.32**).[40] To the extent that we attain this insight and wisdom we transcend the human and resemble the divine (**10.28**, **10.30**).[41]

---

39. The fragments and testimonia on the Milesians provide nothing on this topic. Xenophanes' comments on methods are discussed above pp. 67–68. The Pythagoreans' views must be inferred from (often hostile) testimonia, such as **9.35**.

40. "Thinking" (*phroneein*) and "thinking rightly" (*sōphrōnein*) are closely related in etymology as well as in sense.

41. Many of the ideas sketched in this paragraph have important parallels in Heraclitus's contemporaries Xenophanes and Parmenides.

We gain insight mainly in two ways: inquiry into ourselves (**10.33**) and inquiry, through correct use of the senses (**Group III.E**), into the world around us. At first sight it appears that the senses cannot help us acquire this knowledge (**10.19**, **10.20**, **10.21**, **10.22**, **10.1** [near the end]). But note the qualifications: sight and hearing are unreliable *to those with barbarian souls* (**10.21**), *some* do not know how to hear or speak (**10.20**). Most people fall into these categories, but Heraclitus believes that a wise person can use the senses to gain accurate information. He prefers experiencing things for oneself (**10.35**), but rates hearing lower than sight (**10.36**), perhaps because we can be told falsehoods even by respected authorities (**10.13**, **Group II**). His comments on the sense of smell (**10.37**) indicate that we should use whatever sense is most appropriate in each situation. If all things were smoke or in the darkness of the underworld (**10.38**) we could not see but would distinguish things by smell.

To become wise we must learn to use the senses with insight or intelligence (*noos*).[42] We must also practice inquiry like the Ionian philosophers, but even more widely (**10.34**). Even so, mere learnedness is not the same as wisdom and insight (**9.2**). We must conduct our inquiry systematically (**10.45**), so as to promote right thought, speech, and action (**10.46**), and this requires us to grasp the unity and coherence of the universe and the cooperation of its parts (**10.44**).

Inquiry is difficult (**Group III.F**). It requires work (**10.34**, **10.41**), patience (**10.40**), and hope (**10.39**). **10.39** may mean that unless you have an idea that there is a single principle that governs everything that takes place, you will never think of looking for it and hence will never find it.

10.42 and **10.43** suggest reasons for the difficulty. The principles of nature as a whole or the nature (the basic constitution) of each thing are not obvious. They underlie or are behind all phenomena and must be grasped if we are to understand the phenomena, but we must get past the superficial aspects in order to grasp them. The phenomena are "signs" of the important underlying truths. They do not deliberately hide the truths so as to prevent us from discovering them, but their correct understanding (like the proverbially enigmatic oracular responses given at Delphi) demands careful interpretation.

The *Logos*

Heraclitus's great discovery is that all things that take place or come to be do so in accordance with a *Logos* (**10.1**), which is common (**10.2**) both because it applies everywhere and also because it is objective, and so is available to all humans. This amounts to a claim that the world is governed by a rational principle which humans can come to comprehend. We can comprehend it because we are rational as well, and our rationality is related to the universal rational principle of the *Logos*. A noun related to the verb *legein*, "to speak," *logos* is a thing said, and

---

42. According to **10.128**, perception is needed for our intelligence (*nous*, equivalent to *noos*) to attain its best condition, in which it is fully rational.

hence a word, statement, or story. The close connection between what we say and what we write or think accounts for a further range of meanings: account, agreement, opinion, thought, argument, reason, cause. Perhaps from these last two meanings it gets other senses: relation, ratio, proportion. All these meanings were current in the fifth century. In the fourth it was also used to mean the faculty of reason, general principle, and definition.[43]

None of these meanings adequately describes Heraclitus's *Logos*. It is distinct from what people—even Heraclitus—say or think (**10.47**), so it is not a word, statement, account, opinion, etc., even a (or the) true one. "General principle" probably comes closest to his intent, but it is too abstract a notion, for Heraclitus associates the *Logos* with fire (compare **10.1** and **10.81** and see below page 136) as the active nature in the universe. I have capitalized *Logos* and left the word untranslated when it has its special Heraclitean meaning (**10.1, 10.2, 10.8, 10.47, 10.113, 10.114**). Elsewhere I have translated it and placed "*logos*" in parentheses.

Given the world's vast diversity, if everything happens because of a single principle, that principle must function or be displayed in many different ways. It must be totally general, and so an explanation of a phenomenon in terms of the *Logos* will be at a very general level and will link it to many other phenomena. Such accounts will be unfamiliar to the great majority of people who are unused to thinking in such ways. If Heraclitus "distinguish[es] each [thing] according to its nature" and "say[s] how it is" (**10.1**), it is not surprising that no one understands him.

The words just quoted suggest that Heraclitus believed that when properly used, language represents (or re-presents) reality in the sense that a correct description or account of anything accords with that thing's nature and says how the thing in question is, in that the account itself reflects the nature of that thing. (For an example, see **10.68** above and page 119 note 21.) This belief would account for Heraclitus's riddling and paradoxical expression: that is the only way to express accurately the surprising and complex natures of things and their interrelations. "Nature loves to hide" (**10.42**), and accounts that are too straightforward cannot capture this essential feature of reality. Like reality itself (and like the Delphic oracle), a correct account of reality needs to be interpreted (**10.43**).

One and Many

Heraclitus summarizes his discovery in the pregnant slogan "all things are one" (**10.47**), which he enlarges: "out of all things there comes a unity and out of a unity all things" (**10.48**). These are general principles, to be sure, and subject to widely differing interpretations. To see what Heraclitus means we need to look further, first at the remainder of **10.48**, which introduces three other ways of regarding phenomena. To the opposition between "one" and "all things" are added "whole" and "not whole," "brought together" and "brought apart," and "in tune" and "out

---

43. Guthrie discusses the meanings of *logos* at greater length (Guthrie [1962: 420–24]).

of tune." All four pairs of opposites describe "things taken together." The real nature of the world is simultaneously and equally a unity and a plurality.

We can also understand the claim epistemologically: the world can be regarded either as composed of many distinct things or as a whole. An individual thing is a part of the world; the world as a whole is made up of parts that have their own identities. We tend to think of things and complex processes separately, without paying attention to their interrelations and to the whole of which they are parts. This is a serious error. The correct way to view them involves understanding the whole and recognizing their part in it. This does not deny their individuality; but we can better appreciate a thing's individuality when we know how it is related to other things. Likewise, we can better appreciate the individuality of a process when we understand the stages that constitute it. In both cases, this knowledge is part of understanding that and how all things are one. Likewise, understanding a whole requires knowing how all its parts function, how they do and do not have identity in their own right ("whole[s] and not whole[s]"), how they do and do not join together ("brought together and brought apart"), and how they do and do not work together in various contexts ("in tune and out of tune"). Heraclitus emphasizes unity in diversity more than diversity in unity, for what constantly confronts us is diversity, and our first task is to grasp the underlying unity. This task is also the most difficult because it requires us to learn new ways of perceiving and thinking. Once it is accomplished, we can use the same tools to unpack the unity, to understand how the diversity exists and functions within it.

10.48 says that "things taken together" have opposite qualities. One opposite quality is due to the other: without differing elements there could be no harmony, for harmony is a relation among different things. Likewise, strife, which we think of as destructive, is responsible for the generation of things (**10.5**). **10.49** and **10.78** can be taken in both these ways: either things possess opposite qualities or they possess one quality because they possess its opposite. The second reading of these fragments makes the stronger and more interesting claim and is supported by the images of the bow and the lyre.

We are to imagine a strung bow or lyre which is not being used. The bow consists of a cord and a curved piece of wood. As we look at it, it appears stable and lifeless. What we fail to see is the connection (**10.50**), the tension that makes it a bow, not just a piece of wood and a cord. Moreover, the tension is "backward-turning" or "backward-stretching." The cord and the wood are under equal tension in opposite directions, the cord being pulled apart by the wood and the ends of the wood being pulled together by the cord. The bow's unity and ability to function depend on the tension between the wood and the cord ("out of many, one"), yet the tension cannot exist without the cord and the wood. Further, once we understand how bows function, we can do a better job of designing bows and choosing the types of wood and cord to use, according to their individual qualities ("out of one, many"). The case of the lyre is similar. The bow and the lyre are paradigmatic of how the world works and how we are to understand it. The moral can be applied to all complex things and processes where the whole functions because of the relation of its parts, and the parts contribute to the working of the whole because of their own particular natures. But, as Heraclitus demonstrates, the *Logos* and the doctrine of unity and diversity operate in surprising ways and over a wider range of phenomena than we might expect.

Opposition

The *Logos* guarantees that all things are one, and that one thing is all. Heraclitus expresses this insight paradoxically, in terms of the unqualified opposites "one" and "all." His interest in opposition is wide, and the types of oppositions he treats illustrate how the *Logos* functions in many contexts.

In the first type of opposition (**Group V.A**) a single subject has opposite properties with respect to or in comparison with different types of beings. **10.53** is the clearest case.

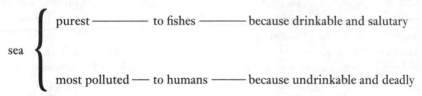

sea
$\begin{cases} \text{purest} \longrightarrow \text{to fishes} \longrightarrow \text{because drinkable and salutary} \\ \\ \text{most polluted} \longrightarrow \text{to humans} \longrightarrow \text{because undrinkable and deadly} \end{cases}$

"Pure" and "polluted" are opposite characteristics that the sea has in a superlative degree. Full understanding of sea water involves knowing both that it is purest and that it is most polluted (and that anything that fails to have these two qualities simultaneously cannot be sea water), but it is insufficient simply to assert that the sea has these opposite qualities; we need to unpack the assertion, pointing out that it has these different characteristics for different kinds of things and explaining why. When we can do this, we know important things about sea water and also about humans and fishes. The other fragments in **Group V.A** can be interpreted along similar lines. Pigs, asses, and oxen have different preferences than humans do, so in each case something has opposite attributes. Mud is both more and less desirable than pure water: more desirable to pigs, less so to humans.

In **Group V.B** a thing has opposite properties in different circumstances. Here it is a matter of objective considerations, not of subjective preferences or judges with different constitutions. **10.61** envisages a case where a disease and the treatment that cures it (surgery or cautery) cause the same kind of pain. In most cases things that cause pain are bad for us and we avoid them, but in some circumstances we choose to suffer something that causes pain because of its other desirable effects.

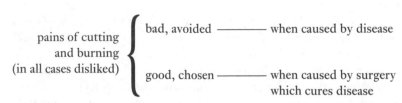

Similarly, a line of writing moves straight across the page, but in view of the shape of each individual letter, it is also crooked (**10.62**).[44] Both are essential aspects of writing. Two fragments included in this section can be taken differently but make sense if analyzed along present lines. The road that goes up the hill, say the Panathenaic Way, which ascends the Acropolis, is the same as the road that goes down it (**10.63**). A road that goes from X to Y also goes from Y to X. Both descriptions are correct but incomplete. Finally, **10.64** contrasts the same river with different waters. If I step into the same river at different times (presumably at the same place) the water that wets my feet is different each time. This is a consequence of the nature of rivers: they are moving water.

In **Group V.C** a single thing has opposite characteristics at different times. **10.69** may proclaim an inevitable law of nature: whatever is cold must at some time become hot. Alternatively, it may make the conceptual point that the only things which can become hot are cold; if they were already hot they could not become hot. It may also describe the physical functioning of the world. (Hot and cold were prominent in Ionian philosophy and play a role in Heraclitus's cosmology [**10.77**].) It can also be seen as making corresponding points about reciprocal processes, such as heating and cooling. **10.70** contains some difficulties, but its general point is similar to that of **10.69**. It begins with a paradox: a single thing has opposite characteristics; but it then resolves the paradox by explaining that the contrasted characteristics belong to the thing at different times, because it changes. The difficulties arise in fitting the explanation to the given pairs of opposites.[45] In **Group V.C** so far we have seen cases where a definite subject now has one characteristic, now the opposite one. The unity of opposites consists in their successively belonging to the same subject. **10.71** extends this idea. Day and night are opposites which alternate, but here there is no subject that undergoes the change. In this case the regular alternation between opposite states is all that is needed to unify the opposites. (See also **Group V.E**.)

Group V.D makes an epistemological point. If all of us were always healthy, we would not know it but would take it for granted in our ignorance of any alternatives. We would not even have a word for health, since the purpose of words is

---

44. On the manuscript reading (see above p. 118 n. 18), **10.62** makes a similar point about carding wheels, though we do not know enough about these ancient devices to be able to understand how the fragment describes them. Carding is the process of straightening wool, part of the preparation of thread to be used in weaving.

45. For one suggestion, see below p. 135.

to distinguish things, to mark them off from others. If all things share a common quality, that quality will not have a name. The point here is that being able to conceive of, understand, and value correctly either of a pair of opposites requires being able to do the same for the other opposite as well.[46]

Group V.E contains fragments important both for the treatment of opposition and for cosmology. **10.74** is least complicated and presents the following picture. Soul dies,[47] ceases to be, when it becomes water; water ceases to be when it becomes earth; but there are also processes in which earth becomes water and water becomes soul.

$$\text{soul} \leftrightarrow \text{water} \leftrightarrow \text{earth}$$

10.75 says the same thing more obscurely, with fire taking the place of soul and sea that of water.

$$\text{fire} \leftrightarrow \text{sea} \leftrightarrow \text{earth}$$

The fiery waterspout (a hurricane funnel illuminated by lightning) is the means by which water from the sea changes into fire.

10.75 emphasizes the idea of measure in change. Sea changes half into fire and half into earth. When earth changes to sea, a conservation principle is at work: for example, two parts of sea become one part of earth, and similarly one part of earth turns into two parts of sea. **10.77** also emphasizes the notion of measured change and the eternity and stability of the overall situation. Since fire, sea, and earth are always being transformed into one another, each of them is always coming to be ("being kindled") and perishing ("extinguished"). All three major components of the *kosmos* are always in existence. The world's current structure is the way it always has been and always will be. Consequently, the world and its order had no origin. Our task is to understand it as it now is.

Group V.E differs from the groups already discussed in that it considers a single opposition, not a type of opposition found in many contexts[48] and in that it presents not two but three contrasted states, each with its own identity and unique role.[49] As in **10.71** there is no identifiable subject that takes on the different qualities and survives the change. Indeed, since the changes take place among the basic forms of matter, there can be no persisting subject of change. When fire becomes water, what was fire is now water, but neither the fire nor the

---

46. Heraclitus's contemporary Xenophanes makes the same kind of point in **7.30**.

47. Death here is not simply a metaphor for change. Heraclitus holds that the soul dies when its fiery nature is (literally) quenched. See **10.104** and below p. 140.

48. For the identification of fire and soul, see below p. 135.

49. In principle there could be any number, not just three. If Heraclitus had adopted Anaximenes' system, he might have had seven (see above p. 52).

water is present throughout the change. There is no way to describe "what was fire" except in terms of what it is at different times. Three factors play a role in analyzing such changes: (a) the different stages of the change (fire, water, earth), (b) the mechanisms or processes of change (for example, rain, fiery waterspout), (c) the regularity, order, and measure of the change.

For Heraclitus, the opposites illustrate the principle of the *Logos*, "out of all things there comes a unity and out of a unity all things" (**10.48**). Since opposite characteristics are normally considered distinct, separate, the furthest apart possible, they seem to present the hardest case for his theory. But if even opposites prove to be "one" the theory has survived an especially difficult challenge. Also, as many opposites are extremes that admit a range of intermediates, if the opposites prove to be "one" then a fortiori all the intermediates are unified too. If hot and cold are "one," so are tepid, lukewarm, etc. Heraclitus considers many kinds of opposition, some physical (**Group V.E**), others conceptual (**Group V.D**), some depending on the point of comparison (**Group V.A**) or the respect in which (**Group V.B**) or time at which (**Group V.C**) a thing is considered. He ranges more widely than the Ionians, who cared principally about the natural world. Moreover, there is no single way to identify or analyze all the kinds of opposition he treats. This is why his enterprise is so difficult. Understanding how the *Logos* works requires finding and analyzing all the cases of unity in plurality and plurality in unity, and these turn up in unexpected settings. Hence the need to inquire into a vast number of things (**10.34**), to pay careful attention (**10.46**), and to acquire the skill of thinking correctly (**10.46, 10.44**). Hence too, learning many things by itself is not enough (**9.2**): it is equally important to know "the one." Finally, we must keep in mind the paradoxical spirit that pervades these fragments. Heraclitus aims to solve the puzzles he finds, but he also takes delight in the manifold complexities of the *kosmos* and the wonderful ways language can convey them.

Cosmological Principles: The *Logos* at Work

Two important features of Heraclitus's *kosmos* are that it is eternal (**10.77**) and that its principal material constituents are fire, water, and earth, which systematically and regularly change into one another (**10.75**). Paradoxically, "changing, it is at rest" (**10.78**): the regularity of change guarantees stability. Otherwise put, change is what is stable. As with the river (**10.64**), the survival and very identity of the *kosmos* is dependent on this change. If the water stopped flowing it would no longer be a river but a long narrow lake. If the basic forms of matter stopped changing, the stable, ordered, regulated *kosmos* would cease to exist. Likewise the "posset" separates into its components unless stirred (**10.79**). Unless it is kept in constant motion, that is, change, it loses its stable identity.

Heraclitus calls water "sea" (**10.75**), thinking of the principal masses that constitute the *kosmos*. Water is found mainly in the sea. Earth is found mainly in the vast mass of it beneath our feet, which we call "the earth." Fire is mostly found (and in its purest form) in the heavens; even the bits of fire we see around us rise up in an effort to reach that place. Thus, like the Ionians,[50] Heraclitus chooses familiar and plentiful materials for his basic forms of matter. Why air does not appear alongside the other three is unclear.[51]

Although the *kosmos* as a whole is ever-living (**10.77**), individual parcels of fire, water, and earth come to be and pass away, are born and die (**10.74**).[52] This may be the point of the obscure **10.89**, **10.90**, and **10.27** as well as of the strange claims that the dead become living and the old young (**10.70**).

Such a system gives no reason to award priority to any of the principal forms of matter. But in similar circumstances Anaximenes called air the basic material, and now Heraclitus declares fire primary: the *kosmos* is an ever-living fire (**10.77**) and all other things are an exchange for fire (**10.80**). The two translations given of **10.80** imply different relations between fire and other things. On the first, the point is that other things can be valued in terms of gold, and exchange can go either way. So much gold is worth so much of something else. Thus, fire can become other things, but they in turn become fire again. So much fire becomes so much water and vice versa. The second translation recalls the ancient practice of coinage in which a gold coin was a piece of gold marked to indicate its weight; its weight determined its value. On this reading, the point of comparison is the persistence of the gold in the coins: the coins are gold. In the same way, other (non-fiery) objects are implied to be not distinct from fire but actually made of fire. They are "coined" out of fire when fire takes on different forms, and will be "exchanged" for fire when the regular process of change brings them around once again into their fiery phase. Neither of these interpretations quite captures the nature of elemental change. Against the first, all things have been and will be fire, but no one who buys a non-golden thing with gold thinks that it has been or will be gold. Against the second, fire does not persist through its changes into water and earth; however, a coin of a given value used to be a lump of gold weighing the same.

Still, however we interpret its identity with other things, fire gets priority among the basic materials, perhaps because the *kosmos* is ever-living (**10.77**). Unlike water and earth, fire has an active, controlling role in the *kosmos* ([**10.81**]: thunderbolt is

---

50. Anaximander is an exception to this generalization, but even for him, once the *kosmos* is generated, its main constituents are familiar substances: fire (especially in the heavens), *aēr* (in the form of clouds), water (especially in the sea), and earth.

51. Given the prominence of air in Anaximenes as well as in the apparent structure of the *kosmos*, it is surprising that Heraclitus omits it. Kahn (1979: 143–45) believes that air is a fourth basic form of matter for Heraclitus, but it is hard to find this doctrine in the fragments (aside from the dubious **10.76**, for which, see the following note).

52. **10.76** reflects Heraclitean ideas, although the mention of air is suspicious and the cycle of change it describes (earth → fire → air → water → earth) is incompatible with that found in **10.74** and **10.75**.

a pure and highly active form of fire). It can be taken as symbolic of the change needed to keep the world going. This conception of fire links it closely with other central features of Heraclitus's philosophy. In the individual, the soul, which makes us alive and directs us, is fiery ("fire" and "soul" are used interchangeably in **10.74** and **10.75**). Further, fire as the all-controller (**10.81**) is somehow associated with the *Logos*, according to which all things happen (**10.1**).

The active nature of the universe is war and strife (**10.82**, **10.83**) (opposition and change), which Heraclitus declares is justice, correcting Anaximander's opinion that the interplay of opposites which prevails in the world is injustice (**5.20**). Events in the *kosmos*, including transformations of one substance into another and changes between opposites, are a necessary and universal war and struggle which is needed to maintain the *kosmos* in a stable condition. Whatever results in a particular case—win or lose—it is part of the overall process that rules the universe with justice. Heraclitus identifies the justice and therefore the strife and war in the universe with fire (**10.84**).

Fire is also associated with God (**10.85**, **10.86**). They both take on different appearances in different situations, but keep their own nature. In a sense, fire is the one behind the many, the unity in all the diversity of the *kosmos*. If **10.87** is correctly brought into the present discussion, then law too forms part of the same cluster of concepts.

We have seen that Heraclitus associates the *Logos*, fire, soul, war, justice, God, and perhaps law. *Logos* is associated with measure as well, since he emphasizes the importance of measure in the orderly changes that go on in the world (**10.75**, **10.77**, **10.91**). In some sense they are the same, the ruling element in the universe, but precisely how they are the same is not clear. When I strike a match and create some fire, I am surely not bringing the eternal *Logos* or God into being. It will not do to demand strict conditions of identity in this context any more than it does when Heraclitus says that day and night are one (**10.71**). In different settings these concepts take on a variety of relations to one another, sometimes being virtually identical and sometimes being almost separate. For example, the burning match is not God, but is related to the cosmic fire (as a part? by resemblance? as an imperfect specimen? as a copy?) and in its small area of active existence it performs functions which both symbolize and are a part of the war and justice that rule the world.

Heraclitus, like the Pythagoreans, lacked conceptual tools and analytical techniques for analyzing such assertions.[53] Broad claims of sameness or identity were easy to make and hard to challenge. This state of philosophy and the Greek language suited Heraclitus's purposes: his approach to the unity of the *kosmos* through the *Logos* required associating ideas rather than analyzing or separating them. He needed to bring things together before bringing them apart again.

---

53. See above pp. 109–10.

Some characteristics are favored over their opposites. War and strife (**10.83**) have opposites in peace and harmony, and it might seem that the *kosmos* is typified as much by peace as by war (compare with **10.86**). Likewise, from God's perspective, which is superior to the human one (**10.28, 10.29, 10.30**), all things are beautiful, good and just, whereas mortals think some things have the opposite, negative qualities (**10.88**). The clear implication is that it is wrong to think anything ugly, evil or unjust, at least when we have gained the correct view of things. (This is a way to avoid conflict with **10.72**.) But why does God think that all things are just rather than that all are unjust or that some are just, others unjust? A possible answer to this serious question is that the order in the *kosmos* is not morally or aesthetically neutral, but good and beautiful. The word "*kosmos*" carries these positive connotations. A static world or a random world would be the opposite. Likewise, the word "*logos*" has connotations of rationality, not irrationality, and is linked with other concepts of positive value, notably justice but also law (which preserves things from anarchy) and soul (which is responsible for life, a condition with positive value).

On the interpretation favored here, Heraclitus puts equal weight on change and on stability, on plurality, and on unity, on difference and on identity: stability is guaranteed by change; change is stable; diverse individual things form a unity; identity is preserved through difference. Other readings are possible. In particular Heraclitus is frequently associated with a doctrine of radical change or "Heraclitean flux." This interpretation can be documented as far back as Plato,[54] who develops it in his dialogues *Theaetetus* and *Cratylus* on the basis of the river fragment (**10.64**), which he cites as follows.

10.125 All things move and nothing remains, and likening existing things to the flow of a river, he says that you could not step twice into the same river.

(Plato, *Cratylus* 402a = DK 22A6)

For Plato's Heraclitus all things are always changing in all respects.

---

54. Plato in turn refers (jokingly?) to a vigorous Heraclitean movement in Ionia (Plato, *Theaetetus* 179d–180c [not in DK]). Also, Aristotle reports that Plato "as a young man became familiar with Cratylus and the Heraclitean doctrines that all sensible things are always flowing (undergoing Heraclitean flux), and there is no knowledge of them" (*Metaphysics* 1.6 987a32–34 = DK 65A3). Aristotle elsewhere speaks of "the extreme doctrine of those claiming to be Heracliteans [Aristotle here coins a verb, "to Heraclitize"], which Cratylus held, who wound up thinking that he should say nothing but only moved his finger, faulting Heraclitus for saying that it is impossible to enter the same river twice; for he thought it could not be done even once" (*Metaphysics* 4.5 1010a10–15 = DK 65A4). In what follows I challenge the view that Heraclitus was a Heraclitean in this sense. These extreme Heracliteans seem to have constructed their philosophy by giving a certain interpretation to Heraclitus's doctrines and carrying them to extremes.

10.126   There is nothing which in itself is just one thing: nothing which you could
rightly call anything or any kind of thing. If you call a thing large, it will
reveal itself as small, and if you call it heavy, it is liable to appear as light,
and so on with everything, because nothing is anything or any kind of thing.
What is really true is this: the things of which we naturally say that they
"are," are in process of coming to be, as the result of movement and change
and blending with one another. We are wrong when we say they "are," since
nothing ever is, but everything is coming to be.

                                   (Plato, *Theaetetus* 152d–e [not in DK], tr. Levett)

In Plato's treatment this theory is shown to imply such a radical instability in
things that they cannot be described. They do not remain the same long enough
for any description to apply. Indeed "every answer, on whatever subject, is
equally correct, both 'it is thus' and 'it is not thus.' . . . <But> one must not use
even the word 'thus'; for this 'thus' would no longer be in motion; nor yet 'not
thus,' for here again there is no motion."[55]

Plato's importance and early date give this interpretation an impressive pedi-
gree, but it is fair to ask how well it fits what we know of Heraclitus from his
fragments, how likely it is that Heraclitus intended all that Plato attributes to
him, and whether the interpretation is due to a misunderstanding or exaggeration of Heraclitus's doctrine (either Plato's own or one that stems from Cratylus
or other Heracliteans).

To begin, there is no reason to attribute to Heraclitus the implications that Plato
draws, that language is impossible because there is insufficient stability in the world
to secure references for words. This is Plato's elaboration and is not presented as
held by Heraclitus or the Heracliteans.[56] On the other hand, Heraclitus's view that
there is constant interchange among the three "elements" (**10.75, 10.77**) suggests
that there is no long-term stability (except for the stability of the very process of
change). The question is, did he believe that there is short-term stability or that
all things are constantly changing? The fragments do not supply a decisive answer.
The existence of constant change among the "elements" requires that some water
is at any moment changing into fire or earth, but not that all water is. Nor does the
predominance of war and strife (**10.82, 10.83**) entail that all things are always in
change, however compatible it is with such a view.

To some extent the answer depends on the changes involved. I see no reason to think that Heraclitus believed that anything large or heavy or white[57] is
undergoing such rapid change that it immediately becomes (or simultaneously
is) small, light, or black. Thus, I see no reason to attribute "Heraclitean flux" to
Heraclitus. On the other hand, he could well have believed in a weaker kind of
flux, in which every object is continually undergoing changes, many of which are

---

55. Plato, *Theaetetus* 183a–b (not in DK), tr. Levett.

56. Plato, *Theaetetus* 181d–e (not in DK).

57. These are Plato's examples at *Theaetetus* 152d, 182d (not in DK).

too small to be noticed. There is nothing to disprove that he anticipated Melissus (**15.10** Section 3) in believing that "iron, although hard, is worn away by contact with the finger, and also gold and stone and anything else we think is enduring." Such a view is compatible with a doctrine of universal change and also with the commonsense view that there is a good deal of stability in the *kosmos*. The iron ring, though constantly being eroded, lasts a long time even though it will eventually cease to be. Such a theory about the nature of things is a natural development from the theories of earlier philosophers, for whom too the *kosmos* was a world of change and motion. Heraclitus did not extend the province of change but came to the paradoxical realizations that stability depends on change and that change is stable.

To return to the river fragment, we now see that it, like **10.78**, stresses identity which persists through, or because of, change. The fragment has always been interpreted as an example: the river is a paradigm. But of what? It is easy to take it as a paradigm for the *kosmos* as a whole, whose identity requires change, primarily the regular interchange of the "elements." It is harder to see it as a paradigm for each individual thing in the *kosmos*. The ring is being eroded; what is worn away is not replaced—though by compensation more iron may be being formed elsewhere. Finally, this interpretation attributes to Heraclitus a view which could easily be exaggerated or extended to the theory of Heraclitean flux.[58] In an obvious sense the Charles River is the same river today as it was yesterday (or a second ago), even though the water at each point of the river's course (or the totality of water in the river) is different at any two different times. In another sense, though, it is not the same river, and it is plain that someone like Cratylus could follow Heraclitus one-sidedly in maintaining that change is universal and stressing the differences this implies rather than the stability Heraclitus found.

Cosmology and Religion

We know few details of Heraclitus's cosmology. The reference to justice in **10.91** makes it likely that he saw the *Logos* at work in the movements of the heavenly bodies. His own astronomical theories are surprisingly naive (**10.92, 10.93**). The following description of his astronomy gives a better picture than the surviving fragments.

10.127 Exhalations arise from earth as well as from sea; those from sea are bright and pure, those from earth dark. Fire is fed by the bright exhalations, the moist element by the others. He does not make clear the nature of the surrounding element. He says, however, that there are in it bowls with their concavities turned toward us, in which the bright exhalations collect and produce flames. These are the stars. The flame of the sun is the brightest and the hottest; the other stars are further from the earth and for that reason give it less light and

---

58. This interpretation is denied by KRS, which argues that Heraclitus did not believe in constant change.

heat. The moon, which is nearer to the earth, traverses a region that is not pure. The sun, however, moves in a clear and untroubled region and keeps a proportionate distance from us. That is why it gives us more heat and light. Eclipses of the sun and moon occur when the bowls are turned upwards; the monthly phases of the moon are due to the bowl turning around in its place little by little. Day and night, months, seasons and years, rains and winds, and other similar phenomena are accounted for by the various exhalations. Thus the bright exhalation, set aflame in the hollow orb of the sun, produces day. The opposite exhalation when it has got the mastery causes night; the increase of warmth due to the bright exhalation produces summer, whereas the preponderance of moisture due to the dark exhalation brings about winter. His explanations of other phenomena are in harmony with this. He gives no account of the nature of the earth, nor even of the bowls.[59]

(Diogenes Laertius, *Lives of the Philosophers*
9.9–11, tr. Hicks = DK 22A1)

The evidence suggests that Heraclitus did not propose specific accounts for all the natural phenomena the Ionians were concerned to explain. His pressing need was to set out a general picture of how the *Logos* works; others could fill in the details. He followed the Ionian approach, accounting for phenomena in terms of understandable processes which do not include the willful actions of anthropomorphic gods.

He was like the Ionians too in not expelling the divine from his system. He even hints that the traditional religion is not wholly wrong but expresses the truth incorrectly, and that religious practices have some benefits (**10.101**). Since God is the *Logos* that governs the world, the *Logos* is analogous to (but not the same as) Zeus, king of the gods, and father of gods and humans (**10.30, 10.82**). Certain cult practices are condemned (**10.96, 10.97, 10.98, 10.99**), especially those having to do with purification, though Apollo's enigmatic oracle (to which Heraclitus may compare his own riddling way of expressing truth[60]) receives respect (**10.43**) and perhaps the raving Sibyl as well (**10.100**).

The Soul

The conception of soul found most often in the Presocratics up to this point has been the "breath-soul," composed of air and having the function of rendering the body it inhabits alive. It departs at death, either to rejoin the cosmic air or (for the Pythagoreans) to be reincarnated. Heraclitus went further than his

---

59. This account, in which exhalations play an important role, is probably based on Theophrastus. But Heraclitus probably posited only one exhalation, to account for the change from water to fire (**10.75**) and Theophrastus mistakenly assimilated his theory to Aristotle's own two-exhalation theory. In any case, Heraclitus's own explanation of night (**10.93**), contradicts one of the functions **10.127** assigns to the "dark" exhalation.

60. See above p. 128.

predecessors in integrating his view of the soul into his cosmology. The soul is fire, as is shown by the substitution of "soul" in **10.74** for "fire" in **10.75**, As the cosmic fire "steers all things" (**10.81**), so the soul directs us. As fire is extinguished when it becomes water, so life ends when the soul becomes wet (**10.103**). If the soul becomes moist, as when a person is drunk (Heraclitus can be surprisingly literal!) it is unable to perform its function of governing our actions (**10.105**)—our vitality is diminished. Conversely, the soul is at its best when dry and in its most fiery state (**10.104**).

Heraclitus apparently believed in an afterlife that depends on the soul's state at the moment of death (**10.106, 10.107, 10.108, 10.109, 10.110**). **10.106** suggests that the soul's purity (degree of fieriness) determines what happens to it at death. Disease debilitates the soul along with the body and perhaps makes it wet and so kills it, whereas the soul of a fighting soldier is (we may suppose) not affected by disease or drink and is made especially fiery by vigorous activity and lust for battle. Heraclitus seems to hold that our soul will have an afterlife only if it is pure when we die. If it becomes wet, it dies too. Souls in general are not exempt from the cosmic cycle of change, and yet Heraclitus gives us hope—and a method—for attaining a good afterlife for our soul. If **10.110** refers to souls of those who die the best deaths, he may hold that they are absorbed into the cosmic fire and so play a part in governing the *kosmos*. On the other hand, the dead body is useless (**10.112**), cast off by its departed soul, decomposing and undergoing elemental change, but no longer the changes accompanying life and caused by the soul. The provocative assertion in **10.112**, which flouts Greek piety and respect for the human corpse,[61] shows how far his doctrines departed from ordinary belief.

The soul is more than a principle of life; it also (and this is new with Heraclitus) has cognitive functions.[62] In **10.21** the soul understands; it interprets the reports of the senses rightly or wrongly. Further, **10.21** may link thought and language. To interpret correctly the testimony of the senses the soul must not be barbarian; it must speak the right language, the universal "language" of the *Logos* so that it can interpret phenomena as manifestations of the *Logos*. The soul also has some connection with anger (**10.124**, but the precise meaning is hard to make out).[63] Finally, **10.114** and **10.113** describe the soul as having a "self-increasing *logos*" and "so deep a *logos*" that its limits cannot be discovered. These fragments may say much the same thing, but what it is is unclear. They may refer to the problem of self-consciousness in which it is possible to generate an infinite regress by regarding mind as both the subject and the object of thought. Or they may associate our soul with the vast amount of fire (that is, the *Logos*) which

---

61. The concern for proper treatment of the dead body is made clear in Sophocles' *Antigone*.

62. See also **10.128**.

63. Heraclitus thus anticipates the two highest parts of Plato's tripartite soul in *Republic* book 4—the rational and the "spirited" (the Greek for this latter word is related to the word for "anger").

governs the universe while itself being a part of the universe. Or, perhaps most likely, they may refer to the link between our rational soul and the rational order of the *kosmos* guaranteed by the *Logos*, with the suggestion that there is no end to the twin quests for unity in plurality and plurality in unity which Heraclitus prescribes as the way to attain wisdom.

The following testimonium offers a physical account of the connection between intelligence and the *Logos*.

10.128   What surrounds us is rational [*logikos*, adj. derived from *logos*] and intelligent . . . According to Heraclitus, we become intelligent by drawing in this divine *Logos* by breathing, and though forgetful when asleep, we again become sensible when we awaken. For during sleep, our intelligence (*nous*) is separated from its natural contact with what surrounds us, since the passages of perception are shut, and only the attachment through breathing—like a root—is preserved. And being separated it loses the power of memory it previously had. When awake again it peeps out through the passages of perception as if through windows, and coming together with what surrounds us, it takes on the power of reasoning. As coals when placed near the fire are altered and glow red, and when removed are extinguished, the portion of what surrounds us which dwells in our bodies as a stranger becomes practically irrational because of the separation, but in virtue of its contact by means of the great number of passages it comes to resemble the whole.[64]

                    (Sextus Empiricus, *Against the Mathematicians*
                    7.127, 129–30 = DK 22A16)

Political Thought

Heraclitus's belief that he alone understands the way the world works, and his contempt for his fellow man presage the anti-establishment, anti-democratic political outlook prominent in his biography and in his fragments. The reports that he resigned a hereditary "kingship" in Ephesus and spurned the Ephesians' request to write laws for them[65] reflect a disgust at political life also expressed in **10.115** and **10.116**. In **10.117**, if it is meant to be a political statement, he rejects the basis on which democracy is founded (see also **10.87**) and proclaims himself an aristocrat in the true sense (the word translated "best" is *aristos*). He does not esteem people for descent from powerful families but values those who are truly "best" through their personal attainments, primarily their success in

---

64. Although contaminated with Stoic ideas, such as the identification of the *logos* with the air we breathe, this interpretation is securely grounded in Heraclitus's text (Sextus quotes three fragments in the immediate vicinity—one in 7.126 and two in 7.132–33, both passages = DK 22A16) and is faithful to Heraclitus's ideas.

65. Diogenes Laertius, *Lives of the Philosophers* 9.2 = DK22A1.

understanding and acting according to the *Logos* (**10.46**). **10.13** further displays his anti-democratic bent: "most people are bad, and few are good."

A number of fragments mention law, crucially **10.51**, which speaks of a single divine law (the *Logos*) that is common to all. The inferential particles translated "for" show that **10.51** is an argument, but its structure is unclear. The *Logos* "nourishes" human laws: like other parts of the *kosmos* they too are manifestations of the *Logos*. Heraclitus's low opinion of humans and their practices make it surprising that **10.51** and **10.119** seem to call on people so strongly and without irony to rely on and defend human laws (or customs). Heraclitus is an unlikely candidate for a conventionalist, one who believes that local traditions should be upheld whatever they are. We expect him to hold that people should obey one person if he is best, but in what sense it is a law to do so (**10.87**)? Not presumably the actual city law; thus, the divine law or *Logos*, or its manifestation in an ideal city law. This in turn suggests a different reading of **10.51**, omitting "its" and taking the law in question to be the divine law. Cities must place complete reliance on the *Logos* as the source of the best possible law code. They must strive to ground their own laws in the universal law of the *Logos*. **10.119** falls into line too. The law the people must champion is not the actual city law but the ideal one. If this interpretation is correct, Heraclitus's contribution to political thought is of fundamental importance. He grounds his views on law and politics in his cosmic theory (his references to war and injustice[66] can be reread in this light), the universal scope of the *Logos* thus providing a metaphysical basis for law and society. To our knowledge he is the first philosopher to extend the range of his philosophy to include these topics, even if the way he expresses his ideas precludes a sustained treatment of them.

Moral Thought

Heraclitus made a fundamental contribution to ethics as well. The Ionians had not shown much interest in moral philosophy, and the moral reflection found in Greek literature before Heraclitus is not philosophical. Homer (above all), Hesiod, the poets of the Archaic period (especially Solon, Tyrtaeus, and Theognis), and the Seven Sages had much to say about the best kind of life to lead, about virtues and vices, about moral choices and other topics studied by ethics, but there is little argument, little attention to what we would call theoretical issues, little self-conscious analysis of ethical language. Much is at the level of prescriptions, frequently in maxims, of what one should do or not do, what sort of goals one should have, what sort of life to live. Aside from the promise of rewards and punishments for just or unjust behavior (as in Hesiod), there was no philosophical attempt to defend morality against immorality.

---

66. See **10.82**, **10.83**, **10.88**, and **10.91**.

Heraclitus too states moral maxims (for example, **10.2, 10.4, 10.17, 10.23, 10.46, 10.120, 10.122, 10.123**). But there is more. The chief questions of Greek ethics which the philosophers of the Classical and Hellenistic periods inherited from the earlier tradition were what is the best life for a person? and what is the best kind of person to be? The answers Heraclitus provides to these questions are characteristically different from answers found in and before his time and are bound up with his doctrine of the *Logos*. For Homer, some of the best human qualities were physical (strength, prowess in battle, beauty), some intellectual (good counsel, wiliness), others material (wealth). Others had to do with one's position (noble lineage, royal power), others with protecting and treating one's family, followers, and city well. The best life was a life spent in the active exercise of these qualities, many of which were not within a person's own power to attain and many of which were considered god given.

For Heraclitus the most important thing to achieve in life is understanding of the *Logos*, which the most famous people from Homer to Pythagoras failed to grasp. Thus, none of Homer's heroes and none of the other paradigms of excellence from the earlier Greek tradition were really good or lived a good life. The supreme excellence is right thinking and wisdom, which consists in knowing "how all things are steered through all things" (**10.44**)—primarily an intellectual virtue, but one manifested in right actions. Heraclitus's wisdom is not only speculative; it has practical implications. Moreover, no one has this wisdom from birth, but whether we attain it or not depends on our own efforts (**10.34, 10.35, 10.39, 10.40, 10.42, 10.43**). Perfect wisdom is either beyond human reach or very difficult to attain (**10.28, 10.29, 10.30**), so the best human life may be one spent in search of perfect wisdom, investigating the world around us and ourselves as well (**10.33, 10.34**). Heraclitus has a motive for understanding the *Logos*, and justifies his claim that wisdom is the best human quality: it is divine, so that by attaining or striving to attain wisdom we become or strive to become godlike. Moreover, since for Heraclitus the divine is not the Olympian gods but the *Logos* itself, the nearer we are to being godlike, the more the *Logos* is actively, consciously, even self-consciously in our soul. Moreover, since Heraclitus associates the *Logos* with the pure cosmic fire, he can maintain that the wisest soul is most fiery (**10.104**), and so reaps the benefits, both in this life and afterwards, of the best souls.

Finally, the famous **10.121** can be taken in different ways, but on any reading it has an important message. It may mean "A person's character, rather than an external divinity, is what determines what happens to him or her," so that we are responsible for our own lives (and for our soul's afterlife). It may also mean "People's characters are their immortal and potentially divine parts," so that we must make great efforts to develop our character as best we can. In particular since our best hope for a good afterlife and perhaps immortality is to learn and live by the *Logos*, our most important aim should be to develop our character to pursue this goal. In this sense whether we succeed in becoming divine beings depends on our character.

11

Parmenides of Elea

Fragments

11.1   (1)[1] The mares which carry me as far as my spirit ever aspired
were escorting me, when they brought me and proceeded along the
    renowned route
of the goddess, which [or, "who"[2]] brings a knowing mortal to all cities
    one by one.
On this route I was being brought, on it wise mares were bringing me,
straining the chariot, and maidens were guiding the way.
The axle in the center of the wheel was shrilling forth the bright sound
    of a musical pipe,
ablaze, for it was being driven forward by two rounded
wheels at either end, as the daughters of the Sun
were hastening to escort <me> after leaving the house of Night
for the light, having pushed back the veils from their heads
    with their hands.   10
There are the gates of the roads of Night and Day,
and a lintel and a stone threshold contain them.
High in the sky they are filled by huge doors
of which avenging Justice holds the keys that fit them.[3]
The maidens beguiled her with soft words   15
and skillfully persuaded her to push back the bar for them
quickly from the gates. They made
a gaping gap of the doors when they opened them,
swinging in turn in their sockets the bronze posts
fastened with bolts and rivets. There, straight through them then,   20
the maidens held the chariot and horses on the broad road.
And the goddess received me kindly, took my
right hand in hers, and addressed me with these words:
Young man, accompanied by immortal charioteers,
who reach my house by the horses which bring you,   25
welcome—since it was not an evil destiny that sent you forth to travel
this route (for indeed it is far from the beaten path of humans),
but Right and Justice. There is need for you to learn all things—
both the unshaken heart of persuasive[4] Truth
and the opinions of mortals, in which there is no true reliance.   30

---

1. The numbers in parentheses are the numbers of the fragments in DK. (1) = DK 28B1.

2. The pronoun can refer to either the road or the goddess.

3. The text is difficult here. The word translated "keys" can also mean "locks," and "that fit them" is a loose rendering of a word which means more literally "alternating" or "in exchange for."

4. The manuscript text of this word varies; another reading is "well-rounded Truth."

But nevertheless you will learn these too—that it is right that
    the objects of opinion[5]
genuinely are, being always, indeed, all things.[6]

11.2   (2) But come now, I will tell <you>—and you, when you have heard the
        story, bring it away—
        about those routes of investigation that are the only ones to be thought of:
        the one, both that "is" and that "it is not the case that 'is not,'"[7]
        is the path of Persuasion, for it accompanies Truth,
        the other, both that "is not" and that "'is not' is right,"[8]   5
        this indeed I declare to you to be a track entirely unable to be
            investigated:
        for you cannot know what is not (for it cannot be accomplished)
        nor can you declare it.

11.3   (3) . . . For the same thing both can be thought of and can be. [Alternative
        translations: "For thinking and being are the same"; "The same thing is for
        thinking and for being."]

11.4   (4) But gaze upon things which although absent are securely present to
        the mind.
        For you will not cut off what-is from clinging to what-is,
        neither being scattered everywhere in every way in order
        nor being brought together.

11.5   (5) For me, it is indifferent where I am to begin from:
        for that is where I will arrive back again.

11.6   (6) It is right both to say and to think that it is what-is: for it is the case
            that it is,
        but nothing is not: these things I bid you to ponder.
        For this is the first route of investigation from which I hold you back,
        And then from that one on which mortals, knowing nothing,
        wander, two-headed: for helplessness in their   5
        breasts steers their wandering mind. They are borne along
        deaf and blind alike, dazed, hordes without judgment

---

5. Another possible translation is "the things that seem." The verb there translated as
"seem" is related to the noun translated as "opinion." The things that seem are the things
that, according to mortal opinions, genuinely are.

6. The last two lines of **11.1** are controversial. I follow Owen's text and interpretation
(Owen [1960]). Other possibilities: "how what is believed would have to be assuredly, pervading all things" (KRS); ". . . all of them passing through all [the tests]" (Lesher [1984]).

7. Alternative translation: "that it is and that it is not possible for it not to be."

8. Alternative translation: "that it is not and that it is necessary for it not to be."

by whom it (namely, what-is) is thought both to be and not to be the same
and not the same; but the path of all[9] is backward-turning.

11.7   (7) For in no way may this ever be defeated, so that things that are not are:
but you, hold your thought back from this route of investigation
and do not let habit, rich in experience, compel you along this route[10]
to direct an aimless eye and an echoing ear
and tongue, but judge by reason the much contested examination   5
spoken by me.

11.8   (8) Just one story of a route
is still left: "is." On this [route] there are signs
very many, that what-is is ungenerated and imperishable,
whole, unique, steadfast, and complete.[11]
Nor was it ever, nor will it be, since it is now, all together,   5
one, holding together: For what birth will you investigate for it?
How and from what did it grow? I will allow you neither to
     say nor to think
"from what is not": for "is not" is not
to be said or thought of. What need would have roused it,
later or earlier, to grow, having begun from nothing?   10
In this way it is right either fully to be or not.
Nor will the force of conviction ever impel anything to come to be
beside it from what-is-not. For this reason neither coming to be
nor perishing did Justice allow, loosening her shackles,
but she [Justice] holds it. And the decision about these
     things is in this: 15
is or is not; and it has been decided, as is necessary,
to leave the one [route] unthought of and unnamed (for it is not a real
route), so that the other [route] is and is genuine.
But how can what-is be hereafter? How can it come to be?
For if it came to be, it is not, not even if it is sometime going to be.   20
Thus generation has been extinguished and perishing cannot be
     investigated.
Nor is it divisible, since it is all alike,
and not at all more in any respect, which would keep it from
     holding together,
or at all inferior, but it is all full of what-is.
Therefore it is all holding together; for what-is draws near to what-is.   25
But motionless in the limits of great bonds
it is, without starting or ceasing, since generation and perishing

---

9. The Greek is ambiguous between "all things" and "all mortals."

10. Alternatively, "rich in experience" can modify "this route."

11. I follow Owen's suggestion (Owen [1960]). In DK, the text of line 4 reads "for it
is complete, steadfast and without end."

have wandered far far away; true conviction repelled them.
Remaining the same and in the same and by itself it lies
and so remains there fixed; for mighty Necessity   30
holds it in bonds of a limit which holds it back on all sides.
For this reason it is right for what-is to be not incomplete;
for it is not lacking; otherwise, what-is would be in want of everything.
What is to be thought of is the same as that on account of which the
    thought is.
For not without what-is, on which it depends, having been
    solemnly pronounced,   35
will you find thinking; for nothing else either is or will be
except what-is, since precisely this is what Fate shackled
to be whole and motionless. Therefore it has been named all things[12]
that mortals, persuaded that they are real, have posited
both to be generated and to perish, to be and not,   40
and to change place and alter bright color.
But since the limit is ultimate, it [namely, what-is] is complete
from all directions, like the bulk of a well-rounded sphere,
equally matched from the middle on all sides; for it is right
for it to be not in any way greater or any lesser than in another.   45
For neither is it the case that what-is-not is—which would stop it
    from reaching
the same—nor is there any way in which what-is would be in
    one way more than what-is
and in another way less, since it is all inviolable;
for equal to itself from all directions, it meets uniformly with its limits.
At this point, I want you to know, I end my reliable account
    and thought   50
about truth. From here on, learn mortal opinions,
listening to the deceitful order of my words.
For they established two forms to name in their judgments,[13]
of which it is not right to name one—in this they have gone astray—
and they distinguished things opposite in body, and
    established signs   55
apart from one another—for one, the aetherial fire of flame,
mild, very light, the same as itself in every direction,
but not the same as the other; but that other one, in itself
is opposite—dark night, a dense and heavy body.
I declare to you all the ordering as it appears,   60
so that no mortal judgment may ever overtake you.

---

12. Some accept a different manuscript reading which would be translated as "wherefore all things are a \<mere\> name."

13. Other manuscripts give a different form of the word rendered "judgment" that requires another translation: "established judgments" (i.e., decided).

11.9   (9) But since all things have been named light and night
and the things which accord with their powers have been assigned to
    these things and those,
all is full of light and obscure night together,
of both equally, since neither has any share.

11.10   (10) You shall know the nature of the *aithēr* and all the signs in the *aithēr*
and the destructive deeds of the shining sun's pure
torch and whence they came to be,
and you shall learn the wandering deeds of the round-faced moon
and its nature, and you shall know also the surrounding heaven,   5
from what it grew and how Necessity led and shackled it
to hold the limits of the stars.

11.11   (11) . . . how earth and sun and moon
and the *aithēr* that is common to all and the Milky Way and
furthest Olympus and the hot force of the stars surged forth
to come to be.

11.12   (12) For the narrower <wreaths> were filled with unmixed fire,
the ones next to them with night, but a due amount of fire is inserted
    among it,
and in the middle of these is the goddess who governs all things.
For she rules over hateful birth and union of all things,
sending the female to unite with male and in opposite fashion,   5
male to female.

11.13   (13) First of all gods she contrived Love.

11.14   (14) Night-shining foreign light wandering around earth.

11.15   (15) Always looking toward the rays of the sun.

11.16   (16) For as each person has a mixture of much-wandering limbs,
so is thought present to humans. For that which thinks—
the constitution of the limbs—is the same
in all humans and every one; for that which is more is thought.[14]

---

14. Other possible translations: "it is the same thing which the constitution of the limbs thinks" (lines 2–3); "the full is thought" (line 4), which can be understood to mean that the *content* of what people think is "the full," i.e., the reality described in *Truth*. The translation given in the text accords better with Theophrastus's account of Parmenides' views on the nature of thought (**11.21**), which quotes **11.16**.

11.17   (17) [That the male is conceived in the right part of the uterus has been
            said by others of the ancients. For Parmenides says:][15]
            <The goddess brought> boys <into being> on the right <side of the
            uterus>, girls on the left.[16]

11.18   (18) As soon as woman and man mingle the seeds of love
            <that come from> their veins, a formative power fashions well
                constructed bodies
            from their two differing bloods, if it maintains a balance.
            For if when the seed is mingled the powers clash
            and do not create a single <power> in the body resulting from the
                mixture,
            with double seed they will dreadfully disturb the nascent
            sex <of the child>.

11.19   (19) In this way, according to opinion, these things have grown and now are
            and afterwards after growing up will come to an end.
            And upon them humans have established a name to mark each one.

11.20   Alone, unmoving, is that for which as a whole
            the name is "to be."
                                                (The "Cornford Fragment"[17] not in DK)

Significance and Life

Parmenides' philosophy marks a turning point in the history of thought. Neither
his style of argument nor his astonishing conclusions could be overlooked even by
those who strongly disagreed with him. Like Heraclitus, Parmenides pushed the
limits of his thinking beyond the range of subjects found in the early Ionian philosophers, and his ideas, like those of Heraclitus, have implications for the entities
and cosmic processes that his predecessors proposed. Whereas his philosophical
predecessors had employed rational criteria in criticizing earlier views and developing their own, Parmenides was the first to make systematic use of another form
of rational thought: the systematic use of argument, deductive argument in particular, to prove his points. Ever since Parmenides' time, rational argument has

---

15. Context in Galen, *Commentary on Book 6 of Hippocrates'* Epidemics, II.46 = DK 28B17.

16. I follow the text given in Gallop (1984).

17. **11.20** is quoted by Plato (*Theaetetus* 180e) and Simplicius. Most editors, including DK, believe that it is a misquotation of **11.8** line 38. Its authenticity was defended by
Cornford (Cornford [1935: 122–23]) and has found influential support. (See McKirahan
[2010].) **11.20** complements the claim in **11.8** lines 38–39 that all words really name
what-is, and mortals invented the many names in their mistaken belief in a world of
change. The point of **11.20** is that the *correct* name for the one existing thing is "to be."

been the principal mode of philosophical discourse, and for good reason. Most philosophical questions cannot be settled simply by empirical means, let alone by appealing to authority. Ideas are only as good as the arguments used to support them. And deductive arguments are particularly compelling. If the premises are true and the reasoning valid, then it necessarily follows that the conclusion is true. Parmenides recognized the compelling force of arguments and employed this new tool to raise basic philosophical questions: What conditions must something satisfy to qualify as a genuine entity? Is reality what our senses tell us it is? How can we tell? He was also the first to undertake explicit philosophical analyses of the concepts of being and coming to be, change, motion, time, and space. And he was the first to use these concepts to analyze the nature of entities, and so in an important sense he is the inventor of metaphysics.

The best piece of information about Parmenides' life[18] indicates that he was born c.515 and lived until at least c.450. He was from the Greek city Elea in southern Italy, as was his follower Zeno, and their distinctive philosophical opinions as well as their philosophical method gave rise to the terms "Eleatic philosophy" and "the Eleatic school."[19] Parmenides was sufficiently respected in Elea to have been asked to draw up a code of laws which were still referred to with respect and were probably still in force over five hundred years later.[20] In the first century CE his statue was placed in a series of statues at Elea that have been associated with a medical school; he may have been its founder, or the school may have liked to promote the idea that Parmenides was somehow connected with it.

Before going further, I should add that Parmenides is probably the hardest Presocratic philosopher to understand and the one about whom there is least consensus, even on basic issues. Recent years have seen an increasing interest in Parmenides, with an even greater divergence of opinion than was found a generation ago. The scope of this book does not allow all sides of the debate to be represented. The interpretation I present here is by no means standard. In many ways it is new. It is bound to be controversial, like all interpretations.

Parmenides' Poem

Parmenides' philosophy is in ways diametrically opposed to Heraclitus's, whom he may have attacked in his writings.[21] He is (implausibly) called the pupil of Xenophanes and said to have had Pythagorean connections, but all this is

---

18. Plato, *Parmenides* 127b–128d (= **12.1**).

19. For reasons to deny that such a school existed, see above p. 78 n. 11.

20. Plutarch, *Against Colotes* 72, 1126A = DK 28A12.

21. Parmenides' conception of things as unmoving and unchanging forms a natural contrast with Heraclitus's world full of plurality and change (especially on the doctrine of Heraclitean flux—see above pp. 137–39). There seem to be some verbal echoes of Heraclitus in Parmenides' writings; for example, compare **11.5** with **10.67**.

shadowy. Parmenides went very much his own way in philosophy. He is best known for a poem written (like some of Xenophanes' poetry and all of Empedocles') in dactylic hexameter, the epic meter of Homer and Hesiod. We are fortunate to possess almost all of the most important section of the work, thanks to Simplicius who in the sixth century CE copied it into his commentary on Aristotle's *Physics* "on account of the rarity of Parmenides' writings."[22] The poetic value of this philosophical work (except for the prologue) is very limited, but Parmenides may have chosen poetry instead of prose because dactylic hexameter as the meter of epic poetry connoted wisdom and authority and was the vehicle of divine revelation (compare 11.1). In addition it is easier to memorize than prose, an important asset in a time when most people were illiterate and oral memory was still the most important vehicle of ideas.

The poem falls into three parts. First 11.1, a prologue in which the goddess announces (lines 28–32) that she will tell Parmenides two things: (a) "the unshaken heart of persuasive truth," and (b) "the opinions of mortals, in which there is no true reliance." These two topics occupy the remaining two parts of the poem whose subjects are, respectively, truth and the opinions of mortals. Parmenides' philosophical importance is due almost entirely to the former part, which I will call "*Truth*," of which many think almost all has survived (seventy-eight or seventy-nine lines are extant). The other part, which I will call "*Opinions of Mortals*,"[23] of which the surviving forty-four lines constitute only a few scraps, seems to have contained a dualistic cosmogony and cosmology that took up topics familiar from the early Ionian philosophers.

The Prologue (11.1)

The prologue proclaims Parmenides a "knowing mortal" and says he received the kind attention of divinities, culminating in a revelation from an unnamed goddess, perhaps to be identified with Persephone, the goddess of the Underworld,[24] who instructs him to "bring it away" (11.2 line 1) to return to "the beaten path of humans" (11.1 line 27) and impart it to his fellow men, as he did in writing his poem. The imagery of light and dark (Day and Night) is prominent, but its interpretation is not quite clear. It seems most likely that Parmenides travels from the light of our familiar world into the darkness of the Underworld. The impressive barrier of the great door signifies the difficulty of the journey and the impossibility, in normal circumstances, to return. Avenging Justice, the gatekeeper, allows

---

22. Simplicius, *Commentary on Aristotle's* Physics 144.25–28 = DK 28A21.

23. The two parts are frequently called "The Route of Truth" and "The Route of Opinion," but the two "routes" of which Parmenides speaks (beginning in 11.2) have different names: "is" and "is not."

24. This identification is ably defended by Kingsley (1999). Others have identified the goddess as a Muse, a goddess who is deliberately anonymous in order to distance her from the traditional Greek deities, and a goddess identical with a priori reason (Granger [2008]).

only those sent by Right to enter. With the approval of Justice as well, Parmenides is brought to the goddess, who promises to teach him two subjects: the truth, and unreliable human opinions. She summarizes the content of these unreliable opinions (lines 31–32): mortals believe in appearances, that is, they believe that what seems to them to be really is and that there is nothing else besides.[25] What this means is as yet obscure, but the indications are clear that the truth is not what we mortals believe and that our trust in appearances will be called into question.

The content and style of Parmenides' thought go oddly with his portrait of his philosophy as a divine revelation. Revealed truth tends to be truth we would disbelieve except for its unimpeachable source. The views that the goddess presents to Parmenides as the truth are indeed things we would disbelieve; he is not expected to accept them simply on the authority of his divine informant but on the strength of the arguments with which she establishes them. Such arguments, we feel, should stand on their own, without needing the support of divine authority. Accordingly some think that the prologue is just a literary show. Others argue that it reports a kind of mystical experience Parmenides actually had. I offer as a suggestion that he is attempting to describe his discovery of the divine power of logic. For the Greeks, many things aside from the Olympian gods were considered divine. In general, anything that exists independently of human will or effort, that is everlasting and that has effects beyond human control might be called divine—such things as rivers, love, and other powers in the universe that occupy prominent places in Hesiod's divine genealogy (see above pages 9–11). Deductive arguments have such power as well. If the premises of a valid deduction are true, the conclusion must also be true, and nothing in human power can make things otherwise. If we accept the premises we must accept the conclusion no matter how little we like it. Now this describes Parmenides' arguments in *Truth*: valid arguments from apparently undeniable premises to conclusions unwelcome to common sense. And it is possible that reflection on the nature of such arguments led Parmenides to recognize their inescapable binding force, their cognitive reliability. It is difficult for us to imagine the magnitude of this discovery, but if the present suggestion is right, Parmenides considered it worthy of divine honor.

Two Routes of Investigation

11.2 begins with a programmatic statement: the goddess will reveal two "routes of investigation" and instructs Parmenides to "bring . . . away" the story—he will be permitted to leave the Underworld and return with the message to the land of the living. The two routes of investigation are "the only ones to be thought of": between them they comprise the only possible ways to go about investigating.

---

25. Lines 31–32 have been taken differently, with "these" (line 31) referring not backwards, to "the opinions of mortals" (line 30), but forward, to the final line and a half of the fragment, which then do not contain just a thumbnail sketch of the false opinions of mortals but the Goddess's endorsement of the cosmology presented in *Opinions of Mortals* as true.

At this point it sounds as if we can expect a treatise on method: perhaps, for example, Parmenides will describe empirical investigation and a priori investigation, or inductive reasoning and deductive reasoning. There may in fact be some connection between the goddess's message and these kinds of investigation, but the way she goes on to describe the two routes does not make this obvious.

The two routes are described in lines 3 and 5 as "the one, both that 'is' and that 'it is not the case that "is not,"'" and "the other, both that 'is not' and that "'is not" is right.'" [26] Of these routes, the first one "is the path of Persuasion, for it accompanies Truth" (line 4), while the second is "a track entirely unable to be investigated." These descriptions prompt several questions. To begin with, "the route that 'is'" and "the route that 'is not'" are strange descriptions of routes; what do the expressions mean? Recall that they are "routes of investigation." So the expressions might mean "the routes that *investigate*, respectively, 'is' and 'is not,'" which might mean that they are methods of verifying a claim that something is or is not or that they are methods of investigating what it is for something to be, or for something not to be. I prefer this last suggestion.

The second question is, why does Parmenides not simply say that one route is true and the other is false? In the first place, the word *alētheiē*, translated "Truth" can also mean "reality," which would fit well here in view of the rest of the poem, especially **11.8**, which derives consequences of "is" that can be taken as criteria which a thing must satisfy in order to be real, or in order to be a genuine, authentic, trustworthy entity. But more importantly, **11.2** lines 7–8 give an argument for "entirely unable to be investigated": "you cannot know what is not . . . nor can you declare it." This shows that the second route has a more radical flaw than that it is simply false. Indeed "you cannot know" does apply to what is false (you cannot know that $2 + 2 = 5$, even if you strongly believe it), but "nor can you declare it" does not (you can say, and say meaningfully, that $2 + 2 = 5$). To understand this second flaw, note that what cannot be known or declared is not the second *route*, but "what is not." This implies that the route "that 'is not'" is closely connected with "*what* is not [italics mine]." I take it that the second route does not straightforwardly investigate what is not, but rather it investigates what it is for something not to be. It cannot investigate what is not, because since it is not, there is nothing to investigate, as a doctor cannot examine your tonsils if you have already had them out. (Parmenides sometimes says "nothing" instead of the more usual "what-is-not" [**11.6** line 2, **11.8** line 10].) **11.2** line 8 makes the analogous point that you cannot even coherently express what-is-not in words. The most likely explanation of this claim is that it depends on a view of language in which words refer to things. If I say "The Golden Gate Bridge is in California" I am talking about the Golden Gate Bridge and about California (two things) and saying that one of them is located in the other. But if I say anything about what-is-not, what am I talking about? If what-is-not is

---

26. These translations are not standard (see above p. 146 nn. 7 and 8), but I think they make best sense in the context of Parmenides' thought.

nothing, then I am talking about nothing. But nothing is not a thing in any sense of the word: and if it is not a thing, it cannot be referred to. Therefore it cannot be expressed in language.[27] Nor, as 11.3 asserts, can it be thought of. *Noein*, the word translated "be thought of" is the word employed in Greek philosophical vocabulary for the strongest or deepest or fullest kind of knowledge. It does not mean just "thinking of" in a casual way, but "knowing fully," "understanding," or "comprehending."[28] The second route is therefore incoherent, a non-starter, "entirely unable to be investigated."

If the route "is not" (impossibly) investigates what it is for something not to be, that is, if it investigates what it is to say that something that is not "is not" (alternatively, if it investigates what it is to say "what-is-not is not") the route "is" will similarly investigate what it is for something to be, that is, if it investigates what it is to say that something that is is (that is, if it investigates what it is to say "what-is is"). But "what-is is" sounds like a tautology, which seems an unsatisfactory beginning for a philosophical theory. However, in its context it should be taken differently.

The route in question is the route "that 'is' and that it is not the case that 'is not.'" The second half of this description is substantiated by the argument in 11.2 lines 7–8 that eliminates what-is-not as a possible topic of study. The same consideration that eliminated what-is-not has the opposite result for what-is: it remains as a possible topic, because what-is is something and therefore can be referred to. And it is possible to go on (as the route does) to investigate what it is for what-is to be. As the original account of the route (which does not mention what-is) indicates, Parmenides' project, which he pursues chiefly in 11.8, is to investigate not the tautology "what-is is," but what must be the case if something (anything) is. In what follows, I interpret "what-is" as a "dummy subject" of the verb "is." The first route of investigation investigates "is," and it proceeds by investigating what is involved in the claim that what-is is, where "what-is" stands for anything that is, considered precisely as something that is, not as anything else. What it is to be a horse is different from what it is to be a chair, but Parmenides does not go into things at that level: he investigates the properties of anything that is only insofar as it is.

The next question concerns "is." Granted that what-is is, what are we saying about what-is when we say that it is? This basic question has received many different answers, the most common ones being (1) that "is" means "exists," (2) that "is" links the subject with a predicate (as in "Eleni is happy"), (3) that

---

27. Referential theories of language have a powerful intuitive appeal, but lead to paradox: to say what is not is to say nothing, but to say nothing is not to speak at all (cf. Plato, *Theaetetus* 189a and *Sophist* 263b). Or, "to 'mean' something is to spear it with a spoken (winged?) word. Then to speak of what is not is to hurl a term at—what? It isn't there" (Furth [1968: 225 n. 27]).

28. The same verb also occurs with this strong meaning at 11.2 line 2, 11.6 line 1, and 11.8 lines 9 (line 8 in the Greek text), 34, and 36. See also p. 62 n. 10 and p. 126 above.

"is" has existential and predicative force: "*x* is *y*" means that subject *x* has predicate *y* and implies that *x* exists, and (4) that "is" reveals the basic nature or essence of a subject, as Anaximenes might have said that all things "are" air.[29] On this view, the elaborate discussion of the first route in **11.8** explicates the requirements something must satisfy in order to exist.

The following discussion is based on the existential interpretation (1), though a good deal of it can be reworked in terms of interpretations (3) and (4). However, this discussion of the various uses of "is" is not meant to imply that Parmenides was conscious of these different possibilities. He was not, it is safe to say, since the earliest attempts to analyze different uses of the verb are found a century after Parmenides, in Plato's *Parmenides* and *Sophist* and in several treatises of Aristotle.[30] Not the least of Parmenides' achievements is that *Truth* can be read in a way free of equivocation on different meanings of "is."[31]

The Route of Mortals

11.6 takes up the main line of development. (**11.4** and **11.5** are placed in between **11.3** and **11.6** in most editions for want of anywhere more suitable, but their relation to the remaining fragments is unclear except that they do not seem to be part of *Opinions of Mortals*). **11.6** begins by summarizing what has been established in **11.2** and **11.3** and also by identifying the subject of "is" for the first time as "what–is" and the subject of "is not" (previously described as "what–is–not") as "nothing." Line 1 means that it is right both to say and to think that the subject of "is" is "what–is." Since what–is–not is nothing, it cannot be said or thought of, and so the route of investigation that "is not" is prohibited.

The goddess next unexpectedly[32] introduces a third route, the route on which mortals wander. Unexpectedly, because in **11.2** she gave the impression that the two routes she described there are the only ones to be thought of. Either the route introduced in **11.6** is identical with one of those mentioned in **11.2** (a view I find unacceptable) or there are three routes to be thought of and the goddess mentioned only two of them in the earlier fragment, saving the other for later (but not much later at all, if, as seems possible, **11.3** immediately followed **11.2** in Parmenides' poem and **11.6** came immediately afterwards). The rejection of the third route occupies the remainder of **11.6** and **11.7**.[33]

---

29. I omit discussion of the veridical use, in which "is" means "is true" or "is the case," which seems to me to be inapplicable to Parmenides' discussion except possibly in 11.2 lines 3 and 5.

30. Especially *Categories*, *De Interpretatione*, *Posterior Analytics*, and *Metaphysics*.

31. For example, there is no need to see Parmenides moving from "*x* is not *F*" to "*x* is not," i.e., "*x* does not exist."

32. Although it is anticipated in **11.6** line 3.

33. Whether there are two routes or three has been the subject of much inconclusive debate. There are strong programmatic reasons to prefer the two-route view, but I think that the text favors the other side.

The goddess characterizes the route in two ways: (a) it is pursued by mortals (that is, normal people) who think that what-is both is and is not the same and not the same, and (b) it is defined by the claim "that things-that-are-not are," in contrast to the first route, defined by the claim "what-is is," and the second route, defined by the claim "nothing [that is, what-is-not] is not."[34] I interpret (a) as follows. Mortals believe that things change (a fig that is green in May ripens and is black in August), which commits them to believing that after a thing changes it is no longer the same as it was before it changed (the fig is no longer green) and yet before and after the change it is still the same thing (it is still the same fig). So it both is and is not the same, and it both is and is not different (i.e., not the same). This is what we do believe, and we are unlikely to make the mistake of thinking that there is anything impossible about its being the same and not the same, in the ways indicated (having different colors at two different times, but being the same fig at both those times). If the goddess supposes that it is objectionable or impossible to think that something can be the same and not the same (as it is impossible for a number to be both even and odd) either she is making an elementary blunder or she has not yet explained why. In fact blunders of this kind were not uncommon in and after Parmenides' time.[35] But as we will shortly see, there is no need to think that she made this mistake.

The goddess dismisses the route of mortals in a series of commands ("hold back," "do not let," "judge") liberally interspersed with abuse. She calls us deaf and blind, describing our eye as unfocused ("aimless") and our ear as full of echoes. We are not literally blind and deaf, but we might as well be, since we neither see nor hear correctly. Nor do we think correctly: our mind wanders without judgment, relying on habit formed from experience, with the result that we are borne along like unthinking hordes. I believe that the goddess is abusing us for misusing our senses and minds, putting too much trust in the former and not using the latter as we should.

The argumentative content of the passage is found only at the end of 11.7: "judge by reason the much contested examination spoken by me," referring to the elimination in 11.2 of the possibility of investigating what-is-not. The unacceptability of the route of mortals is a consequence of the unacceptability of the route "is not," since according to (b) the route of mortals involves the claim that

---

34. 11.7 line 1 declares that it is impossible to refute some claim, which, if it were refuted would have the result that things-that-are-not are. The goddess has previously treated only two theses, the thesis that what-is is and the thesis that what-is-not is not, and has concluded that the latter thesis is inadmissible because what-is-not cannot be spoken or thought of. If anything can be spoken or thought of, then it is not what-is-not; therefore (there being only two possibilities) it is what-is. And as we know, what-is *is*. I therefore take line 1 to mean that the argument against the route that "is not" cannot be refuted, and that this has as a consequence that it cannot be the case that things-that-are-not are. Now this claim is not characteristic of the second route, which is involved with the claim "what-is-not is not." It will, then, be characteristic of the third route, the route of mortals.

35. For a similar one, see 12.1 and discussion on pp. 177–78 below.

things-that-are-not are (which is the plural of "what-is-not is"). The question, then, is how does believing that what-is both is and is not the same and not the same involve the claim that what-is-not is?

We have considered the change that occurs in a ripening fig. Now consider another kind of change. Mortals believe, on the basis of what their senses report, that things come to be and perish. They come to be at one time and perish at a later time. Before coming to be, a thing is not (it does not exist); after it perishes, it is not (it no longer exists), and in between, it is. So mortals suppose that it both is and is not, just as they suppose that the fig is the same and not the same. Neither case involves contradiction.

The goddess makes it clear that this perception-based approach to reality is misguided; we must rely on her "much contested examination." Exactly how the elimination of what-is-not refutes the apparently reasonable and non-contradictory beliefs of mortals is not yet clear. That we learn in 11.8.[36] Here she simply describes them in a way that makes them appear to be hopelessly confused and to represent an incoherent view of reality.

Only now can we begin to discern the force of the goddess's account. Previously she seemed to be making much ado about nothing (what-is-not) and insisting on the tautology that what-is is. Now we have our first hint that this seemingly trivial claim has enormous implications. If it is enough to establish that our senses are unreliable, it follows that we have no good reason to think that reality is anything like the way we perceive things to be. This is a radical challenge to ordinary views and to those of the philosophical tradition as well, since the early thinkers saw the world as a place of change and based their theories at some level on appearances. 11.8 will develop this challenge further.

11.7 has additional importance. It contains the first explicit statement of the contrast between reason and the senses, which immediately became and has since remained one of the focal points of philosophical discussion. Moreover, Parmenides' preference of reason over the senses makes him the ancestor of some forms of rationalism and constitutes an important element in the historical background of Plato's Theory of Forms.

Truth

Next comes the account of the true route. 11.8 is the longest continuous stretch of writing from any Presocratic,[37] and lines 1–49, in which Parmenides expounds his theory, contain the first elaborately structured series of deductive arguments in the history of Western philosophy. This is no accident. Parmenides' thesis is entirely contrary to our beliefs and experience, and he rejects the kinds of evidence on which our opinions about the world are based. Hence he will not find support for his theories in ordinary beliefs about the world and about how we

---

36. See below p. 166.

37. Empedocles fragment 14.58 is sixty-nine lines long, but many lines are incomplete.

come to know things; instead, he uses the divine power of logic to prove them and bases his proofs on truths no one could deny.

He begins by reminding us that there is only one route left to consider (**11.8** lines 1–2), and identifies a number of "signs" along the route (**11.8** lines 2–6). These "signs," which point to the correct interpretation of "is," are attributes of what-is. Some have interpreted them almost as adverbs saying *how* what-is is. To complete our journey along the route we must learn all the signs, so that a full understanding of what-is amounts to knowing all these features and understanding why what-is has them. What-is, that is, anything that is, is ungenerated, imperishable, whole, unique, steadfast, complete, all together, and one. Further, it is now, but never was and will not be, and it holds together. This list is the table of contents for *Truth*, most of which consists of a series of proofs that anything that exists has these attributes.

11.8 lines 6–21: Ungenerated and Imperishable

This section falls into three parts. The first (lines 6–13) contains three arguments to prove that what-is is ungenerated. The next (lines 13–18) concludes that the preceding argumentation has eliminated not only generation but perishing as well (doubtless because parallel arguments hold against the possibility of going out of existence), and it goes on to reaffirm the dichotomy between what-is and what-is-not, which forms the basis for the preceding arguments. The third (lines 19–21) argues against the possibility of generation in the future.

11.8 LINES 6–9: ARGUMENT 1

What-is did not come into existence from what-is-not because what-is-not cannot give rise to anything or foster the growth of anything. Since (as we know from **11.2** lines 7–8 and **11.3**) what-is-not cannot be intelligibly spoken or thought of, generation from what-is-not cannot be coherently conceived.

11.8 LINES 9–11: ARGUMENT 2

What-is was not generated from what-is-not, because if it were so generated, it must have been generated at a certain time. But there is no reason (necessity) for it to be generated at any one time rather than at any other, since that would mean that what-is-not has different attributes at different times. In particular, it would mean that what-is-not supplies a condition (necessity) for coming to be at one time but not at others. But what-is-not has no attributes at any time. Since there is no time at which what-is should come into existence rather than at any other time, and since what-is cannot come into existence at all times, there is no reason to suppose that what-is came into existence at all. This is another application of the Principle of Sufficient Reason.[38]

---

38. For Anaximander's use of the principle, see above pp. 40–41.

11.8 LINES 12–13: ARGUMENT 3

What-is was not generated from what-is-not, because what-is-not cannot give rise to anything in addition to itself. This is the first enunciation of the principle "out of nothing, nothing comes to be,"[39] which was implicit in earlier Greek thought even as far back as Hesiod and which afterwards, because of Parmenides, became a touchstone for subsequent Greek cosmogonies.

These arguments show that coming to be from what-is-not is impossible, which is most obviously relevant in the first stage of a cosmogony. The arguments say nothing of more familiar cases of coming to be, which can be described in terms of changes among already existing things. For more on this point, see below page 166.

11.8 LINES 19–21: ARGUMENT 4

I interpret these lines as follows: "But how can what-is be in the future (hereafter)? How can it come to be in the future? For if it came to be in the future, it is not (now), not even if (as the result of generation in the future) it is sometime going to be."[40] The key to the argument is that if something is going to come to be in the future, it is not now, which means that it is not. And we have learned from the previous arguments that generation from what-is-not is impossible.

11.8 lines 22–25: Indivisible and All Alike

These lines appear to contain an argument, but the argument they contain is hard to make out. As I understand it the basic premise is that what-is is "all full of what-is." The immediate consequence of this premise is that what-is is "not at all more in any respect . . . or at all inferior," which is equivalent to "all alike," which in turn entails "not divisible" (compare line 22), which is equivalent to "holds together" (compare lines 23 and 25 "all holding together"), and "draws near to what-is." "All full of what-is" is another way of saying "fully is" (compare line 11), which means that what-is "is" and is not at all infected with "is not." There are other ways to put the argument together, but the large number of seemingly equivalent ideas here suggests that in this case the goddess's point is not so much to derive a conclusion as to do something else.

---

39. This principle is frequently given in its Latin form, *ex nihilo nihil fit*.

40. The passage is usually taken as an argument that what-is has timeless existence. Line 19 is not given much emphasis. Line 20 says that anything that came to be in the past or that will be in the future is not now, which can hardly describe ordinary things, whose existence stretches from the past into the future. So Parmenides is not describing ordinary things, but a special kind of thing, for example the fact that $2 + 2 = 4$, respecting which we say "two plus two *are* four," but not "two plus two *were four, or will be* four, or *are now* four," They are "timeless" truths. But no argument for this claim is offered, indeed no explanation that this is what is meant, and finally it is hard to reconcile with the statement in line 5 that what-is "is now."

I find it more useful to view the passage as repeating the same point in various ways, trying to get across the meaning of the fundamental truth that what-is is and is not infected with "is not": it "is" *fully*, it "is" all alike, in no respect "is" it any more or any less. It cannot be divided since it "is" all alike: there is no way to distinguish one part of it from another. So it holds together: there is no way to separate it. Looking back to the table of contents in lines 3-6, four of the attributes given there are covered by this discussion: whole, complete, all together, and holding together.

11.8 lines 26–28: Without Beginning or End

This section establishes a straightforward consequence of "ungenerated" and "imperishable": that what-is has no beginning or end in time. Line 26 also seems to assert without proof that what-is cannot move. I will take up the question of its motionless in the next section.

11.8 lines 29–31: The Bonds of Necessity

These lines are frequently taken to assert that what-is is changeless ("remaining the same"), motionless ("in the same"), and unique ("by itself"). Leaving open for now the question whether what-is actually has these attributes (of which the first two are absent from the table of contents in lines 3–6), notice that the passage is less an argument than an account of the results of "mighty Necessity" and the "bonds of a limit." The language of right and justice, necessity and bonds has appeared earlier and will be utilized later on as well. Parmenides uses this language first as a colorful image, but later with increased force to the point that it actually does philosophical work. The notion of necessity with which Parmenides is working is not so much a matter of *logical* necessity (as found in deductive arguments, in which the conclusion follows necessarily from the premises) but of constraint and bonds, which keep something from going anywhere. In context, this amounts to the claim that what-is cannot depart from its nature of "being fully," with no tincture of "is not." The same holds for the claim that what-is is motionless (line 27); it is best taken as part of the imagery of bonds, which hold it fixed, unable to budge from its basic nature as a thing that is. Whether or not what-is is in fact unchangeable, immobile, and unique is certainly not proved in lines 29–31.

11.8 lines 32–33: Complete

Here we have another argument for the attributes "complete" and "whole." Like the previous arguments, this one depends on the radical dichotomy between "is" and "is not" and on the fact that "what-is" fully "is." If what-is is lacking, then it is infected with "is not," and if it is infected with "is not" to any degree however small, it "is not" and so it is not true that it "is." As the goddess puts it, "it is not lacking; otherwise, what-is would be in want of everything."

The goddess here ends her arguments for the attributes of what-is. In the rest of *Truth* (down to line 51) she first (lines 34–41) explores implications of the claim "you cannot know what-is-not . . . nor can you declare it" (**11.2** lines 7–8), so that if you *can* know or declare something, it is not what-is-not, and therefore is what-is. Next (lines 42–49) she uses the memorable image of a sphere to convey her difficult and oft-repeated message in yet another way. Finally (lines 50–51) she announces that her account of what-is has reached its end.

11.8 lines 34–41: The Object of Thought

The train of thought in the first part of this passage (lines 34–38) runs backward from the end to the beginning. Since the only thing that is whole and motionless (in the restricted sense identified above page 161) is what-is, nothing else than what-is either is or will be. Therefore, what-is is in some way a necessary condition for any thinking to take place ("not without what-is . . . will you find thinking"). Thought and therefore also language, in which thought is expressed ("solemnly pronounced" suggests that Parmenides is making this connection between thought and language) depends on what-is in three ways: first, it is a necessary condition for thought; more specifically, second, it is the object of any thought (the only thing we think about; what-is-not cannot be thought of), and third, it is the cause of any thought, in the sense that it is what prompts the thought. These two last claims are expressed in line 34: "what is to be thought of [namely, what-is] is the same as that on account of which the thought is" (that is, the cause of the thought and the object toward which the thought is directed). Therefore, the only thing that can be thought of is what-is.

Lines 38–41 state an immediate consequence of this result: everything we think about and believe to be real is what-is. This is obvious: if what-is is the only possible object of thought and is the only thing that prompts us to have a thought, then if I think, for example, that my brother is out sailing today, then whether or not it is true that he is sailing today, my thought is prompted by what-is and my thought is about what-is, where "what-is" refers to something that is; in this case, it might be my brother (if a human being is the kind of entity that possesses the attributes that **11.8** proves to belong to what-is).[41]

---

41. These lines are usually taken to deny the reality of generation, perishing, motion, and change in general and by extension to deny the reality of the subjects that possess these predicates. But I do not find that the passage denies the reality of anything. It simply lists some things that mortals attribute to the subjects they suppose that they think and speak of. Mortals may be mistaken in what they believe is real, and in believing that the things they believe are real are generated, change color, etc., but the point here is not to assail mortal beliefs; the point is to explain how they come to be.

11.8 lines 42–49: Spatial Metaphors

On the basis of this passage many suppose that what-is is spherical in shape. This would be an unexpectedly specific attribute for what-is to have, and one that is not found in the table of contents in lines 3–6. But this interpretation is not as secure it might appear. In the first place, the goddess does not call what-is a sphere or even compare it to a sphere. Rather she compares it to "*the bulk* of a well-rounded sphere," and specifies the point of comparison: it is "complete from all directions," it is "equally matched from the middle on all sides," it "meets uniformly with its limits," etc. Some of these descriptions are familiar. What-is is complete in the sense established in lines 22–25—it fully "is." And the talk of limits reminds us of the bonds of necessity that maintain what-is as something that "is" and prevents it from becoming infected with "is not." These features of what-is previously had nothing to do with its shape, and I doubt that they do now. The goddess is saying that just as a sphere's bulk (roughly, its spatial extension) is spatially complete, uniform, etc., so what-is is complete, uniform, etc. in its own way, namely in that it fully "is." I interpret the spatial terminology ("from all directions," "from the middle") as metaphorical, not literal, just like the language of bonds, shackles, justice, and routes. I believe that as the goddess reaches the end of her account of *Truth*, she makes a final attempt to communicate her difficult thesis, that what-is fully is.[42]

Further Attributes of What-Is

Some attributes of what-is remain to be considered.

IS NOW, WAS NOT, AND WILL NOT BE

These attributes are stated in line 5, and the argument that what-is has them is found in lines 5–6. Most interpreters understand the goddess to argue that what-is did not exist in the past and will not exist in the future *because it is now*: a very strange argument as it stands, which has provoked some interesting attempts to make sense of it.[43] (After all, most things that are now have existed for some time previous to now and will last for some time into the future.) I propose to construe the argument differently, taking the absence of past and future to follow from the fact that "it is now, all together, one, holding together." "All together" and "holding together" were seen to be ways of expressing that

---

42. On another interpretation, the comparison with the sphere shows that what-is "is the same for all men and for all situations. Whatever varies in accordance with context or viewpoint is not the real but an appearance of it" (Mourelatos [1970/2008: 129]).

43. The prevalent view is that it depends on the timeless existence of what-is (see above p. 160 n. 40). But Parmenides does not explain what he means, and the very fact that he says that it is "now" tells strongly against this interpretation.

what–is fully "is" and has nothing to do with "is not." If past and future involve "is not" in any way, it follows that what–is has no past or future. And we can see why Parmenides might suppose that they do involve "is not." The past was, but *is no longer* (and so is not now) and the future will be, but *is not yet* (and so is not now), and anything that is not now is not. The argument, then, does not need to hold that existing now is incompatible with having existed in the past or being going to exist in the future. Rather it depends on the idea that the very notions of past and future involve "is not" in a way that eliminates them altogether.

CHANGELESS AND MOTIONLESS

These two attributes do not appear in the table of contents unless this is what "steadfast" means (line 4), and no arguments are given to prove that what–is cannot move or change. One way of understanding this situation would be to say that when the goddess says (without proof) that what–is does not move or change, she is expressing in still another way the idea that what–is fully is, and that it cannot move or change from that condition. On the other hand the abolition of past and future implies that in fact what–is cannot either move or change in the sense of moving from one place to another or undergoing other kinds of changes. Moving from one place to another or changing from one condition (say, being hungry) to another (say, being full) take time; you can't be in two places at once, and you can't be both hungry and full at the same time. So if you are full and no longer hungry, you were hungry in the past, not now. Or if you are hungry and after dinner you will be full, you will be full in the future, not now. But we have just seen that past and future are eliminated; what–is has no past or future. Therefore, it cannot undergo motion or change.

STEADFAST

This attribute (literally "not trembling") is listed in the table of contents (line 4), but the word does not recur. It can be taken to mean the same as "unchanging" or "unmoving." If so, it is covered by the consideration in the previous paragraph. It can also mean "calm" or "firm," and so could be a synonym of such attributes as "complete" and "fully is." If so, it is covered by the treatment of those attributes.

UNIQUE, ONE

These attributes are mentioned in lines 4 and 6. The philosophical thesis most often associated with Parmenides is that there is just one, unique thing. This interpretation is found as early as Plato and possibly even earlier. Melissus, a generation after Parmenides, argued clearly that there is only one thing that is, and he has always been regarded as the third and final exponent of Eleatic philosophy, expounding Parmenides' views with only a few disagreements.[44] However

---

44. See Ch. 15.

Parmenides offers no explicit argument that there is only one thing,[45] so if he did hold this very unusual view, it was the only item in his table of contents that he failed to take up. This is truly puzzling.

In the past generation a few scholars[46] have proposed alternative interpretations that deny that Parmenides was a monist of this kind. The interpretation I have given of what-is can fit either approach. According to it, what-is is a short way of referring to anything that is, whatever is. If there is only one thing, then what-is refers only to it; if there are more things, then it refers to each of them. But in that case too what-is (each of them) *is* one: anything that is is a single thing. And this can easily be seen to be yet another way of expressing the idea that what-is fully is, closely related to the claims that it is indivisible and holding together. It has a strong kind of unity in that different parts of it cannot be distinguished as regards the fact that they "are." So on the alternative interpretation the attributes "unique" and "one" are proved in the course of *Truth*.

We are faced with a dilemma. What are we to do when there is a conflict between the text and the tradition? Are we so confident of an interpretation that we can reject the unanimous testimony of antiquity including Plato, whose lifetime could have overlapped with Parmenides' (Parmenides would have been about ninety when Plato was born)? Or are we to accept the authority of tradition when the price of doing so is so high? Clearly it depends on the particular case. In the case of Parmenides my present inclination is to prefer the interpretation that makes best sense of the text. In this particular case we probably have almost all of the relevant original material, and further it is not inconceivable that Plato and his successors (who were influenced by Plato's opinion), who recognized the importance of Parmenides' conclusions but who did not pay careful attention to his actual arguments, misunderstood his assertion that what-is is one to mean that there is only one thing.[47]

Summary: The Nature of What-Is

The entire account of *Truth* is founded on the principles that "is" and "is not" are mutually incompatible, that what-is-not cannot even be conceived of in thought or expressed in language, and that what-is "is" and in no way is it true that what-is "is not": if it were infected in the least degree by "is not," it would no longer be what-is, but would be the unthinkable what-is-not. Many of the attributes of what-is follow immediately and are best seen as redescriptions of this basic feature of what-is. Thus it fully is, it is complete, it holds together, etc. This does not yet tell us anything very precise about what-is. Most importantly, we do not know whether there are one or more such things or whether what-is

---

45. In the first edition of *Philosophy Before Socrates* I believed that an argument for uniqueness could be found in lines 22–25.

46. Notably Curd (1998/2004).

47. Such a misinterpretation could also be ascribed to a conflation of Parmenides with the monist Melissus, who was considered a follower of Parmenides. See Ch. 15. Other explanations are possible as well.

came into being or will perish, whether it moves or changes. For all we know, the goddess could be describing the world as we see it, stressing its ontological foundations but not proposing a theory with any radical implications.

The long stretch of argument in lines 6–21 establishes in several ways that what-is is ungenerated and imperishable, but in the particular sense that what-is did not come to be from and cannot perish into what-is-not. But nothing is said to show that one thing that is cannot come to be from one or more other things that are. In fact, when we talk of something being generated or coming to be, we do not normally think that it comes to be out of sheer nothing. A chair comes to be out of boards, nails, and so forth *that already are*. A baby comes to be when an existing sperm and an existing egg join in the right way in the right circumstances, and already-existing food is subsequently transformed in the mother's body and passed on to the embryo in the appropriate way, etc. So far nothing has been said that excludes the possibility of the familiar world, just as long as we follow Xenophanes and Heraclitus in declaring it to be eternal.[48] As long as the stuff of the world is present, we have not yet seen any reason to suppose that it cannot be mixed and rearranged in ways that account for the changes that our senses tell us go on around us.

What changes the picture is the conclusion that what-is is now but was not and will not be. The objects familiar to us in the world of our experience have duration in time: if they are now, in general they have existed for some time previously and will continue to do so for some time in the future (unless the present moment is the first or last instant of their existence). But if the passage of time necessarily involves what-is-not (in the sense of what-is-not *any more* or *yet*), then temporal duration is eliminated and with it any possibility for change of any sort to occur: no generation or perishing, no motion, no changes in size or qualities or other attributes. It follows that our senses radically mislead us. We assume without reason that they report the truth about reality, but reason disproves what they report. This is what I suggested was the basis of the goddess's objection to the opinions of mortals in **11.6** and **11.7**: our belief that the objects of perception are real commits us to hold the things that are "both to be and not to be the same and not the same" in that we think that they undergo changes of various kinds over time.

Opinions of Mortals

11.8 lines 50–52: Transition to *Opinions of Mortals*

The goddess now proceeds to fulfill her promise (**11.1** lines 28–32) to expound the opinions of mortals. She makes it clear that this route is unreliable (**11.1** line 30) and that her account is deceitful (**11.8** line 52). It purports to be a cosmology proposed by certain unnamed people, which is based on two opposing entities, fire and night. A number of difficult problems immediately arise. First, in what way is the account

---

48. See above pp. 160 and 163 n. 40.

deceitful? Second, whose account is it? Third, what is the purpose of giving a deceitful account; how does this account figure into Parmenides' program?

A general answer to the first question is tolerably clear. Mortals believe in a *kosmos* containing things that move and change, that come to be and perish, and that therefore fail to satisfy the criteria established in *Truth* for things-that-are. It follows from what we have learned that mortals believe that the *kosmos* contains things-that-are-not, and therefore that they believe that what-is-not is. So any account of mortal beliefs will at some level involve what-is-not. Since what-is-not cannot be thought of or expressed in language, any account that purports to describe the world of appearance is misleading, since it does not describe anything at all. We will see specifically how the goddess's account goes astray.

By contrast, the answer to the second is intolerably unclear. No known cosmology matches the account he presents. The Milesians were not dualists but monists either in that they generated the world out of a single substance (Anaximander and probably Thales) or in that they held that all things in the world are composed of a single kind of thing (Anaximenes, with qualifications). Heraclitus may be regarded as a monist as well, with fire (together with its alternate states water and earth) as the single material of which things are made. Xenophanes seems to have proposed a dualist theory, but his basic duality was earth and water, not Parmenides' fire and night. It is doubtful that the Pythagoreans had a cosmology by the time Parmenides wrote, but even if they did there is no reason to suppose that it was the one which Parmenides presents. Nor is any light thrown on this question by traditional views of the world, by Orphic cosmologies known to be earlier than Parmenides,[49] or by other accounts that were in existence in Parmenides' time. I will return to this question (pages 169–70).

An important clue toward answering the third question is found in the final two lines of **11.8**. The goddess declares that she will expound the world "as it appears," that is, the world as the senses present it to us, "so that no mortal judgment may ever overtake you": her account will enable us to withstand all theories that account for mistaken human opinions about the nature of the world. Recall the characterization she offers of mortal opinions: mortals believe "it is right that the objects of opinion genuinely are, being always, indeed, all things" (**11.1** lines 31–32). But how can setting out one deceitful account of the world make us immune to other accounts of the same thing? The answer I propose to this question is that although the goddess's account is deceitful, it is also the best possible account of the world we perceive. It follows that no other account can succeed. Since the best account is deceitful and all other accounts are worse than it, they must be deceitful too.

---

49. The rationalizing cosmology presented in the Derveni papyrus may have some relation to Parmenides' cosmology, but this subject has not yet been adequately explored. In any case the cosmology as it appears in the Derveni papyrus must have been composed after Parmenides (see especially Betegh [2004: chs. 7–8]), although it remains possible that it is based on a pre-Parmenidean Orphic cosmology which is in fact the basis of Parmenides' claims.

Parmenides' strategy, then, is to present an account of the world that is not only better than previous accounts but also can be seen to be the best possible account. He must also make it clear just how his account is deceitful.

11.8 lines 53–55: Foundations of *Opinions of Mortals*

The goddess posits a basic duality of fire (or light—see **11.9**) and night; everything else depends on these two basic things or is reduced to them and their interactions. "All things have been named light and night" (**11.9** line 1). She describes these entities as "two forms . . . of which it is not right to name one— in this they have gone astray." (**11.8** lines 53–54) This has been taken in several ways. (a) Some hold that it is a dualist account. (This interpretation is congenial to the traditional interpretation that Parmenides was a monist in the sense that he believed that there is only one thing. Since only one thing exists, it is wrong to posit two principles.) (b) Some object to the specific dualist account given by the goddess on the grounds that it is wrong to name *even one* of the two principles in question (since neither of them has essential attributes of what-is, such as changelessness and motionlessness).[50] (c) Others object on the grounds that it is correct to name one of the principles she identifies but not the other (since one of them, namely Fire, really exists and is identical with what *Truth* calls what-is, while the other, Night, does not exist, and is identical with what *Truth* calls what-is-not)?[51] I will suggest that it means something else.

11.8 lines 55–61 and 11.9. The basic duality, Fire and Night

Just as what-is has attributes called "signs" (**11.8** line 2), so the two principles of *Opinions of Mortals* have opposing signs. Fire is mild, light, and bright, whereas Night has the opposite qualities: dark, dense, and heavy. No doubt other attributes hold as well. Fire will also be hot and dry and Night cold and wet. Each of these two things is different from the other and identical with itself, its identity and difference being marked by the indicated "signs." The obscure final line of **11.9** may make this point, if we understand it as asserting that neither of the two elements has any share of the other, that is, that they are entirely distinct. Now for the first time we have true elements, distinct basic forms of matter that always preserve their own identity; they may intermingle with each other and form other substances, but under no conditions can they be transformed into each other.

The phenomenal world is full of things composed ultimately of Fire and Night and endowed with properties that stem from the opposed "signs" of the two

---

50. Unfortunately for this interpretation there is nothing corresponding to "even" in the text.

51. Interpretation (c), which seems incompatible with *Truth*, is Aristotle's interpretation (Aristotle, *On Generation and Corruption* 1.3 318b6–7 = DK 68A42, *Metaphysics* 1.5 986b31–987a2 = DK 28A24).

elements. **11.9** lines 3–4 can plausibly be taken as saying either that everything (that is, everything in the phenomenal world other than Fire and Night in their purest form) is a compound of the two elements or that the *kosmos* as a whole is full of the two elements (counting both their pure and their mixed forms). The claim "all is full . . . of both equally" favors the second interpretation, if "equally" refers to an equal amount of fire and night. On this view, the *kosmos* contains an overall balance between the two opposites that is compatible with local variations, so that, for example, the sun will have more fire than it has night.

The important feature of this account for the questions above (pages 166–67) is the emphasis on their mutual opposition. The cosmology depends not just on there being two of them but on their being opposites. I propose that their opposition rather than their duality is both where the goddess's account is superior to previous accounts and where it goes astray.

Whereas one or more of the Milesians were monists in the senses mentioned above, Parmenides thinks that no single principle can give rise to the plurality and opposition observed in the world.[52] A theory that holds that all things were generated from or composed of a single kind of entity with certain definite characteristics (as fire is hot or water wet) has a hard time accounting for things that lack those characteristics or, worse, that have the opposite characteristics. It is notable that fire and night are not just named as such but are described in terms of the opposing characteristics. The principles of the goddess's cosmology are not just two different kinds of matter but are explicitly kinds of matter endowed with definite qualities. This is why he calls them "forms" rather than "things-that-are." They can thus straightforwardly form the basis of accounts of things that are not just fiery and night-like, but of things that are light (in color) and dark, hot and cold, light (in weight) and heavy, and so forth. Further, the emphasis on the characteristics rather than the identity of the basic entities (here it is important that it seems a matter of indifference whether one of them is called fire or light) makes it easier to account for other kinds of entities than traditional monistic accounts could. Water, for example, can be understood as a mixture of fire and night that is darker and heavier than fire but brighter and lighter than night. When fire and night are mixed in the right proportions to produce the right blends of dark and bright, heavy and light, etc., then we have water. These considerations provide ample grounds on which Parmenides could fault not only previous monists for failing to give a satisfactory accounts of opposition,[53] but also Xenophanes, whose dualistic account that posited water and earth as basic substances was unlikely to explain many important features of the *kosmos* satisfactorily.

---

52. Hence Milesian monism is mistaken. Anaximander illegitimately and obscurely derives hot and cold from the *apeiron* (see above pp. 36–37) and Anaximenes' monism involves air in a plurality of states (see above pp. 48–49).

53. This holds even for Anaximenes, for whom the opposition between condensation and rarefaction plays an important role. Anaximenes offers no account of the status of these opposites.

Even if there is good reason to regard the goddess's account as superior to its contemporary rivals, why should Parmenides believe that no better account could ever be proposed? I suggest that he thought the goddess's account was best because it was sufficient to account for the world as it appears and was the simplest account that could do so. A successful monistic account would be simpler, but monistic accounts cannot succeed. Therefore a dualistic account is the simplest. And the goddess's dualistic account succeeds because it straightforwardly accounts for things other than the basic entities in a way that can be adapted with a great deal of flexibility.

Where, then, does it go astray? On the present interpretation—that the "signs" listed beginning at **11.8** line 3 are standards for any thing-that-is and can in principle be satisfied by a plurality of candidates—the failure of the account is not simply that it is a dualistic cosmology or that there is something about fire and night incompatible with their being things-that-are. Nor is there good reason to think that one of them has a better claim than the other to be a thing-that-is. I propose that the text points toward the following objection: that although fire and night taken separately (compare "apart from one another" in **11.8** line 56) may each qualify as a thing-that-is, the cosmology that depends on their forming compounds violates two important conclusions argued for in *Truth*, (a) that what-is is uniform and (b) that what-is does not change.

Regarding (a), the objection is that any account of the *kosmos* must account for plurality. While what-is is indivisible, "all alike, and not any more in any respect, which would keep it from holding together, or at all inferior" (**11.8** lines 22–25), the *kosmos* is "full" of both light and night, and different entities within the *kosmos* are distinguishable from others by the differing proportions they possess of the two ingredients. Thus, it does not "hold together" in the strong sense required by *Truth*. In fact this is inevitable, since the world being described is the world we apprehend by our senses, and our senses distinguish things by contrasts. (For example, if everything were the same color, we would not be able to distinguish anything by sight.)

Regarding (b), the objection is that any account of the *kosmos* must account for change. While what-is is unchanging and immobile, the *kosmos* is full of change and motion. For the reasons mentioned above, a monistic account is unable to account for these features, but a dualist account, which *can* account for them, is flawed for this very reason.

Parmenides might well suppose that the same objection will hold against any possible pluralistic account. But since he also holds that there can be no successful monistic account of the *kosmos* it follows that all possible accounts of the *kosmos* are flawed, but a dualistic account, though false, involves the least possible error.

Cosmology

The total amount preserved from *Opinions of Mortals* is too small to enable us to form anything like a complete picture of the views it contained. The programmatic remarks in **11.10** and **11.11** indicate some of its contents: a cosmogony and cosmology treating the astronomical subject matter obligatory in any such Presocratic treatise. **11.14** and **11.15**, which refer to the moon, form part of this section, as does **11.12**, which is part of a description of the "wreaths," or rings, which are the courses of the celestial bodies.

An interesting feature of the cosmology is the presence of "the goddess who governs all things" (**11.12** line 3), who presumably is the one who generated Love (*Erōs*) first of all gods (**11.13**)—that is, Love was the first god that she generated. We seem to have a theogony as well as, or as part of, the cosmogony, and this reading is supported by ancient references to other gods in Parmenides (War and Discord) and to stories Parmenides told about the gods.[54] Unfortunately we do not know more.

The prominence Parmenides gives to Love ties in with his references to sex (**11.12** lines 4–6), embryology (**11.17**), and the origin of sexual differentiation and of sexual preferences (**11.18**). His discussion of the latter two topics is unusual for a Presocratic. The interest in anatomy and physiology it suggests may be some (slender) support for the ancient tradition that he was a doctor.

Does Parmenides believe that his cosmology is true? On the one hand, it seems clear that he did not believe that the world his cosmology describes is real. That world contains generation and perishing (**11.10** lines 2–3), growth (**11.19**), motion (**11.14**), and other change as well, features that are eliminated by the arguments in **11.8**. This should be good enough reason to hold that his cosmology is not meant seriously as a description of the world, although many people have held that he meant it as such. On the other hand, he holds that it is the best possible account of the phenomenal world, the world of appearances that our senses reveal to us. This gives it value for those of us who care about things as they appear to us, and it leaves the door open for future attempts to discover the truth about our world.

The final belief of Parmenides we will consider is his account of perception and thought, which attempts to find a physical basis for these psychological phenomena.

11.21 Most general theories of sensation are of two kinds. Some make sensation occur by like and others by the opposite. Parmenides, Empedocles, and Plato by like. . . . Parmenides made no general definition, but said only that there are two elements and knowledge is in accordance with the one that exceeds. For if the hot or the cold surpasses, the thought becomes different. Thought that is due to the hot is better and purer, but even this requires a certain balance. . . . [Here Theophrastus quotes **11.16**.] For he speaks of sensation and thought as the same. This is why both memory and forgetfulness are produced from these through their mixture. But he did not at all determine whether or not there will be thought or what will be its arrangement if they are equal in the mixture. But that he makes sensation occur

---

54. Cicero, *On the Nature of the Gods* 1.11.28 = DK 28A37; Plato, *Symposium* 195c (not in DK).

also by the opposite in its own right is clear from the passage where he says that a corpse does not perceive light, heat, and sound, because the fire has left it, but it does perceive their opposites—cold and silence. And in general everything that exists has some knowledge.

(Theophrastus, *On Sensation* 1, 3 = DK 28A46)

This extract is given at length principally to show the level of Parmenides' thinking on these subjects and because it is the first detailed account we have of any treatment of these phenomena. Two implications of the discussion are that the soul, whose presence makes things alive, is fiery and that human (and other) thought depends on the presence of fire and night. Thus, this account of thought makes sense only in the unreal world of mortal opinions and cannot be taken as a clue to how it is possible to have knowledge of the real world of Truth.

This last question is an important one to be sure. If in reality there is no coming to be, perishing, motion, or change, then what is the status of Parmenides himself, the goddess, and the mortals whose opinions he disbelieves? Parmenides can dismiss the last group as part of the unreal world of opinions. And he can dismiss his own body in the same way. But how about his mind, which is having the thoughts? Some have claimed that what-is is identical with thought, translating **11.3** as "for thinking is the same as being," and **11.8** line 34 as "thinking is the same as the object of thought" (where the only possible object of thought is what-is). But apart from these two lines, which can easily be translated differently (as above, pages 146, 148), there is no suggestion that what-is thinks or is identical with thought. Moreover, the whole approach Parmenides takes in *Truth* as well as the absence in the earlier philosophical tradition of any tendency to consider thought as an entity tell against this interpretation. I find it more plausible that he simply did not raise or answer this question.

11.19 appeared in Parmenides' poem "after he had related the ordering of perceptible things"[55] and serves as an appropriate conclusion to *Opinions of Mortals*, stressing that the account covers what occurs "according to opinion," emphasizing change (growth), the time distinctions of past, present, and future, the names applied to all these illusory phenomena, and the fact that the names are the product of human decisions (not due to the nature of reality).

Parmenides' Challenge

The interpretation I have offered agrees with important recent work on Presocratic philosophy that has interpreted Parmenides not as declaring cosmology to be impossible but as establishing criteria that any adequate cosmology must meet. Specifically, the attributes of what-is are taken to be the attributes that any *basic* entity must possess: it must be ungenerated and imperishable, etc. Atoms are a

---

55. Simplicius, *Commentary on Aristotle's* On the Heavens 558.8 = DK 28B19.

good example. The atomic theory of the fifth century[56] held that the things we see in the world are made up of atoms which have always existed and which will never perish. Out of them are formed compounds which *are* generated (when the component atoms come together to form them) and perish (when the compound is dissolved into its constituent atoms). The atoms are the basic entities and they satisfy many of Parmenides' criteria, whereas the compounds, which do not satisfy those criteria, are not basic entities, and on some accounts are not genuine entities at all. I will take up this issue in connection with Anaxagoras, Empedocles, and the Atomists, who proposed the most important cosmologies in the period between Parmenides and Plato.

Concluding Remarks

Parmenides' *Truth* left a lasting mark on philosophy. The present account has been generous in its assessment of this section of his poem. It would be easy to fault him for making our task more difficult than it need be. His language is frequently obscure, as is his argumentation. It is frequently an uphill battle to discern how his train of thought proceeds. There are gaps in the reasoning and extensive use both of terms that may (or may not) be intended as near-synonyms (but how near?) and of figurative, even metaphorical language that needs to be interpreted. Objections can be raised against the arrangement of the arguments, since it is not always clear where one topic leaves off and another begins. In general, it requires a great deal of sympathy to find a way for the arguments go through. My reason for interpreting Parmenides charitably is that only in this way can we appreciate the interest, the potential, and the challenge of his ideas and arguments. Only if we make the effort to unravel his tortuous reasoning and fill in the gaps in ways congenial to his point of view can we hope to understand his enormous influence on philosophy.[57] And enormous it was. With Parmenides Greek philosophy began to become more systematic. Argument played an increasingly important role in the exposition of theories. The subsequent history of Presocratic philosophy is often seen in terms of responses to Parmenides: Zeno and Melissus developed his ideas, while Anaxagoras, Empedocles, and the Atomists (to name only the most important figures) accepted that there is no generation from or perishing into nothing and composed their cosmologies on this basis, even while disagreeing on other points of Eleatic doctrine.

---

56. This is the subject of Ch. 16.

57. One of Melissus's virtues is that he presents his numerical monism in a clearer and more systematic way. See Ch. 15.

12

Zeno of Elea

Parmenides had argued that our senses have no contact with reality—that what-is is one, unmoving, and unchanging, and that it did not come into existence and will not cease to exist. These controversial views were defended by one man and accepted with modifications by another. These two philosophers, Zeno and Melissus, are the subjects of this chapter and Chapter 15.

Life and Relation to Parmenides

Plato is the best source of information on Zeno's age and relation to Parmenides and the purpose and nature of Zeno's work.

12.1 (127a) Once Parmenides and Zeno came to Athens for the (b) Great Pana-thenaic festival. Parmenides was quite an elderly man, very gray, but fine and noble in appearance, just about sixty-five years old. Zeno was then almost forty, of a good height and handsome to see. The story goes that he had been Parmenides' young lover. . . . (c) Socrates and many others <were> eager to listen to Zeno's treatise, for he had then brought it to Athens for the first time. Socrates was then very young. Zeno him-self read it to them. . . . (d) When Socrates had heard it, he asked Zeno to read again the first hypothesis of the first argument. (e) When he had read it, he said, "How do you mean this, Zeno? If things that are are many, they must therefore be both like and unlike, but this is impossible. For unlike things cannot be like, nor can like things be unlike. Isn't that what you are saying?"
—*Zeno*: Yes.
—*Socrates*: Now if it is impossible for unlike things to be like and for like things to be unlike, it is also impossible for things to be many? For if they were many they would have impossible attributes. Is this the point of your arguments—to contend, against all that is said, that things (128a) are not many? And do you think that each of your arguments proves this . . . ?
—*Zeno*: You have well understood the purpose of the whole work.
—*Socrates*: I understand, Parmenides, that Zeno here wants to be identi-fied with you by his treatise as well as his friendship, for he has written in the same style as you, but by changing it he is trying to make us think he is saying something else. For in your poem you declare that the all is one (b) and you do a good job of proving this, while he declares that it is not many, and furnishes many impressive proofs. Now when one of you says it is one and the other that it is not many, and each speaks so as to seem not to have said any of the same things, though you are saying practically the same things, what you have said appears beyond the rest of us.

—*Zeno*: Yes, Socrates, but you have not completely understood the truth of the treatise. . . . (c) It is actually a defense of Parmenides' argument against those who try to (d) make fun of it, saying that if what-is is one, the argument has many ridiculous consequences which contradict it. Now my treatise opposes the advocates of plurality and pays them back the same and more, aiming to prove that their hypothesis, "if there are many things," suffers still more ridiculous consequences than the hypothesis that there is one, if anyone follows it through sufficiently. I wrote it in this spirit of competitiveness when I was young, and then someone stole it, so I did not even have the chance to consider whether it should be made public.[1]

(Plato, *Parmenides* 127b–128d; part = DK 29A11, part = DK 29A12)

Socrates was born in 469. The *Parmenides* makes Socrates "very young" (127c) but old enough for philosophical discussion, hence its stage date can be put c.450. If Parmenides and Zeno were then about sixty-five and forty (127b), they were born c.515 and c.490.

If there is a historical basis for the setting of the *Parmenides*, Parmenides and Zeno may have come to Athens during the quadrennial Great Panathenaia (127a) to expound their philosophy in that public forum.[2] Plato informs us that this was the first appearance of Zeno's book in Athens (127c), but that it had been composed many years before and had been circulated in a pirated edition (128d).

Aside from his visit to Athens the only story told about Zeno is that he plotted against a tyrant, was caught and tortured, but refused to name his fellow conspirators. He was also said to have been the adopted son of Parmenides.

Zeno's Treatise

Zeno wrote his treatise to defend Parmenides' thesis (128c–d), here summarized as "what-is is one" and "there is one" against attempts to refute it by showing its absurd implications. Zeno set out to prove that the opposing view, "things are

---

1. **12.1** must be handled cautiously. The conversation reported in the *Parmenides* certainly did not take place and it is doubtful that Socrates even met Parmenides and Zeno. Still, the detailed information about the ages of the two men is unlikely to be fiction, and they certainly could have visited Athens. In general, the setting is historically plausible. Great festivals were frequented by philosophers and other intellectual and literary figures wanting an audience for their works. Private readings of the sort Plato describes were no doubt common. Further, Plato's account of the purpose of Zeno's work and its relation to Parmenides' ideas is an interpretation, but one that is likely to be correct.

2. See below p. 378.

many" (127e), entails greater absurdities. His book was a series of forty arguments, of which Plato claims to state the first (127d).[3]

Aristotle called Zeno the father of dialectic.[4] Dialectic for Aristotle is an important philosophical technique for sounding out ideas, typically the ideas of an opponent, by getting him or her to state a thesis and then asking questions to draw out its
implications. Dialectical strategy, as discussed in Aristotle's *Topics*, consists in trying to show that the thesis has false or otherwise unacceptable consequences and so
is false, while the opponent defends the thesis by trying to avoid such results. Further, some of Zeno's arguments take the form of antinomies: they derive mutually
contradictory consequences from the hypothesis that there are many things (for
example, the consequence that they are both like and unlike [127e])—an impossible state of affairs, which proves that the hypothesis is false.

Zeno was a master of arguments related to *reductio ad absurdum* ("reduction to
absurdity") or *reductio ad impossibile* ("reduction to the impossible") arguments.
To refute thesis *a*, show that *a* entails *b*, which even the proponent of *a* admits
to be impossible or absurd and therefore false. Since *b* is false and follows from
a, *a* must be false too. Thus *a* is refuted. In the argument cited by Plato we have
an antinomy. The thesis that there is a plurality yields two mutually contradictory consequences: they are like and they are unlike. But it is impossible for
something to be like and unlike. Therefore, the thesis entails an impossibility,
and hence it is false.

Zeno's arguments do not explicitly make the moves from "*b* is impossible" to "*b*
is false" to "*a* is false," nor does the account of their purpose ("to prove that their
hypothesis, 'if there are many things,' suffers still more ridiculous consequences
than the hypothesis 'if there is one' (128d) require these moves. But since the arguments "contend, against all that is said, that things are not many" (127e), they have
the force even if not the form of *reductio* arguments. Zeno did not invent this form
of argument,[5] but he brought it to new heights and prominence.

Some of Zeno's surviving arguments are directed against plurality, some
against motion, one against place, and one against the sense of hearing. Plato's
statement that Zeno's arguments were all aimed against plurality (128d) need not
trouble us, for describing Parmenides' opponents as pluralists may be shorthand
for saying that they deny all Parmenides' claims, just as saying that Parmenides
believed in the one (128d) is a compact way to refer to his views on the nature of

---

3. Proclus, *Commentary on Plato's* Parmenides 694.23–25, Elias, *Commentary on Aristotle's* Categories 109.17–30 (both = DK 29A15).

4. Aristotle, fr. 65 (Rose), quoted in Diogenes Laertius, *Lives of the Philosophers* 8.57
(= DK 29A10), 9.25 (= DK 29A1).

5. *Reductio* arguments are common in Parmenides and underlie both Xenophanes'
arguments against the gods of popular belief and Anaximander's argument that the earth
stays still in the middle of the universe. See above pp. 40–41 and 60–61.

what-is.[6] In that case Plato's statement is incorrect, but understandably so. Alternatively, the arguments about motion, place, and hearing may have constituted part of an attack on plurality. For example, motion requires a plurality of times and places, so by arguing against motion Zeno is arguing against one reason to believe in a plurality of times and places. It is possible that Zeno's book made clear the connections among the targets of his arguments.

In the rest of this chapter I will set out the surviving arguments and discuss them briefly. In several cases I give Aristotle's comments, which provide a useful perspective. Zeno's paradoxes are extremely suggestive philosophically and from the beginning of the last century have received much attention from logicians and philosophers of mathematics and science. They raise mathematical issues which could not be settled until the concepts of the infinitesimal and the mathematical infinite were worked out in the nineteenth century by Bolzano and Cantor, and they raise philosophical issues on which there is still no general agreement.[7]

Arguments against Plurality

The Argument from Like and Unlike

According to Plato (12.1, 127e), Zeno's first hypothesis of his argument against plurality states that "If things that are are many, they must therefore be both like and unlike," and the argument proceeds to claim that it is impossible for what is like to be unlike and for what is unlike to be like; therefore there cannot be many things. I reconstruct the argument as follows. If there are many things, there are at least two. Pick two of them, *a* and *b*. *a* is *unlike b* because *a* differs from *b* in at least one way (*a* is different from *b*, but *b* is not different from *b*). Likewise, *b* is unlike *a*. But *a* is *like a* (since *a* is not different from *a* in any way), and *b* is like *b*. Therefore, *a* and *b* are both like and unlike.

This is by no means a good argument; there is no contradiction unless something is like and unlike the same thing. The argument can be improved to show this. As before, *a* and *b* are unlike each other. But *a* is like *b* (and *b* like *a*) in that both are existing things. Thus *a* is both like and unlike *b*. This argument is not successful either. The contradiction is only apparent since *a* is not both like and unlike *b* in the same respect.[8]

---

6. As we have seen (pp. 164–65), this interpretation of Parmenides is not secure. However, it is the opinion of antiquity, beginning with Plato. Since the bulk of the *Parmenides* is a dialectical exploration of various "hypotheses" related to the view that "if there is a one" or "if one is," Plato's way of expressing Parmenides' claim may be affected by his purpose in the dialogue.

7. Bertrand Russell's interest in Zeno (e.g., Russell [1903, Chs. 42–43] and Russell [1926: Ch. 6]) led to further studies, especially Grünbaum (1968) and the papers collected in Salmon (1970).

8. Not too much weight should be given to this reconstruction, but no other attempt to reconstruct the argument has yet succeeded in making it go through validly.

I begin with this bad argument to show that not all of Zeno's reasoning is sound and not all of his ideas profound. With Zeno as with the other Presocratics it is a mistake to assume that there are brilliant ideas everywhere, however plentiful they may be. Also, this argument gives insight into the level of argument and standards of reasoning that prevailed in the early fifth century, shortly after deductive reasoning was introduced to philosophy and long before the rules of logic were worked out.

The Argument from Large and Small

12.2   Zeno stated that if anyone could make clear to him what the one is, he would be able to speak of existing things.

> (Eudemus, *Physics* fr. 7, quoted in Simplicius, *Commentary on Aristotle's* Physics 97.12–13 = DK 29A16)

Ordinary people believe that there are many things, that there is a plurality which is made up of many individuals, units, or "ones." Some of Zeno's attacks on plurality proceeded by showing that the units on which the conceptions of plurality are founded involve logically unacceptable features.

A number of these arguments are preserved. One of them argues for the antinomy that if there are many things, they are both large and small. In this way it proves that there cannot be many things because if there were, each one of them would have these contradictory attributes. This strategy accords with Zeno's challenge to his opponents in **12.2**.

Zeno argues separately for each limb of the antinomy. He proves first that the many things are small and then that they are large. (In fact, he argues the stronger thesis that [a] they are so large that they are infinite and [b] they are so small that they have no size.) We have the entire argument for (a), but only part of the argument for (b). The proof of (b) came first and the part that is reported went as follows: "Nothing has size because each of the many things is the same as itself and one." The argument for this conclusion is not preserved. Zeno then argues that "anything without size, thickness, or bulk does not exist."[9]

12.3   For if it should be added to something else that exists, it would not make it any larger. For if it were of no size and were added, nothing it is added to can increase in size. And so it follows immediately that what is added is nothing. But if the other thing is no smaller when it is subtracted and it is not increased when it is added, clearly the thing added or subtracted is nothing.

> (Zeno, fragment 2 = DK 29B2)

---

9. Quotation from Simplicius, *Commentary on Aristotle's* Physics 139.9–11 = DK 29B2. It is Simplicius's summary of Zeno's argument and occurs immediately before he quotes **12.3**.

This argument holds for three-dimensional bodies (compare "thickness," "bulk"), and so tells against opponents who have in mind the many objects in the physical world perceived by the senses. Since the conclusion is unacceptable, the many existing things cannot be nothing, and so, by the terms of the argument each must have some size.

The proof of limb (a) of the antinomy, "So large as to be infinite" also has two stages. Zeno next argues for (a) by showing that anything that has any size is infinitely large. He begins with a consequence of the argument given in 12.3.

> **12.4** If it is, each thing must have some size and thickness, and part of it must be apart from the rest. And the same reasoning holds concerning the part that is in front. For that too will have size, and part of it will be in front. Now to say this once is the same thing as to keep saying it forever. For no such part of it will be the last or unrelated to another. Therefore if there are many things, they must be both small and large; so small as not to have size, but so large as to be infinite.
>
> (Zeno, fragment 1 = DK 29B1)

This argument depends on a kind of infinite regress characteristic of Zeno. Take any one of the many existing things. It has some size. Therefore, one part of it ("the part that is in front") can be distinguished from ("must be apart from") the rest. Let A_1 be the original thing and A_2 the part distinguished from the rest. A_2 exists (or else it is not a part of A_1) and so has size. But in the same way we can distinguish a part of A_2 (call it A_3), which exists and has size. And this process has no end, since we never reach a part with no sub-parts.

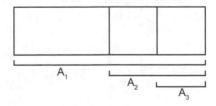

The Argument from Large and Small concludes that the many are (b) so small as not to have size, and (a) so large as to be infinite. The first argument proves that each of the many has no size, which we may take as equivalent to (a), although it does not mention smallness. The second argument (which does not mention largeness) works by dividing up an existing thing (A_1) of limited size. It does not prove that each of the many is infinitely large, but that it has an infinite number of parts. Zeno argues that anything composed of parts is composed of an infinite number of elements, each with positive size. If the sum of an infinite number of positive magnitudes is infinite, it follows that the sum of the parts of A_1 is infinite in size so that A_1, which consists of all its parts, is "so large as to be infinite." I shall postpone criticism of this argument to page 182.

The Argument from Limited and Unlimited

Yet another argument against plurality asserts that "the same things are limited and unlimited."[10] It too is an antinomy. The argument goes as follows.

> **12.5** (a) If there are many, they must be just as many as they are, neither more nor less. But if they are as many as they are, they must be limited. (b) If there are many things, the things that are unlimited, since between things that are there are always others, and still others between those. Therefore the things that are are unlimited.
>
> (Zeno, fragment 3 = DK 29B3)

The first limb (a) of the argument claims that the many things are "just as many as they are, neither more nor less," and therefore limited. The operative principle (though Zeno does not state it) seems to be that there are a definite number of them, and any definite number is a finite number, so there are a limited number of things.

There are different interpretations of the second limb (b). (1) If Zeno is still talking about three-dimensional things with size, it is not clear why he thinks "between things that exist there are always others." Why can't two objects simply touch one another? Could the basis of the infinite regress be the idea that if two things touch, they have a common boundary which belongs neither to the one thing nor to the other and so is yet another thing? (2) The ancient commentator who preserves the argument says, "in this way he proved the unlimited in quantity on the basis of dichotomy [division in two],"[11] a process of division similar to that found in the first limb of the Argument from Large and Small. In that case, the argument may suppose two adjacent existing things A_1, B, with A_1 subdivided as before into A_2, A_3, . . . (where A_2 is half the size of A_1, A_3 half the size of A_2, etc.).

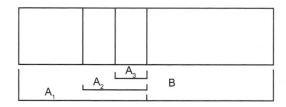

---

10. "Unlimited" and "infinite" translate *apeiron*. I use whichever seems appropriate, but both English words represent the same Greek word and in fact the same notion, which in Zeno's time was still lacking precision (see below p. 183). Partly as a result of reflecting on Zeno's paradoxes, Aristotle (*Physics* books 3 and 6) developed a more precise concept of *apeiron* in which it is appropriately translated as "infinite."

11. Simplicius, *Commentary on Aristotle's* Physics 140.33–34 (= DK 29B3).

The argument can be used to show that things have no adjacent minimum parts, so that a plurality of existing things requires an infinite number of them. This interpretation gives Zeno a valid argument, but the conclusion that it proves is different from what the paradox claimed (that things are unlimited). (3) Zeno is talking not of three-dimensional objects but of mathematical points on a line. Here it is true that between any two distinct points there is a third, and indeed there are an infinite number of points on a line. On this interpretation Zeno discovered a property of densely ordered sets, but there is no evidence that he intended this interpretation of his paradox.

Arguments against Motion

Zeno pressed the Eleatic attack on motion much further than Parmenides. Where Parmenides did not argue directly against motion or change,[12] Zeno offers a number of arguments aiming to prove that our ordinary understanding of motion is incoherent. Aristotle preserves four of his arguments on motion, which he prefaces with the following statement:

> 12.6   There are four of Zeno's arguments about motion that present difficulties
> for those who try to solve them.
> (Aristotle, *Physics* 6.9 239b9–11 = DK 29A25)

The first is called "the Dichotomy," from the process of division employed, or "the Stadium," from a particular use of the argument, perhaps made by Zeno himself, to show that it is impossible to cross a stadium.

The Dichotomy, or The Stadium

> 12.7   First is the argument that says that there is no motion because that which is
> moving must reach the midpoint before the end.
> (Aristotle, *Physics* 6.9 239b11–13 = DK 29A25) (continuation of 12.6)

The argument is spelled out more fully in the following passage.

> 12.8   It is always necessary to traverse half the distance, but these are infinite, and
> it is impossible to get through things that are infinite . . .
> (Aristotle, *Physics* 8.8 263a5–6 [not in DK])

The backbone of the argument lies in the following claims. (a) To move any distance we must first cross half the distance; (b) there are an infinite number of

---

12. See above p. 161.

half-distances; (c) it is impossible to get completely through an infinite number of things; therefore (d) it is impossible to move any distance.

Suppose we want to move from A to B (where A and B are different points). In order to reach B we must first reach A_1, the halfway point, which leaves the distance A_1 to B yet to cover. In order to move from A_1 to B we must first reach A_2, the halfway point, which leaves the distance A_2 to B. There are an infinite number of such steps $A–A_1, A_1–A_2, \ldots$ (equivalently, there are an infinite number of halfway points $A_1, A_2, \ldots$).

A A_1 A_2 B

But it is impossible to cross an infinite number of distances (or to come into contact with an infinite number of points), so the motion from A to B cannot be completed. Therefore, motion is impossible. The argument can also be taken to say that before reaching A_1 we must reach the halfway point of the interval $A–A_1$, etc., so that not only can we not complete a motion, we cannot even begin.

It is natural to think that the argument must be flawed: it has a true premise and a false conclusion. After all, motion does occur, and yet when we move from one point to another we do reach the halfway point before the final destination, and even if there are an infinite number of half-points to reach, somehow or another we manage to do so. We may feel sympathy for Antisthenes the Cynic who, "since he was unable to contradict Zeno's arguments against motion, stood up and took a step, thinking that stronger than any opposition in arguments was a demonstration through what is obvious."[13]

One approach is to point out that some infinite series have finite sums. In particular, the series $\frac{1}{2} + \frac{1}{4} + \frac{1}{8} + \ldots$ adds up to 1. If Zeno thought that it is impossible to cross an infinite number of distances because their sum is infinite, he is just wrong for the particular infinite sets of distances involved in the Stadium and the Achilles (the next argument to be considered), and also for the magnitudes in the Argument from Large and Small (above pages 178–79).

Aristotle takes another approach.

> **12.9**   For this reason Zeno's argument falsely assumes that it is impossible to traverse or come into contact with an infinite number of things individually in a finite time. For both length and time and generally everything that is continuous are called infinite in two ways: infinite in division and infinite with respect to their extremities. Now it is impossible to come into contact with things infinite in quantity in a finite time, but it is possible to do so with things that are infinite in division. For time itself too is infinite

13. Elias, *Commentary on Aristotle's* Categories 109.20–22 (= DK 29A15).

in this way. And so, it follows that it traverses the infinite in an infinite and not a finite time, and comes into contact with infinite things in infinite, not finite times.

(Aristotle, *Physics* 6.2 233a21–31 = DK 29A25)

Aristotle understands Zeno to argue that traversing an infinite number of distances is impossible because it would take an infinite amount of time. Aristotle refutes the argument on the grounds that it confuses two distinct notions of infinity: what is infinite in respect to its extremities (its end points are infinitely far apart), and what is infinite in respect to divisibility (it can be divided without limit). The continuous distance A–B is infinite in respect to divisibility (which is why the process of division by dichotomy is possible) but not in respect to its extremities. The time it takes to move from A to B is also infinite in respect to divisibility but not in respect to its extremities. Time is continuous, and an interval of time can be divided into parts and sub-parts in the same way distance can. If it takes n seconds to move from A to B, it takes $n/2$ seconds to move from A to A_1, $n/4$ seconds to move from A_1 to A_2, etc. So there is no need to suppose that the infinite number of distances needing to be passed in getting from A to B will take an amount of time that is infinite in extent, only one that is (harmlessly) infinitely divisible. Moreover (although this additional point is not made by Aristotle, nor is it necessary for his argument), the total time taken to move from A to B is $n/2$ sec. + $n/4$ sec. + . . . = n sec.

Referring to passages **12.7**, **12.8** and **12.9**, he says,

12.10   This solution is sufficient to use against the person who raised the question (for he asked whether it is possible to traverse or count infinite things in a finite time), but insufficient for the facts of the matter and the truth.

(Aristotle, *Physics* 8.8 263a15–18 [not in DK])

However, nothing in Aristotle's summaries of Zeno's argument suggests that Zeno argued this way. Instead, the argument turns on premise (c) as stated in **12.8**: motion is impossible because "it is impossible to get through things that are infinite," irrespective of how long it takes to do so. And I suppose that he thought that it is impossible to do so because of what it means for there to be an infinite number of things. "Infinite" translates *apeiron*, Anaximander's term for his "unlimited" originative principle (see above page 34). In Zeno's time the word did not have its technical meaning "infinite" but was closer to its etymological meaning "without a limit." Zeno's statement that it is impossible to get through things that are infinite means that it is impossible to reach the end of an endless series, which is necessarily true: it is impossible to reach the end of something that has no end to be reached. For example, we can count as many numbers as we like (1, 2, 3, . . .), but since there is an infinite number of whole numbers, we cannot reach the end of them; in fact there is no end, no largest number. Zeno is correct in saying that

there are an infinite number of halfway points and that we cannot get through
an infinite number of things in the sense that we cannot get through them one
by one. However, this leaves open the question whether there is another way to
achieve the same result. In the present case, the result is reaching the end of the
stadium, point *b*, which is what we would achieve by completing the sequence of
half-distances one by one (were that possible). And the answer to the question is
that there clearly are other ways to reach *b*. For example, if the stadium in question
is the one at Olympia, in which the distance from starting line to finish line is 192
meters, we can cross it by taking steps 1 meter long. We reach the finish line by
taking 192 such steps, and when we have taken those steps, we have in fact passed
all of Zeno's halfway points. Zeno has shown that there is one way of attempting
to cross the stadium which cannot be completed, but he has done nothing to show
that that is the only possible way.

The Achilles

12.11   The second <argument> [see **12.7**] is the one called the Achilles. This is to
the effect that the slowest as it runs will never be caught by the quickest. For
the pursuer must first reach the point from which the pursued departed,
so that the slower must always be some distance in front. This is the same
argument as the Dichotomy, but it differs in not dividing the given magnitude in half.

(Aristotle, *Physics* 6.9 239b14–20 = DK 29A26)

In the Dichotomy the distance is divided into two equal parts each time; the
Achilles points out that the same situation arises for division into other constant
proportions as well. It is understandable that Aristotle says the two arguments
are essentially the same: Zeno describes the race between Achilles, the swiftest
runner, and the slowest runner, (traditionally, but not in Aristotle, identified as
a tortoise) such that there will be an infinite sequence of stages, each one proportionally smaller than the previous one. And the same reasoning that led to
the conclusion that it is impossible to cross the stadium will apply here too: it is
impossible to complete an infinite sequence taking the stages one by one, since
there is no final stage; therefore Achilles cannot catch up with the tortoise

However, Aristotle's interpretation is at odds with his summary of the argument, which does not employ premises anything like those of the Dichotomy.
Zeno concludes that Achilles never catches the tortoise, but there is nothing
about an infinite number of stages in the race or the impossibility of completing
them. This time the argument turns on the words "always" and "never": Achilles never catches up because the tortoise is always ahead. Likewise, as we will
see, the solution to the paradox depends on achieving a correct understanding
of what this claim means. The way Zeno describes the race, there is a sense in
which the tortoise is always ahead: whenever Achilles reaches the position where
the tortoise was at the beginning of some stage of the race, the tortoise is still

ahead (and the race is therefore still going on). But in another sense the tortoise is not always ahead. For example, if the tortoise walks at a rate of one foot per minute and has a head start of one hundred feet, and if Achilles runs at a rate of one thousand feet per minute, and they both run for a minute, then since the tortoise will have moved ahead one foot and Achilles one thousand feet, the tortoise will no longer be ahead; the race will have finished quite some time before the minute ends. In fact, this is just what we would expect. So the interesting question now becomes not how Achilles can catch the tortoise (because this question has an easy answer: he just has to run at his faster pace long enough) but how Zeno managed to raise any doubt that he could.

The argument implies that Achilles has not caught up at the end of any stage of the race, but not that he never catches up. This is possible because, as in the case of the Dichotomy, there is no final stage (by which I mean a stage at the end of which Achilles has caught up). If there were such a final stage, then when Achilles completes it he has caught up, but since the argument implies that at the end of *every* stage Achilles has not caught up, it follows that at the end of the final stage he has not caught up. This would be paradoxical indeed. But since there is no final stage, the problem does not arise. But then, even though it is true that whenever Achilles finishes a stage he has not caught the tortoise, it does not follow that he never catches the tortoise any more than the fact that whenever I finish running a marathon I am tired implies that I am always tired. Likewise the fact that the tortoise is always ahead at the end of every stage does not imply that the tortoise is always ahead. The tortoise is always ahead and Achilles never catches up only in the sense that these situations occur at the end of every stage of the race, not at every instant of time.

The Flying Arrow

12.12   The third argument is the one just stated, that the arrow is stopped while it is moving. This follows from assuming that time is composed of "nows." If this is not conceded, the deduction will not go through.
                            (Aristotle, *Physics* 6.9 239b30–33 = DK 29A27)

Aristotle refers to the following passage.

12.13   Zeno makes a mistake in reasoning. For if, he says, everything is always at rest when it occupies a space equal to itself, and what is moving is always "at a now," the moving arrow is motionless.
                            (Aristotle, *Physics* 6.9 239b5–7 = DK 29A27)

I reconstruct the argument as follows: (1) Whenever something is in a space equal to itself it is at rest. (2) The flying arrow is in a space equal to itself at every instant ("now") of its flight. Therefore (3) the flying arrow is at rest at every instant of its flight. (4) What is moving is always at an instant. Therefore, (5) the flying arrow is at rest during the whole of its flight.

The point of (1) is not terribly easy to make out. The idea may be that if something moves from one place to another, in some sense it occupies a bigger space than if it stays still. For example if an arrow is at rest at position *ab* (where *a* is the butt of the arrow and *b* is the head), the size of *ab* is equal to the size of the arrow. But if the arrow begins its flight at position *ab* and finishes up at position *cd* (where *c* is the final position of the butt and *d* the final position of the head), then in some sense during its flight it has occupied all the space in between, so the space it has taken up extends not just from *a* to *b* but from *a* to *d*, which is larger than the size of the arrow. If this is correct, we can see how the argument is meant to go through. Motion takes time. You can't cover any distance in no time at all, which means that at any instant of time during the arrow's flight, it covers no distance, and this is premise (2), the claim that the arrow is in a space equal to itself at every instant of its flight. Put this result together with premise (1) and we get (3): the arrow is at rest at every instant of its flight. But if something is true of the arrow at every instant during its flight, it is true of it during the whole of its flight, since there is no time during its flight apart from the instants. This is another way of putting premise (4): what is moving is always at an instant. So, since by (3) the arrow is at rest at each instant of its flight, it follows that it is at rest throughout its flight, and therefore it does not move at all.

This is a subtle argument that makes us wonder both when it is that something actually does move from one position to the next and how something can move from one position to another. My answers to these questions are short and simple, and I will state them before going back to Zeno's argument in order to diagnose it. When *does* something move from one position to the next? My answer is that the question is improper, since there is no such thing as the "next" position. Given any two points, no matter how close together, there are other points in between, and the same holds for positions. However, there is no difficulty about telling when something moves from one position to *another*. If I know when it starts to move and how fast it moves, I can tell you when it moves from its starting point to a position any given distance away, no matter how small, and I can tell you when it reaches that position. But I cannot tell you when it moves to the "next" position in the sense of the position that is the minimum distance away, because there just is no minimum distance.

And *how* can something move from one position to another? It does so simply by *being* in all the intermediate positions. This is just what motion is. For something to move continuously from one position to another beginning at one instant and ending at another, is no more and no less than for it to occupy continuously, with no pauses, different positions from the initial position to the final position at all the different times between the initial instant and the final instant. The important point here is that we are talking of motion as something continuous, which means we are assuming that space and time are continuous in the sense that there are no adjacent positions and no adjacent times. There is no mystery about how we get from one moment to the next or from one position to the next because there is no such thing as the next moment or the next position.

Motion, as Aristotle understood, is something that takes place over *intervals* of time. And just as nothing can move any distance in an instant (it requires an interval), so it is wrong to think that anything can be at rest in an instant.[14] Rest is the absence of motion; since motion can occur only over an interval of time, the same holds for rest as well. If you know the precise position of something at an instant, that knowledge does not enable you to say whether that instant occurred during a period of motion or a period of rest, as we all know from putting a DVD player on "pause."

This consideration is relevant to Zeno's argument. It shows that (3) is incorrect. At each instant of its flight the arrow is not covering any distance, but that does not mean that it is at rest. In fact, the arrow is in motion during the whole its flight, since this just means that it is in motion during the whole of its motion. It is covering the entire distance during the whole motion, even though at any instant it does not cover any distance at all.

This gives us material for another objection, that (5) does not follow from (3) and (4) as the argument supposes. In the first place, (4) is controversial: in an important sense a time interval is not composed of instants.[15] But even if we grant (4), we must admit that both (3) and (4) are concerned with the behavior of the arrow at individual instants, whereas (5) is concerned with its behavior over an interval which is in some sense the sum of the instants. In general, it is not safe to infer from the fact that the components of a compound all have some property that the compound has that property too. For example, from the fact that each part of a car weighs less than 500 kg. we cannot safely infer that the whole car weighs less than 500 kg. Likewise, the fact that the arrow does not cover any distance at any instant of its flight does not entail that it covers no distance during the whole of its flight.

Finally, it has been held[16] that this argument is aimed at a theory that time is composed of instants and that motion is "cinematographic," moving in jerks with one still frame for each discrete instant. Those who uphold this interpretation tend to see the argument as sound,[17] but the argument does not depend on such a theory of time, and there is no evidence that such a theory had been proposed.

---

14. *Physics* 239a23.

15. In another sense it *is* composed of instants. It is *not* composed of instants in that there are no adjacent instants: between any two instants, however close we like, there is an interval which contains an infinite number of instants. But it *is* composed of instants in that wherever you look you will find a point—there are no gaps where points are lacking. And similarly in a continuous stretch of time there are no gaps where instants are not to be found.

16. This is the view of Lee (1936), Owen (1957–8/1975/1986), Kirk and Raven (1957), and Guthrie (1965).

17. If the arrow is at rest in each still frame and there is no time in between successive still frames for the arrow to move, then the arrow does not move at all.

The Moving Rows

12.14   The fourth argument is about equal bodies moving in a stadium alongside equal bodies in the opposite direction, the one group moving from the end of the stadium, the other from the middle, at equal speed. He claims in this argument that it follows that half the time is equal to the double. The mistake is in thinking that an equal magnitude moving with equal speed takes an equal time in passing something moving as it does in passing something at rest. But this is false. Let *A*'s represent the equal stationary bodies, *B*'s the bodies beginning from the middle, equal in number and size to the *A*'s, and *C*'s the bodies beginning from the end, equal in number and size to these and having the same speed as the *B*'s. It follows that the first *B* is at the end at the same time as the first *C*, as the *B*'s and *C*'s move alongside one another, and the first *C* has completed the process of coming alongside all the *B*'s but the first *B* has completed the process of coming alongside half the *A*'s. And so the time is half. For each of them is alongside each thing for an equal time. It follows simultaneously that the first *B* has moved alongside all the *C*'s, for the first *C* and the first *B* will be at the opposite ends simultaneously, because both have been alongside the *A*'s for an equal amount of time.

(Aristotle, *Physics* 6.9 239b33–240a17 = DK
29A28) (continuation of **12.12**)

The following diagram[18] represents the starting point of the movement.

	A A A A	
D	*B B B B* →	*E*
	← *C C C C*	

A: stationary bodies
B: bodies moving from *D* to *E*
C: bodies moving from *E* to *D*
D: beginning of stadium
E: end of stadium

The *B*'s and *C*'s move in opposite directions at the same speed. The finish of the movement will correspond to the following diagram

	A A A A	
D	*B B B B*	*E*
	C C C C	

In the time of the movement, the leftmost *C* passes all four *B*'s, whereas the rightmost *B* passes only half the *A*'s and also all four *C*'s. So far, so good. However,

---

18. The diagram is given by Simplicius (quoting Alexander), *Commentary on Aristotle's* Physics, 1016.19–24 (= DK 29A28).

from this situation, according to Aristotle, Zeno wrongly infers that the time the rightmost *B* takes to pass the two *A*'s is half as long as the time the leftmost *C* takes to pass all four *B*'s. This conclusion depends on the premise "each of them is alongside each thing for an equal time," that is, each *C* is alongside each *B* for the same length of time each *B* is alongside each *A*. According to Aristotle, the argument depends on a fallacy: since the *B*'s and *C*'s are moving in opposite directions, a *B* takes only half as long to get past each *C* as it does to get past a stationary *A*. The fallacy is so obvious that some have held that Zeno could not have committed it, but such judgments are dangerous. Equally elementary errors about relative terms occur in Plato's dialogues, written half a century later. Further, the fact that it is a fallacy does not entail that Zeno himself was taken in by it. We recall that he wrote his book in a "spirit of competitiveness" (**12.1**, 128d).

This argument becomes more historically and philosophically significant if the "bodies" are indivisible bodies ("atoms"), and the moving bodies are alongside the stationary ones for a smallest, indivisible unit of time. Zeno then has a good argument against a mistaken ("atomistic") conception of time.[19] However, there is no hint in the sources that Zeno intended the argument in this way. [20] And the argument is not good, since it requires the rightmost *B* be opposite all four *A*'s, whereas in the Atomistic view, it skips over half of them.[21]

---

19. This sort of interpretation is given by Lee (1936), KR, and Owen (1957–1958/1975/1986). "If we say that the first *B* can pass twice as many *C*'s as *A*'s in a given time, what we say entails that if in a given time the first *B* passes one *C*, it also passes half an *A*. But suppose now that any *A* (and therefore any *B* or *C*) is an *infinitesimal* quantity. Then the *B* cannot pass half an *A*: it must pass all or nothing. And since ex hypothesi it *is* moving past the *A*'s, it must pass a whole *A* in the time that it passes one *C*. Yet, as we set up the problem, it would pass twice as many *C*'s as *A*'s in a given time. So when it passes one *C* it also passes two *C*'s." (Owen 1957–1958/1975/1986: 151).

20. Guthrie (1965), Barnes (1979: vol. 1, 291 / 1982: 291), and KRS reject the interpretation for this reason.

21. On this theory, anything that is moving is occupying different places at different times; specifically, if it is moving during all of the period that includes t_1 and t_2, where t_1 and t_2 are successive atoms of time, then it must occupy one place at t_1 and a different place at t_2; otherwise it is not moving in all of the period that includes t_1 and t_2. If, then, the *A*'s, *B*'s, and *C*'s are all adjacent atoms and the *B*'s and *C*'s are moving in opposite directions, then at successive instants we will have the following situations.

    1. Starting position.

$$D \quad \boxed{\begin{array}{c} A\,A\,A\,A \\ B\,B\,B\,B \\ C\,C\,C\,C \end{array}} \quad E$$

Two Remaining Paradoxes

The Place of Place

This argument is reported variously.[22] Its gist is as follows. If place exists, where is it? For everything that exists is in a place. Therefore if place exists, then place is in a place. This goes on to infinity. Therefore, place does not exist.

The target of this infinite regress argument is the existence of place: nothing that exists can have a location. Zeno thus strikes another blow against our conception of the world in which things do have places and against our conception of motion, which involves moving from place to place.

There are several responses. Aristotle and his followers simply denied the premise that everything that exists is in a place. "For no one would say that health or courage or ten thousand other things were in a place."[23] We can then admit that three-dimensional objects have places, but deny that the place of such an object is the kind of thing that has a place. Another reply is to accept the premise and the conclusion that place is somewhere, but to declare that the place of the place of x is just the place of x, so the infinite regress becomes harmless.

The Millet Seed

This argument is preserved in a "theatrical version," a dialogue between Zeno and the Sophist Protagoras, which is probably not the way it originally appeared.

12.15   —*Zeno*: Tell me, Protagoras, does a single millet seed make a noise when it
         falls, or one ten-thousandth of a millet seed?
         —*Prot*: No.
         —*Zeno*: Does a bushel of millet seeds make a noise when it falls, or doesn't it?
         —*Prot*: It does.

---

2. Position after one instant, when each B has moved one atom to the right and
   each C one atom to the left.

$$
D \quad \boxed{\begin{array}{c} A\,A\,A\,A \\ B\,B\,B\,B \\ C\,C\,C\,C \end{array}} \quad E
$$

Note that there is no time when the rightmost B is alongside the leftmost C. Each of them jumps instantaneously from one position to the next and there is no time during the jump when they are opposite each other or midway between the stationary A atoms.

22. Simplicius, *Commentary on Aristotle's* Physics 562.3–6 = DK 29B5 (in DK vol. 2, p. 498), Aristotle, *Physics* 4.3 210b22–23, 4.1 209a23–25, Eudemus, *Physics* fr. 42, quoted by Simplicius, *Commentary on Aristotle's* Physics 563.25–28 (all three testimonia = DK 29A24).

23. Eudemus, fr. 78 (Wehrli) = DK 29A24.

—*Zeno*: But isn't there a ratio between the bushel of millet seeds and one millet seed, or one ten-thousandth of a millet seed?

—*Prot*: Yes there is.

—*Zeno*: So won't there be the same ratios of their sounds to one another? For as the things that make the noise <are to one another>, so are the noises <to one another>. But since this is so, if the bushel of millet seeds makes a noise, so will a single millet seed and one ten-thousandth of a millet seed.

(Simplicius, *Commentary on Aristotle's* Physics 1108.18–25 = DK 29A29)

This argument supports Parmenides by proving one of the senses unreliable. (Analogous arguments hold against the other senses.) Aristotle treats it in connection with the question of how much force it takes to shift a heavy weight.

12.16 It does not follow that if a given motive power causes a certain amount of motion, half that power will cause motion either of any particular amount or in any length of time: otherwise, one man might move a ship, if the power of the ship-haulers is divided into their number and the distance that all of them move it.

(Aristotle, *Physics* 7.5 250a16–19 [not in DK])

Likewise there is a threshold below which no sound is made, and the effect of a single millet seed falling is beneath the threshold. We would explain these states of affairs in terms of friction and the elasticity of air, but Aristotle's criticism is to the point.

Evaluation

The surviving arguments assail elements of our ordinary beliefs that the world contains many things and that it is full of motion and apprehensible by the senses, even if they do not all fit easily with Plato's account in 12.1 of the purpose of Zeno's book—to attack the hypothesis that there are many things. It has been held that some of the arguments tell against Parmenides as much as they do against his critics. Indeed, the conclusion of the Argument from Large and Small—that if each of the many existing things has size then each is infinitely large—contradicts Parmenides' claim that what-is is limited. But the contradiction arises only if Parmenides holds that what-is is limited in respect to size, and the last chapter gave reasons against this view (see above page 163). The nonspatial interpretation of what-is is therefore strengthened by Zeno's argument refuting the possibility of an extended but limited existing thing.

Zeno had a unique role in early Greek philosophy. He did not put forward distinctive views of his own or extend Parmenides' ideas or support them by improved arguments. In the Eleatic team he played on the defensive side. His arguments vary in quality. Aristotle's criticisms show that the paradoxes received attention in antiquity and that Aristotle thought most of them unsound and believed he had adequate solutions.

That is not to say that Zeno is unimportant. His puzzles drove Aristotle to sharpen the conception of the infinite and related ideas. He made later Presocratics (the Atomists and possibly Anaxagoras[24]) sensitive to issues about the minimal size of matter. Zeno's method of argument had a dual legacy in antiquity. His general strategy of constructing arguments on both sides of an issue (for example, that if things are many, they must be both like and unlike) was taken up by Protagoras and became perhaps the most notable weapon in the arsenals of the fifth-century Sophists. His methods of abstract argument were followed in certain fifth-century texts and influenced Plato (the *Parmenides* is a notable example). Insofar as he deserves the title of father of dialectic, he sired an offspring with a long and vigorous life in philosophy and other fields. Finally, his paradoxes, especially those concerning motion, were important because they forced people for the first time to pay attention to the way they conceived of time, space and motion and to either accept Zeno's conclusions or refute them. Frequently refutation was only possible after relevant concepts had been defined precisely and appropriate distinctions drawn. In this century, these paradoxes have provoked a great deal of controversy among mathematicians and philosophers over the nature of space, time, and the infinite. In fact they do raise fundamental questions in these areas, and the attempt to understand them fully has led to much valuable philosophical work.

---

24. Zeno may have been influenced by Anaxagoras rather than vice versa. Our view on this issue depends on what we make of the statement that Zeno wrote his work while a young man (**12.1**, 128d) and on what view we take of the date of Anaxagoras's treatise (see below pp. 198–99). For Zeno and the Atomists, see below pp. 215–16 and 309–11.

13

Anaxagoras of Clazomenae

Fragments

13.1[1] (1)[2] 1. All things were together, unlimited in both amount[3] and smallness.

2. For the small too was unlimited.

3. And when [or, "since"] all things were together, nothing was manifest on account of smallness.

4. For *aēr* and *aithēr* dominated all things, both being unlimited.

5. For these are the greatest ingredients in the totality, both in amount and in magnitude.[4]

13.2 (2) 1. For both *aēr* and *aithēr* are being separated off from the surrounding multitude

2. and what surrounds is unlimited in amount.

13.3 (3) 1. For of the small there is no smallest, but always a smaller

2. (for what-is cannot not be).[5]

3. But also of the large there is always a larger,

4. and it is equal in amount to the small.

5. But in relation to itself, each is both large and small.

13.4[6] (4) 1.These things being so, it is right to suppose that in all things that are being mixed together there are many things of all kinds, and seeds of all things, having all kinds of shapes and colors and flavors;

2. and that humans too were compounded and all the other living things that possess soul;

3. and that there are cities constructed and works built by humans just as with us;

---

1. **13.1–9** and **13.11–17** are all quoted by Simplicius—ample evidence that he had the text (or at least some of the text) of Anaxagoras before him. Guthrie (1965: 332–38) and Barnes (1987/2001: 227–34) quote the full context.

2. The numbers in parentheses are the numbers of the fragments in DK. (1) = DK 59B1.

3. I translate *plēthos* throughout as "amount." Other possible translations of this non-technical word are "number," "multitude," and "quantity."

4. The authenticity of **13.1** sec. 5 has been cast into doubt by Sider (2005: 75–76), who thinks it was written by Simplicius to explain what Anaxagoras means in sec. 4 by the word here translated as "dominated."

5. Many accept an emendation which makes the line read "for what is cannot through division (literally, "by cutting") not be," i.e., it cannot be divided up into parts that do not exist.

6. Many editors divide **13.4** into two or three separate fragments.

4. and that they have a sun and a moon and the rest just as with us;

5. and that the earth grows many things of all kinds for them, the most useful of which they gather into their dwellings and put to use.

6. I have said these things about the separating off, because [or, "that"] separating off would have occurred not only with us, but elsewhere too.

7. But before there was separation off, when [or, "since"] all things were together, not even any color was manifest,

8. for the mixture of all things prevented it—of the wet and the dry, the hot and the cold, the bright and the dark, there being also much earth present and seeds unlimited in amount, in no way like one another.

9. For none of the other things are alike either, the one to the other.

10. Since this is so, it is right to suppose that all things were present in the whole.

13.5   (5) It is right to know that although [or "since"] these things have been separated apart in this way, all things are not at all less or more (for it is not to be accomplished[7] that they be more than all), but all things are always equal.

13.6   (6) 1. And since the portions of both the large and the small are equal in amount, in this way too all things will be in everything;

2. nor can they be separate, but all things have a portion of everything.

3. Since there cannot be a smallest, nothing can be separated or come to be by itself,[8] but as in the beginning, now too all things are together.

4. But in all things there are many things present, equal in amount, both in the larger and in the smaller of the things being separated off.

13.7   (7) . . . and so we do not know either in word or in deed the amount of the things being separated off.

13.8   (8) The things in the single *kosmos* are not separated from one another nor are they split apart with an axe, either the hot from the cold or the cold from the hot.

13.9   (9) 1. As these things are rotating in this way and being separated off by both force and speed,

2. the speed causes the force,

3. and their speed is like the speed of nothing now present among humans, but altogether many times as fast.

---

7. "To be accomplished" translates *anuston*, an unusual word which Parmenides also uses (**11.2** line 7). Here it means something close to "possible."

8. "By itself" means "separate from other things," not "through its own agency."

13.10[9] (10) For how could hair come to be from what is not hair, or flesh from what is not flesh?[10]

13.11 (11) In everything there is a portion of everything except Mind, but Mind is in some things too.

13.12 (12) 1. The other things have a portion of everything, but Mind is unlimited and self-ruled and is mixed with no thing, but is alone and by itself.

2. For if it were not by itself but were mixed with something else, it would have a share of all things, if it were mixed with anything.

3. For in everything there is a portion of everything, as I have said before.

4. And the things mixed together with it would hinder it so that it would rule no thing in the same way as it does, being alone and by itself.

5. For it is the finest of all things and the purest, and it has all judgment about everything and the greatest strength.

6. And Mind rules all things that possess soul—both the larger and the smaller.

7. And Mind ruled the entire rotation, so that it rotated in the beginning.

8. And at first it began to rotate from a small region, but it is <now> rotating over a greater range, and it will rotate over a <still> greater one.

9. And Mind knew all the things that are being mixed together and those that are being separated off and those that are being separated apart.

10. And Mind set in order all things, whatever kinds of things were going to be—whatever were and are not now, and all that are now and whatever kinds of things will be—and also this rotation in which the things being separated off are now rotating—the stars and the sun and the moon, and the *aēr* and the *aithēr*.

11. This rotation caused them to separate off.

12. And the dense is being separated off from the rare and the hot from the cold and the bright from the dark and the dry from the wet.

13. But there are many portions of many things.

---

9. For the context of this fragment, see **13.26**.

10. Some doubt the authenticity of this fragment. It has even been suggested that it may be a fabrication of the source, a scholium (note in the margin of a manuscript) on the text of the Church Father, Gregory of Nazianzus, which is strongly influenced by Aristotle's interpretation of Anaxagoras's. (Schofield [1980: 138–43]). But even on this view, the ultimate source (Aristotle) of the interpretation is quite likely to be correct, since he is thought to have had access to Anaxagoras's book and is unlikely to have misunderstood an obvious point like the one in question here. It is therefore reasonable to take **13.10** as Anaxagorean in thought even if (possibly) not in word.

14. And nothing is being[11] completely separated off or separated apart one from another except Mind.

15. All Mind is alike, both the larger and the smaller.

16. But nothing else is like anything else, but each single thing is and was most plainly those things that are present in the greatest amount.

13.13 (13) 1. And when Mind began to impart motion, separation off proceeded to occur from all that was being moved,

2. and all that Mind moved was separated apart,

3. and as things were being moved and separated apart, the rotation caused them to separate apart much more.

13.14 (14) Mind, which is always, is very much[12] even now where all other things are too, in the surrounding multitude and in things that have come together in the process of separating[13] and in things that have separated off.

13.15 (15) The dense and the wet and the cold and the dark came together here, where the earth is now, but the rare and the hot and the dry went out into the far reaches of the *aithēr*.

13.16 (16) 1. From these things as they are being separated off, earth is being compounded;

2. for water is being separated off out of the clouds, earth out of the water, and out of the earth stones are being compounded by the cold,

3. and these [that is, stones] move further out than the water.

13.17 (17) 1. The Greeks do not think correctly about coming to be and perishing,

2. for no thing comes to be, nor does it perish, but it is mixed together with things that are and separated apart from them.

3. And so they would be correct to call coming to be being mixed together, and perishing being separated apart.

13.18 (18) The sun puts the shine in the moon.

13.19 (19) We call Iris [rainbow] the brightness in the clouds opposite the sun.

---

11. This translation preserves the present tense of the original. Since Anaxagoras cannot mean that Mind (which is already separate from everything else [**13.12** sec.1]) is being separated, or that nothing else undergoes separation (**13.12** sec. 9), he must mean that nothing else attains the complete state of separation which Mind has.

12. The manuscript reading does not make good sense here. In "which is always, is very much," I follow the text of DK.

13. "Come together in the process of separating" is an interpretive overtranslation of *proskrinesthai*, which means literally "separate towards." For discussion, see below p. 223.

13.20 (21) Because of their [the senses'] feebleness we are unable to discern the truth.

13.21 (21a) Appearances are a sight of the unseen.

13.22 (21b) [We are less fortunate than animals in all these respects], but we make use of our own experience and wisdom and memory and skill, and we take honey, milk <cows>, and laying hold <of animals> we carry them and lead <them>.[14]

13.23 (22) Egg white is bird's milk.

Life and Writing

Anaxagoras was born c.500 and died c.428. He was an Ionian, and his philosophy marks a return to the philosophical and scientific interests and style of the Milesians,[15] though he was also keenly aware of and deeply influenced by Eleatic philosophy. He reportedly predicted the fall of a meteorite that occurred at Aegospotami (in the Gallipoli peninsula) in 467 (**13.32**). He moved to Athens, where he lived for thirty years. While there he was an associate of Pericles, the great Athenian statesman. This political connection and his scientific views led to his prosecution and conviction (probably c.450[16]) for impiety, on the grounds that he believed the sun to be not a god but a fiery stone. Anaxagoras thus has the honor of being the first philosopher prosecuted at Athens[17] (Socrates would follow; Aristotle fled to avoid prosecution). Forced to leave Athens, he lived the rest of his life in Ionia, in the city of Lampsacus, near Troy, where he was honored after his death with an annual holiday for children.

He had a reputation for single-mindedly pursuing intellectual inquiry to the extent that (unusual for a Greek of this period) he had no concern with politics or worldly affairs. His commitment to inquiry is displayed in the following incident.

13.24 Once a ram with one horn was brought to Pericles from his country estate, and when the soothsayer Lampon saw the horn growing strong and solid from the middle of the forehead, he said that though there were two

---

14. It is debated how much of this material is Anaxagoras and how much is due to the source (Plutarch, *On Chance* 3 98F).

15. The claim that he was Anaximenes' pupil (Diogenes Laertius, *Lives of the Philosophers* 2.6 = DK 59A1), though chronologically improbable, is true to the spirit of his thought.

16. Some ancient testimonia imply a date of c.430.

17. This title may belong to Protagoras, but the story of his banishment is less secure. See below p. 387.

contending factions in the city (those of Thucydides and those of Pericles), the one who obtained the head would gain power. But Anaxagoras had the skull cut open and showed that the brain had not completely filled its place but was drawn together in a point like an egg in the very spot in the entire cavity where the root of the horn had its origin.

(Plutarch, *Pericles* 6 = DK 59A16)

He wrote a single work, *Physica* ("Studies of Nature") in plain clear prose, with a somewhat hymnic quality, in which he treated the nature and composition of things, the original pre-cosmic state (since for Anaxagoras the *kosmos* had a beginning), the entity (*nous*, which I translate as Mind) that initiated and governed the cosmogonic process, that process itself, and (possibly in considerable detail) the *kosmos* as it is now. In his choice of subject matter and in his general approach, he was a successor of the early Ionian philosophers, and he sustained this tradition by constructing an up-to-date cosmology that takes account of Parmenides' challenge (see above pages 172–73) and perhaps some of Zeno's arguments as well.

Relations to Other Philosophers

Anaxagoras was decidedly younger than Parmenides (born c.515) and somewhat older than Zeno and Empedocles (both born c.490; Empedocles is the subject of Chapter 14). He was strongly influenced by Parmenides, but his relations with the other two philosophers are not clear. The best evidence for the date of Zeno's work is the statement that he wrote his treatise at a young age.[18] Anaxagoras's alleged prediction of the meteorite of 467 may mean that his book had been published by that date.[19] This information does not provide a basis for deciding who wrote first, though I believe that Zeno wrote first and that Anaxagoras constructed his theory partly in response to him.[20] As for his relation to Empedocles, the key text runs as follows.

13.25   Anaxagoras . . . was in age prior to him [Empedocles], but in works posterior.
(Aristotle, *Metaphysics* 1.3 984a11–13 = DK 59A43)

Taken straightforwardly this assertion indicates that Anaxagoras was older than Empedocles, but his book was written (or published) later than Empedocles' work. I think that this interpretation is most likely correct, although in antiquity interpretations were floated that Aristotle meant that Anaxagoras was inferior

---

18. Plato, *Parmenides* 128d (= **12.1**).
19. See below p. 227 and n. 88.
20. Some prefer the reverse ordering.

to Empedocles[21] or that Anaxagoras was "more up to date" than Empedocles, hence superior.[22] Aristotle's statement is thus inconclusive, but Diogenes Laertius reports that Empedocles "heard" Anaxagoras,[23] and the evidence on balance favors an earlier date for Anaxagoras's work.[24] It is reasonable, though, to regard Anaxagoras and Empedocles as contemporaries who in constructing their physical systems were largely concerned with the same problems, which stem from Parmenides. I shall not attempt to point out instances where one of these philosophers may have influenced the other, but I will from time to time show points of similarity and difference between the two systems.

Anaxagoras accepts Parmenides' absolute division between what-is and what-is not (**13.3** section 2) and his consequent denial of coming to be and perishing (**13.17**). Like Empedocles he holds that what appear to be cases of coming to be and perishing are really instances of mixture and separation of existing things. But there is a difference. For Empedocles mixing is sometimes the cause of a compound's coming to be and sometimes the cause of its perishing, and similarly for separation (**14.58** lines 3–5), but for Anaxagoras coming to be is simply mixture and perishing is simply separation.[25]

The ban on coming to be and perishing permeates Anaxagoras's system further than it does Empedocles'. For Empedocles genuine types of substances like flesh and blood are formed out of the four elements and dissolve into them.[26] Anaxagoras prohibits even this sort of coming to be and perishing: the blood or flesh must have been there all along, even if it was not detectable (**13.10**). Counter to appearances there is a portion of everything in everything (**13.6** section 2). The food we eat changes into blood, flesh, and so forth, but these substances do not come to be in either a Parmenidean sense (that is, out of what-is-not) or an Empedoclean sense (out of more fundamental entities). They were already in the food, but in quantities so small as to be invisible (**13.12** section 16). When the

---

21. Alexander, *Commentary on Aristotle's* Metaphysics 27.28–28.3 (not in DK). This reading is rendered less plausible by Aristotle's not infrequent complaints about Empedocles' views. Noteworthy in this connection is Aristotle's description of Anaxagoras as "like a sober man, in contrast with the random talk of his predecessors" (*Metaphysics* 1.3 984b17–8 = DK 59A58), where the predecessors seem to include Empedocles (cf. 1.4 984b31–985a10 = DK 31A39).

22. Alexander, *Commentary on Aristotle's* Metaphysics 68.25–69.3 (not in DK).

23. Diogenes Laertius, *Lives of the Philosophers* 8.56 (= DK 14, 5).

24. See O'Brien (1968).

25. More precisely, perishing is "being separated apart" (**13.17**, sec. 3). Specifically, the destruction of a compound such as an animal is the (not necessarily complete) separation apart of some or all of its component parts (its limbs, tissues, etc . . . and the Basic Ingredients of which they are composed). For the difference between "separation apart" and "separation off," see below p. 222.

26. For these examples, see **14.75** and **14.109**.

food is digested, the (invisible) blood in it becomes (visible) blood in us by a process of separation and mixture. A similar account holds for qualitative changes. When hot food cools, it is not because the hot in it perishes and there comes to be cold which previously did not exist. There was cold already in the hot food, but in an amount too small to be perceptible. Cooling is a process in which the imperceptible cold becomes perceptible and the perceptible hot imperceptible. At another level, things like chairs are assembled (that is, they come to be) out of more fundamental entities: pieces of wood, nails, and so forth, and they can be disassembled (perish) back into their component parts.

The same kind of account holds for natural objects such as the sun, stars, and animals as well. Here again generation is not from what-is-not, but from things that are: more fundamental things, which ultimately are composed of what I call Basic Ingredients. Such events are not genuinely generation and perishing, but further examples of mixing and separation of already existing things.

Thus Anaxagoras accepts the Parmenidean conditions that existing things (which for Anaxagoras include "things" like hot and cold) are permanent and that change cannot involve coming to be or perishing. He posits a plurality of Basic Ingredients, and he assumes that motion is possible. It is plausible to interpret his theory as a response to Parmenides' challenge which takes these starting points. Anaxagoras escapes coming to be and perishing and he accounts for all possible changes by positing a vast number of different kinds of things and by developing an elaborate theory of matter which accounts for the phenomena we observe in the world around us and for the origin of the *kosmos* itself without violating this basic thesis of Parmenides.

Entities and Principles of Anaxagoras's System

Anaxagoras's accounts of the origin of the *kosmos* and of the nature of mind and matter are intimately related and inseparable from one another. They are founded on five kinds of entities and six basic principles. The five kinds of entities are

- Objects and their parts
- Basic Ingredients
- Portions
- Seeds
- Mind

The six principles are the following.

P1. There is no coming to be or perishing.
P2. There are many (perhaps unlimitedly many) different types of Basic Ingredients.
P3. There is a Portion of everything in everything.

P4. Each thing is most plainly those things of which it has the largest Portions.

P5. There are no smallest Portions.

P6. Mind (*nous*) is unmixed with other things and has the following functions: (a) it knows all things, (b) it rules all things, (c) it sets all things in order, and (d) it causes motion.

I shall discuss these entities and principles, and then sketch out the cosmogony and cosmology Anaxagoras based on them.

Entities

Objects and their parts. This category includes ordinary perceptible objects, such as a human being, the earth, and a lump of gold. Also included are the parts of such objects (my right arm, the Pacific Ocean, half of the lump of gold in question) and Portion-Parts (see below page 212). Also included are microscopic objects. The other kinds of entities are posited to account for the generation, existence, and behavior of these. Ordinary objects—including both organic differentiated things such as animals and also apparently uniform, homogeneous things such as a lump of gold—are "mixtures" of Basic Ingredients and Seeds (**13.4** section 1).

Basic Ingredients are the materials out of which macroscopic objects and their parts (also Seeds—see below) are composed. An animal is composed of flesh, blood, and bone (among other things), and these are Basic Ingredients. Perceptible qualities too, such as hot and cold, wet and dry, and colors and flavors, are Basic Ingredients. An animal is composed, then, not only of flesh, etc., but also of Basic Ingredients that endow it with qualities. I shall discuss Basic Ingredients at greater length below in connection with **P1** and **P2**.

The **Portion** of a Basic Ingredient (x) in something (y) is, roughly speaking, how much x there is in y. The Basic Ingredients can be considered as "kinds," "stuffs" and qualities, and the Portion of a Basic Ingredient as the amount or quantity of the Basic Ingredient. If there is more gold than water in an object, or more hot than cold, then the Portion of gold or of hot in it is larger than the Portion of water or cold. Anaxagoras does not make it clear how the sizes of Portions are measured—whether by weight or volume or by one or more other criteria. It is most helpful in understanding Anaxagoras to resist the thoughts that Portions can be separated (as all the bones of an animal can be gathered and separated from the rest of its parts) and that Portions are parts, pieces, or discrete bits (see discussion of **P3**, **P4**, and **P5** below). We would do well to think of liquids mixed together (neglecting their molecular structure) rather than mixtures like salt and pepper. One way of putting the point is that the Portion of x in y is not "how many" bits of x there are in y, but "how much" x.

When the Portion of one Basic Ingredient in something is large enough, that thing is said to be characterized by that Basic Ingredient. For example, a lump of gold is called gold and not iron not because it is pure gold but because it contains a sufficiently large Portion of gold and a sufficiently small Portion of iron.[27] Anaxagoras holds not only that an animal contains Portions of flesh, bone, and blood, but also that everything contains a Portion of *everything* (**P3**).[28] There are Portions of wood and diamond in a human and Portions of hot and wet in ice, although the smallness of these Portions makes them undetectable (**P4**). One of the most distinctive and difficult features of Anaxagoras's system is that each object no matter how small has Portions of everything, so that there are no actually occurring samples of pure substances (no cases where a Basic Ingredient is found without any Portions of other Basic Ingredients), and no end to the analysis of anything into Portions.

Seeds. The extant fragments mention Seeds just twice, once as existing "in all things that are being mixed together" (**13.4** section 1) and once as existing in the original mixture of all things prior to the beginning of the *kosmos* (**13.4** section 8). I suggest that the Seeds are different from both the Basic Ingredients and the Portions, that they are microscopic particles characterized by one or more Basic Ingredients (ingredients like earth and flesh and also ingredients like hot and cold) which are too small to be seen (see **13.1** section 3). They occur in all macroscopic objects. By **P3**, each Seed contains a Portion of everything.

For Anaxagoras's doctrine of **Mind**, see the discussion of **P6** below.

Anaxagoras is committed to separable, countable objects both macroscopic and microscopic. Macroscopic objects include things, such as a lump of gold, a pint of blood, or a bone, which appear to be uniformly constituted of a single Basic Ingredient. They also include non-uniform entities, such as animals, which are obviously constituted of more than one Basic Ingredient (for example, bone, flesh, and blood). One of Anaxagoras's principal innovations is his insistence that apparently uniform objects no less than apparently non-uniform objects are constituted of more than one Basic Ingredient—in fact every object is constituted of all kinds of Basic Ingredients (**P3**).

Anaxagoras also holds that there are microscopic objects, that in fact there is no smallest object, no minimum possible size (**13.1** section 2). These microscopic objects have the same structure as the macroscopic objects, that is, however small one of them is, it is constituted of all kinds of Basic Ingredients. Among the microscopic objects are what Anaxagoras calls "Seeds." So little information is preserved about these "Seeds" that it is unclear whether Anaxagoras acknowledged other microscopic objects, such as might result from dividing and subdividing an object, for example a lump of gold, to the point where the resulting pieces are too small to be seen. He is also committed to nonseparable,

---

27. Here I follow Barnes (1979, vol. 1, 33 / 1982: 339).

28. Mind is the sole exception to this rule (**13.12** secs. 1–4).

noncountable amounts of the Basic Ingredients—the Portions. I shall say more about the nature and interrelations of these types of entities in connection with **P1** and **P6**, but first I shall give a rough illustration of how Anaxagoras viewed the structure of an ordinary macroscopic object.

According to Anaxagoras when we eat a piece of bread it nourishes the body; some of it becomes bone and is added to our bones, some becomes blood and increases (or repletes) the amount of blood, and so forth. Bread can undergo these transformations because it contains some bone, some blood, and so forth. It does not contain small bones or pieces of bone, but some amount of bone, what Anaxagoras calls Portions of those Basic Ingredients. The transformation of bread into bone and other Basic Ingredients of which the body is composed does not involve the bread's ceasing to exist and bone's coming into being as a genuinely new substance (which would violate the Parmenidean requirement, which Anaxagoras accepts, that there is no genuine coming to being or perishing). Instead these changes are explained in terms of the existing Portions of the Basic Ingredients that are present in the original piece of bread. The process of digestion makes manifest some of the Basic Ingredients that are not manifest in the piece of bread. Not all of them: wood is not a product of digesting the bread, but since there is a Portion of everything in everything, there is a Portion of wood in the bread too. However, when the animal dies, it can happen that the process of decay has as products materials that can nourish the growth of trees. Anaxagoras accounts for that possibility in the same way: the animal's body contains Portions of those materials, and those materials contain Portions of wood. But from where did the animal get those Portions? Clearly from the food it ate. Thus the food contains Portions of wood too. (On this point see 13.27 below.) In order to account for all possible changes, both direct and indirect, Anaxagoras posits that everything contains Portions of everything. Every macroscopic object, therefore, contains Portions of all the Basic Ingredients. The appearance of the object is determined by the Basic Ingredients of which it contains the largest Portions. If the object undergoes certain kinds of processes (for example, digestion) different Basic Ingredients become manifest. The same holds for microscopic objects, including Seeds. No matter how small an object is, it contains Portions of all Basic Ingredients, and any of these Portions can undergo processes that make manifest its Basic Ingredient. This theory raises a number of questions which I shall take up in considering the basic principles of the system.

P1. There is no coming to be or perishing. (13.17) Anaxagoras accommodates the Parmenidean ban on generation and perishing, explaining that what ordinarily pass for generation and perishing are cases of mixture and separation of things that already are and will continue to be. This is true uncontroversially for things like tables, which are made by fastening together ("mixing" in a certain way) pieces of wood, glue, and other materials that already exist.

Anaxagoras claims it also holds for plants and animals, which come from seeds[29] containing all the materials (blood, flesh, etc., or bark, sap, etc.) found in the mature individual and which grow by assimilating the same sorts of materials from the nutrients the plant or animal ingests. This view is found in the following passage and in **13.27**.

> **13.26**   In the same seed there are hairs, nails, veins, arteries, sinews, and bones. They are unapparent because of the smallness of their Portions, but as they grow they gradually separate apart. "For how," he says, "could hair come to be from what is not hair or flesh from what is not flesh?"[30] He made these claims not only for bodies but also for colors. For black is in white and white is in black.[31] He posited the same for weights, supposing that light is mixed with heavy and vice versa.
>
> (Scholium on Gregory Nazianzus, *Patrologia Graeca* vol. 36, col. 911 = DK 59B10)

The same also holds for other kinds of changes: from hot to cold, from black to white, and from light to heavy (**13.8**, **13.26**), and also for changes in substance: from bread to hair and flesh (**13.10**). It remains to explain how these changes take place. What actually goes on when a Basic Ingredient that is not manifest in the original object becomes manifest? I will take up this problem in discussing **P4**.

P2. There are many (perhaps unlimitedly many) different types of Basic Ingredients. By Basic Ingredients I mean roughly what corresponds to Empedocles' four elements, even though Anaxagoras's system leaves no room for actually occurring true elements (see the discussion of **P3**). A survey of the fragments yields the following list of Basic Ingredients.

- wet and dry (**13.4** section 8, **13.12** section 12, **13.15**)
- hot and cold (**13.4** section 8, **13.8**, **13.12** section 12, **13.15**)
- bright and dark (**13.4** section 8, **13.12** section 12)
- dense and rare (**13.12** section 12, **13.15**)
- *aēr*, *aithēr* (**13.1** section 4, **13.2** section 1, **13.12** section 10)
- earth (**13.4** section 8, **13.16** sections 1–2)
- cloud, water, stones (**13.16** section 2)
- hair, flesh (**13.10**)

---

29. Aristotle, *Generation of Animals* 4.1 763b30 = DK 59A107. Anaxagoras was interested in questions of biology, including reproduction, but we do not know enough about his views on these matters to be able to say whether he thought of human sperm as being a Seed in his technical sense of the word.

30. This quotation is **13.10**.

31. See **13.33**.

Anaxagoras also speaks of Seeds as ingredients of objects.

- in all things that are being mixed together there are many things of all kinds and seeds of all things with all kinds of shapes and colors and flavors (**13.4** section 1)

The items Anaxagoras mentions reveal his intellectual heritage and his determination to embrace it and to go beyond. The pairs of opposites represent his Milesian forebears—*aēr, aithēr*[32] and earth, along with clouds, water, and stone are reminiscent of Anaximenes (**6.2**). Hair and flesh mark a departure from tradition. These examples suggest a range of things which others had not considered basic. The testimonia mention other Basic Ingredients, including gold, bone, veins, sinews, fingernails, feathers, horn, wood, bark, and (surprisingly) fruit.[33] Further, on the interpretation of Seeds given above (page 202), colors, flavors and possibly shapes (thus, presumably, all perceptible qualities) are yet other Basic Ingredients. Anaxagoras seemingly gives equal billing to all perceptible properties, a novel extension of the Milesian tendency to treat "the hot" and "the cold" as entities.

Aristotle several times discusses Anaxagoras's "elements."[34] The most important passage for present purposes is the one that identifies these "elements" as "the homoeomeries and the opposites,"[35] terms which cover all the Basic Ingredients listed above. In presenting his own physical theory Aristotle defines homoeomeries[36] (literally, "similar part") as "things whose part is synonymous with the whole."[37] In Aristotle's theory, earth, bone, and gold are homoeomeries.[38] Any part of a mass of earth or a lump of gold or a bone is also called earth or gold or bone. By contrast, in non-homoeomerous substances, such as faces

---

32. Aristotle (*On the Heavens* 3.3 302b4–5 = DK 59A43) says that Anaxagoras used this word for "fire," but I suspect that this is Aristotle's conjecture.

33. Simplicius, *Commentary on Aristotle's Physics* 27.14 = DK 59A41and 460.16–19 = DK 59A45, quoted below in **13.27**.

34. Although the notion of element is alien to Anaxagoras's system (see below p. 209), Aristotle can perhaps be forgiven for employing it.

35. Aristotle, *Physics* 1.3 187a25 = DK 31A46. Aristotle more often says just that the homoeomeries are Anaxagoras's elements: *Physics* 3.4 203a20–22 = DK 59A45; *On the Heavens* 3.3 302a31–32 = DK 59A43; *On Generation and Corruption* 1.1 314a17–19 = DK 59A46.

36. Singular, "homoeomery"; the adjective is "homoeomerous."

37. Aristotle, *On Generation and Corruption* 1.1 314a20 = DK 59A46.

38. For some purposes Aristotle distinguishes "elements" (earth, water, air, and fire) from homoeomeries. In these contexts, the homoeomeries are *non-elemental* homoeomeries. Some commentators have wrongly fixed on this special usage; the more general use is needed to account for the examples in Anaxagoras's fragments.

or trees, there are parts (the nose, the roots) that are not called by the same name as the whole.[39] It is almost certain that Anaxagoras did not use the words "homoeomery" or "homoeomerous," and it is likely that Aristotle coined them[40] and applied them to those Anaxagorean Basic Ingredients which in Aristotle's theory are homoeomeries.[41] Since, as P3 implies, there are no true homoeomeries in Anaxagoras's system, Aristotle's use of the term has caused confusion.[42]

The other type of Basic Ingredients according to Aristotle is "the opposites." This term covers the pairs "wet and dry," etc . . . listed above. 13.4 section 1 mentions "Seeds of all things, having all kinds of forms and colors and flavors." On my interpretation of Seeds, 13.4 section 1[43] commits Anaxagoras to yet more Basic Ingredients, which from Aristotle's point of view also come under the heading of "the opposites." For Aristotle, all colors are mixtures of the opposites black and white. Likewise, flavors are mixtures of the opposites sweet and bitter.[44] 13.4 section 1 also mentions "forms," which Anaxagoras probably intends in the sense of "shapes,"[45] but shapes are harder to fit into this account. Anaxagoras may have considered them to be mixtures (in some sense) of straight and round, which might be thought opposites, but he may not be claiming that shapes are among the Basic Ingredients. 13.4 section 1 may only be saying that

---

39. The distinction is first set out clearly by Plato (*Protagoras* 329d [not in DK]), though he does not use the word "homoeomerous."

40. Guthrie (1965: 325).

41. The occurrence of the term "homoeomeries" in this context therefore means "what we Aristotelians call homoeomeries"; it does not mean "what Anaxagoras called homoeomeries" or even "what Anaxagoras believed to be homoeomerous as *we Aristotelians* use the term." It would be wrong to attribute to Anaxagoras—on the basis of the testimony of Aristotle or from the passages of Simplicius, which make the same point (*Commentary on Aristotle's* Physics 460.4–10 = DK 59A45; 27.4–7 = DK 59A41; 27.23–28 = DK 60A5; 65.1–3 = DK 59B3; 155.24–26 = DK 59B1; 156.9–13 = DK 59B5)—any theory of the structure of matter, in particular a "principle of homoeomereity," that "things (namely, "things" like a lump of gold or a clod of earth) are made of parts that are like one another and are also like the whole. These parts are the elements out of which all things are made" (Kerferd [1969]: 491).

42. One way of explaining Aristotle's point is to say that in using these terms to describe Anaxagoras's theory he is employing their denotations, not their connotations.

43. The Greek of 13.4 sec. 1 is tantalizingly ambiguous. It can mean that there are (a) (1) many things of all kinds and (2) Seeds of all things—Seeds which have all kinds of forms, all kinds of colors, and all kinds of flavors; or (less likely) (b) (1) many things of all kinds and (2) Seeds of all things—Seeds which have all kinds of forms, (3) colors, and (4) flavors. It cannot mean that there are (c) (1) many things of all kinds, (2) Seeds of all things, and (3) all kinds of forms, (4) colors, and (5) flavors. I assume that if a Seed can have a particular color or flavor, then that color or flavor is a Basic Ingredient.

44. Aristotle, *On Sense and Sensible Objects* 3–4 (not in DK).

45. The Greek word is *idea*.

the *Seeds* have shapes (which they must have, since they have spatial extension). However this issue is decided, Aristotle's testimony on the types of Anaxagoras's Basic Ingredients confirms the evidence of the fragments.[46]

It sounds odd to modern ears that qualities ("the opposites") should be put on the same footing as substances. (Aristotle, who first clearly distinguished substances from qualities, would agree with us.) But here Anaxagoras continues the Milesian tradition of considering opposites as principles.[47] He views an object, say, a hot lump of gold, as a lump which is, say, gold, hot, heavy, yellow, dry, etc. It contains gold but also hot, heavy, yellow, dry, etc. (I neglect for the moment the complications introduced by **P3**.) The way the lump appears is determined by the Basic Ingredients which predominate in it (**P4**). This way of looking at things is interestingly different from our own and is a conceivable view for Anaxagoras to have proposed.[48] Indeed, it has some plausibility. If we point out that hot is never found by itself, he will agree: in hot, as in everything else, there is a Portion of everything (by **P3**). Still, we might say, there are independently identifiable pieces of bread, earth, and gold, but not so for pieces of hot. Anaxagoras has a reply to this attack too: true, hot is never found except as a hot piece of bread or gold, etc. But equally bread is never found without being hot or cold or some mixture of the two. Just as qualities are not found except in conjunction with substances, so substances are not found without qualities. It is misleading, then, to identify a certain body simply as a lump of gold, on the grounds that gold predominates. The gold has a certain color, texture, shape, temperature, etc., so a full description of it will acknowledge the predominance not only of gold but also of dense, cold, etc. Presumably this is the reason for the plural ("things") in **13.12** section 16.

It would be unwise and also alien to the spirit of Presocratic thought to attempt a complete enumeration of Basic Ingredients. Aristotle asserts that they are infinitely or unlimitedly many,[49] which would indeed follow if Anaxagoras acknowledged all *possible* shapes or colors as Basic Ingredients.

---

46. Some (e.g., Vlastos [1950/1975], Schofield [1980], and Inwood [1986]) hold that the opposites are the only Basic Ingredients out of which everything else including the "homoeomeries" are made. This admittedly simpler interpretation is bought at the price of both rejecting the Aristotelian evidence which supports the present interpretation and overlooking or discounting the evidence in Anaxagoras's fragments that *aēr*, *aithēr*, earth, hair, etc . . . have the same standing as hot, cold, etc.

47. See above pp. 45–46.

48. After Aristotle such a view could not be proposed without an elaborate metaphysics to justify it, but there is no reason why the theory could not have been put forward in the fifth century, before distinctions had been made between substance and attribute and between essence and accident and before the issues had been raised explicitly that led to those distinctions.

49. Aristotle, *Metaphysics* 1.3 984a13 = DK 59A43.

However, not all entities belong at this level. The sun, moon, and stars are fiery stones.[50] Some things, such as humans and animals, are "compounded"[51] of these Basic Ingredients (**13.4** section 2). Cities and "works" (both are mentioned in **13.4** section 3) will be constructed out of the Basic Ingredients in yet different ways.

P3. There is a Portion of everything in everything (**13.6** section 2, **13.11**,[52] **13.12** sections 1, 3; see also **13.8**). By this oft-repeated claim Anaxagoras asserts that there is *some amount* of everything in everything. There is some flesh in bread, some gold in lead, some hot in ice, etc. This is not to say that a piece of ice contains a hot spot, that it is always possible to isolate or identify Portions, only that they are there—like a drop of black paint mixed uniformly throughout a bucket of white paint.[53]

This claim provides for all possible changes. When a hot object becomes cold, the cold does not come into existence (**P1** rules this out) but was already in the object and/or in the environment. The cooling of an object is the concentration of cold in it to the point that the cold overpowers the hot (see discussion of **P4** below); likewise for substantial change.

> **13.27**   Seeing that everything comes to be from everything—if not immediately, at least in sequence (for air comes from fire, water from air, earth from water, stone from earth, and fire again from stone, and when the same food, such as bread, is assimilated, many things of different kinds come to be: flesh, bones, veins, sinews, hairs, nails, and in some cases feathers and horns, and like grows by means of like)—for these reasons he supposed that in the food, even in water if trees are nourished by this, are wood, bark, and fruit. This is why he claimed that all things are mixed in all things.
> (Simplicius, *Commentary on Aristotle's* Physics 460.12–19 = DK 59A45)

Since Simplicius seems to have had access to Anaxagoras's book, there is every reason to accept his account as faithful to Anaxagoras's thought. **13.27** settles two issues which have provoked a great deal of discussion. First, the charge that

---

50. Hippolytus, *Refutation of All Heresies* 1.8.6 = DK 59A42.

51. The term "compounding" is not restricted to organic entities like animals but seems to be synonymous with "separating off," which describes the formation of macroscopic pieces of Basic Ingredients. The formation of earth out of water is "compounding" in **13.16** sec. 1 and "separating off" in **13.16** sec. 2.

52. Mind is the sole exception. See the discussion of **P6**, below.

53. This doctrine does not commit Anaxagoras to a view that there are countable or discrete Portions or particles of flesh in bread, a view that would conflict with **P5**. Like Empedocles (see below pp. 262–63), Anaxagoras does not seem to have been concerned with the ultimate structure of matter, but possibly unlike Empedocles Anaxagoras has a theory that is inimical to there being *any* ultimate structure.

Anaxagoras's theory is *uneconomical*. Since our experience reveals that a given substance can become only a limited number of other things (cheese can become bone and blood, but not chalk), we might suppose that it would be preferable for Anaxagoras to hold that it contains Portions of only *some* things, not of everything.[54] The reply to this charge is twofold. (a) As **13.27** shows, Anaxagoras was concerned to account not only for the changes the cheese undergoes but also for subsequent changes. Some of the bread we eat becomes flesh, but some is excreted with our wastes and can fertilize the earth and so, as nourishment for a tree it can become wood. To cover all such possibilities he postulated a Portion of everything in everything. (b) To investigate all the possible changes of any particular thing would be a very difficult task, quite unlike any research undertaken by any previous Presocratic. Moreover, it is neater, more memorable, and intellectually more (not less) economical simply to make the general pronouncement "a Portion of everything."

Second, **13.27** determines the scope of the two occurrences of "everything" in **P3**. They do not cover all entities: it is implausible to hold that Anaxagoras meant that, say, a rosebush contains a Portion of an octopus. The most plausible interpretations of **P3** in the context of Anaxagoras's theory are that it means that there is a Portion of every Basic Ingredient in every actually occurring entity. That "the opposites" are in everything has not to my knowledge ever been doubted and is confirmed by **13.8**. **13.27** makes it clear that Basic Ingredients like flesh, that are not "opposites" are in everything too. [55]

A corollary of **P3** is that it is impossible to purify anything completely, so no pure substances are found in nature. Any piece of flesh has Portions of all Basic Ingredients—and this is true no matter how small a piece we take. Anaxagoras took this point seriously, as **P5** shows.

It follows that there is no place in Anaxagoras's system for actually occurring elemental or pure substances,[56] and on this point his theory is different from modern chemistry, which holds that impure substances—iron ore, for example— are combinations of pure substances (iron, oxygen, etc.) and that it is possible in theory to isolate samples of these pure substances, that it is possible to give a precise account of a thing's composition in terms of the pure substances that constitute it (so much pure iron, so much pure oxygen, etc.). For Anaxagoras, though, there are no components of this sort. **P3** implies that no such thing as pure gold, water, or blood ever actually occurs, and even in theory there cannot be any such thing. Analysis of a lump of flesh or gold is in a sense

---

54. Cornford makes this thesis the basis of his interpretation of Anaxagoras' theory (Cornford [1930/1975]).

55. On the interpretations of Cornford and Vlastos, Anaxagoras holds that there is a Portion of every *opposite* in every *thing* (Cornford [1930/1975], Vlastos [1950/1975]).

56. Aristotle is thus wrong to say that the homoeomeries and the opposites are "elements" for Anaxagoras (references in p. 206 n. 41 above).

pointless, since at every stage we still have Portions of everything. As he says "things . . . are not separated from one another nor are they split apart with an axe" (**13.8**).

This last consideration points to a potential awkwardness. If flesh and gold both have Portions of everything in them, what makes flesh different from gold? Alternatively, if there is no difference between flesh and gold, Anaxagoras fails to account for the diversity of things in the world, which is a serious flaw in a pluralist of his sort. He addresses these issues in **P4**.

P4. Each thing is "most plainly those things that are present in the greatest amount" (**13.12** section 16), that is, of which it has the largest Portions. Although (by **P3**) there are no instances of pure substances, we identify a macroscopic[57] piece of gold as gold, or a bone as bone because of the Basic Ingredients of which it contains the most. There is more gold (a larger Portion of gold) in a piece of gold than there is in water (although by **P3** there is a Portion of water in the piece of gold too). The word "most" points to a quantitative view. A lump of gold is identified as gold because it contains more gold than anything else—as if it were made, perhaps of 60 percent gold and 40 percent everything else, or perhaps 40 percent gold and 60 percent everything else, but with each other ingredient constituting less than 40 percent of the total. This is not to commit Anaxagoras to the view—which **P5** denies—that all the gold could be isolated, or to the view that there are smallest particles of gold and other Basic Ingredients in the lump. As I noted above, (page 201) Anaxagoras does not explain how to measure the size of Portions.

This move, though intuitively plausible, requires careful treatment. First, it must account for the properties of the lump, which is not only gold but also heavy, yellow, dry, and (at a given moment) cold.[58] Anaxagoras will say that the lump contains more heavy than light, more yellow than other colors, etc. It would be difficult or impossible to place all the properties of the lump of gold, including its being gold, on a single balance sheet which totals to 100 percent, but this is perhaps not a serious objection. Anaxagoras might be content with saying simply that it is yellow because it contains more yellow than any competing quality (where the competitors of yellow are the other colors), and likewise for the rest of its properties. In the case of opposites, there is only one competitor.

---

57. There can of course also be bits of gold (i.e., bits in which there is more gold than other Basic Ingredients) too small to be seen. I take it that **P4** offers an account of macroscopic objects which can be applied straightforwardly to microscopic ones.

58. Gold can change in many of its properties. For example, it can change from cold to hot. It can even be melted and so become wet, while still remaining gold. Failure to account adequately for this consideration vitiates some interpretations of Anaxagoras, notably those of Cornford and Vlastos, in which the nature of other things than the opposites is determined by the relative proportions of the opposites occurring in them (Cornford [1930/1975]: 311, Vlastos [1950/1975]: 338).

Second, what does it mean to say that a lump of gold is composed chiefly of gold? If gold is that which is composed chiefly of gold, then to say that a lump of gold is composed chiefly of gold amounts to saying that it is composed chiefly of that which is composed chiefly of gold. And this puts Anaxagoras on the path to an infinite regress: gold turns out to be that which is composed chiefly of that which is composed chiefly of that which is composed chiefly of. . . . And the same is true for any other substance, such as flesh or bone. But then an even worse result follows. All things turn out to be the same: flesh and blood and hot and cold, as well as gold prove to be that which is composed chiefly of that which is composed chiefly of. . . . To solve this problem, it has been suggested[59] that Anaxagoras means that an (impure) lump of gold has (pure) gold in it. Of course P3 implies that pure gold does not actually exist, but this is not a contradiction, for Anaxagoras need not hold that pure or elemental gold actually exists or could in theory be separated out from actually existing impure gold. It is enough if he treats it as what might be called a factor of analysis (as an economist treats supply and demand, not thinking that they can exist separately but finding it desirable to treat them separately for purposes of analyzing complex actual phenomena).

What, then, *is* gold, apart from its perceptible properties? One answer is: nothing—gold is just its perceptible properties; identify all the thing's perceptible properties and there is nothing more to identify.[60] Another answer is: something—gold is not identical with any or all of its perceptible properties; they can change (the gold can be heated or cooled, melted, painted another color, etc.), but the gold persists.[61] It is clear from the discussion of **P2** that Anaxagoras favors the second reply. Basic Ingredients include substances like gold as well as perceptible properties, and Anaxagoras's theory covers changes in substance as well as changes in quality.[62]

P4 implies that change is a matter of reconstitution. When x ceases to be (an) F and comes to be (a) G the Basic Ingredients which make x be (a) G come to predominate over those that make it be (an) F. How this happens is obscure. Since (by **P5**) there are no smallest Portions, change cannot occur through rearrangement of smallest particles. It must therefore be due to processes that concentrate smaller Portions. For example, in digestion the bone, flesh, etc. which are in a piece of bread but not present in large enough Portions to be visible, are "brought out" so as to become the dominant elements in certain smaller parts,

---

59. This suggestion as well as the regress argument is due to Strang (1963/1975).

60. This is the view of Vlastos (1950/1975: 337).

61. Descartes considers a ball of wax: all of its sensible qualities can change into their opposites when it is heated, and yet it remains wax (R. Descartes, *Second Meditation*).

62. Regarding the further question of what relation gold has to its properties— whether, for example, some properties are essential, so that if *they* change, the gold does not remain gold—there is nothing in the evidence to indicate that it occurred to Anaxagoras.

so that they are expressed as bone and flesh, and added to the bone and flesh already found in our bodies.

The ancient evidence is silent on this subject, but one way to account for this phenomenon is to suppose that the Portion of a given Basic Ingredient in an object is spread throughout the object. (This is actually required by the theory, since if a bone is broken into pieces, there will need to be Portions of every Basic Ingredient in each piece in order to account for all possible changes that that piece may directly or indirectly undergo.) But there is no need for it to be spread uniformly throughout the object. After all, we can reasonably suppose that the fact that in a lump of gold the Portion of water is smaller than the Portion of gold involves there being a smaller concentration of water than gold in any given place. And if different Basic Ingredients can be present in an object in different concentrations, it is reasonable to suppose that a single Basic Ingredient can be more or less concentrated in different parts of the object. The process of digesting bread, then, will make bone manifest by rearranging the concentration of bone so that it becomes dominant in some parts.

I suggest that the Seeds play a role in this process. The bread contains Seeds of bone, flesh, and all other Basic Ingredients (13.4 section 1), microscopic bits of bone, flesh etc . . . which will develop into macroscopic pieces of bone, etc . . . if provided with the appropriate ingredients and environment. In effect, they are focal points for accretion from which macroscopic amounts of bone, etc . . . can grow. Growth takes place through the process of digestion, which somehow rearranges the Portions of Basic Ingredients that are not dominant in the food, so that they become manifest and accrete to the appropriate kinds of Seeds (on the principle of "like to like"[63]), with the result that more bone is added to the Seed of bone, and the Portion of bone in what is left of the bread becomes correspondingly smaller.

I will refer to the additional amount of a Basic Ingredient that becomes manifest as the result of some such process as a Portion-Part. Unlike Portions, Portion-Parts are actual physical constituents of a macroscopic object—not of the original object (there is a Portion of bone in a piece of bread, but no Portion-Part of bone), but of a different object, whether this is an object already in existence before the change in question (in the way that digesting food leads to growth of already existing bones) or an object that comes into existence as the result of a change (as salt is formed by evaporating sea water).

This view of change goes only so far. It accounts for why one thing (or, in the case of food, *part* of one thing) can turn into another, but Anaxagoras owes us an account, or rather an *accounting*, of what happens to the Portions dominant in the original thing. Consider a simplification of what happens when we eat bread.[64] Some bread turns to bone, some to flesh, and the rest becomes bodily

---

63. For the importance of this principle in Anaxagoras' system, see below p. 222.

64. The example is taken from 13.27. For the purposes of the example we should take bread, bone, etc . . . to be Basic Ingredients even if they seem unlikely candidates for Basic Ingredients.

wastes which we excrete. Anaxagoras accounts for its becoming bone and flesh by saying that there were Portions of bone and flesh in the bread to begin with. Conversely, he would say that in any Portion-Part of bone that results from the change, there is a Portion of bread that is smaller than the Portion of bone. The question he needs to face is what happens to *all* of the bread. On the account just given, the Portion of bread in the stuff that does not turn to bone or flesh should become even larger than previously. Digestion would resemble a kind purifying or concentrating. There is no possibility of reaching pure bread, bone, or flesh, but in the simplified account of the products of digestion that I have proposed, the result of digesting an amount A of bread would be on the one hand an amount B of flesh and an amount C of bone and an amount D of excrement, in which flesh, bone and excrement are respectively more concentrated than in the original amount of bread, and there is no bread left. There will be Portions of bread in the flesh, bone, and excrement that result from digesting the original bread, but since these Portions of bread are respectively smaller than the Portions of flesh, bone and excrement in B, C and D it seems that some of the original amount of bread has disappeared, in contravention of principle **P1**. In fact, **13.10** and **13.27** leave it unclear what happens to the excess bread.

Anaxagoras needs to explain not only how, when x becomes y (in the example, when bread becomes bone), what was formerly present in a smaller quantity (y) comes to be present in a larger quantity, but also how what was formerly present in the greatest quantity (x) comes to be present in a smaller quantity (compare **13.12** section 16). The theory is designed to account for the former phenomenon: the tiny amount of bone is added to the bones already in our body. But it does not do well for the former. A satisfactory explanation would have to satisfy Parmenides' requirement that there is no perishing into what is not. Unless we can solve this problem in a way that is consistent with Anaxagoras's theory, this must remain a serious weakness in it.

P5. There are no smallest Portions (**13.6** section 3 with **13.1** sections 1–2 and **13.3** section 1). **P5** is needed for **P3** to get off the ground. To simplify the discussion, suppose that there are only two Basic Ingredients, A and B. Then **P3** implies that in any object X no matter how small there is a Portion of A and a Portion of B. Suppose, further, that as the result of some process of concentrating or refining (as in the digestion and evaporation examples above) some of the A in the Portion of A is concentrated or refined to the point that it is expressed either in some part of X (as in the case of digestion, where some of the Portion of bone originally in the bread is added to the bones already in the animal) or elsewhere (as in the case of evaporation, where some of the Portion of salt in the seawater turns into lumps of salt where there was previously no macroscopic piece of salt). The amount expressed in this way is a Portion-Part of A; call this Portion-Part A_1. **P3** now guarantees that in A_1 there is a Portion of B. If some of the B in the Portion of B in A_1 is similarly concentrated so that it is expressed as a Portion-Part of B (call it B_1), **P3** guarantees that there is a Portion of A in B_1, and so on without limit. Any Portion in an object is less than the object, and so each time a Portion-Part is generated, the Portion of A that it contains is smaller than the Portion of A contained in the previous piece. But since there is no end to the sequence of changes that an object (and its successor Portion-Parts) can undergo and since each change produces smaller Portion-Parts of the original object than the previous one, if there is a lower limit to the size of Portion-Parts or Portions, Anaxagoras's system will founder. If there is a minimum size of Portion-Parts, principle **P3** cannot hold, and without **P3** his way to avoid generation out of what-is-not and perishing into what-is-not must fail.

P5 enables this sequence to continue without end. It guarantees that no matter how small a Portion of something may be, it can generate smaller Portion-Parts and no matter how small a Portion-Part is, it contains smaller Sub-portions, so that we never reach pure pieces of gold, flesh, etc. (see **13.6** section 3).[65]

I believe that **13.3** sections 1–2 contains an argument for **P5**. The argument is incomplete as it stands. Section 1 states the conclusion: "of the small there is no smallest but always a smaller," while section 2 states the premise: "for what-is cannot not be." This premise might well be used to prove that there must be a "smallest," on the grounds that after some point it is impossible to generate still smaller entities; in fact it was one of the arguments used by the fifth century atomists to prove the existence of indivisible atoms (see **16.11**). But this is not the conclusion Anaxagoras draws.

To make the argument go through for Anaxagoras I think it most plausible to bring in **P3**. Suppose we begin with an object X (say, a piece of bread) and that X has smallest Portions. Let the smallest Portion be a Portion of A (say, a Portion of gold) and call it A_1. It follows that there is no Portion smaller than A_1. Suppose now that X undergoes a process that leads to some of the A being expressed as a piece (Portion-Part) of A, which is of course smaller than X. **P3** implies that that piece of A contains Portions of all Basic Ingredients. Let B be one of these Portions, for example, the Portion of A. It follows that B is smaller than A_1. But this contradicts the supposition that A_1 is the smallest Portion of X. Therefore B cannot exist—it's too small. But "what-is (here, B) cannot not be" (section 2). Therefore, given **P3**, the assumption that X has smallest Portions has been shown to lead to a contradiction, and therefore, the hypothesis that X has smallest Portions must be abandoned.

The claim in **13.3** section 3 ("of the large there is always a larger"), can be proved by a related argument if we suppose again that the things under discussion are the Portions and Portion-Parts of a Basic Ingredient in an object (say, a

---

65. This interpretation does not commit Anaxagoras to a doctrine of the infinite physical divisibility of matter. In this respect I agree with Schofield (1980) and Inwood (1986) against the traditional view that the passages cited in support of **P5** imply a doctrine of infinite divisibility. If Anaxagoras's notion of Portions does not involve physically distinguishable parts, there is no need to introduce infinite divisibility into his system.

lump of gold). Here the claim will be that however close to a pure sample of any Basic Ingredient (in this case, gold) we are able to get by repeatedly subjecting it to a process of refining, we never reach a point where we have isolated all of the gold from the original lump.

In its context section 4 ("it [the large] is equal in amount to the small") cannot mean that the Portions of all Basic Ingredients in an object are equally large, since **P4** presupposes the possibility that they are not equally large. On the other hand, it makes perfectly good sense if interpreted as saying that there are as many Portions and Sub-portions of each Basic Ingredient in any object. The original object has one Portion of each Basic Ingredient; when it undergoes a change, the resulting products likewise each have one Portion of each. The sizes of the Portions may differ greatly relative to one another, but the number is equal. This equality is a presupposition of **P5**.

The fragment ends by saying "in relation itself, each is both large and small" (section 5).[66] One way to understand this assertion is to see it as claiming, for example, that the gold in a lump of gold is large (as in section 3) and also small (as in section 1): it constitutes a large Portion of the lump, but there is no lower limit to the size of the Portions of gold in the successive Portion-Parts of any other Basic Ingredient generated from the lump of gold.

Anaxagoras's doctrine that there are no smallest Portions can be seen as a response to Zeno's attack on division of anything into parts (see above pages 178–81). According to Zeno, if the division of a finite-sized object can be carried out infinitely, then the end products left when the division is completed will be infinite in number and will have either no size or positive size. But infinity times zero is zero, and infinity times any positive size no matter how small is infinite. Neither way do we get back to the original finite object. Anaxagoras denies that the process of analysis[67] will ever yield Portions of no size, for he accepts the Zenonian point that that would mean that what-is could cease to be (13.3 section 2). But that does not entail that the end products have positive size. Anaxagoras correctly sees that an infinite process of division is not like a very long process of division, that analyzing something into an infinite number of Portions is not like analyzing it into a very large number of very small Portions. "Of the small there is no smallest, but always a smaller," and "of the large there is always a larger" (**13.3** sections. 1 and 3). In both these statements the word "always" is meant

---

66. I accept the authenticity of **13.3** sec. 5, though some deny it.

67. By "analysis" I mean the manner of considering the Portions and Sub-portions of Basic Ingredients in a given entity. This is presumably a notional activity, unlike division, which (following Zeno) I intend as a physical activity of breaking up an object into separate parts. My thesis is that there are close similarities between Zenonian infinite division and Anaxagorean infinite analysis, that the difficulties Zeno raises for infinite division might be thought to apply to infinite analysis as well, but that Anaxagoras found a way to evade them—a way which can be also applied straightforwardly to cases of infinite division into separate parts.

seriously. An infinite process of division or analysis has no end; it cannot be completed. There *are* no end products, since however far the division or analysis proceeds it can always go farther. And at each stage we have a definite, finite number of parts or Portions, each with a definite, positive size or amount, and the parts or Portions if reassembled reconstitute the original thing (13.5). It appears, then, that Anaxagoras was the first to recognize one of the most important properties of the infinite and to build it into the foundations of his system.

The nature of this "response to Zeno" deserves a comment. Anaxagoras does not *refute* or *contradict* either of the limbs of Zeno's argument; rather he finds a way around them. Zeno's dilemma, that the end products have either no size or some positive size, is a false one, since there are no end products. I find it more plausible that Anaxagoras developed his doctrine of infinite divisibility after thinking about Zeno's arguments than that Zeno composed those arguments in response to Anaxagoras—since they would leave Anaxagoras's theory intact.

P6. The Nature of Mind (13.11, 13.12 sections 1 and 14). The special status of Mind is reflected in its principal functions: knowing, ruling, setting things in order, and causing motion. Unlike Empedocles' four elements (earth, water, air and fire), which have psychological as well as physical attributes, Anaxagoras's "things" are conceived in wholly physical terms. And unlike Empedocles' causes of motion Love and Strife, Anaxagoras's Mind is devoid of moral aspects. On the other hand, Mind is a thinker. For Anaxagoras, all changes are due to mixture and separation, which result from motion, and motion is ultimately caused by Mind. Mind's ability to cause motion in "things" is the basis of its power to put them in order and rule them. It rules them by putting them in order, and it puts them in order by causing them to move. It causes them to move in precisely the way they do because it is a thinking entity that desires certain ends and foresees how to accomplish them. This interpretation results from an examination of Anaxagoras's remarks on Mind.

Mind is the only exception to the principle "a Portion of everything in everything." 13.11 says that there are some things (inanimate things) that do not contain a Portion of Mind, and 13.12 sections 1 and 4 say that Mind is not mixed with anything else. So even in animate things, which do have a small amount of Mind (compare 13.12 section 15 with section 6), the Mind they possess is pure, with no Portions of anything else. Anaxagoras argues for the purity of Mind as follows (13.12 sections 1–4): Mind rules the way it does; if it were mixed with other things it could not do so; therefore, it is unmixed. To understand this argument we need to find out more about how Mind rules.

In the first place, Mind rules all things—animate things (13.12 section 6), the entire *kosmos*, and everything in it (13.12 sections 7–10). It can rule all things because it is always and everywhere, in all things (13.14)—even though it is not in them as a Portion that is mixed with their other constituent Portions—and is thus unlimited (*apeiron*) (**13.12** section 1) in time and space (being present in the unlimited amount of the surrounding multitude [**13.2**] as well as in the unlimited number of existing things). Further, since all Mind is alike (**13.12** section 15), it is unbounded (recall that *apeiron* means "unbounded" as well as "unlimited"—see above page 34) in that it has no internal boundaries: no part is different from another. Moreover, being unmixed with other things, it cannot be affected by other things and consequently it is in a condition to operate on all other things at any time.

I suggest that Mind's unique power of ruling is due to its unique purity and fineness **13.12** section 5). Anything else has positive size and contains limitless numbers of Portions and, potentially, limitless numbers of Portion-Parts of other Basic Ingredients. Since Mind is free of such extraneous baggage it can penetrate and permeate other things right through all their unlimited parts and Portions. Mind's unlimited spatial extent, its extreme fineness and its lack of mixture with other things suggest that Anaxagoras is striving toward the notion of immaterial existence.[68] He lacks the vocabulary and concepts to say that Mind is a pure immaterial force which acts on everything, everywhere. Still, in calling Mind "finest of all things" he is giving it a material attribute. He conceives of Mind as so fine that it penetrates and permeates other things and somehow causes them to move by its presence. Also, like Empedocles' Love and Strife, Anaxagoras's Mind is extended in space and must be physically present to something in order to affect it.

Despite this awkwardness, Anaxagoras was the first philosopher to distinguish clearly between the mover and the moved. Earlier thinkers had conceived of their originating principles as responsible simultaneously for both the material composition and the organization of the *kosmos*. Anaximenes' *aēr*, for example, is always in motion and so causes change, and Heraclitus's fire is somehow identical with soul, god, and the *Logos*.[69] By insisting that Mind is wholly unmixed with other "things" although physically present throughout them, Anaxagoras clearly distinguishes between what causes motion and what is moved—and this is a great conceptual advance. Even if it frequently happens that a material object causes motion, as when my hand makes a book move, the distinction between mover and moved is there, and the same applies even when something moves itself. When I cause myself to move, in a sense mover and moved are identical, but the two aspects of the self-mover can be distinguished in thought even if not physically. Anaxagoras believes that all motion of material things is ultimately traceable to the action of Mind (which is only barely material and which cannot move because, being everywhere, it has nowhere to go), and he would doubtless say that when I move myself, a more careful description of the event would make clear that my mind (the small part of the totality of Mind which is in me and constitutes me as a living, sentient and thinking being) is the mover and my material body is the moved. Thus, the basis of Mind's rule over all

---

68. According to Guthrie (1965: 276–78), followed by Curd (2007: 59) Anaxagoras's Mind is immaterial. According to others, it is material.

69. See above pp. 52, 65–66 and 136.

things is its power of causing them to move, and to move not in a random fashion but in a way that sets them in order (**13.12** section 10). *Diakosmein*, translated "set in order," is closely related to *kosmos*. Mind rules things by moving them so that they form a *kosmos*, an orderly, beautiful arrangement.

The final thing that needs to be accounted for is why Anaxagoras identifies the source of change as Mind rather than a vortex (as with the Atomists, see **16.39**) or some other mechanism. "Mind" (*nous*) is the word standardly used by philosophers for the highest form of reason,[70] so that it is found (if at all) only in humans among mortal creatures. Anaxagoras, however, believes that, as the following passage shows, plants have a certain amount of sensation and thought and feel pleasure and pain, and they possess a share of Mind as well.

> **13.28**   Anaxagoras and Empedocles say that these things [namely, plants] move because of desire. They declare that they have sensations too and feel both pain and pleasure. Anaxagoras said that they are animals [or, "that they have souls"] and that they feel pleasure and pain, using the fall of their leaves and their growth as <the basis of> his argument. Anaxagoras, Democritus and Empedocles held that plants possess mind and knowledge. Anaxagoras held that they also breathe.
>
> (Pseudo-Aristotle, *On Plants* 1.1 815a15–20,
> b16–17; 1.2 816b26 = DK 59A117)

Since he held that plants possess mind, he will doubtlessly have thought that animals do too. Now living things are sources of motion and change (even plants, which convert soil and water into roots, stems and leaves) so Anaxagoras will hold that those motions and changes are due to the activity of Mind. Thus, in identifying Mind as his universal cosmic principle of change, Anaxagoras chooses something already considered responsible for important changes in the sphere of humans and other living things. Since "all Mind is alike, both the larger and the smaller" (**13.12** section 15), that is, both the cosmic Mind and the mind of each living thing, we may infer properties of the cosmic Mind from the workings of living things.

The claim that Mind "has all judgment about everything" (**13.12** section 5) suggests strongly that it is not just a mechanical agent. This idea is strengthened even further by statements that Mind "knew all the things that are being mixed together and . . . separated off . . . and separated apart" (**13.12** section 9) and that Mind "set in order all things"—past, present and future (**13.12** section 10), which suggests that it knows all things in advance and brings about their ordering deliberately and with foresight. If so, we can better appreciate Mind's intellectual aspect. It produces motion and so causes things to change in ways it foresees and thus controls. With unparalleled power and omniscience Mind

---

70. E.g., Plato, *Republic* books 6–7, and Aristotle, *Metaphysics* 12.9 and *Posterior Analytics* 2.19. See also Fritz (1943) and Fritz (1945–46/1975).

brings about the regular and orderly results it desires, through the appropriate mechanical mixtures which it controls, so that the *kosmos* as it is now and has been and will be, is under Mind's control and is arranged as Mind wishes. That the cosmic Mind has desires may be inferred from the desires that humans experience by virtue of being possessed of a small Portion of Mind.

Once we speak of Mind as desiring, or as desiring particular states of affairs and bringing about events so as to achieve its desires, we are in the realm of teleology, in which the reason why something happens or is the case is that the resulting state of affairs is a goal, and events happen and things come to be in order to achieve that goal. It is easy to assume that Mind acts teleologically. According to Plato, Socrates made this assumption when he first learned of Anaxagoras's philosophy, but on reading Anaxagoras's book he soon found that the assumption was incorrect.

13.29   Once I heard someone reading out of a book by Anaxagoras, as he said, and saying that it turns out to be Mind that causes order and is the cause of all things. I was delighted at this account of causation, and I thought it was somehow good that Mind was the cause of everything, and I believed that if it is so, Mind in producing order puts all things in order and establishes each thing in whatever way is best. I thought I had found in Anaxagoras a teacher about causation in things who was after my own mind,[71] and <I thought> that he would tell me first whether the earth is flat or round and then would go on to explain in detail the cause and necessity, stating what was better and that it was better that it be like that. If he revealed this to me I was prepared never to desire any other kind of causation again. I was also prepared to find out in the same way about the sun and moon and the other stars, their relative speeds and turnings and other characteristics—how it is better that each of these act and be affected as they are. For I would never have supposed that after declaring that they are set in order by Mind he would have introduced any cause for them other than that it is best for them to be as they are.

So I thought that by assigning what is best for each of them as a cause for each he would explain what is best for each and the common good for all. And I would not have abandoned my hopes for a great deal, but taking the books with all haste I read them as quickly as I could in order to know as soon as possible what is best and what is worse. But, my friend, I was quickly deprived of this wonderful hope when as I proceeded to read I saw that the man did not make use of Mind at all and did not attribute to it any causation in putting things in order, but used as causes *aērs* and *aithērs* and waters and many other things as well that were out of place.

(Plato, *Phaedo* 97b–98c = DK 59A47)

Aristotle shares Socrates' disappointment. On the one hand he praises Anaxagoras's distinction between Mind and the matter on which it works.

---

71. *Nous*: a play on the word.

13.30   When someone said then that just as Mind is found in animals so it is found
         in nature as the cause of the world and of all its order, he seemed like a sober
         man in comparison with his predecessors who spoke at random. Anaxago-
         ras, we know, clearly maintained these views, but Hermotimus of Clazom-
         enae stated them earlier. Those who believed this posited as a principle of
         things that which is at the same time the cause of beauty and the kind of
         cause from which things acquire movement.
                                (Aristotle, *Metaphysics* 1.3 984b15–22 = DK 59A58)

The reference to beauty implies that Mind is a teleological as well as a motive
principle, though Aristotle says elsewhere that Anaxagoras was unclear on the
difference between thinking of Mind as the cause of movement and as a teleological principle.[72] On the other hand, however, like Socrates, Aristotle says that
Anaxagoras failed to make proper use of Mind as a cause.

13.31   They make hardly any use of their causes except to a small extent. For
         Anaxagoras uses Mind as a mechanism for the making of the *kosmos*, and
         when he is at a loss to say through what cause something necessarily is, then
         he drags Mind in, but in all other cases he makes anything rather than Mind
         the cause of what happens.
                                (Aristotle, *Metaphysics* 1.4 985a17–21 = DK 59A47)

Still, on the interpretation of Mind given above (pages 218–19), not only Plato's
Socrates but also Aristotle may be correct. The world is teleological overall, but
things happen mechanistically. Mind plans the orderly outcome of events and
foresees how to bring the outcome about. The means is mechanical: principally
the action of the vortex. But it is Mind that controls how fast it rotates and what
ingredients (Seeds, for example) are located in each region. In these circumstances we would expect there to be few remarks of a teleological nature and
most of the attention to be spent on the physical processes that lead to the formation of the *kosmos* around us.

   Whether or not Anaxagoras intended the teleological implications of making
Mind his principle of movement must remain an open question. Although Mind's
intellectual and directive powers may be manifested in a general supervision and
control of events in the *kosmos* and of the movements and changes found in living
creatures, the criticism of philosophers who had access to his work proves that he
made little or no use of these considerations in discussing the origins and working
of the world. Their verdict is borne out by what survives of his cosmogony.

---

72. Aristotle, *Metaphysics* 1.7 988b8–11 (not in DK)

Cosmogonic Mechanisms and Principles

Anaxagoras began his book[73] with the pronouncement "all things were together" (**13.1** section 1 and compare **13.4** section 7) in so complete a mixture that nothing was manifest in any part (**13.4** sections 7–8), perhaps not even the *aēr* and *aithēr* that dominated (see below page 225). For an object, or some part of the totality of all things, to be manifest, that is, for it to be perceived as having any definite characteristic, it must have a macroscopic size and contain a greater quantity of that characteristic than of anything else.[74] In the beginning, therefore, no macroscopic part of the mixture of all things had a sufficient concentration of any single "thing" for that "thing" to be manifest (**13.1** section 3). Nevertheless, all "things" (that is, Basic Ingredients) were in the mixture—the hot and the cold, earth, etc. (**13.4** section 8).

The beginning occurred when Mind, which permeated the mixture, initiated a rotational movement (**13.12** sections 7–8). Friends of the Eleatics will immediately object: "What need would have roused it, later or earlier, to grow?" (**11.8** lines 9–10). For if Anaxagoras is not to violate the Principle of Sufficient Reason, he needs to specify some feature of Mind itself or of the state of mixture of all things that accounts for why the rotation began at one time rather than another. There is no evidence on this matter, and it may well be that Anaxagoras simply took the inception of cosmic motion as an unexplained fact.[75]

The rotation began in a small area (**13.12** section 8). As time went on two things happened: (a) ever increasing expansion of the region in which the rotation occurs (**13.12** section 8), and (b) separation of identifiable things out of the mixture (**13.12** sections 11–12, **13.13** sections 1–2). Moreover, the mechanical process of rotation caused the separating to occur (**13.12** section 11, **13.13** section 3) by what we would call centrifugal or centripetal force (**13.9** sections 1–2, where the distinction between the speed and the force which the speed causes is noteworthy). Most likely the speed increased in proportion to the size of the revolving mass, since it is most reasonable to suppose that the original rotation not only occupied a small volume but also was slow. Anaxagoras believes in a cosmogonic vortex in which like is gathered to like. In this way, things were separated off from the indistinct mass of all things together and took on definite characters.

---

73. Simplicius, *Commentary on Aristotle's* Physics 155.26 = DK 59B1; 164.15 (not in DK); 460.26 = DK 59A45; *Commentary on Aristotle's* On the Heavens 608.21 (not in DK).

74. Or a greater quantity than that of any competitor. See above p. 210.

75. The ancient evidence on this point is indecisive. Simplicius reports that "Anaxagoras seemed to say that after all things were together *and at rest* [italics mine] for an unlimited earlier time, *kosmos*-making Mind, wishing to separate the forms (which he calls homoeomeries), put motion into them" (Simplicius, *Commentary on Aristotle's* Physics 1123.21-24 = DK 59A45).

This process doubtless worked similarly to other cases of change in which substances or qualities emerge out of others, such as digestion (see above page 212). Although in the beginning there were no sufficiently large concentrations of Basic Ingredients to form distinct macroscopic objects, there were microscopic concentrations—Seeds—of all Basic Ingredients (13.4 section 8).[76] The "like to like" effect of the vortex caused a rearrangement of the Portions[77] of Basic Ingredients in the whole indistinct mass so that some of the Seeds grew to have macroscopic size. Since the Portions of *aēr* and *aithēr* in the original mixture were the largest (13.1 section 5), there was more of them available than other Basic Ingredients to be added to the Seeds of their kind, and hence it seems that *aēr* and *aithēr* were the first distinguishable things to be separated out of the original mass. Other kinds of things were separated out of the residue of the original mass and out of the *aēr* or *aithēr* as the vortex motion continued to rearrange the Basic Ingredients present in their Portions.

Anaxagoras most frequently speaks of things "separating off" from the mixture, but he also says that they "separate apart," which does not appear to be just a synonym of the more common term (see 13.12 section 9). Perhaps "separating off" refers to the process by which one kind of thing emerges from a different kind of thing,[78] as flesh emerges from bread or as any "thing" emerges from the original mixture. By contrast, "separating apart" is used of the separation caused by the cosmic rotation (13.13 sections 2–3), in which things that result from the process come to occupy different locations. "Separating apart" is also used to describe perishing, where something composed of things "mixed together" is separated apart into its components (13.17).[79] The primary cosmogonic processes, then, are processes of separating—both qualitative and spatial, as we would expect, given the initial state in which all things were mixed together.

Anaxagoras also recognizes a tendency in the opposite direction. A number of places speak of "mixing together" (13.4 section 1, 13.12 section 9, 13.17 sections 2–3). In one place (13.4 section 1) "mixing together" appears to be a complementary description of separating off. When, say, bone is formed out of bread,

---

76. That the Seeds are unlike one another (13.4 sec. 8) is easily explained in terms of differences in their constituent Portions of Basic Ingredients. Infinite analyzability (cf. above p. 215 and n. 67) and the limitless possibilities of variation in the Portions of Basic Ingredients that are not manifest allow ample room for the differences mentioned. These relatively simple accounts of the original mixture and of Seeds are incompatible with the view that Anaxagoras's substances are homoeomerous in Aristotle's sense. Once this view is exploded (see above p. 206 n. 41), the present accounts become possible.

77. It may be more precise to say that the vortex caused a redistribution of the local density of the Portions. See above p. 212.

78. For "separation off" in Anaximander, see above p. 37.

79. This is not to suggest that there are for Anaxagoras any such things as ultimate, smallest components.

the distribution of the Portion of bone in the bread is altered to the point where some of it becomes locally dominant and accretes to one or more Seeds of bone to form an identifiable bit (Portion-Part) of the "thing" in question.

The other occurrences of the term, though, refer to the mixing together of different "things." 13.17 informs us that what we think is a case of coming to be is really a matter of being mixed together and that perishing is really a matter of being separated apart. In that this doctrine applies to the coming to be and perishing of Basic Ingredients like gold and flesh, the point is the same as already discussed. But 13.17 is presented as a general interpretation of coming to be and perishing, so it should apply to other kinds of entities as well. Thus in 13.4, humans and other living beings are said to be "compounded"—presumably, out of Basic Ingredients. The coming to be of a human, then, involves a "compounding" of flesh, bone, etc., and 13.17 requires us to see this "compounding" as a case of "mixing together."[80]

Anaxagoras recognizes mixing together as a process in the world, though he does not explain its relation to the primary processes of separating off and separating apart. In one sense, any separation involves mixture: the very fact that bread is "separated apart" into bone and other things entails that the Portions of bone and of other Basic Ingredients in the bread are re-mixed with Portions of other Basic Ingredients in ways that generate entities in some of which bone is dominant. 13.14 may contain a hint of how to understand this process. It speaks of separating off and also of "separating toward"—in the translation given here, this unusual compound is translated "have come together in the process of separating." It is possible that as different "things" are separated off or apart, the force of the motion throws them together in such a way that they join together and form a compound. Mixing together or "separating toward," then, would not be a different process, but a by-product of the two processes already identified. It would not necessarily take place at random or by chance, since the particular compounds that occur may have been foreseen, and therefore perhaps intended, by Mind, which is the ultimate cause of such compounds.

It is as well that Anaxagoras makes room for processes of combination. If separating off and separating apart were the only processes in the *kosmos*, it would be hard to explain many of the events taking place around us that obviously involve combination, so that the theory would be open to empirical objections. It might be vulnerable to a theoretical objection too. Separating off and separating apart are processes of differentiation—qualitative and spatial. If differentiation proceeds far enough, will things not become so distinct that the changes observed in the *kosmos*, the very changes Anaxagoras's system is designed to explain, can no longer to take place? The principle "a Portion of everything in everything" guarantees that differentiation is never complete. But the principle

---

80. Like "mixing together," "compounding" applies to Basic Ingredients as well as other entities (13.16 sec. 1).

"each single thing is and was most plainly those things that are present in the greatest amount" (**13.12** section 16) again leads to a difficulty. For as the processes of differentiation continue, each thing will come to have greater and greater quantities of what it is "most plainly," and correspondingly less of the others. In these circumstances it will presumably be increasingly difficult for the other things in it to be mixed together so as to be the greatest quantity in any part of the thing, so changes will become more difficult. A case in point can be taken from our present world. Bread can turn directly into bone, but not into gold.[81] Anaxagoras should account for this fact by saying that while there are equal numbers of Portions of flesh and gold in the bread, and although neither is present in sufficiently large an amount as to be visible, still the amount of flesh far exceeds that of gold. The Portion of flesh is far bigger than the Portion of gold. The more there is of one "thing" in another "thing," the easier it should be for the one to change into the other. So if differentiation is carried out far enough without any compensating combination, there is danger that the "things" in the *kosmos* will become separated off and separated apart so far, by the ever increasing force exerted by the ever increasing rotation, that change (aside from motion itself) will cease to occur. Mixture is needed, then, but we may wonder whether the mixtures that are merely byproducts of the primary processes of separation can be enough to stem the tide.

There are two ways Anaxagoras might have guaranteed that mixture continue. First, he might have denied these implications of the quantitative principle (**13.12** section 16), saying that as long as there is a Portion of everything in everything (that is, forever) it is possible to account for all the change we like. His answer here would depend on the explanation he gives of how it is possible for what is present in smaller quantities to come to be present in larger quantities.[82]

Second, he might have held that the amount of matter available for differentiation is unlimited in extent (not just in divisibility), so there is always more undifferentiated material being brought into play. He may well have believed that this was the case. **13.12** section 8 suggests that there is no limit to the volume of material available to undergo the rotatory movement that causes differentiation, and **13.2** section 2 can be taken as making this very point. But the interpretation of both passages is uncertain,[83] and the view under consideration would imply not only that the *kosmos* expands at the periphery but also that the matter at the periphery, as it becomes differentiated through the processes of separating out

---

81. The Portion of gold is too small for this to happen, but Anaxagoras leaves room for there to be a sequence of changes that begins with bread and ends with gold.

82. For difficulties in this area, see above pp. 213–14.

83. **13.2** sec. 2's "unlimited in amount" is Anaxagoras's normal way of referring to the property of infinite analyzability (cf. **13.6** sec. 1), and as for **13.12** sec. 8, anyone who knew Zeno would know that there can be a bounded infinite sequence, as in the Dichotomy argument (above pp. 181–82).

and separating apart, will be affected by the tendency of rotational movement to bring like to like. The vortex action will continually bring more freshly separated earth to the center. But there is no sign or any likelihood that Anaxagoras believed that this was happening.[84] It is therefore necessary to leave this issue unsettled, while acknowledging that it raises one or more difficulties for Anaxagoras's system as we know it.

Cosmogony

Mind initiated a rotatory movement, which caused a force (**13.9** section 2) which separated things off from the original mixture (**13.12** section 11) and separated them apart (**13.13** section 3). As time went on, the rotating area increased (**13.12** section 8), as apparently did the speed and consequently the force and the differentiation. At present the speed of the rotation is much faster than anything found on earth (**13.9** section 3).

13.1, which describes the beginning of the cosmogony, contains an apparent contradiction. In the beginning "*aēr* and *aithēr* dominated all things . . . the greatest ingredients . . . both in amount and in magnitude" (sections 4–5). But since "each single thing is and was most plainly those things that are present in the greatest amount" (**13.12** section 16) *aēr* and *aithēr* must have been apparent in the original mixture, and yet Anaxagoras insists that "nothing was manifest" (**13.1** section 3). I offer the following as a possible solution. In the Greek, the verb "dominated" (**13.1** section 4) is singular, though we would expect it to be plural as it has two subjects, *aēr* and *aithēr*. I suggest that *aēr* and *aithēr* are here treated together as a single subject: *aēr-and-aithēr*. Now if *aithēr* is hot, dry, rare, and bright, and if *aēr* is cold, wet, dense, and dark,[85] *aēr-and-aithēr* would not be marked by any of these qualities, nor would *aēr* or *aithēr* be distinguishable. The Portions of *aēr* and of *aithēr*, like the Seeds of all other Basic Ingredients, were so small in the original mixture as to be indistinguishable (**13.4** sections 7–8), though even so they were the largest ingredients (**13.1** section 5).[86] This is why they were presumably the first to separate off (**13.2** section 1)[87] and so become distinguishable.

---

84. I do not find it likely that it has to do with his views about other worlds (pp. 227–28 below). A connection with his alleged prediction of the fall of a meteorite would be more plausible, but the account of his explanation of meteorites (see **13.32**) seems to exclude this possibility.

85. See above p. 49.

86. See above p. 193 n. 4. The point holds even if **13.1** sec. 5 is not authentic, since it is implied in sec. 4.

87. That they were first to separate off may be supported by **13.2**, which Simplicius (*Commentary on Aristotle's Physics* 155.30 = DK 59B2) says came "a little after" **13.1**, which was the beginning of Anaxagoras's work (see above p. 221 n. 73). However, I hesitate to press

The vortex action will also have separated them apart, so that the lighter, drier, and brighter *aithēr* went toward the periphery and the heavier, moister, and darker *aēr* toward the center. The separating apart of the different constituents of the *kosmos* is also found in **13.15**, which as we would expect has the wet, cold, and dark moving to the center ("here") and their opposites to the periphery ("into the far reaches of the *aithēr*"). These processes still continue, with heavier things being separated off from lighter ones. Out of *aēr* (in the form of clouds) successively denser things are separated off by the force of the vortex (**13.16** sections 1–2).

An important exception to the rule that dense things move to the center is formed by the heavenly bodies which Anaxagoras conceives not as pure, light fire, but as fiery stones. It seems that the speed of the vortex is sufficient in some cases to pick up stones from the earth and whirl them round in the air. Probably only stones are compact enough to undergo this type of motion. Certainly a stone can be thrown upward farther than a handful of water or loose earth (compare with **13.16** section 3).

The gross structure of the *kosmos* is therefore efficiently explained by the vortex with its effects of separating off and separating apart. Moreover, Plato's and Aristotle's complaints (**13.29, 13.31**) are seen to be justified. Mind initiates movement, but afterwards mechanical explanations prevail.

Cosmology

It remains to look at a few of Anaxagoras's most interesting theories about the present world. Anaxagoras's notorious belief that heavenly bodies are masses of stone enabled him to explain meteorites—stones that fall from the sky.

13.32   A huge stone fell from the sky at Aegospotami. And it is still displayed, since the people of the Chersonnese revere it. It is said that Anaxagoras predicted that when there occurred a slip or shaking of the bodies fastened in the heaven, one of them would be torn off and be thrown down and fall. Each of the stars is not in its natural place, since they are made of stone and heavy and shine because of the resistance and breaking of the *aithēr*. They are dragged by force, held tight by the vortex and force of the rotation, as they were kept from falling to the earth at the beginning, when cold and heavy things were being separated off from the whole.

(Plutarch, *Lysander* 12 = DK 59A12)

Anaxagoras was said to have predicted this event, which took place in 467. **13.32** also gives valuable information on how Anaxagoras viewed both the mechanism

---

this interpretation of **13.2**, which requires the present tense of the fragment "are being separated" to be taken as an "historical present," i.e., as equivalent to a past tense.

of the rotation of the heavenly bodies and the source of their brightness. Although it is frequently declared absurd that Anaxagoras could have predicted the fall of a meteorite, he may well have said that the earthen bodies held aloft by the cosmic vortex can sometimes slip and fall to earth. If this assertion (which might loosely be called a general prediction) were widely known when the famous meteorite fell, it would be but a small step to credit Anaxagoras with predicting the event.[88]

Anaxagoras asserts that the moon's light is derived from the sun (**13.18**). He gives the correct explanation of lunar as well as solar eclipses, and he recognizes that rainbows are an effect of sunlight on moisture in the air (**13.19**).

> **13.33** The earth is flat and stays aloft (a) because of its size, (b) because there is no void, and (c) because *aēr* is very strong and so is able to support the earth, which rides upon it.
>
> (Hippolytus, *Refutation of All Heresies* 1.8.3 = DK 59A42)

This testimonium is odd since it gives three apparently independent reasons for the earth's not falling. Reason (a) is hard to make sense of at all. Reason (b) has Eleatic echoes (see **15.9** section 7), but (c), which goes strangely with Anaxagoras's opinions on the cosmological role of the vortex, is pure Anaximenes (see **6.7, 6.8, 6.9**). Perhaps it is best to regard **13.33** as guesswork rather than as based on knowledge of Anaxagoras's text. Following the Ionian tradition, Anaxagoras also has theories about lightning and other meteorological phenomena, earthquakes, the origin of the salt-water sea, the flooding of the Nile, the origins of life, and many questions having to do with biology. Noteworthy among them is his view that the brain is the seat of sensation.[89]

He also speaks of human life "elsewhere" (**13.4** sections 3–6), and he believes that his cosmogonic principles are such that life and the *kosmos* as we know it are not generated uniquely here "with us." The present tenses (**13.4** sections 3–5) indicate that he is not thinking of a series of worlds which succeed one another in time—as in Empedocles' cosmic cycle—but of other places where life is similar to ours right now. This ingenious idea does not fit well with his cosmogony, however. There is only one vortex and therefore only one earth at the center. Accordingly, if Anaxagoras means that there are other worlds contemporary with our own, it is hard to see where they would be located. A number of suggestions have been offered: the other worlds are microscopic worlds contained in our own, or they are worlds created by secondary vortices, each with its own center to

---

88. It would be unsafe to ignore the possibility that Anaxagoras's theory was prompted by the meteorite and that later on people who did not know the order of events gave Anaxagoras credit for predicting it, in other words, that Anaxagoras's explanation of the fact was regarded as a prediction.

89. See Guthrie (1965: 304–18) for discussion and references.

which earth is drawn.[90] The suggestion I find most plausible is that he is thinking of different regions of *this* world—remote and perhaps inaccessible from the region inhabited by and known to the Greeks.

Epistemology

Parmenides' and Zeno's arguments attacked the reliability of the senses as well as our ordinary conceptions about the nature of the world. Anaxagoras developed a physical system which responded to the Eleatics. His claim that the cosmic Mind knows all things (**13.12** section 9) entails that the *kosmos* is rationally comprehensible, and his view that our minds are like the cosmic Mind (**13.12** section 15) entails that we can in principle have knowledge of the *kosmos*. But how can we acquire this knowledge? His answer seems to have involved the use of the senses. He holds that sensation is produced by unlikes acting on unlikes. Something feels hot to the touch when our hand is cold relatively to it. He also holds that since it results from the action of opposites, all sensation involves pain. Since he recognizes that we do not always feel pain when using our senses, he is committed to belief in the fallibility of the senses, more specifically in their frailty—there is a threshold below which they do not function. It is not that they misreport what is the case, but that they may fail to report it. (This view squares well with Anaxagoras's theses that in everything there is a portion of everything and that each single thing is and was most plainly those things of which it contains most.) Anaxagoras states this view generally (**13.20**). Sextus Empiricus, who quotes **13.20**, also paraphrases an example which Anaxagoras used to support the general claim.

13.34   He offers as evidence of their [the senses'] untrustworthiness the gradual change of colors. For if we take two colors, black and white, and then pour out one into the other a drop at a time, our vision will not be able to distinguish the gradual changes, even though they exist in reality.
(Sextus Empiricus, *Against the Mathematicians* 7.90 = DK 59B21)

The weakness of the senses implies that we cannot perceive the complete nature of things, but that is not to say that they are totally misleading and useless for understanding reality. What they tell us has some relation to reality, as the famous pronouncement in **13.21** makes clear. "Appearances are a sight of the unseen" can equally be translated "Phenomena are a vision of what is not manifest." We do not know more about how Anaxagoras thought it was possible to achieve knowledge of the world from our weak senses, but it is an interesting exercise to speculate how he might have thought that our mind operates on the "sight of the

---

90. This last is proposed by Curd (2007: 218–22). Curd also discusses and gives references to the other interpretations (ibid. [212–18]).

unseen" that the senses provide in order to give us knowledge. Still, it is unclear whether Anaxagoras worked out a precise theory of how knowledge is attained.

Conclusion

Anaxagoras's physical theory is more complex than those of his predecessors but comparable to those of Empedocles and the Atomists, who also wrote in response to the Eleatics. Anaxagoras has close connections with his Ionian forebears, as witnessed by his interest in cosmogony and cosmology, the absence of any religious or mystical tendency in his writing, and his determination to give a plausible account of the world around us in terms of a rationally comprehensible set of principles.

The complexities of his system can be attributed to the effects of Eleatic philosophy, which established requirements which Anaxagoras went to great lengths to meet. He did not accept all of Parmenides' views on the nature of reality (in particular, he did not adopt Parmenides' cosmology) but he was apparently convinced (as were Empedocles and the Atomists) by Parmenides' rejection of coming to be and perishing and aimed to construct an account of reality that avoids coming to be and perishing and that also accounts for the origin and present constitution and functioning of the *kosmos*.

The past century has seen a greater number of radically different interpretations of Anaxagoras than of any other Presocratic with the possible exceptions of Parmenides and Empedocles[91]—a remarkable fact given the small number of fragments on which interpretations can be based. Indeed, at present there is no consensus on many of Anaxagoras's central doctrines, such as the kinds of Basic Ingredients, the nature of the Portions and Seeds, whether matter is infinitely divisible, and whether the original mixture of all things was uniform. The interpretation I have presented is based closely on the fragments, in some cases supplemented by appeal to important testimonia, but it should be regarded as an exploration of Anaxagoras's subtle ideas rather than as a definitive account.

---

91. Important contributions in the past thirty years include Barnes (1979/1982), Schofield (1980), Inwood (1986), Furley (1987), Mourelatos (1987), Furth (1991), Graham (1994), Taylor (1997), Sider (2005) and Curd (2007).

14

Empedocles of Acragas

Fragments

On Nature, Book I: The Purifications

14.1[1] (112)[2] Friends who dwell in the great city on the yellow Acragas
on the heights of the citadel, you whose care is good deeds,
respectful havens for strangers, untouched by evil,
hail! I go about among you, an immortal god, no longer mortal,
honored among all, as it seems,   5
wreathed with headbands and blooming garlands.
Wherever I go to their flourishing cities,
I am revered by all—men and women. And they follow together
in tens of thousands, inquiring where lies the path to profit,
some in need of prophecy, while others,   10
pierced for a long time with harsh pains,
asked to hear the voice of healing for all diseases.

14.2 (114) Friends, I know that truth is in the words
I will speak. But very difficult
for men and spiteful is the invasion of conviction into their minds.

14.3 (113) But why do I insist on these matters as if I were accomplishing
　　　something great,
if I am superior to mortal humans who perish many times?

14.4 (128) Nor was there any god Ares among them nor Kudoimos
　　　["battle-din"]
nor King Zeus, nor Kronos nor Poseidon,
but there was Queen Cypris. . . .[3]
Her they propitiated with reverent statues   5

---

1. More than one hundred and fifty fragments of Empedocles survive, quoted in a large number of ancient sources. Since the location in Empedocles' original work(s) is unattested for most of the fragments, any ordering of them is uncertain. The arrangement of the fragments given here is based on the order proposed by Pierris (2005: Appendix, XXVII–XC), the most important exception being **14.58–14.61**, which follow the order proposed by Primavesi (2008). Pierris believes that *The Purifications* constituted the first part of the first book of *On Nature*, a matter on which I do not have fixed views. The location of many fragments, especially the very short ones, is necessarily conjectural. Since the order that sounds best to one person will not necessarily sound best to another, the present arrangement does not pretend to reflect a scholarly consensus.

2. The numbers in parentheses are the numbers in DK. (1) = DK 31B1.

3. This line is incomplete.

and painted figures and unguents with varied odors,
and with offerings of unmixed myrrh and fragrant frankincense,
pouring on the ground libations of yellow honey.
No altar was drenched with the unspeakable[4] slaughter of bulls,
but this was the greatest abomination among humans,   10
to tear out life and devour the noble limbs.

14.5   (130) All were tame and kindly toward humans—
both animals and birds—and friendliness burned brightly.

14.6   (77) leaf-retaining

[Empedocles used this word for evergreens (Plutarch, *Table Talk* 3.2.2 649C).]

14.7   (78) [Empedocles declares that evergreens and continuously
fruiting trees flourish] with bounties of fruits in the air each year.

[Quotation and context from Theophrastus, *On Plants: The Explanations* 1.13.2.]

14.8   (132) Blessed is he who possesses wealth of divine intelligence
but wretched he whose concern is a dim opinion about the gods.

14.9   (115) There is an oracle of Necessity, an ancient decree of the gods,
eternal and sealed with broad oaths,
that whenever anyone pollutes his own dear limbs with the sin of
    bloodshed,[5]
. . .[6] commits offense and swears a false oath
—divinities (*daimones*) who possess immensely long life[7]   5
he wanders away from the blessed ones for thrice ten thousand seasons,
through time growing to be all different kinds of mortals
taking the difficult paths of life one after another.
For the force of *aithēr* pursues them to the sea
and the sea spits them out onto the surface of the earth, and
    the earth into the rays   10
of the shining sun, and he [the sun] casts them into the vortices of *aithēr*.
One receives them after another, but all hate them.
Of these I am now one, a fugitive from the gods and a wanderer,
putting my reliance on raving Strife.

---

4. Reading *arrêtoisi*.
5. Reading *phónôi* with most editors.
6. The first part of this line is not preserved.
7. Lines 4–5 probably elaborate "anyone" in line 3.

14.10   (142) Neither, then, the roofed halls of aegis-bearing Zeus
         nor the house of Hades <? receives> him.

14.11   (125) For from living forms it [? Strife] was making dead ones, changing
         them.

14.12   (126) Wrapping <it> in an alien garb of flesh.

14.13   (148) Mortal-surrounding earth

[This is a description of the body, which surrounds the soul (Plutarch, *Table
Talk* 683E)]

14.14   (153a) In seven weeks

[According to Empedocles this is the time it takes for a fetus to be formed.]

14.15   (117) For I have already been born as a boy and a girl
         and a bush and a bird and a <mute> fish <from the sea>.[8]

14.16   (119) From such honor and how great an amount of bliss . . .

[Apparently describing life before the Fall (Plutarch, *On Exile* 17 607D).]

14.17   (120) We came beneath this roofed cave.

14.18   (116)<The Grace [that is, Love]> loathes Necessity, hard to endure.

14.19   (118) I wept and wailed upon seeing the unfamiliar place.

14.20   (154a) Stirring up distress, pains, deceptions, and laments.

[Of dubious authenticity]

14.21   (121) . . . Joyless place,
         where Bloodshed, Anger, and tribes of other spirits of death
         and squalid Diseases, Rotting, and works of dissolution[9]
         wander in darkness through the meadow of Disaster (*atē*).

14.22   (122) There were the maidens Earth and far-seeing Sun,
         bloody Battle and serious Harmonia,

---

8. The words in brackets are conjectures; the text is corrupt.

9. This line may not belong here.

Beauty and Ugliness, Speed and Slowness,
lovely Truth and dark-haired Unclarity.

14.23　　(123) Growth and Wasting, Sleeping and Waking,
Movement and Fixity, many-crowned Greatness
and Defilement, Silence and prophetic Voice.

14.24　　(124) Alas! Wretched race of mortals! Unfortunate!
Out of such quarreling and groaning were you born.

14.25　　(136) Will you not cease from harsh-sounding bloodshed? Do you not see
that you are devouring each other in the carelessness of your thought?

14.26　　(138) Having drawn off [that is, severed] the soul with bronze.

14.27　　(137) A father lifts up his own dear son who has changed form,
and, praying, slaughters him, committing a great folly. And they
　　are at a loss,
sacrificing him as he entreats them. But he, refusing to hear the cries,
slaughters him and attends an evil feast in his halls.
Likewise a son seizes his father and children their mother,　　　　　　5
and tearing out their life, devour the dear flesh.

14.28　　(145) Therefore, distraught with harsh evils,
you will never relieve your spirit from wretched distress.

14.29　　(135) But what is lawful for all extends far through the wide-ruling
aithēr and through the immense glare.

[This refers to the injustice of killing living things (Aristotle, *Rhetoric* 1.13
1373b6–17).]

14.30　　(143) [It is necessary to cleanse oneself]
after cutting[10] from five springs with the long and pointed bronze.

14.31　　(144) Fast from evil.

14.32　　(140) Keep completely away from laurel leaves!

14.33　　(141) Wretched, wholly wretched! Keep your hands off beans!

---

10. "Cutting" is used here metaphorically to mean "drawing off" (Aristotle, *Poetics* 21
1457b13–16 = DK 31B138), so that the fragment probably refers to an act of killing. The
context, provided by Theon of Smyrna (*Mathematics Useful for Reading Plato* 15.9–11 = DK
31B143) then connects the fragment with the pollution incurred by bloodshed.

14.34   (127) Among beasts they come into being as lions whose lairs are in the
              mountains
              and their beds on the ground, and as laurels among shaggy trees.

[These are the best animals and plants for a *daimōn* to become (Aelian, *Natural
History* 12.7).]

14.35   (146) In the end they are prophets and bards and physicians
              and chiefs among men on earth,
              and from there they arise as gods mightiest in honors.

14.36   (147) Sharing the same hearth and table with other immortals
              relieved of manly distress, unwearied.

(End of Purifications)

14.37   (133) It is not possible to reach and approach <the divine> with our eyes
              or grasp it with our hands, by which the most powerful
              highway of persuasion strikes the minds of men.

14.38   (131) For if, immortal Muse, for any ephemeral creature
              it pleased you that our concerns should come to your thoughts,
              be present once again to me, Kalliopeia, now as I pray,
              as I reveal a good account about the blessed gods.

14.39   (1) But listen, Pausanias, son of wise-minded Anchites.

14.40   (111) You will learn all the drugs there are as a safeguard against evils
              and old age,
              since for you alone shall I bring to pass all these things.
              You will stop the force of the tireless winds that rush
              over the earth and devastate the plowed fields with their blasts.
              And, if you wish, you will arouse their breath again.   5
              You will change black rain into seasonable dryness
              for people, and summer drought you will change
              into tree-nourishing waters that dwell in the sky.
              And you will bring back from Hades the strength of a dead man.

14.41   (5) [Empedocles advised Pausanias] to cover up [his
              teachings] within a voiceless heart (*phrēn*).[11]

---

11. See above p. 62 n. 11. The bracketed material is supplied from Plutarch, *Table
Talk* 8.8.1 728E.

14.42 (4) It is highly typical of evil people to disbelieve what prevails [that is, is the truth];
but learn how the trustworthy reports from our Muse command,
by splitting apart the account (*logos*) in your entrails.[12]

14.43 (2) Narrow are the means of apprehension spread throughout the limbs.
Many wretched things burst in which blunt the thoughts.
People see a tiny part of life during their time
and swift-fated they are taken away and fly like smoke,
persuaded only of whatever each of them has chanced to meet   5
as they were driven everywhere; but everyone boasts that he
   discovered the whole.
These things are not in this way to be seen or heard by men
or grasped with the mind. But you, since you have turned aside to this place,
will learn; mortal cunning has reached no further.

14.44[13] (3b) Nor will it compel you to take away the blossoms of fair-famed honor
from mortals on the condition that you say in rashness more than is
   holy—
and <only> then sit upon the summits of wisdom.
But come, look with every means of apprehension, in whatever way each
   thing is clear,
not holding any sight more in trust than <what comes>
   through hearing,   5
or loud-sounding hearing above the things made clear by the tongue,
and do not at all hold back trust in any of the other limbs,
wherever there is a channel for understanding, but
understand each thing in whatever way it is clear.

14.45[14] (3a) But, gods, avert their madness from my tongue,
and lead a pure stream from holy mouths.
And you, much-remembering maiden Muse with white arms,
I entreat—bring <to me> the things it is right for creatures of a day
to hear, driving your easily-steered chariot from the halls of reverence. 5

Physical Principles

14.46 (6) Hear first the four roots of all things:
shining Zeus and life-bringing Hera and Aidoneus
and Nestis, who with her tears gives moisture to the source of mortals.

---

12. Reading *pélei* and *diatmēthéntes* with the manuscripts.

13. I divide DK fr. 3 into two fragments, since it is implausible to identify the addressee of **14.44** as the Muse who is addressed in **14.45** line 3.

14. See previous note.

14.47   (7) Ungenerated

[Empedocles used this word to describe the elements (Hesychius, *Lexicon* s.v. *agennēta*).]

14.48   (8) I will tell you another thing. There is coming to be of not a
single one of all
mortal things, nor is there any end of destructive death,
but only mixture, and separation of what is mixed,
and nature (*phusis*) is the name given to them by humans.

[Plutarch quotes this fragment to show that Empedocles uses *phusis*, "nature," in the sense of "coming to be" (Plutarch, *Against Colotes* 1111F–12A).]

14.49   (11) Fools. For their thoughts are not far-reaching—
those who expect that there comes to be what previously was not,
or that anything perishes and is completely destroyed.

14.50   (9) Whenever they arrive in the *aithēr* mixed so as to form a man
or one of the wild beasts or bushes
or birds, that is when <people> speak of coming into being;
and whenever they are separated, that <is what they call>
the ill-starred fate of death.
They do not call it as is right, but I myself too assent to
their convention   5

14.51   (15) A man who is wise in his thoughts (*phrēn*) would not divine such
things as this—
that as long as they live what they in fact call life
they are, and have things wretched and good,
but before they took on the fixed form of mortals and after they have
dissolved, they are then nothing.

14.52   (12) For it is impossible to come to be from what in no way is,
and it is not to be accomplished and is unheard of that what is perishes
absolutely.
For it will always be where a person thrusts it each time.

14.53   (13) None of the whole is either empty or over-full.

14.54   (14) Of the whole, nothing is empty; from where, then, could anything
come to be added to it?

14.55   (18) Love.

14.56 (19) Tenacious Friendliness.

14.57 (16) For they are as they were previously[15] and will be, and never, I think,
will endless time be empty of both of these [that is, Strife and Love].

14.58 (17 + Strasbourg papyrus, ensemble a) I will tell a double story. For at
one time they grew to be only one (*232*)[16]
out of many, but at another they grew apart to be many out of one.[17]
Double is the generation of mortal things, and double their decline.
For the coming together of all things gives birth to one [namely,
generation and decline] and destroys it, (*235*)
and the other is nurtured and flies away when they grow apart again.   5
And these never cease continually interchanging,
at one time all coming together into one by Love
and at another each being borne apart by the hatred of Strife.
Thus in that they have learned to grow to be one out of many (*240*)
and in that they again spring apart as many when the one
grows apart,   10
in that way they come to be, and their life is not lasting,
but in that they never cease interchanging continually,
in this way they are always unchanging in a cycle.
But come, listen to my words, for learning increases wisdom. (*245*)
For as I previously said, while declaring the bounds of my words,   15
I will tell a double story. For at one time they grew to be only one
out of many, but at another they grew apart to be many out of one:
fire and water and earth and the immense height of air,
and deadly Strife apart from them, equal in all directions (*250*)
and Love among them, equal in length and breadth.   20
Behold her with your mind, and do not sit with your eyes staring in
amazement.
She is also recognized as innate in mortal limbs.
Through her they have kindly thoughts and do peaceful deeds,
calling her by the appellation Joy and also Aphrodite. (*255*)
No mortal man has seen her spinning   25
among them. But listen to the undeceitful course of my account.
For these [the four elements] are all equal and of the same age,
but each rules in its own province and possesses its own individual
character,

---

15. Reading *ésti gàr hōs páros ēn* (Lloyd–Jones).

16. I give the line numbers in Empedocles' text as reconstructed by Primavesi (2008).
The numbering is based on the identification of the three hundredth line in the poem by
a mark in the margin of the last line in ensemble a of the Strasbourg papyrus (see below
p. 238 n. 18 and p. 256 n. 47).

17. Alternate translation: For at one time one grew to be alone out of many, but at
another it grew apart to be many out of one.

but they dominate in their turn as time revolves. (*260*)
And nothing is added to them or subtracted,   30
for if they were perishing continuously, they would no longer be.
But what could increase this totality? And where would it come from?
And how [or, "where"] could it perish, since nothing is empty of these?
But there are just these very things, and running through one
    another (*265*)
at different times they come to be different things and yet are
    always and continuously the same.   35
{But under Love}[18] we come together into one *kosmos*,
{whereas under Strife it [that is, the ordered whole]
    grew apart, so as} to be many from one,
from which [that is, many things] all things that were and are
    and will be in the future.
have sprouted: trees and men and women, (*270*)
and beasts and birds and fishes nurtured in water,   40
and long-lived gods highest in honors.
{Under her [that is, Strife]} they never cease continually darting
in dense whirls . . .
without pausing, and never . . . (*275*)
but {many} lifetimes before . . .   45
before passing from them . . .
{and never cease} continually darting {in all directions}
for neither the sun . . .
{the onrush full of this} . . . (*280*)
nor any of the others . . .   50
but interchanging in a circle {they dart in all directions}
for at that time the impassable earth runs, and the sun as well
{and the sphere [that is, the celestial sphere]} as large as even now
    {it is judged} by men {to be}
in the same way all these things {were running}
    through one another (*285*)

---

18. At this point begins the section for which the papyrus (for which, see below p. 254) is our only evidence. There are numerous gaps in the preserved text, some of which can be restored with a good degree of confidence from other Empedoclean verses. For the rest, the choice is either to stay close to what the papyrus contains or to fill in the gaps by conjecture informed by one's knowledge of the author's vocabulary, style, and views. The translation I have provided is based on two versions of the Greek text and the accompanying translations: the original publication by Martin and Primavesi (1999), and the text printed in Inwood (2001). Inwood is more conservative, staying closer to the papyrus text, while Martin and Primavesi are more willing to propose ways to restore missing material. The words I have enclosed in curly brackets translate supplements of Martin and Primavesi that Inwood does not include. My purpose has been to offer a readable translation while marking places where there is a good chance that the text translated is not what Empedocles wrote.

{and having been driven away, each of them reached} different
    {and peculiar} places   55
{self-willed}; and we were coming together in the mid-most places
    to be only one.
But when indeed Strife passed through {and reached} the depths
{of the swirl,} and Love {comes to be} in the midst of the vortex,
{then} indeed all these things come together to be only one. (*290*)
{Strive eagerly} so that {my account may arrive}
    not only through ears   60
{and behold} the unerring truths that are around while you
    listen to me.
I shall show you also through your eyes {where they [that is, the
    elements] find} a larger body:
first, the coming together and development {of the offspring}
and all that now still remain of this {generation} (*295*)
both among the {wild species} of mountain-roaming beasts   65
and among the twofold offspring of men, {and also among}
the offspring of root-bearing {fields} and vine-mounting
    {clusters of grapes}.
From these stories bring back to your mind undeceiving evidence,
for you will see the coming together and development
    of the offspring. (*300*)

14.59   (20 + Strasbourg papyrus, ensemble c) {Where Love and Strife have}
        their guiding {counsels} (*301*)
This is very clear in the mass of mortal limbs:
sometimes we come together through Love into one, all the
limbs that have obtained a body, at the peak of flourishing life,
while at other times, split apart through evil Quarrels (*305*)   5
they wander each kind separately on the furthest shore of life.
And it happens the same way for bushes and water-homed fishes
and mountain-dwelling beasts and wing-propelled birds.

14.60   (21) But come, behold this witness of my previous discourse, (*309*)
if anything in the foregoing was feeble in form:
the sun, brilliant to see and hot everywhere,
all the immortal things that are drenched in the heat and shining light,
and rain, in all things dark and cold,   5
and from earth stream forth things rooted and solid.
In Anger they are all apart and have separate forms, (*315*)
but they come together in Love and yearn for one another.
From these all things that were and are and will be in the future
have sprouted: trees and men and women,   10
and beasts and birds and fishes nurtured in water,
and long-lived gods highest in honors. (*320*)
For there are just these things, and running through one another
they come to have different appearances, for mixture changes them.

14.61   (76+ Strasbourg papyrus, ensemble b) This [that is, fire] is found in the
case of heavy–backed shells of sea–dwelling creatures. (*324*)
. . . (*325*)
There you will see earth {dwelling} in the uppermost parts of the flesh
. . . (*327*)
and indeed truly [in the flesh] of stony-skinned tritons and turtles
. . . of horned stags
. . . saying (*330*)

[Quoted to show that for Empedocles fire does not always go up and earth down,
but they are arranged appropriately and usefully (Plutarch, *The Face in the Moon*
14 927F–928A and *Table Talk* 1.2.5 618B).]

14.62   (23) As when painters decorate votive offerings—
men through cunning well taught in their skill—
who when they take the many-colored pigments in their hands,
mixing in harmony more of these and less of those,
out of them they produce shapes similar to all things,   5
creating trees and men and women
and beasts and birds and fishes nurtured in water
and long-lived gods highest in honors.
So let not deception compel your mind (*phrēn*) to believe that
there is from anywhere else
a source of mortal things, all the endless numbers of   10
things that have come to be manifest,
but know these things distinctly, having heard the story from a god.

14.63   (26) They [that is, the four elements] dominate in turn as the cycle
revolves,
and they decrease into one another and grow in their turn, as destined.
For there are just these things, and running through one another
they come to be both humans and the tribes of other beasts,
at one time coming together into a single *kosmos* by Love   5
and at another each being borne apart again by the hatred of Strife,
until they grow together into one, the whole, and become subordinate.
Thus in that they have learned to grow to be one out of many
and in that they again spring apart as many when the one grows apart,
in that way they come to be and their life is not lasting,   10
but in that these never cease interchanging continually,
in this way they are always unchanging in a cycle.

14.64   (Strasbourg papyrus, ensemble d + 139) . . . to fall apart from one
another and encounter their fate
very much against their will, rotting through mournful necessity;
But for those who now have Love . . .

the Harpies will be present with the tokens
   {to be cast in the lottery} of death.
Alas that the pitiless day did not destroy me   5
before I devised with my claws wicked deeds for the sake of eating flesh.
{But now} in vain in this {storm} I wet my cheeks
{for we are approaching} a very deep {whirl,} I think,
{and} although they do not wish it, {tens of thousands of}
   pains will be present in their mind
{to humans,} but we will again mount {you} on {that} account: 10
{when} an untiring flame happened to meet
. . . bringing on a woeful mixture
. . . things that could produce offspring were born
. . . I entered the final place
. . . with a scream and a cry   15
. . . having obtained {the meadow of Disaster}
. . . around . . . earth

14.65   (25) For indeed it is a fine thing to tell twice what one must.

14.66   (24) Joining high points of my story one to another,
       not to complete a single path.

14.67   (22) For all these things—shining sun and earth and heaven
       and sea—are united with their own parts,
       all that are split off and have come to be in mortal things.
       In the same way, all that are more fitted for mixture
       are made alike by Aphrodite and have come to love one another.   5
       But greatest enemies are those which are furthest separated from one
          another
       in birth and mixture and moulded forms,
       in every way unaccustomed to be together and very mournful
       through their birth in Strife,[19] because their births were in anger.[20]

14.68   (32) A joint binds two things (DK) [or, "There is a need for two joints"
       (Inwood)].

[Text and context uncertain.]

14.69   (91) <Water> has a greater affinity with wine, but with olive oil
       it is unwilling <to mix>.[21]

---

19. Reading *neikeogennéteisi*.

20. Adopting Wright's emendation (Wright [1981: 106]).

21. According to Alexander and Philoponus, Empedocles explained these phenomena
in terms of the compatibility of the "pores" in the three substances.

14.70   (33) As when sap from a fig tree curdles and binds white milk.

[A simile for the unifying action of Love, according to Plutarch, *On Having Many Friends* 95A–B.]

14.71   (34) Having glued barley groats with water.

[Probably an illustration of how different elements join to form compounds.]

14.72   (92) [On the question why mules are sterile, Empedocles explains that
               the mixture of seeds becomes thick, although the seed of both the
               horse and the ass is soft. For the hollow parts of each fit together with
               the thick parts of the other, and as a result a hard substance comes
               from soft ones] like copper mixed with tin.[22]

14.73   (93) The brightness of gleaming saffron is mixed with linen.[23]

14.74   (81) Wine is water from grape skin fermented in wood.

14.75   (96) Pleasant earth in her well-made[24] crucibles
               obtained two parts of bright Nestis out of the eight,
               and four of Hephaestus, and white bones came into being,
               fitted together by the divine glues of Harmonia.

The Cosmic Cycle and the Present State of the *Kosmos*

THE SPHERE

[See also **14.60**]

14.76   (27) There neither the swift limbs of the sun are discerned,
               nor the shaggy force of earth nor the sea.
               Thus by the dense concealment of Harmonia is held fast
               a rounded sphere, exulting in its circular [or, "joyous"] solitude [or,
                   "motionlessness"].

14.77   (27a) No dissent or unseemly battle in its limbs.

---

22. This alloy is bronze, a metal harder than either of its ingredients. The bracketed material is supplied from Aristotle, *Generation of Animals* 2.8 747a34–b7.

23. Reading *glaukoîo krókou* and *aktís* with Wright (1981: 123) and Inwood (2001: 254). Cited to exemplify how some things are especially suited to others. Linen readily absorbs dye.

24. Reading *eutúktois*.

14.78   (28) But equal to itself on all sides, and wholly without limit,
        a rounded sphere, exulting in its circular [or, "joyous"] solitude [or,
        "motionlessness"].

14.79   (29) For two branches do not spring from its back
        nor do feet or swift knees or organs of generation,
        but it was a sphere and equal to itself on all sides.

14.80   (134) For he [Apollo, or god in general] is not furnished in his
           limbs with a human head.
        Two branches do not spring from his back.
        He has no feet, no swift knees, no hairy genitals,
        but is only mind (*phrēn*), holy and indescribable,
        darting through the entire *kosmos* with his swift thoughts.   5

INCREASING STRIFE

14.81   (30) [Empedocles says this too about the mastery of Strife.]
        But when great Strife had been nourished in its limbs
        and leapt up to its prerogatives as the time was being fulfilled,
        that is established for them in turn by a broad oath . . .

[Context from Simplicius, *Commentary on Aristotle's* Physics 1184.12–13.]

14.82   (31) [When Strife has again begun to gain mastery, movement again
           occurs in the Sphere.]
        All the limbs of the god trembled, each in turn.

[Context from Simplicius, *Commentary on Aristotle's* Physics 1184.2–3.]

14.83   (37) Earth increases its own form and *aithēr* increases *aithēr*.

[Cited as evidence that Empedocles viewed growth as a matter of addition (Aristotle, *On Generation and Corruption* 2.6 333a35–b1).]

14.84   (90) Thus sweet caught hold of sweet, bitter rushed toward bitter,
        sour went to sour and hot coupled with hot.

[Quoted to illustrate Empedocles' "like-to-like" theory of nutrition (Plutarch, *Table Talk* 4.1.3 663A and Macrobius, *Saturnalia* 7.5.17–18).]

14.85   (38) But come, I shall first tell you the beginning . . .
        from which all that we now look upon came to be clear—
        earth and the sea with many waves and moist air
        and the Titan *aithēr*, squeezing all things round about in a circle.

14.86   (53, 54) [*Aithēr* was borne upward not by Strife, but
sometimes he speaks as if it happened by chance.]
For it sometimes happened to run this way but often otherwise.
[And sometimes he says that fire by nature is borne upward, but]
aithēr sank beneath the deep-rooted earth.

[Context and fragments from Aristotle, *On Generation and Corruption* 2.6 334a1–5.]

CURRENT STATE OF THE *KOSMOS*

14.87   (39) . . . if indeed the depths of earth and plentiful *aithēr* are boundless,
as has passed through the tongues of many and is poured out in vain
from
mouths of men who have seen little of the whole.

[This fragment attacks those like Xenophanes, who believed that the earth
extends downward without limit (Aristotle, *On the Heavens* 2.13 294a21–25).]

14.88   (51) swiftly upward

[Empedocles thus describes the movement of fire, according to Eustathius, *Commentary on Homer's* Odyssey 1.321.]

14.89   (52) Many fires burn beneath the ground.

14.90   (40) sharp-arrowed sun and mildly-shining moon.

14.91   (41) <The sun> after being gathered together traverses the vast heaven.

[Quoted to show that Empedocles regards the sun as a big aggregation of fire
(Apollodorus, quoted in Macrobius, *Saturnalia* 1.17.46).]

14.92   (44) <The sun> shines back toward Olympus with fearless face.

14.93   (42) <The moon> keeps off the sunlight
when it goes above and darkens a portion of the earth
the size of the breadth of the gray-eyed moon.

14.94   (47) For <the moon> gazes straight at the pure circle of her lord [that is,
the sun].

14.95   (43) Thus the sunlight, having struck the broad circle of the moon . . .

14.96   (45) A round alien light spins around the earth.

["Alien" in the sense of "not its own," "belonging to something else," that is, the sun.]

14.97   (46) It spins <around the earth> like the track of a chariot, and around
           the extremity it . . .[25]

[Quoted to show that Empedocles held that the moon's orbit is close to the earth (Plutarch, *On the Face in the Moon* 9 925B). A chariot race in a stadium is meant, in which the chariots would turn as close as possible to the turning posts.]

14.98   (48) Earth makes night by obstructing <the sun's> rays.

14.99   (49) during the desolate blind-eyed night [the air is dark].[26]

14.100   (94) In the depths of a river, a dark color arises from the shadow,
           and is observed as well in deep caves.

[Quoted as Empedocles' explanation of the fact that the deep parts of water are dark, while the shallow parts are bright (Plutarch, *Natural Phenomena* 39).]

14.101   (55) The sea is the earth's sweat.

14.102   (56) Salt is solidified when blasted by the force of the sun.

14.103[27]   (50) Iris [the rainbow] brings wind or a great storm from the sea.

14.104   (71) If your faith in these matters were at all faint—
           <about> how when water, earth, *aithēr*, and sun
           are mixed, as many shapes and colors of mortals came to be
           as now have come to be, fitted together by Aphrodite . . .

14.105   (151) Life-giving Aphrodite

14.106   (73) As then Cypris, busily working on shapes [or, "kinds of things"]
           moistened earth in rain,
           and gave it to swift fire to strengthen . . .

---

25. Following the unmetrical reading of the manuscripts, which I take to be a close paraphrase.

26. The bracketed material is supplied from Plutarch, *Table Talk* 8.3.1 720E.

27. Attributed to "Empedocles or one of the others" by Tzetzes, *Allegories of the Iliad*, book 15 l.85.

LIVING THINGS

14.107   (85) Mildly-shining flame chanced upon a little earth.

[Quoted to show that Empedocles holds that most parts of animals arise through chance.]

14.108   (86) From which [the four elements] divine Aphrodite fashioned tireless
              eyes.

14.109   (98) Earth came together by chance in about equal quantity to these,
              Hephaestus and rain and all-shining *aithēr*,
              anchored in the perfect harbors of Cypris,
              either a bit more or a bit less of it among more of them.
              From them blood came into being and other forms of flesh.   5

14.110   (82) The same things become hairs and leaves and dense feathers of
              birds,
              and scales on stout limbs.

14.111   [In book 2 of Empedocles' *Purifications*][28] For all of them that exist with
              closely packed roots below,
              flourishing with more widely spaced shoots.

(Empedocles fr. 152 Wright [not in DK].)

14.112   (75) . . . all of them that are dense within, while their exterior parts are
              formed in a loose texture,
              because they met with such moisture through the devices of Cypris.

14.113   (83) But in hedgehogs
              sharp-pointed hairs bristle on their backs.

14.114   (79) In this way tall trees first lay eggs in the form of olives.

14.115   (80) Therefore pomegranates and succulent apples are produced late in
              the season.

14.116   (72) How both tall trees and sea-dwelling fishes . . .

14.117   (74) . . . leading the museless tribe of fertile fishes

---

28. Context from Herodian, *Universal Prosody* (see Hunger [1967]).

Origin of Animals in the Phase of Increasing Strife

14.118   (62) Come now, hear these things about how, as fire was being separated,
it raised up the nocturnal shoots of men and women, full of wailing.
For the story is not off the point or ignorant.
First the whole-natured forms rose up out of the earth,
having a portion of both water and heat.   5
These the fire sent up, desiring to come to its like,
and they did not yet show at all the lovely shape of limbs
or a voice or[29] the member native to men.

Anatomy, Sexual Reproduction, Sexual Differentiation

14.119   (63) But the nature of the limbs is rent asunder, partly
in a man's . . .

[This fragment is quoted twice by Aristotle, once with approval, to show that
Empedocles held that the seed of an animal does not come complete from either
parent (*Generation of Animals* 1.18 722b8–12) and once with disapproval to show
that he held that the body of the seed is rent asunder (Ibid., 4.1 764b15–17).]

14.120   (64) Indeed, longing to have sexual intercourse comes upon him
through sight.[30]

14.121   (66) Divided meadows of Aphrodite

[A "disgraceful" expression used of the female genitalia, according to the source,
an anonymous ancient commentator on Euripides, *Phoenissae* line 18.]

14.122   (153) Baubo.

[This was the name of the nurse of Demeter. Empedocles used it for the uterus.]

14.123   (65) They were poured in clean <places>. Some, encountering cold,
become women.

14.124   (67) That which has to do with males came to be in the warmer part of
the earth,
and this is why men are dark and have stronger limbs
and more hair.

---

29. Reading *oút' aû*.

30. Reading *tôi d' epì kaì póthos eîsi di' ópsios ammísgesthai* with Dyer (1974) and
Inwood (2001).

14.125   (69) twice-bearing

[Empedocles used this word to describe women, to indicate that pregnancies last seven or nine months, never eight (Proclus, *Commentary on Plato's* Republic 2 34.26 [Kroll]).]

14.126   (68) On the tenth day of the eighth month <the blood> becomes white pus.

[Empedocles' account of lactation (Aristotle, *Generation of Animals* 4.8 777a7).]

14.127   (70) amnion

[A word used by Empedocles for the membrane that surrounds the embryo.]

PHASE OF INCREASING LOVE

14.128   (35) But I shall return to that path of songs
          that I recounted before, drawing off this account from another one.
          When Strife had reached the lowest depth
          of the vortex, and Love comes to be in the middle of the whirl,
          at this point all these things come together to be one single thing,   5
          not at once, but willingly combining, different ones from
               different places.
          As they were being mixed, myriads of tribes of mortal
               things poured forth,
          but many remained unmixed alternately with those that were being
               mingled—
          all that Strife still held back aloft. For it had not
          entirely completed its blameless retreat from them to the furthest
               limits of the circle,   10
          but some of its limbs remained, while others had departed.
          But however far it kept running out ahead, there followed
               in pursuit
          the gentle immortal onset of blameless Love.
          And immediately things grew to be mortal that formerly had
               learned to be immortal,
          and things previously unmixed <grew to be> mixed,
               interchanging their paths.   15
          And as they were mixed, myriads of tribes of mortal things
               poured forth,
          joined closely together with all kinds of forms, a wonder
               to behold.

14.129   (36) And when they were coming together, Strife was retreating to the
               extremity.

Origin of Animals in the Phase of Increasing Love

14.130 (57) By her [Love] many neckless faces sprouted,
and arms were wandering naked, bereft of shoulders,
and eyes were roaming alone, in need of foreheads.

14.131 (58) [In this situation, the limbs were still] single-limbed [as the result of
the separation caused by Strife, and] they wandered about [aiming at
mixture with one another.]³¹

14.132 (60) Wobbly-footed with countless hands.

14.133 (61) Many grew with faces and chests on both sides,
man-faced ox-progeny, and some to the contrary rose up
as ox-headed things with the form of men, compounded partly from men
and partly from women, fitted with shadowy parts.

14.134 (59) But when divinity was mixed to a greater extent with divinity,
these things began to fall together, however they chanced to meet,
and many others in addition arose continuously.

Perception

14.135 (89) Acknowledging that there are effluences from all things that come to
be . . .

14.136 (88) A single sight [that is, visual impression] comes from both [eyes].

14.137³² (84 and 87) As when someone planning for a journey prepares a lamp,
a flame of blazing fire in the wintry night,
attaching lantern-screens to protect it from all kinds of winds,
scattering the blast of the blowing winds,
but the light springs out, since it is finer,   5
and shines across the threshold with unwearying beams,
in the same way, after Aphrodite had enclosed the primeval fire
in membranes and equipped it with pegs of love
she poured round-eyed Kore in fine-textured garments
that keep back the depth of water that flows around   10
but let the fire pass through since it is finer,
where they are pierced through with marvelous funnels.

14.138 (95) When they first grew together through the devices of Cypris.

---

31. Bracketed material is supplied from Simplicius, *Commentary on Aristotle's* On the
Heavens, 587.18–19.

32. I adopt Rashed's reconstruction (Rashed [2007]).

[Quoted as part of Empedocles' explanation of why some people see better by day and others by night (Simplicius, *Commentary on Aristotle's* On the Heaven 529.26).]

14.139   (99) fleshy twig

[Empedocles thus called the ear (Theophrastus, *On Sensation* 9 = DK 31A86).]

14.140   (100) This is how all [animals] inhale and exhale: in all of them bloodless
              tubes of flesh extend deep in the body.
              At the mouths of the tubes, the furthest extremities of the nostrils
              are pierced through with closely arranged holes, so that they retain the
              blood, but a clear path for *aithēr* is cut through.   5
              Then whenever the delicate blood leaps back from there
              the bubbling air leaps in with a raging swell,
              and when it [the blood] springs up, the animal exhales again, as when a
                  young girl
              playing with a clepsydra of shining bronze
              puts the passage of the pipe against her pretty hand   10
              and dunks it into the delicate body of silvery water,
              no liquid enters the vessel, but the bulk of air,
              pressing from inside on the close-set holes, keeps it out
              until she uncovers the compressed stream. But then
              when the air is leaving, the water duly enters.   15
              In the same way, when water occupies the vessel and the bronze
              mouth and passage is blocked by mortal flesh,
              the air striving eagerly to get in from without restrains the liquid,
              commanding the approaches around the gates of the gurgling strainer,
              until she removes her hand. At that point again, in reverse order,   20
              as the air enters, the water duly runs out.
              In the same way, when delicate blood in violent motion through the
                  limbs
              springs backward to the inmost recesses,
              immediately a stream of air raging in a swell comes in,
              and when the blood swells up, it exhales an equal amount back again.   25

14.141   (101) Hunting with its nostrils the fragments of animals' limbs . . .
              which they were leaving behind from their feet on the soft grass . . .

14.142   (102) So in this way all things have obtained both breathing and the
              sense of smell.

14.143   (104) And to the extent that they happened to fall together at great
              intervals . . . [or, . . . "the finest things happened to fall together"].

[Cited as evidence that Empedocles attributed some events to chance or luck.]

14.144   (109) For by earth we see earth, by water, water,
          by *aithēr*, divine *aithēr*, and by fire, destructive fire,
          yearning by yearning [Love] and strife by mournful Strife.

COGNITION

14.145   (110) If you fix them in your strong intelligence
          and gaze upon them propitiously with pure attention,
          these things will all be very much present to you all your life long,
          and from them you will obtain many others. For these very things
          grow into each kind of character, depending on each person's nature.   5
          But if you reach out for other kinds of things, such as the millions
          of wretched things that are found among men that blunt their thoughts,
          indeed they will quickly leave you as time revolves,
          longing to come to their own dear kind.
          For know that all things possess thought and a
             portion of intelligence.   10

14.146   (106) Wisdom grows in humans in relation to what is present.

[Cited to show that for Empedocles thought and perception work similarly
(Aristotle, *On the Soul* 3.4 427a21–23).]

14.147   (107) For from these [the four elements] all things are joined and
             compounded,
          and by these they think and feel pleasure and pain.

14.148   (105) <The heart is> nurtured in the seas of rebounding blood,
          where most especially is what is called thought by humans,
          for the blood around the heart in humans is thought.

14.149   (103) In this way by the will of chance it thinks all things [or, . . . "all
             things have thought"[33]].

14.150   (108) Insofar as they change and become different, so far, it follows,
          are different thoughts always present to them.

Life and Character

Empedocles' approximate dates are 490–430; he is a contemporary of Zeno and
Melissus, and a generation younger than Parmenides. For his relation to Anaxagoras, see above pages 198–99. He came from Acragas, an important Greek
city in Sicily, and has firm intellectual connections with the western Greek
lands. He visited the city of Thurii in southern Italy shortly after its Panhellenic

---

33. Cf. **14.145** l.10.

foundation in 444, where he may have met such men as Herodotus the historian and Protagoras the Sophist. Southern Italy was home to Pythagorean traditions and other (Orphic) religious beliefs in the afterlife, all of which strongly influenced Empedocles. Finally, Elea, the home of Parmenides, whose philosophical importance for Empedocles was crucial, was also located in southern Italy.

There are many fascinating stories about Empedocles' life and activities, but almost everything they contain is fiction. In fact, we know next to nothing about him. He came from a wealthy and aristocratic background and played an active role in the turbulent political life of the Greek cities in southern Italy. It is likely that as a result he was exiled and may have died in the Peloponnese, although more spectacular stories about his death are told. Most famous is that he leapt into the crater of Mount Etna "wishing to confirm the report about him that he had become a god."[34] He had been hailed as a god by the people of Selinus, a neighboring town of Acragas, for freeing them from a pestilence caused by their polluted river. He diverted two nearby streams at his own expense so as to flush out the unhealthy stream. But this token of reverence hardly accounts for Empedocles' ego and flair for showmanship. In public he wore a purple robe, a gold crown, bronze shoes, and a laurel wreath. He wore his hair long, had a retinue of boys to attend him, and adopted a grave demeanor. He was known as a physician and magician (professions by no means distinct in antiquity). According to a widely known story he kept a woman alive for thirty days without breathing or pulse. In addition he was both a philosopher who articulated a complex and novel theory of the *kosmos*, and a fervent preacher of a doctrine of a fall from a state of original purity and of ultimate redemption. He has been described as a magician and mystic. Not surprisingly he is one of the most difficult Presocratics to understand, and also one of the most interesting.

Writings

His philosophical oeuvre is composed in the epic meter also used by Xenophanes and Parmenides. The genuinely poetic quality of his writing, which has been admired since antiquity, constitutes an obstacle to understanding his literal message, though its figurative and emotional content give it a vividness and urgency unmatched in philosophical writings before Plato. His style suits his purpose, which is not primarily to give an account of the *kosmos*, though it involves this too, but to exhort us to achieve salvation and to show us how. His surviving fragments constitute the largest bulk of material surviving from any Presocratic, but they admit of widely differing interpretations, and readers from the time of Aristotle, who presumably had access to all his writings, have found themselves perplexed. Because of the difficulties and because of the large amount of material,

---

34. Diogenes Laertius, *Lives of the Philosophers* 8.69 = DK 31A1.

my discussion of Empedocles will be more selective, less comprehensive and also more dogmatic than in previous chapters.[35]

Empedocles is said to have composed tragedies, a historical poem on the Persian War, a poem to Apollo, and medical writings as well as philosophical poetry, which will be our exclusive concern and for which two titles are recorded: *On Nature* and *Purifications*.[36] The traditional view holds that these were two separate poems on different, incompatible themes. *On Nature* was a "scientific" poem which treated the elements, Love and Strife, the nature of compounds, the origin and present structure of the *kosmos*, the origin of animal species, and topics in physiology, perception, cognition, and epistemology, while *Purifications* was concerned with the Fall of spirits from a godlike state into mortal creatures, their transmigration, and their hope of ultimate redemption and regaining divine status through the abstention from certain practices and the following of certain rituals. (For want of a better single word, I will refer to these topics as "religious.") On this account the poems not only treat different subjects but also are mutually contradictory, for the "scientific" poem maintains that the only everlasting things are the four elements (earth, water, air, and fire) and the two entities that cause them to move (Love and Strife); all other things are perishable compounds—whereas the "religious" poem requires the spirits to be immortal. Moreover, the development of the *kosmos* in the "scientific" poem, in which the spirits must take part, is thought incompatible with the everlasting divine bliss which is the lot of the redeemed spirits.

This interpretation can be questioned. In the first place a clear distinction between the "scientific" and the "religious" was alien to Presocratic thought (Heraclitus and Parmenides provide the most striking cases of this fact), or indeed to Greek philosophy in general (although the philosophers' notions of the divine were in the main remote from the Olympian gods). The Pythagoreans believed in the soul's immortality and reincarnation. Thus there is no a priori reason why the nature, history, and prospects of the human soul should not form part of a work on the nature, history, and prospects of the *kosmos* and of the elements and compounds within it. Further, if there really is inconsistency, it may not make much difference for our overall interpretation of Empedocles whether

---

35. Diverse accounts abound. See below p. 268 n. 69 for references.

36. It is doubtful that Empedocles titled his poem either *On Nature* or *Purifications*. The former title is attributed to the writings of many of the Presocratics, but the word "nature" is unlikely to have been used in the general sense of "the whole of nature" or "the nature of things" before the time of Aristotle. (At *Phaedo* 96a, Plato seems to treat the expression "on nature" as unfamiliar and requiring explanation, whereas Aristotle and his followers use it as a standard term.) The latter title is not found for Empedocles' poem in sources earlier than the second century CE (Diogenes Laertius, Theon of Smyrna, Hippolytus and Herodian) and is likely to have been attached to it because of the similarity of its theme (or one of its important themes) to other works of that title.

the incompatible features occur in different poems or in different parts of the same poem. Either way we must qualify or restrict our conclusions accordingly. And finally, there may be no inconsistency at all, if we are prepared to accept an appropriate conception of immortality—one bound up with the fate of the elements and devoid of personal identity.

Beginning in the 1980s the traditional view was challenged by a minority of scholars,[37] and its central claim that the "physical" material could not belong to the same poem as the "religious" material was decisively refuted by the publication in 1999 of Empedoclean material that had been lost since antiquity. The text in question, known as the Strasbourg papyrus, was purchased in Egypt, its country of origin, in 1904 and brought to the papyrus collection at the Imperial Library of Strasbourg, where it remained unstudied until the 1990s. Its importance was immediately recognized, and it was soon afterwards published in an excellent edition.[38] It contains seventy-four lines of Empedocles' poetry (many of them only partly preserved). Because of the state of preservation of the papyrus, the lines are not continuous, but four sections are long enough to make some difference to our understanding of Empedocles' thought, and in addition they coincide with, overlap with, or include already-known fragments (**14.58, 14.59, 14.61**, and **14.64**). With the addition of the new material, **14.58** is extended from thirty-six to sixty-nine continuous lines (although some lines are incomplete), thus becoming the longest surviving fragment of any Presocratic. The most striking feature of the new material, and the one that is relevant to the question at hand, is that the section of the papyrus that makes up the last part of **14.58** contains "religious" material, whereas the first part of the fragment is one of the most central sections of Empedocles' "scientific" doctrines. This proves that Empedocles had no difficulty putting both kinds of material in the same poem—in fact, in the same context—only a few lines apart. This discovery does not settle the questions whether there were two poems, one poem referred to by two titles, or one poem known as a whole as *On Nature*, a part of which was known as *Purifications*—and if there were two poems, to which poem each of the surviving fragments belongs, but there is far less at stake in the questions that remain. The challenge now is to reach a satisfactory interpretation of the material we have, ideally one that combines the two aspects of his doctrine. In what follows, I will first present a sketch of Empedocles' "scientific" ideas and then offer an interpretation of his "religious" views which, so far from being inconsistent with the former material, coheres with it to form a whole.[39]

---

37. Osborne (1987a and 1987b) tentatively followed with minor qualifications by Inwood (1992: 8–19 and 2001: 8–19).

38. Martin and Primavesi (1999).

39. This interpretation here is largely the same as the interpretation offered in the first edition of *Philosophy Before Socrates*.

A purification is a means of removing a state of pollution in which an individual, family, or city would find itself as the result of committing a certain kind of forbidden action (manslaughter, for example) or failing to perform a required one (such as a sacrifice). Pollution would be incurred whether or not the improper behavior was done intentionally. Pollution and purification are conceptions of Greek religion, not Greek law. Purification can be achieved through ritual means (sacrifice, pouring libations, or ritual bathing to wash away the stain) or through abstaining from certain kinds of behavior.

The title *Purifications* will therefore refer to the "religious" aspect of Empedocles' work, which describes the pollution and subsequent Fall of divinities from a state of bliss, their successive incarnations in mortal creatures, and the means of purification by which they can be freed from the necessity of rebirth and can return to a condition of blessed happiness.

The Beginning of Empedocles' Poem[40]

The poem begins[41] with an address to his friends in his native city (**14.1**), in which he describes himself as thought of by them as a god, greatly honored, and sought after for his knowledge of medicine, of the future, and of how to make a fortune. His superiority to other humans (**14.3**) enables him to learn directly from a divine source (**14.42** line 2, **14.45**) an otherwise unreachable truth (**14.37**, **14.43**), in particular, knowledge about the gods (**14.38**, **14.8**). He speaks as a seer like Teiresias, confident of his knowledge, assured of its importance, and feeling no need to offer justification. And yet he acknowledges that there are limits to what ordinary mortals can or are willing to understand (**14.43** lines 8–9, **14.2**, **14.42** l.1).

The poem is dedicated to Pausanias, Empedocles' young lover[42] (**14.39**), who is presumably the "you" the fragments frequently address.[43] Empedocles will teach his knowledge to Pausanias to the extent that he will be able to comprehend it, and to that extent Pausanias will be able to transcend the limitations of human experience (**14.43**). Empedocles makes extraordinary claims for the powers this knowledge will bring (**14.40**) and for its value as compared with the

---

40. For purposes of exposition I follow the view of van der Ben (1975), Sedley (1989, 1998), and Pierris (2005)—Inwood (1992: 19; 2001: 19) is more cautious—that the surviving fragments come from one poem, whose opening section was known as *Purifications*. I have arranged the fragments in an order that corresponds to this view.

41. Diogenes Laertius, *Lives of the Philosophers* 8.62 = DK 31A1.

42. Diogenes Laertius, *Lives of the Philosophers* 8.60 = DK 31A1.

43. Some of the fragments refer to a singular "you" and others to a plural "you," which is usually thought to be the citizens of Acragas, as in **14.1**. Some have attempted to use this difference as a basis for assigning the relevant fragments to different works of Empedocles.

misguided concerns of most men (**14.145**). He warns Pausanias not to reveal to others what he learns (**14.41**, **14.44** lines 1–3).

14.9 vividly tells of the origin of the pollution and the punishments it brings. Pollution arises from bloodshed and making false statements under oath.[44] Those who incur this pollution are long-lived *daimones* (singular, *daimōn*) (a looser word for divinity than *theos* "god"). The punishment for these sins is a vast period of exile from the blessed gods, during which the fallen divinity is born and reborn in different forms of life and is driven into exile by each of the four elements in turn. The fragment's intensely emotional tone is explained by Empedocles' own involvement: he is one of the fallen divinities now suffering this awful fate—and so are we, which gives us a powerful motive to heed his earnest message—to become aware of our divine nature, our fate, and the means of our redemption. To comprehend this teaching, we must learn as well the nature and workings of the *kosmos* and our place in it. This is an important link between the "scientific" and "religious" sides of Empedocles' philosophy, as it is between the two sides of Pythagoreanism.[45] Empedocles' overall message is "religious," as the fact that **14.9** appeared near the beginning of his poem[46] shows. Not far from the beginning came the sixty-nine lines of **14.58**, which contain "religious" material. But the "religious" material is embedded in and supported by a cosmology and a physical theory which are highly original and fascinating in their own right. The remainder of this chapter will treat these latter subjects first and afterwards will return to the theme of the divinities and their (our) prospects.

Physical Principles

14.58, which appeared relatively early in Empedocles' treatise,[47] introduces the chief characters and processes of the *kosmos*: four elements (fire, air, water, earth) and two sources of change (Love and Strife), which cause the reciprocal processes of unification and separation. The last section (beginning at line 36), added from the Strasbourg papyrus with its use of the pronoun "we" in lines 36 and 56) also speaks of "our" role in the pageant of cosmic history in a way that makes it clear that it is no longer possible to suppose that Empedocles' statements about "us" and our mournful condition have nothing to do with his physical theory.[48]

---

44. Greek oaths were sworn "by (one or more of) the gods"; to swear falsely is a religious offense that can bring divine wrath on the individual or on his family or entire city.

45. See above p. 110.

46. Plutarch, *On Exile* 17 607C = DK 31B115.

47. In the Strasbourg papyrus there is a mark opposite the final line of the fragment that indicates that it is the three-hundredth line of the text.

48. See also **14.59** line 3: "we come together," a reading also due to the Strasbourg papyrus.

At the elemental level there are four basic substances (line 18). These are eternal (line 35) and fixed in quantity (lines 27, 32–33). They do not change into one another (line 35) or come to be or suffer destruction or undergo change in their basic qualities (lines 31–34). They maintain their identity intact (line 35). Each exists fully, and aside from them (and Love and Strife) there is nothing (line 30). Empedocles calls them not "elements," but "roots" (an evocative term which suggests that they are living sources from which other things grow) to which he gives the names of gods in **14.46**. The Sicilian goddess Nestis (used as another name for Persephone, goddess of the underworld) represents water, Zeus is fire, and Hera and Aidoneus (another name for Hades) probably represent air and earth, respectively.[49] Empedocles uses a range of terms for his elements. Fire is also flame, sun (Helios), "the shining one" (Elektor), and Hephaestus. Water is also called rain and two names (Pontos and Thalassa) which both translate as "sea." Air is Heaven (Ouranos) and *aithēr*. Earth is referred to in several ways (Chthon, Gaia, Aia) which all translate as "earth."

The variation in names raises an important question—did Empedocles conceive of his elements as pure substances? Since he knew that rain is fresh water and sea is salt water,[50] he should recognize that seawater is impure in comparison with rainwater. This way of thinking leads to the concept of perfectly pure water, air, etc.—idealized forms of these materials which perhaps never occur in isolation in the *kosmos* around us but out of which substances we encounter (such as rainwater and seawater) are composed. But the use of "sea" and "rain" indifferently as names for the same element may point to the opposite view, that seawater and rainwater (perhaps other liquids too) are each fully as much water as any of the others, so that the term "water" covers many liquids, and likewise "air" many gases, and "earth" many solids. Alternatively, if Empedocles held that the elements are, properly speaking, "pure," the variety of names by which he calls them may be a deliberate maneuver to avoid identifying any single familiar substance with a pure element. **14.46**, then, may be more than allegory, since ordinary conceptions of the gods are misguided (**14.80**; with lines 4–5, compare **14.145** line 10): the names "Zeus," "Hera," etc. really refer to the elements.

The four roots join to form "mortal" compounds (**14.58** lines 34–35, **14.60** lines 9–12, **14.104**, **14.62**, **14.75**, **14.109**), which, unlike the "immortal" elements (**14.128** line 14), come to be and perish. More properly stated, they are formed by mixture and dissolved by separation of their component elements (**14.48**). The reference to the roots as immortal and to compounds as mortal and as undergoing birth and death (**14.50** line 5; **14.58** line 4) is not simply metaphorical. One of the most familiar contrasts in ancient Greek culture is between the immortality of the gods and the mortality of humans. On the traditional view, the gods

---

49. These identifications have been disputed since antiquity, most recently by Kingsley (1995), who identifies Aidoneus as fire, Zeus as air, and Hera as earth.

50. Cf. **14.101**. **14.102** may refer to the evaporation of seawater to produce salt.

are privileged in a way that humans, who are born and die, are not, but both gods and humans are living beings. Empedocles frequently calls the roots by the names of the Olympian deities, and he describes the roots and their compounds in language suitable for living things. Further, as the fragments (for example, **14.60** and **14.63**) show, living things—plants, animals, and humans—and their parts are his most frequently occurring examples of compounds. This provides another link between the different areas of Empedocles' thought.

Mixing the elements to form compounds and dissolving compounds into separate elements are functions of Love and Strife, respectively (**14.60, 14.59, 14.104, 14.106, 14.112, 14.70**). Love attracts dissimilars to dissimilars, while Strife, in separating dissimilars, attracts like to like. Love and Strife are opposed to one another (**14.58, 14.60, 14.67**), and exist always (**14.57**). When Love fully dominates and Strife is inoperative in the *kosmos*, the totality of the four elements is mixed together into a single, uniform, sphere (**14.76**); conversely, when Strife dominates and Love is unable to do its work, the four elements are separated from one another by being completely segregated into concentric spherical shells with the earth at the center, surrounded in turn by water, air, and fire.

How Empedocles conceived of Love and Strife is problematic. One issue is whether they are something like forces, which operate on matter but are immaterial, as we might expect from statements that compounds are made up of the four elements (not the four elements plus Love and Strife) (**14.58** lines 34–36, **14.60** lines 13–14, **14.63**). But he describes Love and Strife in terms appropriate to material entities with spatial location: "equal in all directions," "among them, equal in length and breadth," and "spinning among them" (**14.58** lines 19, 20, 25–26). Also Love and Strife occupy different parts of the *kosmos* at different stages of its existence (**14.128**). It may be that he conceived of Love and Strife as immaterial forces and that the spatial language just cited is used metaphorically, but I find it more plausible to take this language as evidence of the difficulty of conceiving of an immaterial force in the mid-fifth century.[51] Aristotle aptly complains that Empedocles makes Love and Strife principles "both as movers and as matter (for they are parts of the mixture)."[52] Love and Strife must be physically present among the elements to operate on them, and yet the elements are thought to be the only physical constituents of compounds (cf. **14.75, 14.109**).

Empedocles expresses the relation between Love and Strife and the elements by saying that the latter mix and are separated "by Love," "by the hatred of Strife" (**14.58** lines 8–9), "in Anger" and "in Love" (**14.60** lines 7–8), "through their birth in Strife" (**14.67** line 9), etc.[53]—language suggesting that he thought of Love and Strife as agents, not constituents. And yet they are agents that act by

51. See also above p. 217.

52. Aristotle, *Metaphysics* 12.12 1075b2–7 (not in DK).

53. See also **14.59** lines 2 and 4, **14.67** line 5, **14.104, 14.106, 14.112, 14.75, 14.63** lines 5–6, **14.76**.

their presence: if they depart, their effects do not remain, whereas compounds continue to exist because of the continuing presence of Love, and likewise, the elements remain separate from one another because of the continued presence of Strife (**14.128** lines 7–17.)

Another issue is whether Love and Strife are responsible for all changes that occur in the *kosmos*. It is tempting to think of the elements as inert matter and Love and Strife as what make them move.[54] But such an interpretation runs the risk of anachronism, since earlier philosophers had supposed motion to be an inherent feature of their primary substance, not requiring an external cause. Moreover, the elements seem to have motions due to their own nature: fire and air upward (**14.88**, **14.86**)[55] and, no doubt, water and earth downward,[56] and the whirling vortex motion of the *kosmos* (**14.128** line 4) "compels" the earth to move to the center.

14.151   And so, if the earth is now at rest by compulsion, it came together, brought to the middle by the vortex motion.[57]
(Aristotle, *On the Heavens* 2.13 295a9–10 = DK 59A88)

On the basis of this evidence I conclude that Love and Strife are directly responsible not for all motion but specifically for the mixing and separation of the elements. For a compound to form we need both the correct amounts and proportions of its constituent elements and also of Love (and, I shall argue below, page 276, of Strife) in the right amounts and proportions to unite them in the right way (**14.70** [if the context is given correctly], **14.75**, **14.86**, **14.109**, **14.104**, **14.106**, ?**14.112**).

How, then, do Love and Strife affect the elements? They are not simply mechanical forces. Things under the influence of Love "love one another," while those under Strife's power are "enemies" and "very mournful" (**14.67**). He calls Love by other names (Friendship, Aphrodite, Joy, Harmonia[58]) and declares that she is responsible for kindly thoughts and peaceful deeds (**14.58** line 23). The cosmic unifying force is identical with the familiar force of Love which unites different humans. Love's operation in the *kosmos* is psychological as much as physical. Through her the different elements are attracted to or "yearn for" one

---

54. Aristotle takes this line to identify Empedocles' four elements as "material causes" and Love and Strife as "efficient causes" (*Metaphysics* 1.4 985a29–33 = DK 31A37).

55. The assertion that Empedocles recognizes chance as a cause of motion (**14.86**, **14.109** line 1, **14.143**) is an Aristotelian interpretation which can be disregarded.

56. There is evidence that Empedocles did not state this fact clearly (Aristotle, *On the Heavens* 2.13 295b2–3 [not in DK]).

57. Empedocles is mentioned just below at 295a17 as holding this theory.

58. The basic meaning of this word is "fitting together," "connection," or "joint." For the importance of this concept for the Pythagoreans see above p. 92 and below p. 357.

another (**14.60** line 8). Similarly for Strife, which is also called Quarrels and Hatred and is characterized as destructive, as evil, and as that which operates by hatred, makes the elements bitter and causes them to hate each other. In addition, Love and Strife are moral agents. Love and her effects are good; Strife and its effects are evil. Empedocles' *kosmos* is therefore far from simply a physical environment but has psychological and moral aspects built into it from the very foundations, which further supports the idea that immortal elements and mortal compounds are in some sense living things. This combination of different realms of reality seems odd today, but if we recall the tradition of Heraclitus and the Pythagoreans, it is not out of place in the first half of the fifth century.

The equality of Love and Strife is a striking feature of Empedocles' system and must be understood at the moral and psychological level as well as at the mechanical level. The treatment of opposites given by his predecessors made it unthinkable for Empedocles to attempt to account for strife, hatred, and evil in the world if the only relevant principle was a principle of love, harmony, and good. Opposites are equally powerful and cannot be generated one from the other. Also, since at the mechanical level both separation and union are seen to take place, a principle of separation or unification without a corresponding opposite principle would ultimately lead to a dead end at which all possible separation or unification had occurred. Further, if there were only a single principle, Empedocles would be vulnerable to questions Parmenides had raised: how the cosmic process got started in the first place, and what the original arrangement was like—questions to which Empedocles' everlasting cosmic cycle powered by Love and Strive makes cosmology immune.

Events in the *kosmos* are due to the effects of Love and Strife on the four elements. For cosmology, the mechanical effects of mixture and separation are most important. The two motive principles cause the four material principles to move in various ways. As they move they form temporary ("mortal") compounds which, through the effects of Love and Strife, eventually dissolve into their constituent elements or are transformed into other compounds. Compounds undergo this sort of coming to be and perishing and other changes as well. Growth, for example, is a matter of the addition of more fire, air, water, and/or earth to what was already in the compound. The sum total of earth (for example) in the universe remains constant, but more of this fixed amount is temporarily invested in the growing thing.

The nature of the compounds requires careful attention. First, the terms "elements" and "compounds" are not Empedocles' but come from modern chemistry. The four roots are in important ways comparable to such elements as oxygen and hydrogen[59]; but how far do his compounds resemble chemical compounds?

---

59. However, Empedocles did not analyze his "roots" into anything corresponding to sub-atomic particles, and, unlike modern chemists, he held that they cannot be created, destroyed, split, fused, or transformed into one another.

14.75 gives the ratio of elements in bone: two parts earth, two parts water, and four parts fire. Empedocles does not explain how he arrived at this formula, but the example is helpful nonetheless. It suggests that Empedocles' conception of compounds involves a law of fixed proportions and that a compound such as bone is to be thought of along the lines of a modern chemical compound such as water, which contains a fixed proportion of hydrogen atoms to oxygen atoms. Thus **14.75** would be the ancestor of such formulas as H_2O and CO_2.

14.109 undermines this result, though, since it talks of earth "in about equal quantity" and "a bit more or a bit less" and since it may mean that blood and other forms of flesh, which seem to be different compounds, have the same composition. But **14.109** is unclear: perhaps the slightly different proportions constitute different forms of flesh, each of which has fixed proportions, or perhaps the different proportions are meant to account for variations in the same form of flesh. In any case, there is no reason to think that Empedocles developed systematic methods for discovering the composition of compounds, or that **14.75** and **14.109** are based on anything other than sheer speculation.[60]

Second, how are the elements united in a compound—as a physical mixture, a solution, or a chemical compound? In physical mixtures like salt and pepper, the ingredients come in particles, and each particle preserves its identity in the mixture. They can be separated out of the mixture by mechanical means, since there is no chemical bonding. The different bits just sit next to one another in no determinate order, and there is no definite ratio of the mixture. Any amount of salt can be mixed with any amount of pepper. With solutions like gin and tonic, most of these same characteristics obtain, including the absence of any definite ratio in the mixture. One difference is that it is not a merely mechanical process to separate the ingredients in a solution. There may be some weak bonding effects, but no true chemical bonding. In chemical compounds there are fixed proportions of the ingredients, and the ingredients lose their identity. In H_2O, we do not have two atoms of hydrogen and one of oxygen,[61] but one molecule which does not behave like hydrogen or like oxygen but behaves like water. To recover the constituent elements from the compound is not simply a matter of sorting.

Which, if any, of these three kinds of composites is the mixture of elements which constitutes an Empedoclean compound? Any answer to this question must take into account Empedocles' repeated assertion that the four elements do not perish (**14.58** lines 30–34, **14.60** lines 13–14). They continue to exist in compounds even though they have different appearances. This is also the case in all three of the models of mixture being considered. How mixtures can come to have different properties from their ingredients is suggested by **14.72**, which tells against the salt-and-pepper model, since it shows that some properties of the compound are due to

---

60. The view that blood is composed of all four elements may be connected with Empedocles' theories of perception and thought. See below pp. 283–84.

61. In any case, hydrogen and oxygen do not normally occur in single atoms.

the interaction of the components. Simple juxtaposition is not enough. Apparently more helpful is fragment **14.62**, which likens the formation of compounds out of the elements to colors formed by blending primary colors. When a certain amount of red and yellow are blended to produce a certain shade of orange, neither of the original colors is any longer apparent, but they continue to exist as components of a color whose appearance is different from theirs. Since the original colors cannot be extracted from the compound by a simple mechanical process of separation, this fragment too tells against the salt-and-pepper model. But this interpretation of the fragment is not certain since **14.62** sets out to explain how a small number of basic elements (Greek painters used four basic colors) can combine to produce a vast array of mixtures, not how the pigments blend in forming a mixture. The problem of getting so many mixtures out of so few basic colors is under discussion, not the nature of the mixtures.

Another piece of evidence comes from **14.75** and **14.109**, which identify determinate ratios of the elements in compounds. This evidence points toward the chemical compound model rather than the "gin and tonic" one, though the uncertainties of **14.109** (discussed above page 261) must not be disregarded. Further, the paradoxical description in **14.128** line 14 of the formation of compounds out of pure elements: "immediately things grew to be mortal that formerly had learned to be immortal," explained more straightforwardly in the following line: "things previously unmixed grew to be mixed, interchanging their paths," also points toward the chemical compound model. The immortal elements become mortal by becoming ingredients in temporary compounds. They temporarily lose some of their elemental properties (water does not behave like either hydrogen or oxygen; likewise for Empedocles blood does not behave like fire, air, water, or earth although it is composed of all of them (**14.109**) but in an important sense they continue to exist in the compound.

Finally, **14.75** and **14.109** give Love a role in the compounds themselves, not just in forming them. This strongly suggests that Empedocles thought that we cannot create blood simply by pouring equal amounts of fire, air, water, and earth together and stirring, but that they must be held together in the compound in the appropriate way.[62] This is further evidence for the view that Empedocles' compounds are more like chemical compounds than mixtures or solutions. The role of Love in extant compounds thus corresponds to the modern notion of chemical bonding.

Another question is whether there are "atoms"—smallest bits of fire, air, water, and earth. Such a view is compatible with "gin and tonic" mixtures and with the blending of pigments, as well as with the "chemical compounds" interpretation, and it fits with Empedocles' belief that the four elements are preserved in compounds. Two statements of Aristotle's are illuminating:

---

62. **14.109** is compatible with a theory that blood and other kinds of flesh are made of the same constituents in the same ratios, but bonded differently, thus forming what modern chemists call isomers.

14.152 [How do compounds come to be out of the elements?] For those who talk like Empedocles . . . it must be a matter of composition, as a wall comes to be out of bricks and stones. Also this mixture will be composed of elements which are preserved, placed next to one another close by. In this way, then, there come to be flesh and all the rest.

(Aristotle, *On Generation and Corruption* 2.7 334a26–31 = DK 31A43)

14.153 If the dissolution [of an element into smaller and smaller parts] is going to come to an end, either the end product will be indivisible [atomic] or it will be divisible but will never in fact be divided, as Empedocles means to say.

(Aristotle, *On the Heavens* 3.6 305a1–4 = DK 31A43a)

Although **14.152** seems to argue for atoms, **14.153** excludes them. The two passages are compatible as long as the building blocks in **14.152** are not "atomic" but are the (still divisible) bits which form a given compound. However, it may be mistaken to pursue this issue so far. **14.152** shows that in Aristotle's opinion Empedocles is committed to minimum particles but also that this is Aristotle's opinion; he could not find an explicit statement on the matter in Empedocles' works. And this fact suggests that Empedocles did not push the analysis of the composition of his four elements to that depth. Since Anaxagoras and the Atomists presented theories of the ultimate structure of matter, it is natural to look for one in Empedocles too, but since philosophers of previous generations had not explicitly raised such questions, they may not have occurred to him.

Another feature of Empedocles' understanding of mixture and combination is described in another passage of Aristotle.

14.154 Some believe that each thing is acted on when the last agent—the agent in the strictest sense—enters through certain pores, and they say that this is how we see and hear and use all our other senses. Moreover we see through air and water and transparent substances because they possess pores that cannot be seen because of their smallness but are close together and arranged in rows. Those which are more transparent have these properties to a greater degree. Now some, including Empedocles, declared that this theory applied to certain things—not only to things that act and are acted on, but they also declare that those things undergo mixture whose pores are symmetrical with one another.

(Aristotle, *On Generation and Corruption* 1.8 324b25–35 = DK 31A87)

We will return to the doctrine of pores in connection with Empedocles' theory of perception. For present purposes, the last sentence is most important. Not all substances are equally susceptible to mixture (**14.69**). Mixture is facilitated when the pores of one component are the right size for the projecting bits of the other. Empedocles also accounts for the property of transparency by means of pores. Yet the theory raises difficult questions which he does not seem to have faced. Aristotle makes a number of criticisms that are worth repeating.

14.155   Now as to all who say that processes of being acted on occur on account of movement in the pores, if it takes place even though the pores are filled, the pores are unneeded. For if the whole is acted on in these circumstances, it would be acted on in the same way even if it had no pores but were continuous. . . . But also if these pores are empty (even though there must be bodies in them), the same consequence will follow. . . . In general it is odd to posit the pores. For if the agent does nothing by contact, it will not do it by passing through the pores either. But if it does act by contact, then even if there are no pores, when things are naturally related in this way to one another, they will act and be acted on.

(Aristotle, *On Generation and Corruption* 1.8 326b6–24 [not in DK])

Despite these unclarities and shortcomings, Empedocles' views on the nature of matter are an enormous advance on his scientific predecessors. The first clear distinctions between elements, mixtures, and compounds,[63] the first sketch of analyses of compounds into constituent elements, and the first recognition of the importance of bonding are found in his fragments. The reason for these achievements is to be found in his philosophical predecessors, for Empedocles was keenly aware of the Eleatics, in particular Parmenides, and to a large extent constructed his physical theory with the Eleatic challenge in mind.

Response to Parmenides

Like Anaxagoras,[64] Empedocles was aware of the Eleatic challenge, and his system can easily be understood as an attempt to account for the phenomena of the world around us while preserving the most important lessons of Parmenides' *Truth*. Empedocles was impressed by the force of Parmenides' arguments against generation and perishing. He wholeheartedly accepts Parmenides' thesis that nothing can be generated out of what in no way is, or perish into nothing (**14.49–14.52**). The generation and perishing of compounds is out of and into the elements, and of them there is no generation or perishing, as is maintained in arguments at **14.58** lines 30–35.[65] The arguments in lines 32–33 assume that the four elements exist in their present quantities and point to two reasons why they cannot become more. Increase is impossible, for (a) "what could increase this totality?" (that is, there is nothing aside from the four elements, therefore

---

63. Empedocles' main precursor here is Parmenides, whose conception of elements in *Opinions of Mortals* was noted above (p. 168).

64. See above pp. 198–200.

65. Compare Parmenides' arguments at **11.8** lines 6–21.

nothing is left over which can become any of them), and (b) "where would it come from?" (that is, the place occupied by the four elements is all there is; there is not even any place for anything aside from the them). Analogous reasoning proves that the elements cannot become less, either. This argument is supported by **14.53**,[66] which denies that any part of the whole is "empty or over-full": there are no gaps (places not occupied by any of the elements) in the universe nor are there any "crowds" (places occupied by more than one). The sources do not preserve any argument of Empedocles for these theses, and it would be in keeping with the present interpretation if he did not attempt to prove them but instead proceeded by asserting what his system required.[67]

Love, Strife, and the four elements are the basic principles of the system. They are eternal, not subject to generation and perishing. "There are just these very things" (**14.58** line 34, compare **14.60** line 13), he says, speaking of the four elements; they "are always and continuously the same" (**14.58** line 35)—that is, unchanging—but "running through one another at different times they come to be different things" (**14.58** lines 34–35), that is, compounds. The four elements are different in kind from one another, each with its own attributes (fire is hot, water wet, etc.) (**14.58** line 28), but all of them fully exist. To this extent they satisfy Parmenides' requirements for a thing that is.

Whereas Anaxagoras posited an unlimited number of basic things and held that there are no pure substances (a lump of gold contains more gold than other things, but it contains portions of all other things as well; we call it gold simply because the gold predominates in it, so its properties are apparent; see above page 210), for Empedocles, things are quite different. Instead of positing an unlimited number of permanent basic substances, he posits only four, but this economy has a price: he needs to account for compounds that possess properties different from the elements that make them up.

The position is not straightforward. The difficulty is found in the assertion "at different times they come to be different things and yet are always and continuously the same" (**14.58** line 35): if they come to be different things, how can they remain the same? Indeed, he says "they come to have different appearances, for mixture changes them" (**14.60** line 14). But how is it possible for them to remain the same if they are changed by the mixture they undergo in forming compounds?

A good way to deal with some of these contradictions is to identify a number of different ways in which one thing can "come to be" another, so that the sense

---

66. **14.54**, if it is authentic, may support it too, though it may be a confused recollection of **14.53** and **14.58** l.33.

67. Empedocles' denial of void may well be based on interpreting the prohibited "what-is-not" as void, but the fragments do not make this clear. Melissus argues on this basis against the existence of void (**15.9** secs. 7–10). He holds that what-is is full. He does not argue, however, that it is not *over*-full.

in which the elements "come to be" a compound is different from that in which the compound "comes to be." Thus, the kind of becoming the elements undergo is a matter of coming to be different in their external relations but remaining otherwise unchanged from their former selves, while the kind the compounds undergo is a matter of their coming to existence from something else (namely, the elements). Further, both these kinds of becoming are different from the kind in which something begins to exist without there being a previously existing thing from which it came to exist,[68] so Empedocles' talk of coming to be does not violate Parmenides' prohibition on generation, by which he means generation from what-is-not (see above pages 159–60).

But there is more. Blood is made of equal amounts of all four elements (**14.109**). When some blood "comes to be" out of some earth, some water, some air, and some fire, the result is something with the properties of blood, not of any or all of the four elements. As far as we have any reason to suppose without presupposing the truth of some theory such as Empedocles', the earth, water, air, and fire have ceased to exist and have been replaced by blood. In what sense, then, do these elements exist when they have combined to form blood? Why not say that they simply cease to exist when they become blood; and then when blood disintegrates into earth, water, air, and fire, why not say that these elements came to be? Why not suppose that the four elements are just as "mortal" as their compounds?

This question becomes more pressing when we consider the entire cosmic cycle (discussed below pages 267–80). At one extreme all the earth is together, as is all the water, all the air, and all the fire. At the other extreme, there is a sphere consisting of a total fusion of the elements—leaving no earth, water, air or fire unmixed. So it is not even true that there always exists uncompounded earth, water, air, or fire that can be used to form further compounds. In the period of complete fusion there is only a single compound.

Worst of all is the paradoxical claim that "things grew to be mortal which formerly had learned to be immortal" (**14.128** line 14), with which compare "in that they have learned to grow to be one out of many and in that they again spring apart as many when the one grows apart, in that way they come to be and their life is not lasting, but in that they never cease interchanging continually, in this way they are always unchanging in a cycle" (**14.58** lines 9–13, compare **14.63** lines 8–12).

If this is the best Empedocles can do to put up a theory that preserves the phenomenal world in terms of Parmenidean-like basic entities, Parmenides might well regard his view of reality confirmed rather than refuted. But rather than charge Empedocles with self-contradiction and incoherence, it is more profitable to regard these passages as showing him struggling to express concepts that were beyond the capabilities of the language available to him. The very same kind of questions that were just asked about the relation between the four elements and blood can also be raised about the relation between hydrogen, oxygen, and water.

---

68. Here I follow the approach taken by Inwood (2001: 33–42).

Water does not behave like either hydrogen or oxygen, but like water. A molecule of H_2O is a molecule of water, not some number of molecules of hydrogen or oxygen; the molecules of hydrogen and oxygen that combined to form it no longer exist. So in what sense are hydrogen and oxygen more basic than water? The solution is not as straightforward as it may at first appear when we learn that water is made up of hydrogen and oxygen. It requires knowing what it means to be "made up of," since clearly water is made up of hydrogen and oxygen in a different way from the way that a class is made up of its teacher and students or an orchestra is made up of its musicians. And a full understanding of the relevant sense of this expression cannot be obtained simply by looking in a dictionary but instead requires familiarity with a number of technical and unfamiliar concepts.

Empedocles wanted to express the idea, central to his theory, that some kinds of things are more basic than other (less basic) things, that the latter things depend on the former in ways that the former do not depend on the latter. The claim that the basic things are "always unchanging in a cycle" (**14.58** line 13 and **14.63** line 12) may be a clue to the kind of priority he had in mind. It is reminiscent of Heraclitus's conception of stability and identity through change (above page 137). In one sense, the elements change into compounds and back out of them again, and so are just as mortal as the compounds are. But in another sense the cosmic cycle eventually returns to the same place. We cannot understand the cycle from the Sphere alone; nor can we understand the Sphere itself without knowing about the opposite extreme of the cycle and the intervening phases. From this point of view, what is distinctive about Empedocles' physical theory is that it is viewed as the interaction of four particular basic substances which are fully manifest in their differences only at the (perhaps instantaneous) period of Strife's total dominance.

Finally, Empedocles disagrees with Parmenides' views that the senses and the opinions of mortals are unreliable (**11.1** line 30, **11.6** lines 6–7, **11.7** lines 3–4). That is not to say he finds them wholly trustworthy. They are unable to apprehend the divine (**14.8**, **14.38**). The sense-organs are feeble ("narrow") and impeded by our environment (**14.43** lines 1–2). We tend to generalize on the basis of insufficient experience, and this is the wrong way to go about learning the whole nature of things (**14.43** lines 3–8). Still, used properly the senses can help us gain understanding (**14.44**). Empedocles' distinction between understanding and the senses (most clearly in **14.44** line 8) and his admonition not to prefer any one sense over the others, but to use each appropriately (**14.44** lines 4–7) hardly amount to an epistemology, but they do grant some value to the senses, as is to be expected in a philosopher who preserves the phenomenal world.

Cosmic Cycle

Not only does Empedocles conceive a new approach to traditional questions about the basic form(s) of matter and the source(s) of movement and change, but he also postulates a new kind of system of the *kosmos*, a system governed by the interactions of Love and Strife and the four elements. I will begin this section with a summary of the principal features of the cosmic cycle, reviewing the evidence for the different phases of the cycle, and will then take up a number of related issues. The nature of the cycle is one of the most disputed topics in Empedocles, and despite a large number of detailed studies in the past couple of generations, no consensus has yet been reached. There are two main camps (in each of which there are many variations). Both camps agree that there is an infinitely recurring cycle whose extreme stages are characterized respectively by a total dominance of Love and a total dominance of Strife. One camp maintains the view first proposed in the 19th century and prevalent until the 1960s— that in each turn of the cycle, a *kosmos* is created both in the phase marked by increasing Love (that is, the transition phase from the dominance of Strife to the dominance of Love) and in the phase marked by increasing Strife; in effect, the cosmology under increasing Strife is the reverse of what happens under increasing Love. The other camp denies this double cosmogony, and holds that there is only one, which occurs in the phase of increasing Love. The interpretation given in this chapter belongs to the first camp. I regret that in the scope of this chapter I cannot give the opposing camp the hearing it deserves.[69]

The following text clearly states that Empedocles posited a double cosmogony.

14.156   Some say that the same *kosmos* comes to be and perishes in turn and after
         again coming to be it perishes again, and that this succession is eternal—
         for example, Empedocles, who says that Love and Strife dominate in turn
         and that Love brings all things together into one and destroys the *kosmos* of
         Strife and from it makes the Sphere, and Strife again separates the elements
         and makes this kind of *kosmos*.
                                      (Simplicius, *Commentary on Aristotle's* On the
                                               Heavens, 293.18–294.3 = DK 31A52)

The essential principle of Empedocles' *kosmos* is an eternal pattern of alternate and reciprocal increases and decreases in the influence of Love and Strife over the four elements. At one extreme of the cycle, Love has complete dominance and Strife has none; at the other extreme, Strife dominates all, Love none. At the time of Love's complete dominance, the elements are completely and uniformly mixed and bonded into a single spherical compound, "the Sphere," comprising all the material in the universe. When Strife prevails utterly, there is no mixture at all and the elements are completely separated from one another: all earth in

---

69. My view of the cosmic cycle agrees in its general lines with the interpretations of Guthrie (1965: 167–83), O'Brien (1969), Barnes (1979: vol. 2, 2–7 / 1982: 308–13), Wright (1981), Graham (1988) and Inwood (2001). Several single-cosmology interpretations are discussed by Long (1974), who proposes one more of his own. Also notable are those of KRS and Osborne (1987a).

one mass, and likewise for all water, air, and fire. In between these extreme states, Love and Strife are both on the field. The transition between them is a gradual process in which the one which has dominated steadily loses influence and the other gains until it has complete control. Of the four phases of the cycle, the two extremes are static, the two transition periods dynamic. The processes of increasing mixture and increasing separation which take place in the transition periods have as their limits the states achieved at the extremes, at which no further mixture (in the one case) or separation (in the other) is possible. The elements can interact only during the dynamic transition periods; only then are there formed a plurality of compounds (including living creatures) that come to be, perish, move, and undergo other sorts of changes and interactions. Compounds and living things are formed in both transition periods. The most striking feature of the cycle is that it involves two separate cosmogonies, one in the period of increasing Love and one in the period of increasing Strife, which proceed in reverse directions from one another, the one occurring as the four elements move from complete separation to complete unity and the other occurring as they separate out of the state of complete unification. To what extent the events in successive periods of increasing Love or increasing Strife occur in the same way and in the same order, and to what extent the events in a period of increasing Love or Strife are "reverse playbacks" of the events in the preceding period of Strife or Love is left unclear in the material which we have.[70] Another important feature of the cycle is the perishing of the *kosmos* that occurs in each transition period.[71] The *kosmos* as we know it is not permanent, but doomed—a temporary byproduct of the effects of Love and Strife on the four elements—yet other *kosmoi* will arise in future transition phases, to be obliterated in turn in the periods of complete dominance of Love and Strife.

Empedocles describes the alternation between the dominance of Love and Strife in geographical terms. **14.128** describes the ascendancy of Love from the state in which Strife is dominant ("had reached the lowest depth of the vortex"), crowding Love "to be in the middle of the whirl." Afterwards Love regains dominance in a process that is not instantaneous but gradual. Love expands from its refuge (or prison) at the center, and as it does so it becomes possible for the elements, entirely separate under Strife's complete dominance, to begin forming compounds. During this period, "all these things [the elements] come together to be one single thing [the Sphere], not at once. . . . As they were being mixed, myriads of tribes of mortal things [compounds] poured forth, but many remained unmixed . . . all that Strife still held back aloft. For it had not entirely completed its blameless retreat from them to the furthest limits of the circle. . . ."

---

70. I find a "reverse playback" account implausible, since it would require, for example, such processes as generation, growth, and digestion to go in reverse order.

71. Hence the "double . . . generation of mortal things" and "double their decline" mentioned most prominently in **14.58**.

As Strife retreats, Love pursues it: "however far it [Strife] kept running out ahead, there followed in pursuit the gentle immortal onset of blameless Love." Strife is driven outwards: "when they were coming together, Strife was retreating to the extremity" (**14.129**). When Love dominates everywhere, the elements are merged in a total mixture to form the Sphere which is held fast "by the dense concealment of Harmonia" (**14.76**), where Harmonia is synonymous with Love. Strife is banished at "the extremity," removed from the four elements, awaiting its turn to ascend once again to dominance. There is little information about this phase of the cycle. Afterward Strife gradually gains mastery by causing the elements ("limbs") to move (**14.81, 14.82**) and under Strife's separating influence the elements begin to seek their own kind (**14.83**). While this is happening, Strife is moving inwards, once again crowding Love toward the center until at the end of this phase we have reached the state described at the beginning of **14.128**. This account explains the dual cosmogony as an effect of the oscillating movements of Love and Strife. Love's home base is the center, and Strife's is the periphery. The region in between is territory that is dominated sometimes by Love and sometimes by Strife, and for a good deal of time (during the two intermediate phases) the region in between is occupied by both Love and Strife in reciprocally varying degrees.[72]

The different phases of the cosmic cycle are unevenly set forth in the existing fragments. I have already said something about the transition from the reign of Strife to the reign of Love as described in **14.128**. When Love triumphs completely, there is no longer any separation or any distinct compounds. All that exists of all the elements is blended into a single, featureless, motionless, unchanging sphere, held fast by the bonding force of Love.[73] This state is described in **14.76–14.79**. Very little survives about the other two phases. The next transition stage begins at its appointed time with movement in the sphere (**14.81, 14.82**). As Strife becomes more prominent, the four elements separate (**14.85**). The condition of total Strife is not described in extant fragments, but must be inferred from information in **14.58** (especially lines 8–10, 16–18). The physical process by which this separation happens is called a whirl or vortex (**14.128** lines 3–4), as in Anaxagoras's system (see above pages 225–26). Aristotle declares why a vortex is an appropriate mechanism for Empedocles to use.

---

72. See Graham (2005).

73. Aristotle, followed by Philoponus, complains that the uniformity of the Sphere contradicts the permanence of the four elements and their inability to change into one another. (Aristotle, *On Generation and Corruption* 1.1 315a4–14 [not in DK]; Philoponus, *Commentary on Aristotle's* On Generation and Corruption 19.3–20.4 = DK 31A41). The permanence of the elements can be sustained if we suppose that their identity is preserved in the sphere as it is in "mortal" compounds where, as happens in the sphere (**14.76** lines 1–2), the constituent bits of the elements which form the compounds are not recognizable as such.

14.157   And so, if the earth is now at rest by compulsion, it came together, brought
to the middle by the vortex motion. For all identify this as the cause, judging by what happens in liquids and in the air. For in them the larger and
heavier things are carried toward the middle of the vortex.

(Aristotle, *On the Heavens* 2.13 295a9–13 = DK 59A88)

The circular motion observed in whirlwinds and whirlpools sorts things by
size and weight. This mechanism accounts for why—in the present state of the
kosmos, in which the effects of Strife are widespread and there is considerable,
though not complete, separation of the elements—earth, the heaviest of the four
elements, is in the center and is surrounded successively by water, air, and fire.
Further, there is evidence that the cosmic vortex exists: the circular movements
of the heavenly bodies around the earth. When separation is complete, Strife
reigns supreme and the cycle is ready to continue once again into the transition
to the reign of Love.

The cosmic cycle efficiently accounts for the workings of the *kosmos*. It
requires only the four elements and two motive principles already discussed,
and it does not postulate any properties of Love and Strife aside from their functions of uniting and separating. It makes clever use both of the Anaximandrian
concept of dynamic equilibrium of opposed principles (see above page 44) and
of the Heraclitean concept of stability through change (see above pages 225–26,
also **14.58**). The fact that the elements are immortal and have always behaved in
this cyclical pattern makes it unnecessary to account for how they came to be or
started to behave that way in the first place, so that Empedocles does not fall foul
of Parmenides' use of the Principle of Sufficient Reason (**11.8** lines 9–11).

The general outline of the cosmic cycle is clear, but several of its details
require discussion. (1) Although his system is founded on a cyclical alternation
of Love and Strife, Empedocles says little to explain why the alternation takes
place. **14.81** suggests that there is a set time for Strife (and also, no doubt, for
Love) to prevail, so that the cycle is *regular*, but it offers no physical explanation,
only a reference to "a broad oath" (see also **14.9** line 2), an image reminiscent of
Anaximander's "ordering of time" (**5.20**) and Heraclitus's "ever-living fire . . .
kindled in measures and . . . extinguished in measures" (**10.77**), and perhaps of
Parmenides' "limits of great bonds" (**11.8** line 26, compare to line 31). Aristotle's sour comment on this fragment,

14.158   At the same time he says nothing about the cause of the change except that
it is naturally that way.

(Aristotle, *Metaphysics* 3.4 1000b12–13 = DK 31A30)

is perhaps unfair, since if the alternation of Love and Strife is a basic fact of the
system, it is also a brute fact, incapable of explanation *within* the system. From the
systematic point of view, Aristotle has a point: Empedocles just asserts that that is

how it is. But the reference to an oath (**14.81**)—an unbreakable, sacred principle voluntarily agreed to by the two great equal powers—removes the claim from the level of mere assertion and grounds the system in a transcendental religious conception which can provide the needed guarantee of everlasting stability.

(2) The dual births and perishings of the *kosmos* imply that both generation and perishing are attributable to Love and also to Strife, despite Empedocles' tendency to speak of Love as causing generation and Strife as causing destruction (see, for example, **14.59**, where "quarrels" refers to Strife, **14.67**, and **14.104**). Since *kosmoi* and compounds can no more exist in the Sphere of Love than they can exist in the complete separation under total Strife, for Love to achieve domination involves the perishing of all compounds as well as of the *kosmos* that arose in the transition from Strife to Love; and equally, the formation of the *kosmos* and compounds in the opposite transition phase is due to Strife's breaking up the Sphere of Love.

(3) Although the surviving fragments do not say so, the present *kosmos* is located in the period of increasing Strife.

14.159 He says that the *kosmos* is in a like state both now in the period of [increasing] Strife and previously in the period of [increasing] Love.
(Aristotle, *On Generation and Corruption* 2.6 334a5–7 = DK 31A42)

The elements are now mostly separated, with the vast bulk of each already separate from the others, so Strife must be far along in its advance toward total rule. This situation may account for the prevalence of hostility and war among humans. Since we live in a period of increasing Strife, the present is worse than the past and the future will be worse yet—a view supported by traditional stories about a decline from a golden age.

(4) The cycle is symmetric—there are similar states of the *kosmos* in each transition phase. The strongest evidence for this important feature is **14.159**. It follows that the history of the birth, growth, maturity, decline, and death of the *kosmos* in its present phase is just the reverse of the events that take place in the opposite phase. This fact has two major consequences: it makes Empedocles' work easier, since some events are easier to describe and understand as due to separation and others as due to unification, and it effectively doubles the amount of our knowledge about the specifics of Empedocles' dual cosmogonies.

(5) Although the *kosmos* that occurs in the period of increasing Love is described in outline in **14.128**, Empedocles failed to provide a detailed cosmogony for this phase.

14.160 It is not reasonable to produce an account of coming to be from things which are separated and in motion. For this reason even Empedocles omits an account of coming to be in the period of [increasing] Love. For he would not be able to put together the heaven by constructing it out of separate things and making the compound through Love. For the *kosmos* is composed of separate elements, so that it must have come to be from a single united thing.

(Aristotle, *On the Heavens* 3.2 301a14–20 = DK 31A42)

Such a cosmogony would proceed backward from other Greek cosmogonies which describe the process of differentiation of plurality out of an original unity. Nevertheless, **14.128** indicates briefly that compounds *are* formed in the period of increasing Love, and some of the remarks on the origin of animals refer to this period. Conversely, a cosmogony starting from the Sphere of Love would resemble other cosmogonies and would not present any special problems.

(6) The universe is spherical in all four phases. At the time of Love's total dominance, there is a single spherical compound of all that exists of the four elements (**14.76, 14.78, 14.79**). In the present transition period (and so in the opposite one too) the *kosmos* is also spherical, as witnessed by the cosmic vortex (**14.157**, compare to **14.128** line 4), the statement that in the transition period from total Strife to total Love, Strife was retreating "to the furthest limits of the circle" (**14.128** line 10),[74] and by later accounts of Empedocles' cosmology (for example, **14.164**). It is likely that when Strife has complete rule, the universe is spherical too—with all the earth gathered in a sphere at the center and surrounded by spherical shells of water, air, and fire, as is largely the case now.

(7) While the transition periods are obviously times of change and movement, the extreme phases know no change. In addition, the Sphere of Love[75] is motionless, as **14.78** may say[76] and **14.82** strongly suggests. Aristotle implies that under complete Strife the sphere keeps rotating with the vortex motion which was the mechanical means by which Strife caused the elements to separate.

14.161   This [the vortex] is the reason all who generate the heavens give for the earth's coming together at the center; but they seek the explanation for why it remains. . . . Others, like Empedocles, say that the circular motion of the heavens, which is faster than that of the earth, prevents it like water in cups, and for the same reasons. For when the cup is whirled in a circle, the water, whose natural movement is downward, does not fall down even though it is often underneath the bronze. Although if the vortex did not prevent it . . . where will it move? For it moves to the middle by constraint and stays there by constraint.

(Aristotle, *On the Heavens* 2.13 295a13–24 part = DK 31A67)

---

74. *Kuklos*, the word translated "circle," is frequently used of the spherical vault of the heaven.

75. I shall continue to refer to the *kosmos* during the period of Love's total dominance in this customary way even though the world is spherical in the other periods too.

76. The word in question, *moniē*, can be derived from *monos*, "alone," or from *menein*, "to remain"; hence the alternative translations.

(8) How long do the phases last? **14.159** and the principle of symmetry that it suggests call for the transition periods to have the same length, which must be long enough for the elements to form into a *kosmos* and for the *kosmos* to run its course. Symmetry would also require the periods of total Love and total Strife to have the same length as each other but perhaps not necessarily the same as the transition periods. **14.128** line 5 suggests that the period of total Strife is instantaneous: all things begin to come together at the very moment when Strife has achieved its maximum effect; but it can also be taken simply as saying that the transition to the rule of Love begins after (although not immediately after) Strife reaches its state of dominance. On the other hand, the Sphere of Love is described in ways that make it seem to last more than an instant.

One of the most remarkable discoveries concerning Empedocles since the publication of the first edition of *Philosophy Before Socrates* has been the discovery of important evidence on the relative lengths of the phases of the cycle in a 12th-century manuscript of Aristotle. Like many manuscripts, this one contains scholia (notes in the margins) relevant to the texts it contains.[77] Commenting on some of Aristotle's remarks on Empedocles, the scholia give the following information.

14.162   (a) When Love too came to rest after sixty "times," Strife did not begin to cause a breaking off but remained at rest.

  (b) The breaking apart did not occur immediately after the passing of the sixty "times" in which Love dominated.

  (c) . . . by separation when after one hundred "times" Strife dominates.

(Byzantine scholia on Aristotle's *Physics* and *On Generation and Corruption*. Rashed [2002] [not in DK])

It is reasonable to understand (a) as saying that the length of the phase of ascending Love is sixty "times" and that there was some length of time after that phase concluded (during which we have the Sphere) before the phase of ascending Strife began. That is to say, the duration of the Sphere was not instantaneous. The author of the scholia supposed that during the period of the Sphere, not only the four elements but Love as well were at rest. (b) and (c) indicate that the author employs the word "dominate" for the activity of Love and Strife during the phase in which they are increasing. The one hundred "times" mentioned in (c) are the period in which Love prevails, including the sixty during which Love is ascending to complete power, from which it follows that the duration of Love's total domination during the period of the Sphere is forty "times." **14.81** ("the time . . . that is established for them in turn") indicates that the time of Strife's prevailing is equal to that of Love, which Aristotle confirms:

---

77. The relevant scholia are found in Rashed (2002) and are discussed by Primavesi (2005). I follow Primavesi's interpretation.

14.163 If [Empedocles] is going to determine the alternation [of Love and Strife], he should give some instances where this holds . . . Also, his point about equal times requires some argument.

(Aristotle, *Physics* 8.1 252a27–32 [not in DK])

So the duration of Strife's prevalence is one hundred "times," too. The sources leave it unclear whether Strife's stretch is to be subdivided as Love's is, sixty "times" for the rise to complete dominance and forty for the period of total dominance or in some other way or if, as many hold, Strife exercises total dominance only instantaneously, so that it takes one hundred "times" for Strife to attain total dominance and immediately afterwards the one hundred "times" of Love begin. In any case, the new information enables us to say that the entire cosmic cycle takes two hundred "times."

A remaining question is how long the units are which the scholia refer to as "times." One suggestion, based on Empedocles' occasional use of the term *aiōn* ("lifetime") to designate a lengthy period of time (**9.6** line 6, **14.58** line 45), is that the time unit involved is a human lifetime, which might range from seventy to one hundred years. The length of the entire cosmic cycle would then be somewhere from fourteen thousand to twenty thousand years. Another possibility is based on the figure of thirty thousand seasons during which the fallen divinities take on mortal forms (**14.9** line 6). In Empedocles' time, the Greeks divided the year into three seasons, so that thirty thousand seasons is ten thousand years. If we assume that the divinities are the first compounds formed as Strife begins to gain power and the last to perish before Strife dominates completely, so that thirty thousand seasons, or ten thousand years, is the maximum possible time for a compound to last, then each time unit turns out to be one hundred years.

(9) What happens to Love and to Strife during the period of total dominance of the other? At this point Empedocles' inability to conceive of anything existing without a spatial location causes difficulties. Love and Strife are eternal, so they must always be somewhere. So even when Love is totally dominant Strife must be somewhere, and likewise Love must be somewhere when Strife rules supreme. Yet there is nowhere apart from the region occupied—and occupied without gaps—by the four elements. So even at their periods of no influence, Love and Strife still occupy *some* territory, which means that they are present in some region occupied by one or more of the elements, which means that they are causing their characteristic effects in those regions, since for them to be somewhere is for them to act there. But this implies that there are *no* times at which either is completely dominant, which conflicts with Empedocles' claims that there are such times. Empedocles minimizes this problem by confining Love to "the middle of the whirl" and Strife to "the furthest limits of the circle," but it is a problem that he cannot make vanish completely. A further question arises from the conjecture that during the period of the Sphere, Strife is lurking outside:

the question of what there is outside the region occupied by the elements. Is the *kosmos* only a part of a larger (perhaps infinite) universe?

Another problem arises in connection with the locations of Love and Strife during the transition periods. **14.128** suggests that at any moment during those phases, Love completely controls a determinate volume—a sphere with a definite radius, whose center is the center of the universe—and Strife completely controls the rest—a spherical shell extending from just where Love leaves off to the extremity. But this interpretation seems impossible to maintain, since it implies that at any given moment there is no region of the universe where the effects of both Love and Strife are felt, whereas in our current situation "mortal" compounds are both formed (through Love) and destroyed (through Strife). The geographical implications of **14.128** simply cannot be pursued so far in this direction. Empedocles must allow for regions where neither Love nor Strife is fully in control. It is therefore tempting to suppose that the geographical language of **14.128** is metaphorical and that Empedocles really means that at any moment apart from the total domination of Love or Strife, the effects of both are felt throughout the universe. For example, near the time of Strife's complete control Strife will be present everywhere in nearly full strength and Love will be present everywhere too, though with hardly any strength.[78] Compounds dissolve much more easily than they are formed or held together, but the small amount of Love still left is able to be concentrated sufficiently here and there to overcome Strife locally and to permit compounds to be formed and to stay together at least for a time. But **14.128** lines 8–11 make it difficult to accept such a metaphorical reading as the whole truth: during the increase of Love some things (at least for awhile) are "still held back aloft" so that Strife's power over them is still complete. It therefore seems likely that Empedocles believed that at any moment in the transition periods there is a region where Love holds complete sway, a region where Strife holds complete sway, and one where the effects of both are felt. As Love increases, the first of these regions grows from the center to occupy the entire universe, the second shrinks from occupying the whole universe to occupying as small a space at the extremity as is compatible with the remarks in the previous paragraph, and the third at first grows and then shrinks back to no size at all. Whether it grows so large as to occupy the entire universe is not clear, though this view is compatible with the fragments and is possibly the most satisfying interpretation. Thus, at the midpoint of each transition period Love and Strife have equal power everywhere—the universe is equally balanced between them: the battle is equal.

---

78. This is not to say that Love and Strife can occupy precisely the same spot; a given region may contain some places where Love prevails (where there are compounds) and others where Strife prevails (where the elements are separate). At the moment being described, there are few compounds, and these are distributed through the universe.

Origin and Structure of the Present *Kosmos*

In **14.85** Empedocles promises to tell how the present *kosmos* developed. The following testimonia, not all of them easily reconcilable, give a general picture.

14.164   Out of the first mixture of the elements, the air was separated off, and it flowed around in a circle. After the air, the fire escaped, and since it did not have anywhere else to go, it ran out upward underneath the solid barrier around the air. There are two hemispheres moving in a circle around the earth, one entirely of fire and the other a mixture of air and a little fire, which he believes to be night. The origin of the motion resulted from a chance collection in one region of fire, which weighed heavily. In its nature the sun is not fire but a reflection of fire like that which occurs from water. He declares that the moon was formed separately out of the air which was cut off by the fire. For this air solidified like hail. It has its light from the sun.

(pseudo-Plutarch, *Stromata*, quoted in Eusebius, *Preparation for the Gospel* 1.8.10 = DK 31A30)

14.165   The *aithēr* was separated apart first, fire second, next the earth, and water gushed forth from the earth when it was excessively constricted by the force of the rotation. The air was exhaled from the water and the heaven came to be out of the *aithēr*, and the sun from the fire, and the bodies around the earth were "felted" from the others.

(Aëtius 2.6.3 = DK 31A49)[79]

The overall resemblance as well as the differences between this account and those of earlier Presocratics (especially Anaximander and Anaximenes) are noteworthy.[80] Empedocles is in the same tradition but improves on his predecessors. **14.164** and **14.165** make no mention of Love or Strife, but in both the effects of the vortex are apparent: the four elements are largely separated and the gross structure of the universe is established, with earth in the center, seas on the earth's surface, atmospheric air above that, and the region of fire above that. The heavenly bodies are formed. The *kosmos* has a finite size (**14.87**), and in it the separation of the elements is not complete (**14.88–14.89**). Though some details are obscure, in general the account of the formation and state of the present *kosmos* conforms to Empedocles' physical theory and cosmic cycle.

---

79. 11 **14.164**'s distinction between *aēr* ("air") and *aithēr* does not entail a fifth element. It recalls the distinction, as old as Homer, between the bright upper air (*aithēr*) and the murky lower air (*aēr*) (see above p. 49). Since Empedocles calls one of his four elements "air" and "*aithēr*" indifferently, we should probably think of these as two forms of the same element.

80. See above pp. 36–38 and 55–56.

Empedocles had a considerable interest in astronomy, especially in the sun and moon (**14.91–14.99**). He states that the moon shines with light reflected from the sun (**14.94, 14.96**), gives the correct explanation of solar eclipses (**14.93**), and correctly holds night to be due to the earth's shadow (**14.98**).

Generation of Animals

14.166   The first generations of animals and plants came to be in no way complete, but split apart with parts not grown together. The second generations arose when the parts grew together, and were like images of fantasy. The third were of whole-natured beings. The fourth no longer arose from the elements, such as earth and water, but from each other from that time, in some because the nourishment grew thick and in others because the beauty of the females caused an excitement of the sexual impulse.

(Aëtius 5.19.5 = DK 31A72)

We possess fragments bearing on all four of the stages which this passage identifies (Stage 1: **14.130, 14.131**; Stage 2: **14.132–14.134**; Stages 3 and 4: **14.118**).

Stage 1 occurs in the period of increasing Love.[81] Since Strife is still largely dominant, compounds form with difficulty. Love has enough influence to unite elements to form body parts which "wandered about [aiming at mixture]" (**14.131**, compare to **14.60** lines 7–8) but not enough to unite the body parts into animals.

As Love's influence increases, greater intermixture becomes possible, and we reach Stage 2. In **14.134** I understand the "divinities" to be the four elements and "these things" to be the isolated body parts formed in Stage 1. Previously they "wandered about" but were unable to join together. Now they are able to do so when they "chance to meet." The increased power of Love ensures that they will meet, but still it is an apparently random process which forms monstrous combinations such as minotaurs and centaurs. The following passage is evidence that this same process led to extant types of animals as well.

14.167   Empedocles says that . . . next came together these ox-headed man-progeny, that is, made of an ox and a human. And all the parts that were fitted together in a manner that enabled them to be preserved became animals and remained because they fulfilled each other's needs—the teeth cutting and softening the food, the stomach digesting it, the liver turning it into blood. And when the head of a human came together with a human body, it caused the whole to be preserved, but it does not fit together with the body of an ox, and so it perishes. For whatever did not come together according to the appropriate formula perished.

(Simplicius, *Commentary on Aristotle's* Physics
371.33–372.8 = DK 31B61)

---

81. Aristotle, *On the Heavens* 3.2 300b30 = DK 31B57.

The natural history of humans and other living species thus begins in Stage 2, when limbs happen to form viable combinations. In a viable species the parts "fit together" not only in such a way that the individual can survive (the point of **14.167**), but also in a way that makes reproduction possible, so that the species can continue itself without having to be renewed by further chance combinations of limbs. The situation where animals renew their own kinds apparently represents a still further advance of Love.

The general picture so far requires a few remarks. First, the grotesque picture of body parts being formed and wandering about in isolation from one another is absurd to anyone who thinks of them as organic parts rather than simply as material components. Aristotle, the great teleologist, ridicules this notion of random combinations and says that Empedocles should have admitted "olive-headed vine-progeny" as well[82]—a suggestion we may suppose Empedocles would have accepted. Aristotle argues that the body parts are formed and put together "for an end" and therefore not by chance.[83] In terms of the examples of **14.167**, teeth come to be for the end of cutting and softening the food, and so an animal is an organic whole, made up of parts which cooperate for the survival of the individual and the species. By contrast Empedocles, with his view that survival is due to chance rather than design and is determined by fitness to survive, is more modern than Aristotle, whose teleological approach to nature precludes randomness and chance from playing a significant role.

Second, **14.167** speaks of humans being originally formed in Stage 2, which occurs in the period of increasing Love. Since the world is now in the period of increasing Strife (**14.159**) this is important evidence for the view that the same things occur in both transition phases.

Finally, the claim in **14.167** that humans are formed in Stage 2 together with its obvious implication that from that point onwards humans would reproduce themselves, conflicts with **14.166**, which places sexual reproduction in Stage 4, with the "whole-natured beings" of Stage 3 in between. But the picture is not so simple.

14.118 is devoted to Stage 3, mentioned in **14.166**, and as lines 1–2 of **14.118** indicate, Stage 3 arose before humans did.[84] But it says that the "whole-natured forms" arose first, not third, and that they did so "as fire was being separated." Further, the last two lines strongly suggest that individual limbs had not yet come to be. The obvious place in the cosmic cycle for such a situation to occur is shortly after the breakup of the Sphere of Love, when Strife has little power and the elements are still mostly in a state of mixture, with little differentiation and

---

82. Aristotle, *Physics* 2.8 199b10–13 = DK 31B62.

83. Aristotle, *Physics* 2.8.

84. Simplicius confirms this point: "Empedocles speaks these verses in the second book of the *Physics*, before the articulation of male and female bodies" (*Commentary on Aristotle's* Physics 381.29–30 = DK 31B62).

fragmentation yet occurring. In contrast to the first stage in which individual limbs wandered around, we now have beings in which no distinct limbs are evident (**14.118** lines 7–8). These odd beings made of earth joined with portions of air ("heat"), water, and fire are in some way the ancestors of humans. The word "shoot" in the sense of "sapling" (line 2) suggests that these beings somehow mature into full human form, but it is difficult to imagine how the transformation could come about. Perhaps as the increase of Strife leads to further differentiation these creatures split apart to form familiar kinds of animals.[85] The explicit denial that the "whole-natured forms" had sexual organs (line 8) reveals that sexual reproduction, and probably reproduction in general, was not possible in this stage so that once again Empedocles holds that self-reproducing species occur only during what **14.166** identifies as Stage 4.

In the overall interpretation offered here of symmetry between the two transition periods, all four stages of animal development will occur in each period. The sequence in the period of increasing Love will be $1 \rightarrow 2 \rightarrow 4 \rightarrow 3$, and in the period of increasing Strife it will be $3 \rightarrow 4 \rightarrow 2 \rightarrow 1$.[86] Since our present (fourth) stage is the only one in which animals are able to reproduce their kind, there is a sense in which we live in the highest stage of development, but this is not Empedocles' view. For the increasing dominance of Strife over Love has psychological and moral implications. In important ways the sphere of Love is the best period of existence, in some way a golden age of peace and harmony to be yearned for. And within the present condition of animal nature (Stage 4) life was happier and more harmonious earlier, when Love was more powerful, as described in **14.4** and **14.5**. The thought of an increase in the amount of Strife already present in the world is a grim prospect to be viewed with dread.

Physiology

A doctor as well as a philosopher, Empedocles was famed as the founder of the Sicilian medical tradition which rivaled Hippocrates' school at Cos and was called the empirical school because of its reliance on observation. Empedocles' interest in humans and animals is evident in both his cosmology and his discussion of the principles of his system. His examples of mixtures of the elements are usually ani-

---

85. An account along these lines which some think is related more or less closely to Empedocles' account can be found in Plato, *Symposium* 189e–193d.

86. Some interpreters claim that Empedocles has a single account of the origin of animals extending over both transition periods: Stages 1 and 2 occurring in the period of increasing Love and Stages 3 and 4 in the period of increasing Strife. I consider this reading wholly implausible in view of the gross discontinuity it requires between Stages 2 and 3, when everything is fused in the Sphere of Love, as well as of the evidence of **14.166** that humans arose in the period of increasing Love.

mals or their parts, his standard word for non-permanent compounds is "mortals," and he frequently calls the parts of the universe or the elements "limbs."

Not enough survives from his accounts of animals and plants to make any reconstruction possible, but his biological interests were unusually wide (**14.107–117, 14.119–127, 14.130–134**), he made efforts to relate biological phenomena to his physical theory (**14.61**), and he was keen to identify similarities between plants and animals (**14.110, 14.114**). He developed elaborate theories of many physiological processes, notably reproduction (**14.119–127**), digestion (**14.84**), perception (**14.135–144**) and thought (**14.146–50**), as well as offering speculations on the material composition of bodily parts (**14.75, 14.109**).

Fragment **14.140** contains a fascinating discussion of respiration. The phenomena explained are inhalation and exhalation of air. Where does air go after passing through the nose, how does it enter the body, and what pulls it in and drives it out? Empedocles explains breathing as due to the movement of blood within the body. Little hollow tubes full of blood lead into the body from the interior of the nostrils. When the blood withdraws inwardly, air rushes in to fill the gap and is expelled again when the blood returns to occupy the tubes once more. What makes the fragment so interesting is Empedocles' comparison of this process with the action of a clepsydra, a device made of baked clay which looked something like an old showerhead, perforated at the bottom with many small holes. It could be used to take a measure of water or wine out of a large container and transfer it to a small one—a useful device for serving drinks at parties—but it would also have made a delightful toy for children. Empedocles uses it as a simile, in fact a model for how respiration takes place, and it quite possibly provided the inspiration for his theory. (This is typical of Empedocles' philosophical style. We have already seen him using an analogy taken from a craft—a painter mixing primary colors on a palate [**14.62**]—to account for another natural phenomenon.) The comparison works best if the air we breathe corresponds to the water taken up by the clepsydra, the blood in our bodies to the air in the clepsydra, and the mouths of the internal tubes to the small holes in the clepsydra. The essence of the comparison is that (a) as air in the clepsydra keeps water out, so the blood in our tubes keeps air out, (b) as water enters the clepsydra when the air retreats, so air rushes into the tubes when the blood retreats, and (c) as the water leaves the clepsydra when air returns, so the air is expelled from the tubes when the blood returns. The comparison therefore works at the descriptive level but does not explain the phenomenon of respiration. Empedocles does not suggest that there is anything in us corresponding to the girl or her finger, and there are elements in the clepsydra case which do not apply in the case of breathing. Nothing in respiration corresponds to the clepsydra's ability to retain liquids when the upper opening is blocked. Empedocles does not claim that the air we breathe in is trapped in us. Likewise, nothing in the clepsydra corresponds to the fact that blood does not (normally) get expelled after the air. Though both air and water can pass through the perforations of the clepsydra, something about our structure keeps the blood from flowing out through the tubes (Empedocles might have attributed this fact to blood's being thicker than air and so unable to pass through the tubes' mouths, which are narrower than the rest of the tubes), but the comparison does not explain it.

14.140 is sometimes said to contain a report of a scientific experiment. If so, it is the earliest record of an experiment in Greek science, and one of the few from all antiquity. (In this respect Greek science differs strikingly from modern science.) But Empedocles is not describing anything like a scientific experiment as we now understand the term. First, it occurs as a simile, a literary device. Second, Empedocles does not say that he performed the operation he describes. Third, no properties of a clepsydra could possibly give experimental evidence for a theory of breathing. Fourth, the behaviors of the child and the clepsydra are familiar, whereas an experiment is a procedure whose outcome is unknown before the experiment is performed. Finally, in an experiment, the outcome confirms or refutes a hypothesis; the experiment tests the hypothesis. But belief in the theory of respiration is neither strengthened nor weakened by the comparison with the clepsydra.

On the other hand, the simile of the clepsydra is an analogy, and analogies have an important use in philosophy and science. For example, many phenomena connected with electrical current can be accounted for by comparing electricity with fluid moving through a pipe. The very term "current" reflects this practice. The amount of electricity consumed corresponds to the volume of fluid, and so forth. The analogy does not pretend to explain electrical phenomena, only to provide a model that accounts for some electrical phenomena but not for all. If an analogy is successful enough it can serve as a model of the phenomenon and can be used to predict additional phenomena. Some analogies can be extremely useful for giving a picture of how something that is not fully understood works, and it seems that Empedocles believed that the clepsydra performed this function with respect to respiration. In fact, although Empedocles does not tend to use deductive arguments in connection with his accounts of macroscopic phenomena, he made frequent use of analogies.[87]

Perception and Cognition

Empedocles' discussion of sense-perception relies on his theory of pores, used also to explain properties of mixtures (**14.154**). Physical objects give off effluences—constant streams of particles (**14.135**). (**14.141**, which apparently describes how dogs follow the scents of animals, illustrates how this thesis applies to the sense of smell.) We become aware of the effluences when they strike us and pass through the appropriate pores.

---

87. See **14.62**, **14.70**, **14.72**, **14.97**, and especially **14.137**.

14.168   Empedocles speaks similarly about all the senses and says that perception occurs by a process of fitting into the pores of each sense. This is why they cannot distinguish each other's objects, since the pores of some happen to be too wide or too narrow for the perceived thing, since some objects pass through without coming into contact and others are altogether unable to enter.

(Theophrastus, *On Sensation* 7 = DK 31A86)

Once the effluences have penetrated the proper pores, we become aware of them by virtue of the presence of the elements in the sense-organ, for Empedocles made perception an instance of the principle that like affects like (14.144).

Empedocles' treatment of the senses was the most detailed up to his time,[88] and most of our information concerns his theory of sight. Two mechanisms are instrumental for vision: effluences from visible objects which strike the eye and fire emitted by the eye itself. The latter phenomenon too, which 14.137 describes via a simile,[89] is due to effluences and pores. The pores in the pupil permit the fire to leave the eye while keeping in the water of the aqueous humor. How the emitted fire and the effluences from visible objects interact to enable us to see is obscure. Empedocles was also interested in other issues regarding vision—how we form a single visual image from two eyes (14.136) and why some people see better by day and others by night (14.138). He also had views on why eyes are of different colors and on how mirrors work.

He had a theory of pleasure and pain closely related to his theory of perception:

14.169   We feel pleasure by things that are alike in their parts and mixture, and pain by opposites . . . [so that they are] certain perceptions or accompanied by perception.

(Theophrastus, *On Sensation* 9, 16 = DK 31A86)

Finally, thought works on the principle of like by like (14.146). Thought takes place not in the brain but in the blood around the heart (14.148). In fact 14.148 identifies thought with this blood. Blood is the seat of thought because being composed of all four elements in equal proportions (14.109) it is most receptive, able to be affected by all physical things. Different thoughts are due to differences in the composition of our blood from time to time 14.150.[90] On this crude theory Empedocles cannot distinguish between thought and perception, but

---

88. A lengthy account of his doctrines on perception is found in Theophrastus, *On Sensation* 7–24 = DK 31A86. This passage is translated by Inwood (2001). See also Guthrie (1965: 228–43).

89. For Empedocles' use of analogies, see above pp. 281–82.

90. That there can be differences in composition of the blood is hinted at in 14.109 line 4, "a bit more or a bit less."

he does distinguish between the means of thinking and perceiving on the one hand and the perceiver or thinker on the other: by means of the earth, water, air, and fire in the blood, we, the percipient beings, are able to see earth, water, air, and fire. Even so, it can be objected that we perceive not merely the four elements but also compounds, and Empedocles owes us an account of how this happens.

> **14.170**   For they suppose that we recognize like by like, as if supposing that the soul were the *things*. But these [the four elements] are not the only things, but there are also many others, or rather things composed of the elements are perhaps infinite in number. Now grant that the soul recognizes or perceives what each of these is composed of—still, by what will it recognize or perceive the compound? For example, what is a god or a human or flesh or bone? And likewise for any other compound. For each of these is not simply the elements in any which way, but with some formula and composition, as even Empedocles speaks of bone [**14.75**]. So there is no benefit for the elements to be in the soul unless the proportions and composition are going to be there too. For each one will recognize what is like it, but nothing will recognize the bone or the human, unless these too will be in it. But there is no need to say that this is impossible, for who would wonder whether there is a stone or a man in the soul, and likewise for the good and the not good. And the same holds for the rest.
>
> (Aristotle, *On the Soul* 1.5 409b26–410a13 [not in DK])

Despite the obvious shortcomings of Empedocles' theories of perception and cognition, they are worked out within the terms of his physical theory. In effect he did not consider psychology separate from physiology, which is a part of physics. The fact that Empedocles has much more to say than his forebears did on these subjects may stem from his concerns to rebut Parmenides' rejection of both the senses and the thoughts of mortals. By explaining how our sensations and thoughts arise from interaction between our bodies and the outside world, Empedocles takes an important step toward establishing that our perceptions and thoughts are or can be reliable (see **14.43**, **14.44**, **14.145**). **14.42**, unless it is meant to be purely figurative, may allude to a physical process involved in understanding what our senses apprehend, but it is tantalizingly obscure.

The Fate of the *Daimones*

Empedocles' "religious" teachings I take to be the point of his philosophy; the physical theory, cosmic cycle, and other topics discussed so far set the stage for the account of the *daimones*: their (or, rather, our) initial happy state, original sin and Fall, subsequent sufferings, and ultimate prospects for regaining paradise. This view is supported by the Strasbourg papyrus's supplement to **14.58**, which places the discussion of "our" fate near the beginning of the poem.[91]

---

91. See above p. 256.

14.9 introduces this subject in terms that link it closely with the physical theory: the broad oaths which render the punishment inevitable (lines 1–2) recall (and may be identical with) the broad oath which fixes the time when Strife begins to disrupt the Sphere of Love (**14.81** line 3), the outcast divinities are driven through the rounds of the four elements (**14.9** lines 9–11), and the vortex of the heavens is mentioned (line 11). Three other features of the fragment are noteworthy. First, Empedocles does not present this doctrine as an impersonal observer. He too is suffering the effects of previously incurred pollution and is anguished at his situation (lines 12–14). Second, he attributes his present miserable state to his having placed his "reliance on raving Strife" (line 14, compare to line 4). Strife's evil moral dimension is foremost as the goodness of Love is emphasized in other fragments. Third, the unhappy divinities are exiles from the gods (line 13), having fallen from a happy state of association with "the blessed ones" (line 6).

The happy state of the pure divinities is described in **14.4**: Love (Cypris) reigns supreme (line 3), not Ares, the god of war, or Zeus with his violent thunderbolt, or Kronos, who gained power by castrating his father;[92] bloodshed was unknown, and all animate nature lived harmoniously (**14.5**). This blessed state ended as Strife increased. Killing took place for the first time, and polluted divinities began to suffer the punishment described above (page 256). A number of fragments describe the Fall and unhappy state of a polluted divinity (**14.9–14.10, 14.18–14.24**). As the divinity endures his long exile (**14.9** line 6), he is born into the bodies of living things one after another. Empedocles' doctrine of reincarnation depends heavily on Pythagorean beliefs. He lists his own previous incarnations in **14.15** and describes Pythagoras in a way suggestive of this doctrine (**9.6**). Certain incarnations are better than others (**14.34**) Incarnation as a human is best, and among humans prophets, bards, physicians, and political leaders are closest to the divine (**14.35**). Empedocles himself was a prophet, bard, and physician and played a leading role in politics at Acragas. His claim to be a god (**14.1** line 4)—if it is that[93]—is only an anticipation of his next life, and his close connection with divine functions of prophecy, healing (the work of Apollo and Asclepius), and music (depending on direct inspiration of the Muse) also warrants his claim to knowledge of the divine truth (see **14.38**), which makes him and others like him "blessed" (**14.8**). **14.35** presents the prospect of leaving this vale of tears and returning once again to our former happy state, described wistfully in **14.36**. It is apparent that Empedocles posits a cycle through which the *daimon* progresses, involving an original blessed state, exile, and eventual return.

In a sense which is not made clear, a fallen *daimōn* "grow[s] to be," "[is] born," "come[s] into being," and "in the end" is different kinds of living things (**14.9** line 7, **14.15, 14.34, 14.35**). In speaking of his own past, Empedocles says "*I* [italics mine] have already been born as a . . ." (**14.15**). Thus the fragments imply that the *daimōn* preserves its identity through its incarnations and more strongly

---

92. See above p. 8 and below pp. 463–64.
93. See below p. 287 n. 97.

that a living thing's own identity continues from one incarnation to the next. Further, the *daimōn* is the bearer of personal identity; the body is not. The body is merely "an alien garb of flesh" (**14.12**) which the *daimōn* wears and discards. The *daimōn* occupies the place of the soul (*psukhē*) in the Pythagorean doctrine of reincarnation. By calling it *daimōn* rather than *psukhē*[94] Empedocles stresses our divine nature.

The critical issue in a redemptionist view of this type is what, if anything, we must do to achieve or hasten our salvation. In one sense of the question, **14.9** line 6 implies a negative answer: fallen *daimones* are sentenced to a fixed period of exile: thirty thousand seasons, or ten thousand years,[95] with no time off for good behavior. But the indications that some lives are better than others and that a well-spent life is rewarded by a better next incarnation suggest that Empedocles believed in at least a limited ability to improve our state during our exile by behaving in certain ways.

Most prominent are abstinence from both killing animals and eating meat. Killing, which violates a universal law (**14.29**), is the cause of the *daimones'* Fall (**14.9**) and the cause of continuing pollution. **14.27** explains why we must avoid killing: all living beings are related through reincarnation, so the pollution incurred is the same as if you kill your nearest human relatives. **14.25** draws the implications that all killing is murder, every act of eating meat is cannibalism. **14.26** and **14.30** also seem related to this subject.

Empedocles enjoins other prohibitions as well.

14.171   He teaches his listeners to be continent regarding sexual intercourse with
a woman lest they collaborate and cooperate in the works which Strife produces, always dissolving and destroying the works of Love.

(Hippolytus, *Refutation of All Heresies*, 7.2.9,
printed as a context of DK 31B115)

There are also specific prohibitions against eating (or touching?) laurel leaves and beans (**14.32**, **14.33**), the former doubtless connected with **14.34** and the latter showing Empedocles' Pythagorean connections.[96] In general **14.31** commands us to avoid evildoing. In a positive direction, Empedocles stresses the importance of knowledge about the gods (see also **14.38**, **14.8**).

This is not the place to venture a thorough treatment of these different doctrines, which perhaps are more at home in a history of religion than in a history of philosophy. But it is important to take up the question whether Empedocles'

---

94. Claims like this are not meant to be taken dogmatically, since so much of the original work is lost. Still, the word *psukhē* occurs only once in Empedocles' fragments (**14.26**), and there it means "life."

95. See above p. 275.

96. See above p. 88.

"religious" message is compatible with his physical doctrines. The principal difficulty is how to reconcile the apparently immortal nature of the *daimones* with the two extreme phases of the cosmic cycle, in one of which there are no compounds (including, presumably, the *daimones*) and in the other, where the totality of the four elements is formed into a single compound, there seems to be no place for the gods and *daimones* of **14.9**.

But are the *daimones* immortal? Empedocles says only that they "possess immensely long life" (**14.9** line 5), like the gods (**14.60** line 12, **14.62** line 8). In fact, only Love, Strife (**14.57**), and the four elements (for example, **14.128** line 14) are clearly immortal.[97] As far as the fragments go, the *daimones* can be exceptionally long lasting (yet still "mortal") compounds. The increase of Strife's strength and the breakup of the Sphere are the conditions in which the *daimones* are differentiated—"born"—out of the total mixture of the elements. Likewise, they must perish by the time in the future when the elements become totally separated under Strife. Correspondingly, they can be born at an appropriate time in Love's ascendancy and perish in the universal fusion of the Sphere.

The *daimones* are not indifferent to their fate. At any moment in their careers as fallen divinities, *daimones* yearn for the unity and mutual affection of their parts which occurred before the Fall and even more in the Sphere of Love. It was a gross error to "put [their] reliance on raving Strife" (**14.9** line 14), and their complete dissolution into mutually-hating parts (see **14.67** lines 6–9) under Strife's predominance, although inevitable, is not an end to be desired[98] and fortunately will not last forever—indeed it may be only instantaneous.[99]

This program fits into Empedocles' cosmic cycle in the following way. The Sphere breaks up when Strife's divisive influence is strong enough to keep the totality of all four elements from bonding together any longer in one uniform compound. It breaks up mainly into compounds in which Love strongly prevails so that there is a firmly bonded mixture of all four elements. Since the strong bonding makes these compounds extremely difficult to break up into their constituent elements, the compounds are long-lasting. The "whole-natured forms" of **14.118** line 4 are found at this stage. As Strife waxes and Love wanes, such uniform compounds become more difficult to form and maintain in existence, though not impossible. They can be found wherever Love prevails to a sufficient degree locally, as exceptions to the general conditions of increasing separation of

---

97. In **14.38** line 1, the Muse is called immortal—a conventional epithet—and in **14.1** line 4 Empedocles need not be calling himself an immortal god: "as it seems" (line 5) may well mean that *others* consider him such. In its context, the "immortal things" of **14.60** line 4 ought to stand for the element air.

98. My view that the *daimones'* constant aim is to resist the effects of Strife is my principal disagreement with the interpretation of Inwood (2001: 55–68), to which the present interpretation is otherwise heavily indebted.

99. See above p. 275.

the elements. As Strife nears its state of total dominance, they become increasingly rare until finally at (or shortly before) the moment when Strife crushes Love completely there is no longer enough Love anywhere for them to exist—although the possibility recurs at (or shortly after) the moment when Love's uniting effects are first felt by the elements which had been wholly separated under total Strife. The situation in the transition period leading up to the reign of Love is symmetric, with such compounds becoming increasingly easier to form and maintain until the moment when they are all unified in the Sphere of Love.

Empedocles' description of god (**14.80**) is in keeping with this picture. God strongly resembles the "whole-natured forms." The only important difference between the account of god and the account of the "whole-natured forms" is that in **14.80** god is described as "only mind." But since thought requires the presence of all four elements (**14.148** with **14.109**), it is possible that the "whole-natured forms" *are* gods. For present purposes though, it is enough that gods are the sorts of things associated with the local prevalence of Love in a strong degree. We may suppose that their life, founded on Love and unity, is happy, unwearied, and free of distress (**14.36**), and we may further suppose that the bonding force of Love is so strong in these compounds as to give them "immensely long life" (**14.9** line 5). Even the intrusion of a certain amount of Strife need not sunder the bonds, though it would create circumstances which the deity, a thinking, conscious being, would recognize as inferior to its pristine Strife-less state and would be strongly motivated to remedy, to the extent possible.

In the present period of increasing Strife, although it is increasingly difficult to expel Strife and return to a state where the constituent parts are bound only by Love, it is certainly worth the effort. And even though the effort is ultimately in vain, since Strife *will* separate all the elements, it is in vain "ultimately" only in the limited context of the present transition phase. Strife's period of total dominance will end at the time guaranteed by the "broad oath" of **14.81**. In the following transition period, it once again becomes possible to expel Strife locally.

The Sphere is the best possible condition, but it is not within the capacities of individual mortal compounds to bring it about. On the other hand, some mortal compounds have some power to affect the relative prevalence of Love or Strife within themselves by doing or refraining from certain activities and by thinking friendly or hostile thoughts.

The position of the *daimones* is now clear. They are long-lived divine beings compounded of all four elements, in which Love has great strength. By committing certain sins a *daimōn* introduces Strife into its composition—not enough to disperse its constituents and so destroy it, but enough to disturb the unity that existed before. In punishment the *daimōn* is forced to become living creatures of various kinds. Its goal is to be purified of Strife and return to its state before the Fall, though this is a difficult task to accomplish given the increase of Strife in the universe and also given the nature of animate existence, which involves Strife-increasing sexual reproduction (**14.171**) and the likelihood of committing Strife-promoting actions unwittingly (**14.25**). But it is not a hopeless task, for at present the power of Love in the *kosmos* is still quite strong, since compounds form and stay together quite well and since Love's psychological effects are frequently powerful. Earlier on in human existence it was even easier, to judge by **14.4** and **14.5**.[100] And even though at some point the task does become impossible, until Strife dominates totally there is some Love in the *kosmos*, and hence the possibility and desirability of increasing its local concentration. After Strife's reign it becomes increasingly feasible to secure a local concentration of Love which can produce the complete local fusion of elements which constitutes a blessed god. The *daimōn's* identity continues when it is a god,[101] although the description of deity in **14.80** leaves little room for individuality. On the other hand, personal identity is lost when the gods are absorbed along with everything else into the Sphere of Love.

Until it becomes a god, the *daimōn* will be living things—plants, animals and humans (**14.34**).[102] Presumably every living thing has a *daimōn*. Although some embodiments are better than others (**14.34**, **14.35**), it is hard to see how to construct a sequence of species rank-ordered in terms of desirability or to understand why a notorious carnivore should receive top rank among animals. But if it is correct to think that Empedocles' urgent exhortations to change our way of life are aimed at reducing Strife in us so that we can recover our divine birthright, there must be a direct link between behavior in one incarnation and what form the next incarnation takes, although the surviving information on Empedocles does not state this doctrine explicitly.

Following Empedocles' prescriptions will help us approach as near to the divine ideal of total fusion as is possible in the current stage in the cosmic cycle. Abstaining from killing and eating animals will reduce the amount of Strife in which we are involved (and therefore the amount of Strife that is involved in us) as will abstaining from heterosexual intercourse (**14.171**). The general command "fast from evil" (**14.31**) amounts to a prohibition on participating in works of Strife (compare to **14.28**).

So far we have only a list of acts to avoid—almost a ritual means to purification. But salvation requires knowledge too. Empedocles' stress on knowing the nature of the gods (**14.8**, **14.38**, but see **14.37**) is more than conventional piety. Knowledge of the gods requires learning Empedocles' whole philosophy, since the gods' nature must be understood on the one hand in terms of the cosmic system and the physical theory that underlies it and on the other hand in terms

---

100. These fragments do not conflict with **14.9**, since **14.4** does not establish that bloodshed had not occurred, only that it was (still) considered "the greatest abomination," and **14.5** does not say that there was no Strife at all, only that Love was still more influential.

101. **14.9** and **14.36** make it clear that there is a plurality of gods, so that our *daimōn* is not reabsorbed into a single divine nature at this stage.

102. Will they take on other forms as well? **14.9** describes a passage through the four elements which fallen *daimones* must endure, and it is unclear how these episodes are related to the series of living incarnations.

of the relation between the gods and ourselves, since we have been gods and have the potential to be gods again. We can attain our godhead only through ridding ourselves of Strife, which is partly a matter of what we do and partly a matter of what we know. In particular, we need to know our own nature (including that we are fallen *daimones*) and the nature of Strife and its role in the *kosmos*. We also need to know (presumably at least partly on the basis of the physical theory) which actions are permitted and which are prohibited so that we can attain the purity needed in order to regain our divinity.

Mortal Nature

An interesting aspect of this message is found in the new texts from the Strasbourg papyrus. The previously known fragments speak frequently of the four elements "coming together"—either to form compounds or to be integrated into the Sphere (**14.58** lines 4, 7, **14.60** line 8; **14.109** line 1; **14.128** line 5; **14.129**; **14.63**; lines 3–7; **14.134** line 2; **14.138**). So does the new material (**14.58** line 59), but it also expresses the idea differently, using the first person plural: "We come together into one *kosmos*" (**14.58** line 36); "we were coming together in the mid-most places to be only one" (**14.58** line 56); "sometimes we come together through Love into one" (**14.59** line 3). This way of putting the situation is taken[103] to emphasize that "we" are identical with the elements (at least with the elements as formed into compounds). Especially striking is the indifference with which he uses the first and third persons (first person in **14.58** line 56, third person three lines later). From the long-term cosmic point of view it is indifferent whether we think of things as elements or compounds, and there is no point in being concerned with the history of any particular compound (even the compound which is ourself). Our history does not end with the separation of our constituent elements which we call death. Our *daimōn* will be reborn into other forms of life, and our constituent elements will be intermittently regrouped into other compounds—for a time—and eventually, like everything else, both our *daimōn* and our constituent elements will be absorbed into the Sphere.

Empedocles employs the word "mortal" much more frequently of compounds than specifically of humans or other living things. This tendency to refer to and speak of "mortal" compounds puts our human life in a broader perspective.[104] Humans, animals, and plants are all mortal, are born and die. But the same is true for all compounds of the elements. Mortality is part of our nature not only as living things but also as entities made up of earth, water, air, and fire. But birth and death are not what we tend to think: "There is coming to be of not a single one of all mortal things, nor is there any end of destructive death, but only mix-

---

103. This is the view of Martin and Primavesi (1999), followed by most interpreters since then. Laks (2002) gives different interpretations to the several occurrences of "we."

104. See above p. 260.

ture, and separation of what is mixed" (**14.48**). We are a mixture of elementary ingredients which continue to exist after the temporary compound which we are has ceased to be. The ingredients are immortal even though they temporarily assume mortal forms. So, mortal as we are, we have a direct connection to immortality. In that we "are" our elementary ingredients (**14.63**), we "are" also immortal. This is one of Empedocles' messages.

From the cosmic point of view our current situation is not good. We live in the phase of increasing Strife, and to judge by the degree of separation in which the elements are now found (with almost all earth gathered together, almost all water enveloping the earth, almost all air covering the water, and almost all fire in the heavens) we are nearing the phase of Strife's total domination in which all compounds—even the gods—cease to exist. If the thrice ten thousand seasons of the exile of Empedocles' *daimōn* is not just meant as a large and round figure, but refers to a period of ten thousand years (see above page 275), and if the interpretation given of the chronological figures in the Byzantine scholia (see above page 274) is correct, then Empedocles is telling us that we are indeed on the threshold of the phase of total separation, ten thousand years being the theoretical maximum length of time a compound can exist in the period of increasing Strife.

The thought that the *kosmos* as we know it will shortly vanish from existence must surely be disheartening. By contrast, the idea that we and everything else have a share in immortality—even if not a personal immortality—is sure to be a comforting message for some, and Empedocles may have intended it as such. But it is a message that can be absorbed only by those who have come to understand and accept Empedocles' cosmic system.

Conclusion

Empedocles sparkles like a diamond among the Presocratics—many-faceted and appearing different from different directions. A poet and a politician, a physician and a philosopher, a scientist and a seer, a showman and a charlatan, he was a fallen divinity who proclaimed himself already a god and a visionary who claimed to control nature. It has been well said that "the Hellenic mind has its romantic as well as its classical aspect, and both reach their climax without incongruity in the genius of this remarkable Sicilian. . . . Empedocles sums up and personifies the spirit of his age and race."[105] I have focused mainly on his philosophical and scientific views and only secondarily on his equally remarkable religious message, although I have attempted to defend the two sides of Empedocles' thought from the charge that they contradict one another. It would not be surprising if the same person who was clearly aware of the nature and importance of Parmenides' challenge to our understanding of the world and who developed a cosmic system which met this challenge so effectively also conceived of a doctrine

---

105. Guthrie (1965: 126).

of the role of the individual in this *kosmos*. However, any reconstruction must fill in gaps and smooth out the rough spots caused by materials which join poorly or seem to conflict. For Empedocles leaves crucial questions hanging, and his prophetic style is sometimes too lofty to descend to mean details. Further, his poetic and oracular mode of expression may reflect his manner of thinking. Yet we must keep in mind that it is historically unreasonable to expect much in the way of a detailed, coherent, and consistent account of the *kosmos*: Empedocles' closest forerunners as cosmologists were Anaxagoras, Parmenides (in *Opinions of Mortals*), and Heraclitus, whose accounts, as far as our evidence permits us to judge, were far less complete and detailed than those of Empedocles.

In any case, we must admit that along with Anaxagoras Empedocles extended the realm of natural inquiry, at times saw the need for detailed discussions, and made noble attempts to rescue the study of the *kosmos* from the Eleatic challenge. With Anaxagoras and Empedocles philosophy thus reached a new, higher level. This was apparent to Aristotle, who found it important to discuss the ideas of these men more frequently and extensively than those of any earlier Presocratic even though he had a low opinion of Empedocles.[106] It is not so much that their views on astronomy, physiology, etc. were better than those of their predecessors; their contribution is philosophical more than scientific. This too is part of Parmenides' legacy. The Eleatic challenge compelled later cosmologists to pay attention to the philosophical foundations as they constructed their systems, and the resulting theories have a plausibility lacking in earlier work.

---

106. *Metaphysics* 1.4 985a5 = DK 31A39; *On Generation and Corruption* 1.1 315a3–25 (not in DK); 1.8 326b6–28 (not in DK), 2.6 (not in DK).

15

Melissus of Samos

Fragments

15.1 [Melissus proved through this common axiom that what–is is ungenerated. He writes as follows.[1]] Whatever was, always was and always will be. For if it came to be, it is necessary that before it came to be it was nothing. Now if it was nothing, in no way could anything come to be out of nothing. [Alternative translation of the first sentence: "It always was and always will be what it was." Alternate translation of the second and third sentences: "For if it came to be, it is necessary that before it came to be, there (or, "it") was nothing. Now if there (or, "it") was nothing, not at all could anything come to be out of nothing."]

(Melissus DK 30B1, quoted by Simplicius,
Commentary on Aristotle's Physics 162.23–26)

15.2 Now since it did not come to be, it is and always was and always will be, and it does not have a beginning or an end, but it is unlimited. For if it had come to be it would have a beginning (for if it had come to be it would have begun at some time) and an end (for if it had come to be it would have ended at some time[2]). But since it neither began nor ended, and always was and always will be, it does not have a beginning or end. For whatever is not entire [or, "all"] cannot always be.

(Melissus DK 30B2, quoted by Simplicius, *Commentary
on Aristotle's* Physics 29.22–26, 109.20–25)

15.3 [Just as he says that what came to be at some time is limited in its being, he also wrote clearly that what always is is unlimited in being, saying:] But just as it always is, so also it must always be unlimited in magnitude. [But by "magnitude" he does not mean what is extended in space.]

(Melissus DK 30B3, quoted by Simplicius,
Commentary on Aristotle's Physics 109.29–32)

15.4 [For he himself proves that what–is is indivisible.] For if what–is is divided, it moves. But if it moved, it would not be. [But by "magnitude" he means the distance across its substance.]

(Melissus DK 30B10, quoted by Simplicius, *Commentary
on Aristotle's* Physics 109.32–34) (continuation of **15.3**)

---

1. All of Melissus's extant fragments are preserved by Simplicius. I quote Simplicius's remarks, where relevant. The page and line references to Simplicius's text cover both the fragments and the quoted remarks.

2. Although a better attested manuscript reading yields the translations "it would have begun coming to be at some time" and "it would have ended coming to be at some time," I find it difficult to make sense of this reading.

15.5   [He indicated that he intends what-is to be bodiless, saying:] Now if it is, it
must be one. But being one, it must not have body [or, "a body"]. But if it
had thickness, it would have parts and no longer would be one.

(Melissus DK 30B9, quoted by Simplicius, *Commentary on*
Aristotle's Physics 109.34–110.2 (continuation of **15.4**), 87.6–7)

15.6   [And he put unlimited in being right next to eternity, saying:] Nothing that
has both a beginning and an end is either eternal or unlimited. [And so
whatever does not have them is unlimited.]

(Melissus DK 30B4, quoted by Simplicius, *Commentary*
on Aristotle's Physics 110.2–4) (continuation of **15.5**)

15.7   [From "unlimited" he concluded "one," from the argument:] If it is not
one, it will come to a limit in relation to something else.

(Melissus DK 30B5, quoted by Simplicius, *Commentary*
on Aristotle's Physics 110.5–6) (continuation of **15.6**)

15.8   [Although what is perceived seems clearly to be, if what-is is one, there will
be nothing else besides this. For Melissus says:] For if it is <unlimited>,[3]
it will be one. For if there were two, they could not be unlimited, but they
would have limits in relation to each other.

(Melissus DK 30B6, quoted by Simplicius, *Commentary*
on Aristotle's On the Heavens 557.14–17)

15.9   [Now Melissus speaks thus, summarizing what he has previously said and
introducing the points about motion.]
1. Thus it is eternal and unlimited and one and all alike.
2. And it cannot perish or become greater or be rearranged, nor does it
feel pain or distress. For if it underwent any of these, it would no longer be
one. For if it becomes different, it is necessary that what-is is not alike, but
what previously was perishes, and what-is-not comes to be. Now if it were
to become different by a single hair in ten thousand years, it will all perish
in the whole of time.
3. But it is not possible for it to be rearranged[4] either. For the arrangement
that previously was is not destroyed, and an arrangement that is not does not
come to be. But when nothing either comes to be in addition or is destroyed or
becomes different, how could there be a rearrangement of things-that-are? For
if it became at all different, it would thereby have in fact been rearranged.
4. Nor does it feel pain. For it could not be entire [or, "all"] if it were
feeling pain. For a thing feeling pain could not always be [or, "For it could

---

3. I follow most editors in adding this word, which is not in the manuscripts of
Simplicius.

4. "Arrangement" here translates *kosmos*. "Rearranged" translates a verb whose root
is the word *kosmos*. This section can be taken to deny that the *kosmos* itself, as one particular arrangement, can change.

not always be a thing feeling pain"]. Nor does it have equal power to what is healthy. Nor would it be alike if it were feeling pain. For it would be feeling pain because something is either being taken away or added, and it would no longer be alike.

5. Nor could what is healthy feel pain. For what is healthy and what-is would perish and what-is-not would come to be.

6. And the same argument applies to feeling distress as to feeling pain.

7. Nor is any of it empty [or, "Nor is it at all empty" or, "Nor is anything empty" or, "Nor is anything void" or, "Nor is there any void"]. For what is empty is nothing [or, "For the void is nothing"], and of course what is nothing cannot be. Nor does it move. For it cannot give way anywhere [or, "it has nowhere to give way"], but it is full. For if it were empty, it would give way into the empty part [or, "For if there were void, it would give way into the void"]. But since it is not empty [or, "since there is no void"] it has nowhere to give way.

8. It [or, "There"] cannot be dense and rare. For it is impossible for the rare to be equally full as the dense, but the rare thereby proves to be emptier than the dense.

9. And we must make this the criterion of full and not full: if something yields or is penetrated it is not full. But if it neither yields nor is penetrated, it is full.

10. Hence it is necessary that it is full if it is not empty. Hence if it is full it does not move.

(Melissus DK 30B7, quoted by Simplicius, *Commentary on Aristotle's* Physics 111.18–112.15)

15.10 [After saying of what-is that it is one and ungenerated and motionless and interrupted by no void, but is a whole full of itself, he goes on:]

1. Now this argument is the strongest indication that there is only one thing. But the following are indications too.

2. If there were many things, they must be such as I say the one is. For if there are earth and water and air and fire and iron and gold and the living and the dead and black and white and all the other things that people say are real—if these things really are and if we see and hear correctly, then each of them ought to be just as we thought at first, and it should not change or come to be different, but each thing always ought to be just as it is. But in fact we say that we see and hear and understand correctly.

3. We think that what is hot becomes cold and what is cold hot, that what is hard becomes soft and what is soft hard, and that the living dies and that it comes to be from the non-living, and that all these things come to be different and that what was and what is now are not at all alike, but that iron, although hard, is worn away by contact with the finger, and also gold and stone and anything else that we think is enduring,[5] and <we think> that earth and stone come to be from water.

---

5. I follow Barnes (1979/1982) in omitting the words "so that it happens that we neither see nor know the things that are," which are found in this place in the manuscripts.

4. Hence these things do not agree with one another. For although we say that there are many eternal things that have definite forms and have endurance, we think that all of them become different and change from what we see at any moment.

5. Hence it is clear that we do not see correctly and we are incorrect in thinking that those many things are. For they would not change if they were real, but each one would be just as we thought. For nothing can prevail over what is real.

6. But if it changes, what-is was destroyed, and what-is-not has come to be. Thus, if there are many things, they must be such as the one is.

(Melissus DK 30B8, quoted by Simplicius, *Commentary on Aristotle's* On the Heavens 558.19–559.12)

Life, Work, and Philosophical Connections

Although from the island of Samos in the eastern Aegean, far removed from Elea in western Italy, Melissus is philosophically an Eleatic. The one concrete piece of information concerning when he lived is that as commander of the Samian fleet he won two victories in 441 BCE over the Athenian fleet headed by Pericles. This date makes him probably somewhat younger than Zeno, Anaxagoras, and Empedocles. He was reportedly[6] a student of Parmenides, which is possible but is more likely to be someone's attempt to account for his adoption of Eleatic ideas. He follows the arch-Eleatic in the main but innovates within the Eleatic framework. His treatise, like that of Parmenides, was a systematic series of arguments that deduce the attributes of what-is, but unlike Parmenides he wrote in prose, not verse, made no claims to divine inspiration, and stated his theses and argued for them more lucidly than Parmenides. There are indications (though not proof) that he knew of Anaxagoras and Empedocles.[7] He was approximately contemporary with Leucippus, the originator of the atomic theory, and with Diogenes of Apollonia. He is said (but this is doubtful too) to have been the teacher of Leucippus,[8] and there are traces of Melissus's influence on atomism.

Much of Melissus's work (which may have had a title: *On Nature, or On What-Is*)[9] is preserved in his actual words, and we also possess several summaries of his reasoning.[10] As a result his views and methods are accurately known. He

---

6. Diogenes Laertius, *Lives of the Philosophers* 9.24 = DK 30A1; Aëtius 1.3.14 = DK 30A9. On such matters these sources are unreliable.

7. **15.10**, with its mention of Empedocles' four elements and of some of the opposites mentioned by Anaxagoras (**13.4, 13.26**), may betray familiarity with the doctrines of those two philosophers.

8. Tzetzes, *Chiliades* 2.980 = DK 67A5.

9. Simplicius, *Commentary on Aristotle's* Physics 70.16–17 = DK 30A4.

10. Pseudo-Aristotle, *On Melissus, Xenophanes, and Gorgias* chs. 1–2 = DK 30A5, Simplicius, *Commentary on Aristotle's* Physics 103.13–104.20 (printed in DK, vol 2, pp. 268–70), Philoponus, *Commentary on Aristotle's* Physics 50.30–52.11 (not in DK).

agrees with Parmenides that what-is is ungenerated, imperishable, indivisible, unchangeable, motionless, and uniform. He disagrees on two points, holding that what-is is unlimited and always was, is, and always will be, whereas for Parmenides what-is is spatially limited and has no past or future.[11] Also, Melissus is crystal clear that there is only one thing, whereas Parmenides did not argue this point, and there is some reason to believe that he did not maintain it.

Melissus's Arguments

The first stretch of argument, which occupies **15.1** and the first part of **15.2**, concludes that "whatever was always was and always will be." The argument begins with a short proof that what-is did not come to be (**15.1**), which resembles one of Parmenides' arguments for the same thesis (**11.8** lines 12–13). The rest of **15.2** contains an argument for temporal eternity. The sequence of thought is: (a) if something came to be, it began at some time and therefore it had a beginning. But (by **15.1**) it did not come to be, therefore it does not have a beginning. Therefore, it always has been. And (b) if something came to be, it would have ended at some time, and therefore it has an end. But it did not come to be, therefore it does not have an end. Therefore it will always be.

The argument is inefficient, since the steps involving beginning at some time and ending at some time are not needed. Also, the first sentence of (b) is inadequately justified by the premise translated as "for if it had come to be it would have ended at some time," which is not generally true.[12] Further, both halves of the argument are fallacious, having the form: 'If *a* then *b*, but not-*a*, therefore not-*b*.'[13] And the role of the final clause of **15.2**, "for whatever is not entire [or 'all'] cannot always be," is unclear.[14]

The argument amounts to the following: (a′) what-is did not come to be, therefore it has always been, and (b′) what-is did not come to be, therefore it will

---

11. See above pp. 161 and 163–64. However, Parmenides' limits are not specifically spatial limits (p. 166).

12. For example, the book you are now reading came to be at some time, but has not yet ceased to exist. However, it can be interpreted as meaning that if something came to be, at some time (perhaps in the future) it will cease to exist, in which case it would accord with the view, frequently found in ancient philosophy, that anything that comes to be also eventually perishes. So either the premise is false or it is poorly stated.

13. Aristotle ridicules the argument for this bad reasoning (*Sophistical Refutations* 5 167b13–20 = DK 30A10).

14. In what sense is what-is "entire"? Since prior to **15.2** we know only that what-is did not come to be, Melissus may mean that something that has come to be is not *entirely*, in that there is a time when it did not exist—"is entirely" corresponding to Parmenides' "is fully" (see above pp. 160–61). In that case, the problem about the last clause of **15.2** disappears, but it remains an obscure way of making the rather obvious point.

always be.[15] (a′) is valid if we grant Melissus the presupposition (which he obviously believes) that what-is is at the present time. (b) is clearly invalid, but Melissus is here following Parmenides[16] in assuming that perishing (that is, ceasing to be) is eliminated together with coming to be. In fact a parallel argument to **15.1** can be constructed against perishing, which would then entitle Melissus to the valid (b″): what-is is imperishable (and what-is is at the present time), therefore what-is will always be.

The difference between Melissus's view—that what-is always was, is, and always will be—and Parmenides' view—that what-is exists only now—may be less than it appears. They agree that there is no generation or perishing and that what-is exists at every moment. They differ in that Melissus accepts that there are many moments, while Parmenides admits only one.

15.3 shows that Melissus believed that what-is is unlimitedly large. It is unclear whether we have Melissus's argument for this important thesis. If **15.3** infers unlimited extension from unlimited duration, it is either grossly fallacious or depends on some unstated (and perhaps implausible) premises about the relation between time and space. If the purpose of **15.3** is not to *argue* that what-is is unlimited in size but rather to suggest that unlimited extension follows from a parallel argument to that for unlimited duration, we can take it as an invitation to look back to **15.2** to see whether such an argument can be constructed. If we do so, we should grant that things can have a beginning and end in space as well as in time and that something that has size but whose spatial extension has no beginning or end is indeed unlimitedly large. But on this interpretation Melissus equivocates on "beginning" and "end," since **15.3** requires what-is to have no beginning or end in space, but we have no reason to suppose that it does, since Melissus has only argued that what-is has no beginning or end in time. **15.6** is also relevant, if "unlimited" means "unlimited in size." But again, it gives no reason to think that what-is is in fact unlimited in size. Some hold that **15.2** rules out coming to be in space as well as in time, on the grounds that anything that comes to be must begin to do so at a certain place and cease to do so at another. But Parmenides did not push the parallel between space and time so far, and if this was Melissus's intention, he does not make it clear, since **15.2** is phrased in terms of time, not space.

Unlike Parmenides Melissus argues that what-is is unique:[17] (**15.7**, **15.8**). He states the thesis clearly and offers a clear argument for it: uniqueness is a consequence of unlimitedness (**15.8**, a fuller version of the argument in **15.7**).[18] The

---

15. Contrast **11.8** lines 5, 19–20.

16. In **11.8** lines 6–13, Parmenides argues only against coming into being, but he claims (line 14) to have disproven perishing as well.

17. Melissus is the first to refer to what-is as "the one" (**15.10**, secs. 2, 6).

18. Since this argument requires what-is to be unlimited, Parmenides could not have used it.

argument depends on the doubly unlimited nature of what-is, since there is no objection to there being two unlimitedly large objects, each at a different time, or two eternal objects, each in a different place. Since what-is has no limits in either respect, it occupies all space for all time, which could not be the case if anything else also occupied any space at any time.

15.9 begins by listing the properties treated in **15.1, 15.2, 15.3, 15.6, 15.7, 15.8**, and an additional property, "all alike." The argument for this property goes as follows:

> **15.11** Being one it is all alike. For if it were unalike, being plural, it would no longer be one, but many.
>
> > (pseudo-Aristotle, *On Melissus, Xenophanes, and*
> > *Gorgias* 1 974a12–14 = DK 30A5)

"Alike" is best taken to mean like itself or uniform, being the same throughout, where "throughout" is meant both spatially and temporally. If what-is were spatially non-uniform, it would not be the same throughout; there would be at least two regions of it differing from one another, at least two distinct parts. But then each part would have a separate identity; we would no longer have one thing but a plurality. The same would hold if there were two times at which it were different, that is, if it underwent any kind of change.

The argument is unsatisfactory, no reason being given why a single thing cannot have distinct parts (a stool has four legs and a seat, and yet is one stool). However, it invites further consideration of the nature of (true) unity and of the relation between whole and part. For the notion of unity can be strengthened to make the argument valid,[19] as can the conception of "whole" (along the lines that nothing is whole that can be divided into qualitatively different parts).[20]

Melissus next states more properties of what-is: "it cannot perish or become greater or be rearranged, nor does it feel pain or distress" (section 2). These points are taken up in turn: perishing in section 2, growth and rearrangement in section 3, feeling pain in sections 4–5, and feeling distress in section 6. Sections 2 and 3 offer parallel reasons for their conclusions: what-is cannot perish, become greater, or be rearranged, because if it did it would thereby become different from what it was before, which would violate the unity and uniformity of what-is. (The prohibition on rearrangement may be targeted at theories that account for change as mixture and separation of constituents in order to avoid Parmenides' abolishment of change.) Similar reasoning rules out all other kinds of change. The claim that what-is feels no pain or distress is entirely unexpected, with no known Eleatic

---

19. Cf. Barnes (1979: vol. 1, 204–10 / 1982: 204–10); but this strengthening makes more of the unity of what-is than is warranted by the argument for unity in **15.7** and **15.8**.

20. The argument would then require the additional premise that whatever is one is whole in this sense, which is also unwarranted by the preceding material.

precedents for ascribing or denying psychological attributes to what-is. The motivation for making these points is unclear,[21] but one consequence is to rule out solipsism, the view that only I or only my mind exists.[22]

The final stretch of **15.9** (sections 7–10) identifies what-is with what is full, and what-is-not, or nothing, with what is empty or void,[23] and uses the non-existence of the empty or void to eliminate the possibility of motion. Melissus does not argue as clearly here as elsewhere. On a charitable interpretation, the basis of the argument is that what-is is not empty (or, that there is no void), therefore what-is cannot "give way." Motion, however, requires giving way. Therefore what-is cannot move. On this analysis, there is a good deal of superfluous material in the passage, but the superfluous material contains important ideas.

Most importantly, it introduces into Greek philosophy the conception of the void,[24] which would shortly become one of the bases of the atomic theory.[25] It also analyzes the opposites dense and rare in terms of full and empty, that is, what-is and what-is-not, which eliminates one of the foundations of Anaximenes' theory that the plurality of substances in the world is due to condensation and rarefaction.

And despite its wordiness, Melissus's argument is clearer than the corresponding argument in Parmenides.[26] It achieves its clarity by conceiving what-is more concretely than Parmenides did. For Parmenides, what-is-not is incomprehensible, and his argument against the existence of what-is-not depends on its unintelligibility.[27] Further, for Parmenides what-is-not can have no characteristics at all. In particular it is not the sort of thing that could be extended in space. Void, on the other hand, *can* be conceived of, and Melissus shows that he has conceived of it adequately even while insisting that it does not exist.

Eleatic philosophy entails that sense perception is misleading as a guide to reality. Parmenides knows this and occasionally hints at it,[28] but here again it is Melissus who produces a clear argument (**15.10**). The obvious conflict between what the senses report and what Eleatic logic proves (sections 2–4) forces a

---

21. For a parallel, see the Hippocratic work *The Nature of Man* Chapter 2 sec. 3 (below p. 432).

22. Certain passages in Parmenides (especially **11.3**) might suggest this interpretation of his (but not Melissus's) brand of Eleaticism.

23. For discussion of the concepts of void in play, see Sedley (1982).

24. Unless Leucippus introduced it first and Melissus in **15.9** is arguing against his atomism. For this idea see Graham (2008: 344–47).

25. See below pp. 306–7.

26. **11.8** lines 26–33.

27. **11.2** lines 7–8.

28. **11.6** line 7, **11.7** lines 3–4.

choice upon us: do we prefer reason or the senses? Melissus prefers reason and so rejects the senses (section 5).

15.4 and **15.5** treat the property of indivisibility. **15.4** argues that what-is is indivisible because if it were divided it would move, but this does not explain why what-is moves if it is divided. With the principle of **15.9** section 9 that if x moves then x is not full, **15.4** implies that if what-is is divided, it is not full. Melissus may have in mind a kind of division which physically separates the parts—what, then, is in between? It could only be what-is-not, that is, void—and then motion would be possible (**15.9** section. 7). But of course what-is-not cannot be; and so, neither can be motion.

15.5 can be reconstructed as follows: (a) what-is is one, therefore (b) what-is is without parts, therefore (c) what-is has no thickness, therefore (d) what-is does not have a body. This conclusion seems to contradict the claims that what-is is spatially unlimited (**15.3**, **15.6**) and full (**15.9**, sections 7–10, where "fullness" seems to mean the kind of solidity that applies to bodies). For (1) if what-is has no thickness (if it does not have three dimensions), how can it be spatially unlimited? and (2) if what-is has any extension at all, why can it not be divided into parts?

Melissus might respond to question (1) by saying that bodies have extension and also limits, so something unlimitedly large is not, properly speaking, a body. Nor does it, properly speaking, have thickness, because thickness is a measure of the distance between a body's extremities. If this was Melissus's thought, he again touched on important and difficult conceptual issues—this time concerning measure and extension—without making an effort to clarify them.

Regarding question (2), Melissus cannot say that what-is is empty and so cannot be divided into parts because there is nothing to partition, for what-is is full, not empty.[29] Possibly his declaration that what-is is bodiless and lacks thickness solves the problem. If what-is is incorporeal we have here the first clear reference to incorporeal existence in Greek philosophy. However, this solution is unsatisfactory as it stands, since it leaves open the question how something spatially extended and "full" can be bodiless and lack thickness.[30]

---

29. Commentators are driven to desperate measures here, saying that the fragment is not genuine or that it represents an attack by Melissus on pluralists—an attack which seems to come home against Melissus himself.

30. I take it that thickness means something like bulk or mass. If it means simply possessing a third spatial dimension, Melissus would be saying that what-is is two-dimensional (or one-dimensional), which still does not give any reason why it cannot be divided, and which would yield an interpretation of what-is for which we are totally unprepared by the fragments and testimonia.

Conclusion

Melissus received abuse from Aristotle. "A bit crude" in comparison with Parmenides: "Invalid arguments starting from false assumptions"; "A tiresome argument which gives no difficulty—grant one absurdity and the rest follow"; "But why should his premises be correct? Someone else might assert the exact opposite. For he has not shown that his starting point is correct."[31] Aristotle objects principally to details of Melissus's logic, and Melissus is indeed guilty of committing blunders in his reasoning.

Melissus's writings, however, have the merit of making a version of Eleatic philosophy more comprehensible. The clearly sequenced structure of his work and the short, sharp arguments improve on Parmenides' opaque and oracular verse. In addition, Melissus set up some of his arguments in ways that later philosophers could take advantage of, even in refuting him. The arguments touch on many important philosophical issues that had not previously been raised. Even when he does not explore them himself, he leaves them as a legacy to future philosophers and reveals features of the Eleatic position in need of further discussion. It is plausible that Plato's picture of Eleaticism is actually a conflation of Parmenides and Melissus under the name of the former. If that is so, then Plato's evident respect for the philosophy (both the views and the argumentative method) that he attributed to Parmenides and the immense amount of labor he devoted to responding to it, in ways both positive and negative, is in part a tribute to Parmenides' less well-known follower.

---

31. Quotations from Aristotle, *Metaphysics* 1.5 986b25–27; *Physics* 1.2 185a9–12 (both = DK 30A7); and pseudo-Aristotle, *On Melissus, Xenophanes, and Gorgias* 1 975a3–5 = DK 30A5.

16

Fifth-Century Atomism:
Leucippus and Democritus

The third and most ambitious response to the Eleatic challenge was the atomic theory, invented by Leucippus and developed by Democritus. Leucippus is a shadowy character[1] who we are told was from (a) Miletus, (b) Elea, and (c) Abdera,[2] though these claims could simply reflect the facts that (a) his philosophy continued the Ionian tradition of cosmology, (b) he was keenly aware of the Eleatic challenge, and (c) his pupil Democritus was from Abdera. Of his dates we are equally in the dark. Democritus, born c.460, was his student. It is likely that Leucippus proposed the atomic theory in the decade 440–430. His principal work was called *The Great World System*.

Democritus's birth date is inferred from his own statement[3] that he was young in the old age of Anaxagoras (born c.500), which would make him younger than Socrates. He lived to a ripe old age—perhaps over 100, therefore well into Plato's career and into the time when Aristotle had begun his philosophical work. Born on the Thracian mainland in the remote Greek city of Abdera, which also produced the Sophist Protagoras, Democritus traveled widely in non-Greek lands for study and research. The large number of his writings makes him unique among the philosophers treated in this book. We know the titles of about seventy works, on a wide variety of subjects. The main headings are ethics, natural philosophy, mathematics, music (in the broad Greek sense, which includes language and literature[4]), technical subjects (including medical writings and works on farming, painting, and military strategy) and writings based on his travels. He was later known as the laughing philosopher, allegedly because of his reaction to human follies.

More surviving fragments are attributed to Democritus than to any other Presocratic philosopher, but the great majority are on ethics, and their authenticity and their exact relation to the atomic theory are in many cases doubtful. Our knowledge of atomism depends on testimonia (as opposed to actual fragments) to a greater degree than is the case for our knowledge of the theories of Empedocles and Anaxagoras; unfortunately the Aristotelian tradition which preserves most of our information is hostile to atomism.

---

1. Virtually nothing is known about his life. Epicurus (341–271), the most famous Atomist of antiquity, is reported to have denied Leucippus's existence (Diogenes Laertius, *Lives of the Philosophers* 10.13 = DK 67A2).

2. Diogenes Laertius, *Lives of the Philosophers* 9.30 = DK 67A1.

3. Democritus, DK 68B5.

4. The term "music" was originally used of any art governed by a Muse, such as singing, playing instruments, dancing, and poetry.

Attempts have been made to distinguish between Leucippus's and Democritus's contributions to the atomic theory.[5] In general, it appears that Leucippus, like Empedocles and Anaxagoras, sketched out a physical theory in response to the Eleatics as well as a cosmogony and cosmology which treated additional problems. Democritus then did what had not been done before, and his contribution is a turning point in the history of thought. He accepted the theory essentially as stated by Leucippus, but went on to explain in detail a wide range of natural phenomena, working out elaborate (though not always very clear) accounts of how the five senses function and also how thought and other cognitive activities take place. He also saw (possibly) the need for developing a mathematical basis for his physical theory and (certainly) the need for an appropriate theory of knowledge. Democritus aimed to establish a thoroughgoing atomistic account of all aspects of the world and of humanity to a greater extent than his predecessors seem to have done with their theories. It is a great shame that not one of his works has survived complete—the price, perhaps of doing his work in Abdera instead of Athens, and of championing a theory which was on the one hand apparently despised by Plato (who never mentions Democritus), Aristotle (who argues powerfully against the atomic theory), and the Stoics (who constituted the dominant philosophical movement of the Hellenistic age) and which was on the other hand taken over and adapted by Epicurus, whose pride and influence was such that his followers revered him as The Master and paid no attention to the sources to which he owed almost all his ideas about the natural world. In what follows, little effort will be made to distinguish the contributions of Leucippus from those of Democritus, and I shall speak in general of the Atomists.

Principles of the Atomic Theory

16.1   Leucippus and his associate Democritus declare the full and the empty [void] to be the elements, calling the former "what-is" (*to on*) and the other "what-is-not" (*to mē on*). Of these, the one, "what-is," is full and solid, the other, "what-is-not," is empty [void] and rare. (This is why they say that what-is is no more than what-is-not, because the void is no less than body is.) These are the material causes of existing things. . . . They declare that the differences <among these> are the causes of the rest. Moreover, they say that the differences are three: shape, arrangement, and position. For they say that what-is differs only in "rhythm," "touching," and "turning"—and of these "rhythm" is shape, "touching" is arrangement, and "turning" is position. For A differs from N in shape, AN from NA in arrangement, and Z from N in position.
                                              (Aristotle, *Metaphysics* 1.4 985b4–19 = DK 67A6)

16.2   After establishing the shapes, Democritus and Leucippus base their account of alteration and coming to be on them: coming to be and perishing by means of separation and combination, alteration by means of arrangement and position. Since they held that the truth is in the appearance, and

---

5. Most notably by Bailey (1928) and Graham (2008).

appearances are opposite and infinite, they made the shapes infinite,[6] so that by reason of changes of the composite, the same thing seems opposite to different people, and it shifts position when a small additional amount is mixed in, and it appears completely different when a single thing shifts position. For tragedy and comedy come to be out of the same letters.
(Aristotle, *On Generation and Corruption* 1.1 315b6–15 = DK 67A97)

16.3 Democritus believes that the nature of the eternal things is small substances (*ousiai*[7]) infinite in number. As a place for these he hypothesizes something else, infinite in size, and he calls their place by the names "the void," "nothing" (*ouden*) and "the unlimited" [or, "infinite"] and he calls each of the substances "hing" (*den*) and "the compact" and "what-is." He holds that the substances are so small that they escape our senses. They have all kinds of forms and shapes and differences in size. Out of these as elements he generates and forms visible and perceptible bodies. <These substances> are at odds with one another and move in the void because of their dissimilarity and the other differences I have mentioned, and as they move they strike against one another and become entangled in a way that makes them be in contact and close to one another but does not make any thing out of them that is truly one, for it is quite foolish <to think> that two or more things could ever come to be one. The grounds he gives for why the substances stay together up to a point are that the bodies fit together and hold each other fast. For some of them are rough, some are hooked, others concave and others convex, while yet others have innumerable other differences. So he thinks that they cling to each other and stay together until some stronger necessity comes along from the environment and shakes them and scatters them apart. He describes the generation and its contrary, separation, not only for animals but also for plants, *kosmoi*, and altogether for all perceptible bodies.
(Aristotle, *On Democritus*, quoted by Simplicius, *Commentary on Aristotle's* On the Heavens 295.1–22 = DK 68A37)

16.4 Leucippus . . . did not follow the same route as Parmenides and Xenophanes concerning things that are, but seemingly the opposite one. For while they made the universe one, immovable, ungenerated, and limited, and did not even permit the investigation of what-is-not, he posited the atoms as infinite and ever-moving elements, with an infinite number of shapes on the grounds that they are no more like this than like that and because he observed that coming to be and change are unceasing among the things that are. Further, he posited that what-is is no more than what-is-not, and both are equally causes of things that come to be. For supposing the substance of the atoms to be compact and full, he said it is what-is and that it moves in the void, which he called "what-is-not" and which he declares is no less than what-is. His associate, Democritus of Abdera, likewise posited the full

---

6. *Apeiron.* In previous chapters this word is frequently translated "unlimited."

7. *Ousia,* "substance," is a noun derived from the verb *einai,* "to be." There is a connection in language and meaning between *ousia* and *on* (16.1).

and the void as principles, of which he calls the former "what-is" and the latter "what-is-not." For positing the atoms as matter for the things that are, they generate the rest by means of their differences. These are three: rhythm, turning, and touching, that is, shape, position, and arrangement. For by nature like is moved by like, and things of the same kind move toward one another, and each of the shapes produces a different condition when arranged in a different combination. Thus, since the principles are infinite, they reasonably promised to account for all attributes and substances—how and through what cause anything comes to be. This is why they say that only those who make the elements infinite account for everything reasonably. They say that the number of the shapes among the atoms is infinite on the grounds that they are no more like this than like that. For they themselves assign this as a cause of the infiniteness.

(Simplicius, *Commentary on Aristotle's* Physics
28.4–26 = DK 67A8, 68A38)

16.5   Leucippus and Democritus have accounted for all things very systematically and in a single theory, taking the natural starting point as their own. For some of the early philosophers held that what-is is necessarily one and immovable. For the void is not, and motion is impossible without a separate void, nor can there be many things without something to keep them apart. . . . But Leucippus thought he had arguments which assert what is generally granted to perception, not abolishing coming to be, perishing, motion, or plurality. Agreeing on these matters with the phenomena and agreeing with those who support the one [that is, the Eleatics] that there could be no motion without void, he asserts that void is what-is-not and that nothing of what-is is not, since what strictly is is completely full. But this kind of thing is not one thing but things that are infinite in number and invisible because of the minuteness of their size. These move in the void (for there is void), and they produce coming to be by combining and perishing by coming apart, and they act and are acted upon wherever they happen to come into contact (for in this way they are not one), and they generate <compounds> by becoming combined and entangled. A plurality could not come to be from what is in reality one, nor one from what is really many, but this is impossible.

(Aristotle, *On Generation and Corruption* 1.8
324b35–325a36 = DK 67A7)

There are two types of elements: atoms and void. Atoms are indivisible (the word *atomos* means "uncuttable," "unsplittable") building blocks too small to be seen which move in the void and combine to form compounds, some of which are large enough to be perceived. Atoms are called "full," "solid," "compact," "what-is," and "hing," while void is empty (*kenon*, the word translated "void" means "empty"), "rare," "unlimited" or "infinite," "what-is-not," and "nothing." Among these descriptions of atoms and void which emphasize their strongly contrasting natures, "hing" contrasts with "nothing" as "nothing" minus the negative "not." This translation reflects the Greek, in which *ouden* ("nothing") minus *ou* ("not") gives *den*, a word that neatly makes the Atomists' point.[8]

Atoms

Atoms are eternal (**16.3**) and, as the following passages show, uniform in substance, without perceptible qualities and differing only in their spatial properties—size and shape, the latter illustrated by the letters of the alphabet (**16.1**).

16.6   They declare that their nature is but one, as if each one were a separate piece of gold.
(Aristotle, *On the Heavens* 1.7 275b32–276a1 = DK 67A19)

16.7   Plato and Democritus supposed that only the intelligible things are true (or, "real"); Democritus <held this view> because there is by nature no perceptible substrate, since the atoms, which combine to form all things, have a nature deprived of every perceptible quality.
(Sextus Empiricus, *Against the Mathematicians* 8.6 = DK 68A59)

16.8   Democritus specified two <basic properties of atoms>: size and shape; and Epicurus added weight as a third.
(Aëtius 1.3.18 = DK 68A47)

There are an infinite number of atoms, with an infinite number of shapes moving in infinite void. The Atomists offered arguments for the view that the number of shapes is infinite. (a) Truth is in the appearance; appearances are infinite; therefore the shapes are infinite (**16.2**). (b) They are no more like this than like that; therefore there is an infinite multitude of shapes (**16.4**)—an argument which evidently depends on the Principle of Sufficient Reason, encountered previously in Anaximander and Parmenides.[9]

The infinite number of shapes entails an infinite number of atoms.

16.9   Since the bodies differ in shape, and the shapes are infinite, they declare the simple bodies to be infinite too. But they did not determine further what is the shape of each of the elements, beyond assigning a spherical shape to fire. They distinguished air and water and the others by largeness and smallness.
(Aristotle, *On the Heavens* 3.4 303a11–15 = DK 67A15)

---

8. The Atomists did not invent this word, which was used by the sixth-century lyric poet Alcaeus (fr. 23 [Diehl]).

9. See the discussion following **5.14**; also the discussion of **11.8** lines 9–11 on p. 159 above.

This property in turn, presumably, was thought to entail an infinite amount of void for them to move in (although we do not have any record of arguments that the void is infinite).

Parallel reasoning to (b) would conclude that there are atoms of all possible sizes ("all kinds of . . . differences in size" [**16.3**]). Indeed, one source declares that Democritus believes there can be an atom the size of a *kosmos* (**16.21**). But since there is strong evidence (**16.5**, compare **16.3**, **16.11**) that both Leucippus and Democritus held that the atoms are very small, indeed "invisible because of the minuteness of their size," it is best to hold that Democritus believed that atoms could in principle be any size (which could have led to the interpretation that he believed that some atoms are in fact huge) and yet he, like Leucippus, believed that in fact they are all too small to be seen.[10] This question aside, however, it seems that size as well as shape govern the sorts of compounds in which an atom can be found (**16.9**).

All atoms are made of the same stuff. Moreover this stuff, and consequently the atoms themselves, have no perceptible qualities, unlike the basic substances of earlier theories we have seen. They are not hard or soft, hot or cold, wet or dry, which are properties of macroscopic perceptible compounds of atoms and depend on the atomic structure of the compounds rather than the nature of the individual component atoms.

It is not certain why the Atomists supposed that atoms have no perceptible qualities, but their theory lends itself to some speculations. First, with such atoms it is easier to account for a wider range of changes in quality at the macroscopic level. For example, iron, which is gray, becomes red when heated. If it were composed of gray atoms this change would be hard to explain. But if color depends on atomic structure and movement, we may suppose that heat alters the structure and movement of the atoms in the iron. Second, individual atoms cannot be perceived,[11] hence they cannot have perceptible qualities. Third, since an atom lacks such qualities it can form part of many different compounds with different qualities, as a spherical atom can perhaps in one context be a soul-atom and in another a fire-atom. Fourth, the atomic theory is a beautifully simple theory which rests on a small number of principles. Part of its simplicity resides in the fact that atoms have so few inherent properties.

The atoms are impassive, incapable of being affected or acted upon.

---

10. For further discussion of this point, see Guthrie (1965: 394–95).

11. For the Atomists' account of vision, which depends on atoms being emitted from the perceived object (hence a single atom, which cannot emit other atoms, is invisible), see below pp. 330–31.

16.10   These men [Leucippus, Democritus, and Epicurus] said that the principles
         are infinite in multitude, and they believed them to be atoms and indivisible
         and incapable of being affected because they are compact and have no share
         of void. (For they claimed that division occurs where there is void in bodies.)
                                      (Simplicius, *Commentary on Aristotle's* On the
                                                   Heavens 242.18–21 = DK 67A14)

Also "on account of their hardness the atoms are not acted upon and do not
change" (**16.33**). Since they are quality-less, they cannot change in quality. Nor
can they change in quantity by becoming either more or fewer (which would
involve generation or perishing) or by growing or shrinking. The only sort of
change an atom could suffer would be change in its spatial properties (size and
shape), which is prevented by the absence of internal void (so that it cannot
bend or break). The unique statement that the atoms are also incapable of acting
(**16.33**) must be understood in this context: they cannot cause changes in other
atoms. The contrary claim that "they act and are acted upon whenever they happen to be in contact" (**16.5**) will refer to their behavior not as individual atoms
but as components of compounds.

The atoms' indivisible nature was the subject of a lively debate. The following
passage records some of the Atomists' arguments on the point.

16.11   Those who abandoned division to infinity on the grounds that we cannot
         divide to infinity and as a result cannot guarantee that the division can-
         not end declared that bodies are composed of indivisible things and are
         divided into indivisibles. Except that Leucippus and Democritus hold that
         the cause of the primary bodies' indivisibility is not only their inability to
         be affected but also their minute size and lack of parts.
                                         (Simplicius, *Commentary on Aristotle's*
                                                   Physics 925.10–15 = DK 67A13)

The atoms are indivisible because (a) they cannot be affected, (b) they are so
small, and (c) they have no parts. But all three of these considerations beg the
question. For example, we cannot know that they have no parts unless we already
know that they are indivisible (assuming that "parts" is meant in the only way
that makes sense in the context: parts into which a thing can be divided).

The first part of **16.11**, however, puts these arguments in a different light (if
the reasoning can be attributed to the Atomists). Zeno had shown (The Argument from Large and Small, see above pages 178–79) that unacceptable consequences follow on the assumption that a finite-sized object is infinitely divisible.
Complete the division and either the resulting least parts have no size or they
have some positive size. But either way, the parts cannot be reassembled to form
the original object. If they have no size, when put together they result in something with no size. If they have a positive size, no matter how small, when an

infinite number of them are put together, the result is something of infinite, not finite size. The Atomists dodged this argument.[12] In the absence of a guarantee that bodies are infinitely divisible, they simply declared that they are not, that is, that bodies are ultimately composed of indivisibles. This amounts to hypothesizing the existence of atoms in the absence of a conclusive reason not to do so. The next step would be to describe the atoms so as to corroborate their indivisibility and also explain why we fail to perceive them directly—and the properties mentioned in **16.11** above contribute to this enterprise.

Another passage goes further, arguing that bodies cannot be "everywhere divisible."

16.12   Democritus would appear to have been persuaded by arguments which are appropriate to the science of nature. The point will be clear as we proceed. For there is a difficulty in supposing that there is a body, a magnitude, that is everywhere divisible and that this [the complete division] is possible. For what will there be that escapes the division? . . . Now since such a body is everywhere divisible, let it be divided. What, then, will be left? A magnitude? But that cannot be. For there will be something that has not been divided, whereas we supposed that it was everywhere divisible. But if there is no body or magnitude left and yet the division will take place, either <the original body> will consist of points and its components will be without magnitude, or it will be nothing at all so that even if it were to come to be out of nothing and be composed of nothing, the whole thing would then be nothing but an appearance. Likewise, if it is composed of points it will not be a quantity. For when they were in contact and there was a single magnitude and they coincided, they made the whole thing no larger. For when it is divided into two or more, the whole is no smaller or larger than before. And so even if all the points are put together they will not make any magnitude. . . . These problems result from supposing that any body whatever of any size is everywhere divisible. . . . And so, since magnitudes cannot be composed of contacts or points, it is necessary for there to be indivisible bodies and magnitudes.

(Aristotle, *On Generation and Corruption* 1.2
316a13–b16 = DK 68A48b)[13]

"Everywhere divisible" is different from "infinitely divisible." Dividing a magnitude one meter long in half and then dividing one of these halves in half, and so on, is an infinite division which leaves pieces of positive size: one piece half a

---

12. Aristotle says that "some gave in to [Zeno's arguments] by positing atomic magnitudes" (Aristotle, *Physics* 1.3 187a1–3 = DK 29A22). If Aristotle is referring to the fifth-century Atomists, he may mean that they gave in in the sense that they admitted the logical force of the arguments and avoided them by denying the hypothesis on which they depend—that what-is is infinitely divisible.

13. This passage and its context are well discussed by Sedley (2008).

meter long, one piece a quarter of a meter long, and so on. Dividing the magnitude everywhere—for example, by dividing it into two pieces half a meter long and then dividing both of these pieces into halves and continuing to subdivide each of the products of the previous division—leaves pieces of no positive size. But even though being everywhere divisible is a stronger condition than being infinitely divisible, it rather than infinite divisibility is the antithesis of atomism and hence a view the Atomists need to reject. Thus, **16.12**'s argument is appropriate. If the argument succeeds there is good reason to adopt some kind of atomic theory. However, the argument rests on the assumption not just that a magnitude is everywhere divisible but that division can be carried out in such a way that the magnitude is actually divided at every place, which is quite a different claim and one which proponents of the former need not accept.

As far as the evidence goes, then, the Atomists did not prove that there are atoms. A body can be everywhere divisible even if not actually divided everywhere. But by positing atoms (even without proving that they exist), they avoided the Scylla and Charybdis of Zeno's Argument from Large and Small. This is sufficient to show that physically indivisible bodies are possible, though not enough to escape all of Zeno's arguments. For physical indivisibility of atoms does not guarantee that they are also geometrically indivisible.[14] Atoms have sizes and shapes, and shapes involve spatial extension. For example, Democritus speaks of fire as composed of spherical atoms. A spherical atom may be a very small sphere, but in thought even if not with a knife we can distinguish one part of the sphere from the other. And once we can do this much, others of Zeno's paradoxes take hold—the Dichotomy and the Achilles (see above pages 181–85). We cannot traverse an atom because we would first have to cross half[15] of it, then half the remainder, and so forth.

It is a matter of current controversy whether the fifth-century Atomists believed that atoms are geometrically as well as physically indivisible.[16] The philosophically correct move would be to distinguish between kinds of indivisibility and hold that atoms are geometrically divisible but not physically so. Alternatively and plausibly the Atomists may not have explicitly distinguished among different kinds of indivisibility. (Such distinctions are more at home in

---

14. An atom is geometrically indivisible if we cannot distinguish (even without physical division) the sides from the corners, the center from the edges, the right half from the left half (given its position), and so forth. See Taylor (1999: 164–71) for more detailed discussion. For a different account of kinds of divisibility, see Barnes (1979: vol. 2, 50–51 / 1982: 356–57).

15. Half on the Dichotomy paradox, some larger fraction on the Achilles.

16. Champions of theoretical indivisibility include Guthrie (1965: 396, 503–7) and Furley (1987: 124–31); among the opponents is Barnes (1979: vol. 2, 46–54 / 1982: 352–60). Epicurus seems to have believed that atoms are theoretically divisible into theoretically indivisible parts.

Aristotle than in the fifth century.) They may have conceived of divisibility and indivisibility solely as physical properties and felt free to distinguish parts of atoms in thought without supposing that doing so requires atoms to be divisible in any way. They would then be in a position to admit that atoms are geometrically divisible once the relevant distinctions were made.[17] In fact, as we saw in discussing Zeno, geometrical divisibility to infinity is an illusory problem. There is no need to take any step to oppose it (let alone a philosophically unsound step) because the option Zeno offers between final parts of no size and final parts of some size is misleading: neither of these results will obtain.

The Atomists were aware of the positive Eleatic doctrines of Parmenides and Melissus as well as Zeno's attacks on plurality, and there is no doubt that atomism is a response to the Eleatic challenge. It preserves the world of experience with its change, coming into being, perishing, etc., by saying that these features are due to unchanging atoms which have many of the properties that Parmenides proves belong to what-is. However, the Atomists may have paid more attention to Melissus than to Parmenides. Melissus had said "if there were many things, they must be such as I say the one is" (**15.10** section 2), and some say that the Atomists responded by endowing each of their atoms with the attributes of Melissus's "one." This is true to an extent. Like Melissus's "one," each atom is uncreated and imperishable, therefore eternal. It is continuous and indivisible. It is unchanging in quality; in fact, like Melissus's "one," it has no qualities. Moreover, relative to itself it does not move: its logically distinguishable parts always have the same positions relative to one another. Each atom is, of course, finite in size (unlike Melissus's "one").[18] Atoms are not spatially invariant: different parts have different locations relative to one another. But still, at the level of the individual atom—not considered in its relations to other atoms—there is temporal invariance. Since there is no change or internal motion, an atom is identical with itself throughout its eternal existence.

Void

The void fulfills two main functions. It enables the atoms to move and it makes possible and preserves their uniqueness and identity: "motion is impossible without a separate void, nor can there be many things without something to keep them apart" (**16.5**). Regarding the latter point, Leucippus and Democritus held that if there were no void to separate atoms, all there is would consist of a single infinitely large indivisible mass of matter. "Division occurs where there is void in bodies" (**16.10**).

---

17. Mendell argues ably for this view (Mendell n.d.).
18. See above pp. 298–99.

According to some sources, the Atomists posited that void exists (**16.3, 16.4** and **16.5**[19]). However, they did offer arguments. One, which is another application of the Principle of Sufficient Reason, goes as follows.

16.13 There is no more reason for the "hing" to be than the nothing.

(Democritus, DK 68B156)

The following passage from Aristotle presents four of their reasons for believing in the void, all of which are inconclusive.[20]

16.14 By "void" people mean an interval in which there is no perceptible body. Since they believe that everything that is is body, they say that void is that in which there is nothing at all. . . . So it is necessary to prove[21] . . . that there is no interval different from bodies . . . which breaks up the totality of body so that it is not continuous, as Democritus, Leucippus, and many other natural philosophers say, or that there is anything outside the totality of body, supposing that it is continuous. . . . They say that (1) there would be no change in place (that is, motion and growth), since it does not seem that there would be motion unless there were void, since what is full cannot admit anything else. . . . (2) Some things are seen to contract and be compressed; for example, they say that the jars hold the wine along with the wineskins, since the compressed body contracts into the empty places which are in it. Further (3) all believe that growth takes place through void, since the nourishment is a body and two bodies cannot coincide. (4) They also use as evidence what happens with ash: it takes no less water to fill a jar that contains ashes than it does to fill the same jar when it is empty.

(Aristotle, *Physics* 4.6 213a27–b22 = DK 67A19)

Void is different from air, whose corporeal nature had been hinted at as far back as Anaximenes and was assumed in Empedocles' clepsydra analogy (**14.140**). Nor is it the same thing as space. Consider a fish in a body of water, such as the water in a fish bowl. The water and the fish both occupy space and have locations; they occupy different regions of space and have different locations. Similarly, atoms and void both occupy space and have locations. Where there is

---

19. **16.4** and **16.5** put the Atomists' hypothesis of the existence of void in an anti-Eleatic context.

20. This passage forms part of Aristotle's treatment of the question whether void exists. Aristotle does not believe in its existence, and his refutation (in *Physics* 4.7) of the Atomists' arguments that it does exist is an important part of his support for the opposite view.

21. In this passage Aristotle presents arguments offered in favor of the thesis that void exists and in the present sentence he says that he needs to refute the view that void exists.

void there are no atoms, and where there are atoms there is no void. The atoms move through the void in the same sense as that in which the fish swims through the water. Thus, the water and the void are both *in* space and neither is to be confused with the space in which the fish or atoms move.[22]

But there is also something to be said for Aristotle's interpretation that void is the space or place in which the atoms move (**16.3**). The Atomists said that (unlike water), the void is nothing; but if there is nothing in between atoms, how can atoms be separate? To be separate there must be a gap between them—a region devoid of matter. "Nothing" is a good enough word for a gap, since a gap is nothing material. As with the water and the fish in the fish bowl, both atoms and gaps have locations and occupy space. Regions of space unoccupied by atoms are called void. One solution to the problem would have been to talk of atoms and space instead of atoms and void, but there is no reason to think that the Atomists had a conception of space as such. On the other hand, Aristotle identifies this void as the place of the atoms (not as space) and his conception of place makes this a plausible interpretation.[23]

The Atomists emphasized void's existence and nature with a paradox: Leucippus "asserts that void is what-is-not and that nothing of what-is is not, since what strictly is is completely full" (**16.5**); "what-is is no more than what-is-not, because the void is no less than body is" (**16.1**); "both [what-is and what-is-not] are equally causes of things that come to be" (**16.4**). Further, Democritus calls the void "nothing" (**16.3**), so that nothing exists.

These assertions do more than pose riddles; they fly in the face of the Eleatic challenge. Parmenides had declared that "nothing is not" (**11.6** line 2), and that what-is-not cannot be known or declared (**11.2** lines 7–8), and he had forbidden inquiry along that path (**11.2** lines 5–6). Moreover, Melissus had disproved the possibility of motion on the grounds that motion requires the existence of void and the void is nothing (**15.9** section 7). In this intellectual context it is simply unsatisfactory to assert baldly that "nothing" is one of the physical principles and to declare that nothing exists just as much as "hing."

Some think that calling the void "nothing" is a move to avoid Zeno's Argument from Limited and Unlimited (above pages 180–81), which would entail

---

22. For further discussion of these issues in Melissus as well as in the Atomists, see Sedley (1982).

23. Aristotle declares that proponents of the existence of void conceive of it as "place in which there is no body" (*Physics* 4.7 213b33 [not in DK]). Since Aristotle defines the place of something as "the innermost motionless boundary of what contains it" (*Physics* 4.4 212a20–21 [not in DK]), or, less precisely, as "what contains the thing whose place it is, and is no part of that thing" (*Physics* 4.4 210b34–211a1 [not in DK]), he takes void to be in some sense a potential container of body. Note that on this view the place of an object is not a location in space, but another object which contains it (as an egg carton is the place of an egg).

an infinite number of atoms in a finite area. Zeno argued "if there are many . . . between things that are there are always others, and still others between those. Therefore the things that are are unlimited" (**12.5**). The Atomists can respond that in between the things that are (atoms) is nothing (void), so Zeno's regress fails to take hold.

The void also runs afoul of Parmenides' more abstract reasoning. "Not at all more in any respect . . . or at all inferior" (**11.8** lines 23–24) and "it is right for what-is to be not incomplete; for it is not lacking; otherwise, what-is would be in want of everything" (**11.8** lines 32–33); "For it is right for it to be not in any way greater or any lesser than in another" (**11.8** lines 44–45); "nor is there any way in which what-is would be in one way more than what-is and in another way less" (**11.8** lines 47–48). The Atomists' claim that void is just as much as atoms are is sufficient to meet some of these claims. Although in a sense there is less where there is void than where there are atoms, still, void is on a par with atoms in the relevant respect, that is, being. As for the claim "it is right either fully to be or not" (**11.8** line11), the Atomists simply deny it by distinguishing between the existential interpretation of that principle, which they accept at the atomic level (void and atoms both exist fully) and the predicative interpretation which they could deny (the predicate "full" holds of atoms but not of void, and the predicate "empty" holds of void, but not of atoms).

However, the existence of what-is-not represents a major departure from Eleatic doctrine. I have already discussed the anti-Parmenidean declaration "what-is-not is." In addition, the existence of void goes against Melissus's argument "Nor is any of it empty. For what is empty is nothing, and of course what is nothing cannot be" (**15.9** section 7). As we have seen, the Atomists, while agreeing with the premise that what is empty is nothing, deny the last assertion of the argument and claim that what is nothing (the void) is.

Still, the assertion that "nothing" exists is badly defended. The argument that there is no less reason for "nothing" to be than for "thing" to be would not have impressed Parmenides, who believed there to be a good reason why "nothing" could not be: it cannot be thought or spoken of (**11.2** lines 7–8). But this premise is undefended and need not be accepted if there is no reason to. And Democritus, who has a good deal to say about the void, will reasonably have supposed that there is good reason to reject the premise and to hold that "nothing" is just as much as "thing" (or "hing"). Further he could give as a positive reason for believing in its existence the role it plays in his system.

The assertion that what-is-not is just as much as what-is thus may not simply be a paradox for paradox's sake. It succinctly brings out the fundamental conflict with Parmenides and invites us to consider the role "what-is-not" plays in the atomic theory so that we can judge, by reference to the success of the theory, the merits of the claim that what-is-not (i.e., the void) is.

Can the void be spoken and thought of? In a sense it can, quite obviously. It can be characterized in terms of its roles of occupying space, making possible the motions of atoms, etc. But the Atomists tend to describe it negatively in contrast with the atoms. It is "empty" as opposed to "full," and is "rare" only in an extended use of that word. Although the presence of void is needed to account for certain qualities of compounds, it is more natural to describe those compounds as consisting of atoms more or less separated or atoms arranged in a certain way. If atoms are quality-less, so is the void, and the void per se lacks even the spatial properties of atoms. It has no shape or size of its own (aside from its infinite amount). Thus the Atomists can hold that the void is per se virtually unthinkable and indescribable, and except for the various ways it can be described by contrast with and in relation to the atoms, the only feature it has of its own is infinite extension.

Atomic Motion

The infinitely many atoms are all in motion in the infinite void. As an atom moves it may meet with other atoms of the same kind or of different kinds. Such collisions can result in the atoms rebounding away from one another or in their coming together to form compounds. Before discussing compounds, it will be useful to discuss the atoms' motion.

Aristotle makes several complaints against the Atomists' accounts of atomic motion.

> 16.15   This is why Leucippus and Democritus, who say that the primary bodies are always moving in the void (that is, the infinite) must specify what motion they have and what is their natural motion.
> (Aristotle, *On the Heavens* 3.2 300b8–11 = DK 67A16)

> 16.16   Concerning the origin and manner of motion in existing things, these men too, like the rest, lazily neglected to give an account.
> (Aristotle, *Metaphysics* 1.4 985b19–20 = DK 67A6) (continuation of **16.1**)

> 16.17   For they say that there is always motion. But why it is and what motion it is, they do not state, nor do they give the cause of its being of one sort rather than another.
> (Aristotle, *Metaphysics* 12.6 1071b33–35 = DK 67A18)

It seems certain that they did not specify the nature or cause of the atoms' original motion. Thus, the isolated statement

> 16.18   They say that motion occurs because of the void. For they too say that nature[24] undergoes motion in respect of place.
> (Aristotle, *Physics* 8.9 265b24–25 = DK 68A58)

---

24. This is a word the Atomists used to refer to the atoms.

must mean merely that the void is a necessary condition for motion, not that it is a cause, in the sense of the source of the motion.

However, Aristotle's objections are misconceived. Since atoms and void are eternal and eternally in motion, there was no initial state corresponding to the period in Anaxagoras's cosmogony in which "all things were together" (**13.1**). The Atomists therefore avoid Parmenides' question "what need would have roused it, later or earlier, to grow?" (**11.8** lines 9–10). There is no need to posit a cause of the beginning of motion, since motion has always existed.

Likewise there is no need to talk of an original form of motion. An atom's motion now is determined by its most recent history of contact with other atoms, like the motion of billiard balls after they have collided. If we have perfectly elastic billiard balls and a billiard table with perfectly elastic cushions, and if the balls roll on the table without friction or air resistance, then if the balls are in motion, they will never stop moving unless affected from the outside in the future, and, likewise, unless they have been affected from outside in the past, they have always been moving. There is no initial static condition and no first movement, but at any moment—past, present, or future—their motion is determined by their immediately previous history.

There is good evidence that this was the Atomists' view of atomic motion.

16.19 Leucippus and Democritus said that their primary bodies, the atoms, are always moving in the infinite void by compulsion.
(Simplicius, *Commentary on Aristotle's On the Heavens* 583.18–20 = DK 67A16)

16.20 Democritus, saying that the atoms are by nature motionless, declares that they move "by a blow."
(Simplicius, *Commentary on Aristotle's Physics* 42.10–11 = DK 68A47)

16.21 Democritus says that the primary bodies (these are the compact things) do not possess weight but move by striking against one another in the infinite, and there can be an atom the size of a *kosmos*.
(Aëtius 1.12.6 = DK 68A47)

16.22 These men [Leucippus and Democritus] say that the atoms move by hitting and striking against each other, but they do not specify the source of their natural motion. For the motion of striking each other is compelled and not natural, and compelled motion is posterior to natural motion.
(Alexander, *Commentary on Aristotle's Metaphysics* 36.21–25 = DK 67A6)

These passages agree that the atoms move as the result of striking one another. As **16.19** asserts, this is always the case: an atom is always moving, at all times its movements are due to previous collisions, and there was no first collision. In Aristotelian terminology, such motion is "compelled" as opposed to "natural."

Aristotle's belief in natural motion, a body's motion toward its natural place,[25] and the priority of natural to compelled motion affects several of the sources. The atoms do not have an inherent tendency either to be at rest or to move in any particular direction or toward any particular location, and so in Aristotelian terms they do not have any natural motion.[26]

16.23   They said that moving in virtue of the weight in them, <the atoms> move[27] in respect of place through the void, which yields and does not resist. For they said that they "are hurled all about." And they attribute this motion to the elements as not just their primary but in fact their only motion, whereas things composed of the elements have the other kinds of motion. For they grow and decrease, change, come to be, and perish through the combination and separation of the primary bodies.

(Simplicius, *Commentary on Aristotle's* Physics 1318.35–1319.5 = DK 68A58)

16.24   Democritus holds that there is one kind of motion, that due to pulsation.

(Aëtius 1.23.3 = DK 68A47)

The words translated "are hurled all about" and "pulsation"[28] are etymologically related and presumably refer to the same kind of movement, the bouncing back and forth of the atoms between collisions.

Our discussion of the atoms' original and natural motion leads directly to the vexed question whether they have weight. The evidence is conflicting and problematic: in addition to **16.8** there is also the following.

16.25   Democritus and, later, Epicurus said that all the atoms have the same nature and possess weight, but since some are heavier, when these sink down the lighter ones are squeezed out and move upward, and in this way they say that some things appear light and others heavy.

(Simplicius, *Commentary on Aristotle's* On the Heavens 569.5–9 = DK 68A61)

16.26   Democritus says that each of the indivisibles is heavier according as its quantity is greater.

(Aristotle, *On Generation and Corruption* 1.8 326a9–10 = DK 68A60)

---

25. The four Aristotelian elements have natural places. For example, earth's place is at the center of the *kosmos*, and the natural motion of earth is toward the center. See Aristotle, *On the Heavens* 1.8.

26. I take it that this fact is behind the first clause of **16.20** and the second clause of **16.22**.

27. *Kineisthai*. For Aristotle this word covers motion in place and also other changes, such as the motions listed at the end of this passage.

28. The words are *peripalassesthai* and *palmos*, both derived from the root *pal-*, "to shake."

16.27   Those <who call the primary bodies> solid can rather say that the larger ones are heavier. But since compounds do not appear to behave in this way, but we see many that are smaller in bulk but heavier, as bronze is heavier than wood, some think and say that the cause is different—that the void enclosed within makes the bodies light and sometimes makes larger things lighter, since they contain more void. . . . But those who make these distinctions must add not only that something contains more void if it is lighter but also that it contains less solid.

(Aristotle, *On the Heavens* 4.2 309a1–14 = DK 68A60)

Also **16.21**.

The problem is partly that while most sources assert that atoms have weight, two passages (**16.8, 16.21**) deny it and partly that our concept of weight is different from ancient views. It will help to draw two distinctions. First, atoms may have weight and yet not have it as one of their primary properties (**16.8**). Since atoms are all made of the same uniform stuff, their size and shape will determine how much of that stuff is in them, which will in turn determine their weight (**16.26**).

Second, the word translated "weight" is the noun derived from the adjective that means "heavy," and although "weight" has for us a technical definition (mass multiplied by gravitational acceleration) that involves concepts alien to ancient Atomism, heaviness is a more general and vague term which, depending on the context in which it is found, may or may not be synonymous with weight. In what follows I will continue to speak of weight, but appropriate caution should be observed.

Weight can be understood in different ways, including (a) as a tendency to move or otherwise be affected by a certain force (for example, gravity), or alternatively (b) as a tendency to move in a certain direction (for Aristotle, this direction is toward the center of the *kosmos*, for Epicurus, it is downward), or (c) as a tendency to move in certain ways under certain conditions, differently in different conditions, with no universal tendency to move in any particular direction (this corresponds roughly to our concept of mass). As our treatment of atomic motion has shown, the Atomists hold that an atom's motion at any moment is determined solely by its previous collision with other atoms. No appeal need be made to any immaterial force like gravity, which has no place in ancient atomism. (See below page 324.) However, in certain contexts, such as the *kosmos* we live in, matter does have a tendency to move in a certain direction and in general to display the characteristics we associate with weight—for example, that heavier bodies sink and lighter ones rise and that there is no necessary relation between a body's size and its weight. Some of these phenomena are explained in **16.25** and **16.27**. Others are due to the effects of the cosmogonic vortex, in which like atoms move toward like and the heavier ones toward the center (see below pages 324–25). If this account is correct, the Atomists succeed in accounting for many phenomena of gravity and weight within the confines of their materialistic and mechanistic theory.

If all events are due to the mechanical motion and interaction of atoms in the void, atomism seems to entail a rigid determinism. Perhaps surprisingly, the problems determinism raises both for understanding human actions and for central concepts in ethics were not explored until later in the Greek philosophical tradition. Nevertheless the Atomists and those who discussed their theory did recognize some of its implications for causality. The single surviving sentence of Leucippus bears on this aspect of the atomic theory.

> 16.28 No thing happens at random but all things as a result of a reason and by necessity.
>
> (Leucippus, DK 67B2)

At first sight **16.28** appears to deny the mechanistic picture of the atomistic universe. "No thing happens at random" gives the impression that all things happen for a purpose, and "all things as a result of a reason" suggests that the universe is governed by a purposeful intelligence, much like Heraclitus's rational *logos*. But these impressions are misleading. The key to the fragment is the notion of necessity. Leucippus holds that everything that happens—all movements and interactions of atoms in the void—happens of necessity in that, given the nature of atoms and void and given the positions and motions of the atoms, things cannot happen otherwise. This necessity is blind necessity as opposed to conscious or unconscious plan and purpose. It follows immediately that nothing happens by chance or at random. Moreover there is a reason why everything takes place—not because there is a governing mind but in the sense that every event has an explanation.[29]

Democritus followed Leucippus in this view.

> 16.29 Democritus leaves aside purpose but refers all things which nature employs to necessity.
>
> (Aristotle, *Generation of Animals* 5.8 789b2–4 = DK 68A66)

> 16.30 <Concerning necessity> Democritus <says it is> the knocking against <each other> and the motion and "blow" of matter.
>
> (Aëtius 1.26.2 = DK 68A66)

> 16.31 <Democritus> seemed to employ chance in his cosmogony, but in his detailed discussions he declares that chance is the cause of nothing, and he refers to other causes.
>
> (Simplicius, *Commentary on Aristotle's* Physics 330.14–17 = DK 68A68)

All events are caused by the collisions of atoms, so that chance and purpose form no part of a correct explanation of anything that happens. On the other hand,

---

29. The word translated "reason" is *logos*. This word need not imply the existence of a reasoning agent, only that a reason could in principle be given if one were sought.

the fact that atomic interactions are coincidental in the sense that they are due to purposeless prior events that are beyond perception and so are not humanly predictable gives them an appearance of chance events. This is particularly true of the events that lead to the formation of a *kosmos*. The concurrence of the great number of atoms that have the motions needed to form a cosmic vortex is the result of the prior history of each of the atoms, but the complex interaction of so vast a number of them is beyond our ability to discover.

Compounds

"They declare that the differences <among these> are the causes of the rest. Moreover, they say that the differences are three: shape, arrangement, and position. . . . For A differs from N in shape, AN from NA in arrangement, and Z from N in position" (from **16.1**). It is possible that the use of letters to illustrate properties of the atoms goes back to the Atomists themselves. This analogy is carried further in **16.2**: tragedies and comedies are written with the same letters.[30] These three kinds of differences are of different types. Whereas the first kind (A and N) illustrates differences in shapes of individual atoms, the second explicitly and the third implicitly have to do with the roles of atoms in compounds. The second shows how the same atoms can form different compounds (here think of the syllables "an" and "na"), and the third shows how a single atom can play different roles depending on its immediate context. Both fire and souls are composed of spherical atoms, but that is not to say that souls are fiery or that fire has the attributes of soul. A single spherical atom out of context cannot be identified as either a soul-atom or a fire-atom, and in fact by itself it is neither, though perhaps in the appropriate context it can be either.[31]

Compounds arise when atoms moving through the void come into contact with one another and instead of rebounding become enmeshed.

16.32   These atoms, which are separate from one another in the infinite void and differ in shape and size and position and arrangement, move in the void, and when they overtake one another they collide, and some rebound in whatever direction they may happen to, but others become entangled in virtue of the way their shapes, sizes, positions, and arrangements correspond, and they stay together, and this is how compounds are produced.

(Simplicius, Commentary on Aristotle's On the Heavens
242.21–26 = DK 67A14) (continuation of 16.10)

---

30. It is likely that the analogy in **16.2** comes from an Atomist text, though it could be Aristotle's.

31. Aristotle's unsympathetic report that "Democritus declares the soul to be some kind of fire and hot, for the shapes and atoms being infinite, he says the spherical ones are fire and soul" (*On the Soul* 1.2 403b31–404a2 = DK 67A28), is therefore unfair. Moreover, for all the sources tell us, the atoms which make up souls could be spheres of different sizes from those that make up fire.

16.33   What does Democritus say? That atomic substances infinite in number, not
        different in kind, and moreover incapable of acting or being acted upon are
        in motion, scattered in the void. When they approach one another or collide
        or become entangled, the compounds appear as water or fire or as a plant
        or a human, but all things are atoms, which he calls forms; there is nothing
        else. For there is no coming to be from what-is-not, and nothing could come
        to be from things that are because on account of their hardness the atoms
        are not acted upon and do not change.
                        (Plutarch, *Against Colotes* 8 1110F–1111A = DK 68A57)

Compounds, though composed of eternal atoms, are not permanent. They last
until struck hard enough from outside in the right place by other atoms of sufficient size and appropriate shape, moving with appropriate speed (**16.3**).

   Perceptible qualities of compounds are due to the shape, size, arrangement
and position, and possibly the motions of the quality-less atoms that compose
them. Democritus attempted to apply this general principle to specific cases, as
the following passages show.

16.34   Leucippus and Democritus, calling the smallest and primary bodies atoms,
        <say> that in virtue of differences in their shapes and position and order
        some bodies come to be hot and fiery—those composed of rather sharp and
        minute primary bodies situated in a similar position, while others come to
        be cold and watery—those composed of the opposite kinds of bodies. And
        some come to be bright and shining while others come to be dim and dark.
                   (Simplicius, *Commentary on Aristotle's* Physics 36.1–7 = DK 67A14)

16.35   He makes sweet that which is round and good-sized; astringent that which is
        large, rough, polygonal, and not rounded; sharp tasting, as its name indicates,
        sharp and angular in body, bent, fine, and not rounded; pungent round, small,
        angular, and bent; salty angular, good-sized, crooked, and equal sided; bitter
        round, smooth, crooked, and small sized; oily fine, round, and small.
                         (Theophrastus, *Causes of Plants* 6.1.6 = DK 68A129)

The naïveté of these accounts is less important than Democritus's recognition of the
need to show how the theory could be put to use to explain specific phenomena.

   Void is also invoked to account for certain qualities. In heavy things the atoms
are closely packed, leaving little room for void, and in light things there is more
void (**16.27**). A similar account is given of hard and soft, and an attempt is made
to distinguish the heavy from the hard and the light from the soft in terms of the
position of the atoms.

16.36   Iron is harder and lead is heavier, since iron has its atoms arranged unevenly
        and has large quantities of void in many places . . . while lead has less void
        but its atoms are arranged evenly throughout. This is why it is heavier but
        softer than iron.
                         (Theophrastus, *On Sensation* 62 = DK 68A135)

Equally important, changes in compounds are explained in terms of changes in the spatial relations of atoms: compounds are generated and grow when atoms combine in appropriate ways; they decrease and perish when the atoms separate; they alter (change in quality) when the component atoms change their arrangements and relative positions (**16.2, 16.3, 16.23**). The same explanation also goes for phase changes.

> **16.37** We see that the same continuous body is sometimes liquid and sometimes solid—not suffering this change by means of separation and combination or by turning and touching as Democritus says; for it did not become solid from liquid by being transposed or changing its nature.
> (Aristotle, *On Generation and Corruption* 1.9 327a16–20 = DK 68A38)

The Atomists' aim is clear: to account for the macroscopic phenomenal world in terms of the behavior of the microscopic atoms. They present a two-world theory in which the phenomena in one world are reduced to entities and events in the other. The two worlds are strikingly different: the complex phenomenal world with its many different kinds of things, which behave in many ways, is contrasted with the simple world of atoms, which are made of but a single type of material, which differ only in size and shape, and whose only behavior is to move in place. The claim that all qualities, events, and changes in the phenomenal world can be reduced to changes in the relative positions of eternal, unchanging, quality-less atoms is remarkably ambitious even in the Presocratic tradition, and Democritus's efforts to show how the theory works in detail are unique among the Presocratics.

But this simple picture contains a serious difficulty which is brought out in the following passage.

> **16.38** When Democritus said that the atoms are in contact with each other, he did not mean contact, strictly speaking, which occurs when the surfaces of the things in contact fit perfectly with one another, but the condition in which the atoms are near one another and not far apart is what he called contact. For no matter what, they are separated by void.
> (Philoponus, *Commentary on Aristotle's* On Generation and Corruption 158.27–159.3 = DK 67A7)

The claim is that even in a compound, where atoms are very close to one another, they are separated by void. The reason for this is that atoms are identified only by their spatial extension, and if two atoms fit together perfectly with no gaps—even over a small area of contact, in fact even at a single point—the resulting thing will be uniformly dense, compact, etc., and the two atoms will have become one, (or alternatively, the two atoms will have perished and a new atom will have come to be). Either way the fundamental principle that atoms neither come to be nor perish is violated. And the Atomists, echoing Eleatic sentiments, insist that compounds are not true unities in this sense: "it is quite foolish <to think> that two or more things could ever come to be one" (**16.3**), "a plurality could not come to be from what is in reality one, nor one from what is really many" (**16.5**).

But if atoms cannot come into contact, the doctrine that atomic motion is due to the collision of atoms needs to be radically revised, and all the talk about striking together and blows needs to be explained away. There also needs to be some way to account for why atoms never actually strike one another—perhaps a force of mutual repulsion that acts when the atoms close enough to one another that they would otherwise collide. But there is no talk of forces of any kind in our sources, and it is very implausible that in all the information we have about ancient atomism there is no trace of the existence of such views. It seems better, then, to understand Philoponus as interpreting Democritus rather than reporting his actual views; Philoponus noticed the difficulty which contact between atoms implies for the theory, and he "corrected" Democritus on the point without mentioning the equally great difficulties that his "correction" entailed.

Cosmogony

The origin of the *kosmos* is described in the following passage.

16.39   <Leucippus> declares the universe to be infinite. . . . Of this, some is full and some is empty [void], and he declares these [full and void] to be elements. An infinite number of *kosmoi* arise out of these and perish into these. The *kosmoi* come into being in the following way. Many bodies of all sorts of shapes, being cut off from the infinite, move into a great void. They collect together and form a single vortex. In it they strike against one another and move around in all different ways, and they separate apart, like to like. When they are no longer able to rotate in equilibrium, the fine ones depart into the void outside as if sifted. The rest remain together, become entangled, move together in unison, and form a first spherical complex. This stands apart like a membrane, enclosing all kinds of bodies in it. As these whirl around by virtue of the resistance of the center, the surrounding membrane becomes thin, since the adjacent atoms join the motion when they come into contact with the vortex. And the earth came into being in this way when the atoms moving to the center remained together. And again the surrounding membrane-like thing itself grows because of the accretion of bodies from outside. As it moves in a vortex it acquires whatever it comes into contact with. Some of these become intertwined and form a complex which is at first damp and muddy, but when they have dried out and rotate with the vortex of the whole, they catch fire and form the nature of the stars.
            (Diogenes Laertius, *Lives of the Philosophers* 9.31–32 = DK 67A1)

This passage begins by distinguishing the universe (literally, "the whole") from a *kosmos*: the former is the totality consisting of all the atoms and all the void; the latter is a world-system which is limited both spatially and temporally. There are an infinite number of *kosmoi* scattered randomly through the universe, and they come to be and perish at different times. Though each *kosmos* has its own unique history, since **16.39** is a general account of the origin of *kosmoi*, it follows that *kosmoi* significantly resemble one another.

Many details of the cosmogony are muddy, but the general picture is clear. Atomic collisions and motions sometimes bring a vast number of atoms of different shapes into a region of the universe where they are pretty much isolated from other atoms. The motions and interactions of these atoms create a vortex in which similar atoms move toward one another. The mechanical nature of this sorting is described in the following fragment, which illustrates again[32] Democritus's tendency to employ arguments by analogy—in this case, a correspondence in the behavior of animate and inanimate things.

> **16.40**   Animals flock together with animals of the same kind—doves with doves, cranes with cranes, and likewise for the other irrational kinds. It is the same for inanimate things, as can be seen in the cases of seeds being sifted and pebbles on the shore. For through the swirling and separating motion of the sieve, lentils wind up together with lentils, wheat with wheat, and barley with barley, and through the motion of the waves, elongated pebbles are pushed to the same place as other elongated ones, and round ones to the same place as round ones, as if the similarity in these had some mutually attractive force for things.
>
> (Democritus, DK 68B164)

To return to **16.39**, the rotation of the vortex drives the smaller (therefore lighter) atoms to the periphery, and finally out of the system altogether, while the remaining atoms form a spherical structure ("like a membrane"—a spherical shell, not a solid sphere) which continues to revolve. In the continued rotation, like-to-like separation continues, with the larger, heavier atoms coming together toward the center to form the earth, and the outer shell becoming increasingly thinner as the atoms of which it is composed get dragged into the vortex. But then the outer shell is increased when other atoms in the vicinity are caught up in the whirl. Some of the atoms in the shell form a system which (curiously) is at first moist but later they ignite and thus form the visible stars.

It is worth adding that there is nothing inevitable in this sequence of events. We may imagine that for every time a *kosmos* is formed, there are many times when a sufficiently large number of atoms come together but fail to form a vortex, just hovering in the same area until their interactions cause them to disperse.

The crucial features of this cosmogony are that it results from mechanical atomic movements without purpose or divine agency and that our *kosmos* is not special, only one of an infinite number of similar *kosmoi* with similar histories. That our world is not unique or located at the center of the universe and that we are insignificant from a cosmic point of view are strikingly modern ideas and drastic departures from common sense and from what sense-experience would

---

32. See **16.1**.

lead us to believe. The Atomists' readiness to embrace these counterintuitive consequences of their physical system is a measure of their boldness.

A system that posits an infinite number of worlds naturally invites speculation about their nature. The small amount of information on the ancient Atomists' views on this matter is contained in the following testimonium, which leaves it unclear whether they described the other worlds in detail.

> 16.41   There are an infinite number of *kosmoi* of different sizes. In some there is no sun or moon. In some the sun and moon are larger than ours, and in others there are more. The distances between the *kosmoi* are unequal, and in one region there are more, in another fewer. Some are growing, some are at their peak, and some are declining, and here one is coming into being, there one is ceasing to be. They perish when they collide with one another. Some *kosmoi* have no animals, plants, or any moisture. . . . A *kosmos* is at its peak until it is no longer able to take anything in from outside.
>
> (Hippolytus, *Refutation of All Heresies* 1.13.2–4 = DK 68A40) (The omitted words are translated in **16.43**.)

16.41 states that a *kosmos* perishes when it collides with another—apparently a cosmic vortex can move through the void the way whirlwinds move through the air. But the mention of *kosmoi* which are declining and failing suggests that they can also perish from within, as it were. The final sentence explains the circumstances in which a *kosmos* declines without explaining why those conditions occur. One source of decline might be the condition in which the spherical membrane at the periphery of a *kosmos* vanishes through failing to take in enough atoms from outside to balance the loss of atoms that it suffers through contact with the vortex. This may reflect ancient theories that the bodies of animals deteriorate in old age through loss of the ability to absorb nutrition. If so, the "death" of a *kosmos* could be understood as the final stage in such decline, where its atoms are dispersed—again, through the mechanical motions of its constituent atoms. There is no set life span for a *kosmos*, but the mechanical necessity of atomic interactions guarantees that *kosmoi* must come to an end.

Cosmology

The Atomists paid more attention than many of their predecessors to astronomy. Their views stemmed from a variety of sources as far back as Anaximenes, and they do not seem to have made a consistent effort to explain heavenly phenomena in terms of the behavior of atoms and void, although their theories are compatible with the atomic theory. The following theories are representative.

> 16.42   The orbit of the sun is furthest out, that of the moon is nearest, and the others are in between. All the stars are on fire because of the speed of their motion; the sun too is on fire because of the stars, while the moon has only a small share of fire. The sun and moon suffer eclipses . . . [something is

missing from the text—probably a reference to the ecliptic] because the earth is tilted toward the south. The regions to the north are always covered with snow and are very cold and frozen. The sun is eclipsed rarely, but the moon is eclipsed often because their orbits are unequal.

(Diogenes Laertius, *Lives of the Philosophers* 9.33 = DK 67A1) (continuation of **16.39**)

16.43 In our own *kosmos* the earth came into being before the stars. The moon is lowest, then the sun, then the fixed stars. The planets too have unequal heights.

(Hippolytus, *Refutation of All Heresies* 1.13.4 = DK 68A40) (compare to **16.41**)

Leucippus placed the sun furthest from the earth (**16.42**), Democritus the stars (**16.43**). The Pythagoreans may have previously paid attention to the orbits of the planets (although the planetary theory attributed to Philolaus is probably later),[33] but Democritus had a special interest in the planets (perhaps a result of his travels in the East where he could have gained knowledge of Babylonian astronomy) and wrote a treatise on them. Democritus agreed with Anaxagoras on the nature of the Milky Way and the nature of comets.[34] Both Atomists place the earth at the center of our *kosmos*, and they agree that it is supported by air beneath it.[35] For Leucippus it is flat; for Democritus, concave.[36] Democritus departs from tradition by making the earth not round but oval or oblong, with its length one and one-half times its width.[37] Leucippus interestingly believed that the earth, still under the influence of the vortex, "revolves about the center,"[38] but (again because of the role of the vortex) he failed to go on to make the heavenly bodies stationary and explain their apparent movements as due to the earth's rotation. Democritus explained the angle between the celestial north pole and the zenith as due to the earth's having tilted.[39]

16.44 Because the southerly part of the surrounding is weaker, the earth, as it was growing, tilted in this direction. For the northern parts are intemperate but the southern parts are temperate, which is why it is weighed down in this direction, where it is above average in fruits and growth.

(Aëtius 3.12.2 = DK 68A96)

---

33. See **9.33, 9.34, 9.35** and discussion above pp. 104–5.

34. The Milky Way is the light of stars from which the earth blocks the rays of the sun (Aristotle, *Meteorologica* 1.8 345a25–31 = DK 59A80); comets are a conjunction of planets so near as to be in apparent contact (Aristotle, *Meteorologica* 1.6 342b27–29 = DK 59A81).

35. This view goes back to Anaximenes (see **6.8**).

36. Diogenes Laertius, *Lives of the Philosophers* 9.30 = DK 67A1; Aëtius 3.10.5 = DK 68A94.

37. Democritus, DK68B15.

38. Diogenes Laertius, *Lives of the Philosophers* 9.30 = DK 67A1.

39. Here he disagrees with Empedocles and Anaxagoras, who held that the heavens tilted (Aëtius 2.8.2 = DK 31A58 for Empedocles; Aëtius 2.8.1 = DK 59A67 for Anaxagoras).

Apparently the extra weight of vegetation tended to push the southern part down, while the air there, thinner because of the excessive heat in that region, was less able to support it.

In meteorological matters, Democritus was more consistent in offering atomistic explanations.

16.45   Democritus stated that thunder results from an uneven compound forcing the surrounding cloud to move downward. Lightning is the collision of clouds, as a result of which the atoms that generate fire are filtered through interstices containing much void (a process that involves friction) and collect in the same place. A thunderbolt occurs when there is a violent motion of fire-producing atoms which are very pure, fine, even, and "close-fitted" (the word Democritus himself uses). A waterspout occurs when compounds of fire containing much void are held back in regions with a lot of void and are wrapped in special membranes, and form bodies because of this rich mixture and make a rush toward the depth.

(Aëtius 3.3.11 = DK 68A93)

Democritus wrote works on many scientific subjects, including biology and embryology, but little remains.[40]

The Microcosm

In a famous fragment Democritus calls a human being "a small (*mikros*) *kosmos*."[41] The idea that humans function on the same principles as those that govern the world is hardly new with the Atomists. Earlier Presocratics at least as far back as Anaximenes had exploited it, explaining cosmic phenomena in terms of human phenomena and vice versa. The roots of the idea extend far back into pre-philosophical animistic thought. Although the conception was not new with the Atomists, it had particular force for them since they set out to account for all aspects of the *kosmos*, including animals and human beings, on atomic principles. Their task, then, was to explain how life can arise out of the movement of atoms and how all life's activities can be reduced to atomic behavior. To account for these aspects of the world was perhaps the severest challenge the Atomists faced, and it may be that "microcosm" was their battle cry.

For the origin of life, including human life, Democritus follows Anaximander and other Presocratics in saying that living beings arose from water and mud, a "moisture which gives rise to life."[42] This is all we are told. Living things differ from the inanimate by the presence of soul. For the Atomists, the soul consists

---

40. Representative materials are collected in Taylor (1999: 127–33) and discussed there on pp. 197–99.

41. Democritus, DK 68B34.

42. Aëtius 5.19.6 = DK 68A139.

of spherical atoms because of their mobility. Change and movement are therefore seen to be the key features of living things. The fact that spherical atoms are also the constituents of fire has already been remarked (above page 321). If there is any connection between these two functions of such atoms, it will be that most animals are warm while alive and cold after death. The soul is a material entity. The soul's atoms do not perish at death but disperse from the dead body. They disperse gradually, an idea that makes sense in terms of the likely physical behavior of the atoms and which also accounts for the fact that some vital functions, such as the growth of hair and fingernails, continue for a time after death.[43] Democritus informs us that there were no certain criteria which doctors trusted for determining the end of life.[44]

The spherical atoms which constitute the soul are scattered throughout the body. Their small size and their shape make them most able to move among other atoms without becoming entangled into compounds. In what seems a hopelessly naive way, the Atomists believed that the motions of an animal's body are produced by contact of the easily moving soul-atoms with other atoms in the body. Aristotle's criticism is appropriate.

16.46   Some say that the soul moves the body in which it is found in the same way as it is itself moved, Democritus, for example, who has a view like Philippos the comic poet, who says that Daedalus made the wooden statue of Aphrodite move by pouring quicksilver into it. Democritus speaks similarly, since he says that the indivisible spheres are in motion because their nature is never to stay still, and to draw the entire body along with them and move it. But we will ask if these same things also produce rest. How they will do so is difficult or impossible to state. In general, the soul does not appear to move the body in this way, but through choice of some kind and through thought.
(Aristotle, *On the Soul* 1.3 406b16–25; part = DK 68A104)

Sensation and Thought

The other principal functions of soul are sensation and thought. The Atomists had much to say about sensation in general and the five senses individually. Leucippus proposed a clear but crude theory which Democritus elaborated. Theophrastus's long and critical discussion of Democritus's doctrines[45] provides most of our information. In general, all sensation results from the contact of atoms. Atoms of the perceived object strike atoms in the sense organ, which transmit the sense-impressions to the soul-atoms. In effect, all five senses are reduced to the sense of touch. Thus Democritus makes all sensory objects objects of touch.[46] Since sensation

---

43. Tertullian, *On the Soul* 51 = DK 68A160.

44. Celsus 2.6 = DK 68A160.

45. Theophrastus, *On Sensation* 49–83 = DK 68A135.

46. This is Aristotle's observation (Aristotle, *On Sensation* 4 442a29–b1 = DK 68A119).

depends on the interaction of the sensed object and the sensing animal, the condition of the sensor affects the sensations: sensations are relative to the observer. On the other hand they are not purely relative since they also depend on the sensed object which exists objectively and whose atoms have objective attributes of size, shape, and position. This tension between subjectivism and objectivism is crucial in understanding the epistemology of the Atomists.[47]

Two of the senses, touch and taste, involve direct contact of the sensed object with the body of the sensor. With the remaining three, sight, hearing, and smell, where the object does not normally touch the sense organ, the Atomists need to explain in atomic terms how the object can affect our senses at a distance.

We have seen how Democritus associates different tastes with different atomic shapes (**16.35**) and different tactile qualities with different atomic arrangements (**16.34, 16.36**). No more need be said here about these senses except to point out an objection that Theophrastus makes to the doctrine of taste and which he says applies to the Atomist account of all five senses.[48] Atomic shape is an objective property, and if different tastes are defined in terms of different atomic shapes, taste is objective too. But this view contradicts the relativity of sensations to the sensor. The same thing may taste sweet to some and bitter to others, but an atom cannot be spherical to some and otherwise to others (compare to **16.50**).

Democritus's account of sight is the most interesting account of a sense which takes place at a distance. The Atomists adapted Empedocles' doctrine that physical objects give off films or effluences which enter our body through pores.[49] For the Atomists, the effluences are thin films of atoms which form an image of the object and move through the space between the object and the eye. Leucippus offered a simple theory: these films, which have the shape of the sense object, strike the eye, where they form a reflection of the object in the pupil. In this way vision occurs.[50] Democritus modified this theory.

16.47   The visual impression is not formed directly in the pupil, but the air between the eye and the object is contracted and stamped by the seen object and by the seeing thing. For there is a continual effluence from everything. Then this [air], which is solid and has a different color, forms an impression in the eyes, which are moist.

(Theophrastus, *On Sensation* 50 = DK 68A135)

Good vision requires the parts of the eye to be in good condition. For instance, the "veins" must be straight and dry, to conform in shape to the images or impressions

---

47. See below pp. 333–34.

48. Theophrastus, *On Sensation* 69 = DK 68A135.

49. See above pp. 282–83.

50. Alexander, *Commentary on Aristotle's* On Sensation 24.14–22 9 = DK 67A29.

and to transmit them accurately to the soul-atoms in the body.[51] The mechanics of vision are hard to understand. The nature of the interaction between the film of atoms from the object and the atoms emitted by the eye is especially obscure. The account as we have it leaves many questions open. Why do physical objects not decrease in size as the result of continually losing films of atoms? When we see the Parthenon, how can a film the size of the Parthenon fit into an eye? (Is this why Democritus modified Leucippus' theory and spoke of contraction in the intervening air?) This account explains how a visual impression has the same shape as the object but does not explain how we see colors, and although Democritus says a good deal about color, it is unclear how to fit what he says into his account of vision.

Democritus recognizes four primary colors: white, black, red, and yellow.[52] He associates each of these with certain atomic shapes and arrangements of atoms on the surface of objects. For example, white is associated with smooth atoms in things with hard surfaces, which are bright, conspicuous, and without shadows, and in friable things with easily crushed surfaces white is associated with round atoms set slantwise to one another and in pairs, with the entire arrangement as even as possible. The other colors arise from mixtures of the primaries, and Democritus goes into some detail about how particular blends yield particular colors.[53]

Thought resembles sensation. Both sensations and thoughts are "alterations of the body" and both "take place when images enter from outside."[54] "He makes thought dependent on bodily condition as is appropriate, since he makes the soul a body."[55] Further, thinking arises from the same sort of process as sensations do, especially sight. Apparently the films of atoms that activate thought are not in all cases the same as those that activate the sense organs, though those too affect thought after the sense organs transmit them to the soul. But since not all thinking is reflection on present sensations, some of the films entering from outside affect the soul directly, not through the mediation of the senses. The atoms in these films may be too fine to be noticed by the senses.[56] A similar account is offered of dreams.[57]

The naïveté of these attempts to explain the phenomena of sensation and thought does not need to be stressed. They raise many questions which they seem unable to answer, and they are open to many obvious objections. From

---

51. Theophrastus, *On Sensation* 50 = DK 68A135.

52. These were the four basic colors used by Greek painters. Compare 14.62 and p. 262 above.

53. Theophrastus, *On Sensation* 73–82 = DK 68A135. However, Aristotle reports that Democritus held that "things get colored by 'turning'" (*On Generation and Corruption* 1.2 316a1–2 = DK 68A123).

54. Aëtius 4.8.5, 4.8.10 = DK 67A30.

55. Theophrastus, *On Sensation* 58 = DK 68A135.

56. This interpretation follows Guthrie (1965: 452–53).

57. Plutarch, *Table Talk* 8.10 735A–B = DK 68A77.

our information about these theories[58] it appears that the Atomists failed to face several important issues. They reduce all thought and sensation to movements of the soul-atoms but do not say why some movements are perceived as sounds, others as tastes, and others as thoughts. They do not clearly distinguish between mental events and the concomitant bodily states. Their assimilation of thought to perception, and to vision in particular, makes it hard to see how they can account for non-pictorial thinking. Also, they do not account for the voluntary and apparently undetermined nature of some thought but seem to think that our thoughts are determined by the atomic films striking us at a given moment. Cicero makes fun of this flaw: "If I begin to think of the island of Britain, will its film of atoms fly to my breast?"[59]

Although these theories are easy to criticize, we must recall that Leucippus and Democritus were the first philosophers to attempt so detailed an account of thought and perception. They performed an important service by exploring how far a purely materialist theory of cognition can go. The questions their accounts left open and the objections others made to their views stimulated further thought on the subject and pointed out to later investigators (notably their harsh critics Aristotle and Theophrastus) many important problems that needed to be tackled.

Knowledge

The philosophies of Anaxagoras, Empedocles and the Atomists respond to the Eleatic challenge by postulating a more fundamental level of reality which conforms in some degree to the demands of the Eleatics and which also accounts for the sensible phenomena which the Eleatics rejected. These accounts raise important questions not only about the nature of reality but also about our knowledge of reality. For if one goal of the exercise is to rescue the senses and the sensible world, and if doing so requires explaining them as mere epiphenomena of a realm of reality which is inaccessible to the senses, does it not follow that the senses and the world they reveal are unredeemed? And if another goal is the empiricists' aim to ground knowledge in the reports of sense perception, is it not fatal if the basic entities prove to be in principle imperceptible? For the system will rest upon things whose existence and behavior are not known through the principal avenue of knowledge.

These issues are more pressing for the Atomists than for Empedocles or Anaxagoras, whose basic things are in some sense perceptible. Democritus paid them due attention. He wrote a work called *Canon* or *Canons*,[60] which opposed

---

58. Our information depends almost entirely on the hostile Aristotelian-Theophrastean tradition and may not always be fair to the Atomists.

59. Cicero, *Letters to his Friends* 15.16.1 = DK 68A118.

60. Epicurus's work on epistemology had the same title.

scientific demonstration and contrasted the senses unfavorably with the mind as sources of knowledge,[61] and one called the *Confirmations* in which "he promised to attribute to the senses the power of conviction."[62]

It is deeply frustrating that little remains of Democritus's work on this subject. Even the descriptions of the works just mentioned seem to conflict with one another, and the situation is no better with the other material we possess. The problem is partly due to the nature of our sources. Sextus Empiricus (second century CE), to whom we owe much of our information, tries to make Democritus into a fellow skeptic, but does so by quoting him out of context. Immediately after the sentence quoted at the end of the previous paragraph, he goes on to say that Democritus's theory of perception does not provide a basis for certain knowledge: perception depends on interaction between our body and atoms from the perceived object, and since the atomic composition of both our body and the object is subject to change, our perceptions are not sufficiently stable for exact understanding.

16.48   Nonetheless he is found condemning them [the senses]. For he says, "We in fact understand nothing exactly [or, "exact"], but what changes according to the disposition both of the body and of the things that enter it and offer resistance to it."

(Democritus DK 68B9 and context from Sextus Empiricus, *Against the Mathematicians* 7.136 = DK 68B9)

Further, some of Democritus's epistemological discussion was cast in the form of a dialogue between mind and the senses (see 16.57), which makes it extremely difficult to assess his commitment to either side.

In general, the atomic theory provides a variety of viewpoints from which to approach epistemological issues, and our severely limited sources may simply not add up to a coherent theory just because their contexts have been lost. In what follows I attempt to make sense of the extant information by fitting it into the framework of the atomic theory developed earlier in this chapter. Two principal distinctions govern the following discussion: that between the objective and subjective components of sensation (see above page 330) and that between judgment of perceptible qualities, based on the senses, and judgment of atoms and the void, based on the mind.

16.49   There are two kinds of judgment, one legitimate and the other bastard. All the following belong to the bastard: sight, hearing, smell, taste, touch. The other is legitimate and is separate from this. When the bastard one is unable

---

61. Sextus Empiricus, *Against the Mathematicians* 8.327 = DK 68B10b, 7.138 = DK 68B11.

62. Ibid. 7.136 = DK 68B9.

to see or hear or smell or taste or grasp by touch any further in the direction of smallness, but <we need to go still further> toward what is fine, <then the legitimate one enables us to carry on>.[63]

(Democritus DK 68B11)

16.50   By convention [or, "custom"], sweet; by convention, bitter; by convention, hot; by convention, cold; by convention, color; but in reality, atoms and void.[64]

(Democritus DK 68B9)

Knowledge of atoms and void is legitimate because it is objective and based on what exists in reality. The senses yield bastard judgment because they reveal perceptible qualities, which are properties not of atoms but of compounds. Worse, these qualities are not even objective properties which compounds have in their own right but result from interaction between the perceived object and the observer's sense organs. How an object appears differs from perceiver to perceiver and in the same perceiver from time to time, depending on the condition of the sense organ, so that there is no objective reason to attribute any particular quality to a given object. Such attributions are only "by convention." Thus, the senses fail to produce legitimate judgment for three separate reasons: they have a subjective component; their objects are compounds, not the primary entities atoms and void; and the qualities they perceive are not the basic atomic properties—shape, order, and position.

Some of Democritus's remarks so emphasize the difficulty of going beyond appearances to reality that he has seemed to some a thorough skeptic about the possibility of knowledge:[65] in addition to **16.48**, also the following.

16.51   A person must know by this rule [*kanōn*: measuring stick, standard] that he is separated from reality.

(Democritus, DK 68B6)

16.52   In fact it will be clear that to know in reality what each thing is like is a matter of perplexity [or, . . . "that people are at a loss to know in reality what each thing is like"].

(Democritus, DK 68B8)

---

63. This fragment trails off into corruption, but there is general agreement about the sense of what is missing.

64. The contrast between "by convention" (*nomos*) and "in reality" recalls that between *nomos* and *phusis* which was prominent in other intellectual contexts in the late fifth century. See Ch. 20.

65. Notably Barnes (1979: vol. 2, 253–58 / 1982: 559–64). Asmis (1984: 337–50) casts him as a skeptic about humans' capacity to attain knowledge since we must employ the senses, but as possibly holding a rationalist belief in the ability of reason to attain truth without the use of sense perception. Guthrie (1965: 454–65) does a good job of posing the problems and setting out the evidence.

16.53 In reality we know nothing about anything, but for each person opinion is a reshaping [of the soul-atoms by the atoms entering from without].
(Democritus, DK 68B7)

16.54 Either nothing is true, or at least to us it is unclear [or, "hidden"].
(Aristotle, *Metaphysics* 4.5 1009b11–12 = DK 68A112)

16.55 In reality we know nothing, for truth is in the depths.
(Democritus, DK 68B117)

On the other hand, there is good evidence that Democritus was far from a skeptic, as in reports like the following.

16.56 It is because these thinkers suppose intelligence to be sensation, and that, in turn, to be an alteration, that they say that what appears to our senses must be true (or, "real").
(Aristotle, *Metaphysics* 4.5 1009b12–15 = DK
68A112) (continuation of 16.54)

Also "truth is in the appearance" (16.2).[66] The apparent contradiction[67] between these claims and the previously quoted fragments makes for severe difficulties in understanding the Atomists' epistemology. I suggest that 16.2 and 16.56 reflect Democritus's view that sensations do have an objective basis in reality (being caused by the atoms of the perceived object) and are not simply arbitrary fictions of our mind. Sensations, which are the effects of atomic interactions, really exist. "True" here may mean "based in reality."

Democritus also recognizes a genuine form of judgment alongside the obscure judgments due to the senses. And although atoms and void are imperceptible, the Atomists claim to have grasped the truth. How this can happen is suggested by the report[68] that Democritus approved of Anaxagoras's assertion (13.21) "Appearances are a sight of the unseen." Perception of macroscopic phenomena constitutes the first step in acquiring knowledge of the microscopic reality.

In what appears to be a moment of self-awareness, Democritus portrays the senses as addressing the mind in a dialogue or legal suit, as follows.

---

66. Another passage attesting this view is Aristotle, *On the Soul* 1.2 404a28–29 = DK 68A101.

67. The fact that 16.56 occurs in Aristotle just after 16.54 has been taken to prove that Aristotle did not think that the two statements are contradictory (Guthrie [1965: 460]), but it is quite likely that Aristotle took them out of different contexts in Democritus.

68. Sextus Empiricus, *Against the Mathematicians* 7.140 = DK 59B21a.

16.57   Wretched mind, do you take your evidence from us and then throw us
        down? Throwing us down is a fall[69] for you!

                                                        (Democritus, DK 68B125)

Mind's reply should be that the senses provide the necessary starting point for
inquiry. They perceive things that do not *really* exist (as atoms and void really
exist [16.50]), and so cannot really be known (the best kind of knowledge the
senses can give us is "bastard" [16.49]).[70] Even though the resulting theory
reveals the shortcomings of the senses, it could not have been reached without their help. Moreover, sensible attributes include shape, size, position, and
arrangement (conspicuously absent from 16.50), the primary qualities of the
atoms. And even though we cannot perceive atoms and void, still our sensations
have an objective basis in compounds of atoms which although not basic entities,
certainly exist. As 16.2 shows, the behavior and appearance of sensible compounds are grounds for inferences to the nature and behavior of their constituent atoms. Again, "appearances are a sight of the unseen." Thus sensible reality
constitutes the data which the atomic theory is to account for. Finally, far from
simply discrediting the senses, the atomic theory explains how and why they go
wrong and how they are related to truth and reality.

    We have no information on how the Atomists believed it is possible to move
from the level of sense experience, in which we are separated from reality and
believe in qualities which have no real existence, to the level of reason, in which
we possess secure, objective knowledge of the truth of things. Thought, like the
senses, depends on films of atoms and on the condition of the atoms in the thinking soul. It has been suggested that the mind has direct awareness of atoms by
virtue of their striking its atoms, but this does not explain how the senses provide
the evidence the mind uses in grasping the truth of things. Some process of reasoning is needed to get from the one kind of grasp to the other, and it is doubtful
that so crude a materialist theory as fifth-century atomism could come close to
accounting for such a mental process.

The Gods

Since all sensation and thought result from our contact with atoms from outside
us, and since we have conceptions of gods, there must be a basis in reality for
these conceptions. Democritus therefore recognized the existence of gods, but
the sources leave his actual views on this subject unclear. The most interesting
information is the following statement.

---

    69. The word is a technical term for a fall in wrestling.

    70. For a good discussion of this point and a more extended treatment of the ques-
tion of Democritus's skepticism (which agrees with the present interpretation), see Curd
(2001), especially pp. 159–69.

16.58 Democritus says that certain images of atoms approach humans, and of them some cause good and others evil, and as a result he prayed "to meet with propitious images." These are large and immense, and difficult to destroy though not indestructible. They indicate the future in advance to people when they are seen and emit voices. As a result people of ancient times, upon perceiving the appearances of these things, supposed that they are a god, though there is no other god aside from these having an indestructible nature.

(Sextus Empiricus, *Against the Mathematicians* 9.19 = DK 68B166)

The impression given in this passage, that the images themselves are gods, is confirmed by other sources, but according to other reports[71] Democritus also said that the gods are things that are the source of these images in the same way that other physical objects emit films of atoms which affect our mind and senses. The ability of these images to predict the future must be a concession to ordinary superstitious belief, since it is hard to square with the atomic theory. The extremely long-lasting but not eternal nature of these gods seems to show that Democritus was willing to accommodate his theology to common belief only within limits. No atomic compound is completely imperishable.

Ethics

Most of the fragments attributed to Democritus concern ethical matters, though the authenticity of many of the ethical fragments is disputable. Democritus seems to have thought that the atomic theory provided a physical basis for ethics.

16.59 Cheerfulness arises in people through moderation of enjoyment and due proportion in life. Deficiencies and excesses tend to change suddenly and give rise to large movements in the soul. Souls that undergo motions involving large intervals are neither steady nor cheerful . . . .

(Democritus, DK 68B191)

This fragment must be taken in connection with the following statement.

16.60 The goal of life is cheerfulness, which is not the same as pleasure . . . but the state in which the soul continues calmly and stably, disturbed by no fear or superstition or any other emotion. He also calls it well-being and many other names.

(Diogenes Laertius, *Lives of the Philosophers* 9.45 = DK 68A1)

---

71. Cicero, *On the Nature of the Gods* 1.12.29 = DK 68A74; Clement of Alexandria, *Stromata* 5.88 = DK 68A79.

The references in **16.59** to movements in the soul and large intervals seem to refer to the atoms which constitute the soul. Not that all movement of the spherical soul-atoms is bad: they remain the most mobile atoms of all and the functioning of the soul depends on their movements. Despite this likely link with Atomism, we have no indication that Democritus attempted to prove that cheerfulness corresponds with or is caused by a particular condition of the soul-atoms, and his ethical views taken by themselves can be adopted by people who do not accept the atomic theory.

16.59 and **16.60** identify a particular physical condition of an individual's soul as the goal of his or her life and give an indication (cheerfulness) by which we can recognize whether our soul is in this state. The remainder of the fragment (not quoted here) specifies certain ways of thinking and behaving (avoid envy, consider yourself fortunate in comparison with the truly wretched, etc.) that contribute to a life aimed at this goal. The identification of the objective physical basis of cheerfulness or well-being as the goal of life accords with Democritus's distinction between cheerfulness and pleasure. Not all pleasures are to be pursued.

16.61   Accept nothing pleasant unless it is beneficial.

(Democritus, DK 68B74)

16.62   To all humans the same thing is good and true, but different people find different things pleasant.

(Democritus, DK 68B69)

What is beneficial is what helps attain or maintain a state of well-being, the one thing that is good for all. Still, pleasure is not altogether divorced from cheerfulness. Some pleasures are beneficial and we should pursue them. As for the rest, it is within our power to master them.

16.63   Brave is not only he who masters the enemy but also he who masters pleasures. Some are lords of cities but slaves of women.

(Democritus, DK 68B214)

We even have the capacity to reform ourselves so as to take pleasure in beneficial things.

16.64   Nature and teaching are closely related. For teaching reshapes the person and by reshaping makes <his> nature.

(Democritus, DK 68B33)

In this fragment, *metarhusmein*, translated "reshape," will designate an alteration in the *rhusmos* or "rhythm" (the Atomists' technical term for shape)[72] of the configuration of the soul's atoms. When these atoms are rearranged, the soul

---

72. See **16.1**.

undergoes a significant alteration: its very nature (its atomic structure) is affected. The word *phusiopoiein*, translated "makes <his> nature," is found only here. Doubtless an invention of Democritus, the word boldly puts his point that we can be affected at the most fundamental level by our experiences and it contributes as well to the interpretation of this point in terms of the atomic theory. In this way what we find pleasant depends on our soul's state, and since we can affect this, we can also determine our pleasures.

16.65   Best for a person is to live his life being as cheerful and as little distressed as possible. This will occur if he does not make his pleasures in mortal things.

(Democritus DK 68B189)

16.66   All those who make their pleasures from the belly, exceeding the right time for food, drink, or sex, have short-lived pleasures—only for as long as they eat or drink—but many pains.

(Democritus DK 68B235)

We are to "make our pleasures" from the things that promote and preserve the objective, lasting state of true cheerfulness. Thus Democritus the laughing philosopher is no simple hedonist but the proponent of a naturalistic ethics based on his physical theory and also on both the real condition and the potentialities of human nature.

Many of the ethical fragments can be read in the light of this connection between physical theory and ethics. It is easy to relate Democritus's counsels of moderation, prudence, doing right rather than wrong, and obeying rather than disobeying the laws to this view of the goal of life. However, it is not clear that he worked out a detailed ethical system, as some have claimed.[73]

How Far Atomism?

The atomic theory is a theory about the nature of physical reality. However, it is possible to develop atomistic philosophical interpretations of other phenomena as well. Some later Greek philosophers held that time is not continuous, but composed of time-atoms: indivisible minimum instants, and likewise for spatial extension ("place") and motion.[74] I mentioned earlier (pages 309–12) the

---

73. For an interesting attempt to construct an ethical theory out of the fragments and relate it to the atomic theory and to fifth-century medical doctrines, see Vlastos (1945–46/1975). There is a persuasive account of Democritus's ethics, its relation to his physical theory, and its location in the context of the moral thinking of the fifth century in Ferrar (1988: Ch. 6).

74. Simplicius says that the Epicureans believed in atomic units of all these types (*Commentary on Aristotle's Physics* 934.23–30 [not in DK]). See discussion in Long and Sedley (1987 vol. 1: 51–52).

controversy whether the fifth-century Atomists believed that atoms are mathematically as well as physically indivisible, and it is possible that Epicurus was following Democritus in his atomistic view of time.

One interesting fragment survives which is relevant to the question of indivisible spatial magnitudes.

> **16.67**   If a cone is cut by a plane parallel to the base, what should we think about the surfaces of the segments? Do they prove to be equal or unequal? If they are unequal they will make the cone uneven, with many step-like notches and rough spots, but if they are equal the segments will be equal, and the cone will appear to have the character of a cylinder, being composed of equal, not unequal circles, which is most absurd.
>
> (Democritus, DK 68B155)

The difficulty is that the fragment states the dilemma but does not indicate Democritus's solution. Clearly enough, an atomistic view of space would compel him to say that the apparently smooth surface of a cone is really (that is, at the atomic level) jagged,[75] but in that case there is no real dilemma at all. In the end it must be admitted that the fragment as it stands is compatible with spatial atomism but cannot be used as evidence that Democritus advocated that view.[76]

It is reasonable to press on to ask what the subject matter of geometry is for Democritus. For he was a mathematician of note. He is credited with stating, though not proving, the theorems that the volume of a cone is one-third that of a cylinder with the same base and height and that the volume of a pyramid is one-third that of a prism with the same base and height.[77] Is geometry somehow related to the atomic theory or is it a separate subject, not intended to describe physical reality at all, whether compounds, atoms, or the void?[78] Given Democritus's interest in the shapes of atoms, it seems to me likely that geometry, viewed as the analysis of magnitudes, which include shapes, was not meant to be without application in the physical world in general or to atoms in particular. That geometry applies to the atoms themselves becomes almost inescapable on the interpretation of atoms as geometrically divisible though physically indivisible (see above pages 311–12).[79]

---

75. This would not hold for a cone-shaped atom, but there is no reason to suppose that Democritus was speaking specifically of atomic shapes here.

76. For further discussion, see Sedley (2008).

77. Archimedes, *Method* 430.2–9 in vol. 2 of Heiberg's edition (Leipzig, 1913), printed in a note at DK vol. 2 p. 174.

78. This latter view is held by Furley (1987: 129–31). It accords with and is to some extent dependent on Furley's belief that Democritean atoms are theoretically indivisible.

79. In this interpretation I agree with H. Mendell, who discusses the issues more fully in Mendell (n.d.)

The Fate of the Atomic Theory

The view that matter is composed of atoms did not, of course, die with Democritus. In fact, there is a historical link between fifth-century atomism and today's atomic theory. But it is far from true either that once discovered, the atomic theory gained universal acceptance or that 20th-century atomic theory closely resembles the atomism of Leucippus and Democritus. In what follows I shall briefly sketch a few of the most important stages in the history of responses to and developments in the atomic theory, both in antiquity and in modern times.

Plato. Although Plato mentions many of his philosophical predecessors and contemporaries, he never refers to Democritus by name. Nevertheless, some points of contact have been found between the Atomists' cosmogony and that given in Plato's *Timaeus*, and the "geometrical atomism" of that dialogue may owe some of its inspiration to Democritus. Still, the differences between the two thinkers are profound. Plato's idealism makes beauty, goodness, and order the foundations of a grand teleological scheme which is the antithesis of Democritus's non-moral, mechanical materialism.

The Aristotelian tradition. Aristotle wrote a treatise (now lost) on Democritus. He, his commentators, and Theophrastus knew of fifth-century atomism and frequently discussed it. Their attitude is in general hostile and their discussions mostly consist of unsympathetic criticisms based on their own system, which is incompatible with atomism.

Epicurus (341–271). Democritus had a number of followers during his lifetime and after his death. The most important was Epicurus, who founded a school of philosophy in Athens. Like other philosophers of the Hellenistic period, Epicurus's chief interests were in ethics, but the physical theory on which his entire philosophical system rested was Leucippus's and Democritus's atomic theory with a few modifications. There are only a finite number of atomic shapes; atoms are physically but not theoretically indivisible, though they have theoretical parts which are indivisible; weight is a fundamental property of atoms; atoms had an original motion in which they were falling at equal velocities in parallel downward trajectories through the void; the initial collisions resulted from occasional uncaused "swerves." In the area of human action, the swerve, as the only kind of atomic movement not caused mechanically (and therefore in theory predictably) by interaction with other atoms, becomes the key to account for free will. The gods are located in the tracts of the universe between *kosmoi*—remote and unconcerned with human events and therefore wrongly considered as figures of awe and dread. As with Democritus, the soul is composed of atoms and disperses at death; Epicurus inferred from this thesis that there is no afterlife to fear. This is not the place to go further into Epicurean philosophy, but from what has been said it is clear that atomism remained a vital part of the Greek intellectual tradition long after the end of the Presocratic period. In this respect it is unique among the Presocratic systems.

Modern atomic theory. Epicurus's atomism was revived in the 17th century by Descartes' opponent Gassendi, and in the 18th century it was common ground that matter was composed of ultimate units which are hard, unchanging, and endowed with shape and weight. The classical chemical theory of the 19th century continued to envisage atoms as the smallest units of matter, and the distinction between atoms and molecules is a recognizable development of the ancient distinction between atoms and compounds. The idea that atoms have physically separable parts (electrons, protons, etc.) is anathema to the ancient atomic theory, but the obvious response is that what corresponds to Democritus's unsplittable atoms are what we (incorrectly) call subatomic particles. The most important differences between ancient and modern atomic theory therefore are not in the splittability of the modern (so-called) atom. Rather they are to be found in the nonmaterialistic aspects of the modern atom. Nothing in the ancient theory corresponds to the forces which bind the atom together or which bind atoms together into molecules, and the thought that in some sense matter and energy (a concept absent in the ancients) are equivalent is incomprehensible to the thought of Democritus.

In addition, the atomic theory is accepted for different reasons now. In the fifth century it was presented as one response among others to the Eleatic challenge. Those few who accepted it will have done so for philosophical reasons or because they found the theory satisfactory, or at least preferable, to its rivals as a device for explaining many aspects of the world. But the theory was supported by a priori reasoning rather than empirical evidence. In this, ancient atomic theory was no worse than other ancient theories of the ultimate nature of reality. There is no need to do more than state that by contrast modern atomic theory is based on empirical evidence and has gradually emerged as the hypothesis that has best withstood experimental and theoretical challenges. It is subject to further extension and modifications, and even to wholesale revision on the basis of further theoretical and experimental work. Thus ancient and modern atomic theory, while historically related, are different not only in detail but also in approach, but here as elsewhere much of the philosophical ground covered by the modern theory was first explored and seen to be fertile by the keen-sighted ancients.

17

Diogenes of Apollonia

Fragments

17.1   (1)[1] In my opinion, a person beginning any discourse must present a starting point [or, "principle"] which is indisputable and an explanation [or, "style"] which is simple and serious.[2]

17.2   (2) [In *On Nature*, the only one of his works that has come into my hands, he proposes to give many proofs that in the principle he posits there is much intelligence. Immediately after the introduction he writes the following.][3]

1. In my opinion, to sum it all up, all things that are are differentiated forms of the same thing and are the same thing.

2. And this is manifest. For if the things that are now in this *kosmos*—earth, water, air, fire, and all the rest that are seen to exist in this *kosmos*—if any one of these were different from another, being different in its own nature, and if it were not the case that, being the same thing, it changed and was differentiated in many ways, they could not mix with each other in any way nor could help or harm come to one from another, nor could a plant grow from the earth nor an animal or anything else come to be, unless they were so constituted as to be the same thing.

3. But all these things, being differentiated out of the same thing, come to be different things at different times and return into the same thing.

17.3   (3) [In what follows he shows that in this principle there is much intelligence.]

For without intelligence it [the "same thing" of **17.2**] could not be distributed in such a way as to have the measures of all things—winter and summer, night and day, rains and winds and good weather. If anyone wants to think about the other things too, he would find that as they are arranged, they are as good as possible.

17.4   (4) [He continues as follows, saying that men and the other animals live and have soul and intelligence from this principle, which is air.]

Moreover, in addition to the preceding indications, the following too are important. Humans and animals live by means of air through breathing. And this [air] is both soul and intelligence for them, as will be displayed manifestly in this book. And if this departs, they die and their intelligence fails.

---

1. The numbers in parentheses are the numbers of the fragments in DK. (1) = DK 64B1.

2. Diogenes Laertius, who quotes this fragment (*Lives of the Philosophers* 9.57 = DK 64A1), says that it was the beginning of Diogenes' book.

3. **17.2–17.5** are quoted by Simplicius (*Commentary on Aristotle's* Physics 151.28–153.17 = DK 64B2–B5), some of whose comments on them are here put in brackets.

17.5   (5) [Then, a little later he continues clearly.]

1. And in my opinion, that which possesses intelligence is what people call air, and all humans are governed by it and it rules all things.

2. For in my opinion this very thing is god, and it reaches everything and arranges all things and is in everything.

3. And there is no single thing that does not share in this.

4. But no single thing shares in it in the same way as anything else, but there are many forms both of air itself and of intelligence.

5. For it is multiform—hotter and colder, drier and wetter, more stable and possessing a sharper movement, and unlimitedly many other alterations are in it, both of flavor and of color.

6. And the soul of all animals is the same thing, air hotter than the air outside in which we are located, but much colder than the air near the sun.

7. This heat is not identical in any two animals, since it is not identical even in any two humans, but it differs—not greatly, but so that they are similar.

8. Moreover, it is impossible for any of the things that are being differentiated to be exactly like one another without becoming the same thing.

9. Now since the differentiation is multiform, also the animals are multiform and many and are like one another in neither shape nor way of life nor intelligence, on account of the large number of their differentiations.

10. Nevertheless, all things live, see, and hear by means of the same thing, and all get the rest of their intelligence from the same thing.

17.6   (6) [And next he shows that the sperm of animals has the form of air, and thoughts come into being when air occupies the whole body through the veins, together with blood. In the course of this discussion he gives an accurate anatomy of the veins. In these words he is clearly seen to say that the principle is what people call air.[4]] This is an account of the blood vessels in humans. There are two very large ones. These run through the belly alongside the backbone, one on the right side and one on the left. Each goes toward the leg on the same side, and up toward the head alongside the collar bone through the throat. From these, blood vessels extend through the entire body, from the vessel on the right to the parts on the right and from the vessel on the left to the parts on the left. The largest two go next to the backbone to the heart, and others, a little higher up, go through the chest under the armpit to the hand on the same side. One of them is called the splenetic vessel, the other the hepatic. Each of them is divided at the extremity, one part going to the thumb, the other to the palm, and from these, tiny vessels with many branches go to the rest of the hand and to the fingers. Other tinier vessels extend from the first vessels—from the one on the right side, to the liver, from the one on the left side, to the spleen and kidneys. The vessels that go to the legs branch at the junction of the legs

---

4. The account of the veins is preserved in Aristotle, *History of Animals* 3.2 511b30–512b11 = DK 64B6.

and run through the entire length of the thigh and are visibly thick. Another one runs inside the thigh and is smaller and less thick than the other. Then they go next to the knee, to the shin and the foot in the same way as the ones that go to the hands, and they arrive at the sole of the foot, and from there they divide and go to the toes. Many tiny vessels branch off from them in the belly and ribs. Some go to the head through the throat and are visibly large in the neck. Many others branch off from the end of each of them and go to the head, some crossing from the right side to the left and others from the left side to the right. They end at each ear. On each side there is another vessel in the neck next to the large vessel, a little smaller than it, to which most of the vessels that come from the head are connected. These too go through the throat on the inside, and from each of them others go under the shoulder blade to the hands, and they are visible next to the splenetic and hepatic vessels as other vessels that are a little smaller. These are the ones that [physicians] lance when there is pain under the skin. If there is pain in the region of the belly, they lance the hepatic and the splenetic vessels. Others begin from these and go to the breasts. There are others, tiny ones, that go from each of these through the spinal marrow to the testicles. Others go under the skin, through the flesh, to the kidneys and end at the testicles in men and in women at the uterus. The vessels from the belly are at first wider, and then they become narrower until they cross from right to left and from left to right. These are called the spermatic vessels. The thickest blood is absorbed by the fleshy parts of the body; the excess goes to these regions [the genital organs] and becomes thin, hot, and foamy.

17.7   (7) And this very thing is an eternal and immortal body, and by means of it some things come to be and others pass away.

17.8   (8) But this seems clear to me, that it is large and strong and eternal and immortal and knowing many things.

Dates and Life

Next to nothing is known of Diogenes' life. He was probably active in the two decades after 440, which would place him later than Empedocles and Anaxagoras and contemporary with Melissus and Leucippus. In what follows, I follow the commonly held view that Diogenes knew the theories of these four philosophers, but not those of Democritus.[5] Though there are other cities of the same name, his birthplace was probably the Apollonia on the Black Sea, a colony of Miletus with whose foundation Anaximander was associated. Although only a few fragments survive, Diogenes was well known. His doctrines were influential and are echoed in Aristophanes and Euripides as well as in medical writers.

---

5. Certainty on this issue is impossible, and it has been held, for example, that Melissus's philosophy is a response to Leucippus and Diogenes.

He may have been a physician himself. His longest fragment is **17.6**, a detailed account of the veins in the human body, and he may well be the Diogenes whom Galen names as the author of a treatise in which he "collected the diseases and their causes and remedies."[6] His "simple and serious" (**17.1**) style places him alongside Anaxagoras in the Ionian prose tradition.

The Material Principle, Air

The hints we are given about the order of the fragments[7] suggest that Diogenes postponed identifying the material principle until he had discussed certain metaphysical issues.

Empedocles had avoided coming to be and perishing by saying that apparent cases of coming to be and perishing are really mixture and separation of four basic kinds of "things." Anaxagoras had posited a large (perhaps infinite) number of types of basic ingredients, which drove coming to be and perishing even further away. But if the world consists of a plurality of radically different things, it is not easy to understand how they can interact and affect one another. Accordingly Diogenes argues for material monism: all things (and he singles out Empedocles' four elements for specific mention) are modifications of a single basic substance (**17.2**).[8]

More explicitly than Anaxagoras,[9] Diogenes considers the order in the universe to be the result of intelligence and argues that since everything is arranged in the best possible way, it follows that what caused the arrangement is intelligent (**17.3**). This is the clearest indication in Presocratic philosophy of a teleological view of the workings and structure of the world.

Diogenes accepts the Eleatic prohibition against coming to be and perishing (**17.9**, below), and unlike Anaxagoras and Empedocles he declares that plurality and change are due to differentiations or alterations of a single basic substance (**17.2** sections 2–3), air. Most scholars think that Diogenes' arguments that the principle is air are what he refers to in **17.4** as "the preceding indications" and that they are lost. I find it more likely that Simplicius, who quotes **17.2** through **17.5** in a single passage, did not omit so crucial a part of the account, and that "the preceding indications" are the arguments for a single intelligent material principle (**17.2–3**), arguments that do not specify what the principle is, and "the following" establish that the principle is air. The train of thought is: all things are made of the same stuff; this stuff is intelligent; therefore, all intelligence is

---

6. Galen, *On Medical Experience* 22.3 (Walzer [1944]) (not in DK).

7. See above p. 343 n. 2 and the comments that preface **17.2** and **17.3**.

8. The Milesians are traditionally called material monists, although in my view the only predecessor of Diogenes whom this title might properly describe is Anaximenes. Graham holds that Diogenes is the first material monist (Graham [2008: Ch. 10]).

9. See above pp. 219–20.

due to the presence of this stuff (implicit conclusion); in humans and animals, intelligence, like life, is due to the presence of air; therefore, air is the stuff of which all things are made.

Air takes on other forms "when condensed and rarefied and when it changes in its attributes."[10] The first two of these mechanisms come from Anaximenes, who, however, held that other attributes are due to these two.[11] Other attributes of air mentioned in the fragments are hot, cold, dry, wet, stability and mobility, flavor and color (**17.5** section 5), but the evidence does not say whether these are primary modifications of air or effects of condensation and rarefaction.

In any case, the assertion that air is modified by condensation and rarefaction is of particular interest after Parmenides' dictum that it is "not at all more in any respect, which would keep it from holding together, or at all inferior, but it is all full of what-is" (**11.8** lines 23–24) and Melissus's argument that "it cannot be dense and rare" (**15.9** section 8) "nor is any of it empty" (**15.9** section 7), so that there is no void. Leucippus, as we have seen, argued for the existence of void.[12] Diogenes too holds that void exists (**17.9**, below). Despite the uncertainty as to whether Diogenes wrote before or after Melissus or Leucippus, or who was responding to whom, in the post-Parmenidean philosophical scene, the idea that condensation and rarefaction entail the existence of non-being, thus of void, could have occurred to anyone. I find it most plausible that Diogenes followed Leucippus in accepting the existence of void and that one of the main functions of void in his theory was to provide a basis for the differentiation of air, so that (as for the Atomists[13]) void makes plurality and change possible. Thus, Diogenes agrees with the Eleatics (as against Anaxagoras and Empedocles) that reality is in a sense one, but the price of his material monism is admitting (as Anaxagoras and Empedocles did not need to do) the existence of void.

Anaxagoras held that Mind is unmixed with and unlike anything else, and yet it rules all things. Diogenes strongly disagreed. And where Anaxagoras did not explain how Mind effects its control, the reasoning found in **17.2** section 2 leads to the conclusion that the governing substance must be a modification of the same stuff of which everything else is composed (**17.5** sections 1–2).

Like Anaxagoras's Mind, Diogenes' principle is intelligent (**17.5** section 1).[14] The word he uses (*noēsis*, here translated "intelligence" and "thought") is related to Anaxagoras's word for Mind (*nous*). Even though not all things are intelligent,

---

10. Theophrastus, quoted by Simplicius, *Commentary on Aristotle's* Physics 25.5–6 = DK 64A5.

11. See above pp. 52–53.

12. See above p. 314.

13. See above p. 312.

14. Also Simplicius's comments that preface **17.2** and **17.3**.

their ultimate material identity with thought (air) enables them to be affected by the intelligent ruler of the universe.

In keeping with the early Ionians Diogenes asserts that the eternal, immortal (**17.7**) primary substance which governs and rules all things is divine (**17.5** section 2). He seems to argue from air's divinity to air's possessing intelligence and governing all things (**17.5** sections 1–2). The attributes with which the divine air is endowed form an impressive list (**17.5** sections 1–2, **17.7**, **17.8**) which makes explicit the implications of hints on the divine nature of the originating substance found in earlier thinkers including Anaximander and Heraclitus.

Although air is intelligent and all things are forms of air, not all things are intelligent. Only living things can be intelligent. What makes animals and humans alive—their soul—is air, for when we stop breathing we die (**17.4**). Diogenes successfully integrates this pre-philosophical conception of the breath as the soul or animating principle into his system as a rational, material basis for the distinction between inanimate and animate beings (compare **17.5** sections 6, 10).

The air that is soul is hot, since warmth is characteristic of the living. Further, by identifying the directive cosmic intelligence with air Diogenes accounts for the intelligence of humans and animals through their breathing,[15] which maintains them in contact with the cosmic air. Under the heading of intelligence he includes the sense faculties (**17.5** section 10).

If all animals have souls consisting of warm air, and if warm air is the cosmic intelligence that rules all things and makes them turn out in the best possible way, why are some kinds of animals less intelligent and less well endowed in other ways than other animals? Diogenes sought to answer this question by talking of small differences in the forms of animating air possessed by different animals (**17.5** sections 7, 9). In fact, it is clear that there are differences in the nature of animating air not only from species to species, but even from individual to individual (**17.5** section 7). The variation in the forms of air which animate different individuals of the same species is not great—presumably it differs less among individuals of a single species than among individuals of different species.

The place of **17.5** section 8, the earliest statement of the principle of the identity of indiscernibles, in Diogenes' train of thought is uncertain. It may serve as a ground for the claim that different animals have different amounts of heat.

Cosmogony and Cosmology

Diogenes also concerned himself with standard topics in cosmogony and cosmology. In addition, he had a deep interest in physiology (especially embryology) and provided physiological accounts of perception and cognition. I shall mention his most interesting ideas in these fields, though our information on them is almost entirely second hand.

---

15. For a similar idea in Heraclitus, see **10.129**.

He accepted the Atomists' view that the *kosmos* is surrounded by infinite void, and although the evidence is conflicting, he probably agreed with the Atomists that in the infinite void there are an infinite number of *kosmoi* which come to be and pass away.

17.9   Air is the element. There are infinite *kosmoi* and infinite void. The air, by being condensed and rarefied, is generative of the *kosmoi*. Nothing comes to be from or perishes into what-is-not. The earth is round and is supported in the center [of the *kosmos*] and has undergone its process of formation through the rotation resulting from the hot and the solidification caused by the cold.

    (Diogenes Laertius, *Lives of the Philosophers* 9.57 = DK 64A1)

17.10   All things are in motion and there are infinite *kosmoi*. His account of cosmogony is the following: the whole is in motion and comes to be rare in one place, dense in another. Where the dense part chanced to come together it formed the earth by revolving, and the other things in the same way. The lightest things occupied the highest location and produced the sun.

    (Pseudo-Plutarch, *Stromata* 12 = DK 64A6)

This information together with **17.5** sections 1–2 implies that a *kosmos* is formed when some of the intelligent, divine, unlimited air causes itself to differentiate, some being rarefied and the rest condensed. Most of the details of Diogenes' cosmology are borrowed from other Presocratics. In particular, the notion of a cosmogonic principle that is a self-starter hearkens back to Anaximenes rather than to any of the post-Parmenidean cosmogonies. Contemporary references include the Atomist beliefs in infinite void and infinite *kosmoi* (**17.9**), which are not eternal but eventually return to their pre-cosmic state (**17.2** section 3), and an elaboration of Anaxagoras's idea that the heavenly bodies are stones:[16] Diogenes specifies them to be pumice,[17] a very light stone (it floats on water) which is porous, the better to contain fire and let it shine through.

A detailed but inaccurate account of the blood vessels is preserved (**17.6**), which shows Diogenes' interest in human anatomy. This account should be compared with the discussion of blood vessels in Chapter 11 of the Hippocratic work *The Nature of Man* (below page 437).[18]

---

16. See above p. 226.

17. Aetius 2.13.5 = DK 64A12; 2.20.10 = DK 64A13; 2.25.10 = DK 64A14.

18. For discussion of the importance of this fragment, which has been otherwise neglected, see Lloyd (2006).

Perception and Cognition

Theophrastus gives a long account of Diogenes' views on perception and cognition.

> **17.11**   Diogenes attributes the senses, as well as life and thought, to air. . . . The
> sense of smell is due to the air around the brain. . . . Hearing occurs when
> the air in the ears is set in motion by the air outside and is passed on toward
> the brain. Sight occurs when things are reflected in the pupil, and the
> reflection, being mixed with the air inside, produces sensation. Evidence
> of this is the fact that if the veins [in the eyes] become inflamed, it [the
> reflection?] is not mixed with the air inside and we do not see, although
> the reflection is there just the same. Taste occurs in the tongue because of
> its rare and soft nature. Concerning touch he declared nothing, neither its
> functioning nor its objects. . . . The interior air, which is a small part of god,
> is what perceives. Evidence of this is that often when we have our mind on
> other matters we neither see nor hear.
>
>   (Theophrastus, *On Sensation* 39–42 = DK 64A19)

This passage mostly speaks for itself. Diogenes' distinction between the external
conditions needed for sensation (reflection in the pupil) and the actual occurrence of sensation is worth noting, as is his identification of the perceiving and
thinking element in us with god, that is, the cosmic air. Theophrastus goes on to
report physiological accounts (in which air is prominent) of other related cognitive functions.

> **17.12**   Pleasure and pain arise in the following manner: pleasure whenever a large
> amount of air is mixed with the blood and makes it light, being in accor-
> dance with its nature and penetrating the whole body; and pain whenever
> the air is contrary to its nature and is not mixed, and the blood coagulates
> and becomes weaker and denser. Similarly also boldness and health and the
> opposites. . . . Thought, as was said, is due to air that is pure and dry. For
> moisture hinders the mind. For this reason thought is diminished when we
> are asleep, drunk, or full. . . . This is why children are foolish. . . . They are
> also prone to anger and in general easily roused and changeable because air,
> which is great in quantity, is separated by small intervals. This is also the
> cause of forgetfulness: when the air does not go through the entire body,
> people cannot comprehend.
>
>   (Theophrastus, *On Sensation* 43–45 = DK
>   64A19) (continuation of **17.11**)

Although the idea that a wet soul is less efficient than a dry one goes back to
Heraclitus,[19] this is the most thorough and consistent attempt before Democritus to work out a physical basis for mental phenomena. Diogenes is classified

---

19. **10.104–10.106.**

together with the Atomists as holding that sensations are relative to the individual since they are affected "by our opinion and [bodily] conditions."[20] Still, there is an objective element in them, since they also depend on external conditions, for instance the reflection of an external object in the pupil.

Conclusion

Diogenes proposed an updated form of Milesian cosmology, perhaps out of dissatisfaction with the complexities of the post-Parmenidean pluralistic systems of Anaxagoras, Empedocles, and Leucippus. Though he made some important innovations, he largely proceeded by exploiting existing ideas and synthesizing them in new and more effective ways. He was aware of the Eleatic challenge and met it by skillfully deploying elements of the philosophies of Anaxagoras and the Atomists, though not following either system blindly. The resulting physical theory has strong links with his Milesian forebears, Anaximenes in particular, as well as echoes of other Ionians: Xenophanes and Heraclitus. In the context of the second half of the fifth century, Diogenes' aim to return to the simplicity of the beginnings of the Presocratic tradition is breathtaking in its ambition. It is a pity that the evidence available to us is too scanty to tell how successfully he carried out his mission. What we know of the fundamentals of his theory leads me to think that he had the materials to construct as plausible a system as any other Presocratic.

---

20. Aetius 4.9.8 = DK 64A23.

18

Philolaus of Croton

Fragments[1]

18.1   (1)[2] Nature in the *kosmos* was joined from both unlimiteds and limiters, and the entire *kosmos* and all the things in it.

18.2   (2) 1. It is necessary that the things that are be all either limiters or unlimited or both limiters and unlimited;
2. but not in all cases only unlimited.[3]
3. Now since it is evident that they are neither from things that are all limiters nor from things that are all unlimited,
4. it is therefore clear that both the *kosmos* and the things in it were joined together from both limiters and unlimiteds.
5. The behavior of these things in turn makes it clear.
6. For those of them that are from limiters limit, those that are from both limiters and unlimiteds both limit and do not limit, and those that are from unlimiteds will evidently be unlimited.

18.3   (3) There will not be anything that is going to know at all, if all things are unlimited.

18.4   (4) And in fact all the things that are known have number. For it is not possible for anything at all either to be comprehended or known without this.

18.5   (5) In fact, number has two proper kinds, odd and even, and a third kind, even-odd, from both mixed together. Of each of the two kinds there are many forms, of which each thing itself gives signs.

18.6   (6) 1. Concerning nature and *harmonia* this is how it is:
2. the being of things, which is eternal—that is, in fact, their very nature—admits knowledge that is divine and not human,
3. except that it was impossible for any of the things that are and are known by us to have come to be
4. if there did not exist the being of the things from which the *kosmos* is constituted—both the limiters and the unlimiteds.
5. But since the principles are not similar or of the same kind, it would be completely impossible for them to be brought into order [or, "for them

---

1. I give all the fragments recognized as authentic by Huffman (1993), and except where noted I follow his text.

2. The numbers in parentheses are the numbers of the fragments in DK. (1) = DK 44B1.

3. I follow Huffman in omitting DK's addition "or only limiting."

to be kept in an orderly arrangement (*kosmos*)"] if *harmonia* had not come upon them in whatever way it did.

6. Now things that are similar and of the same kind have no need of *harmonia* to boot, but those that are dissimilar and not of the same kind or of the same speed must be connected together in *harmoniai*[4] if they are going to be kept in an orderly arrangement (*kosmos*).

18.7 (6a) The magnitude of the *harmonia* is the fourth plus the fifth. The fifth is greater than the fourth by a 9:8 ratio. For from the lowest string to the second string is a fourth, and from the second string to the highest string is a fifth, but from the highest string to the third string is a fourth, and from the third string to the lowest string is a fifth. What is between the third string and the second string is a 9:8 ratio; the fourth has a 4:3 ratio, the fifth a 3:2 ratio, and the octave a 2:1 ratio. Thus the *harmonia* is five 9:8 ratios plus two half tones, the fifth is three 9:8 ratios plus one half-tone, and the fourth two 9:8 ratios plus one half-tone.

18.8 (7) The first thing that was joined, the one in the middle of the sphere, is called the hearth.

18.9 (17) The *kosmos* is one. It began to come to be right up at the middle, and from the middle <it came to be> in an upward direction in the same way as it did in a downward direction and the things above the middle are symmetrical with those below. For in the lower <regions> the lowest part is like the highest part <in the upper regions>, and similarly for the rest. For both <the higher and the lower> have the same relationship to the middle, unless they have been moved to another location. (based on Huffman's translation).

18.10 (16) Some *logoi* are too strong for us.

18.11 (20) [Philolaus correctly called] the number 7 motherless. [For it alone is of a nature neither to generate nor to be generated.]
[Context taken from John the Lydian, *On the Months* 2.12.]

18.12 (13) The head <is the location> of intellect, the heart of soul and sensation, the navel of the taking root and growth of the first <part>, the genital organs of the depositing of seed and of generation. The brain contains the principle of man, the heart <contains the principle> of animals, the navel that of plants, and the genital organs that of them all. For they all both flourish and grow from seed.

---

4. This is the plural of *harmonia*. I accept the manuscript reading *harmoniais*.

Life and Writing

Philolaus was born in Croton (the city in southern Italy where Pythagoras settled) sometime in the middle of the fifth century and lived into the fourth. Estimates of his birth vary from 470 to 430. I think that a date close to the end of this period is indicated by the level of sophistication of his ideas. Plato tells us that he visited Thebes—where he taught Cebes and Simmias, two of the principal speakers in the *Phaedo*[5]—and that he held that suicide is wrong. This visit occurred before Socrates' death (in 399). He also taught Eurytus (for whom see **9.22** and **9.23**). There is reason to think that Plato met him on a trip to Sicily c.388. He was a Pythagorean, and his book is the earliest authentic Pythagorean text we know of. Plato is reported to have obtained a copy of it and is libelously alleged to have copied the *Timaeus* from it. We are fortunate to possess a number of fragments from it, which have been recently established as genuine[6] and which give Philolaus an important place in the history of philosophy.

Philolaus's ideas differ significantly from Aristotle's reports of some aspects of Pythagorean thought,[7] perhaps because on those points Aristotle used other Pythagorean sources.[8] His work shows the influence of Parmenides and is reasonably read as a response to Anaxagoras and to the Atomists. It contains a level of abstraction not found in earlier thinkers (Parmenides and Melissus would be the closest rivals) which has close connections with the late Platonic work *Philebus*. Philolaus was interested in mathematics and harmonic theory, astronomy, and medicine, pursuits that establish him as one of the *mathēmatikoi* (see above pages 88–89).

The Nature of Reality

Philolaus began his book with **18.1**, which claims that three things are "joined" from unlimiteds and limiters: nature in the *kosmos*, the entire *kosmos*, and all things in the *kosmos*. (Contrast these principles with those mentioned in Aristotle's accounts of Pythagorean thought: limit and unlimited.) Adopting the approach associated with Eleatic thinkers, Philolaus establishes these theses by argument. **18.2** and **18.3** establish that the *kosmos* and all the things in it are joined from both limiters and unlimiteds, and **18.6** sections 2–4 establish that nature in the *kosmos* is constituted out of the same.

---

5. Plato, *Phaedo* 61d = DK 44B15.

6. Huffman (1993). This book is the starting point for all discussion of Philolaus. Huffman places Philolaus's birth around 470.

7. Aristotle mentions Philolaus only once and attributes to him a saying (**18.10**) whose relation to Pythagorean thought is unclear.

8. Huffman holds that Philolaus was Aristotle's principal source on Pythagorean thought and that the discrepancies between Aristotle's reports and Philolaus's fragments are due to misunderstanding on Aristotle's part.

I take **18.2** section 1 to mean that every entity is either a limiter or an unlimited or an unlimited limiter (something joined together from one or more unlimiteds and one or more limiters). It also presupposes or implies that there are entities of all three of these kinds—which is verified by **18.2** section 6. **18.2** section 2 follows from **18.3**. **18.3** presupposes that there are knowers and declares that if all things are unlimited there will not be any knowers. It follows that not all things are unlimited, and this is what **18.2** section 2 declares. Philolaus's purpose in stating **18.2** section 2 is to criticize those who had held that things are all unlimited. This could be directed at Anaximander or at Anaxagoras, a more contemporary figure, many of whose Basic Ingredients (see above page 204) would count for Philolaus as unlimiteds.

18.2 section 3 begins a new stretch of argument, whose conclusion is **18.2** section 4 (which restates two of the three theses of **18.1**). **18.2** section 4 follows from **18.2** section 3, which in turn follows from **18.2** section 6, whose function is announced in **18.2** section 5. The argument goes as follows. The desired conclusion is that the *kosmos* and all the things in it are joined together from unlimiteds and limiters. This is shown by the way things behave: things derived from limiters limit, things derived from both limiters and unlimiteds both limit and do not limit, and things derived from unlimiteds are unlimited. Philolaus distinguished between "things" and what "things" are derived from. I will call these "products" and "principles." He holds in **18.2** section 5 that we can infer the nature of the principles of a product from the nature (behavior) of the product. So since according to **18.2** section 6 there are things (products) that limit, things that are unlimited, and things that both limit and do not limit, it follows in **18.2** section 3 that there are corresponding kinds of principles, and therefore, in **18.2** section 4, that it is not the case either that all principles are limiters or that all are unlimited.

18.6 section 2 identifies the "being" of a thing with its nature and says two things about it: it is eternal, and it admits divine but not human knowledge; it is beyond our ken. Since **18.6** section 3 acknowledges that there are some things that we know, it follows that the being of these things (which is eternal) is different from the things themselves (which come to be). Also, **18.6** section 4 admits that we know something about the being of a thing: we may not know what the being of a given thing is, but we do know that none of the things we know could have come to be without the being of the things from which the *kosmos* is constituted. It goes on to identify those constituents of the *kosmos* as the limiters and the unlimiteds. And this entails the remaining thesis of **18.1**, that nature in the *kosmos* (that is, the "being" of the *kosmos*) was joined from both unlimiteds and limiters.

The highly abstract nature of this discussion finds its match in the Presocratics only in Parmenides and Melissus. After reading it we have no idea what Philolaus takes to be the principles of the *kosmos*. Neither did he; in fact, **18.6** section 2 asserts that this is beyond human capacities to know. But it is possible to understand how he thought the world works.

The key concepts so far are limiters, unlimiteds, and "being." If we want to understand the "being" or nature of a block of ashwood, for example, we note that it is made of ashwood and that it has a certain size and shape. Ashwood per se has no size or shape. It is a material that can be found in or formed into a wide variety of sizes and shapes. Since any piece of ashwood has *some* size and shape, ashwood per se never exists on its own. Neither do sizes or shapes. Philolaus holds that the particular block of ashwood under consideration is a compound of an unlimited (ashwood) and limiters (including the particular size and shape it has). Now consider ashwood itself (the unlimited). It too can be regarded as a compound of limiters and unlimiteds. For example, as a species of wood it involves an unspecified (unlimited) generic substance, wood, and specifications (limiters) that determine it to be the particular kind of wood that is ashwood. For another example, ashwood is composed of various fibers and other kinds of matter, arranged in a definite structure. On this analysis the component materials are the unlimiteds, and the structure is determined by the relevant limiters. Further, consider the particular shape or size of the ashwood block (the limiters). They too can be regarded as compounds of limiteds and limiters. By itself neither shape nor size is definite. So we can think of size per se and shape per se as unlimiteds that when limited become definite sizes and shapes.

This is the way Philolaus looks at things in the *kosmos* and indeed how he looks at the *kosmos* itself. His approach is more general than that of the Atomists, for example, who simply analyzed things into atoms and void. For one thing, it does not commit him to any particular physical theory. For another, it is an analysis that applies to more than just physical objects. Consider the tuning of a lyre, a Pythagorean example (see above pages 91–92) employed by Philolaus himself (18.7). If we pluck a string of any given length under suitable tension, we hear a note. If we stop the string at any place along its length and pluck it on either side of the stop, we hear a different (higher) note. The note depends both on the string (the unlimited) and where it is stopped (the limiters). If it is limited in appropriate places, the notes produced form concordant intervals. A system of concordant intervals is a "tuning" (*harmonia*). I shall return to this shortly below.

Philolaus holds that a thing can be analyzed into limiters and unlimiteds that can themselves be analyzed into other limiters and unlimiteds. He refers to the limiters and unlimiteds that constitute a thing as its principles (*arkhai*), **18.6** section 5. The "being" of things, then, cannot be known, because knowing it involves knowing the limiters and unlimiteds of which it and its constituent limiters and unlimiteds are composed, and there is no telling how far back such an analysis goes. (The gods may know this, but we humans do not.) It is possible that the analysis ends somewhere. If it does, we will have reached limiters and unlimiteds that are ultimate in that they cannot be analyzed further. An ultimate unlimited would not be determinate in any way. It would not have size or shape or structure of any kind and would not even be any kind of thing. This constitutes a good reason for supposing that there is only one ultimate unlimited. One will do the job, since it can be operated on by all possible limiters to produce all possible products. In addition, even if we supposed that there were more than one, there would be no way to tell them apart or even to tell that they are more than one. Therefore by the Principle of the Identity of Indiscernibles they would be the same thing. **9.31**, if it is due to Philolaus, may indicate that the first products from the ultimate unlimited include time, breath, and void.

The last two sections of **18.6** introduce a further element into the analysis of entities: *harmonia*. The basic idea is clear enough: limiters and unlimiteds do not form products simply by being thrown together. They must be joined together in the way appropriate to form the product in question. The way in which a string and the places where it is stopped form concordant intervals is different from the way in which ashwood and size and shape go together to form an ashwood block. **18.1** says that they are "joined" from their constituent limiters and unlimiteds, and **18.6** sections 5–6 say that the limiters and unlimiteds must be connected in *harmonia*. In fact, the word translated "joined" is related to *harmonia*, which literally means "joint" or "joining." Note that *harmonia* is not a force that binds limiters and unlimiteds together. Rather it "come[s] upon" them when they are in an orderly arrangement (*kosmos*). The expression "comes upon" is tantalizing, and unfortunately it is all we have on the important question of how limiters and unlimiteds join together when they are "harmonized" so as to produce other entities. The passage and the word *harmonia* itself suggest that the unlimiteds and limiters do not lose their identity when they form products, but that the *harmonia* is a *harmonia of* the still existing unlimiteds and limiters; the *harmonia* supervenes upon them. The association of *kosmos* with *harmonia* is typically Pythagorean (see above page 93), but here it is given a more precise meaning. **18.1** also makes clear that the *kosmos*, the entire world, is a *harmonia* as well, joined together out of all limiters and unlimiteds in a complex variety of ways.

In **18.7** *harmonia* is used in a different sense, equivalent to octave. The "joining" which is the interval of the octave is analyzed further into subintervals: the fifth and the fourth. The octave is the sum of the fifth and the fourth (for example, the intervals C–G and G–C′ sum to the octave C–C′). As the Pythagoreans had known before Philolaus, these intervals correspond to the ratios 2:1, 3:2, and 4:3. If we add the intervals corresponding to 3:2 and 4:3, we get the interval corresponding to 2:1, and in fact the product of those two ratios is equal to 2:1. If adding intervals is represented by multiplying the ratios, then subtracting intervals is represented by dividing them. This is how Philolaus arrives at 9:8 as the ratio "between the third string and the second string," that is, the difference between F and G, one whole tone. This takes the numerical analysis of intervals significantly further than the original Pythagorean discovery of the numerical analysis of only the three primary intervals.

A related use of the word *harmonia* is found in the following passage.

18.13   Some, following Philolaus, think that it [the mean] is called harmonic because it accompanies every geometric *harmonia*, and they say that the cube is a geometric *harmonia* because it is joined together in three dimensions as equals times equals times equals. For this mean is reflected in every cube: in every cube there are 12 sides, 8 angles, and 6 surfaces. Therefore 8 is the harmonic mean of 6 and 12.

(Nicomachus, *Introductio Arithmetica* 2.26.2 = DK 44A24)

Philolaus is here said to have had knowledge of the harmonic mean.[9] The example given has to do with the number of edges, angles, and surfaces on a cube (12, 8, and 6, respectively, where 8 is the harmonic mean of 12 and 6). Another example of a harmonic mean is found in the musical intervals: 4/3 (which corresponds to the interval of a fourth) is the harmonic mean of 2 and 1, which numbers represent the ratio of the octave.

Cosmogony and Cosmology

Philolaus held that the unique *kosmos* (**18.9**) was generated (**18.1, 18.8, 18.9**). The following account may indicate that he also held that it perishes.[10]

18.14   Philolaus says that the destruction is twofold, caused both by the heavenly fire rushing down and by lunar water that has been poured forth by the revolution of the air, and the exhalations of these are nourishment of the *kosmos*.

(Aëtius 2.5.3 = DK 44A18)

The first thing to be formed was the hearth that occupies the central position (**18.8**). From there it developed symmetrically (**18.9**). The Pythagorean cosmology described in Chapter 9 (above pages 103–6) may actually be due to Philolaus.[11] One of the obstacles to this claim is that while Philolaus says that the first thing formed was the central hearth (**18.8**), the cosmology described by Aristotle says it was "the one" (**9.26**). However, **18.8** says that what is called the hearth is "the one in the middle of the sphere." This suggests two ways to hold that Aristotle is describing Philolaus's system. First, he may have misunderstood

---

9. If *a*, *b*, and *c* are numbers, then *b* is the arithmetic mean of *a* and *c* if $c - b = b - a$; *b* is the geometric mean of *a* and *c* if $a/b = b/c$; and *b* is the harmonic mean of *a* and *c* if $b = (2ac)/(a + c)$. Apparently the harmonic mean was discovered later than the other two means mentioned here, and we must suppose that Philolaus knew the other two means as well.

10. The meaning of this testimonium is unclear; it may refer not to the perishing of the entire *kosmos* but to wide-scale disasters on earth.

11. Huffman argues for this thesis (1993: 202–88). An important consideration in its favor is that the sources describe only one Pythagorean cosmology, whose basic features (earth in orbit around a central fire; ten celestial bodies) are attributed explicitly to Philolaus. Against it is the fact that some ancient discussions of Pythagorean cosmology attribute some views to Philolaus and others to "the Pythagoreans," and even attribute views to "some Pythagoreans including Philolaus," as if there were other Pythagoreans who held other views.

Philolaus's assertion and focused on "one" rather than "hearth." Second, Philolaus may have actually identified the hearth, as the first thing generated, with the number 1 in the Pythagorean way of thinking that identifies (in some sense of that word) marriage with the number 5 (see above pages 93–95).

Philolaus was concerned with the order of the heavenly bodies (**9.33** and **9.34**), and he may have established the correct order of the planets (a result attributed to "the Pythagoreans"[12] but not specifically to Philolaus). The following passages show that he had distinctive views on the sun and moon as well as on the orbits of these bodies and of the earth around the central fire.

18.15 Philolaus the Pythagorean says that the sun is like glass, receiving the reflection of the fire in the *kosmos* and passing the light and heat through toward us, so that what resembles the sun is <first> the fiery material in the sky, <second> the one that comes from it and is like a mirror, and third the radiance from the mirror spread in our direction by reflection. For in fact what we call the sun is this, like an image of an image.

(Aëtius 2.20.12 = DK 44A19)

18.16 Some Pythagoreans including Philolaus say that the moon appears earthlike because it is inhabited all about, just like our earth, but with animals and plants that are bigger and more beautiful. For they are fifteen times more powerful and do not excrete any wastes, and their day is as many times [that is, fifteen times] as long [as a day on earth].

(Aëtius 2.30.1 = DK 44A20)

18.17 Others say that the earth is stationary, but Philolaus the Pythagorean says that it revolves around the fire in an inclined circle, like the sun and moon.

(Aëtius 3.13.2 = DK 44A21)

His speculations in **18.16** about life on the moon are to be compared with Anaxagoras's views on humans living "elsewhere" (**13.4** sections 3–6, see above pages 227–28). Yet another contribution to astronomy is found in the following testimonium, which shows an interest in calendrical phenomena: the length of the year and the number of years—known in antiquity as a "great year"—that coincides with an exact number of lunar months.

18.18 There is also a [great] year of Philolaus the Pythagorean that is 59 years long, in which there are 21 intercalary months. . . . Philolaus proposed that the natural year has 364 1/2 days.

(Censorinus, *On the Day of Birth* 18.8 = DK 44A22)

---

12. See above p. 104 n. 47.

The Human Body

18.19   Philolaus says that our bodies are constituted out of hot. For he suggests on
the basis of the following kinds of reasons why they have no share of cold.
Sperm is hot, and this is what constructs the animal; the place into which
it is deposited, the womb, is hotter than the sperm and like it. And what is
like something has the same power as it. But since the thing that constructs
has no share of cold, it is clear that the animal that is constructed also comes
to be like that. He also mentions the following point regarding the construction of the animal. Immediately after birth the animal draws in air
from without, which is cold. Then it sends it out again as if it were a debt.
Indeed, this is why there is a desire for air from without, so that our bodies,
which are too hot, by the drawing in of breath from outside are cooled by it.
He says, then, that the constitution of our body depends on these things.

He says that diseases are due to bile, blood, and phlegm, and that these
are the origin of diseases. He says that the blood is made thick when the
flesh is squeezed inward, but that it becomes thin when the vessels in the
flesh are dilated. He says that phlegm results from rain. Bile, he says, is a
serum of the flesh. The same man creates a paradox about this; he says that
bile is not even assigned to the liver, but that it is a serum of the flesh, and
although most say that phlegm is cold, he hypothesizes that it is hot by
nature, for phlegm comes from *phlegein* ["to burn"]. Therefore things that
are inflamed are inflamed because they have a share of phlegm. He hypothesizes these things as the origins of diseases, while excesses of heat, food,
and cooling also have a contributory effect, as well as deficiencies of these
things and things like these.

(Anon. Londiniensis 18.8 = DK 44A27)

This passage treats the constitution of the human body ("out of hot") and the origin of disease. The explanation of breathing and the fact that breathing is the first
thing an animal does after birth has been compared to the Pythagorean account
of cosmogony in which "from the unlimited it draws in time, breath and void"
(**9.31**)—an account that may be due to Philolaus.[13] It is not clear just how this
account of the human body is related to his analysis of things in terms of limiters and unlimiteds. Hot will be an unlimited, but it is hard to see how the various
parts and structures of a living being can be formed and made to function simply
by limiters acting on a single unlimited. The account of diseases as due primarily
to (a bad condition of) blood, bile, and phlegm gives Philolaus a significant role
in the history of ancient medicine. It is worthwhile to compare his account of the
makeup of the human body and origin of diseases with those given in the Hippocratic medical treatises translated in the Appendix of this book.

---

13. Huffman may be correct in thinking that it is part of Philolaus's cosmogony (Huffman [1993: 43, 47, 212–14]), but the evidence is not conclusive.

Knowledge and Number

Philolaus has interesting things to say about what must be the case in order for knowledge to be possible (**18.3** and **18.4** in addition to **18.6** sections 2–3). We have seen that according to **18.6** sections 2–3 humans cannot know the "being" of things—the complete account of their harmonious composition of limiters and unlimiteds at all levels of analysis—although we do have knowledge of some things, including "things that come to be." **18.3** claims that if all things were unlimited, then nothing could know at all, which implies that nothing could be known. This view, which has Parmenidean echoes,[14] is consistent with the interpretation proposed above (pages 356–57), that Philolaus's system requires there to be an ultimate principle that is wholly unlimited. Since it has no definite characteristics (only the potential to take on any possible characteristic), such a thing could not be known. If everything were like that, nothing could be known, nor, therefore, could there be a knower.

According to **18.4**, a necessary condition for anything to be known is that it "have number." Thus, we have two criteria of intelligibility: in order to be intelligible a thing must not be purely unlimited (**18.3**) and it must "have number" (**18.4**). Philolaus's claim is different from the views Aristotle ascribes to the Pythagoreans, that things *are* numbers, or that they are *composed of* numbers, etc. (See above page 96.) It cannot be excluded that Philolaus asserted one or more of those views as well, but I do not think it is very likely. When he talks about the nature of things, he speaks of limiters and unlimiteds, not numbers.

The fragments do not say precisely how number is related to intelligibility. However, it is plausible that the two fragments are connected: things can be known *because* they have number. But then we must ask *how* they "have number." In the first place, anything that "has number" is not wholly unlimited, and so is limited in one or more ways. It is possible that Philolaus simply identified limits with numbers, but it is not clear that all possible limits have anything to do with number or that all limiters operate in a way that can reasonably described as imparting number to their products. The general Pythagorean practice of associating things with numbers any which way (see above pages 93–95) does not seem to suit Philolaus's careful approach, and it is likely that he has something more specific in mind. **18.7** provides a hint. The concordant intervals and their various relations are intelligible because they are associated with ratios (*logoi*) of whole numbers in a particular way. They are not identical with those ratios, let alone with numbers themselves. The ratio 3:2 is in fact the ratio of the lengths of a string (any string), which when plucked produces notes that make the concordant interval of a fifth. If this counts as "having number," then it is reasonable to think that anything that has one or more definite numerical relations as basic properties can be described as "having

---

14. Parmenides held that what-is is limited (**11.8** lines 26, 31, 47, 49) and is intelligible (**11.8** lines 34–41).

number." This calls for a more general notion of number than simply the positive integers. (Conceivably, the reference to the "many forms" of even and odd "of which each thing itself gives signs" (**18.5**) is an indication that Philolaus attempted to make a suitable generalization or at least saw the need to do so.) This view might well have been held by a Pythagorean in the late fifth or early fourth century. It can claim to be following the Pythagorean tradition of giving importance to numbers, while abandoning the excessive enthusiasm about numbers that was rife in earlier generations and making room for the more abstract conceptions of limiters and unlimiteds to be the principles of Philolaus's system. This interpretation also makes sense of the following statement.

18.20   The Pythagoreans declare that *logos* <is the criterion of truth>—not <*logos*> in general, but [the *logos*] that arises from the mathematical sciences, as Philolaus too used to say.
                    (Sextus Empiricus, *Against the Mathematicians* 7.92 = DK 44A29)

Logos means "reason," but it also means "ratio." If Philolaus used the word in the broad sense of "ratio" sketched above and if he also conceived of ratios as numbers, then since he held that things are made intelligible by possessing number we can understand why he called *logos* the criterion in the sense of something that can be used to determine the truth. Finally, the obscure statement that some *logoi* are too strong for us (**18.10**) may refer to the limitations of human knowledge identified in **18.6** section 2.

Other surviving evidence proves that not only number but also mathematics in general was important for Philolaus.

18.21   Geometry is the origin and the mother-city of the other <mathematical sciences>.
                    (Plutarch, *Table Talk* 781E = DK 44A7a)

This passage shows that he thought about the relations among different branches of mathematics. If this testimonium is taken as an historical claim—that the Greeks developed geometry before other mathematical fields—it may well be the first appearance of this view.

The curious statement that the number 7 is motherless (**18.11**) is taken to refer to the fact that 7 is alone among the numbers up to 10 in being a prime number that has no multiple less than or equal to 10. The sources[15] link this with mystical Pythagorean identifications of numbers with the Olympian gods (for example, 7 is identified with Athena, who had no mother and, being a virgin, no children), but it is not clear that Philolaus went in for this kind of thinking.

---

15. Collected and translated by Huffman (1993: 335–37).

Life and the Soul

Since the Pythagoreans were known for their belief in the post mortem existence of souls and their transmigration into the bodies of other humans, animals, and even plants,[16] it is not surprising that Philolaus expresses views on the nature of the soul. What is surprising is that what we are told about Philolaus's views on the soul has nothing to do with transmigration and may even be taken to show that Philolaus did not accept this important Pythagorean tenet.

The remarkable fragment **18.12** identifies four different parts of the body as the location of different kinds of faculties characteristic of living things and for the first time presents plants, animals, and humans in a hierarchy that depends on the faculties they possess. The first of these approaches was subsequently adopted by Plato and the second by Aristotle, although Plato and Aristotle differ from Philolaus in important respects. Philolaus distinguishes between intellect, soul, and sensation, whereas Plato and Aristotle place intellect and sensation among the capacities of the soul. All living things (plants, animals, and humans) possess genital organs and are capable of "taking root" and growing; animals and humans, but not plants, have soul and sensation; humans alone possess intellect. The status of the soul in this scale—as occupying an inferior position to intellect—is striking. Whereas for Aristotle all living things—even plants—possess soul, for Philolaus possession of soul is characteristic of the complex kind of living things that animals and humans are. It is possible that there is an echo here of the concept of the "breath-soul"[17]—the concept of the soul as the vital breath which we expire upon dying and thus cease to move. (Absence of motion is evidently characteristic of dead humans and animals, and less obviously so for plants.) However, it is difficult to imagine how this concept of soul is compatible with the kind of soul that survives the death of a human and that can enter other living bodies. Further, if we can make use of Empedocles as evidence for Pythagorean beliefs about transmigration,[18] we run into another difficulty. Empedocles claims that in previous incarnations he was a plant as well as other humans and other kinds of animals (**14.15**). But how can this be, if plants are excluded from possessing soul? In view of these problems, it is tempting to hold that Philolaus abandoned the Pythagorean belief in transmigration. If this is correct, it is another way in which he deviated from the mainstream of that tradition.

The following testimonium gives further information about Philolaus's concept of the soul.

18.22   Philolaus <said that the soul> is a *harmonia*.
(Macrobius, *Scipio's Dream* 1.14.19 = DK 44A23)

---

16. See above pp. 84–87.

17. See above p. 53.

18. Empedocles' relation to the Pythagoreans is a vexed question. In general, it seems there must be some connection, but it is impossible to be sure how close the connection is.

This appears to be an obvious consequence of Philolaus's view that every orderly compound is a *harmonia* (**18.6** section 5). But a *harmonia* is a joining together of limiters and unlimiteds, so we are entitled to ask what limiters and unlimiteds are the constituents of the soul and in what sense a soul can be identical with a *joining together* (as opposed to the constituents joined together in the correct way). Other difficulties arise in connection with the doctrine that the heart is the location of the soul as the head is the location of the intellect (**18.12**), which may make the soul appear more of a physical entity (that is, a set of limiters and unlimiteds joined together in a *harmonia*) than if it were somehow associated with the entire body.[19] Along the lines of this interpretation Huffman has proposed that the soul is a *harmonia* of very fine material elements located in the heart which are in continual motion, and their motion is transmitted to the rest of the body.[20] If this interpretation is correct, then it is even harder to see how Philolaus could believe in the soul's survival after death. On the other hand, so little information about his understanding of the nature of the soul survives that it would be rash to do more than point out some consequences and tendencies of the materials we have without going so far as to claim that he was aware of them or accepted them.

Conclusion

An adequate estimation of Philolaus's importance has only recently become possible with the publication of Huffman's excellent edition of his fragments with its commentary on the fragments and its extensive introduction. As yet there is no consensus about his doctrines, their philosophical significance, or their place in the history of Greek philosophy. This chapter contains a sketch of a new interpretation that differs in some respects from Huffman's. On any account, Philolaus turns out to be a more interesting philosopher than used to be thought and we may expect to see more attention devoted to him in the future.

---

19. This other view of the soul as a *harmonia* is discussed both by Plato (the *Phaedo* 86b–e and 92a–95a) and Aristotle (*On the Soul* 407b27–408a18). It is usually held that this other view is Pythagorean.

20. Huffman (1993: 329).

19

Early Greek Moral Thought and
the Fifth-Century Sophists

The Presocratic philosophers[1] are remembered mainly for their attempts to understand the physical world—how it functions, how it came to be the way it is, what it is made of. After Xenophanes and Parmenides they were forced to take up problems of logic, metaphysics, epistemology, and philosophy of mind. Noticeably absent from this list are moral, political, and social philosophy. Indeed, the ancient tradition has it that these philosophical areas remained untouched until Socrates (469–399) began to explore them.

> 19.1   From the earliest philosophy down to the time of Socrates . . . numbers and movements were treated and the source from which all things arise and into which they return. Those philosophers diligently investigated the sizes of the stars, their distances and paths, and all heavenly matters. Socrates, however, was first to call down philosophy from the sky, establish it in the cities, and even bring it into homes. He compelled it to investigate life and customs and things that are good and evil.
>
> (Cicero, *Tusculan Disputations* 5.4.10 [not in DK])[2]

However, this picture is incorrect. As we have seen, many of the Presocratics expressed opinions on questions in moral, political, and social philosophy.[3] Moreover, serious treatment of such questions goes much further back—to the beginnings of Greek literature, in the poems of Homer and Hesiod, which date to the eighth century, some three hundred years before Socrates. Among the issues Homer and Hesiod raised are the nature of the best kind of life for a man (and for a woman), the relation between humans and gods, what actions are virtuous, whether (and why) a person should be virtuous, the relation between the individual and society, and the best kind of ruler. (This list could be far

---

1. The distinction between Presocratics and Sophists is not neatly drawn, since Democritus was born a decade after Socrates and Philolaus probably later than that, and since the earliest Sophists were born a generation before him. I will continue to use the term "Presocratic" for thinkers from Thales to Democritus and Philolaus who were mainly concerned with issues of the kinds treated already in this book, as opposed to the Sophists, whose principal interests were somewhat different. Even so there is overlap, since Democritus, for example, had serious interests in ethics and possibly even anthropology; and of the Sophists, Gorgias had interests along Eleatic lines, and Hippias did work in mathematics and cosmology.

2. Cicero presents a similar idea at *Academica* 1.4.15 (not in DK).

3. Notably Xenophanes, Heraclitus, the Pythagoreans, Empedocles, and Democritus.

longer.) In the Archaic period (roughly 750–480), poets such as Tyrtaeus, Solon, Theognis, and Pindar enshrined traditional Greek ethical thought and raised questions and offered solutions of increasing sophistication. This moral tradition was continued in the fifth century by such authors as the historians Herodotus and Thucydides and especially by the tragedians Aeschylus, Sophocles and Euripides, whose treatments of moral issues are among the most sensitive and profound of any conceived in ancient Greece. Nevertheless, this work was something different from moral philosophy.

The first people who can properly be said to have done work in moral philosophy were the fifth-century Sophists. These thinkers engaged in seminal discussions in the areas of moral, political, and social philosophy and raised a host of issues in other philosophical areas as well, such as philosophy of language and epistemology. Some also engaged in scientific speculations familiar from the Presocratic tradition, and one pursued themes associated with the Eleatics.[4] The chief Sophists overlapped in time, in their travels and in their interests, so as a result it is hard to identify clear cases where one Sophist is reacting to another. We get a picture of mutual influence colored by professional rivalry. It is equally hard to identify a set of doctrines held by all the Sophists. Instead of a "school" of thought, they constituted a more broadly defined "movement" whose common points include goals and methods as well as subject matter.[5] Whether the Sophists should be called philosophers, however, is a controversial issue which I will take up at the end of this chapter.

The present chapter sets the stage by sketching some issues prominent in the pre-philosophical moral thought of the Archaic period, and then considers the nature and general features of the Sophistic movement, prior to surveying the most important Sophists and taking up some of the most significant philosophical issues they raised. The next chapter focuses on the *nomos–phusis* debate, to which Sophists and others as well contributed.

Early Greek Moral Thought

Aretē and *Agathos*

These two basic concepts of Greek morality are closely related and not straightforwardly translatable into English. As an approximation, *aretē* can be rendered "excellence" or "goodness" (sometimes "virtue"), and *agathos* as "excellent" or "good." The terms are related in that a thing or person is *agathos* if and only if it

---

4. Gorgias, in his work *On What-Is-Not, or On Nature*. See below pp. 393–97.

5. *The Sophistic Movement* is the title of an excellent book by G. Kerferd (1982), which makes an ambitious effort to rehabilitate the Sophists as serious philosophers. The present treatment is more conservative, the result of my skepticism about the value of Plato's exposition of allegedly Sophistic doctrines.

has *aretē* and just because it has *aretē*. The concepts apply to objects, conditions, and actions as well as to humans. They are connected with the concept of *ergon* (plural, *erga*), which may be rendered as "function" or "characteristic activity." A good (*agathos*) person is one who performs human *erga* well, and similarly a good knife is a knife that performs the *ergon* of a knife well. The *ergon* of a knife is cutting, and an *agathos* knife is one that cuts well. Thus, the *aretē* of a knife is the qualities or characteristics a knife must have in order to cut well. Likewise, if a human *ergon* can be identified, an *agathos* human is one who can and on appropriate occasions does perform that *ergon* well, and human *aretē* is the qualities or characteristics that enable him or her to do so. The classical discussion of these concepts occurs after our period, in Aristotle,[6] but he is only making explicit ideas that go back to Homer and which throw light on much of the pre-philosophical ethical thought of the Greeks.

This connection of concepts makes it automatic, virtually an analytic truth, that the right goal for a person—any person—is to be or become *agathos*. Even if that goal is unreachable for someone, the *aretē–agathos* standard still stands as an ideal against which to measure one's successes and failures. However, there is room for debate over the nature of human *erga*, both whether there is a set of *erga* applicable to all humans and relevant to *aretē* and, supposing that there is such a set of *erga*, what those *erga* are. The existence of the *aretē–agathos* standard makes it vitally important to settle these issues, for otherwise human life is left adrift with no standards of conduct.

Homer's Legacy

In the *Iliad* the heroic ideal is well known and widely accepted as the standard by which a warrior is to be measured. It consists of several attributes, some of which we would consider external and some internal to the person. Some are thought to form part of a person's inherent nature while others can be acquired. The ideal Homeric hero is male and well born (the nobler, the better; the best have a god or goddess as a parent or ancestor). He is a ruler and is wealthy, beautiful, excellent at fighting, excellent at counsel, excellent in leadership, brave, strong, generous to friends and harsh to enemies, reverent to the gods, and aware of his worth and of his position in society and anxious to maintain and improve it. The expectation is that these qualities go together, and little attempt is made to analyze this ideal to determine whether, say, anyone could be a hero without being beautiful. The circumstances in which this ideal is typically expressed are the activities of war. Fighting is normally hand-to-hand combat in which two warriors fight to the death. The competitive virtues are paramount, especially courage. On the other hand, within the army the cooperative qualities of counsel and leadership have great importance. Counsel is given in circumstances where the leaders cooperate

---

6. Aristotle, *Nicomachean Ethics* 1.7.

to decide on a course of action, and effective leadership requires behaving so as to merit the respect, loyalty, and obedience of those being led. Also, despite the unbridgeable gulf between mortal humans and immortal gods, humans can hope for a lesser kind of immortality by achieving fame and so being remembered by others. This was achieved through epic poetry which recorded the "glorious deeds of men" and was memorized and performed for the entertainment and edification of future generations. Above all Homer's *Iliad* and *Odyssey* served as a powerful and widely known source of ideals which many of the philosophers saw as outdated and needing to be replaced. (See **7.3–7.13, 10.16**.)

The *Iliad*, an epic of war, focuses on the warrior and ruling caste which occupies the highest male positions in Homeric society, but to a small extent in the *Iliad* and much more in the *Odyssey*, the poet shows us other aspects of the life of that semi-mythical world. There are virtues and appropriate modes of behavior not only for warriors and rulers but also for wives, children, parents, servants, bards, and the lesser nobles who are of local importance but not to be ranked with the heroes of the *Iliad*. The cooperative and passive values of affection, hospitality, loyalty, patience, and endurance receive almost as much attention as the competitive and active virtues of courage, strength, and cleverness.

The account just given picks out only a few features of the rich and varied world of the Homeric epics. The moral scene Homer presents is appropriate to the society it represents and quite alien to our own. It is the starting point for subsequent moral speculation which no one in the later Greek tradition could quite forget. The development of Greek moral thought through the Archaic and Classical periods can be seen as the gradual replacement of the competitive by the cooperative virtues as the primary virtues of conduct and as the recognition and increasing recognition of the significance of people's intentions as well as their actions.[7]

Rapid change in Greek society in the Archaic and Classical periods called for new conceptions of the ideal human and the ideal human life and activities. The Archaic period saw different kinds of rulers from the Homeric kings, and individual combat gave way to the united front of a phalanx of hoplites (heavily armed warriors). Even though the Homeric warrior-king was no longer a possible role in society, the qualities of good birth, beauty, courage, honor, and the abilities to give good counsel and rule well remained. Nevertheless, the various strands of the Homeric heroic ideal began to unravel. In particular, good birth, wealth, and fighting ability no longer automatically went together. This situation forced the issue: what are the best qualities we can possess? What constitutes human *aretē*? The literary sources contain conflicting claims about the best life for a person, the best kind of person to be, and the relative merits of qualities thought to be ingredients of human happiness. In one way or another these different

---

7. This is an important theme in A.W. H. Adkins' influential book, *Merit and Responsibility* (Adkins [1962]).

conceptions of human excellence have Homeric origins, though they diverge from Homer's conception and from one another.

Lack of space makes it impossible to present the wealth of materials that bear on this subject.[8] I will confine discussion to two representatives of the aristocratic tradition who wrote at the end of the Archaic period. Pindar shows how the aristocratic ideal had survived and been transformed from the Homeric conception and how vital it remained as late as the early fifth century, and Theognis reveals how social, political, and economic reality was undermining that ideal.

Pindar

In the late sixth and early fifth centuries Pindar composed odes to celebrate victors in athletic competitions, including the those held at the Olympic festival. His patrons, the victorious athletes, were wealthy, sometimes royal, and frequently aristocratic. Pindar champions an ideal that these people would tend to adopt for their own, so his poetry is a valuable source for the aristocratic mentality of his time—a set of traditions and attitudes with which the democratic tendencies of the fifth century had to cope and which continued to exert pressure, if not always an articulate voice, in the moral debates of the late fifth century.

Pindar unsurprisingly gives prominence to the athletic ideal with its emphasis on success. Victory at the games brings glory to a person for the rest of his life, also to his family, descendants, and city. Defeat is shameful, disgraceful. But the glory of victory (especially when spread abroad by the talents of a poet like Pindar) brings lasting fame and praise, two of the chief components of happiness, which is the supreme goal of life. Athletic competition was a form of divine worship and took place in such sanctuaries as Olympia and Delphi as part of religious festivals, and Pindar insists that success in the games and in other fields is a mark of the gods' favor and cannot be gained without their assistance. However, it also requires valor, effort, daring, strength, and wealth (which are also gifts of the gods). The gods control all human things and can give and take away happiness at will. Since humans are frail and their destiny is shaky, it is important to be reverent to the gods, who alone can make prosperity long-lasting. Hence, in evaluating persons, actions, and qualities, it is important to judge by what happens in the end. Despite the uncertainty of the future, Pindar is sure of the consequences of success: humans find good fortune hard to bear. It brings envy, slander, and mockery from others and tends to make the fortunate person proud, over-confident, and arrogant. The jealousy of other humans can be dealt with, but arrogance (*hubris*) brings divine retribution. The gods bring down the proud. Therefore it is necessary to resist the impulses to go too far, to be moderate in good fortune, and to know your limits as a human being.

---

8. Many of the most important passages are from poets of the Archaic period, such as Mimnermus, Tyrtaeus, Solon, Pindar, and Theognis.

There is no single passage that expresses all the elements of this complex system of values, but the following are representative.

19.2   Wide is the strength of wealth
        when, mixed with stainless virtue
        and granted of destiny, mortal man leads it home,
        most dear companion . . . .
        Even power granted of God
        is carried the better for wisdom . . . .
        This man is praised of the wise,
        I speak what men say.
        He ministers a mind that outruns his years;
        speech also; for daring he is the eagle
        of wide wings among birds;
        in games, strength, like a wall;
        among the Muses he goes lightfooted from birth;
        he has approved himself a subtle charioteer.
        To all splendors in his own land he has dared
        the entrance; now God, favoring, makes perfect his power,
        and hereafter, you blessed sons of Kronos,
        may you grant him in action as in deliberation
        such things to have; let no autumn storm blast
        of winds break the bloom.
        The great mind of Zeus guides
        the angel in men he loves.
                        (Pindar, *Pythians* 5 [not in DK], tr. Lattimore)

19.3   The crucial strength is given of the gods to men;
            but two things only there are that minister to the brightest bloom of life
                as wealth blossoms:
        success and the good speech that a man hears of himself.
        Strive not to become Zeus; you have everything
        if destiny of such splendors befall you.
        Mortals must be content with mortality.
                        (Pindar, *Isthmians* 5 [not in DK], tr. Lattimore)

Pindar was far from a moral philosopher. Instead of argument he uses mythological archetypes to support the values he promotes and the advice he offers. No doubt his moral precepts do not form a tidy system—perhaps not even a consistent one. Sometimes they are banal to the point of vacuousness: "Praise the good," he says with all seriousness. But overall he recommends an aristocratic ideal of life appropriate for his time, a sophisticated, updated version of the Homeric ideal in which noble birth, beauty, wealth, strength, daring, and success in competitive situations (athletics more than war, but Pindar often mentions military exploits) are prominent as are excellence at counsel and government.

Even such aesthetic qualities as appreciation for and support of music, festivals, and other lovely enterprises are quite at home in the Homeric ideal (one thinks of the Phaeacians in *Odyssey*, books 6–8). What is new is the occurrence of such quiet, cooperative virtues as gentleness, righteousness, discretion, honesty, and modesty as well as explicit advice to avoid excess and to be moderate. Nevertheless, in the world of Pindar's victorious aristocrats as in Homer's elite warrior caste the comfortable assumption is that all the desirable qualities hang together reasonably coherently and (with the gods' will) can be attained in a lasting way.

Xenophanes

Pindar's contemporary Xenophanes demonstrates that in the decades around the turn of the fifth century there was no uniformity in moral ideas. In contrast to Pindar's piety we find Xenophanes rejection of the Olympian gods;[9] in contrast to Pindar's athleticism, Xenophanes complains that athletes receive more recognition and respect than they deserve and in fact more than Xenophanes himself receives; in contrast to his elitism, Xenophanes promotes social coherence. The following two poems illustrate his stance. The first begins with an idealized description of preparations for a drinking party (*sumposion*) and ends with prescriptions for the behavior appropriate to such an occasion: reverence, moderation in drinking, and piety. The poem contains "a progression from a description of material circumstances to the spiritual qualities conveyed by them to the demands of moral seriousness the latter give rise to. . . . It is a lesson in moral sensitizing . . . beyond the level of conventional entertainment and piety with which it began."[10] On the other hand, it is not clear how Xenophanes reconciles his reference to the plural gods with his rejection of Olympian polytheism in favor of a single god. I think it most likely that he chose not to introduce his reformist views into a poem written for social settings that will surely have included people who wanted to enjoy themselves without being subjected to controversial new-fangled ideas.

19.4 For now the floor is clean, and the hands of all,
    and the cups. He is putting on the woven wreaths,
    another is offering fragrant myrrh in a bowl,
    a mixing bowl stands full of joy,
    another wine, gentle and scented of flowers, is at hand in wine-jars   5
    and boasts that it will never betray us.
    In the middle, frankincense is sending forth its holy scent.
    There is cold water sweet and pure.
    Golden loaves of bread are served and a magnificent table

---

9. See above pp. 59–61.
10. Lesher (1992: 54).

is laden with cheese and rich honey.   10
In the center an altar is all covered in flowers
and the rooms are full of song and good cheer.
Cheerful men should first sing a hymn to the god
with well-omened words and pure speech.
When they have poured an offering and prayed to be able to do
    acts of justice   15
(for indeed these are the first things to pray for),
it is not going too far (*hubris*) if you drink only as much as
    permits you to reach
home without assistance (unless you are very aged[11]).
Praise the man who after drinking behaves nobly
in that he possesses memory and aims for excellence (*aretē*).   20
and does not relate battles of Titans or Giants
or Centaurs—the fictions of our fathers—
or violent conflicts in which there is no use,
but it is good always to have high regard for the gods.
           (Xenophanes fr. 1 = DK 21B1)

In the following poem Xenophanes elevates wisdom (more precisely, the kind of wisdom that he has) over strength. In Homer wisdom in the form of good counsel was valued. The aged king Nestor received great respect even though he was no longer an excellent warrior. But his advice was subordinate to fighting; he typically offers recommendations about fighting and battle tactics. Xenophanes repositions his own kind of wisdom (which is wisdom of a different sort from Nestor's) on the scale of values.

Xenophanes claims that however proud a city may be of its successful athletes, their attainments do nothing to improve either its political or its economic condition, whereas Xenophanes' wisdom has those positive results. Clearly enough athletic success had positive results for the successful athletes: in some cities they received free meals for life at public expense and the honors bestowed upon them would have reinforced their social position and possibly have advanced it. Any benefits accrued to the athlete, not to his city. On the other hand, the advice Xenophanes offers (for example in lines 13–24), which emphasizes the cooperative virtues of moderation and reverence and which discourages telling stories that may hold up the antisocial brawling of gods as models for human behavior, is intended to benefit others by showing them how best to live, what attitudes to have, and how to behave toward one another. In view of his doubts about the possibility of attaining certainty[12] we need to distinguish this wisdom from knowledge of things which Xenophanes declares humans cannot know (7.27), but this

---

11. The point is not that the elderly are encouraged to drink themselves into a stupor but that they need assistance getting about in any case.

12. See 7.27.

caution need not be seen as a criticism. Xenophanes might well have held that the obscure topics on which he declares that certainty cannot be reached[13] do not include suggestions for proper behavior.

19.5   If anyone were to achieve a victory
     at Zeus's sanctuary at Olympia by the streams of Pisa
     in a foot race or the pentathlon or in wrestling
     or the painful art of boxing
     or the frightful contest they call the pankration,   5
     he would be more glorious in the eyes of the citizens.
     They would grant him a seat of honor at the games,
     he would enjoy meals at public expense
     and a gift from the city for his children to inherit.
     Even if he were to be victorious with horses he would
        obtain these things,   10
     though he is not as worthy of them as I. For superior to the strength
     of men or horses is my wisdom.
     But these ways are misguided and it is not right
     to put strength ahead of wisdom, which is good.
     If an excellent boxer were among the people   15
     or someone excellent at the pentathlon or in wrestling
     or in the foot race (which is the most highly honored
     display of strength of all men's deeds in the contests)
     that would not make a city be any more in a state of *eunomia*.[14]
     A city will find little joy in a person   20
     who wins in the contests by the banks of Pisa,
     since this does not fatten the city's storerooms.
                 (Xenophanes fr. 2 = DK 21B2)

Theognis

A person reading Pindar would hardly suspect that the heyday of the aristocracy would soon be over. Already in Athens a century earlier Solon's political reforms (594) had severely limited traditional aristocratic rights and had given a political voice and role to a much larger segment of the community. While Pindar was writing his poetry, the Athenians adopted Cleisthenes' democratic reforms (508) designed to put an end to the concentrations of power through which aristocratic families had dominated the Athenian political scene. Moreover, in sixth century Athens under Peisistratus and his sons, and in a multitude of other city-states as well, a kind of monarchy called "tyranny" (the word *turannos* originally meant "absolute ruler" or "monarch," without any necessarily negative connotations;

---

13. See above pp. 67–68.

14. *Eunomia* is found where the laws are good and people abide by them. For the importance of *eunomia* see **20.15**.

frequently these "tyrants" were enlightened rather than "tyrannical," as we use
the word) had wrested influence from the aristocratic families and had recognized the growing wealth and importance of the commercial classes.

The increase in wealth and the shift in its distribution which had begun by the
seventh century led to profound changes in the social and political scenes in the
sixth and forced a wedge in among the complex of qualities which traditionally
constituted aristocratic *aretē*. Pindar's unified picture in which wealth, power, and
noble birth tend to go together became ever less true to contemporary reality.

The aristocratic response to this changed situation receives its clearest
expression in the poems attributed to Theognis and composed in the sixth and
early fifth centuries. Even less than with Pindar can we find a consistent set
of views advocated in these poems, but among the most frequently recurring
themes are the view that money does not make the man, that many undeserv-
ing people are now rich and many deserving people (deserving because of their
birth and social background) are now poor. It is noteworthy how Theognis
plays on the different connotations of uses of the primary terms of value, *agathos* and *aretē*, and their opposites *kakos* and *kakia*: morally good vs. evil; well-
born, noble vs. low-born; and politically and socially powerful vs. powerless.
Since the traditional positive attributes no longer regularly all went together,
it was important to decide which are most important, indeed which are the
essential ingredients of human *aretē*.

19.6   We look for rams and asses and horses, Kyrnos,
           that are well bred, and a person wants to get offspring
           from good [*agathos*] stock. But a noble man does not mind marrying
           a lowly [*kakos*] woman of a lowly [*kakos*] father, if her father gives him a
               lot of money.
           Nor does a woman refuse to be the wife of a lowly [*kakos*] man
           who is rich, but she prefers wealth to goodness [*agathos*]. . . .
           They honor money. And so a noble man marries into a lowly [*kakos*]
               family,
           and a lowly [*kakos*] man into a good [*agathos*] one. Wealth has
               mixed the race.
           So do not be surprised, son of Polypais, that the race of the citizens
           is becoming obscure, since nobility is being mingled with the
               low [*kakos*].
                                                            (Theognis lines 183–92 [not in DK])

19.7   It is easier to beget and raise a child than to instill
           good thoughts in it. No one yet has devised a way
           to make the fool wise and a bad [*kakos*] person good [*agathos*] . . . .
           If intelligence could be fashioned and put into a man,
           never would a bad [*kakos*] person come from a good [*agathos*] father,

> obeying wise words. But never will he make
> a bad [*kakos*] man good [*agathos*] by teaching.
>
> > (Theognis lines 429–38 [not in DK])

19.8   Kyrnos, a good [*agathos*] man keeps his good judgment always fixed.
   He has courage whether he is found among the bad [*kakos*] or the good
   [*agathos*].
   But if god grants livelihood and wealth to a bad [*kakos*] man,
   in his folly he is unable to hold back his bad [*kakos*] nature.

> > (Theognis lines 319–22 [not in DK])

The Sophists

Sources

The controversial nature of the Sophists makes for special difficulties in the source materials. Very little survives of their writings: the only complete works are two short rhetorical display pieces by Gorgias. Also, the Sophists lack the kind of doxographical tradition which the Presocratics possess, probably because of Aristotle's low opinion of them. Since he did not consider them serious philosophers, neither he nor his followers made systematic surveys of their views as they did for other early thinkers.[15] There was virtually no interest in the Sophists in the post-Aristotelian period until the so-called Second Sophistic movement of the second and third centuries CE. From this period there is a work by Flavius Philostratus entitled *Lives of the Sophists*, which contains brief sections on most of the principal fifth-century Sophists. This work, however, reflects the interests of the Second Sophistic movement which were rhetorical rather than philosophical.

The most extensive information about the Sophists and the Sophistic movement comes from Plato's dialogues, several of which are either named after individual Sophists[16] or refer to the Sophists and their doctrines.[17] If Plato were reliable, we would know a great deal more about the Sophists than if we ignore him, and this very fact has led some to follow him too incautiously. But Plato, following Socrates, is hostile to the Sophists. In the dialogues where individual Sophists appear, they are always defeated by Socrates in philosophical discussion. And when Plato treats them as a group, he insults and ridicules them rather than giving them serious philosophical consideration.[18] Moreover, Plato is no serious historian of philosophy but uses others' ideas as springboards for his own philosophical thought. In these circumstances, it is extremely dangerous to follow blindly his treatment of the philosophical ideas raised by the Sophists.

---

15. See above pp. 3–4.

16. *Protagoras, Gorgias, Greater Hippias, Lesser Hippias, Euthydemus.*

17. Especially *Apology, Laches, Meno, Theaetetus,* and *Sophist.*

18. Especially in *Meno* 91a–92c (not in DK) and *Sophist* 221c–226a (part = DK 79,2)

In what follows I adopt a middle course between refusing to use Plato at all and using him uncritically. When allowances are made for irony, humor, exaggeration, and bias, Plato gives us an idea of Sophistic education and methods and also portraits of many of the chief Sophists that seem broadly accurate. On the other hand, I adopt a cautious approach in dealing with Plato's treatment of certain Sophistic ideas—in particular, Protagorean relativism as found in the *Theaetetus* and the political and social ideas presented in Protagoras's long speech early in the *Protagoras*.[19] While Plato may be paraphrasing Protagoras's own writings, it seems to me more likely that he is developing Protagoras's ideas for his own purposes and is unreliable about the details of Protagoras's own thought.

Since Socrates is the chief speaker in almost all of Plato's works, a serious problem in Platonic studies is how far the words he puts into Socrates' mouth contain Socrates' own ideas and how far they contain Plato's, and to what extent Plato's ideas are developments of Socrates'. A similar problem arises for the Sophists, but with them it is more complicated since the positions Plato ascribes to them usually come under devastating attack. My view is that Socrates and Plato are deeply indebted to the Sophists in matters of method and approach for many of the philosophical issues they discuss and for some aspects of their own ideas. Perhaps because their nearness made Plato unable to see his debt, and perhaps because he deliberately set out to distance the Sophists from Socrates, Plato never credits the Sophists for these points of agreement. On the other hand, where there is disagreement, he is only too ready to subject the Sophists' ideas—or his development of their ideas—to searching examination. This fact in itself is evidence that Plato and Socrates forged their own philosophical views through reflection on the Sophists, though this is not the place to pursue such ideas. As for the particular passages containing Plato's extensive treatments of philosophical theses of individual Sophists, it is best to take them up in connection with Plato himself.[20] In matters of doctrine the present treatment will tend to stick to non-Platonic materials.

What Is a Sophist?

Strictly speaking, Sophists were itinerant educators who operated independently and charged fees. Different Sophists taught different ranges of subjects, but all taught rhetoric, the art of constructing and delivering public speeches, which was seen as the key to success in public and private life. They were professional rivals, competing for fame, wealth, and pupils. Their shared interest in rhetoric

---

19. The *Theaetetus* and *Protagoras* passages are discussed below at pp. 389–92 and 418–19, respectively.

20. The commentaries of C. Taylor on Plato's *Protagoras*, T. Irwin on the *Gorgias*, and J. McDowell on the *Theaetetus*, (Taylor [1976], Irwin [1979], McDowell [1973]) are recommended for philosophical exposition of the issues raised in those dialogues.

and related issues led them to develop philosophical theses, and their rivalry led them to challenge each other's views and formulate competing ones. Their contributions to philosophy are best understood in this light.

The Sophists were in the center of late fifth-century intellectual life. The issues they raised and discussed came to be prominent in the minds of all thoughtful people and widely known to the general public. Virtually every major author of the period makes reference to Sophistic themes, so that it narrows the ground artificially if we consider only the testimonia and fragments of the Sophists themselves. The intellectual scene, which has been called the Sophistic Movement, included in its penumbra the tragedian Euripides, the historian Thucydides, the comic poet Aristophanes, the philosophers Socrates and Plato, and the chief fifth- and fourth-century orators such as Lysias and Demosthenes, to mention only the most prominent. Nevertheless, we must turn to Protagoras and his like for the clearest idea of what a Sophist was. With a core definition in mind, we are in a position to relate others more or less closely to the heart of the movement.

Sophistic Education

Before the mid-fifth century, education in Greek city-states did not last long or go far. The normal education of a young, free Greek boy consisted of physical training, arithmetic, and "music" in the broad Greek sense of the word, which included learning how to read and write and reading and memorizing works of the great poets, especially Homer, in addition to learning how to play musical instruments. This basic education was completed by age fourteen and was typically conducted by slaves. The Sophists were free men who offered a program of higher studies for those who had completed the normal curriculum and who could pay for it. The subjects the various Sophists offered to teach included astronomy, meteorology, and other scientific subjects; questions about being and becoming; legislation, and various arts.[21] Plato makes Protagoras say that other Sophists force their students to study arithmetic, geometry, and "music," whereas he, Protagoras, teaches just what they want to know—how to succeed in public and in private life.[22] In addition, many Sophists were interested in the Greek language and in literary criticism, and it is likely that they taught these subjects too.

The range of interests found in the Sophists is as wide as can be imagined in classical Greece. Plato mocked Hippias for his expertise as a metalworker, jeweler, and weaver. Hippias, Antiphon, and Protagoras all contributed to geometry.[23] But it is useful to distinguish between an individual Sophist's interests and the subjects he was prepared to teach. Hippias, as far as we know, did not

---

21. Plato, *Sophist* 232b–e (part = DK 80B8).

22. Plato, *Protagoras* 318d–e = DK 80A5.

23. For Protagoras, see **19.22**. For Hippias and Antiphon, see below pp. 399–401.

offer weaving in his curriculum, and Protagoras's interest in geometry in no way conflicts with his boast not to require his students to study that subject and to teach them only what they want to learn.

Protagoras's boast and Gorgias's claim to teach only rhetoric stem from the competitive nature of the Sophist's profession. Each aimed to market himself so as to bring the most fame and money and attract the greatest number of students. One of their techniques was the practice of giving public displays of their brilliance, for which they charged admission.[24] In these displays they would deliver a speech on an announced topic or invite the audience either to choose from a list of topics on which they were prepared to speak or to propose any topic at all. These displays would naturally take place in public settings where the largest admission-paying crowds could be found as well as the most potential students. Accordingly, Hippias was well known at the Olympic festival and Gorgias spoke at Olympia, at the Pythian festival at Delphi, and at the theater in Athens.

Paying pupils would attend smaller classes of the kind portrayed vividly (and amusingly) in Plato's *Protagoras*.[25] Fees could be high, which makes it probable that the price was not for a single class but for a whole course. The excitement aroused by the prospect of attending such a course, associating with a famous person like Protagoras, and joining the band of his students is well brought out by Plato in his depiction of the young Hippocrates.[26]

Rhetoric and *Aretē*

For our purposes the most important subject taught by Sophists is hinted at by Protagoras in words put into his mouth by Plato.

> **19.9**   My boy, if you associate with me, the result will be that the very day you begin you will return home a better person, and the same will happen the next day too. Each day you will make constant progress toward being better.
>
> (Plato, *Protagoras* 318a = DK 80A5)

Shortly afterward, he says more specifically what he teaches each of his pupils:

> **19.10**   Good counsel concerning his personal affairs, so that he may best manage his own household, and also concerning the city's affairs, so that as far as the city's affairs go he may be most powerful in acting and in speaking.
>
> (Plato, *Protagoras* 318e–319a = DK 80A5)

---

24. At Plato, *Greater Hippias* 286a–b = DK 86a9, Hippias advertises such a performance. See also, for example, Plato, *Cratylus* 384b = DK 84A11.

25. Plato, *Protagoras* 314a–316b (not in DK).

26. Plato, *Protagoras* 310a–311a (not in DK).

In short, Protagoras taught his students how to succeed in public and private life. What he claimed to teach is, in a word, *aretē*. That this was his boast follows from the intimate connection between *agathos* and *aretē* as well as from the fact that a person with *aretē* is one who enjoys success, as measured by current standards. Anyone with the abilities Protagoras claimed to teach had the keys to a successful life in fifth-century Athens.

In fact, the key to success was rhetoric, the art of public speaking, which has a precedent in the heroic conception of *aretē*, which included excellence in counsel. But the Sophists' emphasis on rhetoric must not be understood as hearkening back to Homeric values. Clear reasons why success in life depended on the ability to speak well in public can be found in fifth-century politics and society.

The fifty-year period beginning with the end of the Persian War in 478 was the supreme moment of Athens. The city enjoyed military supremacy in the Aegean, and as leader of an alliance of Greek city-states which soon became an Athenian empire, Athens became wealthy and by far the most powerful and influential Greek *polis*. The rulers of Athens controlled the destiny of most of Greece. At this time, and particularly after 458, Athens had as its form of government a radical form of democracy. State officials and jury men were paid—an unusual practice in the ancient world—so that participation in government was possible for the poor as well as the rich. Further, most officials were not elected but appointed by lot, and it was not permitted to hold such offices repeatedly. The result of this state of affairs in which there was no continuity and no opportunity for anyone to gain much experience in ruling the state or become entrenched in office was that political power shifted away from these officials principally to the Assembly, the body of all adult male citizens, which discussed and decided issues of interest to the state. In the Assembly any member could speak on any issue, and political power came to be a matter of speaking convincingly. We see the type of speeches made there in Thucydides' *History of the Peloponnesian War*, which contains many public addresses.[27] The decisions of the Assembly, which, as Thucydides makes clear, might be based on emotion or hysteria, were the final determiners of action. Pericles, the supreme political figure in Athens from 444 to 429, owed his success largely to his personality and intelligence as manifested in his public speaking. After his death his unworthy successors were called

---

27. Since there were no transcripts of proceedings, Thucydides cannot be reporting the actual words spoken, but he gives in general a faithful picture of the subjects discussed and the styles of speaking actually used. Thucyidides' own statement of what he is doing in the speeches runs as follows: "As for the speeches delivered by the several statesmen before and during the war, it proved difficult for me to report the exact substance of what was said, whether I heard the speeches myself or learned of them from others. I have therefore made the speakers express primarily what in my own opinion was called for under the successive circumstances, at the same time keeping as close as possible to the general import of what was actually said" (Thucydides 1.22.1 [not in DK]).

"demagogues" from their ability to lead the people, typically in unwise paths, through their ability to speak effectively.

Rhetorical ability was important in the private sphere too. Athens was a litigious society, and anyone might have to appear in court, as prosecutor or as defendant. It is easy to see how success or failure in court can be regarded as essential to success or failure in one's personal life. Three features of the Athenian legal system are relevant. First, there were no lawyers. As plaintiff or defendant you spoke on your own behalf. Your speech could be written by a speech writer, but the delivery and cross-examination of witnesses were done by you. Second, there was no public prosecutor. Prosecutions were conducted by the private citizen who made the complaint. Finally, the size of juries tended to be large. The jury which condemned Socrates to drink hemlock was 501 strong. In these circumstances, pleading a case demanded rhetorical skills.

That is not to say that every kind of success depended on rhetoric. It could not make you successful in a craft like carpentry and would not on its own make you a successful military commander. Nor is it plausible that every student of Protagoras could have become another Pericles. Protagoras acknowledged that natural aptitude was required over and above diligence.

19.11   Teaching requires nature and training.

(from Protagoras DK 80B3)

19.12   Learning must begin at an early age.

(from Protagoras DK 80B3)

19.13   Art (*tekhnē*) without practice and practice without art are nothing.

(Protagoras DK 80B10)

19.14   Education is not implanted in the soul unless one reaches a greater depth.

(Protagoras DK 80B11)

Protagoras recognized that he could not make a silk purse out of a sow's ear, but he claimed to be able to develop a (sufficiently young) person's abilities to the greatest extent possible.[28]

Pericles was an effective counselor in part because he could speak well but also by dint of his personality, experience, and intelligence. To a large extent these last three factors cannot be taught, but rhetoric can be offered as a *tekhnē*, a technical art or skill which has rules of its own and which can be instilled through training and practice. In these ways rhetoric is like medicine, carpentry, and other technical arts, but it is different in its seemingly universal applicability.

---

28. See Plato, *Protagoras* 326e–328d (not in DK) for further development of this line of thought.

Debates can arise on any conceivable subject, including technical ones, and rhetorical skill can be turned to the topic at hand whatever it may be. The story goes that Gorgias used his rhetorical skill to convince medical patients to undergo surgery when physicians failed to persuade them.[29] Socrates turned the tables on the Sophists, arguing that if rhetoric has no specific subject matter, then so far from being a universal art, it should not be considered an art at all.[30] And even if we grant that rhetoric is an art that can be taught, it remains controversial whether *aretē* can be taught and in what *aretē* consists.

The Meaning of the Word "Sophist"

The English words "sophism," "sophistry" and "sophist" have negative connotations. A sophism is a fallacious piece of reasoning; sophistry is the technique of using fallacious arguments, and so forth. These English words come directly from Greek equivalents with many of the same associations. Aristotle matter-of-factly defines a sophistical argument as one that appears sound but is not, sophistry as what appears to be wisdom but is not, and Sophists as those who specialize in such arguments and as those who make money from what appears to be wisdom but is not.

In the Platonic dialogue named after him, Protagoras proclaims himself a Sophist by profession, though he admits that it is risky to make such an admission.[31] Clearly the meaning of the term altered from Protagoras's time to Aristotle's. No one went around boasting that he dealt in specious arguments and inviting people to pay him to teach them what is not real wisdom, and when Protagoras describes his profession he certainly does not do so in such terms.[32] What, then, does the word *sophistēs*, "sophist," mean?

It is based on the adjective *sophos*, used originally to describe a person skilled in a particular craft, and extended to mean generally knowledgeable or wise. The ending *-istēs* added to the stem produces a noun which means "one who exercises wisdom," that is to say, a specialist in wisdom. This word is analogous to *kitharistēs*, one who plays the kithara or lyre, an expert at the art of playing the lyre. The self-importance of anyone who called himself an expert in wisdom was probably not lost on the Greeks of the fifth and fourth centuries, who had a keen sense of the ridiculous, but the word is older than the fifth-century Sophists, and was first applied to poets, musicians, seers, and sages—those who had special knowledge and insight and the gift of communicating it to others (though as far

---

29. Plato, *Gorgias* 456b (= DK 82A22).

30. Plato, *Gorgias* 449c–458b (not in DK); *Protagoras* 311b–313a (not in DK) and 318a–319a (part = DK 80A5).

31. Plato, *Protagoras* 316c–317c (not in DK).

32. Plato, *Protagoras* 318a–319a (not in DK) and 328b = DK 80A6; *Gorgias* 449a–b (not in DK) and 459d–460a (not in DK).

as we know, no one before Protagoras called *himself* a *sophistēs*). Protagoras is not wholly off the mark when he says that "the sophistic art is ancient," going back to Homer and Hesiod,[33] although the wisdom Protagoras and his fellow Sophists claimed to teach was different from the lessons that could be learned from the earliest Greek poets.

The fifth-century figures who usurped the word and the resistance they met from upholders of traditional morality and from philosophers of the stature of Socrates and Plato are responsible for the negative associations of "sophist" and related words, which became so closely identified with Protagoras and his kind that their more general associations were mostly lost. They came to be associated with illegitimate reasoning, with arguments that appear to prove a point but are fallacious. The influence of Socrates and Plato, assisted by widespread hostility reflected in authors as diverse as the comic poet Aristophanes and the soldier and gentleman Xenophon (who compares Sophists to whores for the way they sell their wares to any buyer and amidst other salvos against them says "it is sufficient for each of them to be called a Sophist, which is an insult, at least to those who have good judgment"[34]) is responsible for the change of connotations from the honorific to the disreputable.

Hostility to the Sophists

The main charges against the Sophists are of two different sorts. First the charge of prostituting themselves. Plato emphasizes the money-making aspect of the Sophist's work, which he uses as one of his chief criteria for determining that Socrates was not a Sophist. This charge contains two elements: the Sophists teach *aretē* for money, and they teach it to anyone who pays. Both elements have aristocratic origins. Traditionally *aretē* was learned from one's family and friends and came as the result of a long process of socialization beginning in infancy. Such training and background can hardly be bought. Further, according to the aristocratic mentality most people are not of the right type, the appropriate social background, to aspire to *aretē*. Pindar expresses these thoughts in the following lines.

19.15   The wise man knows many things in his blood;
         the vulgar are taught.
         They will say anything.
         They clatter like crows against the sacred bird of Zeus.
                    (Pindar, *Olympians* 2.86–88 [not in DK], Lattimore's translation)

The second principal charge is reflected in Aristotle's definitions of the terms "sophist," etc., cited above (page 381). According to it, the Sophists are masters

---

33. Plato, *Protagoras* 316d = DK 25, 1.
34. Xenophon, *Memorabilia* 1.6.13 = DK 87A3; *On Hunting* 6.13 (not in DK).

of dishonest arguments. Their stock in trade is fallacious reasoning. They have no regard for the truth, but specialize in eristic, the practice of using any and all means, fair and foul, to win a dispute. They "make the weaker argument stronger," the catchphrase for gaining victory with a case that deserves to lose. To understand the basis for these claims we must look more closely at the rhetorical training the Sophists offered. Here the most important feature is the practice of arguing both sides of a case—pro and con.

"Antilogic"—The Method of Two Arguments

19.16   Protagoras was the first to declare that there are two mutually opposed arguments on any subject.

(Diogenes Laertius, *Lives of the Philosophers* 9.51 = DK 80A1)

In any deliberation there are conflicting considerations and an advocate aims to present one side as convincingly as possible. This is the situation in the arenas for which the Sophists prepared their pupils to compete—the courts and the Assembly. Like us, the Athenians believed that a defendant is entitled to present a case for the defense, and a good defense will be as strong as the circumstances make possible. In matters of public policy there are usually several options and reasons for and against each, and it is normally unclear which option will prove best. According to the ideas of Athenian democracy, presenting the strengths and weaknesses of each side in public debate is the best way to reach a good decision. The case is similar where the goal is to ascertain the truth rather than to gain victory for one's side. We are in the best position to recognize the truth when all views have been represented as well as possible.

We are familiar with attacks on defense attorneys for getting their clients off too lightly, and we are aware of politicians who use half-truths and faulty logic. These charges are no different from the stock accusation in fifth-century Athens that the Sophists made the weaker argument stronger.[35]

19.17   Protagoras made the weaker and stronger argument and taught his students to blame and praise the same person.

(Stephanus of Byzantium, s.v. Abdera = DK 80A21)

19.18   This is making the weaker argument stronger. And people were rightly annoyed at Protagoras's promise.

(Aristotle, *Rhetoric* 2.24 1402a24–26 = DK 80A21)

---

35. In *The Clouds* Aristophanes takes this charge one step further, staging a mock–sophistical debate between the Stronger, or Just Argument and the Weaker, or Unjust Argument, which is won, as we would expect, by the latter.

The Sophists taught their pupils the art of "antilogic": arguing as strongly as possible for both sides of a case, thus (where one side was weaker than the other) "making the weaker argument stronger." The training involved debates or mock trials in which students would gain experience in public speaking, including presenting arguments for whichever side of the case they were assigned. Closely related are the "display speeches" of Gorgias, the *Praise of Helen*, which argues that Helen of Troy should not be blamed for forsaking her husband Menelaos to sail to Troy with Paris, and the *Defense of Palamedes*, which presents a speech Palamedes might have used to defend himself against the false accusation of Odysseus that he tried to betray the Greek camp to the Trojans.[36]

An example of "antilogic" is the *Twofold Arguments*, an anonymous collection of arguments which present considerations on both sides of certain issues: Are Good and Bad the same or different?; likewise for Fair and Foul, Just and Unjust, True and False; Do wise and sane people say and do the same things as fools and the insane?; Can wisdom and virtue be taught?[37] The section on True and False exemplifies the style of arguing.

19.19   (1) Twofold arguments are also stated concerning the false and the true, of which one declares that true *logos* [speech, statement] and false *logos* are different from one another, and others that they are the same. (2) And I say the following. First, that true and false *logos* are expressed in the same words. Second, when a *logos* is spoken, if events have occurred the way the *logos* is spoken, the *logos* is true, but if they have not occurred, the same *logos* is false. (3) Suppose it accuses someone of sacrilege. If the deed took place, the *logos* is true, but if it did not take place, it is false. And the *logos* of the defendant is the same. And the courts judge the same *logos* to be both false and true. (4) Next, if we are seated one next to the other, and we [each] say "I am an initiate of the mysteries," we will all say the same thing, but only I will be true, since in fact I am <the only> one <who is>. (5) Now it is obvious that the same *logos* is false whenever falsehood is present to it and true whenever truth is, in the same way a person is the same individual as a boy and as a youth and as an adult and as an old man. (6) It is also stated that false *logos* and true *logos* are different from one another, differing in name just as they differ in fact. For if anyone asks those who say that the same *logos* is both false and true which of the two [namely, false and true] the *logos* that they are stating is, then if it is false, clearly they [the true *logos* and the false *logos*] are two [and therefore not the same]. But if it is true, this same *logos* is also false. And if anyone has ever spoken or borne witness of things that are true, it follows that these same things are false. And if he knows any man to be true, also he knows the same man to be false. (7) As a result of

---

36. Much of the *Praise of Helen* is translated in **19.20**.

37. In the last sections of this work the author argues that officials should not be appointed by lot (as was done at Athens), discusses the power of the rhetor, and gives tips for developing the memory.

the argument they say these things because if the thing occurred the *logos* is true, but if it did not then it is false. Therefore it is not their name that differs, but the fact of the matter. (8) Moreover, if anyone should ask the jurors what they are judging (since they are not present at the events), (9) these people too agree that the *logos* with which falsehood is mixed is false, and that with which truth is mixed is true. This is the entire difference.

(*Twofold Arguments* DK 90, 4)

The Power of Persuasion

Argument is for the sake of persuasion, and persuasion is the key to success in the arenas (courts and Assembly) for which Sophists trained their pupils. Peithō ("Persuasion") was a goddess, and Gorgias's display piece the *Praise of Helen* speaks of her power.

19.20 (5) I will set forth the reasons for which it was likely that Helen's voyage to Troy took place. (6) She did what she did through the will of Fate and the designs of the gods and decrees of Necessity or because she was taken by force, persuaded by words (*logoi*), or conquered by Love. . . . (8) Not even if speech (*logos*) persuaded and deceived her soul, is it hard to make a defense against this charge and free her from blame, as follows. *Logos* is a powerful master which by means of the smallest and most invisible body accomplishes most divine deeds. For it can put an end to fear, remove grief, instill joy, and increase pity. I will prove how this is so. (9) But it is to the opinion of my audience that I must prove it. I both consider and define all poetry to be speech (*logos*) with meter. Those who hear it are overcome with fearful shuddering, tearful pity, and mournful yearning, and over the good fortunes and ill-farings of other people and their affairs the soul experiences a feeling of its own, through the words (*logoi*). Come now, let me shift from one argument (*logos*) to another. (10) Inspired incantations bring on pleasure and bring away grief through words (*logoi*). For conversing with the soul's opinion the power of incantation charms, persuades, and changes it by witchcraft. Two arts of witchcraft and magic have been discovered— errors of the soul and deceptions of opinion. (11) All who have persuaded or who persuade anyone of anything do so by fashioning false *logos*. For if on all subjects everyone had memory of the past, <a conception> of the present, and foreknowledge of the future, *logos* would not be similarly similar as it is for people who, as things are, cannot easily remember the past, consider the present, or divine the future. Thus, on most matters, most people make opinion an adviser to their soul. But opinion is fallible and uncertain and involves those who make use of it in fallible and uncertain successes. (12) What, then, keeps us from supposing that Helen too, against her will, came under the influence of *logoi* just as if she had been taken by the force of mighty men? For it was possible to see how persuasion prevails, which lacks the appearance of necessity but has the same power.[38] For *logos*, which persuaded, compelled the soul, which it persuaded, both to believe what was said and to approve what was done. Therefore, the one who persuaded, since he compelled, is unjust, and the one who was persuaded, since she was compelled by *logos*, is wrongly blamed. (13) As to the fact that persuasion added to *logos* makes whatever impression it likes on the soul, one should attend first to the accounts (*logoi*) of the astronomers, who replace one opinion with another and so make things incredible and unclear seem apparent to the eyes of opinion; second, to compulsory competitions which use speeches (*logoi*) in which a single *logos* written with art (*tekhnē*) but not spoken with truth delights and persuades a large crowd; and third, to contests of philosophers' accounts (*logoi*), in which is revealed how easily the swiftness of thought makes our confidence in our opinion change. (14) The power of *logos* has the same relation (*logos*) to the order of the soul as the order of drugs has to the nature of bodies. For as different drugs expel different humors from the body, and some put an end to sickness and others to life, so some *logoi* cause grief, others joy, some fear, others render their hearers bold, and still others drug and bewitch the soul through an evil persuasion. (15) It has been stated that if she was persuaded by *logos* she did not do wrong but was unfortunate. . . . (21) By my account (*logos*) I have removed ill fame from a woman. I have stayed faithful to the rule (*nomos*) I stipulated at the beginning of my *logos*. I have attempted to put an end to the injustice of blame and the ignorance of opinion. I wanted to write the *logos* as a praise of Helen and an entertainment for myself.

(Gorgias DK 82B11)

Sections 11 and 13 contain the germs of interesting philosophical theses. Section 11 begins with the tantalizing assertion that all persuasion involves falsehood. What, then is Gorgias's view of truth? Can rhetoric never be used to convince people of the truth? It moulds people's opinion, which can be swayed because it is by nature fallible and uncertain. Gorgias implicitly contrasts opinion with knowledge, which is infallible and certain. He associates truth and falsity with the means by which we achieve knowledge and opinion. Knowledge is based on memory (in the case of things in the past), awareness (for things in the present), and foreknowledge (for things in the future). Memory, awareness. and foreknowledge must be true, whereas persuasion depends on something else—speech (*logos*), which cannot produce in us the infallible and certain state of knowledge and so is called false. Truth and falsity, then, are not attributes of beliefs or propositions which they have independently of how they are reached.

Section 13 identifies three types of occasions for persuasion. The second includes the public forums for which the Sophists prepared their pupils. The first and third include scientific and philosophical settings, which naturally

---

38. The text of this sentence is corrupt. I follow Diels's suggestions (DK vol. 2, p. 291).

include the settings at which the theories of the Presocratic philosophers were presented and debated. Rhetoric is useful on these occasions, for where the topic is obscure, rhetoric can persuade people this way or that. In the occasions mentioned, the truth is not clear; we have to do with opinion, not secure knowledge, and hence persuasion through rhetorical ability can prevail, bending the audience's opinions. In such cases the power of speech is compelling, more so than the mere truth of a particular theory. It can be used for good or evil, and those under its influence have no power to resist.

The Individual Sophists

The following five men were the most celebrated Sophists of the fifth century.

Protagoras

Born c.490 in Abdera, the birthplace of Democritus, Protagoras claimed to be the first to proclaim himself a Sophist and to charge fees for the education he offered.[39] He grew wealthy from his profession. He visited Athens at least twice[40] and probably did so frequently. He was a friend of Pericles, and doubtless through Pericles' influence he was asked to draft a constitution for Thurii, the Panhellenic city in South Italy founded in 444 under the leadership of Athens. He died c. 420 after practicing his profession over forty years.[41] There are reports that he was tried at Athens and either condemned to death or banished for his agnosticism regarding the gods and that his books were collected and burned in public.[42]

The portrait of him in Plato's *Protagoras* is, despite the touch of vanity and pride it accords him, not unflattering. (Some have found him preferable to Socrates in that dialogue.) He wrote several works, most importantly *On Truth*, known alternatively as *The Throws*, that is, arguments which will throw an opponent (the title is a term from wrestling), the *Antilogies* ("Contrary Arguments"), and *On the Gods*, which contained the following apparently agnostic assertion.

19.21   Concerning the gods I am unable to know either that they are or that they are not or what their appearance is like. For many are the things that hinder knowledge: the obscurity of the matter and the shortness of human life.

(Protagoras DK 80B4)

---

39. Plato, *Protagoras* 317b, 349a (both = DK 80A5).

40. Plato, *Protagoras* 310e (not in DK).

41. Plato, *Meno* 91e = DK 80A8.

42. Plato, (*Meno* 91e = DK80A8), however, declares that he never ceased to enjoy a good reputation.

In many ways he was the intellectual leader of the Sophistic movement. A highly successful teacher of rhetoric, he claimed to teach *aretē*, the key to success in life. In some sense he may have invented Greek grammar: he is said to have been the first to distinguish the tenses of verbs[43] and the three grammatical genders.[44] He raised objections to mathematics.

> **19.22**   It is not true that geometry studies perceptible magnitudes . . . For perceptible lines are not the kind of things the geometer talks about, since no perceptible thing is straight or curved in that way, nor is a circle tangent to a ruler at a point, but the way Protagoras used to say in refuting the geometers.
>
> (Aristotle, *Metaphysics* 3.2 997b34–998a4 DK 80B7)

> **19.23**   Protagoras says of mathematics, the subject matter is unknowable and the terminology distasteful.
>
> (Philodemus of Gadara, *On Poetry* PHerc 1676, col. 1.12–13 [not in DK])

With Protagoras is most closely associated the doctrine that there are two arguments on any subject. Moreover, his assertion "A human being is the measure of all things" (**19.24**), which was the starting point for a relativistic approach to philosophy, can serve as an emblem for the whole Sophistic movement.[45]

Protagorean Relativism

If, as Gorgias says, certainty is often unattainable and we are at the mercy of persuasion—if, that is to say, knowledge is for practical purposes unattainable and we are forced to rely on easily swayed opinions—what counts is what we believe, or are made to believe. This is the case in courts and in the Assembly. The jury did not witness the crime and bases its verdict on arguments brought by the prosecution and the defense. The Assembly does not have foreknowledge of the effects or the correctness of its decisions, but must decide what to do on the basis of arguments. In either case (and analogically in scientific and philosophical discussions) what matters is the decision. From the orator's pragmatic point of view the best case is the one for which there are the strongest arguments, which need not be the one based on truth. For what decides is a number of individual people, not the facts of the matter.

Protagoras encapsulated this view in the most famous dictum of the Sophistic era.

---

43. Diogenes Laertius, *Lives of the Philosophers* 9.52 = DK 80A1.

44. Aristotle, *Rhetoric* 1407b7–8 = DK 80A27.

45. For Protagoras's contribution to the *nomos–phusis* debate, see below pp. 418–19.

19.24 A human being is the measure of all things—of things that are, that they
are, and of things that are not, that they are not.

(Protagoras DK 80B1)

The precise translation is debated. Is the subject humans as a whole or an individual human? (The most common translation is "Man is the measure.") Is he
(are they) *a* measure or *the* measure? What is the scope of "things"? What sorts
of judgments are involved—just whether a thing exists or does not exist, or more
broadly what is and what is not true to say about it? Certainty on these matters
cannot be hoped for, and different answers lead to different philosophical interpretations. I favor the translation given, which accords with the rhetorical and
educational aspects of Protagoras's profession as follows. The individual person,
not the facts of the matter, is the practical standard for determining what is the
case. Each member of the jury or Assembly is the target of the orator's skills.
The truth may be as you say, but that is irrelevant if you cannot convince the
appropriate people.

On the basis of this pragmatic advice to aspiring public speakers, an elaborate
philosophy was developed.[46] If each person is the determiner of truth and falsity,
then any judgment any person makes is true. If I judge the wind to be hot and
you judge it to be cold, we are both correct. Moreover, in declaring that the wind
is hot I am not contradicting you, but stating something that is true too. The
wind is both hot and cold. On the basis of this kind of case, Protagoras drew the
surprising conclusion that contradiction is impossible.

19.25 IIe was the first to use in dialectic the argument of Antisthenes that attempts
to prove that contradiction is impossible.

(Diogenes Laertius 9.53 = DK 80A1)

19.26 The people in Protagoras's circle made powerful use of this argument.

(Plato, *Euthydemus* 286c2–3 = DK 80A19)

These doctrines were backed up by theories about the nature of perception
and the nature of the relation between perception and judgment. Perceptions
depend on features of the thing perceived and on features of the individual who

---

46. This section depends more on Platonic material than the rest of the chapter. Without Plato and sources familiar with Plato, we have little more than Protagoras's dicta "a
human being is the measure" and "it is impossible to contradict" (Diogenes Laertius, *Lives
of the Philosophers* 9.53 = DK 80A1), which are insufficient to reconstruct Protagoras's
views. Whether or not Protagoras actually developed these ideas as Plato and the subsequent tradition assert he did must remain obscure, but the topic is so important that it
requires treatment despite its shaky credentials.

does the perceiving and so are both objective and subjective.[47] Both the condition of the sense organ and the nature of the object affect our perceptions. If honey tastes sweet to a healthy person and bitter to a sick person, it does so because of the way it reacts with their taste organs. Likewise, if it tastes bitter to me now and sweet later, the difference will be due to a change in my taste organs. Further, judgments are based on perceptions. If our judgments about the honey's taste or the warmth or coldness of the wind differ, they do not conflict, because they are really assertions about our own private perceptions. "The wind is hot" boils down to "The wind feels hot to me, now," and this statement does not contradict your claim "The wind is cold," which boils down to "The wind feels cold to you, now." We can go one step farther: the wind is both hot and cold. While it cannot be perceived as either hot or cold in the absence of a perceiver, it has objective features which cause it to be perceived as hot by a perceiver in the appropriate condition and as cold by a perceiver in a different condition.

Perceptions are incorrigible in the sense that each of us is the unique authority about the content of his or her own perceptions. No one else can offer considerations that will force a person to perceive things differently. Since judgments are based on perceptions, they are incorrigible too. And since reality, how things are, is manifested through perception and expressed in judgments, things are as they seem to a person and no one can be a judge of how things seem, or therefore of how they are, to anyone else. Thus, truth is relative to the individual. This is the doctrine of Protagorean relativism. It is a philosophical theory that is simultaneously epistemological and ontological, that is, a theory about the nature and basis of our judgments and also about the nature of reality.

Protagorean relativism is most plausible for the type of cases considered—judgments based directly on perceptions and which express the content of those perceptions. It is also plausible for ethical judgments, since it is notoriously difficult to find objective standards of good and bad, right and wrong. In fact, certain forms of ethical relativism were current in fifth-century Greece and will be taken up in the next chapter.

Perceptual and ethical judgments apart, how plausible is relativism? If I think that $2 + 2 = 5$, does that make it true? If I think I can survive a fall from the roof of the Parthenon, does that guarantee that I will? If I think Protagorean relativism is false, does that make it false? These and related issues are taken up in Plato's brilliant treatment of Protagorean relativism in the *Theaetetus*.[48] For now, I will take up just one problem the theory raises—a problem for the Sophists themselves.

If everyone's beliefs are true, how can one belief be better than another? If Protagorean relativism assures me that my opinion on a given subject is true, what could induce me to reject it in favor of another? These questions, which suggest that persuasion and education are impossible, attack the foundations of the Sophists' program.

---

47. This view of perception was shared by the Atomists. See above p. 350.

48. Plato, *Theaetetus* 152a–172b, 177c–179c (neither passage in DK).

The beginnings of an answer are given in the following passage of the *Theaetetus*.

19.27   I do say that the truth is as I've written: each of us is the measure of the things that are and the things that are not. Nevertheless, there's an immense difference between one man and another in just this respect: the things that are and appear to one man are different from those that are and appear to another. As for wisdom or a wise man, I'm nowhere near saying there's no such thing; on the contrary, I do apply the word "wise" to precisely this sort of person: anyone who can effect a change in one of us, to whom bad things appear and are, and make good things both appear and be for him. . . . Remember the sort of thing you were saying before: to a sick man what he eats appears, and is, bitter, whereas to a healthy man it is, and appears, the opposite. Now what must be done isn't to make either of them wiser, because that isn't even possible; nor is it to accuse the sick one of being ignorant because he makes the sort of judgments he does, and call the healthy one wise because he makes judgments of a different sort. What must be done is to effect a change in one direction; because one of the two conditions is better. In education too, in the same way, a change must be effected from one of two conditions to the better one; but whereas a doctor makes the change with drugs, a Sophist does it with things he says.

It's not that anyone ever makes someone whose judgments are false come, later on, to judge what's true: after all, it isn't possible to have in one's judgments the things that are not, or anything other than what one's experiencing, which is always true. What does happen, I think, is this: when, because of a harmful condition in his mind, someone has in his judgments things that are akin to that condition, then by means of a beneficial condition one makes him have in his judgments things of that same sort—appearances which some people, because of ignorance, call true; but I call them better than the first sort, but not at all truer.

And as for the wise . . . where bodies are concerned, I say it's doctors who are the wise, and where plants are concerned, gardeners—because I claim that they, too, whenever any of their plants are sick, instill perceptions that are beneficial and healthy, and true too, into them, instead of harmful ones. My claim is, too, that wise and good politicians make beneficial things instead of harmful ones seem to their states to be just. If any sort of thing seems just and admirable to any state, then it actually is just and admirable for it as long as that state accepts it; but a wise man makes the beneficial things be and seem just and admirable to them, instead of any harmful things which used to be so for them. And according to the same principle the Sophist is wise, too, in that he can educate his pupils in that way.

(Plato, *Theaetetus* 166d–167c = DK 80A21a, tr. McDowell)

All judgments are true, but not all are equally good or beneficial. If I judge that honey tastes bitter, my judgment is true, but my sick condition in which honey tastes bitter is not as good as one in which it tastes sweet. Even in my sickness I believe it is better for me to be in a state where honey tastes sweet, so I am willing to submit to the directions of a physician who can change my condition so that honey tastes sweet to me. Likewise in public debates. Everyone has an (equally true) opinion about what is the just, good and beneficial thing to do, but not all opinions are equally good or beneficial. A statesman can induce the citizens to abandon bad and harmful opinions and adopt good and beneficial ones in their place, and instead of using medicines he uses persuasion.[49] Education too is possible since it consists in leading pupils to have good and beneficial judgments and in training them to persuade others to adopt such judgments in place of the ones they hold.

Gorgias

Also born c.490, Gorgias was from Leontini in Sicily. He is said to have lived over one hundred years. Like other Sophists he traveled and gave public performances of display pieces written for such occasions. He would speak on any subject the audience proposed. He also taught students and received handsome fees. His flowery rhetorical style caught the fancy of the Athenians when he represented Leontini on a diplomatic mission in 427, and it had some lasting influence on Greek prose even though its strong emphasis on rhyme, rhythm, alliteration, wordplay, and precisely balanced clauses was ultimately thought to be excessive.[50] Gorgias claimed to teach rhetoric, not *aretē*, and for that reason it has been claimed that he was not a Sophist.[51] Gorgias held that rhetoric can be used for both good and evil but is morally neutral in itself. It is a means, not an end, indeed a means by which its possessor can gain power and achieve whatever ends he or she adopts.[52] When the nature of the Sophistic claim to teach *aretē* is understood (above pages 378–81), Gorgias's move is seen as a way to put himself above his rivals, a strategy in positioning himself in the competitive educational market. But, as has been well said, "rhetoric was in the curriculum of every Sophist, [and] Gorgias must have put it more prominently in his shop window than any of the others."[53] Gorgias was associated with Empedocles, who also came from Sicily, and with certain Sicilian rhetoricians. He composed many speeches, also display pieces such as the surviving *Praise of Helen* and *Defense of Palamedes*, a technical treatise on rhetoric, and a remarkable work entitled *On What-Is-Not, or On Nature*, which employs reasoning of the Eleatic type to argue for theses which outdo even those of Parmenides.

---

49. **19.20** sec. 14.

50. **19.20** may give a faint idea of some of these features, which are difficult or impossible to bring out in translation.

51. Plato, *Meno* 95c = DK 82A21; *Gorgias* 449a, 459d–460a, cf. 465c (none of these passages in DK). For the claim that Gorgias was not a Sophist, see Dodds (1959: 6–7).

52. Plato, *Gorgias* 456c–457c (not in DK).

53. Guthrie (1969: 272).

GORGIAS, *ON WHAT-IS-NOT*

The Sophistic interest in rhetoric, persuasion and grammar naturally led to discussion of the relations between thought, language and reality. Before Plato the most important document is Gorgias's *On What-Is-Not, or On Nature*, two summaries of which survive. The title parodies the title standardly given to the works of the Presocratics, *On Nature*, and especially the title of Melissus's work *On Nature, or On What-Is*. In a style reminiscent of the Eleatics, particularly Gorgias's contemporary Melissus, Gorgias argues for three theses: (a) nothing is, (b) even if something is, humans cannot comprehend it, and (c) even if it is comprehensible, it cannot be expressed or communicated to another.

Gorgias's essay has aroused a great deal of controversy, first over the question whether it is meant as a serious contribution to philosophy and second (by those who answer the first question affirmatively) over the nature of its contribution.[54] My view is that Gorgias did not believe any of the theses he argues for, and that the fallacies in some of his arguments are so blatant that he must have been aware of them. These are reasons for thinking that Gorgias intends his work as a parody of a certain type of argument that was current, specifically the kind of argumentation we find in Melissus.[55]

The fact that the same sort of argument could be used to prove these obviously false propositions as was used to prove propositions which the Eleatics seem to have intended seriously casts doubt on their methods and on the conclusions that derive whatever plausibility they have from the arguments on which they are based. Parody can have devastating effects. In addition Gorgias may have had a serious purpose: perhaps to challenge the apparent invincibility of close deductive arguments, and perhaps to point to flaws in some of Parmenides' and/or Melissus's basic assumptions. Either of these achievements would have been both an important contribution to the current debate on correct philosophical method. Further, by undermining the power of one kind of reasoning Gorgias may have intended to boost the importance of rhetorical persuasion as a source of belief. Also, even if Gorgias's intent was not philosophical and even if his arguments do not convince, the work nevertheless raises important philosophical issues which

---

54. Kerferd (1982: 93–100) takes Gorgias seriously, Guthrie (1969: 192–200) less so. Curd (2006) interprets the argument for thesis (a) as proving that the very grounds that Parmenides uses to prove that what-is is also establish that what-is-not is. So "G. targets the Eleatic logical requirements for what-is: that is, for what it is to be a metaphysically basic entity. G.'s argument . . . purports to demonstrate that Parmenides' requirements are self-defeating, for they allow the reality of what-is-not just as they demonstrate the reality of what-is." In effect Parmenides' reasons for rejecting what-is-not "provide a way to undermine his assertions, and to show that . . . what-is-not has as much claim to be as what-is" (quotes from Curd [2006: 188, 193]).

55. The work is dated to the late 440s (Olympiodorus, *Commentary on Plato's* Gorgias, p. 112 = DK 82A10), which makes it contemporary with the likely date of Melissus's writings.

Plato and later philosophers took up. To this extent Gorgias's work has an important place in the history of philosophy. For this reason I present it in full.[56]

19.28   (66) He concludes as follows that nothing is: if <something> is, either what-is is or what-is-not <is>, or both what-is and what-is-not <are>. But it is the case neither that what-is is, as he will show, nor that what-is-not is, as he will justify, nor that both what-is and what-is-not are, as he will teach this too. Therefore, it is not the case that anything is. (67) And in fact, what-is-not is not. For if what-is-not is, it will be and not be at the same time. For in that it is considered as not being, it will not be, but in that it *is* not being, on the other hand, it will be. But it is completely absurd for something to be and not be at the same time. Therefore, it is not the case that what-is-not is. And differently: if what-is-not is, what-is will not be, since they are opposites, and if being is an attribute of what-is-not, not-being will be an attribute of what-is. But it is certainly not the case that what what-is is not, and so neither will what-is-not be. (68) Further, neither is it the case that what-is is. For if what-is is, it is either eternal or generated or eternal and generated at the same time. But it is neither eternal nor generated nor both, as we will show. Therefore it is not the case that what-is is. For if what-is is eternal (we must begin at this point), it does not have any beginning. (69) For everything that comes to be has some beginning, but what is eternal, being ungenerated, did not have a beginning. But if it does not have a beginning it is unlimited, and if it is unlimited it is nowhere. For if it is anywhere, that in which it is is different from it, and so what-is will no longer be unlimited, since it is enclosed in something. For what encloses is larger than what is enclosed, but nothing is larger than what is unlimited, and so what is unlimited is not anywhere. (70) Further, it is not enclosed in itself, either. For "that in which" and "that in it" will be the same, and what-is will become two, place and body (for "that in which" is place, and "that in it" is body). But this is absurd, so what-is is not in itself, either. And so, if what-is is eternal it is unlimited, but if it is unlimited it is nowhere, and if it is nowhere it is not. So if what-is is eternal, it is not at all. (71) Further, what-is cannot be generated either. For if it has come to be it did so either from a thing that is or from a thing that is not. But it has come to be neither from what-is (for if it is a thing that is, it has not come to be, but already is), nor from what-is-not (for what-is-not cannot generate anything, since what generates anything must of necessity share in existence). Therefore it is not the case that what-is is generated either. (72) In the same ways, it is not both eternal and generated at the same time. For these exclude one another, and if what-is is eternal it has not come to be, and if it has come to be it is not eternal. So if what-is is neither eternal nor generated nor both together, what-is would not be. (73) And differently, if it is, it is either one or many. But it is neither one nor many, as will be shown. Therefore it is not the

---

56. I give a translation of the version in Sextus Empiricus, *Against the Mathematicians* 7.65–86 = DK 82B3. The shorter summary in pseudo-Aristotle, *On Melissus, Xenophanes, and Gorgias*, Chs. 5–6 (not in DK), is preferable at some points.

case that what-is is. For if it is one, it is either a quantity or continuous or a magnitude or a body. But whichever of these it is, it is not one, but being a quantity, it will be divided, and if it is continuous it will be cut. Similarly if conceived as a magnitude it will not be indivisible. And if it chances to be a body, it will be three dimensional, for it will have length, width and depth. But it is absurd to say that what-is is none of these. Therefore it is not the case that what-is is one. (74) Further, it is not many. For if it is not one it is not many either. For the many is a compound of individual ones, and so since <the thesis that what-is is> one is refuted, <the thesis that what-is is> many is refuted along with it. But it is altogether clear from this that neither what-is nor what-is-not is. (75) It is easy to conclude that neither is it the case that both of them are, what-is and what-is-not. For if what-is-not is and what-is is, then what-is-not will be the same as what-is as regards being. And for this reason neither of them is. For it is agreed that what-is-not is not, and what-is has been shown to be the same as this. So it too will not be. (76) However, if what-is is the same as what-is-not, it is not possible for both to be. For if both <are>, then they are not the same, and if <they are> the same, then <it is> not <the case that> both <are>. It follows that nothing is. For if neither what-is is nor what-is-not nor both, and nothing aside from these is conceived of, nothing is.

(Gorgias DK 82B3)

It is instructive to compare the arguments in this part with those of the Eleatics, especially sections 69–70 with Melissus (**15.1, 15.2, 15.3,** and **15.6**), section 71 with Parmenides (**11.8** lines 12–13), and sections 73–74 with Zeno (**12.4**). Parmenides believed that the only possible approaches were the two alternatives which he considered: "is" and "is not," and he rejected the latter, leaving the former. Gorgias now offers refutations of both alternatives, leaving a wholly negative conclusion: Nothing is.

The second and third parts of Gorgias's essay break new ground.

19.29   (77) Next in order is to teach that even if something is, it is unknowable and inconceivable by humans. For if things that are thought of, says Gorgias, are not things-that-are, what-is is not thought of. And reasonably so. For just as if things that are thought of have the attribute of being white, being thought of would be an attribute of white things, so if things that are thought of have the attribute of not being things-that-are, not to be thought of will necessarily be an attribute of things-that-are. (78) This is why the claim that if things that are thought of are not things-that-are, then what-is is not thought of is sound and preserves the sequence of argument. But things that are thought of (for we must assume this) are not things-that-are, as we will show. Therefore it is not the case that what-is is thought of. Further, it is completely clear that things that are thought of are not things-that-are. (79) For if things that are thought of are things-that-are, all things that are thought of are—indeed, however anyone thinks of them. But this is apparently false. For if someone thinks of a person flying or chariots racing in the sea, it is not the case that forthwith a person is flying or that chariots are racing in the sea. And so, it is not the case that things that are thought of are things-that-are. (80) In addition, if things that are thought of are things-that-are, things-that-are-not will not be thought of. For opposites have opposite attributes, and what-is-not is opposite to what-is. For this reason, if being thought of is an attribute of what-is, not being thought of will assuredly be an attribute of what-is-not. But this is absurd. For Scylla and Chimaera and many things-that-are-not are thought of. Therefore it is not the case that what-is is thought of. (81) And just as things that are seen are called visible because they are seen and things that are heard are called audible because they are heard, and we do not reject visible things because they are not heard or dismiss audible things because they are not seen (for each ought to be judged by its own sense, not by another), so also things that are thought of will be, even if they may not be seen by vision or heard by hearing, because they are grasped by their own criterion. (82) So if someone thinks that chariots race in the sea, even if he does not see them, he ought to believe that there are chariots racing in the sea. But this is absurd. Therefore it is not the case that what-is is thought of and comprehended.

(Gorgias DK 82B3) (continuation of **19.28**)

Gorgias argues that there is no necessary correlation between thought and reality. It is possible to think of a human flying even though no human flies. It is possible to think of Scylla even though Scylla does not exist. Further, the first sentence of section 79 seems to establish a condition for there to be a correlation between thought and reality: if the object of thought exists, it must have the attributes with which thought invests it. If I think of a chariot racing in the sea and no chariot is racing in the sea, I am not thinking of a real chariot and attributing to it something that is not true of it. Rather, what I am thinking of—a chariot racing in the sea—does not exist. This is an interesting philosophical position which invites serious discussion, but to discuss it seriously requires a great deal of work in the fields of philosophy of language and philosophy of mind—work which was not done by Gorgias or by anyone earlier than or contemporary with him.

The same can be said about the third and final part of Gorgias's essay.

19.30 (83) But even if it should be comprehended it cannot be expressed to another. For if things-that-are are visible and audible and generally perceptible and in fact are external objects, and of these the visible are comprehended by vision and the audible by hearing and not vice versa, how can these be communicated to another? (84) For that by which we communicate is *logos*, but *logos* is not the objects, the things-that-are. Therefore it is not the case that we communicate things-that-are to our neighbors, but *logos*, which is different from the objects. So just as the visible could not become audible and vice versa, thus, since what-is is an external object, it could not become our *logos*. (85) But if were not *logos*, it would not have been revealed to another. In fact, *logos*, he says, is composed of external things, that is, perceptible things, falling upon us. For from encountering flavor there arises in us the *logos* which is expressed with reference to this quality, and from the incidence on the senses of color arises the *logos* with reference to color. But if so, it is not the *logos* that makes manifest the external <object>, but the external <object> that comes to be communicative of the *logos*. (86) Further, it is not possible to say that *logos* is an object in the way visible and audible things are, so that objects that are can be communicated by it, which is an object that is. For, he says, even if *logos* is an object, it anyway differs from all other objects, and visible bodies differ most from *logos*. For the visible is grasped by one organ, *logos* by another. Therefore it is not the case that *logos* makes manifest the great number of objects, just as they do not reveal the nature of one another.

(Gorgias DK 82B3) (continuation of **19.29**)

Gorgias raises explicitly the questions how the senses are related to their objects and how one sense is related to another. What can be seen—colors, for example—cannot be heard, and vice versa. Speech is audible and therefore cannot communicate visible things. Moreover, speech is different and of a different kind from the external things it attempts to communicate—even the audible things. Therefore, it cannot communicate them. Section 85 presents a causal theory of language. Speech arises as the result of our being affected by external sensible objects. But then it is backward to say that speech displays the object, rather it is the object that makes speech intelligible.

Again we find a host of interesting and important philosophical arguments and theses, and again there is no reason to suppose that Gorgias did any more philosophical work than we see here, no clear reason to suppose that he even thought that there was more work to be done. Not until Plato took up these and related issues in such dialogues as *Cratylus*, the *Theaetetus*, and the *Sophist*, or at least not until he posited his theory of Forms in the *Phaedo*, do we find the beginnings of the philosophical labor required to untangle them and provide a satisfactory treatment.

Prodicus

A generation younger than Protagoras and Gorgias, Prodicus was probably born c.460 and was still alive when Socrates died (399). He came from Ceos, an Aegean island near Attica. He visited Athens on embassies from Ceos, traveled widely, and like Gorgias grew wealthy from his public presentations and teaching. Plato makes Socrates say that Prodicus was his teacher,[57] in particular on the topic of the correctness of names, in which he was concerned to draw fine distinctions in the meanings of words.[58] The following examples (or parody examples) indicate his style and the range of his subject matter.

---

57. Plato, *Protagoras* 341a; *Meno* 96d (neither passage in DK); *Cratylus* 384b = DK 84A11.

58. See Plato, *Protagoras* 337a–c = DK 84A13 for an example—or parody—of this art.

19.31   When Critias had said this, Prodicus said "You are right, Critias. Those who are
present at discussions of this kind should listen to both speakers impartially but
not equally—for they are not the same thing, but it is necessary to listen to both
with impartiality, but not to respect them equally, but to respect the wiser one
more and the more ignorant one less. And, Protagoras and Socrates, I myself
think you should agree to dispute about arguments but not to quarrel about
them—for friends dispute with friends with goodwill, whereas adversaries and
enemies quarrel with one another. This is the best way for your conversation to
proceed, for this is the best way for you who are speaking to gain the esteem—
but not praise—of us who are listening—for esteem is in the hearts of the audience and is genuine, while praise is frequently only in their words, which are
false and contrary to their opinion. Further, this is how we the listeners will get
enjoyment but not pleasure—for enjoyment occurs when we learn something
or use our intelligence in thinking, while we get pleasure from eating or engag-
ing in some other pleasant bodily activity."

(Plato, *Protagoras* 337a1–c4 = DK 84A13)

19.32   In *On the Nature of Man* Prodicus named the burnt and scorched element in
the humors phlegm (from *pephlekthai* [a form of a verb meaning "burn"]),
using the word in a nonstandard way, while preserving the same understanding of the thing as others have.

(Galen, *On the Natural Faculties* 2.9.50.4–12 Kühn = DK 84B4)

Socrates also asserts that Prodicus was a teacher to whom he sent philosophically infertile people who could not benefit from his own teaching.[59] Evidently
Socrates considered Prodicus's work valuable and also easier to comprehend
than his own difficult message. A possible link is the interest in definition that
characterized both men's work. Where Socrates was interested in understanding the nature of things (for example, understanding what friendship is), Prodicus examined the meanings of words. But there is a close connection between
asking what friendship is and asking for a definition of the word "friendship."
Recognizing the importance of distinguishing the meanings of words (of near-
synonyms in particular) is basic to philosophy as well as to lexicography, and
Socrates may have thought that Prodicus could teach students things that would
be useful in case they cared to return to him for more advanced study.

   Like Protagoras Prodicus asserted that contradiction is impossible. The
grounds for his claim are different from those of Protagoras.

19.33   There is a reference to the paradoxical view of Prodicus that contradiction
is impossible. What does this mean? It goes against everyone's judgment
and opinion. For in both practical and intellectual matters we are constantly
conversing with people who contradict us. He says dogmatically that contradiction is impossible because if two people contradict one another they

---

59. Plato, *Theaetetus* 151b = DK 84A3a.

are both speaking, but they cannot both be speaking with reference to the same fact. He says that only the one who speaks the truth is reporting the fact as it is, while the person who contradicts him does not state the fact.

(Didymus the Blind, *Commentary on Ecclesiastes* [not in DK])

One of his display pieces, the *Choice of Herakles*, an exhortation to choose a life of virtue over one of vice, is summarized by Xenophon, who though a loyal admirer of Socrates also had a high regard for Prodicus.[60] Evaluations of this piece have run from the wildly enthusiastic to the opposite extreme.[61]

Prodicus was reputed to be an atheist and offered the following naturalistic account of the origin of religion.

19.34 The ancients believed that the sun and moon, rivers and springs, and in general everything that benefits our life were gods because of the benefit deriving from them.

(Sextus Empiricus, *Against the Mathematicians* 9,18 DK 84B5)

19.35 He says that the gods worshipped by men neither exist nor have knowledge, but that the ancients exalted crops and everything else that is useful for life.

(PHerc. 1428 col. 19.12–19 [not in DK])

This criticism of Greek religion is in line with the anthropological interests current in the fifth century and is found also in Protagoras's long speech in Plato's *Protagoras*.[62] Prodicus might well have been one of the most impressive figures of the fifth century, but given the paucity of evidence we can only be tantalized by the scraps of his reputation.

Hippias

Like Prodicus, Hippias was a member of the second generation of Sophists.[63] He was born in Elis, the district of the Peloponnese in which the Olympic festival took place, and he represented Elis on official missions. In an amusing passage[64] Plato portrays him vividly as a polymath whose range of learning goes well beyond the other Sophists, extending to metalwork, jewelry, shoemaking,

---

60. Summary in Xenophon, *Memorabilia* 2.1.21–34 = DK 84B2. As evidence for Xenophon's interest in Prodicus, there is the story that while a prisoner in Boeotia Xenophon obtained release on bail to attend one of Prodicus's presentations (Philostratus, *Lives of the Sophists* 12 = DK 84A1a).

61. Guthrie (1969: 277–78).

62. Plato, *Protagoras* 321c–322c = DK 80C1.

63. We cannot be more precise about his dates, except that he was still alive when Socrates was put to death in 399.

64. Plato, *Lesser Hippias* 368b–e = DK 86A12.

weaving, epic and tragic poetry, prose writing, metrics, musical theory, and orthography. To this list of subjects we may also add arithmetic, geometry, astronomy, painting, sculpture, genealogy, and history. His memory was phenomenal—he boasted that he could repeat a list of fifty names after hearing it only once—and he taught memory techniques as part of his curriculum. Like other leading Sophists he traveled widely and earned a great deal of money from his teaching and his performances. He made a name for himself by speaking at the Olympic festival on a range of prepared topics and offering to answer any question anyone might put to him. He made a significant contribution to geometry by discovering the quadratrix, a curve used to solve the problem of how to trisect any angle and which was also employed in attempts to square the circle, that is, to construct a square equal in area to a given circle. He compiled the first list of Olympic victors, which was an important contribution to chronology and historiography. (According to tradition, the Olympic festival was first held in 776 and was celebrated every four years, thus providing a way of dating events that could be used throughout Greece, for example, "the third year of the forty-seventh Olympiad.") In addition he seems to have done important work in the history of philosophy and science. He was probably the first to collect passages of poets and philosophers and group them under various headings, thus beginning the doxographical tradition continued by Aristotle and his followers. The following is his own description of this work.

> **19.36** Some of these things may have been said by Orpheus, some by Musaeus—in short, in different places by different authors—some by Hesiod, Homer, or other poets and some in prose works by Greeks or foreigners. From all of them I have collected the most important ones that are related, and I will compose out of them this original and multiform account.
>
> (Clement of Alexandria, *Stromata* 6.2.15 = DK 86B6)

Some samples of Hippias's work have survived, including the statements that Thales believed that amber possesses soul,[65] and that Mamercus, the brother of the poet Stesichorus, studied geometry.[66]

Among his prose discourses was one set after the fall of Troy, in which the young Neoptolemus asks the aged Nestor how a young man can acquire the best reputation, and Nestor responds with suitable advice for life. He also wrote a work entitled *The Names of Peoples*. For possible contributions of Hippias to the *nomos–phusis* debate, see **20.2** and **20.20**.[67]

Despite these substantial achievements, Plato presents him alone among the Sophists as a vain, pretentious, self-advertising fellow with extremely limited

---

65. See above p. 30. Diogenes Laertius cites Hippias as a source for this information.

66. Proclus, *Commentary on the First Book of Euclid's* Elements, 65.11–14 = DK 14, 6a.

67. Both passages occur in conversations with Socrates in a work by Xenophon. How closely they reflect the actual views of Hippias is impossible to say.

philosophical talent. He seems to take Hippias less seriously than other Sophists but does not present him as unscrupulous or immoral. One is left with the suspicion that for all his success and erudition, he did not pose as much of a threat to Socrates and Plato as other Sophists did.

Antiphon

If, as I suppose, Antiphon the Sophist is identical with Antiphon of Rhamnous, the Athenian orator and politician,[68] he was born c.480 and executed in 411 for taking part in the oligarchic regime known as the Four Hundred. We possess several of his speeches, including the *Tetralogies*, oratorical exercises consisting of groups of four speeches—opening and closing speeches for the prosecution and for the defense on fictitious charges of murder. These speeches are samples of the Sophistic rhetorical instructional technique known as antilogic. Antiphon is not mentioned by Plato. As an Athenian (Rhamnous is a village in Attica), Antiphon is unlike the other Sophists treated here, since he could—and did— have a political career in Athens. He resembles the "Presocratic" philosophers in that he had theories (some of them primitive in comparison with other contemporary views) on astronomical, meteorological, medical, and biological subjects and on the origin of the present state of the *kosmos*. Some of his fragments on these subjects are ascribed to a work entitled *On Truth*. This work of Antiphon's probably contained his attempt to square the circle, which Aristotle criticized for being based on principles inappropriate to geometry.[69] If we believe Xenophon, Antiphon scorned Socrates for not charging fees and for not taking part in political life and attempted to show him up in front of his followers in order to win them away from him.[70]

For our purposes Antiphon's most important fragments, also from *On Truth*, are his contribution to the *nomos–phusis* debate.[71] In addition, there was a moral (or moralizing) work *On Concord* to which numerous fragments, some of them deeply pessimistic, are ascribed. Antiphon was interested in practical psychology; there is a story that he set up a kind of clinic in Corinth where he "advertised that he could treat the distressed by means of words (or, "speeches": *logoi*), and inquiring the reasons <for their distress> he would address the afflicted with soothing words."[72]

---

68. Their identity is disputed. For arguments against, see Guthrie (1969: 285–86 and 292–94). For arguments for, see Kerferd (1982: 49–50), with references.

69. Aristotle, *Physics* 1.2 185a14–17 = DK 87B13; *Sophistical Refutations* 11 172a7 (not in DK).

70. Xenophon, *Memorabilia* 1.6 (not in DK).

71. See below pp. 408–11.

72. Pseudo-Plutarch, *Lives of the Ten Orators*, p. 833C–D = DK 87A6.

Were the Sophists Philosophers?

I end this chapter with a topic many have thought important. From the fifth century the Sophists have often been considered intellectual charlatans, purveyors of faulty reasoning and out to gain victory rather than reach the truth. In these ways they fare badly against philosophers, whose selfless search for truth transcends all other concerns. Plato, for whom the type of the philosopher was Socrates, sharply contrasts Socrates' manner and methods with those of the Sophists. Socrates claimed to know nothing, to have no positive doctrine to impart, whereas the Sophists claimed to be experts on everything and taught their knowledge to others. They grew rich from their profession, while Socrates, who did not offer formal instruction and did not charge people fees for associating with him, remained poor. Their claim to teach *aretē* was suspect and based on a superficial and ill-thought-out conception of human good. Their methods were dishonest in emphasizing rhetorical tricks over real knowledge. Their technique of arguing both sides of an issue was no more likely to lead to a concern for the truth than their emphasis on swaying crowds rather than convincing thoughtful individuals.[73] On this account the Sophists are the antithesis of philosophers, and the opprobrium cast by Plato remains to this day.

Looked at more broadly, however, Socrates can be seen as a Sophist, or as a product of the Sophistic movement. True, he did not take fees for teaching, but this aspect of the matter, which Plato stresses heavily, has no importance for our assessment of the intellectual relations between Socrates and the Sophists. In fact, these relations are very close. Socrates as well as the Sophists dealt in *logoi*—arguments and reasoning. If Socrates reacted against certain Sophistic doctrines, so did the Sophists themselves. There is little uniformity in their views and frequently they took up opposing positions on a single issue.[74]

Socrates challenged the Sophists on basic issues. What is *aretē*? Can it be taught? What constitutes a good or successful life for a person? Do the Sophists, or any other humans for that matter, really have the knowledge and wisdom they claim to have? It is important to recognize that these questions were central ones not only in Socrates' thought but in the Sophists' as well, and that the Sophists were Socrates' most important precursors, contemporaries, and opponents on these topics. Without the Sophists these issues would not have had the same importance for Socrates or even the same meaning. Moreover, by using *logoi* to refute the Sophists Socrates followed Sophistic practice. He excelled in arguments and developed his own methods of reasoning and techniques of argument (the "Socratic method"). In doing so he was outdoing the Sophists at their own game and inventing new moves in it, but he was still playing the same game.[75]

---

73. Plato, *Gorgias* 458e–459b (not in DK).

74. Most notably in the *nomos–phusis* debate, discussed in Ch. 20.

75. It has even been held that the method of questions and short answers that is so characteristic of Socrates was widely used by the Sophists. See Kerferd (1982: 32–34).

If Socrates' tools and methods, as well as the issues he addressed fall within the range of the Sophists, perhaps he can be distinguished from them by his intentions. Socrates' goal was to improve the souls of those who conversed with him, whereas the Sophists showed people how to gain reputation, power, and wealth. Even here, though, the differences are not as great as they may appear. For Socrates, improving the soul is the most important thing anyone can do.[76] Success in this arena constitutes success in life. The Sophists for their part also held that the ends they promoted made for success in life. The difference comes down to one of criteria for success, but the overall goal, "living well," is the same.

Another possible way to separate Socrates from the Sophists is to say that Socrates aimed for the truth while the Sophists aimed for victory in argument. In that they taught rhetoric, it is true that they aimed to train effective, that is, successful and victorious, speakers. The same can be said of the Sophists' own speeches. But how are we to treat the Sophists' contributions to the *nomos–phusis* debate and other philosophical topics? By now it should be clear that we would be naive simply to follow Plato and declare that the Sophists were not philosophers because they taught for pay, etc. Plato's testimony is suspect because it is self-serving. Plato was out to dissociate Socrates from the Sophists but the ways he did so fall short of proving that they were not philosophers.

Another approach to this issue starts from the position that the Sophists were primarily educators. Since they taught rhetoric, their interest in the nature of language is predictable. Since they taught how to win in debate, they might be expected to work out a pragmatic, relativistic conception of knowledge and truth. Since they were concerned with legislation and political power, it is unsurprising if they formulated views on the nature of political power and its relation to law and custom. All these are appropriate themes for display speeches. Moreover, since the Sophists were rivals, they would be quick to learn one another's views on these matters, formulate objections to them, and devise new, superior theories—the better to attract audiences and pupils. Let us suppose that their primary intention in doing this philosophical work was to advance their own standing as Sophists, to increase their wealth, fame, and importance. Is this sufficient reason to refuse to call them philosophers?

Before answering this question let us take another tack. The material presented in this chapter and the next shows that the Sophists raised important issues in a number of fields of philosophy and in some cases gave those issues philosophically interesting treatment. There are grounds, therefore, for asserting that the Sophists did some philosophy. If doing philosophy qualifies a person as a philosopher, then at least some Sophists were philosophers.

This answer may be all that is required. On the other hand, those who feel that philosophers must be aiming at the truth in the philosophical matters they take up, or at least that they must care in a certain way about the arguments and theses they construct and champion may still have reservations about calling the Sophists

---

76. Plato, *Apology* 30a–b (not in DK).

philosophers. Gorgias's *Praise of Helen*, which contains interesting philosophical ideas about truth and falsity, knowledge and opinion, speech and persuasion, was composed as a kind of entertainment (**19.20** section 21). Part of the intention of the work is to demonstrate the power of *logos* (a self-serving thesis for a teacher of rhetoric), and the philosophically interesting material may be subordinate to this end. For all we know, Gorgias wrote *On What-Is-Not, or On Nature* in the same spirit. It is likewise possible that Protagoras did not really believe that a human being is the measure of all things but simply articulated that view and perhaps expanded it into a whole relativistic philosophy in order to dignify his profession and attract students. It is even possible that the Sophists who contributed to the *nomos–phusis* debate were simply staking out positions which they could use to show off their brilliance and from which they could assault the stances adopted by their rivals. It is thus possible that the Sophists were no more concerned with the truth of the philosophical positions they adopted or the soundness of the arguments they advanced than modern public relations firms need to be about the claims they make for the products they promote. And this consideration may give us qualms about designating the Sophists as philosophers.

But for all we know, they may have cared passionately for the views they expressed. If the fact that someone does philosophical work is not sufficient grounds for calling that person a philosopher and we need to know his or her attitudes and intentions as well, we must admit that we are not in a position to judge. In this matter as in many others concerning the Sophists of the fifth century, opinions will continue to vary.

20

The *Nomos–Phusis* Debate

In Greece and especially in Athens, the second half of the fifth century was a period of unmatched intellectual liveliness. A profusion of ideas were floated, discussed and fought over by such distinguished figures as the tragic poets Sophocles and Euripides, the comic poet Aristophanes, the historians Herodotus and Thucydides, numerous orators, the later Presocratics (above all, Democritus), the Sophists, and, of course, Socrates and his associates. The fact that in most cases these ideas were presented in public settings, from the theater, Assembly, and law courts to the great festival of Olympia, proves that the general public was exposed to and presumably understood and entered into the debate. The surviving writings give a vivid picture of the intellectual scene—the issues, the manners of treatment, and the range of solutions that were in the air.

One topic in particular was discussed frequently and in a variety of contexts: the contrasting concepts *nomos* (plural, *nomoi*), which can be translated "law," "custom," and "convention," and *phusis*, "nature" and the ways of interpreting the contrast between them. These concepts themselves are interesting and complex in their own right, but more importantly, they were thought to be the keys to understanding a wide range of issues that stemmed from sources as varied as the Presocratic philosophical tradition and the practical politics of running an empire. These issues include the following: Do gods exist in nature or only by custom? Does human society exist as a result of human nature or of convention? Is morality natural or only a product of custom? Are the optimal political arrangements for a state determined by the facts of human nature alone, or should laws be introduced to provide a control on nature? Am I better off to follow the dictates of *nomos* or those of *phusis*?

There is a large and diverse body of source materials from fifth- and fourth-century writers on what is known as the *nomos–phusis* debate, some found in the philosophical writings of the Sophists, some in the works of Plato and Aristotle, and some in dramatic, historical, and political writings of the period. The present chapter will present some of this material in order to display a number of the ways in which the terms of the debate were conceived and to show both how certain issues were conceptualized and discussed in terms of these notions and how thoroughly the debate penetrated Greek intellectual life. Three passages from Plato are summarized and discussed but not translated since they are comparatively long and readily available. I have drawn materials from authors as late as Aristotle in order to make the selection as representative and useful as possible. This purpose conflicts with the title of this book, but excluding all fourth-century material would leave the picture awkwardly incomplete. Constraints of space require the passages to speak for themselves more than elsewhere in this book, but since they speak loud and clear this should not prove a serious disadvantage.

The Terms of the Debate

Nomos

There is no single English equivalent for *nomos*. It is related to the verb *nomizō* ("think," "believe," "practice") and originally meant what people (or a people) believe or practice—their customs, which, especially in early times, had the force of laws. Indeed, before the existence of written law codes, a distinction between custom and law would have been hard to draw. *Nomos* has prescriptive force: it is not simply what is believed, but what is believed to be right, not just the ways of life a people practices, but what it practices as the right way of life. The word was extended to cover laws formally enacted and enforced by the state. In this usage it retains its prescriptive force: people are under an obligation to obey the laws.

A passage from Herodotus's *Histories* illustrates some of the ways the Greeks regarded *nomos*.

> 20.1   If all humans were told to select the best *nomoi* from all that are, each people
>   would upon consideration choose its own. . . . There is a vast amount of
>   evidence for this fact, including the following. When Darius was king of the
>   Persian Empire he summoned the Greeks who were at his court and asked
>   how much money it would take for them to eat the corpses of their fathers.
>   They responded that they would not do it for any price. Afterward Darius
>   summoned some Indians called Kallatiai, who do eat their parents, and
>   asked in the presence of the Greeks, who understood through interpreters,
>   for what price they would agree to cremate their dead fathers. They cried
>   out loudly and told him to keep still. That is what people's customs are and
>   I think Pindar was right when he wrote that *nomos* is king of all.
>
>   (Herodotus, *Histories* 3.38 [not in DK])

This passage shows the prescriptive force of *nomos* as well as another feature frequently associated with *nomos*—variability. It was well known that *nomos*, in the sense of custom or customary beliefs or practices, differs among different peoples. Herodotus proves that the strange ways of foreign folk were a fascinating topic for the Greeks, since much of his popular *Histories* is given over to ethnographic accounts of Persians, Egyptians, Scythians, and other peoples. An earlier reference to this topic is found in Xenophanes' brief mention of how different peoples conceive of their gods (**7.6**). Moreover, *nomos* in the sense of the positive written law of a state was known to all Athenians to be the product of human contrivance and capable of being created, abolished or changed by the Assembly. Thus, even for a single people *nomos* was different at different times, as the following statement of the Sophist Hippias recognizes.

> 20.2   How can anyone suppose that laws are a serious matter or believe in them,
>   since it often happens that the very people who make them repeal them and
>   substitute and pass others in their place?
>
>   (Xenophon, *Memorabilia* 4.4.14 [not in DK])

Phusis

Phusis, standardly translated "nature," has several philosophical usages. Some of these have been brought out in connection with the Presocratic philosophers, the conventional name for whose writings was *Peri Phuseos* (*On Nature*). Of primary concern here is the sense of the basic nature of an individual or type of thing, in contrast to its acquired characteristics. In this way a thing's *phusis* is its permanent or essential characteristics, or how it would be if it were not interfered with. A second relevant use is found in the phrase "by nature," which comes close to "in reality" or "as things really or fundamentally (perhaps despite appearances) are."

The Antithesis between *Nomos* and *Phusis*

The contrast between *nomos* as variable, impermanent, and artificial and *phusis* as necessary, universal, and permanent was a commonplace. In arguing for his thesis that "by nature all people, foreigners and Greeks alike, are naturally similar in all respects," Antiphon offers as evidence "things that are by nature (*phusis*) necessary to all humans," such as breathing through the mouth and nostrils, laughing when happy and crying when sad, hearing with our ears, seeing with our eyes, working with our hands and walking with our feet.[1] In the same vein, Aristophanes refers to love (and adultery!) as necessities of nature.[2] Things that are "by nature" are necessary; also *phusis*, in the sense of the nature of something, implies that some features of that thing are necessary, those it has by virtue of being the type of thing it is. For example, Socrates has some features by virtue of being a human. Being a human, he has human nature, the nature of a human being. As a result, he has characteristics, for example, breathing through the mouth and nostrils, which he shares with all other humans. These features are universal and permanent—they belong to all humans whenever and wherever they may live.

The nature of the contrast between *nomos* and *phusis* can be construed variously. It is related to the contrast between the prescriptive (how things ought to be) and the descriptive (how things are), though it is not the same, since some attributed a prescriptive dimension to *phusis* as well as to *nomos* (if things are such and such by nature, that is how they ought to be). Among other aspects of the *nomos–phusis* antithesis is the contrast between appearance (how things seem to someone) and reality (how things are in fact). Another is the opposition between the artificial or man-made and the natural. Yet another is that between the contingent or accidental, and the necessary.

In addition, the interplay of *nomos* and *phusis* was conceived in different ways. Some saw them as hostile to one another, each prescribing situations and behavior the other proscribes. Others saw them as complementing one another, *phusis* providing a range of options and *nomos* determining which of these to adopt.

---

1. Antiphon DK 87B44 B.
2. Aristophanes, *The Clouds* lines 1075–76 (not in DK).

Still others claimed that *nomos* is based on *phusis*, thus employing the terms of the debate while undermining the dichotomy between them. We even find the phrase "*nomos* of *phusis*"—"law of nature" in the sense of "what nature prescribes" as opposed to the *nomos* which humans establish.[3]

Finally, different writers expressed different evaluations and preferences. Some held it best to follow *nomos* because it permits us to live in civilized society; without *nomos* we would be reduced to a state of nature where life is, in the memorable words of the 17th-century philosopher Thomas Hobbes, solitary, poor, nasty, brutish, and short. Others saw *nomos* as a conspiracy of the weaker to defeat the naturally stronger, who have a natural right to rule and do what they wish. A superior person should follow the dictates of *phusis* rather than those of *nomos*. Again, the view was expressed that we should follow *nomos* when others are looking and *phusis* when they are not. And some "realists" believed that as *phusis* is necessary and inevitable, considerations of *nomos* are simply irrelevant. The rest of the chapter will show how the *nomos–phusis* debate was explored and exploited in the fifth and fourth centuries.

Champions of *Phusis*

Antiphon

"Most of the things that are just according to *nomos* are established in a way which is hostile to *phusis*." This statement, which is emblematic of much of the *nomos–phusis* debate, occurs in the middle of a long fragment of Antiphon which brings out the contrast between *nomos* and *phusis* in several ways as he subverts the *nomoi* of a state, arguing that it is most advantageous to follow the prescriptions of *phusis* whenever we can get away with it.

20.3   (1) Justice is a matter of not transgressing what the *nomoi* prescribe in whatever city one is a citizen. A person would make most advantage of justice for himself if he treated the *nomoi* as important in the presence of witnesses and treated the decrees of *phusis* as important when alone and with no witnesses present. For the decrees of *nomoi* are extra additions, those of *phusis* are necessary; those of the *nomoi* are the products of agreement, not of natural growth, whereas those of *phusis* are the products of natural growth, not of agreement. (2) If those who made the agreement do not notice a person transgressing the prescriptions of *nomoi*, he is free from both disgrace and penalty but not so if they do notice him. But if, contrary to possibility, anyone violates any of the things which are innate by *phusis*, the harm is no less if no one notices and no greater if all observe. For he does not suffer harm as a result of opinion but as a result of truth.

This is the entire purpose of considering these matters—that most of the things that are just according to *nomos* are established in a way that is hostile

---

3. Plato, *Gorgias* 483e (not in DK).

to *phusis*. For *nomoi* have been established for the eyes as to what they must (3) see and what they must not, and for the ears as to what they must hear and what they must not, and for the tongue as to what it must say and what it must not, and for the hands as to what they must do and what they must not, and for the feet as to where they must go and where they must not, and for the mind as to what it must desire and what it must not. Now the things from which the *nomoi* deter humans are no more in accord with or suited to *phusis* than the things which they promote.

Living and dying are matters of *phusis*, and living results for them from what is advantageous, dying from what is not advantageous. (4) But the advantages which are established by the *nomoi* are bonds on *phusis*, and those established by *phusis* are free.

And so things that cause pain, at least when thought of correctly, do not help *phusis* more than things that give pleasure. Therefore it will not be painful things that are advantageous rather than pleasant things. For things that are truly advantageous must not cause harm but benefit. Now the things that are advantageous by *phusis* are among these . . . .

<But according to *nomos*, those are correct> who defend themselves after suffering (5) and are not first to do wrong, and those who do good to parents who are bad to them, and who permit others to accuse them on oath but do not themselves accuse on oath. You will find many of these cases hostile to *phusis*. They permit people to suffer more pain when less is possible and to have less pleasure when more is possible and to receive injury when it is not necessary.

(Antiphon DK 87A44 A, col. 1, 6–col. 5, 24)

Though Antiphon stops short of advocating that we all replace *nomos* with *phusis* as a standard for behavior, he maintains from a variety of viewpoints that *nomos* and what *nomos* prescribes are opposed to *phusis* and what is advantageous according to it, and he asserts that what is advantageous by *phusis* is beneficial and hence truly advantageous. The decrees of *nomos* are extra additions—products of agreement, not natural growth; those of *phusis* are necessary and products of natural growth, not agreement. Anyone who violates *nomos* will be punished only if caught, whereas anyone who violated *phusis* (which is impossible) would suffer equally whether observed or not. *Nomos* is associated with (mere) belief or opinion; *phusis* with truth or reality. Toward the end of the passage Antiphon contrasts things that are naturally advantageous with those that are advantageous by *nomos* and suggests that things that give pleasure and joy are naturally advantageous and those that cause pain and grief are naturally disadvantageous, whereas what is advantageous by *nomos* is at least as likely to cause pain as pleasure.

The passage requires some interpretation. First, a word about the nature of the necessity of *phusis*. We are told both that it is impossible to violate the decrees of *phusis* and that if we did we would suffer harm. Then *nomos* is said to make dictates contrary to *phusis*. Finally, pleasure and pain seem to be criteria respectively of what is in accordance with and what is contrary to *phusis*. When Antiphon asserts that the dictates of *phusis* cannot be violated, it may seem that he is thinking of laws of nature, like the law of gravity. If this were so, it is hard to see what role *nomos* could play. No society has as its custom or law that people must break the law of gravity!

We get further if we start from the end of the passage. There are naturally advantageous things, like life, and naturally disadvantageous things, like death. *Phusis* tells us to pursue the former and avoid the latter. If we violate these decrees of *phusis* the results will be bad for us, since we will have fewer advantageous and more disadvantageous things. Pleasure and pain are natural indicators of the advantageous and disadvantageous. Therefore *phusis* calls for a hedonistic approach to life. *Nomos*, on the other hand, is frequently contrary to *phusis*. It decrees that we shall not always (or even usually) pursue our own pleasure and avoid pain. Therefore, if we obey the dictates of *nomos* rather than those of *phusis* we are inhibited from pursuing our real advantage and will experience less pleasure and/or more pain than necessary. Violating *phusis* therefore brings its own penalties in the form of less pleasure or more pain. *Nomos*, however, works differently. Since it is artificial, penalties for transgressing its decrees do not follow inevitably. You must be caught and convicted first. Hence the cynical remark at the beginning of the fragment. Even so, if justice according to *nomos* were rendered effectively, it might still be worth one's while to obey *nomos*. The penalties for transgressing the dictates of *nomos* are typically painful. Therefore, if *nomos* were enforced perfectly, going against it could be made to bring a greater amount of pain (or a lesser amount of pleasure) than would come from following the dictates of *phusis*. That is, *nomos* could exploit the naturally advantageous and disadvantageous to the point where people would maximize their natural advantage and minimize their natural disadvantage by following *nomos*. Antiphon's reply to this thought is contained in the following passage from the same fragment.

20.4   Now if some assistance came from the *nomoi* for those who submitted to these conditions and some damage to those who do not submit but resist, (6) obedience to the *nomoi* would not be unhelpful. But as things are, it is obvious that the justice that stems from *nomos* is insufficient to aid those who submit. In the first place, it permits the one who suffers to suffer and the wrongdoer to do wrong, and it was not at the time of the wrongdoing able to prevent either the sufferer from suffering or the wrongdoer from doing wrong. And when the case is brought to trial for punishment, there is no special advantage for the one who has suffered over the wrongdoer. For he must persuade the jury that he suffered and that he is able to exact the penalty. And it is open to the wrongdoer to deny it. . . . (7) However convincing the accusation is on behalf of the accuser, the defense can be just as convincing. For victory comes through speech.[4]

(Antiphon DK 87A44 A, col. 5, 25–col. 7, 15)
(continuation of **20.3**)

---

4. The last part of the text is uncertain.

Nomos does not prevent harm from being done but only comes into play after the fact. Even then it is no guarantee. When a case comes to court, the victim has no particular advantage over the wrongdoer, since what wins the case is not truth but persuasion.[5]

Antiphon is possibly the earliest advocate of hedonism in Greek philosophy.[6] He distinguishes what is advantageous according to *phusis* from what is so according to *nomos*, says that what is truly (that is, presumably, according to *phusis*) advantageous is beneficial, not harmful, and seems to identify things that give joy and are pleasant with that is advantageous according to *phusis* and things that cause distress and are painful with what causes harm and is therefore, presumably, disadvantageous according to *phusis*. Things that result in death are disadvantageous and things that result in living are advantageous.

This position is not well worked out, and Antiphon's remarks raise many questions and seem open to several serious objections. However, his treatment contains features that are important in the history of moral philosophy. The move to ground the concept of advantage in *phusis* amounts to an attempt to provide a naturalistic basis for ethics, and the identification of life and death as standards for judging advantage and disadvantage has the effect of offering objective criteria for ethical judgments.

Callicles

A more satisfactory development of these ideas is found in Socrates' encounter with Callicles in Plato's *Gorgias*. In a memorable speech (482c–484c), of which the following is a summary, Callicles maintains that some are superior by *phusis*, hence better people, and that they can and should use their superiority for their own selfish advantage.

Phusis and *nomos* are in most things opposed to one another. By *phusis* everything that is worse is more shameful, but by *nomos* this is not so. By *phusis* it is both worse and more shameful to suffer injustice than to commit it, and both better and less shameful to commit injustice than to suffer it, whereas by *nomos* it is worse to suffer injustice but more shameful to commit it. Justice and injustice here are understood as characterizing respectively what is prescribed and what is forbidden by *nomos*. What *phusis* prescribes and forbids is quite different. In fact, *nomos* is a conspiracy of the weak against the strong. The majority of people are weak. They realize that they would be unable to resist the strong if everyone were free to pursue his or her own advantage, since the stronger would get a larger share. Hence the weak majority establish *nomoi* which declare it unjust and shameful to have a larger share. They are willing to settle for equal shares for

---

5. At this point we almost expect an advertisement for Antiphon's skills as a speech writer and Sophist. See above p. 401.

6. Unless Democritus's fragments were written earlier. See above pp. 337–38.

all, for they see that in this way they will have more than they would if the strong were allowed to pursue their own advantage. What *nomos* declares to be just and unjust is to the advantage of the weak and to the disadvantage of the strong, but by *phusis* it is just for everyone to be able to pursue his or her own advantage and consequently for the strong to have more than the weak. This is the *nomos* of *phusis*. A truly strong person will see through the sham of *nomos*, will succeed in pursuing his own natural advantage, and will become master.

Callicles subsequently explains his view more fully (488b–492c). If you are superior by *phusis*, you are better, wiser, braver and more powerful. *Phusis* calls for you to be free to pursue and enjoy your natural advantage and gratify your desires without restraint. You will not be restrained by other people or by *nomos*, or by your desires either. The successful life, the life of *aretē* and happiness, is a life spent in the unhindered satisfaction of one's desires.

Callicles' challenge to conventional *nomos*-based morality is powerful and thoroughgoing. It provoked some of Plato's most profound moral thinking (in the *Republic* as well as the *Gorgias*). For our purposes, its importance is its conception of the advantages of *phusis* and its way of seeing *nomos* as a deliberate subversion of *phusis*. All people are by nature egoists; all pursue their own advantage—even the weak pursue theirs in establishing *nomos*, since they believe that they will fare better under the restraints imposed by *nomos* than under the freedom permitted by *phusis*. The primary command of *phusis* is to pursue your own advantage by satisfying your desires. It is good to satisfy your desires, and a person who is able to satisfy them is better than one who is not. Thus Callicles' position is not merely a descriptive account of human nature and behavior but a normative account of the way people ought to behave.

Political power is also relevant, though as the discussion in the *Gorgias* goes, it is left unclear whether it is a means to the satisfaction of one's desires or is itself the object of desire. Nevertheless, the connection between desires and advantage is an important addition to the position of Antiphon and one which makes hedonism more plausible (though the egoistic view I have attributed to him does not necessarily point toward hedonism). In fact, Callicles goes on to make this connection (495a), though under pressure from Socrates he withdraws from his doctrine of extreme hedonism (499b).

Thrasymachus

Callicles is mainly concerned with contrasting what is just by *phusis* with what is just by *nomos*, to the advantage of the former. In the first book of Plato's *Republic*, Thrasymachus offers a position that is superficially similar: justice is the advantage of the stronger (338c). He illustrates this thesis by saying that the ruling (that is, stronger) power in any city enacts laws to its own advantage (338d–339a). This assertion is apparently intended as a descriptive claim about how things actually are in the world, but when Socrates points out that rulers are fallible and sometimes make mistakes about their own interest, so that following the laws does not promote the ruler's advantage (339b–e), Thrasymachus says that a "true ruler" would never make such a mistake (340d–e). This implies that regardless of what the laws actually command, justice consists in promoting the advantage of the rulers.

In developing this position Thrasymachus later asserts that justice consists in pursuing other people's good (343c) and injustice in pursuing your own advantage (344c). Injustice is more advantageous than justice (344a). And he caps his position by placing injustice under the heading of virtue and wisdom and regarding it as honorable and strong (348e–349a).

Thrasymachus turns conventional morality on its head. The ultimate standard, as with Callicles, is one's own advantage. Both maintain the normative claim that we should pursue our advantage. But Thrasymachus differs from Callicles on a crucial matter. For Callicles, pursuing your advantage is natural justice, whereas for Thrasymachus pursuing your advantage is always unjust. So whereas Callicles recommends being just while at the same time substituting one notion of justice for another, Thrasymachus holds that there is only one notion of justice but also that justice is to be avoided, not pursued. Another difference between Thrasymachus and Callicles is that Thrasymachus drops Callicles' interpretation of one's advantage as the unrestrained fulfillment of one's desires. Thrasymachus's position is thus more general than Callicles' and it cannot be refuted just by attacking hedonism. It raises sharply the question why anyone should be just rather than unjust, that is, why we should act to the advantage of others rather than to our own. More generally, it challenges us to consider why we should care about anyone else and whether we have any social responsibilities and obligations. Moreover, since it is put generally in terms of our interests or advantage, it calls for an answer to the question what our interests and advantage really are—since like Thrasymachus's fallible rulers we too may make mistakes in thinking that something is to our advantage. In addition, analogous questions arise in the political sphere. What are the responsibilities of rulers to subjects and vice versa, and what are the corresponding rights? Also, what are appropriate standards for the relations among different states? Is it right for the stronger to prevail, as Thrasymachus asserts actually happens (343d–344c)? Or are there other considerations as well, deriving either from the nature of the state or from the rights and advantages of the individuals who compose it? Plato takes up these questions in a serious way in the remainder of the *Republic* and they have remained central topics ever since in social, moral and political philosophy.

Antiphon, Callicles, and Thrasymachus mount an impressive attack against justice and against the prescriptions of *nomos* in general. The attack is based on the claim that *phusis* calls for each of us to pursue our own interests and advantage; and where *nomos* conflicts with *phusis* (which is usually the case) and so tells us to act against our own interests and to our disadvantage, we should follow *phusis* rather than *nomos* whenever we can get away without being observed

(Antiphon), or if we are sufficiently clever to see through the sham of *nomos* and sufficiently strong to have our own way (Callicles), or if we are sensible and pursue *aretē* and happiness (Thrasymachus).

Thucydides

This way of looking at things was not confined to philosophical discussion but played an important part in the practical politics of the late fifth century, where it was used to justify imperialism and brutality. In two notable passages of his *History of the Peloponnesian War*, Thucydides presents debates in which considerations of strength and advantage are used to the exclusion of justice, mercy, and forgiveness. The first takes place in the Athenian Assembly. In 428 Mitylene, a city-state subject to Athens, had revolted along with most of the island of Lesbos. The Athenian army had put down the revolt, and the Assembly had passed a decree that the adult males of the defeated city should be put to death and the women and children enslaved. The next day there was a change of heart, so the Assembly was summoned to discuss the matter again. In the debate, which concluded with a decision to rescind the brutal decree of the previous day, Cleon spoke in favor of carrying out the decree.

> 20.5   You do not see that your empire is a tyranny, and that you have unwilling subjects who are continually plotting against you. They obey you not because of any good turns you might do them to your own detriment, and not because of any good will they might have, but only because you exceed them in strength. . . . In sum I say only this: if you follow my advice, you will do justice to the Mytileneans and promote your own interests at the same time. But if you see the matter differently, you will not win their favor; instead, you will be condemning yourselves: if they were right to rebel, you ought not to have been their rulers. But then suppose your empire is not justified: if you resolve to hold it anyway, then you must give these people an unreasonable punishment for the benefit of the empire, or else stop having an empire so that you can give charity without taking any risks.
>
> (Thucydides 3.37.2, 40.4 [not in DK], Woodruff's translation)

In his reply, Diodotus, who spoke for the opposite side, showed no more concern for mercy and justice than Cleon, thus indicating that political advantage was indeed foremost in the Athenians' minds.

> 20.6   Our dispute, if we are sensible, will concern not their injustice to us, but our judgment as to what is best for us. Even if I proved them guilty of terrible injustice, I still would not advise the death penalty for this, unless that was to our advantage. Even if they deserved to be pardoned, I would not have you pardon them if it did not turn out to be good for the city. In my opinion, what we are discussing concerns the future more than the present. And as

for this point that Cleon insists on—that the death penalty will be to our advantage in the future, by keeping the others from rebelling—I maintain exactly the opposite view. . . . But we are not at law with them, and so have no need to speak of justice. We are in council instead, and must decide how the Mytileneans can be put to the best use for us.

(Thucydides 3.44.1–4 [not in DK], Woodruff's translation)

The second episode occurred in 416 when the Athenians attacked the island of Melos, which although originally a Spartan colony was neutral in the war. The Athenians intended to bring it into their empire. Thucydides presents a discussion between envoys of the Athenians and the Melian leaders about the Athenian ultimatum: become a subject state or suffer destruction. The Athenians begin by saying that the basic fact of the situation is the relative strength of the two sides.

20.7   *Athenians*: For our part, we will not make a long speech no one would believe, full of fine moral arguments—that our empire is justified because we defeated the Persians, or that we are coming against you for an injustice you have done to us. And we don't want you to think you can persuade us by saying that you did not fight on the side of the Lacedaemonians in the war, though you were their colony, or that you have done us no injustice. Instead, let's work out what we can do on the basis of what both sides truly accept: we both know that decisions about justice are made in human discussions only when both sides are under equal compulsion; but when one side is stronger, it gets as much as it can, and the weak must accept that.

(Thucydides 5.89 [not in DK], Woodruff's translation)

The Melians reply that justice is to everyone's advantage since even Athens may someday be at the mercy of others.

20.8   Well, then, since you put your interest in the place of justice, our view must be that it is in your interest not to subvert this rule that is good for all: that a plea of justice and fairness should do some good for a man who has fallen into danger, if he can win over his judges, even if he is not perfectly persuasive. And this rule concerns you no less than us: if you ever stumble, you might receive a terrible punishment and be an example to others.

(Thucydides 5.90 [not in DK], Woodruff's translation)

Nevertheless, the Athenians dismiss this consideration as irrelevant to the present. The subsequent dialogue demonstrates how remote considerations of justice had become.

20.9   *Melians*: So you would not accept a peaceful solution? We could be friends rather than enemies, and fight with neither side.

> *Athenians*: No. Your enmity does not hurt us as much as your friendship
> would. That would be a sign of our weakness to those who are ruled by us;
> but your hatred would prove our power.
> *Melians*: Why? Do your subjects reason so unfairly that they put us, who
> never had anything to do with you, in the same category as themselves,
> when most of them were your colonies, or else rebels whom you defeated?
> *Athenians*: Why not? They think we have as good a justification for control-
> ling you as we do for them; they say the independent cities survive because
> they are powerful, and that we do not attack them because we are afraid.
>   (Thucydides 5.94–97 [not in DK], Woodruff's translation)

The Melians decide to resist the Athenians and place their hopes in the gods
and the Spartans. The Athenians respond to the first of these hopes that it is a
requirement and law (*nomos*) of *phusis*—applying to gods as well as humans—
that the strong shall rule.

20.10   *Athenians*: The favor of the gods should be as much on our side as yours.
Neither our principles nor our actions are contrary to what men believe
about the gods, or would want for themselves. Nature always compels gods
(we believe) and men (we are certain) to rule over anyone they can control.
We did not make this law, and we were not the first to follow it; but we will
take it as we found it and leave it to posterity forever, because we know that
you would do the same if you had our power, and so would anyone else. So
as far as the favor of the gods is concerned, we have no reason to fear that
we will do worse than you.
                    (Thucydides 5.105.1–3 [not in DK], Woodruff's translation)

As to the Spartans, the Athenians claim that not much help can be expected from
them, since they more than most people act to their own advantage.

20.11   Of all the people we know, they are the ones who make it most obvious that
they hold whatever pleases them to be honorable, and whatever profits them
to be just.
                      (Thucydides 5.105.4 [not in DK], Woodruff's translation)

And to the Melian assertion that it is to the Spartans' advantage to assist Melos,
the Athenians—correctly, as events prove—reply that the Spartans will not
think it to their advantage to undergo such a risk. The Athenians conclude by
saying that fear of disgrace (a typical moral consideration) is a foolish motive for
action; the best results come from assessing the strength of the parties involved
and acting accordingly.

20.12   Do not be distracted by a sense of honor; this destroys people all too often,
when dishonor and death stand before their eyes. Many have been so overcome by the power of this seductive word, "honor," that even when they
foresee the dangers to which it carries them, they are drawn by a mere word

into an action that is an irreparable disaster; and so, intentionally, they fall
into a dishonor that is more shameful than mere misfortune, since it is due
to their own foolishness. You must guard against this if you are to deliberate
wisely, and you must not think it unseemly for you to submit to a city of
such great power, which offers such reasonable conditions. . . . Remember
what is usually the best course: do not give way to equals, but have the right
attitude toward your superiors and use moderation toward your inferiors.
(Thucydides 5.111.3–5 [not in DK], Woodruff's translation)

The political realism espoused by the Athenian envoys was put to the test when
the Melians decided to fight for their liberty rather than submit to the Athenian
demands, and after an easy victory the Athenian army inflicted the terrible punishment they had threatened.

Conclusion

The champions of *phusis* are agreed on the universality of nature or of human
nature and find in *phusis* a standard for determining the advantage of an individual or a community. The writers so far considered, with the possible exception of Antiphon, claim a prescriptive force for the decrees of *phusis*: we, or our
community, should pursue our own natural advantage. Moreover, all humans
and communities tend to be in competition with one another, so that my pursuing my advantage tends to conflict with you pursuing yours, and it is to my
advantage for you not to attain yours.

If the competitive aspect of this view is set aside, the egoism which remains is
in fact common ground in Greek moral thought. Even Socrates, Plato and Aristotle held that a person's chief goal is his or her own happiness. And these three
philosophers also agreed with the proponents of *phusis* that not the unstable
prescriptions of variable *nomos* but facts about human *phusis* are the correct basis
for determining what we should do and how we should live.

Defenses of *Nomos*

Nevertheless, a case could be made for *nomos* as well. The following passages
show some of the arguments that were used.

Critias

Critias champions *nomos* outright: without *nomos*, life would be insupportable
and civilized society nonexistent; *nomos* raises human life above the beasts.

20.13   There was a time when human life was without order,
         on the level of beasts, and subject to force;
         when there was no reward for the good
         or punishment for the bad.

And then, I think, humans established
nomoi as punishers, so that justice would be the mighty ruler
of all equally and would have violence (*hubris*) as its slave,
and anyone who did wrong would be punished.

(Critias DK 88B25 lines 1–8)

Protagoras

The idea that humanity advanced from a primitive state to civilization was common in the fifth and fourth centuries and found expression in many writers,[7] among them Plato, who puts into the mouth of Protagoras a "myth" of human progress[8] which most scholars take to have a basis in Protagoras's own thought and which makes *nomos* an important part of civilization while possibly also linking *nomos* with *phusis*.

In the beginning, says Protagoras, humans received as gifts from Prometheus technical ingenuity and fire, through which they developed speech and provided themselves with shelter, clothing and food. They lived a scattered life, without cities, because they did not have the "political art," the skills needed for civilized life. As a result many were killed by wild beasts and there was danger that the human race would be annihilated since they could not cooperate even for defense. To prevent their destruction Zeus gave humans two further gifts: *aidōs* (a sense of shame and respect for others) and *dikē* (a sense of right and justice), which enabled them to have political order and to form bonds of friendship and union. Everyone is expected to have some share of *aidōs* and *dikē*. Without them a person cannot lead a civilized human life.

Moreover, Protagoras continues, after concluding the myth,[9] it is to everyone's interest that all citizens develop their moral character and so there is a continuous process of moral and social education which takes place from infancy to adulthood, with family, friends, teachers, and the institutions of the city itself all taking part. Each city establishes *nomoi* to guide the lives of its citizens in paths of *aretē* and through education and threat of punishment molds and compels the citizens to rule and be ruled in accordance with them.

For Protagoras, the moral qualities *aidōs* and *dikē* make civilized life possible for humans, and *nomoi* establish patterns of civilized life, there being many possible patterns and many different sets of *nomoi*. In interpreting Protagoras's myth, most commentators distinguish between technical ingenuity on the one side and *aidōs* and *dikē* on the other, saying that the first is innate and part of human nature, that is, we have it by virtue of our *phusis*, whereas *aidōs* and *dikē* are not innate but supplement *phusis*. It is also possible that Protagoras intends *aidōs* and *dikē* as part of human nature and uses the device of the myth to show

---

7. See Guthrie (1969: 60–63, 79–84) for source material.

8. Plato, *Protagoras* 320c–323a = DK 80C1.

9. Plato, *Protagoras* 324d–326e (not in DK).

that if human nature lacked these moral qualities life as we know it would not be possible. If this latter interpretation is accepted, the *nomoi* of a community have some basis in human nature, that is, in (distinctively human) *phusis*.

The *Anonymus Iamblichi*

An even clearer defense of *nomos* by showing its basis in *phusis* occurs in a work by an unknown author extracts of which are preserved in the *Protrepticus* of the fourth-century CE author Iamblichus. This work is known as the *Anonymus Iamblichi* and is thought to date from c.400 BCE.

20.14   (6.1) No one should set out to maximize his own advantage or suppose that power used for one's advantage is *aretē* and obedience to *nomoi* is cowardice. This is the most wicked thought and it results in everything diametrically opposed to what is good: evil and harm. For if humans were by *phusis* unable to live singly but yielding to necessity came together to live with one another and discovered all their life and their contrivances for living, but it is impossible for them to live with one another and to conduct their lives in the absence of *nomoi* (since that way they would suffer more damage than they would by living alone)—on account of these necessities *nomos* and justice are kings among humans, and in no way can they depart. For they are firmly bound into our *phusis*.

           (*Anonymus Iamblichi* fr. 6 = DK 89, 6 vol. 2 402.21–30)

In his attack on *nomos* as a conspiracy of the weak to hold down the strong (above pages 411–12), Callicles implies that *nomos* does have important benefits for the weak, who constitute the vast majority of people. This line of thought is carried farther by the *Anonymus Iamblichi*, which denies that a Calliclean strong individual could ever gain dominance.

20.15   (6.2) If, then, someone were born who had from the beginning the following sort of *phusis*: invulnerable in his flesh, not subject to disease, without feelings, superhuman, and hard as steel in body and soul—perhaps one might have thought that power used for personal advantage would be sufficient for such a person, since such a person could be scot-free even if he did not subject himself to the law (*nomos*). But this person does not think correctly. (6.3) Even if there were such a person, though there could not be, he would survive by being an ally of the laws (*nomoi*) and of justice, strengthening them and using his might for them and for what assists them, but otherwise he could not last. (6.4) For it would seem that all people would become enemies of a person with such a nature (*phunti*, related to *phusis*), and through their own observance of *nomos* and their numbers they would overcome him by craft or force and would prevail. (6.5) So it is obvious that power itself— real power—is preserved through *nomos* and justice.

           (*Anonymus Iamblichi* fr. 6 = DK 89, 6, vol. 2
           402.30–403.10) (continuation of **20.14**)

A number of authors praise the benefits that *nomos* brings. Here too, the *Anony-mus Iamblichi* states the case powerfully, contrasting *eunomia* (a condition where the *nomoi* are good and people abide by them) and *anomia* (the opposite of *euno-mia*), which he seems to conceive as a condition in which each person pursues his or her own advantage in competition with others.

20.16   It is worthwhile to learn these facts about *eunomia* and *anomia*—how big the difference is between them, and that *eunomia* is the best thing both for the community and for the individual and *anomia* is the worst, for the greatest harm arises immediately from *anomia*. Let us begin by indicating first what results from *eunomia*.

(7.1) In the first place, trust arises from *eunomia*, and this benefits all people greatly and is one of the great goods. For as a result of it, money becomes available and so even if there is little it is sufficient, since it is in circulation, but without it not even a great deal of money would be enough. (7.2) Fortunes and misfortunes in money and life are managed most suit-ably for people as a result of *eunomia*. For those enjoying good fortune can use it in safety and without danger of plots, while those suffering ill for-tune are aided by the fortunate through their mutual dealings and trust, which result from *eunomia*. (7.3) Through *eunomia*, moreover, the time people devote to *pragmata* [a word which can mean "government," "public business," or "troubles"] is idle, but that devoted to the activities of life is productive. (7.4) In *eunomia* people are free from the most unpleasant con-cern and engage in the most pleasant, since concern about *pragmata* is most unpleasant and concern about one's activities is most pleasant. (7.5) Also when they go to sleep, which is a rest from troubles for people, they go to it without fear and unworried about painful matters, and when they rise from it they have other similar experiences and do not suddenly become fearful. Nor after this very pleasant change [that is, sleep] do they expect the day to bring poverty but they look forward to it without fear directing their con-cern without grief toward the activities of life, lightening their labors with trust and confident hopes that they will get good things as a result. For all these things *eunomia* is responsible. (7.6) And war, which is the source of the greatest evils for people, leading as it does to destruction and slavery—this too comes more to those who practice *anomia*, less to those practicing *eunomia*. (7.7) There are many other goods found in *eunomia* that assist life, and also from it comes consolation for our difficulties.

These are the evils that come from *anomia*. (7.8) In the first place, people do not have time for their activities and are engaged in the most unpleasant thing—*pragmata*, not activities—and because of mistrust and lack of mutual dealings they hoard money and do not make it available, so it becomes rare even if there is much. (7.9) Ill fortune and good fortune minister to the opposite results [from what occurs under *eunomia*]: good fortune is not safe in *anomia* but is plotted against, and bad fortune is not driven off but is strengthened through mistrust and the absence of mutual dealings. (7.10) War from outside is more frequently brought against a land, and domestic faction comes from the same cause, and if it did not occur earlier it happens then. Also it happens that people are always involved in *pragmata* because of plots that come from one another, which force them to live constantly on guard and to make counterplots against each other. (7.11) When they are awake their thoughts are not pleasant, and when they go to sleep their receptacle [that is, sleep] is not pleasant but full of fear, and their awakening is fearful and frightening and leads a person to sudden memories of his troubles. These and all the previously mentioned evils result from *anomia*.

(7.12) Also tyranny, so great and so foul an evil, arises from nothing else but *anomia*. Some people suppose—all who do not understand correctly— that a tyrant comes from some other source and that people are deprived of their freedom without being themselves responsible but compelled by the tyrant when he has been established. But they do not consider this correctly. (7.13) For whoever thinks that a king or a tyrant arises from anything else than *anomia* and personal advantage is an idiot. For when everyone turns to evil, this is what happens then. For it is impossible for humans to live without *nomoi* and justice. (7.14) So when these two things—*nomos* and justice—are missing from the mass of the people, that is exactly when the guardianship and protection of them passes to a single person. How else could solitary rule be transferred to a single person unless the *nomos* had been driven out which benefited the mass of the people? (7.15) For this man who is going to destroy justice and abolish *nomos* which is common and advantageous to all, must be made of steel if he intends to strip these things from the mass of the people, he being one and they many. (7.16) But if he is made of flesh and is like the rest, he will not be able to accomplish this, but on the contrary if he reestablishes what is missing, he might be a solitary ruler. This is why some people fail to notice this occurring when it does.

(*Anonymus Iamblichi* fr. 7 = DK 89.7, vol. 2
403.11–404.32) (continuation of **20.15**)

Other Defenses of *Nomos*

Some turned the tables on *phusis*. Instead of viewing *nomos* as variable and *phusis* as fixed, they declared that *phusis* (here in the sense of one's natural abilities) varies with the individual, whereas *nomos* (here, typically, the positive law in force in a given community at a given time) holds uniformly for all.

20.17 (15) All the life of the people in cities both great and small is run by *phusis* and by *nomoi*. Of these, *phusis* is without order and private to each individual but the *nomoi* are common, in order, and the same for all. Now *phusis*, if it is wicked, often has low desires. This is why you will find people of that sort doing wrong. (16) The *nomoi*, on the other hand, desire what is just and good and advantageous, and they aim for this and when it is found, this is published as a common command, equal and similar for all, and this is *nomos*. There are many reasons why all ought to obey it, especially because every law is a discovery and gift of the gods, a decision of sensible people,

a correction of voluntary and involuntary wrongdoing, a common commitment of the city according to which all in the city ought to live. . . . (20) I
will say nothing new or clever or odd, but what you all know as well as I
do. If any of you wants to investigate what is the reason and what causes
the Council to meet, the people to gather in the Assembly, the courts to be
filled, the previous magistrates to yield their place willingly to the new ones,
and all the things to take place through which the city is run and preserved,
you will find the *nomoi* and the fact that everyone obeys them, since if they
were abolished and everyone were given the opportunity to do whatever he
wished, not only is it goodbye to the constitution, but also our life would be
no different from that of wild beasts.

(pseudo-Demosthenes 25.15–16, 20 [not in DK])

20.18   Nothing is more hateful to a city than a tyrant, because then in the first
place there are no common *nomoi*, but a single person holds power after
taking the *nomos* into his own possession. And this situation is no longer
equal for all. But when *nomoi* are written both the weak and the wealthy
have equal justice, and when slandered the fortunate is able to make the
same case as the weaker and the lesser person defeats the great man if he has
justice on his side. That is freedom.

(Euripides, *Supplices* 429–38 [not in DK])

Unwritten *Nomoi*

Even if customs and enacted laws were known to vary from place to place and
from time to time in a given place, the Greeks of the Classical period did not
lose consciousness of the earlier tradition that laws are god given. Early lawgiv-
ers such as Lycurgus of Sparta and Solon of Athens received greater reverence
than was usually accorded to humans. Moreover, some *nomoi* were felt to be
universal either in the sense that all peoples at all times actually recognize them
or that they should recognize them even if they do not. These *nomoi*, sometimes
called unwritten laws, were thought to have a divine origin and to take prece-
dence over (possibly faulty) human laws. The most famous assertion of the existence and priority of these laws is made by Antigone in Sophocles' play of that
name (written in 441), when she defends her action of burying her brother in
defiance of King Creon's decree.

20.19   For me it was not Zeus who made this proclamation, nor was it Justice who
dwells with the gods below who established these *nomoi* among humans. And
I did not suppose that your proclamations had power enough that you, a
mortal, could prevail over the gods' unwritten and secure practices [*nomima*,
derived from *nomos*]. For they live not just now and yesterday, but always
forever. No one knows when they appeared. I did not out of fear of the will of
any man intend to pay a penalty before the gods for transgressing them.

(Sophocles, *Antigone* 450–60 [not in DK])

The concept of unwritten laws is developed and defended in a dialogue between Socrates and Hippias, as reported by Xenophon.

20.20   *Socrates*: Do you know of any unwritten laws, Hippias?

Hippias: Yes, the ones uniformly observed in every country.

Soc.: Could you say that humans made them?

Hip.: How could they, since they could not all have come together and they do not speak the same language?

Soc.: Then who do you suppose are the ones who made these laws?

Hip.: I think that the gods made these laws for men. For among all men the first law is to revere the gods.

Soc.: Is it not also the law everywhere to honor parents?

Hip.: Yes, that is too.

Soc.: And also that parents shall not have sexual intercourse with their children nor children with their parents?

Hip.: This does not seem to me to be a law of God.

Soc.: Why so?

Hip.: Because I notice that some transgress it.

Soc.: Yes, and they do many other things against the laws. But surely those who transgress the laws established by the gods pay a penalty which in no way can a person escape, as some, when they transgress the laws established by humans, escape punishment, either through not being noticed or by violence.

Hip.: And what penalty, Socrates, are parents and children who have intercourse with one another unable to avoid?

Soc.: The greatest, by Zeus! For what greater penalty could people incur in producing children than producing them badly?

Hip.: How, then, do these people produce children badly, since the fathers and mothers may both be good people?

Soc.: Because, by Zeus, the parents must not only be good; they must also be at their physical peak. Or do you think that those who are at their peak have seed similar to that of people who have not yet reached that condition or have passed it?

Hip.: By Zeus, it is unlikely that it is similar.

Soc.: Which is better then?

Hip.: Clearly, the seed of people at their peak.

Soc.: Therefore, the seed of those not at their peak is not sound?

Hip.: It is unlikely, by Zeus.

Soc.: In these conditions, then, they should not produce children?

Hip.: Certainly not.

Soc.: Therefore those who produce children in such circumstances produce them as they should not.

Hip.: I think so.

Soc.: What other people, then, will produce children badly if not they?

Hip.: I share your opinion on this, too.

Soc.: Again, is it not everywhere customary to repay good deeds with good deeds?

Hip.: It is customary, but this custom too is transgressed.

Soc.: Don't those who transgress it pay a penalty in being bereft of good friends and being compelled to pursue people who hate them? Or is it not true that, whereas those who benefit the people they have dealings with are good friends, those who do not do such people good deeds in return are hated for their unkindness, while they pursue such people most of all because of the great benefits of having dealings with them?

Hip.: By Zeus, Socrates, all this smacks of the gods. For I accept that laws which themselves contain punishment for those who break them, come from a better law-giver than man.

                                        (Xenophon, *Memorabilia* 4.4.19–25 [not in DK])

Xenophon's idea of unwritten laws is not altogether clear. First, they are said to be observed in every country. Next, when it is admitted that they are not actually observed everywhere, they are said to be universally valid, that is, they ought to be observed everywhere even if they are not. With this change, we can no longer determine what laws are unwritten laws simply by finding customs that are followed by all people without exception. Socrates suggests a different criterion (reminiscent of Antiphon's assertion about the inevitability of paying a penalty for violating the dictates of nature, see **20.3**), that although punishment for breaking manmade *nomoi* can sometimes be avoided, transgressions of unwritten laws are always punished. His discussion of incest and ingratitude points toward the idea that violating unwritten laws brings retribution inevitably, as a natural and automatic consequence. But it is hard to see how this analysis could be extended to cover some of Xenophon's other examples (such as honoring one's parents), let alone the Sophoclean case of burying a dead brother.

Aristotle recognizes two sorts of unwritten laws: the universal *nomoi* so far discussed, as opposed to the *nomoi* of particular states, and also the beliefs of a particular state, based on its customs and traditions, which supplement its written laws.

20.21   *Nomos* is (a) particular and (b) common. I call (a) particular the written *nomos* in accordance with which a city is administered and (b) common all the unwritten principles which appear to be agreed upon among all peoples.
                                        (Aristotle, *Rhetoric* 1.10 1368b7–9 [not in DK])

20.22   I call *nomos* (a) particular, (b) common. (a) Particular *nomos* is that which each people establishes as applying to themselves, and this is (1) unwritten and (2) written, whereas (b) common *nomos* is that in accordance with *phusis*.
                                        (Aristotle, *Rhetoric* 1.13 1373b4–6 [not in DK])

In the latter case Aristotle is working with two different aspects of *nomos: nomos* as law (written legislation) and *nomos* as custom. Moreover, in the latter passage he equates universal laws with natural laws and in what follows cites Antigone's case as an example of a natural law. Now Sophocles did not make Antigone describe the unwritten laws as "natural," but in the context of the *nomos–phusis* debate, the association of the universal with the natural was easy and automatic.

So far, the unwritten law is superior to and nobler than written law. It is frequently called divine and is sometimes said to have been authored by the gods in contrast to mutable, fallible, and perhaps self-interested human law. However, the window it opens for arguing in court against the legal prescriptions of the state did not go unnoticed by Sophists and other rhetoricians. By Aristotle's time it was possible to see the contrast as the source of simply one more debating move.

20.23   The broadest rhetorical commonplace for forcing people to utter paradoxes is that derived from what is according to *phusis* and according to *nomos*, as Callicles is described as saying in the *Gorgias* and all the men of old believed that it happened. For they held that *phusis* and *nomos* are opposites, and justice is fine and noble according to *nomos* but not fine and noble according to *phusis*. Therefore a person speaking according to *phusis* should be answered according to *nomos*, and a person speaking according to *nomos* should be brought to (considerations of) *phusis*. Both ways it results that they utter paradoxes. They considered what is according to *phusis* to be true and what is according to *nomos* to be what the many believe.
        (Aristotle, *Sophistical Refutations* 12 173a7–16 [not in DK])

Moreover, people could invoke "unwritten laws" whenever it suited their advantage. By the end of the fifth century, appeal to the concept of unwritten law, which began as a way of invoking a higher authority when human laws were evil, had fallen to a tool that might be used to defend any illegal action. That it was actually employed in that way is suggested by an Athenian decree passed at the end of the fifth century:

20.24   The magistrates must not make use of unwritten law, even in a single case . . . No law can be established for an individual person unless the same law applies to all Athenians.
        (quoted in Andocides, *On the Mysteries* 87 [not in DK])

Moreover, at this time the Athenians were engaged in revising their laws and inscribing them on stone tablets and setting them up in public so that anyone could consult them who wished.[10]

It hardly needs saying that the unwritten "law of nature" that the strong should rule the weak, put forward by Callicles and expressed elsewhere too, was

---

10. The decree is quoted in Andocides, *On the Mysteries* 83–84 (not in DK). See references and discussion in MacDowell (1962: 194–99).

an ideology that would support tyranny and subvert organized life as known to the Greeks.

Conclusion

The *nomos–phusis* debate had no winners or losers. The notions of *nomos* and *phusis* were sufficiently broad and loose to leave room for many positions to be staked out, most of them with something to recommend them. In this fertile field of discussion the seeds of many philosophical problems, views, and approaches were sown. But the *nomos–phusis* debate was the common property of Classical Greece, not the private field of the philosophers. As we have seen, the contributors to the debate included playwrights, historians, and orators, and the ideas involved played an important role in practical politics and in the courts.

The debate also has a considerable philosophical legacy. The wide range of answers given to the questions it raised and the variety of approaches taken invite reflection on how to proceed with complex and interwoven issues like these. Socrates made crucial contributions in recognizing the importance of accurate and agreed upon definitions of key terms and discovering that such definitions are difficult to find and require a great deal of work in their own right.

The debate also had an important effect on Plato. Plato is our most important single source for the debate, not because he had an antiquarian interest in it, but because he believed the issues needed further treatment. He disagreed with many of the views that had been expressed but was in agreement with others. It is probably not too great an exaggeration to say that one of the most important bases for his ethical work in dialogues up to and including the *Republic* was his (and Socrates') reflections on issues raised by or implicit in the *nomos–phusis* debate.

The legacy extends much further. Many of the issues raised for the first time in the context of the debate have remained important both for philosophers and for reflective people in general. Why should I be just? Is morality artificial or natural? What is human nature? What is the origin of society? What are the bonds of society? What is the relation between obeying the law and being good? What is the nature of our obligation to obey the law, and what limits does it have? Many current theories on these topics have their earliest ancestors in the fifth- and fourth-century context of the *nomos–phusis* debate.

Appendix

Some Contemporary Texts

Introduction

Presocratic philosophy is frequently treated separately from other areas of Greek thought in the sixth and fifth century, and it is easy to take away the impression that in their own times the Presocratic philosophers had little influence on anyone aside from one another. That this impression is false can be easily shown by reference to other surviving works from this period, both poetry and prose. The purpose of this final chapter is not to collect such references and traces of influence but to present some texts that show how Presocratic thinking had effects in two very different areas of Greek thought: medicine and religion. Space considerations require the texts to speak for themselves; I will provide only a brief introduction.

The first three texts, *The Nature of Man*, *Ancient Medicine*, and *The Art*,[1] come from the collection of about sixty works known as the Hippocratic Corpus. Although associated with the name of Hippocrates (a contemporary of Socrates and the founder of a medical school on the island of Cos) the authors of the works in the collection are unknown, and they were written over a span of centuries. The works I have included are dated to the late fifth century, roughly contemporary with Empedocles, Anaxagoras, Democritus, and Philolaus. All works in the collection are on medical topics and range from practical treatises on how to set fractures to works on anatomy, the diagnosis and prognosis of sickness, methods of treatment and advice to physicians, as well as theoretical treatises, such as the three presented here.

Early medicine was not a theoretical subject; rather it was a practical art or craft. Because its purpose was to treat individual patients (diagnosing their illnesses, trying to palliate or cure them, or prescribing regimens for them that would prevent illness), it was not amenable to constructing theories at a high level of generality. On the other hand and quite possibly at least partly through the intellectual influence (or pressure) of Presocratic thought, medicine (or at least one way of doing medicine—there were other, more traditional approaches as well) came to be interested in giving rational, theory-based accounts of itself. From the fifth century, the study of medicine associated with the name Hippocrates was based on theories about the constitution and workings of the human body and the nature of sicknesses, their causes, and their cures. Like the Presocratics the Hippocratic writers reject traditional beliefs that the gods play an active role in the aspect of the world that concerns them. In addition to proposing theories on these subjects, some of

---

1. My translations are based on the editions of Jouanna (Jouanna [1975], [1988], [1990]), which differ in many places from the texts used in earlier translations. To my belief, the present translations of *The Nature of Man* and *The Art* are the first English translations to use Jouanna's texts.

the works, including the three presented here, take up questions of method and
justification more explicitly and in greater detail than we find in the materials on
the Presocratics, making important contributions to the understanding of scientific method and stressing the importance of experience and observation. Moreover, they display the disagreement on the nature, aims, and goals of medicine
that was going on in the late fifth century, even on the question whether the art of
medicine actually exists, and they play an important role in the vigorous debates on
these topics. Finally, the works included in the Hippocratic Corpus are complete
treatises—unlike the writings of the Presocratics, none of which is preserved in its
entirety. This fact together with the large overlap of subject matters and interests
makes these texts important for our understanding of Presocratic thought as well
as its contemporary influence.

The Nature of Man takes up a variety of topics. It begins by objecting strongly
to the kind of accounts of the constitution of the human body that we would
expect to have from a Presocratic who believes that all things have a single material constituent (earth, water, air, or fire), and also raising parallel objections to
the accounts of doctors who hold that the body is made up of blood or bile or
phlegm. The text goes on to argue that such accounts cannot be true and to claim
that the body is made up of not one but several constituents: blood, phlegm, yellow bile, and black bile—which came to be known as the four humors. Health
occurs when the humors are blended and balanced in the right amounts, disease
when they are separate. The treatise presents evidence and arguments that these
substances are found in the body (arguments that, however, fall short of proving
that they are its basic constituents), and proofs that the evidence contradicts the
rival claim that the body is composed of only one of the humors. It talks of the
waxing and waning of these elements during the four seasons of the year and so
explains the prevalence of different sicknesses in different seasons. It gives some
general considerations on how to cure sickness (prominently the principle that
opposites cure opposites), what causes sickness (including factors external to the
individual, such as the climate and the season of the year, as well as factors that
vary from individual to individual, such as diet and exercise), and how to diagnose sicknesses. It contains an elaborate although fanciful account of the blood
vessels and brief accounts of the progress and causes of certain ailments, ending
with a classification of fevers.

Ancient Medicine defends the theory and practice of the ancient and honorable
art of medicine against newfangled theories and practices introduced by those
who adopt "hypotheses" such as the hot, the cold, the wet, or the dry, claiming
that one or two of these is the cause of human sickness and death. The author
acknowledges that not all practitioners of what he claims to be the true medical
art are equally good but insists that the discoveries that medicine has made in the
past and the methods by which it has made them are correct and that they are
the correct basis for further research. Primitive humans were unable to endure
a diet of raw grain and meat and gradually learned how to turn those naturally
occurring products into edible and healthy food. Medicine arose in the same

manner—by finding ways to alter a healthy person's diet so that it would be suit-able for those who suffer from different sicknesses. In general, sick people need "weaker" food than healthy people, but this is not true in all cases. Therefore medicine is a difficult specialty requiring precise knowledge. Even so, medicine is not an exact science. Perfection is rarely achieved; we should not demand it but should praise doctors who make few and small mistakes. After discussing different eating habits, the author returns to his original topic, raising theoretical and practical objections against those who investigate medicine from a hypoth-esis, pointing out that their approach is too simple to account for differences between our reactions to different but closely related kinds of food. Experience has shown that it is not the amount of something like "the hot" that determines the effects of a substance on us, but the blend of its "affective qualities" (such as salty, bitter, and sweet). However, the author recognizes "the hot" as an affective quality, and the theory he presents appears open to some of the same objections as he raises against the simpler views of his predecessors. The author goes on to consider different health problems in the light of this theory, treating colds, runny eyes, and discharges in the throat, among others. He returns again to the rival theory, saying that it "tends toward philosophy in the same way as Empe-docles or others who have written about nature from the beginning, stating what a human is, how humans first came to be, and from what elements they are con-stituted," and asserting that this kind of knowledge is irrelevant to a doctor and that medicine is actually the best source of knowledge on these topics.

The Art is a highly rhetorical polemical work which contains a number of argu-ments both against unidentified opponents—apparently not specialists in med-icine—who claim that medicine is not an art at all and against those who blame doctors for refusing to treat hopeless cases. It offers a definition of medicine as "delivering sick people entirely from their pains, limiting the violence of sick-nesses, and not attempting to cure those who have succumbed to their sicknesses, and doing these things in the knowledge that medicine is capable of all this" and argues that, thus understood, medicine does exist and that it is an art. In doing so, the author contrasts art with luck and spontaneity, admitting that luck plays a role in recovering from sickness but denying that spontaneous events (which he iden-tifies as events that happen without a cause) exist, since every event has a cause. Cases where illness is cured without the help of doctors do not prove that the art does not exist but only that sometimes sick people stumble upon the cures that the art prescribes—and the cases where they do not recover simply proves their ignorance of the art. To the argument that medicine is not an art because some-times patients die, the counterargument is given that when patients die it is their own fault for not following the doctor's instructions. The defense of doctors for not treating mortal diseases turns on the point that some sicknesses are incurable, in other words that medicine has limits; fatal cases are beyond those limits; and no expert in any art attempts to do things that do not fall under the art in question. The final section of the work divides sicknesses into two categories: those that can be observed and those that cannot be observed because they are located in the interior of the body. The author, who optimistically supposes that the treatments of observable sicknesses have already been discovered, devotes most of this section to a discussion of "obscure" sicknesses and the methods for obtaining perceptible evidence of their nature in order to make diagnosis. The methodology favored is more empirical than in the other two works.

These texts show close connections with the ideas of the Presocratics, who treated the origin and physical constitution of humans and other living things along with those of other physical objects. Understanding the nature of life and death was part of their goal, and some of them had things to say on medical and related topics (Empedocles, Democritus, Diogenes, and Philolaus in particular). But the Hippocratic texts insist that the art of medicine is different from the general study of the nature of things and point out the complexity of the human body and the variety of conditions it can have as well as the variation among individual humans and what is good and bad for them. Medicine's expert practitioners know how to take these individual circumstances into account. Medicine is an art or craft whose foundations have been established on a sound basis, and although there is still much to be learned, full knowledge will be attained by following the methods that brought it to its present state. One can imagine a Presocratic thinker saying something of the same kind about knowledge of the physical world.

The Derveni papyrus is a different kind of work. Discovered in 1962 and published in 2006,[2] it is a document, written on papyrus, which was burnt on a funeral pyre in the fourth century BCE. (Imagine a rolled up newspaper partially burned in a fire, whose outer pages are destroyed, as are the top and bottom of the remaining pages, in which the fire, heat, and subsequent handling have created holes of varying sizes.) The papyrus contained an Orphic poem on the origin of the gods together with an interpretation of the poem which has close affinities with Presocratic philosophy. The surviving text is divided into twenty-six columns, none of which is complete, the first three containing only a few words and letters. My translation, which is based on the text of the 2006 publication, indicates gaps in the text and adopts conjectures proposed by others which I regard as plausible. The actual wording of the text is still controversial and its interpretation even more so.

Orphism was a Greek religious cult that differed from popular ancient Greek religion in several ways. It was associated with Orpheus, a mythological figure who descended into Hades and returned alive. Orphism considered human souls to be divine and immortal but condemned to undergo successive bodily incarnations through metempsychosis. Orphism promoted a way of life which guaranteed eventual release from these incarnations as well as freedom from punishment after death for acts committed during life. It also required devotees to go through secret initiation ceremonies. Importantly, it was based on sacred texts attributed to Orpheus, which discussed the origin of gods and of human beings.

---

2. Kouremenos, et al. (2006).

The Derveni papyrus contains fragments of one such Orphic theogony, dated to the late sixth century. The theogony is written in epic hexameters (also used by Homer, Hesiod, Xenophanes, Parmenides, and Empedocles) and narrates a succession story parallel to the one given by Hesiod in his *Theogony*.[3] According to the Derveni theogony Night gave birth to Heaven (Ouranos), who became the first king. Kronos was next and took over the kingship from Ouranos. Finally Zeus became king and arranged the *kosmos* into the form it now has. Most important for our purposes, the Derveni papyrus not only quotes the theogony but also provides a commentary on it which interprets it as an allegorical account of a cosmology that has important resemblances and connections with the cosmologies of the Presocratics. The Derveni papyrus explicitly mentions Heraclitus, quoting one of his fragments,[4] and details of the cosmology associated more or less closely with Anaxagoras, although in my opinion the connections are not as strong as some have claimed.

The Nature of Man, Chapters 1–15

Chapter 1

(1) This account is not suitable for anyone to hear who is used to listening to people talking about human nature more deeply than concerns medicine. I do not in the least maintain that a human being is air, fire, water, or earth, or anything else that is not an obvious constituent of humans. I leave these views to those who wish to assert them. (2) In my view, however, people who do say such things do not have correct knowledge. For they all have the same opinion even though what they say is not same; nevertheless, they employ the same reasoning, saying that what exists is a single thing and this is the one and the all. But they disagree in the names they give it, one saying that this one and this all is air, another saying that it is water, another fire, and another earth, and each chooses evidence and proofs for his account that are worth nothing. Since they all share the same opinion but say different things, it is clear that they know nothing. (3) You can recognize this best if you are present at their debates. When the same men debate one another in front of the same audience, victory in the discussion never goes to the same man three times in a row, but now one person wins, now another, and now the one who happens to speak most fluently in front of the crowd—whereas when a person claims to have correct knowledge on a subject, the speech he gives should prevail every time, provided that he knows the facts and presents them correctly. (4) But in my opinion such people in their stupidity overthrow themselves in the terminology they use in their accounts and resurrect the theory of Melissus!

---

3. See Ch. 2 above.
4. **10.91.**

Chapter 2

(1) About these people I have said enough. As for doctors, some of them say that human beings are blood, others that they are bile, and some that they are phlegm. (2) These people too employ the same reasoning: they say that there is a single thing—naming it whatever each of them pleases—and that this changes its appearance and affective qualities when it is constrained by the hot and the cold, and becomes sweet and bitter, white and black, and in short it changes in all kinds of ways. (3) But in my opinion this is not at all how these things are. Now most doctors maintain views of this kind or very similar ones, but I say that if a man were a single thing he would never feel pain. For if he were a single thing there would not be anything that could make him feel pain. Further, if he were to feel pain, the remedy would have to be a single thing; but as it is, there are many. And the reason is that there are many constituents in the body that give rise to sickness when they are heated and cooled and dried and moistened by one another contrary to nature. And so there are many kinds of sickness and many remedies. (4) I think that a person who declares that man is only blood and nothing else should prove that it neither changes its appearance nor becomes different in all kinds of ways, but that there is a period of the year or of a person's life in which it is obvious that blood is the only constituent of a person. For it is plausible that there is some period in which what it is is apparent in its own right. And I say the same things concerning anyone who declares that a human being is only phlegm or bile. (5) For I will demonstrate that the things I declare humans to be, both by convention (*nomos*) and by nature (*phusis*), are always the same, whether a person is young or old and whether the season is hot or cold, and I will provide proofs and will present the necessary conditions for the growth and decrease of each in the body.

Chapter 3

(1) Now in the first place, generation must not originate in a single thing. How could a single thing engender anything without being combined with something else? Further, not even a single offspring can result if the things combined are of different kinds and have different affective qualities. And again, generation cannot occur unless the hot stands in an appropriate and equal relation to the cold and the dry to the wet, but one—the stronger—far exceeds the other—the weaker. How, then, is it likely that anything will be engendered from a single thing when it is not even generated from more than one thing unless it happens that they are appropriately related for blending with one another? (2) Since this is the nature of everything else and of man as well, man must not be a single thing, but each of the things that contribute to generation must preserve in the body the particular affective quality it contributed. (3) Moreover each of them must revert to its own nature when a person's body dies: wet to wet, dry

to dry, hot to hot, and cold to cold. (4) Such too is the nature of living things and of everything else as well: all things are generated in a similar way and all things perish in a similar way, for their nature is composed of all those things that were stated earlier and it perishes in the ways that have been stated—each thing reverting to the same thing from which it was composed.

Chapter 4

(1) The body of a person has in itself blood, phlegm, yellow bile, and black bile, and these things are the nature of his body, and it is through these that he feels pain or is healthy. (2) He is healthiest when these are fittingly related in their blending, in their affective qualities and in their amount, and when they are thoroughly combined. He feels pain when a larger or smaller amount of any of these is isolated in the body and not united with all the rest. For when any of them is separate and stands apart by itself, not only must the place from which it departed become diseased but also the place where it stands and to which it has flooded must cause pain and discomfort since it is overfull. For even when more of any of them flows out of the body than the amount that is superfluous, the evacuation causes pain. But if it is inside the body that the evacuation and change in place and separation from the others occurs, according to what has been said it is wholly necessary for it to cause a double pain—both in the region from which it departed and in the place where it produced an excess.

Chapter 5

(1) Since I said that I will show that the things I declare a man to be are always the same both by convention and by nature, I declare them to be blood, phlegm, yellow bile, and black bile. (2) I declare first, that their names are different by convention, none of them possessing the same name, and second, that their appearances are different in nature, phlegm having no similarity to blood nor blood to bile nor bile to phlegm. For how could they resemble one another when their colors appear different when seen and they do not appear similar when we touch them with the hand? For they are not hot, cold, dry, or wet in the same degree. Since they are so different from one another in appearance and affective qualities, they must not be a single thing, if in fact fire and earth are not a single thing. (3) From the following considerations you can understand that these are not all a single thing but that each has its own affective qualities and nature: if you give a person a drug that expels phlegm, he will vomit phlegm; if you give him a drug that expels bile, he will vomit bile. Black bile is purged similarly if you give him a drug that expels black bile. And if you injure a part of his body so as to make a wound, his blood will flow. And these events will occur every day and every night, in winter and summer, as long as he is able to draw breath in and breathe it out again or until he is deprived of one of these congenital elements.

And the things I have mentioned are the congenital elements. How could they not be congenital? (4) In the first place a human being obviously has all these in him perpetually, as long as he is alive. In the second, he was born from a human being who has them all and was nourished in a human being who has them all— all the things I am declaring and am proving.

Chapter 6

(1) Those who say that man is a single thing seem to me to be reasoning as follows: seeing people taking drugs and perishing through excessive purgings, some of them vomiting bile, others phlegm, they thought that man is whatever they saw the person evacuating as he died. And those who say that man is blood employ the same reasoning: observing people whose throat has been cut with the blood flowing out of their body, they think that this is the person's soul. And they employ this evidence in their discussions. (2) But in the first place no one who has died by excessive purgings has ever done so through being purged of bile alone. Rather, when anyone takes a drug that expels bile, he first vomits bile and afterward phlegm. Then in addition to these, such people vomit black bile and finally pure blood. They suffer the same effects through drugs that expel phlegm. First they vomit phlegm, then yellow bile, then black bile, and finally pure blood, and at that point they die. (3) For when the drug enters the body it first expels the component of the body that is closest to its nature and then it expels and purges the others too. When things that are planted or sown enter the earth, each of them attracts the constituent in the earth that agrees with its own nature (there being sour, bitter, sweet, and salty, in fact, all kinds), it first attracts to itself the greatest amount of the one that agrees most with its nature, and then it attracts the others as well. Drugs too do something of this sort in the body. Those that expel bile first purge bile that is purest and subsequently bile that is mixed; the drugs for phlegm first expel phlegm that is purest and afterward phlegm that is mixed. And in the case of people whose throat has been cut the blood at first flows very hot and very red but afterward as it continues to flow it looks more like phlegm and bile.

Chapter 7

(1) In winter phlegm increases in humans, for of the constituents of the body this is the most wintry in nature since it is the coldest. (2) A proof that phlegm is the coldest is that if you touch phlegm, bile, and blood you will find phlegm to be coldest. It is also the most viscous and except for black bile it is expelled with the greatest violence. All those that require violence become hotter by the force of the violence. But nevertheless even despite all these considerations phlegm is obviously the coldest by its own nature. (3) That winter fills the body with phlegm you can tell from the following considerations: in winter people's spit and mucus contain the most phlegm, and especially during this season there

occur white swellings and other sicknesses characterized by phlegm. (4) In the spring phlegm continues to be powerful in the body and the blood increases because the cold weather decreases and rains come after; the blood increases because of the rains and the warm days, since these conditions of the year are most like its nature, since blood is both wet and hot. You can tell this from the following considerations. In spring and summer people suffer most from dysentery and nosebleed, and they are hottest and red. In the summer the blood continues to be powerful, and bile increases in the body and lasts into the fall. (5) In the fall there is a decrease in blood, since the fall is opposite to its nature, but bile prevails in the body during the summer and fall. You can tell this from the following considerations. In this season people spontaneously vomit bile and the evacuations resulting from taking drugs are full of bile. It is also clear from people's fevers and complexions. In summer phlegm is at its weakest, since the season, being dry and hot, is opposed to it in nature. In the fall blood reaches its minimum in humans, since the fall is dry and is already beginning to cool us. Black bile is most plentiful and powerful in the fall. (6) When winter comes bile decreases because of the cold and phlegm increases again because of the large amount of rain and the length of the nights. (7) The human body contains all of these continually but the change of the seasons makes them vary in quantity, each in its turn and according to its nature. (8) For as every year has a share of all things: hot things and cold, dry things and wet (for without all the constituents of this *kosmos* nothing could last any length of time, but if any one of them were absent, everything would disappear, for from the same necessity, all things are combined and are nourished by one another), similarly if any of these congenital elements were absent from a person, he could not live. (9) During the year sometimes winter is powerful, sometimes spring, sometimes summer, and sometimes fall, and in the same way in a person sometimes phlegm is powerful, sometimes blood, and sometimes bile—first yellow and then what is called black bile. (10) The clearest evidence is if you give the same person the same drug four times in a year, you will find that his vomit is most full of phlegm in the winter, wettest in the spring, fullest of bile in the summer, and blackest in the fall.

Chapter 8

(1) Since this is the case, all the sicknesses that increase in the winter ought to decrease in the summer, all that increase in the summer ought to leave off in the winter except those that do not come to an end in a period of days. (I will discuss the period of days below.) In the fall we should expect relief from all the sicknesses that arise in the spring, and in the spring we should expect relief from those that occur in the fall. But it is important to know that any sickness that exceeds these seasons will last a year. In fact a doctor's stance with regard to sicknesses should be that each of them has strength in the body during the season that is most in accordance with its nature.

Chapter 9

(1) It is important to know in addition that all sicknesses caused by repletion are cured by evacuation and all that arise from evacuation are cured by repletion; all that arise as the result of exertion are cured by relaxation and all sicknesses caused by excessive idleness are cured by exertion. (2) In sum, a doctor must act to counter the sicknesses that have become established, as well as <taking into consideration> the individual constitutions, seasons, and ages and must relax what is tense and make tense what is relaxed, since in this way the part that is suffering will be relieved. In my opinion, cures consist in this. (3) Some sicknesses arise from our regime, others from the breath we inhale in order to live. The diagnosis of each should be made in this way: when many people catch the same sickness at the same time, the cause should be attributed to what is most common and especially to that which we all use. This is what we breathe. For it is obvious that our different regimes are not the cause when the sickness strikes everyone in turn, both young and old, women and men, and likewise drunkards and teetotalers, people who eat barley bread and those who eat wheat bread, and those who exert themselves a lot and those who do so only a little. The regime cannot be the cause when people with all different regimes catch the same sickness. (4) But when all kinds of sicknesses occur at the same time, it is clear that each person's regime is the cause of his sickness and that the therapy should be brought about by opposing the cause of the disease, as I have stated elsewhere, and by altering the regime. For it is obvious that the ingredients of the person's accustomed regime do not suit him—either all of them or most of them or at least one of them. So it is necessary to find them out and change them and conduct the therapy—taking into consideration the person's age and constitution, the season of the year, and the manner of the sickness, removing some things, adding others, as I said some time ago—and in each case to pay attention to the age, the season, the individual constitution and the sickness both in the use of drugs and in the regime. (5) But when there is an epidemic of one sickness it is clear that the cause is not people's regime but what we breathe, and it is clear that this causes distress because it contains an unhealthy exhalation. At this time the following recommendations should be given to people: not to change their regime since it is not the cause of the sickness, but to make sure that their body is very lean and weak by gradually abstaining from the food and drink they are used to, for if they change their regime suddenly there is a risk that something untoward will take place in their body as a result of the change. This is how one should deal with the regime when it is clear that it does not harm the person. As to the air, patients should make sure that the influx into the body is as little as possible and as different as possible, moving as far as possible from the places where the sickness is established and reducing their weight. For in this way they will minimize the need to breathe deeply and rapidly.

Chapter 10

(1) Sicknesses arising in the strongest part of the body are the most dangerous. If they remain where they begin, the whole body must suffer, since its strongest part is suffering; and if they move from the strongest part to any of the weaker parts, they are difficult to get rid of. (2) Those that move from weaker to stronger parts are easier to get rid of, since the humors that flow into them are easily driven back by the strength of those parts.

Chapter 11

(1) The thickest blood vessels have the following nature. There are four pairs in the body. One of them extends from the back of the head through the neck, along the exterior of the spine on either side, goes along the haunches to the legs and then passes through the shins to the outer side of the ankles and reaches the feet. Therefore for pains in the back and haunches it is necessary to let blood from behind the knees and the outer side of the ankles. (2) The second pair extends from the head alongside the ears through the neck. They are called the jugular veins. Then they pass along either side of the spine internally, alongside the loins to the testicles and thighs, through the back of the knee internally, and then through the shins to the ankles on the inner side and to the feet. Therefore for pains in the loins and testicles it is necessary to let blood from behind the knees and the inner side of the ankles. (3) The third pair passes from the temples through the neck, under the shoulder blade, and then they meet in the lung; the one on the right then crosses over to the left and goes under the breast into the spleen and kidney, while the other crosses from the left to the right as it leaves the lung and goes under the breast into the liver and kidney. Both terminate at the anus. (4) The fourth pair goes from the front of the head and the eyes, under the neck and the clavicles, and then through the upper arms to the elbows, then through the forearms to the wrists and fingers, then from the fingers back through the palms of the hands and the forearms up to the elbows and through the lower side of the upper arms to the armpits, and leaving the upper ribs one of them arrives at the spleen, the other at the liver, and then passing above the belly both terminate in the genital organs. (5) This is the nature of the thick vessels. In addition, from the abdomen there are many vessels of all kinds that go throughout the body and distribute the body's nutriment. There are also vessels that proceed from the thick vessels (both the exterior and the interior ones) into the abdomen and the rest of the body and communicate with one another, some proceeding from the interior outward and others from the exterior inward. (6) It is important to bear these considerations in mind when letting blood. It is also important to take care to make the incision as far as possible from the places where the pains usually occur and the blood collects. In this way it is least likely

that there will suddenly be a big change. and you will change the habit so that blood will no longer collect in the same place.

Chapter 12

(1) People who spit up a lot of pus when they do not have fever, people whose urine has a sediment with a lot of pus but without any associated pain, and people over thirty-five whose stools are chronically bloody, as in dysentery— all these have sicknesses due to the same cause. (2) They must have lived lives of exertion, effort, and hard work when they were young, and afterward when relieved from their labors they must have become corpulent with a great deal of soft flesh very different from what it was before, and there is a big differ-ence between the portion of the body that existed before and what has been added to it, with the result that they do not correspond. (3) Now when people in that condition catch a sickness, they escape for the moment, but later, after the sickness, in time their body wastes away and blood full of serum flows through their blood vessels wherever it finds a broad passage. (4) If it rushes into the lower intestine the stools become quite similar to how it was in the body, for since the path is downward it does not stay long in the intestine. (5) But when it flows into the chest it becomes purulent, for since the evacua-tion occurs in an upward direction and it lodges in the chest for a long time, it rots and is putrefied. (6) When it discharges into the bladder the heat of that region makes it white and it becomes separated. The thinner part of it rises upward to the surface while the thicker part sinks downward. This is what is called pus. In children kidney stones are formed because of the heat of this region and of the body as a whole, while they are not formed in men because of the body's coldness. It is important to know well that we are hottest on the first day of our life and coldest on the last. The body is hot when it is grow-ing and has difficulty in evacuating, but when it begins to wither and the flux occurs easily, it becomes colder. By this reasoning, to the extent that people grow the most on the first day of their life, the hotter they are at that time, and to the extent that they decline the most on their last day, the colder they are on that day. (7) Most people who have the kind of disposition mentioned above recover their health spontaneously within forty-two days in the season when they begin to decline. When the sickness lasts longer than that season, they become healthy in a year unless they are harmed by something else.

Chapter 13

All sicknesses arising from something small and all those whose causes are well known have the safest prognosis. Their treatment should be effected by oppos-ing the cause of the sickness, for this is how to get rid of the thing that causes the sickness in the body.

Chapter 14

(1) When a sandy deposit or bladder stone is found in the urine, this is due to abscesses on the thick vessel with the formation of pus. Then since the abscesses did not burst quickly, stones grew from the pus by concretion, and these pour through the vessel into the bladder along with the urine. (2) When the urine is merely bloody the vessels are injured. (3) When the urine is thick and contains small hair-like pieces of flesh, it is important to know that these come from the kidneys. (4) When the urine is clear but a bran-like sediment occasionally appears in it, the bladder has psoriasis.

Chapter 15

(1) Most fevers are due to bile; there are four kinds apart from those that occur in connection with distinct pains. They are named continued, quotidian, tertian, and quartan. (2) The one called continued results from the purest bile in the greatest quantity. It has the briefest crises, since the body does not cool off for any length of time and so it quickly wastes away, since it is heated by the action of a great deal of heat. (3) Next in order after continued fevers, quotidian fevers result from the greatest quantity of bile and remit most quickly of the others but last longer than continued ones to the extent that they are caused by less bile and because the body has some respite [since the patient does not have fever continuously], whereas in continued fevers it has no respite at all. (4) Tertian fevers last longer than quotidians and result from less bile. The longer the respite that the body has in tertians than in quotidians, the longer lasting this fever is than the quotidian. (5) The same account holds for quartan fevers in other respects, but they are longer lasting than tertians to the extent that they have a smaller share of bile that causes the heat, and the body has longer to cool off. They have an additional feature due to black bile—their long duration and the difficulty met in getting rid of them. For black bile is the most viscous of the constituents of the body and the one that stays longest in the places where it settles. You can know by this evidence that quartan fevers contain black bile. People catch quartans mainly in the fall and when they are between twenty-five and forty-two years old. Black bile is dominant in this age span more than any other and in the fall more than any other season. But as for those who catch a quartan fever outside of this season and age range, it is important to know that the fever will not last long unless the person is harmed by something else.

Ancient Medicine

Chapter 1

(1) All those who have undertaken to speak or write on the subject of medicine basing their account on a hypothesis they have adopted—whether this be the hot, the cold, the wet, the dry, or anything else they may wish—and

restricting the primary cause of human sicknesses and death by hypothesizing one or two things as the same cause for all of them, are obviously mistaken in many things they say, and they are particularly to be faulted for doing so in connection with an existing art to which everyone turns at the most critical times and whose craftsmen and practitioners they hold in the highest honor. (2) Some practitioners are bad, others are far better—which would not be the case if medicine did not exist at all and if nothing in it had been thought through or discovered; instead everyone would be equally inexperienced and ignorant in it, and everything that has to do with the sick would be managed by chance. But in fact it is not like that, but just as practitioners of all the other arts differ greatly one from another in manual ability and judgment, so too in the case of medicine. (3) For this reason I have considered there to be no need of a newfangled hypothesis as there is for things that are unapparent and puzzling: anyone who undertakes to say anything about them has to make use of a hypothesis—for example things in the heavens or under the earth—and if anyone were to describe and understand those things as they actually are, it would not be clear either to the speaker himself or to those who hear him whether what he says is true or not. For there is nothing to which a person can refer in order to obtain clear knowledge.

Chapter 2

(1) But medicine has long had everything, including a principle and method that has been discovered, through which many sound discoveries have been made over a long period of time and the remaining ones will be made if someone adequate for the work, who knows the past discoveries, investigates using them as his starting points. (2) But anyone who discards and rejects them and undertakes to investigate everything with a different method and manner and says that he has discovered something has been deceived and keeps being deceived. For it is impossible. What necessitates its impossibility I will attempt to prove by stating and proving that the art exists. From this it will be evident that discoveries cannot be made in any way different from this. (3) Above all it seems to me that a person speaking about this art must say things that lay people can understand. It is inappropriate to investigate or speak about anything other than the afflictions from which they themselves are sick and suffer. But since they are lay people, it is not easy for them to learn both how their afflictions come to be and cease and the causes of their growth and decline, but when these things have been discovered and are explained by another, it is easy. The only thing that happens is that when he hears them, each person recalls the things that happen to him. But if anyone fails to coincide with the judgment of lay people and to put his audience into this kind of disposition he will fail to coincide with the truth. And for these same reasons, therefore, there is no need for a hypothesis.

Chapter 3

(1) For in the beginning the art of medicine would not have been discovered or looked for (since there would have been no need for it) if it were beneficial for sick people to have the same diet and employ the same things as healthy people eat, drink and use in their diet in other ways, and if different things were not better for them than these. (2) But as things are, necessity itself compelled people to look for and discover medicine, because it was not beneficial for the sick to be given the same things as the healthy just as it is not beneficial now. (3) And going back even further, I think that even the regime and food that healthy people now use would not have been discovered if it were sufficient for humans to eat and drink the same things that cows, horses and all animals other than humans do—plants, fruit, brush and grass. For they feed on these and grow and live their lives without suffering, requiring no other food. In fact I believe that in the beginning humans too used this kind of food, whereas our present diet was discovered and skillfully devised over a long period of time. (4) For since they underwent much severe suffering because of their strong and bestial diet, ingesting raw and unblended substances with strong affective qualities—the kinds of sufferings that they would nowadays endure, meeting with intense pain, sickness and speedy death, in those days they probably suffered less because they were used to this kind of food, but they suffered violently even then, and most of them—the ones with rather weak natures—probably perished while the stronger lasted longer, just as nowadays some recover easily from strong food while others do so after much suffering and trouble. In my opinion this was the need that drove these people to look for food suited to their nature and to discover the food we now use. (5) Therefore from wheat they produced wheat bread by soaking, winnowing, grinding, sifting, kneading and baking, and from barley they produced barley bread. And by performing many other operations on it they boiled, roasted, mixed and blended the strong unblended substances with the weaker ones, fashioning them all with a view toward the nature and capacity of humans, believing that if they are too strong our nature will be unable to dominate them if they are ingested, but that these will be the causes of suffering, sicknesses and death, whereas the ones that our nature can dominate will be the causes of nourishment, growth and health. (6) What name could more justly or appropriately be given to this discovery and investigation than medicine, because it has been discovered for the health, preservation and nourishment of humans as a change from that diet from which there came suffering, sickness and death?

Chapter 4

(1) But it is not unreasonable if this is thought not to be an art. For where no one is a lay person but everyone is knowledgeable because they use it by virtue of necessity, no one should be called a specialist. (2) And yet it was a great discovery

and one that required much thought and skill. And even now those who are in charge of training and exercise are continually making discoveries through the same method, investigating what to eat and drink in order best to dominate them and be at one's strongest.

Chapter 5

(1) Let us also consider what is commonly agreed to be medicine—the art that was discovered for the sick, which has both a name and specialists as well: does this too aim at any of the same things, and what was its origin? In my opinion, as I said at the beginning, no one would even have looked for medicine if the same diet suited both the sick and the healthy. (2) In fact, those who do not make use of medicine even now, whether foreigners or certain Greeks, have the same diet as the healthy do, although they do so with a view toward pleasure, and they would not refrain from anything they desire or reduce their consumption. (3) But since those who looked for and discovered medicine had the same idea as the people I discussed previously, they first reduced the number of these foods and, instead of quite a large amount, gave very little. (4) But since this proved sometimes to be sufficient for some of the sick and obviously helped them—although not for all, but some were in such a condition that they could not dominate even a little food, and such people seemed to be in need of something weaker—they discovered gruels by mixing small quantities of strong ingredients with a lot of water and removing their strength by blending and boiling. (5) For those who could not dominate even gruels they took away even these and arrived at liquid diets, taking care that they should be moderate in their blend and quantity and administering food that was neither more than necessary nor inadequately blended nor too little.

Chapter 6

(1) It is important to know this well, that when people whom gruels do not help in sickness, but just the opposite, consume them, their fever and pains become acute, and it is clear that what has been administered becomes nourishment for the sickness and makes it become worse and makes the body waste away and grow weak. (2) All people in this condition who take dry food, either barley bread or wheat bread, even if only a little, are harmed ten times worse and more conspicuously than people who drink gruel—for no other reason than the strength of the food in relation to their condition. (3) And anyone who is benefited by drinking gruel and not eating is harmed far more if he eats much than if he eats little, and even if he eats a little he will suffer. So all the causes of suffering are reduced to the same thing: the strongest foods do the worst and most obvious harm to humans, whether healthy or sick.

Chapter 7

(1) What then is the difference between the way the person reasoned who is called a doctor and is by common consent a craftsman, who discovered a regime and nourishment for the sick, and the way the person who originally, out of that savage and bestial diet, discovered and prepared the nourishment for all people, which we still employ? (2) It is obvious to me that the method of investigation is identical and the discovery is one and the same. The one aimed to remove all foods which, when ingested, human nature in a state of health could not dominate because of their bestial and unblended character, while the other aimed to remove all foods that each person's condition at a given time cannot dominate. (3) How then does the one differ from the other except in that it has more varieties and that it is more complex and laborious? But its origin was the other one, the one that came first.

Chapter 8

(1) If we consider the diet of the sick in relation to the diet of the healthy, we will find it is no more harmful than the diet of healthy people is in relation to that of beasts and other animals. (2) Take a man who is suffering from a sickness that is neither difficult nor unbearable but not completely benign either, but that will be clearly noticeable if he makes a mistake in his diet—if he wants to eat bread, meat or something else that healthy people benefit from eating and he eats not much, but much less than he could if he were healthy. Also take another person, who is healthy but whose nature is neither extremely weak nor extremely strong—if he eats something that would be beneficial for an ox or horse to eat and would make it strong (bitter vetch, barley, or something else of that kind), eating not much, but much less than he might. The healthy person who does this will suffer no less and will be in no less danger than that sick person who was administered wheat bread or barley bread at the wrong time. (3) All this is evidence that the true art of medicine may be discovered in its entirety if pursued with the same method.

Chapter 9

(1) If it were as simple as it has been described and all the stronger foods caused harm and the weaker ones benefited and nourished both the sick and the healthy, it would be an easy matter; people wanting to leave plenty of room for safety would need to direct patients toward the weakest kind of food. (2) But as things are, it is no smaller an error and it does no less harm to a person if he is administered less food and weaker food than is sufficient. For the force of hunger enters powerfully into a person's nature to disable him, weaken him, and kill him. Many other kinds of troubles are due to depletion, different but no less severe than

those due to repletion. (3) This is why the work of a doctor is much more complicated and demands more precision. For it needs to aim at a measure, but you cannot discover any other measure, number or weight than bodily perception to refer to in order to have precise knowledge. This is why it is a lot of work to learn so precisely that you make but small errors on one side or the other. (4) And I would strongly praise the doctor who makes but small mistakes; perfect accuracy is rarely seen. In my opinion most doctors have the same experience as bad steersmen. When they make a mistake in steering their boat in calm weather they are not noticed, but when a big storm and a violent wind overtakes them it is apparent to everyone that they lost their ship through ignorance and error. (5) In the same way when bad doctors, who are in fact the majority, treat people who have no severe problem and nothing terrible would happen to them even if one made the biggest mistakes (indeed there are many such sicknesses, and they occur much more often than serious ones do), if they make mistakes in these cases they are not noticed by lay people; but when they meet with a major, strong and dangerous sickness, then their mistakes and lack of skill are noticed by everyone. The punishment is not far off in either case, but comes quickly.

Chapter 10

(1) That no less severe problems result from depletion at the wrong time than from repletion can be learned well by referring to the healthy. Some of them benefit by eating once a day and they prescribe this for themselves because of the benefit they gain, whereas others benefit by having lunch as well, on account of the same necessity. For thus it is beneficial to them, though not for those who adopt either of those regimes for pleasure or some other chance reason. (2) For most people it makes no difference whether they stick to their habit, whichever practice they adopt—eating once a day or having lunch as well. But there are some who cannot easily recover if they deviate from the regime that is beneficial for them, but whichever regime they normally follow, they suffer terribly if they change for a single day or even less. (3) For those who have lunch when it is not beneficial to them immediately become heavy and sluggish in both body and mind, and full of yawning, drowsiness and thirst. If they have dinner as well they suffer wind, colic and diarrhea, and for many this has been the beginning of a major sickness even if they have eaten in two sittings the same amount of food they are used to consuming in one, and no more. (4) On the other hand, if a person who is used to eating lunch and it is beneficial for him to do so—if he does not eat lunch as soon as it is time, he immediately feels a severe weakness, trembling and faintness. Moreover, his eyes are sunken, his urine is yellower and warmer, his mouth bitter and his internal organs seem to hang; there is vertigo, despair and lack of energy. These are all the symptoms. And when he tries to eat dinner he finds the food less pleasant and he cannot digest as much as when he dined after having lunch. These very foods descend accompanied by colic and noise and inflame the belly. These people

sleep badly and have disturbed and turbulent dreams, and for many of them this has been the beginning of sickness.

Chapter 11

(1) It is important to consider the causes through which these things happen to them. For the person used to eating only once a day, the cause, I think, is that he did not wait long enough for his belly to get the full benefit of the food eaten the day before, to dominate it, discharge it, and rest, but he ingested new food while it was still boiling and fermenting. Bellies of this kind digest much more slowly and require more relaxation and rest. (2) On the other hand, for the person who is used to having lunch, the cause is that he did not get new food as soon as he needed it and had consumed the previous food and no longer was benefiting from it. He declines and wastes away from hunger—since I attribute to hunger everything I say such a person suffers. (3) I say also that everyone else who is healthy but goes without food for two or three days will suffer the same effects that I have said occur in those who go without their lunch.

Chapter 12

(1) I declare that the kinds of natures that are affected quickly and strongly by mistakes <in their diet> are weaker than the others. A weak person is very close to a sick person, only the sick person is even weaker and he is the one who is prone to suffer more when he misses the right measure in anything. (2) Since the art requires such precision, it is difficult to achieve perfect accuracy every time. But there are many things in medicine that have reached this degree of precision, and I will discuss them below. This is why I deny that this ancient art should be rejected as nonexistent or as not well investigated just because it has not achieved precision in all things; rather, because it has been able from a state of great ignorance to come close to the highest standards of accuracy through reasoning, we should admire its discoveries as having been discovered well and correctly and not by chance.

Chapter 13

(1) I want to return to the account of those who investigate the art in the new way, on the basis of a hypothesis. For if it is something hot, cold, dry or wet that harms a person, and a person who gives correct treatment must use the hot against the cold, the cold against the hot, the dry against the wet, and the wet against the dry, give me someone who is not strong by nature but rather weak. Suppose he eats wheat that he takes from the threshing floor raw and unprepared, and also raw meat, and suppose that he drinks water. If he follows this diet, I know well that he will suffer many terrible things; he will feel pain, his body will be weak, his belly

will be ruined, and he will not be able to live for long. (2) What assistance should be prepared for a person in that state? Hot, cold, dry, or wet? Clearly it must be one of these. For if what causes the harm is one of them, it is appropriate to relieve it by the opposite, according to their account. For the most certain and obvious medicine is to remove the diet the person has been using and to give him bread instead of wheat, boiled meat instead of raw, and for him to drink some wine afterward. If he makes these changes, he cannot fail to become healthy unless he is completely ruined by his diet over a long time. What then will we say? That he was suffering from the cold and we benefited him by administering these things, which are hot? Or the opposite? (3) I think that I have posed a difficult puzzle for the person asked this question. Did the one who prepared the bread remove the hot, the cold, the dry, or the wet from the wheat? Anything that has been put in the fire and dipped in water and processed in many other ways, each of which possesses its own affective qualities and nature, loses some of the properties it had and has gained others by blending and mixing.

Chapter 14

(1) I know this too, that it makes a difference to the human body whether the bread is made of sifted or coarse flour or of unwinnowed or winnowed wheat, or whether it is kneaded with much water or little or is well kneaded or unkneaded or is overbaked or underbaked, and thousands of other considerations as well. The same holds for barley bread too. Each of these things has strong affective qualities that are not at all like one another. (2) How could anyone who has not considered these things or who considers them but does not understand them be in a position to understand the effects that these things have on people? A person is affected and altered by each one of them in one way or another, and on these depends the life of everyone, whether healthy, recovering from sickness, or sick. Surely nothing else could be more useful or necessary to know. (3) And since the people who first discovered these things discovered them by investigating them well in relation to human nature, through appropriate reasoning, they even believed the art worthy to be attributed to a god, as is still believed now. They did not believe that it is the dry, the wet, the hot or the cold or any other such thing that causes harm or that a person needs, but rather the strong ingredient of each thing, the ingredient that is more powerful than human nature. They believed that what does harm is that which our nature is unable to dominate, and this is what they sought to remove. Now among sweet things the strongest is sweetest, among bitter things the strongest is bitterest, and among sour things the strongest is sourest: of each constituent the extreme degree. (4) For they observed that these things are also found in humans and harm them. For salty, bitter, sweet, sour, astringent, bland, and thousands of other things are found in a person, with all kinds of affective qualities, amounts, and strengths. When they are mixed and blended with one another they are not noticeable nor do they cause a person pain. But when any of them separates off and comes to be by itself, it

then becomes noticeable and causes a person pain. (5) On the other hand, of all the foods that are unsuitable for us and harm humans when they are ingested, every one of them is either bitter and unblended or salty or sour or something else untempered and strong, and this is why we are troubled by them just as we are troubled by the things that separate off in the body. (6) Everything a human eats or drinks, such foods clearly have the smallest share of an unblended and predominant flavor of this kind—wheat bread, for example, and barley bread and things that follow suit, which the person is used to eating all the time in large quantities, with the exception of things that are prepared and made for pleasure and indulgence. These foods even when they are ingested in very large amounts cause the least disturbance and the least separation of the affective qualities contained in the body, but they are chiefly responsible for strength, growth, and nourishment, for no other reason than that they are well blended and contain nothing unblended or strong but have become a single simple whole.

Chapter 15

(1) I, at least, am at a loss as to how those who maintain that account and lead the art away from this method to a hypothesis are going treat people in accordance with what they hypothesize. For they have not, I suppose, discovered anything that is hot in and of itself or cold or dry or wet that has nothing in common with any other type. (2) Rather, I suppose that they have available the same foods and drinks that we all use, but they attribute to one of them that it is hot, to another that it is cold, to another that it is dry, and to another that it is wet. But it is pointless to tell a sick person to take something hot, since he will immediately ask what. And so it will be necessary either to speak nonsense or to have recourse to one of these things that are known. (3) But if one hot thing happens to be astringent, and another hot thing is bland and another causes agitation—for there are many other hot things that have many other powers opposed to one another—it will surely make a difference whether we administer one of them that is hot and astringent or one that is hot and bland or one that is cold and astringent together—for this kind of thing exists too—or one that is cold and bland. (4) For as I know, a completely opposite effect results from each member of these pairs, not only in human beings but also in leather, wood, and many other things that are less sensitive than humans. For it is not the hot that possesses a strong affective quality but the astringent, the bland, and everything else I have mentioned, and they affect humans both internally and externally, whether eaten and drunk or applied externally as ointments and plasters.

Chapter 16

(1) In fact, I believe that of all the affective qualities cold and heat are least powerful in the body, for the following reasons. As long as the cold and the hot are in the body in a state of mixture with one another, of course they do not cause

pain; blending and moderation come to the cold from the hot and to the hot from the cold. But it is when either of them is isolated that it causes pain. (2) At this critical moment when the cold comes on and causes the person some pain, very quickly the hot comes to be present all by itself, coming from within the person without the need for any assistance or preparation, and it accomplishes this result in both the healthy and the sick. (3) Further, if a healthy person wants to chill his body in winter either by taking a cold bath or in some other way, the more he does this (supposing that his body is not completely frozen) the hotter his body becomes when he puts on his clothes and goes inside. (4) But if he wants to warm himself strongly with a hot bath or a big fire and afterward puts on the same clothing and if he spends his time in the same place as when he was chilled, he will feel far colder and will shiver more besides. (5) Or if someone who is fanning himself because of stifling heat and is creating cold for himself in this way stops doing this, the burning and stifling heat he will feel be ten times as great as it would be for a person who does no such thing. (6) And here is a much stronger piece of evidence. All who have walked through snow or another kind of cold feel especially cold in their feet, hands, or head. And how greatly they suffer at night from burning and itching when they are covered and in a warm place! Some even get blisters like people burned by fire. And they do not suffer this until they have become warm. So readily does each of these affective qualities succeed the other. I could mention thousands of other examples. (7) And as to the sick, is it not in people who shiver that fever breaks out most acutely? And it is not so strong but even stops after a short time, and besides, it is harmless for the most part. And as long as it is present the person is hot through and through, and passing through the whole body it ends up mainly in the feet, where the shivering and chill are most violent and long lasting. And again, when a person sweats and the fever departs, he is chilled much more than if he had not caught it in the first place. (8) Therefore, whenever the extreme opposite of something comes quickly and spontaneously removes its power, what major or severe result can occur? Or why is there need of much help against it?

Chapter 17

(1) Someone might say: "but people who have causus fever, pneumonia, or other powerful sicknesses are not quickly relieved of the heat, nor is the cold present in these cases to counteract the hot." (2) I consider that this is my most important piece of evidence that people do not have fever simply because of the hot and that this is not the only cause of the harm, but the same thing is both bitter and hot, or sour and hot, or salty and hot, or thousands of other things—and the cold in turn occurs together with other affective qualities. (3) Therefore these are the things that cause damage. The hot is present too, but as an auxiliary, with strength corresponding to that of the leading agent, getting more intense and increasing along with it but possessing no more power than is appropriate.

Chapter 18

(1) It is clear from the following examples that this is so, looking first at very obvious things we have all frequently experienced and that we will <experience> in the future. (2) In the first place, in all of us who catch colds and have a discharge running from the nostrils, this is usually more acrid than that which previously occurred and passed through the nostrils each day, and it makes the nose swollen, inflamed, and extremely hot and burning; if you put your hand on it and the cold lasts quite a long time, the area, which is hard and without flesh, even breaks out in sores. How does the burning heat depart from the nose? Not when the discharge is occurring and there is inflammation, but when it is thicker, less acrid, concocted and more mixed with the kind that occurred previously—that is when the burning heat stops. (3) But people whose colds are obviously due to chilling alone with no other concurrent cause get relief in this way: by warming themselves after being chilled and cooling off after the burning heat; this must happen rapidly, and there is no need of any coction. (4) All other colds, which I say are due to the acridity and absence of blending of the humors, subside in the same way, by coction and blending.

Chapter 19

(1) All the discharges that turn toward the eyes, since they contain many kinds of acrid matter, produce ulceration in the eyelids, and in some cases corrode the cheeks and the region under the eyes wherever the discharge reaches and break the membrane around the eyeball and eat through it. Pain, burning heat and extreme inflammation prevail—until when? Until the discharges are concocted and become thicker, and produce rheum. Coction results from their being mixed and blended with one another and boiled together. (2) Further, all the discharges that turn toward the throat that result in hoarseness, sore throat, erysipelas and pneumonia initially secrete discharges that are salty, moist and acrid, and the sicknesses are strengthened because of them. But when they become thicker and concocted and free from all acridity, that is when the fevers stop, as well as the other things that make the person feel pain. (3) Of course we must regard these things as the causes of each condition, since when they are present such a condition has to occur and when they change into another blend it has to cease. (4) Therefore all the discharges that are due solely to pure heat or chill and have no share of any other affective quality will stop when the person changes from hot to cold or from cold to hot. And he changes in the way I have previously said. (5) Moreover, everything else that humans suffer is due to affective qualities. For on the one hand, when the kind of bitterness is secreted that we call yellow bile, what nausea, burning heat and weakness occur! When freed from this, sometimes even by purging, whether spontaneous or drug induced, if one of these happens at the right time people are manifestly freed from both their pains and the heat. But as long as these things are unsettled and unconcocted and unblended, there

is no way to stop either the pains or the fevers. And those people affected by acrid and pungent acidities—what frenzy, gnawings in the viscera and chest, and hopelessness! And it does not stop until they are removed by purging, smoothed down and mixed with the others. (6) Undergoing coction and alteration, becoming thinner or thicker so as to go through many kinds of humors of all sorts and end up in one kind (which is why the crises and the number of time periods is so important in such cases)—hot and cold are least suited of all the affective qualities to undergo. For they can neither rot nor thicken. How, then, will we say that this exists—that blendings of hot and cold with different things have different affective qualities, since the hot will not lose its warmth when mixed with anything other than the cold, and the cold will not lose its coldness when mixed with anything other than the hot? (7) But as for all the other things in a human, the more things they are mixed with the milder and better they become. And a person is in the best condition of all when these are being concocted and are calm and do not show any affective quality of their own.

Chapter 20

(1) I believe I have given a sufficient proof of these matters. But some doctors and wise people claim that no one who does not know what a human is can know medicine, but anyone who is going to treat humans correctly must learn this. The account of these people tends toward philosophy in the manner of Empedocles or others who have written about nature from the beginning, stating what a human is, how humans first came to be and from what elements they are constituted. (2) But I think that everything that has been said or written about nature by wise people or doctors has less to do with the art of medicine than with painting. And I think that clear knowledge about nature can come from no other source than medicine. A person can learn this subject when he correctly understands all of medicine—until then it seems to me that he is far from being able to do so. I mean this inquiry, to know accurately what humans are and through what causes they come to be and the rest. (3) But this is what I think necessary for a doctor to know about nature and to make a great effort to know if he intends to perform any of his duties: what a human is in relation to what he eats and drinks, what he is in relation to the rest of his lifestyle, what effect each thing has on each person, and not just like this: "eating cheese makes people suffer because it causes suffering in a person who is replete with it," but he must know what suffering it causes and why and to which of the constituents of a person it is unsuited. (4) For there are many other foods and drinks that cause suffering but which affect people differently. For example, grant me that unmixed wine drunk in large quantities affects people in a certain way; everyone upon seeing this will recognize that this is the affective quality of wine and that it is responsible by itself, and we know on which of the constituents of a human it has this effect most intensely. (5) This is the kind of truth I want to be apparent about everything else as well. For cheese (since this is the example I used) does

not harm all people equally, but some people can be filled with cheese without being harmed at all. In fact there are even some whom it benefits by giving them amazing strength, while others have difficulty in recovering from eating it. (6) Therefore, the natures of these people are different—differing in the particular constituent of the body that is hostile to cheese and is stirred up and set in movement by it. Those in whom this humor is present in a greater amount and in whose body it is more powerful are likely to suffer more harm. But if it were bad for every human nature, it would harm everyone. And if anyone were to know this he would not suffer.

Chapter 21

(1) Further, in recovery from sickness and in long-lasting sicknesses as well, there occur many serious disturbances, some spontaneously and others resulting from whatever may have been administered. (2) But I know that most doctors, just like lay people—if patients happened to do something unusual on the day in question—if they bathed or took a walk or ate something different, regardless of whether or not it was better for all these things to be administered, nonetheless they attribute the cause to one of these, being ignorant of the cause and prescribing abstention from what may in fact be the most useful thing. (3) But one must not do this, but know what effect a bath taken at the wrong time can have, or what effect fatigue can. For the harm that comes from either of these things is never the same, nor is that which results from repletion or from eating this or that kind of food. Anyone who does not know how each of these is related to human beings will not be able to know their effects or employ them correctly.

Chapter 22

(1) But seems to me to be necessary to know as well all the afflictions of people that are due to affective qualities and all those that are due to configurations. What do I mean by this? I declare that an affective quality is the extreme degree and strength of the humors, and I call configurations all the internal parts of a person, some of them being hollow and tapering from wide to narrow, others spread out, others solid and round, others broad and hanging, others stretched, others long, others dense, others loose textured and swollen, others spongy and porous. (2) Now which of these can best attract and draw moisture to themselves from the rest of the body—those that are hollow and spread out, those that are solid and round, or those that are hollow and taper from wide to narrow? I suppose that these are the ones that taper from hollow and wide to narrow. (3) It is necessary to learn these matters, judging by things outside the body that are obvious. You cannot suck up water when your mouth is wide open, but you can when you stick our your lips, draw them in, and compress them, and if in addition you use a tube you can easily suck up whatever you want. Further, cupping instruments which are applied taper from a wide part to a narrower part, and

are designed for the purpose of drawing and attracting material out of the flesh, and there are many other things of this kind. (4) The internal parts of the person that have this kind of nature and configuration are the bladder, the head, and, in women, the uterus. And these things obviously draw liquids more than the others and are full of liquid that has come from elsewhere. (5) Parts that are hollow and spread out are best of all at receiving liquid that flows over them, but cannot they attract it so well. The parts that are solid and round cannot attract it or receive it if it flows over them, because it will slide around them and will have no place on which to remain. (6) Parts that are spongy and porous, like the spleen, lung, and breasts, are best at absorbing liquid with which they are in contact, and these most of all will become hard and increase in size when liquid is added. For they cannot be evacuated every day as happens if the moisture is in a cavity and this cavity surrounds it. But when one of these drinks liquid and receives it into itself, the empty and porous parts—even the small ones—are filled everywhere, and it becomes hard and dense instead of soft and porous and neither concocts it nor discharges it. These effects are due to the nature of its configuration. (7) Everything that produces wind and flatulent colic in the body tends to cause noise and rumbling in the hollow and roomy parts such as the belly and chest. For when the wind does not fill a part so completely that it remains immobile but it can undergo changes and movements, both noise and noticeable movements necessarily result. But parts that are fleshy and soft are where it produces numbness and fullness, as occur in places that are obstructed. (8) When the wind comes up against a part that is broad and blocks its way and collides with it, and when this part is neither strong by nature so as to able to endure the force without suffering harm, nor soft and porous so as to receive the blow and yield, but is tender, swollen, full of blood, and dense (for example the liver), on the one hand, because of its density and breadth it resists and does not yield—but the oncoming blast increases and becomes more powerful and rushes against what resists—and on the other, because of its tenderness and the blood it contains it cannot be free from suffering. In fact, it is through these causes that the most acute and frequent pains occur in this region as well as the greatest number of abscesses and tumors. (9) These same things occur intensely under the diaphragm as well, but much less so, because although the diaphragm is broad in extension and blocks the way, its nature is more sinewy and strong. This is why it is less painful, although pains and tumors occur in these regions as well.

Chapter 23

In addition there are many other kinds of configurations both inside and outside the body, and they differ greatly from one another as to the afflictions they produce in both the sick and the healthy. For example heads that are small or large; necks that are thin or thick, long or short; bellies that are long or round; and many thousands of others. It is necessary to know how all these configurations differ in order to guard against them by knowing the cause of each of the afflictions.

Chapter 24

(1) Concerning the affective qualities, it is necessary to consider what each of the humors can do by itself to a person, as I said above, and how the humors are related to one another. This is what I mean, for example: if a sweet humor were to change into another kind, not as the result of blending but changing all by itself, what sort of humor will it become first? Bitter, salty, astringent, or sour? Sour, I think. Therefore a sour humor is the most appropriate of the remaining ones to administer if in fact the sweet humor is the most appropriate of all. (2) If a person could succeed by investigating externally in this way he would always be able to select the best of all; and the best one is always the one that is furthest from the one that is inappropriate.

The Art

Chapter 1

(1) Some people have made an art of bad-mouthing the arts, not because they think that they will achieve the goal I mention but in order to show off their own knowledge. (2) But in my opinion the purpose and the proper work of the intelligence is to discover something that has not yet been found, which when found is better than if it had not been discovered, and also to bring to completion things that are half complete. But to be eager to vilify through an art of dishonorable discourses the discoveries of others, not correcting their mistakes but slandering before the ignorant the discoveries of those who know, seems to be no longer the purpose and proper work of the intelligence but more a denunciation of nature than a lack of knowledge of the art. For in fact the following behavior is suited to people who are merely ignorant of the art: to pander to the wicked tendency of ambitious but totally unable people to slander the achievements of their neighbors when they are successful and to find fault with them when they are not. (3) Now for people who attack the other arts in this manner, I leave the work of stopping them to those who care to do so, who concern themselves with the arts in question and who are able. The present discourse will oppose the people who proceed in this way against medicine, taking courage from the people it is criticizing, being well supplied with material from the art which it aims to defend and able because of the wisdom in which it has been educated.

Chapter 2

(1) In my opinion there is no art at all that is nonexistent. For it would be absurd to suppose that any of the things that exist is nonexistent—what reality connected with nonexistent things could a person observe and consequently announce that they exist? For if it is possible to see nonexistent things just as it is to see existing things, I do not know how anyone could think that those very things are nonexistent that could be seen with the eyes and grasped with the mind, that they exist.

(2) We might fear that it is not so, but in fact it is existing things that are always seen and comprehended, while nonexisting things are neither seen nor comprehended. Now comprehension occurs from the moment when the corresponding arts are taught, and every single art is seen in consequence of a certain form.[5] (3) But I think that they have taken even their names because of their forms, since it is absurd to suppose that their forms arose from their names, for the names are due to the legislation of nature whereas the forms are due not to legislation but to growth.

Chapter 3

(1) Anyone who does not understand these matters sufficiently well from what I have said may receive clearer instruction in other discourses. But about medicine—since that is the subject of this discourse—I will make a demonstration of its existence. (2) First of all I will define what I hold medicine to be: delivering sick people entirely from their pains, limiting the violence of sicknesses, and not attempting to cure those who have succumbed to their sicknesses, and doing these things in the knowledge that medicine is capable of all this. (3) The rest of my discourse will be devoted to proving that it accomplishes these things and that it is able do so continually. In demonstrating that the art exists, I will simultaneously refute the arguments of those who believe that they are vilifying it on whatever point each of them may think he is successful.

Chapter 4

(1) The starting point of my discourse is something on which everyone will agree. For it is agreed that some patients are healed by medicine. But the art is faulted because not all are healed, and those who speak the worse of it on the grounds that some people are overcome by their sicknesses declare that those who escape do so by luck and not through the art. (2) Now I do not deny that there is a place for luck, but I hold that failure mostly occurs when sicknesses are treated badly, whereas success occurs when they are treated well.[6] (3) Further, how is it possible for those who have been healed to attribute the cause of their recovery to anything other than the art, if in fact they were healed while making use of it and obeying its instructions? For in cases where they entrusted themselves to the art they were unwilling to look to luck alone. (4) And so they are freed from referring their cure to luck but not freed from referring it to the art. For in cases where they entrusted themselves to it and had confidence in it, they considered its reality and recognized its power when its work was complete.

---

5. In this passage "form" refers to the visual appearance of the relevant phenomena.

6. This point depends on double meanings of the words for bad luck (failure) and good luck (success).

Chapter 5

(1) My opponent will say that many sick people have been cured in the past without making use of a doctor, and I do not disbelieve the claim. (2) But I think that it is possible for people who do not employ a doctor to stumble upon medicine—not, of course, to the point of knowing what is correct and incorrect in it, but to the point that they may chance on the same kinds of cures in the course of treating themselves that they would have received if they had employed doctors. (3) And this is a powerful proof of the reality of the art—that it exists and is important—that even those who do not believe it exists are in fact preserved by it. (4) For it is necessarily the case that those who do not employ doctors but have fallen sick and been cured know that they were cured either by doing something or by not doing something. For they were healed either by fasting or excessive eating, or by drinking more than usual or by thirst, or by bathing or not bathing, or by physical exertion or rest, or by sleeping or staying awake, or by a combination of all these. (5) And because they were benefited, it is necessarily the case that they have comprehended what it was that benefited them, and likewise in cases where they were harmed they must recognize what it was that harmed them. For not everyone is capable of comprehending what things are distinguished by bringing benefit and what by bringing harm. Now if the patient is in a position either to praise or find fault with any element of his regime as responsible for his cure, all these matters belong to medicine. And the mistakes are no less evidence that the art exists than the benefits that it brings about. For the things that were beneficial were beneficial because they were administered correctly, while the things that caused harm have caused harm because they were not yet administered correctly. (6) But wherever the correct and the incorrect have each of them a limit, how would this not be an art? For I, at least, declare that art is absent in cases where nothing is either correct or incorrect, but in any domain where both of these (that is, correctness and incorrectness) are found, art can no longer be absent.

Chapter 6

(1) In addition, if cures through drugs purgative or astringent were the only resource available to the medical art and to doctors, it is my discourse that would be in need of a cure. (2) But in fact it is obvious that the most highly praised doctors cure people by means of special regimens and other kinds of treatment that no one could claim not to be part of the art—not only a doctor but even a layperson without a knowledge of medicine who heard it said. (3) Now since there is nothing useless in good doctors or in the medical art itself, and since the forms of treatments and drugs are found in most things that grow naturally or are made, no one who is cured without a doctor can any longer with correct reasoning attribute the cause to spontaneity. (4) For under examination, spontaneity is clearly proved to be

nothing, since everything that happens will be found to happen because of something, and in cases where there is a "because of something" spontaneity obviously has no reality except a name. But because it is concerned with cases where there is a "because of something" and where the outcome can be known in advance, the art of medicine evidently has and always will have a reality.

Chapter 7

(1) This might be a response to those who attribute health to luck and remove it from the art. But as to those who eliminate the art on the basis of cases where the patients die, I wonder what worthwhile argument induces them to establish the weakness of will of the dying as blameless and the intelligence of people who have practiced the art of medicine as blameworthy, as if doctors can give orders that they should not, but it is not possible that patients can disobey their orders. (2) In fact it is far more likely that patients cannot obey their doctor's orders than that doctors give wrong orders. (3) For the latter have a sound mind in a sound body when they attempt to cure, and they take into account both the present circumstances and features of past cases that are similar to the ones at hand so as to be able to say how they relieved the illnesses. One the other hand, the patients submit to the doctor's commands not knowing what they are suffering or what is its cause or what will result from their present condition or what occurs in similar cases, but suffering pain at the present time, fearing the future, and full of the sickness, empty of nourishment, wanting to take things that will have an immediate effect against the sickness rather than things that are conducive to health, not because they are in love with death but because they cannot endure. (4) Is it likely that people in this condition follow their doctors' orders or that they do different things from what they were ordered to do, or that doctors who are in the condition explained above give wrong orders? (5) Is it not far more likely that they give correct orders and that the others, as you would expect, are incapable of obeying and through disobedience meet with their death—and that people who reason incorrectly attribute the causes of death to those who are not at all responsible and let off those who are?

Chapter 8

(1) Some people also blame the art of medicine because of doctors who are unwilling to attempt to cure patients who have succumbed to sickness, claiming that the sicknesses that they do attempt to cure would be healed by themselves, while the doctors do not touch sicknesses requiring a great deal of help, and that if the art existed it would have to cure all sicknesses equally. (2) Now if the people who say these things were to blame doctors for refusing to take care of them on the grounds that they are out of their minds, their complaints would be more reasonable than they are. For anyone who demands that an art or that nature be capable of things that do not fall under it is suffering from a kind of ignorance that is

closer to madness than to lack of learning. (3) For it is possible for us to work with skill on things that we can master by the instruments of nature or of the arts, but not on other things. So whenever a person is suffering from a malady that is too much for the instruments of medicine, of course we must not expect that it can be mastered by medicine. (4) For example, of the caustic agents used in medicine, fire burns most intensely, while there are many others that burn in a lesser degree. Now when the sicknesses are stronger than the weaker caustic agents, clearly they are not for this reason incurable; but is it not evident that they are incurable when they are stronger than the strongest caustics? As to things on which fire operates, is it not clear that the sicknesses that do not succumb to this require another art and not this one in which fire is an instrument? (5) The same account also holds for all the other instruments that assist medicine in its work. I declare that the doctor who succeeds in the use of every one of all these instruments should hold not the art but the power of the sickness responsible. (6) Those who blame doctors who do not attempt to cure people who have succumbed are encouraging them to undertake cases that do not concern them no less than cases that do, and when such people encourage doctors to do these things, they are admired by those who are doctors in name but they are the laughingstock of those who are doctors by virtue of the art as well. (7) However, doctors who are experienced in this art do not need foolish people either to blame them or to praise them; they need people who have calculated the point that the activities of practitioners reach if they are complete and short of which they fall if they are defective, and further, which of the defects are to be attributed to the craftsmen and which to the subjects on whom they practice their art.

Chapter 9

(1) Matters that fall under the other arts will be for other times and other discourses to establish. But as to those that fall under medicine—what their nature is and how they are to be judged—my previous discussion expounded some of them and my present discussion will expound others. (2) Some sicknesses—although not many—are located in places that are not hard to detect for those who have sufficient knowledge of this art, while others—and there are many of them—in places that are not obvious. (3) Some break out on the skin and are obvious by their color or because there is swelling. They present hardness and moisture for the senses of vision and touch to perceive, and the senses perceive as well which of them are hot, which are cold, and likewise for each of the qualities whose presence or absence makes them be the kinds of sicknesses that they are. (4) Now in all sicknesses of this kind the cures should be unerring, not because they are easy but because they have been discovered. However, they have been discovered not by those who wanted to but by those by those who had the ability. And the ones who have the ability are those whose education is not irrelevant and whose nature is not averse to hard work.

Chapter 10

(10) Thus it is necessary for the art to be successful against sicknesses that are obvious, but it must not be at a loss even against ones that are less obvious. These are the ones that are directed against the bones and the body cavities. (2) The body contains not one cavity but several: there are two that receive the food and discharge it and others, more than these, which the people who concern themselves with these things know. (3) All the parts of the body that have rounded flesh which they call muscle contain a cavity. For everything that is not naturally joined together but is covered with skin or flesh is hollow and is full of breath when healthy and full of serum when sick. The arms have this kind of flesh, as do the thighs and the lower legs. (4) Further, the same kinds of cavities are found in parts that are not fleshy as have been shown to occur in the fleshy parts. For the part that is called the trunk, in which the liver is sheltered, and the circle of the head, in which the brain is located, and the back, adjacent to which is the lung, contain every one of them an empty space that is full of natural partitions. In some cases nothing keeps them from containing vessels full of many substances, some harmful to their possessor, while others are actually beneficial. (5) Also, in addition to these parts there are many vessels and tendons that are not hanging free in the flesh but are stretched along the bones and bind the joints together, and the joints themselves in which rotate the connections of the movable bones. The interior of every one of these is foamy and contains chambers whose existence is proved by the serum that flows out in great quantities when they are opened wide, causing intense pain.

Chapter 11

(1) It is impossible for anyone to know any of these things I have mentioned by seeing them with his eyes. This is why they have been both named obscure by me and judged so by the art. But although they are obscure they have not for that reason gained mastery; in fact, they have been mastered as far as possible. And it is possible, to the extent that the nature of the patients presents itself for examination and the nature of the investigators is suited for the investigation. (2) For it requires more labor and no less time to find these things out than if they were seen by the eyes, since everything that escapes the sight of the eyes is mastered by the sight of the intelligence. (3) And all the sufferings the sick endure because their sickness is not seen quickly are due not to the people who treat them but to the nature of the patient and the sickness. For since the doctor could not see the troubled part or find it out by hearing, he pursued the investigation through reasoning. (4) In fact, even the information that people suffering from obscure sicknesses try to report about their sicknesses to those who are treating them, they report in a state of belief, not of knowledge. If they had knowledge they would not have fallen ill. For it is the same intelligence that knows the causes

of sicknesses and knows how to treat them with all the treatments that prevent the sicknesses from becoming more severe. So, since it is not even possible to hear a clear and unerring account in the information reported, the person who is providing treatment must look elsewhere as well. (5) Therefore it is not the art but the nature of the body that is responsible for this slowness. For the art thinks it right to treat an illness only after perceiving it and taking into consideration how it may conduct the treatment not by rashness more than by judgment and with mild measures rather than violent ones. While as for the nature of the body, if it holds out until the sickness has been seen, it will also hold out until it has been cured, whereas if the body is mastered by the sickness during the time when the sickness is under investigation because of the patient's slowness in going to the doctor or because of the rapidity of the sickness, the body will perish. (6) For if the sickness starts at the same time as the treatment it is not more rapid, but it is if it gets a head start. It gets a head start both because of the body's imperviousness, on account of which sicknesses dwell in places that are not open to view, and also because of the negligence of the patients, which adds to the problem. They are not willing to be treated when they are catching the sicknesses but only when they have already caught them. (7) And yet it is more fitting to marvel at the power of the art when it puts someone who has an obscure sickness back on his feet than to marvel when it does not attempt to treat impossible cases. Certainly nothing of this kind is found in any other art that has been discovered to date. Those that employ fire are idle when fire is not present and those whose activities require things to be seen and that operate on bodies in which mistakes are easy to correct—some of them working with wood, others with leather, and others—the majority of them—with bronze, iron, and ingots of similar metals—their products, which are made of these materials and produced with their help and are easy to correct when mistakes are made, nevertheless are not produced with greater speed than necessary or by taking shortcuts, and if any instrument is missing the work comes to a halt. Even in these cases slowness is contrary to profit, but all the same it is preferred.

Chapter 12

(1) But medicine—deprived of the ability to see anything relevant to internal suppurations or sicknesses of the liver or kidneys or any of the sicknesses in the body cavity, by means of vision, with which everyone sees all things most satisfactorily—has nevertheless found other means that contribute to its work. (2) Using as criteria the clarity or roughness of the voice, the rapidity or slowness of the breath, and sometimes the smell, sometimes the color, and sometimes the thinness or thickness of the discharges that in each person are accustomed to flow through the outlets that are provided, it infers the parts of the body of which these things are signs and what has gone wrong with those parts and what can go wrong with them. (3) But when not even nature is willing to send these

informants of her own accord, the medical art has discovered ways of compulsion by which nature is forced to let them go without herself being damaged. And when nature is relieved, she reveals to those who know the art what needs to be done. (4) In the first place the art forces the innate phlegm to change into some pus by means of bitter foods and drinks, in order, on the basis of something seen, to form a judgment about things that it had no way of seeing. Also, by means of uphill walks and running it compels the breath to denounce the things that it can. It also forms judgments by inducing sweating through the methods already mentioned and by steam rising from hot water. (5) Some discharges through the bladder too are more satisfactory at revealing a sickness than ones that come out through the flesh. Therefore medicine has also discovered drinks and foods that become hotter than the things that cause heat in diseases and so make those things waste away and cause them to be excreted via a passage where they would not have been excreted without this treatment. (6) Now of the things that are excreted and that report information, some are brought forth by one means and others by another, and different ones pass through different passages, and so it is not surprising both that it takes more time to reach conviction about them and that there is less time to treat them, since in these cases the information is being interpreted indirectly to the intelligence that treats them.

Chapter 13

(1) That medicine contains in itself ample resources for speeches to defend itself, and that it is right for it not to attempt to cure sicknesses for which there is no correct remedy, or, alternatively, that for those sicknesses which it does attempt to cure it provides error-free treatment, is shown both in the arguments I have given and in the public presentations of those who have knowledge of the art, which they are happier to give in their deeds than in their speeches, since they have not made a careful study of speaking but believe that most people place more personal conviction in what they see than in what they hear.

The Derveni Papyrus, Columns IV–XXVI[7]

Column IV

. . . In the same way, Heraclitus [? using as evidence][8] things that are common, [overturns] things that are private, saying like an [? astronomer], "the sun . . . by its nature is the width of a human foot, not exceeding [? in size the limits of its width. Otherwise] the Erinyes, [the ministers of Justice] will find him out . . . .

---

7. I have not translated the remains of the first three columns, which contain only isolated words and phrases.

8. I use the conventions of three dots and square brackets to indicate gaps in the text. Three dots indicate a gap which I do not attempt to fill. Square brackets indicate supplements that seem likely. Question marks indicate supplements that are less certain.

Column V

... for them we enter the oracular shrine to [? inquire], for the sake of those who are seeking oracles, whether it is right ... Why do they disbelieve in the terrors of Hades? Since they do not understand dreams or any of the other things, what examples would be the grounds for their belief? [? For] overcome by error and pleasure as well they [neither] learn [nor] believe. Disbelief and failure to understand [? are the same thing. For if] they [neither] learn nor understand [it is not possible that they will believe] even when they see . . . .

Column VI

... prayers and sacrifices propitiate the [souls], and [the incantation] of the magi is able to remove the divinities that are in the way; divinities that are in the way [? are the enemies of souls]. For this reason the magi [perform] the sacrifice as if they are paying a penalty. On the offerings they pour water and milk, and from these they also make libations to the dead. They offer countless round knobby cakes because the souls too are countless. Initiates make a preliminary sacrifice to the Eumenides in the same way as the magi do, for the Eumenides are souls. On account of these things anyone who is going to sacrifice to the gods first [? must sacrifice] a bird . . . .

Column VII

... a hymn saying sound and lawful things. For [. . .] in the poem, and it is not possible to say [. . .] of words and the things that have been spoken. The poem is [alien] and enigmatic for people. [Orpheus] himself did not want to utter riddles that may be contested, but great matters in riddles. In fact he is narrating a holy discourse from the first word to the last, as [he shows] in the easily understood [verse]. For after bidding them to "put doors on their ears" he says that [he is not legislating for the] many ... those [pure] in hearing ...

Column VIII

... he shows [in this] verse:

> who were born from Zeus, the [exceedingly mighty] king.

And how they begin he shows in this:

> When Zeus from his father took the prophesied rule
> and the strength in his hands, and the glorious divinity.

Angle brackets enclose material that is not in the Greek and is added for reasons of style. Parentheses are used for Greek words and English synonyms.

It is not noticed that these words are transposed. This is how they should be taken: "When Zeus took the strength from his father and the glorious divinity." When taken this way . . . not that Zeus hears [his father] but that he takes the strength [from him]. If taken [the other way he might seem to have taken the strength] contrary to the prophesies . . . .

Column IX

. . . So he made the [strength] belong to the most powerful just as a son belongs to his father. But those who do not understand what is said think that Zeus takes both the strength and the divinity from his own father. Now knowing that when fire is mixed up with the other things it agitates the things that are and prevents them from combining because of fomentation, he removed it far enough for it not, once it is removed, to prevent the things that are from being compounded. For whatever is kindled is dominated, and when dominated it is mixed with the other things. But regarding the words "he took in his hands," he was speaking in riddles as he was with the other things [? that previously appeared unclear, but which have been understood] with complete certainty. [Speaking in riddles,] then, he said that Zeus [took] by force [the strength and the] divinity just as if . . .

Column X

. . . and speaking; for it is [not] possible to speak without uttering. But he thought that speaking and uttering are the same. Also speaking and teaching mean the same thing. For it is impossible to teach without speaking whatever is taught through speech. Also, teaching is thought to take place through speaking. Therefore teaching was not considered separate from speaking, nor speaking from uttering, but uttering, speaking and teaching [mean] the same. Thus [nothing prevents] "all-uttering" and "teaching all things" from being the same thing. By calling her "nurse" he says in riddles that whatever the sun dissolves [by heating] the night [combines by cooling] . . . whatever the sun heated.

Column XI

. . . of Night. [He says] that she "proclaims oracles from the [innermost shrine (*aduton*)]," intending that the depth of the night is "never setting" (*aduton*). [For] it does not set as the light does, but the sunlight overtakes it as it remains in the same place. Further, "proclaim oracles" and "assist" mean the same thing. But it is important to consider what "assist" and "proclaim oracles" apply to. "Believing that this god proclaims oracles, they come to find out what they should do." [After this] he says:

[And she] proclaimed all that it was [right] for him [to accomplish] . . .

Column XII

. . . The next verse goes as follows:

> In order that he might [? rule] on the lovely dwelling place of
> snow-clad Olympus.

Olympus and time are the same thing. Those who think that Olympus and the heaven are the same are completely mistaken. They do not understand that the heaven cannot be longer rather than wider, but if someone were to call time long he would not be completely mistaken. Whenever he wanted to say "heaven" he added the epithet "wide," while whenever <he wanted to say> ["Olympus"] he never <added> "wide," [but "long"]. By saying that it is "snow-clad" he virtually [? likens time to what is] snowy; what is snowy [? is cold and] white . . .

Column XIII

> When Zeus, having heard the prophecies from his father.

For he did not hear this, but it has been shown in what way he heard. Nor does Night give orders, but he makes it clear by saying as follows:

> He swallowed the genital organ, who was first to spring out of the *aithēr*.

Because in all his poetry he is speaking in riddles about things, it is necessary to discuss each word individually. Seeing that people believe that generation depends on the [genital organs] and that without the genital organs there is [no] coming to be, he used this <word>, likening the sun to a genital organ, since without the sun it would be impossible for the things that are to come to be as they are . . . .

Column XIV

. . . spring out of the brightest and hottest, which had been separated from himself. So he says that this Kronos was born to Helios (Sun) and Gē (Earth) because it was through the sun that he <Kronos> was the cause of their <the things that are> striking they were caused to strike against one another. This is why he says, "who did a great deed."

And the next verse,

> Ouranos (Heaven), son of Evening, who was the first of all to reign.

Mind that strikes (*krouonta*) <the things that are> against one another he named Kronos and says that he did a great deed to Ouranos, since he deprived him of the kingship. He named him Kronos from his deed and <he named> the other things according to the [same] principle. For when all the things that are [? were not yet being struck, Mind,] as [? defining (*horizōn*)] nature, [? received the designation Ouranos. He says that he] was deprived [of his kingship] when the things that are [? were being struck].

Column XV

. . . [? in order to prevent the heat from] striking them <the things that are> against one another and [in order to] make the things that are separate for the first time and stand apart from one another. For when the sun was being separated and confined in the middle, <Mind> coagulated them and it holds them fast, both those above the sun and those below. And the next verse:

> After him in turn <reigned> Kronos, and then Zeus wise in counsel.

He means something like "from that time is the beginning from which the present rule reigns." It is related [that Mind,] by striking the things that are against one another and setting them apart toward their present reconfiguration, [did] not [make] them become different things, but things with different [qualities]. The words "and then [Zeus wise in counsel" make it clear] that it <Mind> is not different but the same. And he indicates this: "counsel . . . royal honor."

Column XVI

It has been shown [that] he called the sun a [genital organ]. He also says that the things that are now come to be from things that exist:

> Of the genital organ of the first born king, on which all
> the immortals grew, blessed gods and goddesses,
> and rivers and lovely springs, and all other things
> that had then been born, and he himself, therefore, came to be alone.
> [He is now] king of all things [and will be] in the future.

In these verses he indicates that the things that are existed always and the things that are now come to be from things that exist. As for <the phrase>, "he himself, therefore, came to be alone," in saying this he shows that Mind, being alone, is worth everything [as] if the others were nothing. For without Mind it is not possible for the things that are now to be [? through them]. [Further in the next verse after this he said that Mind] is worth everything:

> [? Clearly] Mind and [? the king of all things are the] same thing.

Column XVII

It existed before it was named. Then it was named. For air was a thing that is before the things that are now were formed, and it always will be. For it did not come to be, but it was. Why it was called air has been shown above. It was thought to have come to be because it had been named Zeus, as if it previously were not a thing that is. And he said that this will be "last" because it was named Zeus, and this will continue to be its name until the things that are now are formed into the same state in which they were previously floating as things that are. He [shows] that it is because of this <namely, air> that the things that are came to be such, and, having come to be, [? again] in this. . . . He indicates in the following words:

> Zeus is the head, [Zeus the middle], and from Zeus all things [? are
> fashioned].

Head . . . he speaks in riddles . . . head . . . comes to be the beginning of formation . . . is formed

Column XVIII

. . . and the things moving downward . . . saying . . . that this [earth] and all other things are in the air, being breath. Now Orpheus named this breath Moira [Fate]. Other people commonly say "Moira has spun for them" and "all that Moira has spun will be," speaking correctly but not knowing what either Moira or spinning is. For Orpheus called intelligence Moira, for this appeared to him the most suitable of the names that all people had given, since before it was called Zeus there existed Moira, the intelligence of the god, always and everywhere. But when it had been called Zeus, [it was thought] that he had come to be, even though he existed before without being named. [This is why he says] "Zeus came to be first." . . .

Column XIX

. . . the things that are are called each one after what dominates. According to the same principle all things were called Zeus. For air dominates all things as much as it wishes. In saying "Moira spun" they are saying that the intelligence of Zeus sanctioned the way in which the things that are, the things that come to be, and the things that will be should come to be and be and cease. He likens the air to a king—for among the names that are spoken this appeared to be appropriate to it—saying as follows:

> Zeus the king, Zeus the ruler of all, he of the bright thunderbolt.

He says that he is [king] because one [of the authorities <namely, the royal author-ity>] has power over [? all the others] . . . and accomplishes all things . . . .

Column XX

. . . of people in cities, after performing the sacred rites, they saw. I wonder less that they do not understand. For it is impossible to hear what is being said and to learn it at the same time. But people who <have heard the rites> from a person who makes the holy rites his craft deserve to be wondered at and pitied: wondered at because before they performed the rites they think they will gain knowledge, but after performing them they go away before gaining knowledge, without even asking further questions, as if they had gained knowledge of the things they saw or heard or learned; and pitied because it was not enough that they spent their money in advance, but they go away deprived of their judgment as well. Before performing the rites they hoped that they would gain knowledge, but after performing them they go away deprived even of their hope . . . .

Column XXI

. . . nor the cold to the cold. By saying "jump" he shows that divided up into small pieces, they were moving and jumping in air, and as they were jumping the pieces of each kind were set together with one another. They continued to jump until each of them came to its like. Aphrodite Ourania (Heavenly Aphrodite) and Zeus, "aphrodizing" and jumping, *Peithō* (Persuasion) and *Harmonia* ("joining") are established as names of the same god. A man mingling with a woman is com-monly said to aphrodize. Since the things that are now were mingled with one another, <the god> was named Aphrodite, and <he was named> *Peithō* because the things that are yielded to one another; yielding and persuading are the same thing. <He was named> *Harmonia* because he joined many of the things that are to each of them. For they existed previously [too], but were named as coming to be after they were separated apart . . . .

Column XXII

[so] he named all things similarly, in the best way he could, knowing the nature of men, that they do not all have a like <nature> or want the same things. When they have power, each of them says whatever may come to his heart, whatever they may happen to want, never the same things, out of greed, and some things out of ignorance too. Gē (Earth), Mētēr (Mother), Rhea, and Hera are the same; she was called Gē by custom, Mētēr because all things come to be from her, Gē and Gaia according to each person's dialect. She was named Demeter as in Gē Mētēr—a single name from both, because they are the same. It is also said in the Hymns, "Demeter Rhea Gē Mētēr Hestia Dēiō." For she is called Dēiō

because she was ravaged (*edēiōthē*) in the mingling. He will make it clear [. . .] in the verses that she [? is born]. <She is called> Rhea because many and . . . animals grew . . . from her.

Column XXIII

This verse is composed in a way that makes it misleading, and it is unclear to the many, although for those who understand correctly it is very clear that Oceanos is air and air is Zeus. Therefore it was not another Zeus that "contrived" Zeus, but Zeus himself contrived for himself "great strength." But those who do not understand suppose that Oceanos is a river because he added the epithet "wide-flowing." But he indicates his own meaning in customary words that are in current use. For people say that those who have great power "have flowed big." The next <verse>,

He inserted the sinews of silver-eddying Achelous.

[gives] the name Achelous to water . . . .

Column XXIV

. . . are equal measured from the middle, but those that are not circular cannot be equal-limbed. This makes it clear:

which shines for many mortals over the boundless earth.

Someone might suppose that this verse was said in a different sense, namely that if <the moon> is full, the things that are appear more than before it was full. But he does not mean that it is shining, for if this is what he meant he would have said not that it shines "for many" but "for all" at once—both those who work the land and those who sail when it is time for them that they should sail. For if there were no moon, people would not have discovered how to reckon the seasons or the winds . . . and everything else . . . .

Column XXV

. . . and brightness. But those of which the moon <is composed> are the whitest of all, divided according to the same principle, but they are not hot. There are others too now in air floating far from one another, but by day they are invisible because they are dominated by the sun, while at night it is evident that they are. They are dominated on account of their smallness. Each of them floats in necessity in order for them not to come together with one another. Otherwise all that have the same property as those from which the sun was formed would come together in a mass.

If the god did not want the things that are now to exist, he would not have made the sun. But he made it the sort and size of thing as is related at the beginning of the account. The following <words> he composes as a blind, [not] wanting everyone to understand. He indicates in the following verse:

> [but when the mind] of Zeus [contrived all] deeds.

Column XXVI

. . . "of mother" because Mind is the mother of the other things. "Good" because she is good. He makes it clear in the following verses as well that he means good.

> Hermes, son of Maia, messenger, giver of good things.

He also makes it clear in the following:

> At Zeus's threshold are placed two jars
> of gifts such as they give—one of evils, one of goods.

Those who do not understand the word suppose it is "of his own mother." But if he wanted to show the god "wanting to mingle in love of his own mother," by altering the letters he could have said "of his mother," for in that way it would become "of his own," and he would be her [son].

Bibliography

L'Année Philologique and The Philosopher's Index are important bibliographical resources for work on early Greek philosophy. Most of the work in this field appears in journal articles, and these annual bibliographies cover the most important journals in the fields of classics and philosophy. In most cases they provide summaries of articles and information on book reviews as well as bibliographical information. In addition, the following bibliographies cover the period treated in this book.

Bell, G. G., Jr., and Allis, J. B. (1991) Resources in Ancient Philosophy: An Annotated Bibliography of Scholarship in English, 1965–1989, Metuchen, NJ.

Classen, C. J. (1985) "Bibliographie zur Sophistik," Elenchos 6: 75–140.

Navia, L. E. (1990) Pythagoras: An Annotated Bibliography, New York.

Paquet, L., Roussel, M., and Lafrance, Y. (1988–1989) Les Présocratiques: bibliographie analytique (1879–1980), 2 vols., Montreal.

Paquet, L., Lafrance, Y., and Longpré, H. (1995) Les présocratiques: bibliographie analytique, 1450–1879 : III Supplément, Montreal.

Šijaković, B. (2001) Bibliographia Praesocratica, Paris.

Extensive bibliographies are also contained in the following:

Guthrie (1962, 1965, and 1969)
Barnes (1979/1982)
Mourelatos (1974/1993)

Works Referred To and Selected Other English-Language Publications

Aaboe, A. (1972) "Remarks on the Theoretical Treatment of Eclipses in Antiquity," Journal of the History of Astronomy 3: 105–18.

Adkins, A.W. H. (1960) Merit and Responsibility, Oxford.

Allen, R. E., and Furley, D. J. (1975) Studies in Presocratic Philosophy, vol. 2, Eleatics and Pluralists, London.

Anton, J. P., and Kustas, G. L. (eds.) (1971) Essays in Ancient Greek Philosophy, Albany.

Anton, J. P., and Preus, A. (eds.) (1983) Essays in Ancient Greek Philosophy, vol. 2, Albany.

Asmis, E. (1984) Epicurus' Scientific Method, Ithaca, NY.

Bailey, C. (1928) The Greek Atomists and Epicurus, Oxford.

Barnes, J. (1979/1982) *The Presocratic Philosophers*, London, 2 vols., 1979; revised edn., 1982, 1 vol..

———. (1987/2001) *Early Greek Philosophy*, Harmondsworth, UK, 1987; 2nd revised edn., 2001.

Ben, N. van der. (1975) *The Proem of Empedocles' Peri Physios: Towards a New Edition of All the Fragments*, Amsterdam.

Betegh, G. (2004) *The Derveni Papyrus*, Cambridge.

Bowen, A. C., and Goldstein, B. R. (1994) "Aristarchus, Thales, and Heraclitus on Solar Eclipses: An Astronomical Commentary on P. Oxy. 53.3710 cols. 2.33–3.19," *Physis. Rivista internazionale di Storia della Scienza* 31.3: 689–730.

Brumbaugh, R., and Schwartz, J. (1980) "Pythagoras and Beans: A Medical Explanation," *Classical World* 73: 421–2.

Burkert, W. (1972) *Lore and Science in Ancient Pythagoreanism*, Cambridge, MA.

Burnet, J. (1930) *Early Greek Philosophy*, 4th edn., London.

Caston V., and Graham, D. W. (2002) (eds.) *Presocratic Philosophy: Essays in Honor of Alex Mourelatos*, Aldershot.

Cherniss, H. F. (1935) *Aristotle's Criticism of Presocratic Philosophy*, Baltimore.

Conche, M. (1996) *Parménide*, Paris.

Cornford, F. M. (1930) "Anaxagoras' Theory of Matter," *Classical Quarterly* 24: 14–30 and 83–95 (reprinted in Allen and Furley [1975]: 275–322).

———. (1935) "A New Fragment of Parmenides," *Classical Review* 49: 122–3.

———. (1939) *Plato and Parmenides*, London.

Coxon, A. H. (1986/2009) *The Fragments of Parmenides*, Assen/Maastricht, 1986; rev. and expanded edn., Las Vegas, 2009.

Curd, P. (1998/2004) *The Legacy of Parmenides*. Princeton 1998; 2nd edn., Las Vegas, 2004.

———. (2001) "Why Democritus Was Not a Skeptic," in Preus 2001: 149–69.

———. (2006) "Gorgias and the Eleatics," in Sassi (2006): 183–200.

———. (2007) *Anaxagoras of Clazomenae*, Toronto, Buffalo, and London.

———, and Graham, D. (2008) *The Oxford Handbook of Presocratic Philosophy*, Oxford.

Diels, H. (1879) *Doxographi Graeci*, Berlin.

Dillon, J., and Gergel, T. (2003) *The Greek Sophists*, London.

Dodds, E. R. (1959) *Plato, Gorgias*, Oxford.

Dover, K. J. (1974) *Greek Popular Morality in the Time of Plato and Aristotle*, Oxford.

Dyer, R. (1974) "Empedocles, fr. 64 (= Plut. *Quaest. Nat.* 21. 917C)," *Mnemosyne* 27: 175–76.

Ferrar, C. (1988) *The Origins of Democratic Thinking*, Cambridge.

Fowler, D. H. (1987) *The Mathematics of Plato's Academy*, Oxford.

Frankfort, H., and others (1949) *Before Philosophy*, Harmondsworth.

Fritz, K. von (1943) *"Nous* and *Noein* in the Homeric Poems," *Classical Philology* 38: 79–93.

———. (1945–46) *"Nous, noein,* and Their Derivatives in Pre-Socratic Philosophy (excluding Anaxagoras)," *Classical Philology* 40: 223–43, 41: 12–34 (reprinted in Mourelatos (1975/1993): 23–85).

Furley, D. J. (1967) *Two Studies in the Greek Atomists,* Princeton.

———. (1987) *The Greek Cosmologists, vol. 1, The Formation of the Atomic Theory and Its Earliest Critics,* Cambridge.

———. (1989) *Cosmic Problems: Essays on Greek and Roman Philosophy of Nature,* Cambridge.

———. and Allen, R. E. (1970) (eds.) *Studies in Presocratic Philosophy, vol. 1, The Beginnings of Philosophy,* London.

Furth, M. (1968) "Elements of Eleatic Ontology," *Journal of the History of Philosophy* 6: 111–32 (reprinted in Mourelatos [1974/1994]: 241–70).

———. (1991) "A 'Philosophical Hero'? Anaxagoras and the Eleatics," *Oxford Studies in Ancient Philosophy* 11: 95–129.

Gallop, D. (1984) *Parmenides of Elea,* Toronto, Buffalo, and London.

Godley, A. D. (1981) *Herodotus,* vol. 1, Cambridge, MA.

Graham, D. W. (1988) "Symmetry in the Empedoclean Cycle," *Classical Quarterly* 38: 297–312.

———. (1994) "The Postulates of Anaxagoras," *Apeiron* 27: 77–121.

———. (2005) "The Topology and Dynamics of Empedocles' Cycle," in Pierris (2005): 225–44.

———. (2006) *Explaining the Cosmos: The Ionian Tradition of Scientific Philosophy,* Princeton.

———. (2008) "Leucippus's Atomism," in Curd and Graham 2008: 333–52.

Granger, H. (2008) "The Proem of Parmenides' Poem," *Ancient Philosophy* 28: 1–20.

Grote, G. (1888) *A History of Greece,* London.

Grünbaum, A. (1968) *Modern Science and Zeno's Paradoxes,* London.

Guthrie, W. K. C. (1962) *A History of Greek Philosophy, vol. 1, Earlier Presocratics and Pythagoreans,* Cambridge.

———. (1965) *A History of Greek Philosophy, vol. 2, The Presocratic Tradition from Parmenides to Democritus,* Cambridge.

———. (1969) *A History of Greek Philosophy, vol. 3, The Fifth-Century Enlightenment,* Cambridge.

Heath, T. L. (1913) *Aristarchus of Samos, the Ancient Copernicus: A History of Greek Astronomy to Aristarchus,* Oxford.

———. (1921) *A History of Greek Mathematics,* Oxford.

Heidel, W. A. (1941) *Hippocratic Medicine: Its Spirit and Method,* New York.

Hermann, A. (2004) *To Think Like God. Pythagoras and Parmenides. The Origins of Philosophy,* Las Vegas.

Hippocrates (1922–1988) *Selected Works*, 6 vols., Loeb Classical Library, Cambridge, MA, and London.

Huffman, C. (1993) *Philolaus of Croton: Pythagorean and Presocratic*, Cambridge.

Hunger, H. (1967) "Palimpsest-Fragmente aus Herodians ʽκαθολική προσωδία,'" *Jahrbuch der Österreichischen byzantinischen Gesellschaft* 16: 1–33.

Hussey, E. (1972) *The Presocratics*, London.

Inwood, B. (1986) "Anaxagoras and Infinite Divisibility," *Illinois Classical Studies* 11: 17–33.

———. (1992) *The Poem of Empedocles*, Toronto, Buffalo, and London.

———. (2001) *The Poem of Empedocles*, revised edn. Toronto, Buffalo, and London.

Irwin, T. (1979) *Plato*, Gorgias, Oxford.

Jaeger, W. (1947) *The Theology of the Early Greek Philosophers*, Oxford.

Jarratt, S. C. (1991) *Rereading the Sophists. Classical Rhetoric Refigured*, Carbondale and Edwardsville, IL.

Jones, W. H. S. (1946) *Philosophy and Medicine in Ancient Greece*, Baltimore.

Jouanna, J. (1975) *Hippocrate*, vol. 2 part 1: *De l'ancien médécine*, Paris.

———. (1988) *Hippocrate*, vol. 5 part 1: *Des vents, De l'art*, Paris.

———. (1992) *Hippocrate, De Natura Hominis, Corpus Medicorum Graecorum* 1, 1, 3, Berlin.

Kahn, C. H. (1960) *Anaximander and the Origins of Greek Cosmology*, Indianapolis.

———. (1979) *The Art and Thought of Heraclitus*. Cambridge MA.

———. (2001) *Pythagoras and the Pythagoreans: A Brief History*, Indianapolis.

Kerferd, G. (1969) "Anaxagoras and the Concept of Matter before Aristotle," *Bulletin of the John Rylands Library* 52: 129–43 (reprinted in Mourelatos [1974/1993]: 489–503).

———. (1982) *The Sophistic Movement*, Cambridge.

Kingsley, P. (1995) *Ancient Philosophy, Mystery, and Magic: Empedocles and Pythagorean Tradition*, Oxford.

———. (1999) *In the Dark Places of Wisdom*, Inverness, CA.

———. (2003) *Reality*, Inverness, CA.

Kirk, G. S. (1954) *Heraclitus: The Cosmic Fragments*, Cambridge.

———. (1955) "Some Problems in Anaximander," *Classical Quarterly* 5 (1955), 22–38 (reprinted in Furley and Allen [1970]: 323–49).

Kirk, G. S., and Raven, J .E. (1957) *The Presocratic Philosophers*, Cambridge.

Kirk, G. S., Raven, J. E., and Schofield, M. (1983) *The Presocratic Philosophers*, 2nd. edn. Cambridge.

Knorr, W. R. (1975) *The Evolution of the Euclidean Elements*, Dordrecht and Boston.

———. (1982) "Infinity and Continuity: The Interaction of Mathematics and Philosophy in Antiquity," in Kretzmann 1982: 112–45.

Kouremenos, T., Tsantsanoglou, K., and Parassoglou, G. M. (2006) *The Derveni Papyrus*, Florence.

Kretzman, N. (1982) *Infinity and Continuity in Ancient and Medieval Thought*, Ithaca, NY, and London.

Laks, A. (2002) "Reading the Readings: On the First Person Plurals in the Strasburg Empedocles," in Caston and Graham (2002): 127–37.

Lattimore, R. (1947) *The Odes of Pindar*, Chicago.

———. (1955) *Greek Lyrics*, Chicago.

Lee, H. D. P. (1936) *Zeno of Elea*, Cambridge.

Lesher, J. H. (1984) "Parmenides' Critique of Thinking," *Oxford Studies in Ancient Philosophy* 2: 1–30.

———. (1992) *Xenophanes of Colophon*, Toronto, Buffalo, and London.

Lloyd, G. E. R. (1966) *Polarity and Analogy: Two Types of Argumentation in Early Greek Thought*, Cambridge.

———. (1970) *Early Greek Science: Thales to Aristotle*, London.

———. (1978) *Hippocratic Writings*, Harmondsworth.

———. (1979) *Magic, Reason, and Experience: Studies in the Origin and Development of Greek Science*, Indianapolis.

———. (1987) *The Revolutions of Wisdom: Studies in the Claims and Practice of Ancient Greek Science*, Berkeley.

———. (1991) *Methods and Problems in Greek Science*, Cambridge.

———. (2006) "Diogenes of Apollonia: Master of Ducts," in Sassi (2006): 237–57.

Lloyd-Jones, H. (1971) *The Justice of Zeus*, Berkeley.

Long, A. A. (1974) "Empedocles' Cosmic Cycle in the 'Sixties'," in Mourelatos (1974/1994): 397–425.

———, ed. (1999) *The Cambridge Companion to Early Greek Philosophy*, Cambridge.

Long, A. A. and Sedley, D. (1987) *The Hellenistic Philosophers*, 2 vols. Cambridge.

MacDowell, D. (1962) *Andocides*, On the Mysteries, Oxford.

Mackenzie, M. M. (1988) "Heraclitus and the Art of Paradox," *Oxford Studies in Ancient Philosophy* 6, 1–37.

Mansfeld, J., and Runia, D. (1997, 2009) *Aetiana, vols. 1 and 2*, Leiden and New York.

Marcovich, M. (1967) *Heraclitus*, Merida, Venezuela.

Martin, A., and Primavesi, O. (1999) *L'Empédocle de Strasbourg (P.Strasb. gr. Inv. 1665–1666)*, Berlin and New York. (in French, with an English summary).

McDiarmid, J. (1953) "Theophrastus on the Presocratic Causes," *Harvard Studies in Classical Philology* 61: 85–156.

McDowell, J. (1973) *Plato*, Theaetetus, Oxford.

McKirahan, R. (2001) "Anaximander's Infinite Worlds," in Preus 2001: 49–65.

——. (2008) "Signs and Arguments in Parmenides B8," in Curd and Graham 2008: 189–229.

——. (2010) "Parmenides B8.38 and Cornford's Fragment," *Ancient Philosophy* 30: 1–14.

Mendell, H. (n.d.) "Democritean Mathematical and Physical Shapes and the Emergence of Fifth-Century Geometry," unpublished.

Miller, M. (1983) "The Implicit Logic of Hesiod's Cosmogony: An Examination of *Theogony*, 116–133," *Independent Journal of Philosophy* 4: 131–42.

Mouraviev, S. (1999–) *Heraclitea*, Sankt Augustin (Germany). Multivolume work in progress.

Mourelatos, A. P. D. (1970/2008) *The Route of Parmenides*, 1st edn., 1970, New Haven; revised and expanded edn., 2008, Las Vegas.

——. (1974/1993) (ed.) *The Pre-Socratics. A Collection of Critical Essays*, Garden City, NY, 1974; rev. edn. 1994.

——. (1987) "Quality, Structure, and Emergence in Later Presocratic Philosophy," *Proceedings of the Boston Area Colloquium in Ancient Philosophy* 2: 127–94.

——. (2008) "The Cloud-Astrophysics of Xenophanes," in Curd and Graham (2008): 134–68.

Neugebauer, O. (1957) *The Exact Sciences in Antiquity*, 2nd edn., Providence.

O'Brien, D. (1968) "The Relation of Anaxagoras and Empedocles," *Journal of Hellenic Studies* 88: 93–113.

——. (1969) *Empedocles' Cosmic Cycle*, Cambridge.

——. (1981) *Theories of Weight in the Ancient World, vol. 1, Democritus, Weight and Size*, Leiden.

Osborne, C. (1987a) "Empedocles Recycled," *Classical Quarterly* 37: 24–31.

——. (1987b) *Rethinking Early Greek Philosophy: Hippolytus of Rome and the Presocratics*, London.

Ostwald, M. (1969) *Nomos and the Beginnings of the Athenian Democracy*, Oxford.

Owen, G. E. L. (1957–8) "Zeno and the Mathematicians," *Proceedings of the Aristotelian Society* 58: 199–222 (reprinted in Allen and Furley [1975]: 143–65 and in Owen [1986]: 45–61).

——. (1960) "Eleatic Questions," *Classical Quarterly* N.S. 10: 84–102 (reprinted in Owen 1986: 3–26).

——. (1986) *Logic, Science, and Dialectic: Collected Papers in Greek Philosophy*, Ithaca, NY.

Panchenko, D. (1994) "Thales' Prediction of a Solar Eclipse," *Journal of the History of Astronomy* 25: 275–88.

Parker, R. (1995) "Early Orphism," in Powell (1995): 483–510.

Pendrick, G. J. (2002) *Antiphon the Sophist*, Cambridge.

Pierris, A., ed. (2005) *The Empedoclean Kosmos: Structure, Process and the Question of Cyclicity*," Patras, Greece.

Prichard, J. B., *Ancient Near Eastern Texts Relating to the Old Testament*, 2nd. edn., Princeton, 1955.

Powell, A. (1995) *The Greek World*, London and New York.

Preus, A. (2001) (ed.) *Before Plato: Essays in Ancient Greek Philosophy VI*, Albany.

Primavesi, O. (2005) "The Structure of Empedocles' Cosmic Cycle: Aristotle and the Byzantine Anonymous" in Pierris (2005): 245–64.

———. (2008) *Empedokles, Physica I*, Berlin.

Rashed, M. (2002) "La Chronographie du système d'Empédocle: Documents byzantins inédits," *Aevum antiquum* N.S. 1, 237–59.

———. (2007) "The Structure of the Eye and its Cosmological Function," in Stern-Gillet and Corrigan (2007): 21–39.

Riedweg, C. (2005) *Pythagoras: His Life, Teaching and Influence*, Ithaca, NY.

Robinson, T. M. (1987) *Heraclitus*, Toronto.

de Romilly, J. (1992) *The Great Sophists of Periclean Athens*, Oxford.

Runia, D. T. (2008) "The Sources for Presocratic Philosophy," in Curd and Graham (2008): 27–54.

Russell, B. (1903) *The Principles of Mathematics*, London.

———. (1926) *Our Knowledge of the External World*, revised edn., London.

Salmon, W. (1970) *Zeno's Paradoxes*, Indianapolis.

Sambursky, S. (1956) *The Physical World of the Greeks*, London.

Sassi, M. M. (2006) (ed.) *The Construction of Philosophical Discourse in the Age of the Presocratics*, Pisa.

Schiappa, E. (1991) *Protagoras and Logos*, Columbia, SC.

Schofield, M. (1980) *An Essay on Anaxagoras*, Cambridge.

Seaford, R. (2004) *Money and the Early Greek Mind*, Cambridge.

Sedley, D. (1982) "Two Concepts of Vacuum," *Phronesis* 27: 175–93.

———. (1989) "The Proems of Empedocles and Lucretius," *Greek, Roman, and Byzantine Studies* 30: 269–96.

———. (1998) *Lucretius and the Transformation of Greek Wisdom*, Cambridge.

———. (2008) "Atomism's Eleatic Roots," in Curd and Graham (2008): 305–32.

Sprague, R. K. (1972) *The Older Sophists*, Columbia, SC.

Sider, D. (2005) *The Fragments of Anaxagoras*, 2nd edn., Sankt Augustin.

Snell, B. (1953) *The Discovery of Mind: Greek Origins of European Thought*, Oxford.

Stern-Gillet, S., and Corrigan, K. (2007) (eds.) *Reading Ancient Texts, vol. 1, Presocratics and Plato*, Leiden and Boston.

Stokes, M. C. (1971) *One and Many in Presocratic Philosophy*, Washington, DC.

Strang, C. (1963) "The Physical Theory of Anaxagoras," *Archiv für Geschichte der Philosophie* 45:101–18 (reprinted in Allen and Furley [1975]: 361–80).

Szabó, A. (1978) *The Beginnings of Greek Mathematics*, Dordrecht and Boston.

Tarán, L. (1965) *Parmenides. A Text with Translation, Commentary, and Critical Essays*, Princeton.

Taylor, C. C. W. (1976) *Plato*, Protagoras, Oxford.

———. (1997) "Anaxagoras and the Atomists," in *The Routledge History of Philosophy*, London and New York, vol. 1: 208–43.

———. (1999) *The Atomists: Leucippus and Democritus*, Toronto, Buffalo, and London.

Urmson, J. O. (1990) *The Greek Philosophical Vocabulary*, London.

Vernant, J.-P. (1982) *The Origins of Greek Thought*, Ithaca, NY.

Vlastos, G. (1945–6) "Ethics and Physics in Democritus," *Philosophical Review* 54: 578–92 and 55: 53–64 (reprinted in Allen and Furley [1975]: 381–408).

———. (1950) "The Physical Theory of Anaxagoras," *Philosophical Review* 59: 31–57 (reprinted in Allen and Furley [1975]: 323–53).

Waerden, B. L. van der. (1954) *Science Awakening*, Groningen.

Walzer, R. (1944) *Galen on Medical Experience*, Oxford.

Warren, J. (2007) *Presocratics*, Stocksfield.

Waterfield, R. (2000) *The First Philosophers*, Oxford.

West, M. L. (1966) *Hesiod*, Theogony, Oxford.

———. (1971) *Early Greek Philosophy and the Orient*, Oxford.

White, S. A. (2008) "Milesian Time, Space, and Matter," in Curd and Graham (2008): 89–133.

Wöhrle, G. (2009) *Die Milesier: Thales*. Traditio Praesocratica vol. 1, Berlin.

Wright, M. R. (1981) *Empedocles: The Extant Fragments*, New Haven.

Concordance with Diels-Kranz,
Die Fragmente der Vorsokratiker, 6th edn.[1]

DK	This Volume	DK	This Volume	DK	This Volume
The Seven Sages		58B22	9.39	22B3	10.91
10,3	4.1	58B26	9.29	22B4	10.56
		58B28	9.28	22B5	10.96
Thales		58B30	9.30, 9.31	22B6	10.92
11A5	4.4	58B35	9.37	22B7	10.37
11A9	4.2	58B36	9.32	22B8	10.52
11A10	4.3	58B40	9.11	22B9	10.55
11A12	4.7, 4.8, 4.10	58C3	9.16	22B10	10.48
11A14	4.9	58C4	9.14, 9.15	22B11	10.15
11A22	4.11	58C6	9.17	22B12	10.64
				22B13	10.54
Anaximander		**Xenophanes**		22B14	10.98
12A1	5.1	21A12	7.8	22B15	10.97
12A9	5.3, 5.20	21A29	7.1	22B16	10.111
12A10	5.3, 5.6, 5.11, 5.18	21A30	7.14	22B17	10.3
12A11	5.3, 5.8, 5.12,	21A32	7.9, 7.20	22B18	10.39
	5.13, 5.15	21A33	7.24	22B19	10.20
12A15	5.5	21A38	7.22	22B20	10.90
12A16	5.4	21A39	7.26	22B21	10.27
12A18	5.10	21A40	7.21	22B22	10.40
12A21	5.9	21A44	7.23	22B23	10.72
12A23	5.16	21B1	7.3, 19.4	22B24	10.107
12A26	5.14	21B2	19.5	22B25	10.108
12A27	5.7	21B7	9.1	22B26	10.25
12A30	5.17, 5.19	21B8	7.2	22B27	10.109
12B1	5.20	21B11	7.4	22B28	10.17
		21B14	7.5	22B29	10.4
Anaximenes		21B15	7.7	22B30	10.77
13A5	6.1	21B16	7.6	22B31	10.75
13A6	6.7	21B18	7.29	22B32	10.30
13A7	6.2, 6.9, 6.10, 6.11	21B23	7.11	22B33	10.87
13A10	6.5	21B24	7.12	22B34	10.22
13A14	6.12	21B25	7.13	22B35	10.34
13A17	6.13	21B26	7.10	22B36	10.74
13A20	6.8	21B27	7.18	22B37	10.57
13A21	6.14	21B28	7.19	22B39	10.18
13B1	6.3	21B29	7.15	22B40	9.2
13B2	6.6	21B30	7.17	22B41	10.44
		21B32	7.25	22B42	10.16
Pythagoras and the		21B33	7.16	22B43	10.120
Pythagoreans		21B34	7.27	22B44	10.119
14,1	9.8, 9.12	21B35	7.28	22B45	10.113
14,2	9.7	21B38	7.30	22B46	10.19
14,8	9.13			22B47	10.45
14,8a	9.10	**Heraclitus**		22B48	10.68
14,10	9.9	22A1	10.127	22B49	10.117
18,2	9.14	22A6	10.125	22B49a	10.66
45,3	9.22, 9.23	22A16	10.128	22B50	10.47
58B4	9.19, 9.25, 9.35	22B1	10.1		
58B5	9.26, 9.38	22B2	10.2		
58B8	9.21, 9.27				

---

1. For information on abbreviations used in this concordance, see p. xviii.

DK	This Volume
22B51	10.49
22B52	10.118
22B53	10.82
22B54	10.50
22B55	10.35
22B56	10.5
22B57	10.71
22B58	10.61
22B59	10.62
22B60	10.63
22B61	10.53
22B62	10.89
22B63	10.110
22B64	10.81
22B65	10.85
22B66	10.84
22B67	10.86
22B67a	10.102
22B68	10.101
22B69	10.99
22B70	10.6
22B71	10.9
22B72	10.8
22B73	10.23
22B74	10.7
22B75	10.26
22B76	10.76
22B77	10.103
22B78	10.28
22B79	10.29
22B80	10.83
22B82	10.58
22B83	10.59
22B84a	10.78
22B84b	10.41
22B85	10.124
22B86	10.10
22B87	10.11
22B88	10.70
22B89	10.24
22B90	10.80
22B91	10.65
22B92	10.100
22B93	10.43
22B94	10.91
22B95	10.123
22B96	10.112
22B97	10.12
22B98	10.38
22B99	10.93
22B100	10.94
22B101	10.33
22B101a	10.36
22B102	10.88

DK	This Volume
22B103	10.67
22B104	10.13
22B107	10.21
22B108	10.14
22B110	10.122
22B111	10.73
22B112	10.46
22B113	10.31
22B114	10.51
22B115	10.114
22B116	10.32
22B117	10.105
22B118	10.104
22B119	10.121
22B120	10.95
22B121	10.115
22B123	10.42
22B124	10.60
22B125	10.79
22B125a	10.116
22B126	10.69
22B129	9.3
22B136	10.106

Parmenides

28A46	11.21
28B1	11.1
28B2	11.2
28B3	11.3
28B4	11.4
28B5	11.5
28B6	11.6
28B7	11.7
28B8	11.8
28B9	11.9
28B10	11.10
28B11	11.11
28B12	11.12
28B13	11.13
28B14	11.14
28B15	11.15
28B16	11.16
28B17	11.17
28B18	11.18
28B19	11.19

Zeno

29A11	12.1
29A12	12.1
29A16	12.2
29A25	12.6, 12.7, 12.9
29A26	12.11
29A27	12.12, 12.13
29A28	12.14
29A29	12.15

DK	This Volume
29B1	12.4
29B2	12.3
29B3	12.5

Melissus

30A5	15.11
30B1	15.1
30B2	15.2
30B3	15.3
30B4	15.6
30B5	15.7
30B6	15.8
30B7	15.9
30B8	15.10
30B9	15.5
30B10	15.4

Empedocles

31A30	14.158, 14.164
31A42	14.159, 14.160
31A43	14.152
31A43a	14.153
31A49	14.165
31A52	14.156
31A67	14.161
31A72	14.166
31A86	14.139, 14.168, 14.169
31A87	14.154
31B1	14.39
31B2	14.43
31B3a	14.45
31B3b	14.44
31B4	14.42
31B5	14.41
31B6	14.46
31B7	14.47
31B8	14.48
31B9	14.50
31B11	14.49
31B12	14.52
31B13	14.53
31B14	14.54
31B15	14.51
31B16	14.57
31B17 + Str.a	14.58
31B18	14.55
31B19	14.56
31B20 + Str.c	14.59
31B21	14.60
31B22	14.67
31B23	14.62
31B24	14.66

DK	This Volume	DK	This Volume	DK	This Volume
31B25	14.65	31B78	14.7	31B134	14.80
31B26	14.63	31B79	14.114	31B135	14.29
31B27	14.76	31B80	14.115	31B136	14.25
31B27a	14.77	31B81	14.74	31B137	14.27
31B28	14.78	31B82	14.110	31B138	14.26
31B29	14.79	31B83	14.113	Str. d	14.64
31B30	14.81	31B84	14.137	+ 31B139	
31B31	14.82	31B85	14.107	31B140	14.32
31B32	14.68	31B86	14.108	31B141	14.33
31B33	14.70	31B87	14.137	31B142	14.10
31B34	14.71	31B88	14.136	31B143	14.30
31B35	14.128	31B89	14.135	31B144	14.31
31B36	14.129	31B90	14.84	31B145	14.28
31B37	14.83	31B91	14.69	31B146	14.35
31B38	14.85	31B92	14.72	31B147	14.36
31B39	14.87	31B93	14.73	31B148	14.13
31B40	14.90	31B94	14.100	31B151	14.105
31B41	14.91	31B95	14.138	31B153	14.122
31B42	14.93	31B96	14.75	31B153a	14.14
31B43	14.95	31B98	14.109	31B154a	14.20
31B44	14.92	31B99	14.139		
31B45	14.96	31B100	14.140	**Ion of Chios**	
31B46	14.97	31B101	14.141	36B2	9.5
31B47	14.94	31B102	14.142	36B4	9.4
31B48	14.98	31B103	14.149		
31B49	14.99	31B104	14.143	**Philolaus**	
31B50	14.103	31B105	14.148	44A7a	18.21
31B51	14.88	31B106	14.146	44A13	9.24
31B52	14.89	31B107	14.147	44A16	9.33
31B53	14.86	31B108	14.150	44A17	9.34
31B54	14.86	31B109	14.144	44A18	18.14
31B55	14.101	31B110	14.145	44A19	18.15
31B56	14.102	31B111	14.40	44A20	18.16
31B57	14.130	31B112	14.1	44A21	18.17
31B58	14.131	31B113	14.3	44A22	18.18
31B59	14.134	31B114	14.2	44A23	18.22
31B60	14.132	31B115	14.9, 14.171	44A24	18.13
31B61	14.133, 14.167	31B116	14.18	44A27	18.19
31B62	14.118	31B117	14.15	44A29	18.20
31B63	14.119	31B118	14.19	44B1	18.1
31B64	14.120	31B119	14.16	44B2	18.2
31B65	14.123	31B120	14.17	44B3	18.3
31B66	14.121	31B121	14.21	44B4	18.4
31B67	14.124	31B122	14.22	44B5	18.5
31B68	14.126	31B123	14.23	44B6	18.6
31B69	14.125	31B124	14.24	44B6a	18.7
31B70	14.127	31B125	14.11	44B7	18.8
31B71	14.104	31B126	14.12	44B13	18.12
31B72	14.116	31B127	14.34	44B16	18.10
31B73	14.106	31B128	14.4	44B17	18.9
31B74	14.117	31B129	9.6	44B20	18.11
31B75	14.112	31B130	14.5		
31B76	14.61	31B131	14.38	**Anaxagoras**	
+ Str. b		31B132	14.8	59A12	13.32
31B77	14.6	31B133	14.37	59A16	13.24
				59A42	13.33

Index of Passages Translated

Subject Index